THE
NEW
ENCYCLOPEDIA
OF
ORCHIDS

THE NEW ENCYCLOPEDIA OF ORCHIDS

1500 SPECIES IN CULTIVATION

Isobyl la Croix

Foreword by **Phillip Cribb**
Photographs by **Manuel Aubron**

To Eric

Page 3: *Dendrobium cuthbertsonii* is a colorful miniature orchid from New Guinea characterized by warts on the upper leaf surface. These may serve to store water.

Published in 2008 by
Timber Press, Inc.

The Haseltine Building
133 S.W. Second Avenue, Suite 450
Portland, Oregon 97204-3527
timberpress.com

Designed by Christi Payne
Printed in China
Fourth printing 2019

Library of Congress Cataloging-in-Publication Data

La Croix, I. F.
The new encyclopedia of orchids : 1500 species in cultivation / Isobyl la Croix. -- 1st ed.
p. cm.
Includes bibliographical references and index.
ISBN-13: 978-0-88192-876-1
1. Orchids--Encyclopedias. 2. Orchid culture--Encyclopedias. I. Title.
SB409.L23 2008
635.9'344--dc22

2007038802

A catalog record for this book is also available from the British Library.

CONTENTS

FOREWORD

Few authors of orchid books have a broader knowledge and experience than Isobyl la Croix, whose name is well-known to aficionados of tropical African orchids. She has been the author, or co-author, of a series of authoritative books and articles on tropical African species: *Epiphytic Orchids of Malawi* (1983), *Orchids of Malawi* (1991), *Flora Zambesiaca Orchidaceae* (1995, 1998), *African Orchids in the Wild and in Cultivation* (1997). Isobyl trained as a botanist at the University of Edinburgh where she came under the influence of Peter Davis, one of Britain's most influential plant taxonomists, and there she first came into contact with and developed a deep passion for tropical orchids. After graduation, she and her husband spent 22 years in the tropics, mainly in Africa, collecting, studying, and growing orchids. Since her return to the United Kingdom, she has edited the influential *Orchid Review*, the doyen of orchid journals. Her broad knowledge of orchids is put to good use in this encyclopedic account of the family.

The Orchidaceae is the largest family of flowering plants with an estimated 25,000 or more species, making the identification and naming of orchids a difficult art. Furthermore, recent studies of orchid DNA have led to a radical reassessment of orchid classification that has had many repercussions for orchid names. Consequently, many traditional concepts at both the species and genus levels have been changed, and long-accepted names have been dumped and new names learned.

Photographs are the easiest way for the nonspecialist to access orchid identities, but their utility depends upon their accurate and current nomenclature. This encyclopedia provides the means whereby orchid enthusiasts can easily and quickly name a wide range of species from every continent. The information provided for each species is concise and accurate, providing names, synonymy, short descriptions, distributions, cultivation, and notes on similar species.

This encyclopedia arrives at a critical time for orchid specialists, when the sweeping changes in orchid nomenclature are beginning to impact orchid growers, for example, through the international registration of orchid hybrids. New hybrids cannot be registered unless their parents are known. The identity of the parents is, therefore, critical to having a new hybrid name accepted or not. Isobyl la Croix's deep and extensive knowledge of orchids, as scientist, horticulturist, orchid journal editor, and orchid hunter, reflected in her concise but critical text, places her in an ideal position to make the decisions on whether to accept or reject the proposed changes in orchid nomenclature, some with more convincing evidence to back them than others.

Phillip Cribb

PREFACE

The first problem with a book of this kind is to decide what to include. With an estimated 25,000 orchid species, selection must be rather rigorous and information must be brief. Wherever possible, I have gone to regional floras and monographs to find out habitat details, although with widely distributed species, these may not apply to the entire range.

Many of the most widely grown orchids are hybrids, which are not included here. If there are 25,000 species, there are over 100,000 hybrids and the numbers are constantly increasing. Many of those that are registered, and perhaps even awarded, will not enter general cultivation. Also a lot of those that are now widely available in garden centers and supermarkets are unnamed.

With the development of mass production of orchids by meristem culture, many people have worried that the range of orchids available in commerce would become more limited. Fortunately this does not seem to be happening. Interest in orchid species is growing and specialist nurseries attend orchid shows all over the world with a good selection of unusual and interesting plants. Information on many of these is not easy to come by so I hope that readers will find what they are looking for here. For anyone wanting more information, there are monographs on most of the important horticultural genera; these are listed in the Bibliography. Also, there are many articles in orchid journals such as *The Orchid Review*, *Orchid Digest*, and *Orchids*.

Acknowledgments

Even Manuel Aubron's comprehensive collection of photographs could not cover everything and I should like to thank those who filled the gaps as well as offering help and advice in other ways. I particularly thank (in alphabetical order) Folbert Bronsema, Marcos Campacci, Bob Campbell, George Carr, William Cavestro, Jim Comber, Jim Cootes, Phillip Cribb, Mary Gerritson, Johan Hermans, Harold Hills, Eric la Croix, Sharon Laurent, Marilyn Light, Chuck McCartney, Michael MacConaill, Steve Manning, Henry Oakeley, Peter O'Byrne, Ron Parsons, Joyce Stewart, Juan Carlos Uribes, Mark Whitten, Cassio van den Berg, Gab van Winkel, and Jeff Wood. Extra thanks must go to Joyce, who wrote the account of *Dendrobium* and helped to check the slides, and to Phil Cribb for writing the foreword.

I should also like to thank Anna Mumford, Linda Willms, and others at Timber Press for their patience over the long gestation of this book.

Rare in cultivation, the magnificently flowered *Chloraea magellanica* is one of the southernmost orchids, found in the wild in grassland and open scrub in Patagonia and southern Chile.

1 INTRODUCTION

The Orchidaceae is one of the two largest plant families. No one knows how many genera and species comprise the family, but a fair guess is about 900 genera and 25,000 species.

Over the years there have been many attempts at classification and these have inevitably changed with greater knowledge of the plants and the discovery of new scientific techniques. In recent years, the development of DNA analysis has led to greater emphasis on relationships between plants. Some of the results have been surprising—some species that were thought to be closely related have been found to be only distantly connected and vice versa. Results can, however, be interpreted in different ways, and the old division between "lumpers" and "splitters" remains—some botanists take a broad view of a particular genus whereas others hold the view that even small differences should be recognized at generic level. Here, I have followed the findings of the *Genera Orchidacearum* project. This is a series of six volumes, coordinated at the Royal Botanic Gardens, Kew, but involving specialists from all over the world. Not everyone may agree with all its findings, but it forms a consistent reference point.

In *Genera Orchidacearum*, the orchid family is divided into five subfamilies: Apostasioideae, Cypripedioideae, Orchidoideae, Vanilloideae, and Epidendroideae. The Apostasioideae is accepted as being the most primitive of the subfamilies; there are only two genera, *Apostasia* and *Neuwiedia*, neither of which is in general cultivation and so are not included in this book.

The Cypripedioideae comprises the slipper orchids, of which there are five genera, *Cypripedium*, *Mexipedium*, *Paphiopedilum*, *Phragmipedium*, and *Selenipedium*. *Selenipedium* is not included here because plants are often several meters tall, with relatively small flowers, and so are rarely cultivated.

Most terrestrial orchids, both temperate and tropical, belong to the Orchidoideae. Vanilloideae consists of 15 genera of which the best known is *Vanilla*. This leaves Epidendroideae, which includes most of the widely grown epiphytic orchids (and some terrestrial ones). Both the Orchidoideae and Epidendroideae are divided into numerous tribes and sometimes subtribes; I have given these as it is often useful to know how various genera are related.

It may seem strange that the orchid family is so large yet so many orchids are rare and hard to find. However, although it is large in terms of number of species, the numbers of individuals is another matter. Orchids never dominate a landscape in the way that grasses, for example, do. A few species of orchid are widespread, but many more are very local, occurring perhaps in only one small area. These are obviously vulnerable to destruction of, or changes to, their habitats.

Why Orchid Names Change

Orchid-growers—indeed all gardeners—tend to get upset when a familiar name is changed and I am sure that many think that botanists just do it as a whim. There are, however, good reasons for most changes. Probably the commonest is the Law of Priority, which states that the earliest name published after 1753 (when Carl Linnaeus published *Species Plantarum*) must take precedence. Sometimes an early name was simply overlooked, perhaps because it was published in a rather obscure journal. Sometimes, particularly in the case of a widespread plant, the same species was described several times from different parts of its range. Plants from the extreme ends of their range may look surprisingly different, but further collecting from the intermediate areas often shows that there is a complete gradation and that these apparently different plants represent just one variable species.

Increasing knowledge may also lead to name changes. Many African epiphytes were originally described in the genus *Angraecum* but in the early 20th century, German botanist Rudolf Schlechter (1872–1925) divided it into a number of genera, such as *Aerangis* and *Jumellea*, many of which are recognized to this day. These early changes were based on morphology, the appearance of the plant and, in particular, the characteristics of the column. More recent name changes based on DNA analysis sometimes result in species that look on the outside rather dissimilar

Named *Restrepia cucullata* in 1845 by John Lindley, considered by many to be the father of orchid botany, this South American native was re-named *Barbosella cucullata* by Rudolf Schlechter in 1918 and is still known by that name today.

Like most commonly grown orchids, *Cattleya intermedia* has resupinate flowers, that is, the ovary twists 180 degrees as the flower opens so that the showy lip ends up at the bottom.

being placed in the same genus. An example of this is the transfer of some species from *Orchis* to *Anacamptis*.

Name changes may take a long time to come into common use. *Paphiopedilum* was described by German botanist Ernst Pfitzer in 1886, but as late as the 1960s, species now universally known as *Paphiopedilum* were often still listed as *Cypripedium* in nursery catalogs.

What Is an Orchid?

Flowering plants are divided into two major groups, the Dicotyledons (dicots) and Monocotyledons (monocots). Monocots have, among other things, leaves that are usually distinctly longer than broad, with parallel veins, and flowers with their parts in threes or multiples of three. Like daffodils, tulips, snowdrops, and many other familiar flowers, orchids are monocots. They have three sepals, which may or may not resemble the petals, and three petals. One of the petals, though, is specialized to form the lip or labellum, which almost always differs from the other two in size and shape and often in color, and sometimes has a nectar-containing spur at the base. Orchids have an inferior ovary, that is, the ovary lies below the flower. In an orchid bud, the lip is at the top of the flower but in most orchids, the ovary twists through 180 degrees and so by the time the flower opens, the lip ends up at the bottom of the flower, where it may act as a landing platform for pollinators. Flowers like this are called resupinate. Sometimes, however, the ovary twists through 360 degrees and, in some orchids, it does not twist at all. In both these cases, the lip will be at the top of the open flower; these flowers are known as nonresupinate.

In the slipper orchids, the lip is modified to form an inflated pouch and the two lateral sepals are joined together behind the pouch to form what is known as a synsepal. (Some orchids in subtribe Pleurothallidinae also have joined or partly joined lateral sepals.)

The ancestral orchid flower would have had three stamens and three stigmas. In orchids, these are joined into a single structure known as the column or gynostemium and this is the most significant feature distinguishing orchids from other monocots. In subfamilies Orchidoideae, Vanilloideae, and Epidendroideae, the stamens and stigmas have each been reduced to one. Slipper orchids have two stamens; the third stamen has become modified into the staminode, a prominent shieldlike structure in the center of the flower. Orchid pollen is aggregated into masses called pollinia. These are usually attached to a sticky structure known as the viscidium, which adheres to some part of a visiting insect or bird and is transported to another flower, where it is deposited on the stigma. Orchids have many strange adaptations to ensure pollination; there is no space to go into these here.

Within this basic structure, there is almost infinite variation—in size, color, and shape. The Central American *Platystele jungermannioides* has leaves 2 mm long and flowers barely 2 mm across, while mature plants of the Asiatic *Grammatophyllum speciosum* are estimated sometimes to weigh more than one ton. As for color and shape, a glance through the photographs in this volume shows the range there.

Although the pollen grains in orchids are joined into waxy, or mealy, masses, the seeds are extremely small and dustlike. Unlike in almost all other plants, there is no food reserve for the developing embryos, and germination and subsequent growth depend on an association with a fungus, known as mycorrhiza. Lack of suitable mycorrhiza is undoubtedly one factor in the unpredictable distribution of many species. Some species of orchid require one kind of fungus for the seed to develop and another kind to sustain the adult plant.

When orchids are propagated artificially, it is necessary to supply the nutrients that in nature would be provided by the appropriate fungus. This can be done by sowing the seed in a nutrient gel in sterile conditions. For more detail, see the list of "cultural" references in the bibliography.

How Orchids Grow

Orchids have two types of growth, sympodial and monopodial. Sympodial orchids, such as bulbophyllums, have a specialized stem called a rhizome that produces shoots from axillary buds. These shoots have a determinate growth; that is, in a new growing season, they do not increase in size but instead completely new shoots arise from the rhizome. Many sympodial orchids have pseudobulbs, swollen stems that serve as food and water reserves and come in many shapes, from globose in, for example, *Coelogyne cristata*, to club-shaped in cattleyas or canelike in some epidendrums and dendrobiums. The pseudobulbs may be set close together so that the plant forms a mat or they may be well-spaced out on the rhizome, forming long chains. Not all orchids with a sympodial growth habit have pseudobulbs; for example, paphiopedilums and pleurothallids have none. The inflorescences may be terminal on the pseudobulb, arise from its base, or arise from the axils of sheathing leaves. Because of their growth habit, sympodial orchids are much more easily divided than are monopodial species.

Coelogyne cumingii showing sympodial growth. E. la Croix

Monopodial orchids have no rhizome, and the stem has indeterminate growth with new leaves developing from the same growing point; vandas are an example of this, as is *Angraecum* (see photo of *A. birrimense* on page 47.) Although some monopodial orchids develop long stems, that is not always the case. Often the amount of annual growth is very short and the plant remains small. Inflorescences arise along the stem, usually from leaf axils; often roots also arise along the stem. At the end of the resting season, new growth resumes from the top of the stem. The stem in monopodial orchids may branch, often at the base, so that the plant eventually forms a clump.

Epiphytes and Terrestrials

Epiphytic orchids grow on trees; they are not parasitic but use the trees as a platform. Often the roots are thick, surrounded by a layer of dead cells called the velamen, which is able to absorb water. When epiphytes have thin roots, they often grow surrounded by moss and lichen. Many epiphytic orchids have to survive for weeks, if not months, without rainfall; even in equatorial forests, there tend to be wet and dry seasons. Epiphytic orchids are predominantly tropical and subtropical.

A few epiphytic orchids seem to be linked to specific trees in the wild, but most are apparently not particular, although many have a preference for rough-barked trees, possibly because these are easier for the roots to cling to and for the wind-blown seeds to lodge there. Many species do, however, tend to grow on a particular part of the tree; some habitually grow on trunks or large, low branches where the shade will be heavy, while others are twig epiphytes, growing in the canopy where, even in dense forest, they will receive more light.

Telipogon latifolius, seen here in habitat in Ecuador, is a twig epiphyte in cloud forest.

Lesser butterfly orchid, *Platanthera bifolia*, is native to three continents—Europe, Africa, and Asia—where it grows in acid moorland and in woodland. E. la Croix

Terrestrial orchids, as the name implies, grow in soil, like most other plants. They grow both in temperate and tropical parts of the world, but are most prevalent where part of the year is unfavorable to plant growth. In temperate regions, this is winter while in the tropics and subtropics, it is usually the dry season. Some tropical terrestrials are evergreen, but most are deciduous and spend the unfavorable part of the year underground, perennating by corms, tubers, or fleshy roots. In northern Europe and much of North America and Canada, they remain underground in winter and grow and flower in spring and summer. In southern Europe and other parts of the world with a Mediterranean climate, where the winter is wet and rarely severe and the summer is hot and dry, many species are winter green, flowering in spring and dying back in summer.

Lithophytic orchids grow on rocks and boulders. Sometimes they are essentially epiphytes and their roots cling to the bare rock. In other cases, they grow in a thin layer of moss and detritus on top of a rock and their growth habit is more like that of a terrestrial. A few species of orchid seem to be consistently lithophytic, but most use it as an alternative habitat.

It has been estimated that about half of all orchids are epiphytic and half terrestrial, but the proportions vary greatly in different parts of the world. In the tropics, most orchids are epiphytic, but the further one goes from the equator, the higher is the proportion of terrestrials. In cool-temperate regions, including Europe, there are no epiphytic orchids.

Where Orchids Grow

Orchids can be found on every continent except Antarctica; a few species even grow inside the Arctic circle. They are, however, found in the greatest numbers, both of species and individuals, in the tropics. Epiphytic orchids, by definition, need trees to grow on (although in parts of tropical America they can colonize fence-posts), so they are particularly vulnerable to deforestation, whether that is commercial logging, large-scale clearing for plantation crops, or felling by individuals for subsistence farming and firewood.

Orchids also need a climate without a prolonged unfavorable season. Although many epiphytes have storage organs, such as pseudobulbs and thick, fleshy leaves, few are equipped to survive without moisture for very long periods. Altitude is very important; probably the richest environments for orchids are montane forest and cloud forest. In these regions, even when there is no rain, daily mist and cloud bring moisture to the plants.

In general, terrestrial orchids dislike competition from other plants. Species can be found on embankments and road cuttings and in short grassland. The chalk downs in England, where sheep were traditionally grazed, were rich in orchids. When there is no grazing, the grass grows long and becomes invaded by scrub, with the result that the orchids die out. In Africa and Australia, many orchids (and other geophytes) flower much more profusely after a fire—some species only ever flower after a fire. Several factors are probably involved but one is likely to be that the fire burns off the mat of dead and decaying vegetation that tends to accumulate. Montane grassland is often rich in terrestrial orchids, as are bogs and marshes.

2 CULTIVATION

While it is never possible to replicate exactly the conditions in which wild orchids grow, a knowledge of their natural habitats is always helpful. Most orchids in cultivation are epiphytes, or hybrids derived from epiphytes. So, outside the tropics and subtropics, they must be grown in a heated glasshouse or inside a house. Unless a greenhouse comes with double or triple glazing, some sort of insulation will be necessary. The most usual is bubble plastic—the kind with large bubbles is more effective. This has a limited life-span as it tends to deteriorate with time but should last for several years.

Temperature

The conditions in which orchids are grown are conventionally known as warm, intermediate, and cool. The limits are defined by the minimum night temperatures that are provided. Warm-growing orchids require a night minimum of 18–21°C (65–70°F) and ideally a day maximum of 26°C (79°F), although it seems to do no harm if this is exceeded on occasion. Intermediate orchids should have a night minimum of 13–18°C (55–65°F) and again an ideal maximum of 26°C. Cool-growing orchids should have a night minimum of 10–13°C (50–55°F) and a day maximum of 21°C (70°F). Whatever the temperature range, it is important that there should be a day-lift in temperature of at least 5°C (10°F).

In the tropics, distance from the equator has little effect on temperature and so the temperature requirements of orchids depend on the altitude at which they grow in the wild. A large orchid house can be divided into two or three sections, each with a different temperature range. If this is not possible, the widest range of orchids can be grown in intermediate conditions. No greenhouse will have exactly the same temperature throughout; there are always warmer spots and cooler spots and the observant grower will discover these. So some warm-growing orchids are often successful in the warmer parts of an intermediate greenhouse while the same applies in reverse to cool-growing ones.

In tropical and subtropical areas, where the problem is likely to be too much heat (and light), orchids are often grown in shade houses. These are usually made from poles with a thatched or shade-cloth roof and sometimes shade-cloth curtains on the sides.

There is no room here to go into the different methods of heating a glasshouse, except to say that it is always wise to have some kind of back-up heating. For example, electrical heating of some kind is probably the most widely used, but power-cuts can and do happen. In an emergency, a few paraffin heaters kept in reserve can save a whole collection.

Containers and Mounts

In the tropics and subtropics, orchids can be grown outside as garden plants, but elsewhere they are grown in pots or baskets or mounted on slabs of bark or tree fern.

Although *Habenaria carnea* is not easy to find, this tropical terrestrial is well worth growing for its showy flower dominated by a large trilobed lip. W. Cavestro

Pots can be plastic or clay; which is used is mainly a question of personal preference as each kind has advantages and disadvantages. Plastic pots are cheap, easily obtained, light, easy to clean, and tend to retain moisture. Clay pots are heavier and therefore more stable, dry out more quickly, and keep the roots cooler when it is very hot. Because clay and plastic pots require different watering regimes, it is better to use one kind or the other, or at least to group pots of a particular kind together.

In recent years, transparent plastic pots have become popular, particularly for *Phalaenopsis* species and hybrids. The roots of many orchid species photosynthesize when exposed to the light, but it is rather doubtful whether green roots provide much additional nutrient in the case of plants such as *Phalaenopsis* with large, broad leaves. However, these pots do enable the grower to see whether the roots are in good condition and may be worth using for that alone.

Baskets can be made of wood or plastic mesh. They are essential for plants like stanhopeas and draculas, where the flowering shoot grows downwards—the spaces between the slats or mesh must be large enough to allow the developing inflorescence to pass through. Baskets, particularly wooden ones, are also useful for species with a rambling growth habit, like some species of *Bulbophyllum* and *Coelogyne*, where the plants can grow on the outside of the container as well as inside.

Some orchids, such as species of *Aerangis*, dislike having their roots confined, and these usually do better when mounted on a slab of bark (usually cork), which is the closest approximation to how they grow in the wild. Plants with arching inflorescences, or which flower below the leaves, look more attractive when mounted. When mounting an orchid, it is best to chose a time when the roots are actively growing—easily seen by their bright green tips. Spread out the roots, place a small pad of moss on top to retain moisture while the plant is becoming established, and tie them on firmly; this is important because if the roots move around, they will not adhere to the mount. What material is used to tie them on is a matter

Ornithocephalus ciliatus, with its fan of leaves, can be grown either on a mount or in a small pot filled with fine epiphyte compost. The roots should be allowed to dry between waterings but should not remain dry for any length of time.

of personal preference. Some people use fishing line, which is very unobtrusive, but is difficult to handle and if pulled too tight, can cut into the roots. Strips of stocking or tights are good, as they are slightly elastic and are easy to tie firmly. However, there is nothing wrong with fine string; it looks unsightly to start with but once the roots have become attached, it can be removed.

A mount is usually suspended vertically by a wire hook through a hole bored at one end, but it can also be hung horizontally, with a hook at each end, in the form of a raft. This may well be preferable in many cases, as in the wild, more orchid species grow on horizontal branches than on vertical trunks, but it is rather less convenient to arrange. Once a plant has become attached to its mount, it is impossible to remove it without damaging the roots. If a plant grows too big for its original mount, both plant and mount can be tied on to a larger slab.

Compost

The important characteristics of a suitable orchid compost are that it should retain some moisture but also be free-draining and have air spaces between the particles. A soggy, stagnant compost will soon kill any orchid, whether epiphytic or terrestrial. Which potting compost is used depends largely both on personal preference and availability. In the past, osmunda fiber was widely recommended but it has become scarce and expensive. Now, the most widely used composts are based on chopped bark, usually pine or fir bark mixed with coarse perlite or perlag and sometimes charcoal. This can be bought ready-mixed or growers can mix their own. Orchid bark usually comes in three grades: fine bark is used for seedlings and plants with thin roots; medium or standard grade, which is suitable for most mature orchid plants; and coarse, used for large, thick-rooted plants. However, good quality bark is becoming hard to obtain; partly composted bark, such as is sold as mulch or decorative top-dressing in garden centers, is not suitable. Poor quality bark tends to decompose quickly.

More recently, chopped coconut husk has become available. This is usually compacted into bales and must be thoroughly soaked before use, both to remove any salt and tannin and, because when dry, it is difficult to re-wet. The best thing is to put some in a bucket, fill this from a rainwater butt if possible (if not, use tap water), leave it overnight, drain it, and repeat the process; the following day it will be ready for use. Coconut husk can be mixed with perlite but is satisfactory—probably better—on its own. The pieces are usually about a centimeter square and aeration is good. It retains more moisture than bark and so plants will need less frequent watering.

Some growers are very successful with inorganic mixtures such as rockwool and pumice. These come in various forms from different manufacturers. They have the advantage over organic media in that they do not decompose and so plants need to be less frequently repotted. Inorganic and organic composts require different watering regimes and so, as with clay and plastic pots, it is better to use one or the other or at least to group plants in similar composts together.

Some suitable epiphyte composts

- 3 parts bark chips, 1 part coarse perlite or perlag, 1 part horticultural charcoal
- Chopped coconut husk, well washed
- 1 part chopped sphagnum moss, 1 part coarse perlite
- Rockwool, following manufacturer's instructions

Terrestrial Composts

Terrestrial orchids need different composts. Almost all growers have their own favorite mixes, which suit their own conditions. Again, it is vitally important that whatever compost is used, it is free-draining. Many terrestrial

In the wild, *Masdevallia tovarensis* grows as an epiphyte in the forests of Venezuela, but in cultivation, this old but very popular species is usually grown in small pots in a free-draining compost.

orchids grow naturally in marshes, but there will always be some water movement, even if very slight. Stagnant water is fatal.

Some suitable terrestrial composts

- 3 parts fibrous peat substitute, 2 parts coarse perlite, 2 parts coarse grit, 1 part horticultural charcoal
- 3 parts sterile loam, 3 parts coarse grit, 2 parts sieved oak or beech leaf mold, 1 part fine orchid bark
- 3 parts Seramis (clay granulate), 2 parts bark/perlite/charcoal epiphyte mix, 2 parts chopped leaf mold

Repotting

Repotting is necessary when a plant has outgrown its pot or when the compost has broken down. Ferns should never be allowed to grow in a pot with an orchid as they quickly break down an organic compost. Ideally, plants should be repotted when they are just starting into growth but in an emergency they can be repotted at any time. Some orchids react badly to disturbance, but it is better to risk that than to leave a plant in a soggy medium.

Repotting gives an opportunity to cut away dead roots; these are easily distinguished as they are soft to the touch and usually brownish, whereas a healthy root is firm and white or gray. It is also a good time to divide a plant if it has become too large or if divisions are wanted for some reason. However, plants should not be divided without good reason as many flower better when they are large. Always use a pot that is just big enough to contain the plant's roots and, in the case of sympodial orchids, allow for one or two years of new growth. If the pot is too large, parts of the compost that are not penetrated by roots become sodden.

If a plant is not making growth but looks otherwise healthy, it is often worth repotting it; new compost sometimes seems to kick-start the plant, even though the original compost does not appear to have deteriorated.

Watering and Humidity

When to water is one of the most frequently asked questions by new growers, but it is impossible to give hard-and-fast rules about this as so much depends on other factors such as temperature, the type and state of the compost, pot size, and whether a plant is growing actively. Plants with thick roots need less-frequent watering than plants with fine roots. As a (very) rough guide, orchids in pots should be watered once or twice a week in summer, perhaps only every two weeks in winter. It is always advisable to give plenty of water at a time and let the compost almost dry out before watering again; small amounts of water given frequently are not a good idea. Mounted plants should be sprayed daily in summer—perhaps more than once a day in very hot weather. A few orchids seem to keep growing year-round but most have a resting season, usually in winter, and should be kept cooler and drier at this time. Sometimes this is essential for a plant to set flowers.

Even though in the wild rain falls both in the day and at night, orchids in a greenhouse should be watered in the morning so that the plants can dry before nightfall, when the temperature drops. Any water lying in the leaf axils is liable to become a focus for bacterial or fungal rot.

Relative humidity is also important. Ideally it should be at least 70 percent, certainly not below 50 percent. In a greenhouse, the humidity can be kept high in various ways, by misting or by a machine such as a hydrofogger. Different manufacturers provide equipment for automatic misting. Also, the old-fashioned method of keeping the floor wet still works! Keeping the humidity high is less easy when orchids are grown in a house, on a table or windowsill, as no one wants mold growing over the curtains. Grouping plants together helps and so does standing them in a saucer or tray on pebbles or chippings of some kind, so that these can be kept wet but the orchid pot is not actually standing in water.

Water quality is important as orchids are intolerant of water containing a high proportion of mineral salts, as is the case with tap water in some areas. If possible, rain water should be used, but if this is not practicable, reverse osmosis units are said to remove up to 98 percent of dissolved salts. Water companies should be able to let customers know the composition of their water. Hard water does not seem to be too harmful but can lead to a deposit of calcium salts on the leaves, which both looks unsightly and can block the pores in the leaves.

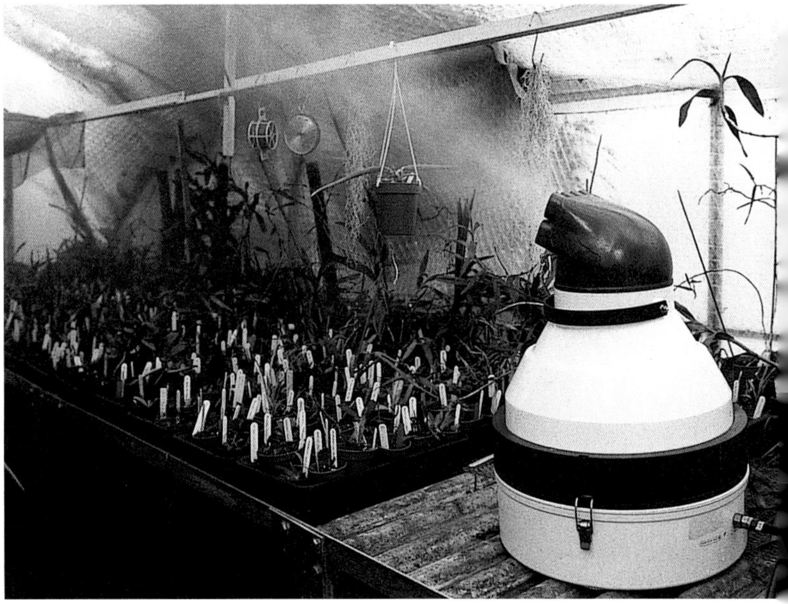

A hydrofogger raises humidity in a greenhouse by producing a very fine misty fog. E. la Croix

Water used on orchids should be at the ambient temperature of the orchid house. In winter, water used straight from the mains is too cold and leads to black spotting on the leaves. It is a good idea to have a drum or tank of water standing in the greenhouse—there is usually room under the staging—and water from that using a submersible pump of the kind used in ponds. Once watering is finished, the tank can be filled from the mains and by the next day should be at the greenhouse temperature again. This method has the added advantage that any chlorine in the water will come out overnight.

Watering Terrestrial Orchids

Most terrestrial orchids like plenty of water while they are actively growing but when dormant, they should be kept almost dry as the tubers or fleshy roots rot very quickly if kept too wet. On the other hand, they can shrivel if kept absolutely dry, particularly if it is too warm. It is better to move plants to a cooler place until signs of new growth are seen. It is will do no harm to turn out a dormant tuber from its pot from time to time to see whether it is in good condition. The new growth of most orchids is susceptible to rot, even more so with terrestrials. It is best to water round the edge of a pot, so avoiding getting water on the leaves. Small watering cans, such as are used for house plants, are easier to handle than standard-size ones.

Like most terrestrial orchids, the pink butterfly orchid, *Anacamptis papilionacea*, requires a dry rest period from the time its leaves die back until signs of new growth appear.

The final point to remember about watering for both epiphytes and terrestrials is, if in doubt, don't. More orchids are killed by overwatering than underwatering.

Fertilizing

In the wild, orchids receive little in the way of fertilizer. Epiphytic orchids, like other green plants, produce carbohydrates by photosynthesis, but for other minerals, they depend on what is dissolved in rainwater. Small amounts of nitrogen probably dissolve in rain as it falls, while other minerals are absorbed in small quantities from bark as it breaks down and from exudates from leaves as the rain passes through the canopy. Almost all terrestrial orchids grow in poor soil, low in minerals, whether acid or alkaline.

There are numerous fertilizers specially formulated for orchids, and with these the manufacturer's instructions given on the packet or bottle should be followed. There is nothing wrong with using "ordinary" fertilizers sold for garden plants or house plants, but in this case, they should be used at a quarter to a third of the recommended strength. Some growers use dilute solutions on the "weakly, weekly" principle; others use a weak solution in perhaps three waterings out of four. It is important to flush out pots with plain water at regular intervals as otherwise mineral salts tend to accumulate in the compost. This leads to burning of root tips and blackening of leaf tips. This is even more likely to happen in orchids that are fertilized when they are not growing, for example, in winter.

Types of Fertilizer

Nitrogen, phosphorus, and potassium (N–P–K) are known as the essential elements and are supplied in all fertilizers, although in varying proportions. The composition is usually expressed as a ratio on a packet, for example, 30–30–30 indicates a balanced fertilizer with equal amounts of the major nutrients; 30–10–10 indicates a high-nitrogen fertilizer, while 10–10–30 is one that is high in potassium. Many growers use a high-nitrogen fertilizer in spring when orchids are growing vegetatively and change to a high-potassium one (sometimes sold as blossom-booster) later in the year. I am not sure how necessary this is; after all, the minerals available to wild orchids are unlikely to change throughout a year. Orchids grown in bark need a high-nitrogen fertilizer as the bacteria and fungi that break down bark use up nitrogen. The source of nitrogen should be nitrates rather than urea; this information should be given on the packet.

Trace elements such as magnesium and iron are also important but most fertilizers contain these. One element that is not always included is calcium, presumably on the basis that it will be present in the water supply. In soft water areas, or when reverse osmosis is used, this should be applied in the form of calcium nitrate.

Light and Shade

Few orchids thrive in direct sunlight, and in summer, some form of shading on a greenhouse is necessary. The simplest way to provide this is by painting the greenhouse with white paint made for the purpose. This should be on sale in any garden center. Once dry, the paint is resistant to rain but will gradually wear off in the course of a year and needs to be reapplied every spring. Blinds and shade netting are most effective on the outside of a greenhouse, but depending on the structure of the greenhouse and its position (that is, if it is exposed to a lot of wind), this is not always possible, in which case they should be fixed inside.

Elleanthus species, seen here in habitat, make good landscape plants for tropical and subtropical gardens where they can be provided with light shade and year-round moisture.

There will be variations in light intensity within any greenhouse. Plants such as vandas, with high-light requirements, can be suspended near the glass while those that need low light can be placed in the shade of other plants or even under the staging. In the wild, many orchids grow in surprisingly dark places, where a light meter gives no reading at all, but most grow in moderate or dappled shade. Terrestrial orchids, even though they may be growing in the open, usually get some degree of shade from the surrounding vegetation.

In cultivation, if a plant is grown in too much shade, the leaves become dark green and luxuriant but the plant will be rather leggy and may not flower. In too bright light, the leaves may scorch or be small and yellow-green or tinged with red, but the plant will probably flower well. However, such a situation is not good for the plant's long-term health.

Orchids grown as house plants need to be carefully placed. A south-facing windowsill is probably the best in winter but will be too hot and bright in summer, as may a west-facing one. While net curtains will provide some shade if no other aspect is available, it is better to place the plants on a table slightly back from the window.

Artificial Light

Growing orchids entirely under artificial lighting seems to be commoner in America than in Europe, perhaps because of energy costs. The practice has much to recommend it as it gives the grower virtually complete control over the conditions and allows places like cellars and attics to be used as growing areas.

Several manufacturers make "grow lights," specially designed for optimum plant growth. Energy for plant growth can only be produced by light that a plant can absorb, which lies in the blue and red parts of the spectrum. Cool white or "daylight" fluorescent lamps supply this, and incandescent light bulbs produce light in the red part of the spectrum (which helps to trigger flowering) so a combination of the two kinds is satisfactory. When artificial lighting is used, the lights are usually attached to a wooden structure hung on chains from the ceiling, which can be moved up and down as required. Four 40-watt fluorescent tubes and four 8-watt incandescent bulbs should be satisfactory. The lights should be 15–45 cm above the leaves, with light-loving plants, such as cattleyas, being nearest the light. Lights also give off heat, so good ventilation is necessary in an enclosed area.

Lady orchid, *Orchis purpurea*, is one of many hardy species that can be grown in the open garden in temperate regions. It is shown here growing in its native habitat on well-drained chalky soil in woodland.

Ventilation

Where orchids grow in nature, there is almost always some air movement. In an enclosed greenhouse, even with opening vents, fans are beneficial. Most kinds can be used as fan-heaters or as fans only.

Hardy Orchids

These are plants that can be grown outdoors, in an alpine house, cold frame, or frost-free greenhouse in cool-temperate regions. Some need to be grown under glass because, although they can withstand low temperatures, they are intolerant of winter wet. Some hardy orchids come from temperate regions, others from high altitudes in the tropics. An example of the second group is *Pleione*, which must be kept cool and dry in winter. Many European orchids, such as species of *Dactylorhiza*, *Ophrys*, and *Orchis*, can be grown in the open garden, taking account of their natural habitats, for example, whether they grow in acid or alkaline soil. In regions usually with wet winters, people often prefer to grow them in pots and keep them under glass in winter.

3 PESTS AND DISEASES

Pests

Prevention, as always, is better than cure, so any new plant should be thoroughly checked before it is added to a collection. Some growers keep new acquisitions separate for a week or two but often this is not practicable. Keep a greenhouse as clean as possible and remove dead leaves and flowers (and dead plants) regularly. Also inspect plants regularly; it is usually possible to remove, say, a few scale insects or aphids manually before they have a chance to build up into a serious infestation. If things have progressed beyond that stage, pests can be controlled by either biological or chemical means.

Biological Control

Almost all greenhouse pests are themselves attacked by a parasite or a predator. The big advantage of using a biological control is that harmless and beneficial insects are not affected. The main drawback is that such predators are never 100 percent effective—it is not in their own interest to eradicate their food supply completely. Various types of parasite and predator are available commercially; the firms advertise in the horticultural press.

Chemical Control

Chemical controls, or pesticides, are either contact or systemic. Contact pesticides are sprayed on a plant and kill any insect that they touch. It is necessary therefore to spray both the underside as well as the top of the foliage and even so, pests lurking in a sheath or leaf axil may escape. Systemic pesticides are absorbed by a plant and so kill only pests that are actually feeding on it. They may seem an obvious choice, but they do not always work; for example, although an infestation of scale is very damaging, an individual scale insect takes in so little sap that it is unaffected by a systemic insecticide. Because of government regulations and safety concerns, the range of insecticides and fungicides available to the amateur grower changes and gets smaller every year and there is no point in listing names of specific products here. All garden centers carry a range of pesticides; the grower has to see which ones are recommended for a specific purpose and carefully follow the instructions, including the safety instructions.

Scale Insects

Although several species of scale insects may attack orchids, all have a waxy, water-repellent shield, which means that insecticides carried in water are ineffective. Scale insects look like miniature limpets and, although the adults do not move, the larvae do. A small infestation can be dealt with easily by wiping plants with cotton-wool dipped in methylated spirit (rubbing alcohol). If the infestation is too extensive, there are available insecticides.

Mealy Bugs

Mealy bugs are related to scale insects and are easy to see as they have a white, waxy covering. They can be controlled by the same insecticides as scale insects. A species of ladybird also acts as a predator. It however, needs a constant temperature of about 21°C (70°F) to thrive and be effective so may not be practicable for many growers to use.

Spider Mites

Red spider mites are probably the worst orchid pests because they are so small that the first sign of their presence is usually the damage they have caused. The undersides of the leaves develop a silvery appearance and later turn brown. Spider mites tend to be more prevalent when humidity is low. In winter, they hibernate in webs, often on the greenhouse frame, so washing the frame at this time of year with dilute bleach is helpful. Biological control can be provided by a predatory mite, which attacks all stages of the life cycle: egg, nymph, and adult. It is best introduced in spring when the number of spider mites will be rising. Pesticides are also available, but do not harm the eggs, so a spray must be repeated after 10 days, when the eggs have hatched.

False spider mite is also a pest of orchids and can be controlled by the same pesticides and by neem oil.

Aphids

Aphids are not as serious a pest of orchids as of some other plants, but they get into greenhouses through vents and open doors, and home in on new growth and developing flower buds. They are killed by almost any insecticide, but if the grower is watchful, it is usually possible to rub them off before the numbers build up. The worst thing about aphids is that they carry viruses.

Vine Weevils

Vine weevils tend to be a more serious pest of garden plants but if one gets into a greenhouse, it can cause damage in the form of circular holes eaten out of leaves, which is unsightly. The grubs can cause fatal damage, though, as they feed on roots and tubers. They are not likely to affect epiphytic orchids growing in bark or rockwool, but can attack terrestrials growing in soil or a peat-based compost. A parasitic nematode controls both grubs and adults, as do insecticides. The adults feed at night and the sound of their crunching jaws sometimes gives away their presence.

Slugs and Snails

I have never heard of an orchid grower who has not been troubled by slugs and snails at some time. Damaged leaves and flowers and trails of slime make their presence obvious. These pests can climb and also abseil, so mounted plants are not safe; in fact the back of a mount is a favorite hiding place. Slug pellets of various kinds are readily available, as is a liquid formulation that can be sprayed on mounted plants, although these do not seem to work on the tiny garlic snails. Various nonchemical controls can be used, such as a saucer of beer on the greenhouse floor or on the staging. Some people claim that a segment of orange skin placed upside down is effective, but I have never found this to work. As good a method as any is to walk round the orchid house in the evening and look for slugs and garlic snails on the plants.

Woodlice

Woodlice (pill bugs) mainly feed on decaying vegetable matter but also attack growing tips of roots. They hide on the backs of mounts and under a pot or saucer on the greenhouse floor, and will enter pots (presumably via the drainage holes) particularly if a compost has started to break down. Good hygiene helps, but they are also susceptible to most insecticides.

Bacterial and Fungal Diseases

Not many fungal and bacterial diseases are specific to orchids, but they can cause serious, often fatal, damage. They are usually caused by overwatering or allowing water to lodge in the crown of a plant, particularly when the temperature is low and ventilation is poor. Any damaged tissue should be cut out with about 1 cm of the adjoining healthy tissue, and the wound treated with Physan® (quaternary ammonium compounds) or dusted with sulfur or cinnamon powder. In a terrestrial orchid, when rot is evident it is usually too late to save the plant but epiphytic orchids may branch from lower down the stem.

Viruses

Several viruses attack orchids. The commonest is cymbidium mosaic virus (CMV), which does not only attack cymbidiums. The symptoms of viral infection are irregular pale patches on a young leaf that later turn brown or black. Yellow streaks on a leaf, or color breaks or distortions on a flower, are other symptoms. Viruses are transmitted from one plant to another by sap-sucking insects such as aphids and also by using a knife or pruning shears contaminated by sap from an infected plant or repotting into an affected pot. Knives and pots should always be sterilized after use. There is no cure for viruses and plants should be destroyed. Several firms offer tests for viruses, and kits that growers can use themselves are now available.

Physiological Damage

Not all marks on orchid leaves are caused by disease. Brown marks can be caused by sun scorch; these are unsightly and remain until the leaf is shed. Yellowing of leaves can be caused by too bright light or by mineral deficiency, when the discoloration tends to be more blotchy, with the veins often remaining green. The commonest mineral deficiencies are magnesium and iron. These can be treated by magnesium sulfate (epsom salts) or iron sequestrene, both of which are readily available from garden centers. Sprinkle a teaspoonful on the surface of the compost and water it in.

Cold water on leaves, particularly in winter, can cause black spotting—new leaves appearing in spring will be unmarked. Black leaf tips are usually a sign of a build-up of mineral salts in the compost. Trim these off as they look unsightly.

New leaves sometimes display horizontal corrugations; this is most prevalent in *Miltoniopsis* but also occurs in other genera. It is caused by the compost being too dry and the humidity being low. Sadly, these folds remain for the lifetime of the leaf in question.

4 CONSERVATION AND PROPAGATION

Conservation

A section on conservation has become almost obligatory in all orchid books. Most people know that orchids are covered by the Convention on International Trade in Endangered Species (CITES), which covers the movement of orchids from one country to another. Most orchids are on Appendix 2 and require import permits and export permits from the country of origin. All slipper orchids and several other species are on Appendix 1, where restrictions are severe. Information can be obtained on the website www.cites.org.

Most countries also have their own laws concerning protection of orchids (and other rare plants) within the country. Obviously, these vary from one country to another and sadly, in some cases they are honored more in the breach than in the observance.

Orchids were brought into CITES in an attempt to stop overcollection for the horticultural trade; species of *Paphiopedilum* in particular were being collected to extinction. Although overcollection has severely affected some species, for orchids in general, loss of habitat is the commonest and most serious threat. The destruction of rain forest is what comes first to most people's minds, but in the developed world, housing and shopping developments, and road and airport building have meant that many orchids have vanished under tarmac.

There are two basic ways in which orchids can be conserved: *in-situ* and *ex-situ*. In the latter, orchids are grown in an artificial situation such as a botanic garden or a private collection. If species become endangered or even extinct in the wild, at least they may survive in cultivation and, if conditions change, may eventually be returned to their original habitats. In *in-situ* conservation, plants are conserved in their natural habitats. This is the ideal situation, but we do not live in an ideal world. There is little point in returning plants to the wild if they are going to be dug up or buried under concrete or their trees felled. All growers can help *ex-situ* conservation by growing their orchid species as well as possible, propagating them, and passing plants around. The more people who are growing a particular species, the more likely it is to survive.

Propagation by Division

Orchids can be propagated in a number of ways. The simplest of these is division, certainly for plants with sympodial growth. When a plant has been in the same pot for a year or two, quite often the stems or pseudobulbs in the center will die, with those around the edges making new

Coelogyne cristata, seen here in habitat in Nepal, requires cool to intermediate growing conditions and, because it has a sympodial growth habit, can be propagated by division.

growth. When this plant is repotted and dead matter is cut away, it will have naturally divided itself into two or more plants. Plants where there are no dead pseudobulbs can still be divided but do not make the divisions too small; most new plants should have at least three growths.

Monopodial orchids are less easy to divide. Those that branch at the base and form clumps are not too difficult, and plants such as vandas, which produce roots along the stem, can be cut in half. This is often done when a plant becomes too tall and straggly. The top part is potted up in the usual way and with luck, the basal part will branch and form a new shoot.

Propagation by Backbulbs

Cymbidiums and some other orchids can be propagated from leafless backbulbs, as long as there is a resting bud at the base. Remove loose sheaths, let the pseudobulb dry for a day or two, then plant it for about a third of its length in sharp sand or perlite, and keep it moist and cool. In a few months, a new shoot should have appeared. When roots have also developed (the pseudobulb will then feel firm in the compost), the orchid can be potted up in the usual way.

Propagation by Keikis

A keiki is the term given to a young plant that develops on an inflorescence or sometimes on top of a pseudobulb. Some kinds of orchid are particularly prone to doing this. *Dendrobium nobile* and its hybrids develop plantlets along the stem instead of flowers if the plants are not kept cool and dry after buds have set; *D. kingianum* tends to do the same. Sometimes *Phalaenopsis* species and hybrids produce one or two keikis among the flowers. If these are to be used for propagation, they should be left in place until the roots are 2–3 cm long and growing actively. They should then be cut off using a sterile knife and potted up as usual. If the roots are allowed to grow too long, they are less likely to become established.

Propagation by Seed

Orchids are pollinated when pollinia are transferred from the anther of one orchid to the stigma of (usually) another orchid of the same species. In the wild, pollination of almost all orchids is carried out by insects, and the flowers have many adaptations, some bizarre, to ensure this. In a greenhouse, the grower has to take the insect's place. Using something like a cocktail stick, it is not difficult to transfer pollen from one flower to another. It is always better to involve two different plants, but this is not always possible. While some orchids are self-sterile, others are not and it is always worth an attempt with a rare orchid. If pollination has been successful, the ovary starts to swell. If it soon turns orange and remains soft, the capsule will be empty. If the ovary does not start to change color until it has been on the plant for several months, that is a sign that it is starting to ripen. If it is harvested then, wrapped in tissue paper, and kept in a warm place, it should soon split and the seed can be collected.

Dendrobium kingianum with a keiki. E. la Croix

As already mentioned, orchid seeds are like dust and consist of little more than an embryo with a few cells surrounding it. In the wild, they must have the presence of mycorrhizal fungi to provide the nutrients they need to develop. In cultivation, seeds are sown on nutrient gel in sterile conditions. This requires a lot of patience and attention to detail, and while some amateur growers are successful, most pass their seed to a commercial firm. Young plants in flask are exempt from CITES regulations (although they may need a phytosanitary certificate) so this is an easier way of bringing plants in from another country. Before this method of artificial propagation was developed, growers had some success by scattering seed around the base of the parent plant or, I believe, sometimes on a moss-covered brick. All the 19th-century hybrids must have been raised in this way.

Meristem Propagation

If someone wants to propagate a particular form or clone of an orchid, this must be done by vegetative means as seed-produced plants are likely to show considerable variation. Meristem propagation, which involves multiplying a growing point in similar sterile conditions to when seed is sown, has meant that desirable cultivars can be multiplied very cheaply. Meristem propagation, however, is much more widely used for hybrids than species.

5 A-Z OF ORCHIDS

Acampe Lindley

TRIBE: Vandeae
SUBTRIBE: Aeridinae
ETYMOLOGY: From Greek *akampes*, rigid, presumably referring to the brittle flowers
DISTRIBUTION: 6 species in India, Southeast Asia, China, tropical Africa, and Madagascar

Robust epiphytic, occasionally lithophytic, monopodial plants with stout roots and branched or unbranched, woody stems, often forming large clumps. Leaves distichous, leathery or almost fleshy. Inflorescences axillary, branched or unbranched. Flowers small to medium-sized, often scented, usually yellow and brown; sepals and petals similar; lip saccate or spurred. Pollinia 4, in 2 unequal pairs.

CULTIVATION: Because of their size, species of *Acampe* are best accommodated in a basket, in a coarse bark-based mix. They require bright light and warm or intermediate temperatures, with plenty of water while in growth. Keep them drier in winter while they are resting.

Acampe carinata (Griffith) Panigrahi

SYN. *Acampe papillosa* (Lindley) Lindley

Large epiphyte to ca. 90 cm tall, with roots arising from nodes. Stem long, branched, scandent. Leaves 7–15 × 1–2 cm, oblong. Inflorescence densely many-flowered, 3–3.5 cm long. Flowers scented, ca. 1–1.5 cm across; sepals and petals yellow spotted with brown; lip trilobed, papillose in the basal half, white with purplish spots at base; spur conical.

Tropical low altitude woodland, ca. 300 m (1000 ft.)

Nepal to Thailand

Acampe ochracea (Lindley) Hochreutiner

SYN. *Acampe dentata* Lindley

Robust epiphyte with stout roots. Stems woody, to 1 m long. Leaves thick, recurved, to 22 × 2.5 cm. Inflorescence branched, loosely many-flowered, to 22 cm long. Flowers 6–12 mm across, scented, pale yellow blotched with brown, the lip white with brownish marks; spur cylindrical, 3–4 mm long.

Tropical low altitude woodland, ca. 500 m (1650 ft.)

Sri Lanka, northeastern India to Vietnam

Acampe rigida (Buchanan-Hamilton ex J. E. Smith) P. F. Hunt

Stem erect, 60–90 cm long, branched or unbranched, often forming large clumps. Leaves 15–45 × 3.5–5 cm, stiff, strap-shaped. Inflorescence 5–20 cm long, branched, densely many-flowered. Flowers fleshy, scented, 12–18 mm across; sepals and petals yellow, barred with red-brown; lip white, spotted with red; spur short.

Tropical woodland, 1200–1250 m (4000–4100 ft.)

India to Malaysia

SIMILAR SPECIES: *Acampe praemorsa* (Roxburgh) Blatter & McCann, from India to Myanmar and Sri Lanka, differs only in minor details as does *A. pachyglossa* Reichenbach f. (syn. *A. renschiana* Reichenbach f.) from tropical Africa and Madagascar.

Acanthephippium Blume

TRIBE: Collabieae
ETYMOLOGY: From Greek, *akantha*, thorn, and *ephippion*, saddle, referring to the saddle-shaped lip
DISTRIBUTION: About 12 species from tropical Asia, as far east as Fiji

Sympodial terrestrial orchids closely related to *Calanthe* and *Phaius* with big ovoid pseudobulbs and thick roots. Leaves apical, usually several (most often 3), large, petiolate, pleated. Inflorescences racemose, few-flowered, much shorter than the leaves. Flowers showy, cup-shaped, with a waxy texture, usually yellowish or pink, often scented; sepals joined, enclosing the petals and lip, petals free, lip trilobed. Column short and stout, with a long foot that is joined to the lateral sepals forming a mentum; pollinia 8.

CULTIVATION: Plants should be grown at intermediate temperatures in pans, in a well-drained terrestrial compost, in a shady situation. They should be watered and fertilized freely while in growth. While resting, plants should be kept drier and cooler. They are said to dislike disturbance and so should only be repotted when really necessary.

Acanthephippium javanicum Blume

Pseudobulbs large, almost cylindrical, to 25 cm long, 2- to 4-leaved. Leaves elliptic or oblong, to 60 × 18 cm. Inflorescence 3- to 6-flowered. Flowers ca. 5 cm long, 3.5 cm across, pale yellow and pink, with red streaks inside; lip with a basal callus of yellow, toothed keels.

In deep shade in forest on rich soil, 400–1100 m (1320–3600 ft.)

Borneo, Java, peninsular Malaysia, Sumatra

SIMILAR SPECIES: *Acanthephippium splendidum* J. J. Smith from New Guinea.

Acanthephippium mantinianum Lindley & Cogniaux

Large plants with conical pseudobulbs to 15 × 5 cm. Leaves to 60 × 15 cm, thin-textured. Inflorescence erect, to 15 cm long, up to 6-flowered. Flowers scented, ca. 2.5 cm across, yellow, striped with red, with a golden yellow lip.

Shady situations in mountainous regions, 500–1500 m (1650–5000 ft.)

Philippines

Acanthephippium striatum Lindley

Pseudobulbs tapering, to 20 cm tall. Leaves 2–3, elliptic, to 26 × 10 cm. Inflorescence 3–4 cm tall, 2- to 5-flowered. Flowers rather thin-textured, ca. 3 cm long, white or pale pink, streaked with red or violet inside; lip with a basal callus of smooth lamellae.

Heavy shade in forest on rich soil, 650–1650 m (2150–5410 ft.)

Borneo, Bhutan, India, peninsular Malaysia, Vietnam

SIMILAR SPECIES: *Acanthephippium sylhetense* Lindley, which occurs from India to Japan, is similar but larger, with scented yellow flowers spotted with red.

Acampe carinata

Acanthephippium splendidum. P. O'Byrne

Acanthephippium sylhetense. R. Parsons

Acanthephippium mantinianum. J. Cootes

Acianthera Scheidweiler

TRIBE: Epidendreae
SUBTRIBE: Pleurothallidinae
ETYMOLOGY: From Greek *akis*, point or beak, and *anthera*, anther
DISTRIBUTION: More than 200 species from Mexico, Central and South America and the Antilles, with most in Brazil

Acianthera is often treated as a subgenus of *Pleurothallis*, but DNA evidence suggests that it is a genus in its own right. Plants are tufted or creeping epiphytes, lithophytes, or sometimes terrestrials, the stems enclosed in sheaths, lacking an annulus, 1-leafed at apex. Inflorescences 1- to several-flowered, usually apical but sometimes arising directly from the rhizome. Flowers resupinate; sepals usually fleshy, pubescent on outside; lateral sepals joined at least to halfway, sometimes to the apex, occasionally forming a tube with the dorsal sepal; petals short; lip thick, sometimes with a basal claw hinged to the column-foot.

CULTIVATION: Species of *Acianthera* can be grown in a fine bark or a sphagnum-perlite mixture, or mounted on a slab of bark of tree fern. They require cool or intermediate temperatures (depending on altitude of origin), shade, high humidity, and good ventilation throughout the year.

Acianthera johnsonii (Ames) Pridgeon & M. W. Chase

SYN. *Pleurothallis johnsonii* Ames

Plants shortly creeping or forming clumps. Stems 3–11 cm tall. Leaf erect, elliptic, to 14 × 5 cm. Inflorescence 3–8 cm long, few-flowered. Flowers mottled purple, lip yellow, mottled with purple; sepals to 16 mm long.

Epiphytic, or terrestrial in cloud forest, 1200–1600 m (4000–5300 ft.)

Mexico, Central America

Acianthera prolifera (Herbert ex Lindley) Pridgeon & M. W. Chase

SYN. *Pleurothallis prolifera* Herbert ex Lindley

Rhizome creeping; stems to 20 cm long. Leaves to 8 × 4 cm, leathery, ovate. Inflorescence few- to many-flowered, shorter than leaves. Flowers purple or maroon, sepals 9 mm long.

Epiphytic in cloud forest, ca. 1500 m (5000 ft.)

Brazil, Guyana, Venezuela

Acianthera sicaria (Lindley) Pridgeon & M. W. Chase

SYN. *Acianthera alpina* (Ames) Pridgeon & Chase; *Pleurothallis sicaria* Lindley, *P. alpina* Ames

Stems tufted, 10–30 cm long. Leaves 6–13 × 1–3 cm, ovate, the margins running like wings on to the stem. Inflorescence 2–3 cm long, few-flowered. Flowers yellow, green, or brownish with red or purple stripes; sepals to 12 mm long.

Epiphytic in rain forest and cloud forest, 600–2000 m (2000–6600 ft.)

Central and South America, Trinidad

Acianthus R. Brown

MOSQUITO ORCHIDS, MAYFLY ORCHIDS
TRIBE: Diurideae
SUBTRIBE: Acianthinae
ETYMOLOGY: From Greek *akis*, point, and *anthos*, flower
DISTRIBUTION: About 20 species in Australia, New Zealand, New Caledonia, and the Solomon Islands

Small, terrestrial orchids with globose tuberoids and a single heart-shaped or ovate leaf near the base of the stem. Most species form colonies. Inflorescences erect, unbranched, few- to several-flowered, arising from between the leaf lobes. Flowers small, rather dull-colored, insectlike and pollinated by small flies; dorsal sepal erect or arched, lateral sepals and petals spreading; lip entire, usually heart-shaped, with 2 nectar-secreting glands at the base. Pollinia 4.

CULTIVATION: In the wild, most species grow in shady situations with high humidity, at least in the growing season. Most of the colony-forming species grow well in cultivation. They should be planted in a group in a pan with a gritty, free-draining, slightly acid, loam-based compost and kept in a cool house or alpine house. Plants are dormant in summer, when they should be kept on the dry side but not allowed to dry out completely. The tubers sprout in late summer, produce the leaf, and then flower. Plants should be watered freely when in growth, that is, from late summer to late spring. Repot and divide if necessary when dormant.

Acianthus caudatus R. Brown

MAYFLY ORCHID

Leaf 3–4 cm long, heart-shaped, dark green above, purple below. Inflorescence to 25 cm long, 1- to 9-flowered. Flowers dark purple with an unpleasant smell; sepals 30–35 mm long, tapering to long, narrow points; petals small, spreading; lip ovate, to 7 × 4 mm. Flowering late summer–autumn. This species is said to be more difficult to grow than most of the colony-forming species.

Open forest

Endemic to central and southeastern Australia

Acianthus exsertus R. Brown

MOSQUITO ORCHID

A colony-forming species. Leaf to 4 × 2.5 cm, dark green above, purple or green below. Inflorescence to 20 cm long, to 20-flowered. Flowers small, greenish or purplish; sepals ca. 10 mm long, narrow, the dorsal erect, the laterals deflexed; lip ca. 5 × 4 mm, ovate, with a rough line running from base to apex. Flowering spring–summer. Easily grown.

Forest, especially near the coast on sandy soil

Endemic to temperate central and eastern Australia, including Tasmania

Acianthera johnsonii

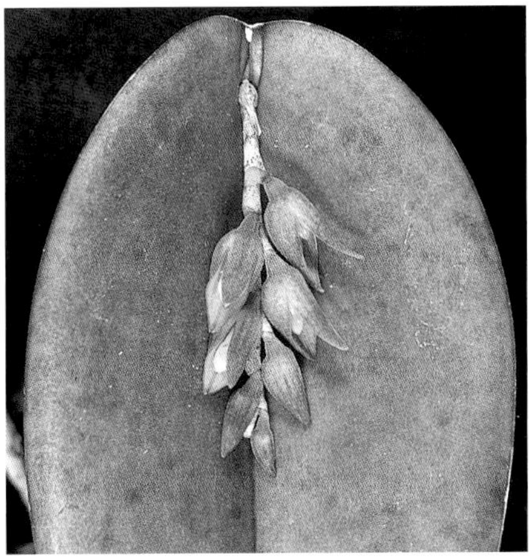
Acianthera prolifera

Acianthera sicaria

Acianthus caudatus. R. Parsons

Acianthus fornicatus R. Brown
PIXIE CAPS
Leaf to 4 × 2 cm, heart-shaped, dark green above, purple below. Inflorescence to 20 cm long, to 14-flowered. Flowers small, grayish green to purplish; sepals ca. 10 mm long, the dorsal broad, ovate, laterals very slender, deflexed, sometimes crossing below lip; lip dark purple, the margins warty. Easily grown.

Forms large colonies in moist forest

Endemic to eastern Australia

Acineta Lindley

TRIBE: Maxillarieae
SUBTRIBE: Stanhopeinae
ETYMOLOGY: From Greek *akinetes*, immobile, referring to the lip, which is fused to the column
DISTRIBUTION: About 20 species in tropical America from Mexico to Peru

Large epiphytic, lithophytic, or rarely terrestrial plants; pseudobulbs clustered, laterally compressed, ovoid to cylindrical, usually grooved or wrinkled, 1- to 4-leaved. Leaves thick, ribbed or pleated, stalked. Inflorescences basal, usually pendent, unbranched, with large floral bracts. Flowers large and showy, waxy in texture, scented, cream to yellow or maroon, marked with red; sepals incurved; lip trilobed, fleshy, fixed to the column-foot, concave or saccate at the base; side lobes erect, larger than the midlobe; disc with simple or complex calli. Pollinia 2.

Many species look very similar, and detailed examination of the lip is necessary to distinguish them.

CULTIVATION: Because of the pendent inflorescences, plants should be grown in baskets, like *Stanhopea* species. They require cool to intermediate conditions and moderate shade. They should be planted in a coarse bark-based compost, and watered and fertilized freely while in growth. While resting, they should be moved to a brighter position and sprayed only enough to stop the pseudobulbs from shriveling.

Acineta alticola C. Schweinfurth
Pseudobulbs to 17 × 7 cm. Leaves to 58 × 10 cm. Inflorescence pendent, sometimes suberect at first, 17–33 cm long, to 15-flowered. Flowers yellow, the petals sometimes with brownish spots; lip with a simple, fleshy callus.

Epiphytic or occasionally terrestrial in open forest 500–2500 m (1650–8250 ft.), sometimes as low as 100 m (330 ft.)

Venezuela

SIMILAR SPECIES: *Acineta erythroxantha* Reichenbach f., from the Andes in Colombia and Venezuela, has yellow flowers with a complex callus on the lip.

Acineta chrysantha (Morren) Lindley & Paxton
SYN. *Acineta warszewiczii* Klotzsch
Pseudobulbs ca. 8 × 4 cm, ovoid, usually 4-leaved. Leaves to 45 × 7 cm. Flowers fleshy, cup-shaped, long-lasting, vanilla-scented, to 6 cm across, yellow, the petals dotted with red; lip golden-yellow dotted with red, saccate at the base.

Cloud forest, 1600–2000 m (5300–6000 ft.)

Costa Rica, Guatemala, Peru

Acineta superba (Kunth) Reichenbach f.
Pseudobulbs to 13 × 5.5 cm, ovoid or ellipsoid. Leaves to 65 × 12 cm. Inflorescence 20–70 cm long, to 15-flowered. Flowers to 8 cm diameter, cup-shaped, variable in color, usually golden-yellow to yellow-ochre with maroon dots, or yellow-bronze heavily marked with red or brown; lip fleshy with a complex callus.

Cloud forest, 1800–1900 m (6000–6300 ft.)

Panama to Suriname and Ecuador

Ada Lindley

TRIBE: Maxillarieae
SUBTRIBE: Oncidiinae
ETYMOLOGY: Named for Ada of Caria, sister of Artemis, in Greek mythology
DISTRIBUTION: 16 species in Central and South America

Sympodial epiphytes and lithophytes; pseudobulbs usually laterally flattened with leafy bracts, 1- or 2-leaved at apex. Leaves dark green, linear or strap-shaped, folded at the base. Inflorescences axillary, racemose, with papery bracts. Flowers not opening wide but often showy, green, brown, yellowish, or bright orange-red; sepals free, linear-lanceolate, pointing forwards; petals similar but smaller; lip entire, acuminate, recurved, with a callus of 2 ridges, lacking a spur. Pollinia 2, attached to a heart-shaped stipes, viscidium 1.

The species with red and orange flowers are thought to be pollinated by hummingbirds.

CULTIVATION: Species of *Ada* are usually grown in pots. They require cool to intermediate conditions, with high humidity, good air movement, and plenty of water while in growth and flowering and a drier rest. Most flower in winter or spring.

Ada aurantiaca Lindley
SYN. *Ada lehmannii* Rolfe
Pseudobulbs to 10 cm long, 1- or 2-leaved at the apex. Leaves to 30 cm long. Inflorescence to 35 cm long, arching, 7- to 18-flowered. Flowers semi-tubular, nodding, bright orange to red, about 3.5 cm long. The form previously known as *A. lehmannii* has a white lip.

Cloud forest, 1500–2500 m (5000–8250 ft.)

Colombia, Venezuela

SIMILAR SPECIES: *Ada bennettiorum* Dodson from Peru has bright red flowers.

Aerangis Reichenbach f.

TRIBE: Vandeae
SUBTRIBE: Aerangidinae
ETYMOLOGY: From Greek *aer*, air, and

angos, vessel, probably referring to the spur

DISTRIBUTION: About 50 species in Africa, Madagascar, and the Mascarene Islands with 1 species also in Sri Lanka

Small to medium-sized epiphytic, occasionally lithophytic, plants; stems short to long and woody; roots numerous, often thick and fleshy. Leaves distichous, thick-textured, often oblanceolate, bilobed at the apex, sometimes scattered with small black dots. Inflorescences unbranched, axillary, long or short, few- to many-flowered. Flowers white to cream, sometimes tinged with green, yellow, or salmon-pink, usually night-scented; sepals and petals free, subsimilar, usually lanceolate and acute, spreading, reflexed or less often cup-shaped; lip entire, often similar to the sepals and petals, with a long or short, pendent spur.

CULTIVATION: In the wild, most species grow in warm, humid, shady situations and do well in intermediate conditions but there are exceptions, which are mentioned in the species descriptions. All grow and look better when mounted but those with thin roots, such as *Aerangis hyaloides*, need frequent spraying.

Aerangis arachnopus

(Reichenbach f.) Schlechter

Stem short. Leaves to 20 × 5.5 cm, oblanceolate, unequally and obtusely bilobed at the apex. Raceme pendent, 30–60 cm long, rather loosely to about 15-flowered. Flowers white, strongly pink-tinged; sepals 14–18 × 3 mm, spreading; petals shorter, reflexed; lip 12–14 × 2–3 mm, acuminate, deflexed, spur 6–7 cm long.

Epiphytic in shade in lowland evergreen forest

West and Central Africa

Aerangis articulata (Reichenbach f.) Schlechter

SYN. *Aerangis calligera* (Reichenbach f.) Garay

Acineta superba. J. Stewart

Ada aurantiaca

Aerangis arachnopus. E. la Croix

Stem to 30 cm long; leaves to 15 × 5 cm, dark green, rather fleshy, oblong to oblanceolate. Raceme 15–25 cm long, to about 18-flowered. Flowers white; sepals and petals 12–20 × 4–5 mm, elliptic; lip 12–20 × 5 mm, oblong, acute; spur 10–20 cm long; anther-cap with a beak in center.

Epiphytic in humid evergreen forest, 0–1400 m (4600 ft.)

Madagascar, Comoro Islands

SIMILAR SPECIES: *Aerangis modesta* (Hooker f.) Schlechter, from Madagascar and the Comoro Islands, is slightly smaller and the apical flowers of the raceme open first. *Aerangis stylosa* (Rolfe) Schlechter, also from Madagascar and the Comoro Islands, has gray-green leaves, often with red margins.

Aerangis biloba (Lindley) Schlechter

Leaves obovate, bilobed at apex, to 18 cm long, 3–6 cm wide near tip, dark green with black dots. Raceme arching to pendent, 10–40 cm long, to 10-flowered. Flowers white, 3–4 cm across; spur pinkish, 5–6 cm long. Flowering autumn–winter.

Epiphytic in forest and woodland

West Africa

Aerangis brachycarpa (A. Richard) Durand & Schinz

Stem usually short. Leaves several, to 25 × 6 cm, obovate, rather fleshy, dark green often dotted with black. Racemes arching or pendent, to 40 cm long, up to 12-flowered. Flowers white, sometimes slightly pink-tinged; sepals and petals 20–45 × 2–8 mm, narrowly lanceolate, acuminate, the lateral sepals and petals reflexed; lip 20–45 × 5–10 mm, lanceolate, acuminate, deflexed; spur straight, 12–20 cm long; column slender, to 8 mm long. Flowering in autumn.

Epiphytic in forest, 1500–2300 m (5000–7600 ft.)

Widespread in East, Central, and southwestern tropical Africa

SIMILAR SPECIES: *Aerangis confusa* J. Stewart, from Kenya and Tanzania, has smaller flowers and a shorter spur (4–6 cm)

Aerangis citrata (Thouars) Schlechter

Short-stemmed plants with fine roots. Leaves elliptic, to 12 × 3.5 cm, bright, glossy green. Raceme to 25 cm long, 12- to 18-flowered. Flowers all facing the same way, flat, 15–18 mm diameter, creamy white to pale yellow; sepals and petals ovate; lip fan-shaped, emarginate, 8–10 mm long, 7–10 mm wide near apex; spur 3 cm long, swollen at apex.

Epiphytic in humid evergreen forest, 0–1500 m (5000 ft.)

Madagascar

Aerangis distincta J. Stewart & la Croix

Leaves ± triangular, deeply bilobed at apex, the lobes acute. Racemes arching or pendent, to 25 cm long, 2- to 5-flowered. Flowers white, the tips of the sepals and petals pink; sepals 40–65 mm long, lanceolate, acuminate; petals similar but ca. 10 mm shorter; lip to 45 mm long, 9 mm across near base, constricted at about halfway into a long, narrow tip; spur pink, straight, 15–23 cm long. This species has the largest flowers of any in genus *Aerangis*. Flowering summer or autumn.

Epiphytic in riverine forest, 650–1750 m (2150–5800 ft.)

Malawi

SIMILAR SPECIES: *Aerangis carnea* J. Stewart, from southern Tanzania and northern Malawi, has smaller flowers with a much shorter spur (5–6 cm). Plants offered for sale under this name are almost always *A. distincta*. *Aerangis splendida* J. Stewart & la Croix, from Malawi and Zambia, has larger, glossy dark green leaves obtusely bilobed at the tip, large, pure white flowers, and a long, coiled spur.

Aerangis ellisii (Reichenbach f.) Schlechter

SYN. *Aerangis alata* H. Perrier, *A. caulescens* Schlechter, *A. platyphylla* Schlechter

A large species with woody stems up to 80 cm long, becoming pendent. Roots numerous, stout. Leaves to 15 cm long, oblong, light green, slightly fleshy. Racemes spreading to pendent, to 40 cm long, 12- to 18-flowered. Flowers white, sometimes tinged with salmon, the sepals often winged on the back; sepals and petals reflexed, 15–22 mm long, ovate; lip similar, spur straight, 11–18 cm long. Flowering in autumn.

Var. *grandiflora* J. Stewart has larger flowers and a spur 18–27 cm long.

Epiphytic in humid evergreen forest or lithophytic on rocky outcrops, 300–1800 m (1000–6000 ft.)

Madagascar

SIMILAR SPECIES: Plants offered for sale as *Aerangis cryptodon* (Reichenbach f.) Schlechter are usually *A. ellisii*. *Aerangis cryptodon* has 2 teeth in the mouth of the spur and the top of the column has 2 toothed wings that overtop the anther.

Aerangis fastuosa (Reichenbach f.) Schlechter

A small species with short stem and fine roots. Leaves to 8 × 4 cm, oblong, fleshy, dark green. Racemes 2–6 cm long, to 6-flowered. Flowers glistening white, not opening wide, large for the size of plant; sepals and petals 20–30 × 10 mm, oblong to almost round, obtuse; lip similar but slightly longer, spur 6–8 cm long, sometimes coiled.

Epiphytic in humid evergreen forest, 1000–1500 m (3300–5000 ft.)

Madagascar

Aerangis hyaloides (Reichenbach f.) Schlechter

SYN. *Aerangis pumilio* Schlechter

Stem short, roots fine. Leaves to 7

Aerangis articulata

Aerangis biloba

Aerangis splendida. E. la Croix

Aerangis ellisii

Aerangis fastuosa

× 2 cm, elliptic, glossy dark green. Racemes 5–7 cm long, 5- to 20-flowered. Flowers glistening white, cup-shaped; sepals to 8 × 1.5 mm; petals similar, slightly wider; lip to 8 × 2 mm; spur 5–12 mm, swollen at apex.

Epiphytic on small trees in evergreen forest, 1000 m (3300 ft.)

Madagascar

Aerangis kirkii (Reichenbach f.) Schlechter

Stem short. Leaves to 15 × 3 cm, narrowly oblanceolate, the apex deeply bilobed, dark gray-green, leathery, often longitudinally ridged. Racemes arching or pendent, to 17 cm long, up to 6-flowered. Flowers white, sometimes tinged with pink; sepals spreading, 18–15 × 4–7 mm, ovate-lanceolate, acuminate; petals smaller, also usually spreading; lip to 20 × 8 mm, oblong, apiculate or acuminate; spur 6–7.5 cm long, pendent. In cultivation, this species does better in warm conditions.

Epiphytic on small trees and bushes in coastal and riverine forest, 0–450 m (1500 ft.)

Kenya, Tanzania, Mozambique

Aerangis kotschyana (Reichenbach f.) Schlechter

Stem usually short; roots stout, to 9 mm diameter. Leaves to 20 × 8 cm, obovate, often with wavy margins, the apex unequally bilobed, dull, dark green often with black dots. Raceme arching or pendent, to 46 cm long, to 20-flowered. Flowers white, pinkish in center, ca. 5 cm across; sepals spreading; petals reflexed; lip fiddle-shaped, to 25 × 23 mm, with 2 crests in the mouth of the spur; spur pinkish, 12–25 cm long, with a corkscrew twist. Flowering autumn–winter. Plants do better grown in intermediate to warm conditions.

Epiphytic in woodland, 450–1350 m (1500–4500 ft.)

Widespread in tropical Africa

Aerangis luteoalba (Kraenzlin) Schlechter var. *rhodosticta* (Kraenzlin) J. Stewart

Small plants with slender roots. Leaves to 15 × 1.5 cm, narrowly strap-shaped, glossy dark green. Racemes arching to pendent, to 35 cm long, the flowers all in the same plane. Flowers creamy white, 2–3 cm across; sepals and petals spreading; lip to 20 × 15 mm, obovate; spur 2–4 cm long, incurved, slightly thickened towards apex; column short and stout, bright red. The typical variety, from DR Congo, has a white column but does not seem to be in cultivation.

Epiphytic on twigs and small branches, often in riverine forest, 1250–2200 m (4100–7260 ft.)

Widespread in East and Central Africa

Aerangis macrocentra (Schlechter) Schlechter

SYN. *Aerangis clavigera* H. Perrier

Stems short. Leaves to 20 × 3.5 cm, lanceolate, dark green or gray-green. Racemes pendent, 12- to 30-flowered. Flowers slightly drooping, white with a pinkish brown spur; sepals and petals reflexed, to 10 × 4 mm, oblong, obtuse; lip broader, oblong, acute; spur 5–6 cm long, swollen at apex.

Epiphytic in humid evergreen forest and moss forest, 0–1500 m (5000 ft.)

Madagascar

Aerangis mystacidii (Reichenbach f.) Schlechter

Short-stemmed plants, variable in size. Leaves 4–23 × 1–5 cm, oblanceolate, apex unequally bilobed, dark green, leathery. Racemes arching or pendent, to 20 cm long, few- to many-flowered. Flowers white, often tinged with pink in the center and on the spur; sepals 7–14 × 2–5 mm, oblong, apiculate; petals similar, strongly reflexed; lip 7–14 × 3–8 mm, oblong, acute; spur 6–8 cm long, incurved, slightly swollen towards apex.

Evergreen forest, often riverine forest, high rainfall woodland, 60–1800 m (200–6000 ft.)

East Africa from Malawi to South Africa

SIMILAR SPECIES: *Aerangis appendiculata* (De Wildeman) Schlechter, from southeastern and south-central Africa, is smaller in all parts with a spur 4–6 cm long. *Aerangis mooreana* (Rolfe ex Sander) P. J. Cribb & J. Stewart, from Madagascar and the Comoro Islands, has flowers similar to larger specimens of *A. mystacidii*, but the dorsal sepal is markedly smaller than the other floral parts, the spur is 7–9 cm long, and the flowers may be white or pink. Larger-flowered specimens of *A. mystacidii* are sometimes offered for sale as *A. mooreana*.

Aerangis punctata J. Stewart

Very small plants with flattened, verrucose roots. Leaves 2–4, to 3.5 × 12 mm, elliptic, dull gray-green dotted with silver. Inflorescence 1-flowered. Flowers white, sometimes tinged brownish, ca. 4 cm across, large for the size of plant; sepals and petals spreading; lip to 22 × 9 mm, ovate, acuminate; spur pendent, 10–12 cm long, funnel-shaped at the mouth, then slender. This little species should always be mounted on bark or a branch.

Epiphytic in humid, evergreen forest, 1000–1500 m (3300–5000 ft.)

Madagascar

SIMILAR SPECIES: *Aerangis monantha* Schlechter, also from Madagascar, is often confused with *A. punctata*. It is also very small but the roots are not verrucose, and the leaves are glossy and bronze-green without silver dots. It has long been known as *A. curnowiana*. *Aerangis fuscata* (Reichenbach f.) Schlechter (syn. *A. umbonata* Schlechter), from Madagascar, has

Aerangis luteoalba var. *rhodosticta*

Aerangis mystacidii. E. la Croix

fine roots, reddish-green leaves that can be up to 8 cm long, and larger flowers, 5–6 cm across.

Aerangis thomsonii (Rolfe) Schlechter

Stem woody, 10–100 cm long; roots numerous, to 9 mm diameter. Leaves up to 20, distichous, strap-shaped, to 28 × 4.5 cm, dark green. Raceme arching, to 30 cm long, 4- to 10-flowered. Flowers white; lateral sepals and petals reflexed; sepals to 32 mm long, lanceolate or elliptic; lip to 25 × 8 mm, elliptic-lanceolate; spur pendent, flexuous, 10–15 cm long. This high-altitude species requires cool, airy conditions in cultivation.

Epiphytic on trunks and branches in heavy shade in upland forest, 1600–2600 m (5300–8600 ft.)

Ethiopia, Kenya, Tanzania, Uganda

Aerangis verdickii

(De Wildeman) Schlechter

Short-stemmed plants with many fleshy roots to 9 mm diameter. Leaves to 20 × 5 cm, fleshy, pale gray-green, sometimes purple-tinged, the margins usually undulate. Racemes to 40 cm long, 4- to 15-flowered. Flowers white, sometimes green-tinged, very strongly scented at night; sepals 11–22 × 3–8 mm, ovate or oblong, the lateral sepals and petals reflexed; lip 11–20 × 5–9 mm, oblong, with 2 ridges in the mouth of the spur; spur 12–20 cm long, pendent, slightly flexuous, slender but slightly thickened towards apex. In cultivation, this species requires more light than most species of *Aerangis* and should be kept rather dry when not in active growth.

Epiphytic, occasionally lithophytic, in woodland, usually in hot, rather

Aerangis punctata

dry areas, 100–1800 m (330–6000 ft.)

Widespread in eastern and south-central Africa

SIMILAR SPECIES: *Aerangis somalensis* (Schlechter) Schlechter, from East Africa, also grows in dry areas but has darker gray-green leaves with darker reticulate veining, a slightly smaller flowers, and a spur 10–15 cm long.

Aeranthes Lindley

TRIBE: Vandeae

SUBTRIBE: Angraecinae

ETYMOLOGY: From Greek *aer*, air, and *anthos*, flower

DISTRIBUTION: Madagascar, Comoros Islands, Mascarene Islands, Zimbabwe

Short-stemmed monopodial epiphytes with slender roots. Leaves usually strap-shaped. Inflorescences simple or branched, 1- to many-flowered, usually pendent, the peduncle often long and wiry. Flowers green, yellowish green, or greenish white, rarely white, usually translucent; dorsal sepals and petals free, lateral sepals joined to column-foot; lip entire, attached in front of the mouth of the spur; spur long or short (rarely absent), sometimes swollen at the tip. Column long or short; pollinia, stipites, and viscidia 2.

CULTIVATION: Most species grow well at intermediate to warm temperatures but need shade, high humidity, and good ventilation. Because their fine roots dry out quickly, they are better potted in a fine to medium bark compost, rather than mounted, but the pots must be hung up when the plants are in flower because of the long, pendent inflorescences.

Aeranthes caudata Rolfe

SYN. *Aeranthes imerinensis* H. Perrier

Stem to 15 cm long, covered with old leaf bases. Leaves several, 20–30 × 2.5–3.5 cm, strap-shaped, the edges slightly wavy. Inflorescence pendent, 50–100 cm long, 3- to 8-flowered. Flowers green; sepals 10–12 cm long, including a long, slender tip; petals similar but smaller; lip 5 cm long; spur slender, 1 cm long.

Epiphytic in humid, evergreen forest, 700–1500 m (2300–5000 ft.)

Madagascar, Comoro Islands

SIMILAR SPECIES: *Aeranthes ramosa* Rolfe from Madagascar has smaller, darker green flowers.

Aeranthes grandiflora Lindley

Leaves to 15 × 4 cm, strap-shaped, light green, the edges often wavy. Inflorescence pendent, to 50 cm long, few-flowered, the peduncle covered by dry sheaths. Flowers cream, greenish white, or greenish yellow; sepals and petals ovate at the base, then tapering abruptly into a long, slender acumen; sepals 8–9 cm long including the acumen, 1.5 cm wide at the base, petals slightly smaller; lip 5 cm long, 2 cm wide at the base, with a long acumen; spur 1.5 cm long, swollen at the tip.

Epiphytic in humid, evergreen forest, 0–1200 m (4000 ft.)

Madagascar, Comoro Islands

SIMILAR SPECIES: *Aeranthes arachnites* Lindley has smaller, greener flowers.

Aerides Loureiro

TRIBE: Vandeae

SUBTRIBE: Aeridinae

ETYMOLOGY: From Greek *aer*, air, and *eides*, resembling, referring to the epiphytic habit

DISTRIBUTION: 20–30 species from India through Asia to New Guinea and the Philippines

Monopodial epiphytes, usually large, often with long stems, erect at first but usually becoming pendulous with age; roots numerous, many aerial. Leaves in 2 rows, leathery, strap-shaped. Inflorescences axillary, densely many-flowered, sometimes branched, often numerous. Flowers showy, scented, usually white with pink or purple, occasionally yellow; sepals and petals spreading, the laterals partly joined to the column-foot; lip entire or trilobed, spurred at the base, the spur usually pointing forwards.

CULTIVATION: Because of their numerous aerial roots, plants are usually grown in baskets in an open, coarse epiphyte mix. Most species need bright light and plenty of water and high humidity. The temperature requirements depend on the place of origin but most plants will grow in intermediate to warm conditions.

Aerides houlletiana Reichenbach f.

Medium-sized to large plants. Inflorescence to 40 cm long, pendent, densely many-flowered. Flowers to 25 mm across, scented, yellow-brown with purple markings, lip cream, magenta in center, the midlobe fringed. This is a warm-growing species.

Lowland forest, 0–700 m (2300 ft.)

Cambodia, Thailand, Vietnam

Aerides lawrenciae Reichenbach f.

Large plants to 1 m tall Leaves to 30 × 5 cm, unequally bilobed at the tip. Inflorescence pendulous, to 30 cm long, densely many-flowered. Flowers ca. 4 cm in diameter, the largest in the genus, white, the segments purple-tipped; sepals and petals ± oblong, lip side lobes erect, midlobe rectangular, the edges finely toothed; spur conical, incurved, green.

Epiphytic in bright situations, up to 500 m (1650 ft.)

Philippines (Mindanao Island)

Aerides multiflora Roxburgh

SYN. *Aerides affinis* Lindley

Plants erect or pendent. Stems to 25 cm long. Leaves numerous, to 35 × 2 cm. Inflorescence 15–30 cm long, occasionally branched, densely many-flowered. Flowers scented, 2–3 cm across; sepals and petals white to pinkish purple, the tips sometimes spotted purple; lip light purple; sepals and petals oblong to orbicular; lip clawed, abruptly bent down, convex; side lobes erect, midlobe ovate, callus bilobed, spur ca. 5 mm long, pointing forwards.

Aeranthes caudata

Aeranthes grandiflora

Aeranthes ramosa

Aerides lawrenciae

Aerides houlletiana

Aeranthes arachnites

Aerides multiflora

Epiphytic in tropical and subtropical forest, 200–660 m (660–2170 ft.)
India through Southeast Asia, Java, Philippines

Aerides odorata Loureiro

Plants to 1 m tall. Stems pendent, branched. Leaves 15–30 × 2–5 cm, oblong to strap-shaped. Inflorescences numerous, pendent, unbranched, densely many-flowered. Flowers strongly scented, 15–25 mm across, purple or white, often tipped with purple, spur greenish yellow at tip; lip trilobed, almost surrounding the column, with 2 small appendages near the mouth of the spur; midlobe short, incurved, the margins sometimes finely dentate; spur hornlike, incurved.
Epiphytic in subtropical forest in low valleys, 360–710 m (1200–2350 ft.)
India through Southeast Asia to Philippines

Aerides rosea Loddiges ex Lindley & Paxton

Robust plants with stout stems to 25 cm long. Leaves 15–35 × 2.5–4.5 cm, oblong, bilobed, channeled above and keeled below. Inflorescence occasionally branched, to about 60 cm long, densely many-flowered. Flowers 1.5–4 cm across, white and amethyst-purple, the lip amethyst-purple dotted with white; lip trilobed, ± trowel-shaped; spur funnel-shaped, ca. 4 mm long.
Epiphytic on tree trunks in forest, 1500 m (5000 ft.)
Northeastern India, Myanmar, China, Thailand, Laos, Vietnam

Aganisia Lindley

SYN. *Acacallis* Lindley
TRIBE: Maxillarieae
SUBTRIBE: Zygopetalinae
ETYMOLOGY: From Greek *aganos*, desirable
DISTRIBUTION: 3 species from Trinidad to tropical South America
Small epiphytes with small, 1- to 2-leaved pseudobulbs set well apart on a climbing rhizome. Leaves pleated, petiolate. Inflorescences arising from base of pseudobulb, few- to many-flowered. Flowers bluish to white and yellow; sepals and petals free, spreading, subsimilar; lip trilobed. Column short; pollinia 4.
CULTIVATION: Because of their scandent habit, plants are better mounted but can be grown in a shallow pan in a fairly fine compost. They require intermediate or preferably warm conditions, with shade, high humidity, and good air movement. They should be watered throughout the year but allowed to dry out between waterings.

Aganisia cyanea (Lindley) Reichenbach f.

SYN. *Acacallis cyanea* Lindley
Pseudobulbs ovoid, to 5 cm long, 1- to 2-leaved. Leaves to 20 cm long. Inflorescence longer than leaves, loosely few- to several-flowered. Flowers showy, scented, ca. 6 cm across; sepals and petals lavender-blue; lip kidney-shaped, violet-blue, red-brown in the center.
Epiphytic in lowland forest, often near a river
Brazil, Colombia, Peru, Venezuela

Aganisia pulchella Lindley

SYN. *Aganisia brachypoda* Schlechter
Pseudobulbs slender, 2–3 cm long, 3–5 mm wide. Leaves with 3 prominent veins, lanceolate, to 25 cm long including a petiole to 7 cm long. Inflorescence to 12 cm long, unbranched, loosely 2- to 8-flowered. Flowers showy, 3–4 cm across, sometimes scented, white, the lip purplish at the base with a yellow callus.
Wet forests, 400–1000 m (1320–3300 ft.)
Trinidad to Brazil

Alamania Lexarza

TRIBE: Epidendreae
SUBTRIBE: Laeliinae
ETYMOLOGY: Named for Lucas Alamán (1792–1853), a botanical collector and prominent literary and political figure in Mexico
DISTRIBUTION: 1 species in Mexico
Dwarf plant with creeping rhizome and small, clustered, ovoid pseudobulbs, 2- or 3-leaved at apex. Inflorescence terminal, unbranched. Sepals and petals subequal, narrow, erect or spreading. Lip joined to base of column, similar to sepals, lacking a spur.
CULTIVATION: Grow in pots or mounted in cool (minimum winter temperature 5°C (41°F)), well-ventilated, humid conditions. Keep drier in winter but do not let plants dry out completely.

Alamania punicea Lexarza

SYN. *Epidendrum puniceum* (Lexarza) Reichenbach f.
Leaves oblong-elliptic, leathery or fleshy, to 2.5 × 1 cm. Inflorescence borne on leafless pseudobulbs, 1- to several-flowered. Flowers large for the size of plant, showy, 1–2 cm across, bright red, the lip yellow at the base.
Epiphytic or lithophytic in forest, 1500–2000 m (5000–6600 ft.)
Mexico

Amesiella Garay

TRIBE: Vandeae
SUBTRIBE: Aeridinae
ETYMOLOGY: Named for Oakes Ames (1874–1950), founder of the orchid herbarium at Harvard University
DISTRIBUTION: 3 species from the Philippines, 1 first described in 1907 and the other 2 in 1998 and 1999
Small, short-stemmed epiphytes with fleshy roots. Leaves several, thick-textured. Inflorescences to 5-flowered. Flowers large for the size of plant, white or cream; sepals and petals subsimilar, spreading, the lateral sepals joined to the column-foot; lip trilobed with a long, slender spur. Rostellum trilobed; pollinia 2, stipes and viscidium 1.
CULTIVATION: Plants require intermediate conditions with high humidity but good drainage and air movement.

Aerides odorata

Aganisia cyanea. R. Parsons

Amesiella philippinensis

Alamania punicea. R. Parsons

Amesiella monticola

They can be grown either mounted or potted in a medium bark-based compost.

Amesiella philippinensis (Ames) Garay

SYN. *Angraecum philippinense* Ames

Plants 3–6 cm tall. Leaves to about 7 × 2.5 cm, rather pale green. Inflorescence 3–5 cm long, to 5-flowered. Flowers ca. 6 cm in diameter, creamy white with yellow marks in the throat; spur to 7 cm long.

Epiphytic in forest, 400–1400 m (1320–4600 ft.)

Philippines

SIMILAR SPECIES: *Amesiella monticola* J. E. Cootes & D. P. Banks has glistening white flowers, rarely with yellow marks, a longer spur (to 11 cm), and occurs at higher altitudes in central Luzon Island (1800–2200 m (6000–7260 ft.)). *Amesiella minor* Senghas is smaller in all its parts.

Amitostigma Schlechter

TRIBE: Orchideae

SUBTRIBE: Orchidinae

ETYMOLOGY: From Greek *a*, not, *mitos*, a thread, and *stigma*, stigma, meaning not *Mitostigma*, a name which had been used for a genus in the Asclepiadaceae

DISTRIBUTION: Almost 30 species from China, India, Japan, Korea, Myanmar, and Vietnam

Terrestrial herbs with small, ellipsoid tubers. Leaf usually single, narrowly oblong or elliptic, acute, basal or on lower half of stem. Inflorescences erect, 1- to few-flowered. Flowers white, pink, mauve, purple, rarely yellow, the lip often with deeper purple marks; sepals and petals free; lip lobed, spurred.

CULTIVATION: Various species are cultivated in China and Japan. Grow in a standard terrestrial compost, in a cool glasshouse or alpine house, in moderate shade, with plenty of water while in growth. Keep plants dry when they die back after flowering.

Amitostigma faberi (Rolfe) Schlechter

Plants to 20 cm tall. Leaf 2–6 cm long, 2–10 mm wide, linear to narrowly oblong. Inflorescence 2- to 8-flowered. Flowers to 1 cm across, purplish, the lip darker with a greenish-white base; lip 4-lobed, 6–8 mm long; spur slender, 5–6 mm long. Flowering summer.

Terrestrial in rocky soil on hillsides or on mossy rocks in forest, 2400–3000 m (7900–9900 ft.)

China

Amitostigma keiskei (Maximowicz) Schlechter

Plants 5–15 cm tall. Leaves oblong, to 7 cm long. Inflorescence 1- to 3-flowered. Flowers 1 cm across, mauve with 2 lines of purple spots at the base of the lip, rarely white; lip deeply 4-lobed; spur short. Flowering summer.

Damp places in mountains or on wet, mossy rocks

Japan

Anacamptis Richard

TRIBE: Orchideae

SUBTRIBE: Orchidinae

ETYMOLOGY: From Greek *anacampto*, to bend back, referring to the reflexed pollinia, or the spur, or the reflexed tips of the floral bracts

DISTRIBUTION: About 12 species in Europe, western Asia, and North Africa

Terrestrial orchids with globose, unlobed tubers and leafy stems. Leaves unspotted. Inflorescences densely or loosely few- to many-flowered, pyramidal or cylindrical. Flowers smallish, usually pink to lilac; dorsal sepal and petals usually forming a hood, lateral sepals spreading; lip spurred, trilobed or entire. Pollinia 2, viscidia 1 or 2.

Until recently, this genus comprised only 1 species, *Anacamptis pyramidalis*, but molecular work has indicated that several species previously included in *Orchis* should be placed here. These look very similar to *Orchis* species but the flowering stems have sheathing leaves, which are absent in *Orchis*.

CULTIVATION: Most species grow on well-drained alkaline soils, either chalk or limestone. They can be grown in pans in a standard terrestrial compost with added limestone or naturalized in short grass (the grass must be kept short either by grazing or cutting before and after the plants are in growth). Most species develop a rosette of leaves in winter, which remains green throughout the winter and dies back after (or sometimes during) flowering in early spring.

Anacamptis coriophora (Linnaeus) R. M. Bateman, Pridgeon & M. W. Chase

SYN. *Orchis coriophora* Linnaeus

BUG ORCHID

Plants 15–60 cm tall. Leaves mostly basal, to 15 cm long. Inflorescence oblong to cylindrical, densely many-flowered. Flowers reddish brown, pink, or greenish with an unpleasant smell; sepals and petals forming a hood; lip trilobed with a decurved, conical spur. Flowering spring–early summer.

Damp grassland

Europe, North Africa, Near East

Anacamptis laxiflora (Lamarck) R. M. Bateman, Pridgeon & M. W. Chase

SYN. *Orchis laxiflora* Lamarck

JERSEY ORCHID; LOOSE-FLOWERED ORCHID

Plants 20–100 cm tall. Leaves lanceolate. Inflorescence ovoid to cylindrical, loosely 6- to 20-flowered. Flowers pink, lilac, or purple-red; lip trilobed, usually white in center; spur to 2 cm long, pointing upwards. Flowering spring–early summer. This species naturalizes well in damp gardens.

Swampy meadows

Europe north to Belgium (including Channel Islands), North Africa, western Asia

SIMILAR SPECIES: *Anacamptis palustris* (Jacquin) R. M. Bateman, Pridgeon & M. W. Chase (syn. *Orchis palustris* Jacquin, *O. laxiflora* subsp. *palustris* (Jacquin) Bonnier & Layens) has a denser inflorescence and a more deeply divided lip.

Anacamptis longicornu (Poiret) R. M. Bateman, Pridgeon & M. W. Chase

SYN. *Orchis longicornu* Poiret

LONG-SPURRED ORCHID

Plants 10–35 cm tall. Leaves bright green, in basal rosette. Inflorescence laxly several-flowered. Flowers purple (rarely pink or red), lip white, spotted purple, with 3 shallow lobes and a long (16 mm), upcurved spur. Flowering late winter–early spring.

Dry grassland, roadside banks, open woodland

Western Mediterranean, North Africa

SIMILAR SPECIES: *Anacamptis champagneuxii* (Barnéoud) R. M. Bateman, Pridgeon & M. W. Chase is usually less robust with a shorter, fewer-flowered inflorescence.

Anacamptis morio (Linnaeus) R. M. Bateman, Pridgeon & M. W. Chase

SYN. *Orchis morio* Linnaeus

GREEN-WINGED ORCHID

Amitostigma keiskei. R. Parsons

Anacamptis coriophora

Anacamptis laxiflora

Anacamptis morio

Plants 10–40 cm tall. Leaves oblong to lanceolate, to 9 cm long. Inflorescence to 8 cm long, pyramidal to oblong, loosely 5- to 25-flowered. Flowers purple, rarely pink or white; sepals with conspicuous green veins; lip trilobed, paler with dark spots in the center; spur horizontal or upcurved, about the same length as lip. Flowering in early summer.

Grassland on basic soil

Europe, western Asia

Anacamptis papilionacea (Linnaeus) R. M. Bateman, Pridgeon & M. W. Chase

SYN. *Orchis papilionacea* Linnaeus

PINK BUTTERFLY ORCHID

Plants 15–40 cm tall. Basal leaves lanceolate, to 18 cm long. Inflorescence loose or dense, 4- to 14-flowered. Flowers purple, sepals and petals with darker veins; lip 12–25 mm long, fan-shaped, usually paler than rest of flower, with darker spots or stripes; spur conical, curving down. Flowering spring.

Dry grassland and open woodland

Southern Europe, North Africa

Anacamptis pyramidalis (Linnaeus) Richard

PYRAMIDAL ORCHID

Plants 20–60 cm tall. Basal leaves in a rosette, withered by flowering time. Inflorescence densely many-flowered, pyramidal at first, becoming cylindrical later. Flowers pale to deep pink, rarely white; lip ca. 9 × 10 mm, deeply trilobed; spur 10 mm long. Flowering summer.

Chalky grassland

Europe, North Africa, western Asia

Ancistrochilus Rolfe

TRIBE: Collabieae

ETYMOLOGY: From Greek *ankistron*, hook, and *cheilos*, lip, referring to the shape of the lip midlobe

DISTRIBUTION: 2 species in West and Central Africa

Sympodial plants with clustered, round to pear-shaped pseudobulbs, 2-leaved at apex. Leaves deciduous, pleated, thin-textured, lanceolate to elliptic, acute. Inflorescences arising from base of pseudobulbs, unbranched, 1- to 5-flowered. Flowers showy, large for size of plants, white or pink; sepals and petals spreading, subsimilar; lip trilobed; side lobes erect, midlobe narrowly lanceolate, recurved. Column long, pollinia 8.

CULTIVATION: Grow in shade at intermediate or warm temperatures in a shallow pot in a bark-based compost with additional leaf mold or composted bark. The inflorescences start to appear before the leaves. Water freely while pseudobulbs and leaves are developing but after the leaves have fallen, give only enough water to stop the pseudobulbs from shriveling. Plants are prone to rot if given too much water during the resting period.

Ancistrochilus rothschildianus O'Brien

Pseudobulbs pear-shaped, ca. 5 cm in diameter. Leaves 10–40 × 2–7.5 cm. Sepals and petals pale to deep pink, lip deep purple. Flowering usually in autumn and winter.

Epiphytic on large branches of evergreen forest trees, 500–1100 m (1650–3600 ft.)

West Africa eastwards to Uganda

RELATED SPECIES: *Ancistrochilus thomsonianus* (Reichenbach f.) Rolfe from Nigeria and Cameroon has smaller pseudobulbs (2.5 cm diameter) and larger flowers (7–9 cm across) with white sepals and petals and a purple lip midlobe.

Ancistrorhynchus Finet

SYN. *Cephalangraecum* Schlechter

TRIBE: Vandeae

SUBTRIBE: Aerangidinae

ETYMOLOGY: From Greek *ankistron*, hook, and *rhynchos*, beak, referring to the rostellum, the end of which is bent upwards like a hook

DISTRIBUTION: About 15 species in tropical Africa

Small to fairly large epiphytes, usually short-stemmed. Leaves distichous, linear or strap-shaped, the apex unequally bilobed and the lobes often toothed. Inflorescences arising at base of plant, short and dense, almost round, with large bracts. Flowers small, white, the lip marked with green or yellow; sepals and petals similar; lip oblong, ovate or orbicular, entire or trilobed, spurred; spur wide-mouthed and usually swollen again at apex, straight or S-shaped.

CULTIVATION: Plants require intermediate to warm, shady, and humid conditions. They can be mounted on bark or grown in a pot with a free-draining epiphyte compost. Plants should be kept slightly drier in winter but not allowed to dry completely.

Ancistrorhynchus capitatus (Lindley) Summerhayes

Short-stemmed plants. Leaves to 40 × 3 cm, forming a fan, linear, acutely bilobed at apex, each lobe with 2 or 3 acute teeth. Flowers white, lip with a green blotch, in dense, globular raceme; lip ovate, concave, ca. 5 mm across; spur to 11 mm long, almost straight. Flowers usually open in early spring.

Epiphytic in heavy shade in evergreen forest, 500–1300 m (1650–4300 ft.)

West Africa across to Uganda

SIMILAR SPECIES: *Ancistrorhynchus cephalotes* (Reichenbach f.) Summerhayes from West Africa has leaves partly folded, with the apical lobes not dentate; the inflorescence is surrounded by large, chaffy bracts. *Ancistrorhynchus clandestinus* (Lindley) Schlechter, also from West Africa, has long, narrow, leathery leaves to 180 × 3.5 cm, often pendent, very unequally bilobed at the apex.

Angraecopsis Kraenzlin

TRIBE: Vandeae

SUBTRIBE: Aerangidinae

ETYMOLOGY: From *Angraecum* and Greek *opsis*, like, meaning resembling *Angraecum*

Anacamptis papilionacea

Anacamptis pyramidalis

Ancistrochilus rothschildianus

Ancistrorhynchus capitatus. E. la Croix

DISTRIBUTION: 15–20 species in tropical Africa, Madagascar, the Mascarene Islands, and the Comoro Islands

Short-stemmed, monopodial epiphytes with fine roots. Leaves usually linear, oblanceolate or strap-shaped, often curved and twisted at the base to face one way. Inflorescences axillary, unbranched, few- to many-flowered. Flowers small, green, white, or yellow-green, sometimes scented; lateral sepals usually longer than dorsal sepal and petals; lip spurred, usually trilobed but occasionally entire.

CULTIVATION: In the wild, most species grow in shady, humid situations, and this is what they prefer in cultivation. They need an intermediate to warm greenhouse and can be mounted on slabs or grown in pots in a standard epiphyte mix. They should be kept slightly cooler and drier in winter.

Angraecopsis amaniensis Summerhayes

Dwarf plants with many roots clinging to bark. Leaves 2–4, to 4 cm long, bluish green, rather fleshy. Inflorescence to 7 cm long, densely many-flowered. Flowers yellow-green, sweetly scented; dorsal sepal and petals ca. 5 mm long, lateral sepals 7 mm long; lip lanceolate, 7 mm long, obscurely trilobed at the base; spur 9 mm long.

Epiphytic (rarely lithophytic) often at a low level on trees in high-rainfall woodland, usually 1000–1500 m (3300–5000 ft.)

East and east-central Africa from Kenya to Zimbabwe

SIMILAR SPECIES: *Angraecopsis breviloba* Summerhayes has a shorter spur and comes from Kenya and Tanzania.

Angraecopsis gracillima (Rolfe) Summerhayes

Leaves several, to 15 × 2.5 cm, curved, lying in one plane. Inflorescence to 20 cm long, 4- to 15-flowered. Flowers ca. 1 cm long, white, the base of the sepals and petals orange; lip trilobed, side lobes reflexed; spur slender, parallel to ovary and pedicel, ca. 4 cm long. Flowering in winter.

Epiphytic in deep shade in forest, often near a stream, 1500–1850 m (5000–6100 ft.)

DR Congo, Kenya, Uganda, Zambia

Angraecopsis parviflora (Thouars) Schlechter

Short-stemmed plants with fine roots. Leaves several, pendent, 6–25 × 0.5–1.5 cm, dark green, rather fleshy, linear or strap-shaped, slightly curved, unequally and acutely bilobed at the apex. Inflorescence 5–10 cm long, densely 10- to 15-flowered, the flowers clustered near the tip. Flowers greenish white, very small; lip 4 mm long, trilobed near base; spur ca. 1 cm long. Flowering in early winter.

Epiphytic in deep shade at a low level in forest, often near a river, 600–1800 m (2000–6000 ft.)

Tropical Africa, Madagascar, Mascarene Islands

Angraecum Bory

TRIBE: Vandeae

SUBTRIBE: Angraecinae

ETYMOLOGY: The Latinized form of the Malayan word *angurek*, used for any orchid with aerial roots

DISTRIBUTION: More than 220 species in Africa, Madagascar, Comoro Islands, Mascarene Islands, and Seychelles with 1 species in Sri Lanka

Large or small monopodial plants, epiphytic, lithophytic, or more rarely terrestrial; stems long or short, covered with old leaf bases. Leaves variable in shape, usually distichous. Inflorescences axillary, 1- to many-flowered, rarely branched. Flowers from very small to very large, usually white, green, or yellowish. The white-flowered, long-spurred species are moth-pollinated and almost all are strongly scented after dark. Sepals and petals subsimilar, usually spreading. Lip entire or obscurely trilobed, concave, the base more or less surrounding the column, with a long or short spur. Column short, cleft in front; rostellum bifid; pollinia, stipites, and viscidia 2.

Angraecum calceolus and *A. eburneum* are the only *Angraecum* species that occur both on Indian Ocean islands and mainland Africa. Not a great deal of hybridization has been done with this genus, although several of the larger Madagascar species, particularly *A. eburneum*, *A. magdalenae*, and *A. sesquipedale*, have been used.

CULTIVATION: Many species of *Angraecum* grow in shady situations and do well in intermediate to warm conditions. Small and trailing species can be mounted, but most grow well when potted in a standard epiphyte mix; the thicker the roots, the coarser it should be. Long-stemmed species such as *A. birrimense* and its allies should be given a moss pole to climb. Most species require high humidity, although they should be kept drier while not in active growth.

Angraecum aporoides Summerhayes

SYN. *Angraecum distichum* Lindley var. *grandifolium* (De Wildeman) Summerhayes

Stems branched, 20–30 cm long, forming large clumps and becoming pendent, leafy along their length; roots fine. Leaves distichous, overlapping, to 2.5 × 1 cm, bright green, fleshy, laterally flattened with a groove along the upper surface. Flowers ca. 1 cm across, white, scented, arising along the stem, mainly towards the apex; sepals and petals spreading; lip 4 × 5 mm, spur 6–7 mm long, straight, slender. Flowers off and on through year.

Epiphytic in lowland rain forest, in deep shade

West and Central Africa

SIMILAR SPECIES: *Angraecum distichum*

Angraecopsis amaniensis. E. la Croix

Angraecopsis gracillima. E. la Croix

Lindley is more widespread in West and Central Africa and is like a smaller version of *A. aporoides*, with leaves to 1 cm long, smaller flowers, and spur 5–6 mm long. *Angraecum bancoense* Van der Burg is smaller still, with sepals only 2 mm long. It is known from Cameroon, Congo, and Ivory Coast.

Angraecum birrimense Rolfe
Stems to 2 m long, slightly flattened. Leaves distichous, to 15 × 4.5 cm, oblong-lanceolate, unequally and obtusely bilobed at the apex. Inflorescence usually 2-flowered. Flowers to 12 cm across, scented; sepals and petals pale green, lip white with a green mid line; sepals and petals narrowly lanceolate, lip suborbicular to almost square, 3–4 cm long and wide, with an apicule 1–1.5 cm long; spur

Angraecum distichum

to 5 cm long, tapering from a wide mouth.

Epiphytic in lowland evergreen forest

West Africa

SIMILAR SPECIES: *Angraecum eichlerianum* Kraenzlin, from West and Central Africa, has 1- to 4-flowered inflorescences and an emarginate lip, with the lower margins projecting beyond the apicule.

Angraecum calceolus Thouars

Stems woody, to ca. 10 cm long, sometimes branched and forming clumps; roots numerous. Leaves numerous, to 22 × 2.5 cm, strap-shaped. Inflorescence to 25 cm long, branched, each branch several-flowered. Flowers pale yellow-green, ca. 15 mm across; lip ovate, very concave, to 7 mm long, including an acumen ca. 2 mm long; spur to 12 mm long, slender but slightly swollen at the tip, often pointing upwards. Flowering summer–autumn.

Although found at low altitudes, this species grows well in intermediate conditions and likes good light.

Epiphytic in coastal forest, 30–60 m (100–200 ft.)

Mozambique, Madagascar, Mascarene Islands, Comoro Islands, Seychelles

Angraecum compactum Schlechter

Stems 15–25 cm tall. Leaves several, 5–13 cm long, strap-shaped, often slightly wrinkled transversely. Inflorescence 1-flowered. Flowers 4.5–5 cm across, scented, pure white with a green spur; lip ovate; spur slender from a wide mouth, 12–13 cm long. Flowering summer.

Epiphytic in forest, 700–2000 m (2300–6600 ft.)

Madagascar

SIMILAR SPECIES: *Angraecum elephantinum* Schlechter, also from Madagascar, has narrower floral segments and a spur with a narrow mouth.

Angraecum didieri Baillon ex Finet

Stems to 15 cm long; roots warty. Leaves several, to 4.5 × 1 cm, strap-shaped, leathery. Inflorescence 1-flowered, sometimes with a rudimentary second flower. Flowers white, 4–7 cm across; lip 23–32 × 12–15 mm, ovate, very concave; spur slender, 8–15 cm long.

Epiphytic in forest, 0–1500 m (5000 ft.)

Madagascar

Angraecum eburneum Bory

Robust plants 30–75 cm tall, forming large clumps. Leaves numerous, stiff, strap-shaped, distichous, to 50 × 7 cm. Inflorescence erect, 30–75 cm long, up to 20-flowered. Flowers 7–8 cm in diameter; sepals and petals greenish white; lip white, shell-shaped, held uppermost; spur usually 6–7 cm long, slender, tapering from a wide mouth. Flowering in winter.

Four subspecies and 1 variety are recognized, differing in distribution and proportions of flower. Subsp. *eburneum*, from Madagascar, Mascarene Islands, Seychelles, and Comoro Islands, has a lip 35 × 30 mm. Subsp. *giryamae* (Rendle) P. J. Cribb & Senghas from East Africa has a broader lip, to 35 × 50 mm. Subsp. *superbum* (Thouars) H. Perrier (syn. *Angraecum superbum* Thouars, *A. brongniartianum* Reichenbach f.) from Madagascar has larger flowers with a lip 40 mm long and a prominent median keel. Subsp. *xerophilum* H. Perrier from Madagascar is a smaller plant with leaves to 15 cm long and smaller flowers with the lip broader than long (20 × 35 mm) and a spur 7–8 cm long.

Lithophytic or epiphytic, 0–400 m (1320 ft.), but most often near the coast

East Africa, Madagascar, Comoro Islands, Mascarene Islands, Seychelles

SIMILAR SPECIES: *Angraecum longicalcar* (Bosser) Bosser (syn. *A. eburneum* var. *longicalcar* Bosser) from central Madagascar is larger with the inflorescence to 100 cm long and has larger flowers; the lip is 50 mm long, including an acumen 18 mm long, and 60–65 mm wide, and the spur is 35–40 cm long.

Angraecum equitans Schlechter

Compact plants 9–10 cm tall; stems to 10 mm diameter, sometimes branched, densely leafy. Leaves 3–6 × 1–2 cm, spreading, fleshy, curved, keeled. Inflorescence short, 1- to 3-flowered. Flowers white, scented, ca. 4 cm across; pedicel and ovary 4 cm long, the ovary 4-angled; lip to 20 × 15 mm, ovate, concave; spur 8–11 cm long, very slender from a wide mouth. Flowering spring–summer.

Epiphytic on moss and lichen-covered trees, ca. 2000 m (6600 ft.)

Madagascar

Angraecum florulentum Reichenbach f.

Stems 15–30 cm long, slightly flattened, sometimes branched. Leaves numerous, distichous, to 7 × 1.5 cm, narrowly lanceolate, rather fleshy, light green. Inflorescence to 5 cm long, 2- to 4-flowered. Flowers white, strongly scented, 4–5 cm in diameter; lip 23 × 6 mm, concave; spur 9–10 cm long, very slender.

Epiphytic on tree trunks in forest

Comoro Islands, perhaps Madagascar

Angraecum germinyanum Hooker f.

Stems to 70 cm long, sometimes branched, leafy. Leaves to 9 × 1.5 cm, narrowly lanceolate. Inflorescence ca. 3 cm long, 1-flowered. Flowers with the lip on top, all white or with sepals, petals, and spur tinged with green or brown; sepals and petals narrowly lanceolate, long acuminate; dorsal sepal to 60 × 5 mm, lateral sepals to 80 × 5 mm, petals to 70 × 3 mm; lip 45–60 mm long, including an apicule 10–27 mm long, very

Angraecum birrimense. E. la Croix

Angraecum calceolus. J. Hermans

Angraecum compactum

Angraecum eburneum

concave, shell-shaped; spur 8–12 cm long, very slender from a wide mouth.

Epiphytic in humid forest, 800–1000 m (2640–3300 ft.)

Comoro Islands

Angraecum infundibulare Lindley

Stems somewhat flattened, almost winged, occasionally to 10 m long in the wild. Inflorescence 1-flowered. Flowers green with a white lip, strongly scented, 15 cm long from tip of dorsal sepal to lip apex; lip to 8.5 × 5.5 cm, oblong, with an apicule 1 cm long; spur 10–20 cm long, slender from a funnel-shaped mouth.

Epiphytic in forest, usually in hot, humid areas, 1150–1300 m (3800–4300 ft.)

West and East Africa

Angraecum leonis (Reichenbach f.) Veitch

Stems short. Leaves 4–5, fleshy, bilaterally flattened, spreading and recurved, to 20 × 2.5 cm. Inflorescence to 10 cm long, 2- to 4-flowered. Flowers fleshy, white, scented, 5–10 cm across; spur 7–15 cm long, slender with a wide mouth. Plants from the Comoro Islands have much larger flowers than those from Madagascar. Flowering spring.

Epiphytic in forest, usually on trunks, 0–1500 m (5000 ft.)

Madagascar, Comoro Islands

Angraecum magdalenae Schlechter

Stems short, 25–30 cm tall, branching at base. Leaves forming a fan, oblong, to 30 × 5 cm. Inflorescence arising below leaves, to 10 cm long, 1- to 2-flowered. Flowers white with a spicy scent, 10 cm across; lip 5 × 4 cm, almost round to obovate, acuminate; spur 10–11 cm long, S-shaped, tapering from a wide mouth. Flowering spring–autumn.

Var. *latilabellum* Bosser has a broader lip and is epiphytic in humid, high-altitude forest.

Lithophytic on rocky outcrops, 800–2000 m (2640–6600 ft.)

Madagascar

Angraecum mauritianum (Poiret) Frappier

Stems 25–40 cm long, rather flattened, branched near base. Leaves numerous, distichous, to 6 × 1.5 cm. Inflorescence 1-flowered. Flowers white; sepals to 20 × 4 mm, the dorsal slightly shorter than the laterals; petals to 12 × 3 mm; lip 15 × 7 mm, lanceolate; spur 8 cm long.

Epiphytic in humid evergreen forest, 200–1400 m (660–4600 ft.)

Madagascar, Mauritius, Réunion

Angraecum rutenbergianum Kraenzlin

Stems 4–12 cm tall; roots rough but not warty. Leaves several, to 6 × 0.7 cm, linear. Inflorescence 1-flowered. Flowers to 6 cm across, white, the spur greenish towards the tip; lip to 35 × 18 mm, ± elliptic; spur 6–14 cm long, very slender. Flowering summer.

Epiphytic in humid evergreen forest or lithophytic on shaded rocks, ca. 1500 m (5000 ft.)

Madagascar

Angraecum scottianum Reichenbach f.

Stems 30–40 cm long, becoming pendent; roots finely warty. Leaves numerous, 6–10 × 0.5 cm, terete, grooved on upper surface. Inflorescence to 10 cm long, 1- to 4-flowered. Sepals and petals ca. 25 long, sepals 4 mm wide, petals slightly narrower. Lip ca. 3 cm long, 4 cm wide, concave, transversely oblong; spur 9–15 cm long, slender from a wide mouth. Flowering spring–autumn.

Epiphytic on trunks and lower branches

Comoro Islands

Angraecum sesquipedale Thouars

COMET ORCHID

Robust plants to 120 cm tall, usually forming clumps; roots stout, to 1 cm diameter. Leaves numerous, distichous, to 40 × 7 cm, strap-shaped. Inflorescence shorter than leaves, usually 1- to 4-flowered. Flowers creamy white, fleshy, to 22 cm across, strongly scented at night; lip to 9 × 4.5 cm, oblong or fiddle-shaped; spur 30–35 cm long, slender. Flowering in winter.

Var. *angustifolium* Bosser & Morat (syn. *Angraecum bosseri* Senghas) is a smaller plant with narrower leaves and 1-flowered inflorescences. It is usually terrestrial in dry, deciduous forest.

Epiphytic or lithophytic in coastal forest, 0–100 m (330 ft.)

Madagascar

Angraecum viguieri Schlechter

Stems 15–30 cm tall; roots arising at base of stem, densely warty. Leaves dark green, narrowly strap-shaped, 10–15 cm x 1.5–2.5 cm. Inflorescence 1-flowered. Flowers to 15 cm across; sepals, petals, and spur pinkish brown or yellow-brown, lip white, to 70 mm long plus an acumen 15–25 mm long, to 50 mm wide, concave; spur 9–13 cm long, slender from a wide mouth. Flowering spring.

Epiphytic in evergreen forest, ca. 900 m (3000 ft.)

Madagascar

Anguloa Ruíz & Pavón

TULIP ORCHIDS, CRADLE ORCHIDS

TRIBE: Maxillarieae

SUBTRIBE: Maxillariinae

ETYMOLOGY: Named for Don Francisco de Angulo (fl. 1790), Director-General of Mines in Peru, who studied the local flora

DISTRIBUTION: 9 species and 4 natural hybrids in Venezuela, Ecuador, Colombia, Bolivia, and Peru with center of speciation in Colombia

Angraecum leonis

Angraecum scottianum

Angraecum sesquipedale

Angraecum magdalenae. E. la Croix

Large plants, usually terrestrial on slopes but occasionally epiphytic; pseudobulbs clustered on a short rhizome. Pseudobulbs ellipsoid, grooved, antero-posteriorly compressed, 3- to 5-leaved at apex. Leaves deciduous at onset of new growth, large, broadly lanceolate, plicate, tapering to a grooved petiole. Inflorescences basal, 1-flowered, occasionally 2-flowered. Flowers large, with medicinal scent, fleshy, cup-shaped; sepals and petals erect, subsimilar; lip variably motile, trilobed.

Anguloa has been crossed with the related genera *Lycaste* and *Ida* to form the hybrid genera ×*Angulocaste* and ×*Lycida*.

CULTIVATION: Grow in pots in intermediate temperatures and light shade, in a bark/sphagnum or perlite/sphagnum mixture. Plants should be kept dry after the new pseudobulbs have matured but given plenty of water and fertilizer while in growth. It is important that water should not get on to the new growth. Flowers from May to July (late spring–late summer) in northern temperate greenhouse culture.

Anguloa cliftonii J. Farmer

Pseudobulbs clustered, to 15 × 6.5 cm. Leaves 4–5, to 70 × 20 cm, oblanceolate. Inflorescence 10–15 cm long. Flowers large, to 9 cm long, cup-shaped but more open than most in the genus, yellow, lateral sepals falcate, petals with dark red reticulation at the base; lip yellow with red-orange bars and spots at base, goblet-shaped.

Terrestrial, ca. 1800 m (6000 ft.)

Colombia

Anguloa clowesii Lindley

Pseudobulbs to 23 × 7 cm. Leaves 3–5, to 70 × 20 cm. Inflorescence to 30 cm long. Flowers large, 7–8 cm long, lemon to golden yellow; lip boat-shaped, white in type specimen, but yellow with orange tips in the more commonly seen forma *flava*.

Usually terrestrial, sometimes epiphytic, at 1800–2000 m (6000–6600 ft.)

Colombia, Venezuela

Anguloa uniflora Ruíz & Pavón

Pseudobulbs 13 × 8 cm. Leaves 3–5, to 90 × 24 cm. Inflorescence to 11 cm long. Flowers 7 cm high; sepals and petals cream, lateral sepals flushed with pink; lip tubular, lateral lobes yellow-orange. This species was confused with *Anguloa virginalis*, *A. eburnea*, and *A. tognettiae* for many years.

Terrestrial or lithophytic in forest margins or scrubby grassland, 1400–2250 m (4600–7300 ft.)

Peru

Anguloa virginalis Linden ex B. S. Williams

Pseudobulbs 19 × 7 cm. Leaves 3–5, to 70 × 17 cm. Inflorescence to 45 cm tall. Flowers to 8.5 cm long, white, speckled with pale to dark pink dots especially on petals and lip, laterally flattened; lip tubular but kinked at basc.

Terrestrial and lithophytic on forest margins and open grassland, 1750–2400 m (5800–7900 ft.)

Bolivia, Colombia, Ecuador, Peru, Venezuela

Anoectochilus Blume

TRIBE: Cranichideae

SUBTRIBE: Goodyerinae

ETYMOLOGY: From Greek *anoektos*, open, and *cheilos*, lip, referring to the spreading lip apex

DISTRIBUTION: About 50 species in India, Southeast Asia, the Pacific Islands, and Australia

Terrestrial herbs with creeping, fleshy stems, rooting at nodes. Leaves in a loose rosette, petiolate, usually ovate or elliptic, velvety, the veins usually white, gold, or purplish. Inflorescences terminal, unbranched, erect. Flowers small, inconspicuous; sepals free, the dorsal forming hood with petals; lip spurred, clawed at base, the apical part lobed, spreading. Column short.

These plants are known as "jewel orchids," grown for the beauty of their leaves rather than flowers.

CULTIVATION: Plants require shade, high humidity, and usually intermediate conditions. The compost should be based on fine bark or sphagnum moss and should not be allowed to dry out completely. In the past, jewel orchids were often grown in Wardian cases.

Anoectochilus setaceus Blume

SYN. *Anoectochilus roxburghii* (Wallich) Lindley

Leaves ca. 5 × 3.5 cm, ovate, purplish with a network of gold veins; underside purple. Inflorescence to 20 cm tall, few-flowered. Flowers pinkish brown; lip white, the mesochile fringed. This is probably the most commonly cultivated species, usually sold as *Anoectochilus roxburghii*.

In dark gullies at the edge of forest, 330–1200 m (1100–4000 ft.)

Tropical Asia

SIMILAR SPECIES: *Anoectochilus regalis* Blume from southern India and Sri Lanka has slightly larger flowers with the lip deeply fringed. It may be synonymous with *A. setaceus*.

Anoectochilus sikkimensis King & Pantling

Leaves to 12 × 10 cm, broadly ovate, dark green with white to yellow reticulate veining. Inflorescence 5–16 cm long, few- to many-flowered. Flowers green and white.

Undergrowth of forest, 900–1500 m (3000–5000 ft.)

Eastern Himalayas

SIMILAR SPECIES: *Anoectochilus brevilabris* Lindley is very similar and may be synonymous, in which case *A. brevilabris* is the older and therefore the valid name.

Anguloa cliftonii

Anguloa clowesii

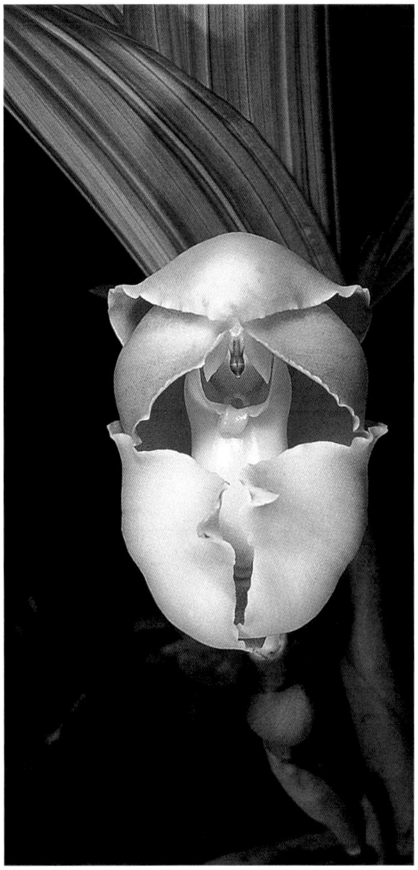

Anguloa uniflora

Anoectochilus sikkimensis. J. Hermans

Anoectochilus setaceus. G. van Winkel

Ansellia Lindley

TRIBE: Cymbidieae
SUBTRIBE: Cyrtopodiinae
ETYMOLOGY: Named for John Ansell (d.1847), who collected the type specimen on Fernando Póo
DISTRIBUTION: 1 variable species widespread in tropical and South Africa

Large sympodial epiphyte, rarely terrestrial or lithophytic; pseudobulbs clustered, canelike, with several nodes, ridged lengthways, yellow or yellow-green, leafy towards the apex. Roots of 2 kinds: stout roots which grow down and cling to the substrate, and fine, erect roots around the base of the plant. Inflorescence terminal, branched. Sepals and petals free, spreading. Pollinia 4, in 2 pairs.

In the past, several species, subspecies, and varieties have been described, but all the variation in flower size and color is continuous and there are no consistent links between particular forms and geographical distribution.

CULTIVATION: Plants can grow very large and need to be planted in baskets or clay pots, in a coarse bark mix. They do well in intermediate or warm conditions, with bright light and plenty of water while in growth. They should be kept almost dry in the resting period, apart from occasional spraying to prevent the pseudobulbs from shriveling.

Ansellia africana Lindley

SYN. *Ansellia gigantea* Reichenbach f., *A. nilotica* (Baker) N. E. Brown, and many others
LEOPARD ORCHID

Pseudobulbs canelike, to 60 × 2–3 cm. Leaves several, ± distichous, dark green, 15–50 × 1.5–5 cm, narrowly strap-shaped. Inflorescence loosely many-flowered. Flowers 4–5 cm across, usually pale to deep yellow spotted or blotched with light brown to deep chocolate-maroon, but some forms are plain yellow or greenish yellow with no spotting while others are so heavily blotched as to look almost black. The more heavily blotched flowers tend to be the largest. Sepals 15–35 × 5–10 mm, elliptic; petals similar but slightly smaller. Lip 20–25 mm long, trilobed, with 2 or 3 central keels; side lobes erect, midlobe round, apiculate. Column 10–12 mm long.

Usually epiphytic in dry, open woodland, often in forks of trees, but occasionally in forest, usually at altitudes of 0–700 m (2300 ft.) but occasionally up to 2200 m (7260 ft.)

Tropical Africa, South Africa

Arachnis Blume

SCORPION ORCHIDS
TRIBE: Vandeae
SUBTRIBE: Aeridinae
ETYMOLOGY: From Greek *arachnis*, spider, referring to the spidery flowers
DISTRIBUTION: 11 species from Sikkim to mainland Asia, Indonesia, Philippines, and the Pacific Islands

Long-stemmed, scrambling epiphytic or terrestrial plants related to *Vanda* and *Renanthera*; stems branched, rooting along their length, becoming bare and woody at the base. Leaves in 2 rows, thick-textured, strap-shaped. Inflorescences axillary, borne towards top of stem, sometimes branched, erect or pendent. Flowers scented, often with brown bands; sepals and petals spreading, subsimilar, narrow at the base and widening towards the apex; lip hinged to the base of the column by a short strap, trilobed, side lobes broad, erect, midlobe fleshy with a raised central ridge and a fleshy callus below the apex. Pollinia 4.

Species of *Arachnis* have been used in hybridization. The cross with *Vanda* is known as ×*Aranda* and the genus has also been used in more complex hybrids. These hybrids are popular in the cut flower trade in Singapore.

CULTIVATION: Most species require warm temperatures, bright light, and high humidity throughout the year. Because of their size, they are usually grown in clay pots in a coarse compost, with a support such as a moss pole to climb up. Usually, plants do not flower until they are quite large.

Arachnis flos-aeris (Linnaeus) Reichenbach f.

Lithophytic or epiphytic plants climbing high into trees, stems to 10 m long. Leaves to 20 × 5 cm, oblong, bilobed at the apex. Inflorescence simple or branched, to 150 cm long, becoming pendulous, loosely many-flowered. Flowers 10 cm across, yellow blotched and banded with reddish brown; sepals and petals linear, spathulate; lip much shorter, 1.5–2 cm long, side lobes brown, midlobe yellow, obovate.

Lowland forest, 100–300 m (330–1000 ft.)

Borneo, Java, Malaysia, Sumatra, Thailand, Philippines

SIMILAR SPECIES: *Arachnis longisepala* (J. J. Wood) Shim, Soón & A. L. Lamb has flowers 5 cm across. It is endemic to Borneo (Sabah) where it grows in hill forest at 600–800 m (2000–2640 ft.).

Arachnis hookeriana (Reichenbach f.) Reichenbach f.

Shorter plants than *Arachnis flos-aeris*. Inflorescence to 60 cm long, erect, unbranched. Flowers ca. 8 cm across, creamy white or pale yellow finely dotted with purple, the lip purple or purple-striped.

Terrestrial on sandy soil and scrambling through coastal scrub

Borneo, Malaysia, Sarawak, Vietnam

Arethusa Linnaeus

TRIBE: Arethuseae
SUBTRIBE: Arethusinae
ETYMOLOGY: From Arethusa, a river nymph, referring to the wet habitat where the species grows
DISTRIBUTION: 1 species in Canada and United States

Slender terrestrial plants with underground corms. Leaf single,

Ansellia africana

Arachnis flos-aeris. P. O'Byrne

linear, appearing after flowering. Inflorescence erect, slender, 1-flowered, rarely 2-flowered. Flowers showy; sepals and petals subsimilar, the sepals ± erect, the petals projecting forwards; lip obscurely trilobed with a short basal claw, reflexed, the disc with a fringed crest. Pollinia 2.

CULTIVATION: *Arethusa* tends to be difficult and short-lived in cultivation. Plants seem to do best grown in a pot in a compost of live sphagnum moss and peat or peat substitute and kept constantly moist. Pots can be plunged in a wet place outside in summer and brought into a cool greenhouse or alpine house in winter.

Arethusa bulbosa Linnaeus

DRAGON'S MOUTH

Leaves to 20 × 1 cm, grasslike. Inflorescence to 40 cm tall. Flowers to 5 cm long, pale to deep pink, occasionally white; lip to 45 mm long, obovate, marked with deep purple and with a fringed yellow crest. Flowering late spring–summer

Acid bogs and wet meadows

Northeastern Canada and United States

Arachnis longisepala. P. O'Byrne

Arethusa bulbosa. R. Parsons

Arpophyllum Lexarza

BOTTLEBRUSH ORCHIDS

TRIBE: Epidendreae

SUBTRIBE: Laeliinae

ETYMOLOGY: From Greek *harpe*, sickle, and *phyllon*, leaf, referring to the curved leaves of *A. spicatum*, the type species of the genus

DISTRIBUTION: 4 species from Central and northern South America and Jamaica

Epiphytic, terrestrial, or lithophytic plants with a thick rhizome; pseudobulbs narrowly cylindrical, with papery sheaths at the base, 1-leafed at apex. Leaves stiff, fleshy, narrowly lanceolate to strap-shaped, curved. Inflorescences terminal, erect, unbranched, densely many-flowered. Flowers small, pink to purple; sepals spreading, ovate to triangular; petals smaller than sepals; lip entire, saccate at the base. Pollinia 8.

CULTIVATION: Grow potted in a coarse, free-draining compost in intermediate conditions with high humidity and good light. Water throughout the year, giving less water after flowering. Plants flower best when pot-bound.

Arpophyllum giganteum Hartweg ex Lindley

HYACINTH ORCHID

Large plants 70–100 cm tall; pseudobulbs to 20 × 1 cm, enclosed in papery sheaths. Leaves to 55 × 2 cm, strap-shaped. Inflorescence 25–40 cm long. Flowers to 2 cm across, nonresupinate, pink to magenta.

Three subspecies are recognized. Subsp. *giganteum* occurs from Mexico to northwestern Venezuela. Subsp. *alpinum* (Lindley) Dressler (syn. *Arpophyllum alpinum* Lindley) comes from southeastern Mexico and Central America and has a shorter, looser inflorescence. Subsp. *medium* (Reichenbach f.) Dressler has a distribution similar to subsp. *alpinum*.

Epiphytic in rain forest, 700–1850 m (2300–6100 ft.)

Mexico south to Colombia and Venezuela

Arpophyllum spicatum Lexarza

Plants to 1 m tall. Leaves fleshy, narrow, V-shaped in cross-section, curved. Inflorescence to 15 cm long. Flowers pink, the lip darker.

Epiphytic, lithophytic, or terrestrial in open forests, 1000–2400 m (3300–7900 ft.)

Mexico south to Colombia and Venezuela

Arundina Blume

TRIBE: Arethuseae

SUBTRIBE: Arethusinae

ETYMOLOGY: From Latin *arundo*, reed, referring to the reedlike stems

DISTRIBUTION: 1 variable species throughout tropical Asia

Terrestrial plants with reedlike stems clustered on a short rhizome. Leaves grasslike, sheathing at the base. Inflorescence terminal, several-flowered. Sepals and petals free, spreading, sepals lanceolate, acute, the petals broader. Lip obscurely trilobed, clasping column, the margins undulate. Pollinia 8.

CULTIVATION: *Arundina* is widely planted in tropical and subtropical gardens and has become naturalized in some places, for example, Hawaii. Plants like a well-drained compost rich in organic matter and plenty of water while actively growing (which may be all year round) in full sun or light shade. Clumps can be divided after flowering.

Arundina graminifolia Blume

SYN. *Arundina chinensis* Blume, *A. speciosa* Blume, and many others

Stems 50–250 cm tall, sometimes branched, leafy in the upper half. Inflorescence 30–40 cm long, the flowers open in succession 1 or 2 at a time. Flowers showy, like a small *Cattleya*, scented, short-lived; white, mauve, or pink, the lip usually darker with a yellow blotch; sepals to 4 cm long.

Grassy hillsides, by roadside, 200–1420 m (660–4700 ft.)

Widespread in tropical Asia

Ascocentrum Schlechter

TRIBE: Vandeae

SUBTRIBE: Aeridinae

ETYMOLOGY: From Greek *askos*, bag, and *kentron*, spur, referring to the large spur

DISTRIBUTION: 13 species in Asia from the Himalayas to Borneo

Monopodial epiphytes related to *Vanda*. Stem often short but can reach 30 cm long. Leaves in 2 rows, fleshy, usually recurved, narrowly strap-shaped, often V-shaped in cross-section. Inflorescences axillary, erect or spreading, several- to many-flowered. Flowers small, usually brightly colored and showy; sepals and petals similar, spreading; lip entire or trilobed, fixed to the base of the column, side lobes small, midlobe tonguelike; spur shorter than the pedicel and ovary. Column short, pollinia 2.

Ascocentrum species have been widely used in hybridization. The cross with *Vanda* has given the important hybrid genus ×*Ascocenda*.

CULTIVATION: Plants can be grown in pots or baskets or mounted on slabs or rafts. They require intermediate to warm conditions, bright light, and plenty of water while in active growth.

Ascocentrum ampullaceum (Roxburgh) Schlechter

Stem unbranched, to 16 cm tall, rooting at base. Leaves numerous, distichous, overlapping, to 14 × 1 cm, strap-shaped. Inflorescence shorter than leaves, several- to many-flowered. Flowers 15–18 mm across, rich rose-red; lip entire, to 7 mm long; spur to 9 mm long, slightly swollen near the tip.

Epiphytic in forest, 330–1100 m (1100–3600 ft.)

Nepal to Indochina

Ascocentrum curvifolium (Lindley) Schlechter

Stems woody, sometimes branched at base. Leaves distichous, strongly recurved, 10–30 cm long, linear.

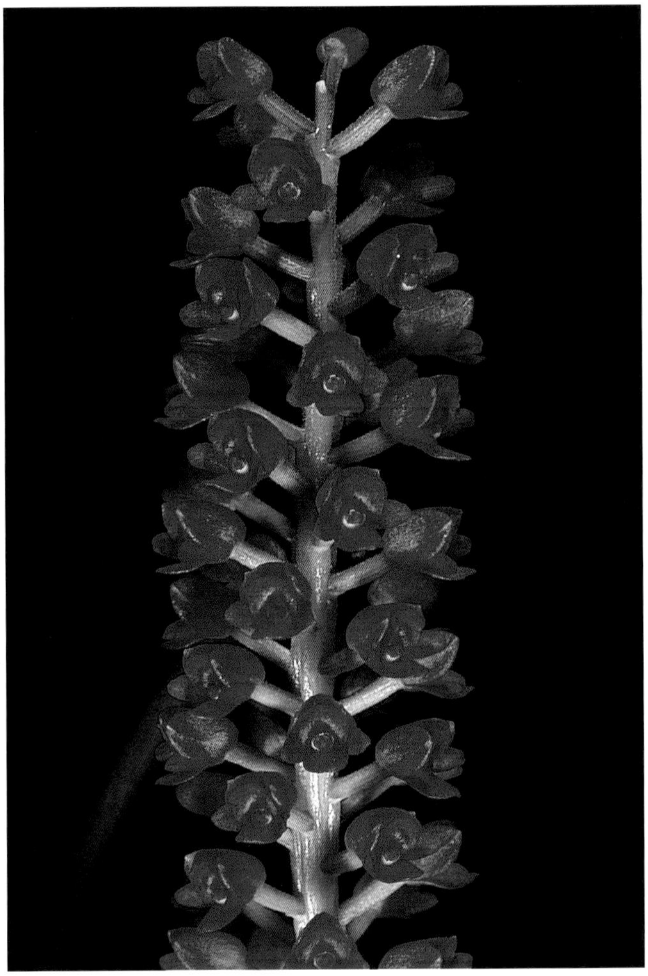
Arpophyllum giganteum

Ascocentrum ampullaceum

Arundina graminifolia

Ascocentrum curvifolium

Inflorescence shorter than leaves, densely many-flowered. Flowers 20–27 mm across, sepals and petals orange to scarlet, lip golden yellow, spur orange, column red, anther-cap purple; lip obscurely trilobed, 6 mm long; spur straight, slightly swollen at tip, 6 mm long.

Epiphytic in forest

Myanmar, Laos, Thailand

Ascocentrum garayi Christenson

Leaves about 10 cm long, rigid, straight. Inflorescence to 25 cm long, densely many-flowered. Flowers bright orange; lip trilobed, side lobes erect, obtuse, midlobe concave, rounded at apex, at an angle of 90 degrees to the spur.

Most plants in cultivation as *Ascocentrum miniatum* belong to this species, which differs mainly in its straight, not recurved leaves and concave lip midlobe.

Epiphytic in forest

Thailand, Vietnam

Ascocentrum miniatum (Lindley) Schlechter

Stems erect, to ca. 30 cm tall. Leaves ca. 10 cm long, narrowly strap-shaped, fleshy, V-shaped in cross-section, recurved. Inflorescence to 25 cm long, densely many-flowered. Flowers bright orange-red, 12 mm across; lip trilobed, side lobes erect, acute, midlobe strap-shaped, decurved, shallowly notched; spur pendent, swollen towards apex. See note after *Ascocentrum garayi.*

Epiphytic in forest, 0–1200 m (4000 ft.)

Java

Ascoglossum Schlechter

TRIBE: Vandeae

SUBTRIBE: Aeridinae

ETYMOLOGY: From Greek *askos*, bag, and *glossa*, tongue, referring to the saccate lip

DISTRIBUTION: 1 species from Philippines to Solomon Islands

Medium-sized to large monopodial epiphyte related to *Renanthera* and *Ascocentrum*. Leaves distichous, strap-shaped. Inflorescence axillary, usually branched, many-flowered. Sepals and petals subsimilar, reflexed. Lip trilobed with a saccate spur at the base, side lobes erect, midlobe small, ovate. Pollinia 4, in 2 pairs.

CULTIVATION: Plants do well in baskets or mounted on a large slab of bark in warm conditions, in good light, with high humidity throughout the year.

Ascoglossum calopterum (Reichenbach f.) Schlechter

SYN. *Saccolabium calopterum* Reichenbach f., *Ascoglossum purpureum* (J. J. Smith) Schlechter

Stems erect. Leaves to 20 × 2.5 cm, stiff, rather fleshy. Inflorescence longer than leaves, densely many-flowered. Flowers showy, pale to deep purple, ca. 2.5 cm across.

High-level epiphyte in rain forest, 0–600 m (2000 ft.)

Moluccas, New Guinea, Philippines, Solomon Islands, Sulawesi

Aspasia Lindley

TRIBE: Maxillarieae

SUBTRIBE: Oncidiinae

ETYMOLOGY: From either Greek *aspasias*, glad or delightful, or Aspasia, wife of Pericles

DISTRIBUTION: 8 species in tropical America

Epiphytes or lithophytes forming clumps on short rhizomes; pseudobulbs ellipsoid to oblong with a short stalk at the base, laterally flattened, with 1 or 2 leaf-bearing sheaths at the base, 1- or 2-leaved at the apex. Leaves lanceolate to strap-shaped. Inflorescences arising from leaf sheaths, shorter than leaves, erect, unbranched, 1- to several-flowered. Flowers showy; sepals free, spreading; petals shorter and broader than sepals; lip joined to column at base, lacking a spur, the free part at right angles to the column, entire or obscurely trilobed, narrow at the base, broad at the apex, the margins often undulate. Pollinia 2.

CULTIVATION: Plants can be grown in pots or baskets in a standard epiphyte compost, or mounted on slabs, but they seem to flower better if pot-bound. They require intermediate temperatures, shade, and high humidity, but should be kept drier for some weeks after flowering.

Aspasia epidendroides Lindley

SYN. *Aspasia fragrans* Klotzsch

Pseudobulbs to 7–20 × 1–4 cm. Leaves 15–30 cm long, 2–5 cm wide. Inflorescence 10–25 cm long, few-flowered. Flowers to 3.5 cm across, scented, variable in color; sepals yellow-green to bronze, with chocolate or violet bands; petals mauve or bronze, lip white to cream with purple blotches in center; disc yellow.

Epiphytic in damp forest, 0–1100 m (3600 ft.)

Central America to Colombia

Aspasia lunata Lindley

Pseudobulbs to 6 cm long, strongly flattened. Leaves to 20 cm long. Inflorescence 9–10 cm tall, 1- to 3-flowered. Flowers ca. 7.5 cm across; sepals and petals greenish, banded and blotched with brown; lip white, marked with purple in center.

Brazil

Aspasia principissa Reichenbach f.

Pseudobulbs 15–20 cm long. Leaves to 25–40 cm long. Inflorescence 20–30 cm tall, 1- to 3-flowered. Flowers to 7.5 cm across; sepals and petals green with longitudinal red-brown stripes; lip white, yellowish in center.

Epiphytic in very wet forest, 0–500 m (1650 ft.)

Central America to Colombia and Brazil

SIMILAR SPECIES: *Aspasia variegata* Lindley, from Central and South America and Trinidad, has slightly

Ascocentrum miniatum

Aspasia epidendroides

Ascoglossum calopterum. P. Cribb

Aspasia lunata

smaller flowers, the sepals and petals with brown or maroon banding at base.

Barbosella Schlechter

SYN. *Barbrodria* Luer
TRIBE: Epidendreae
SUBTRIBE: Pleurothallidinae
ETYMOLOGY: Named for João Barbosa Rodriguez (1842–1909), who studied Brazilian Orchidaceae
DISTRIBUTION: About 20 species in the West Indies, Central and South America

Small epiphytic or lithophytic herbs, forming clumps or creeping; stem erect, covered by 1 or more sheaths, 1-leafed. Leaves linear to oblong, fleshy or leathery. Inflorescences erect, 1-flowered, arising from a papery sheath at the leaf insertion. Dorsal sepal free, lateral sepals joined to form a synsepal. Petals free, sometimes fringed. Lip shorter than the sepals, fleshy, strap-shaped to ovate, hinged at the base to the column-foot, sometimes with a ball-and-socket joint, sometimes simply. Column usually winged, hooded, with a foot; pollinia 4, stigma not lobed.

CULTIVATION: Most species come from fairly low altitudes and require temperatures in the range of 12–25°C (54–77°F) with moderate shade, high humidity, and good air movement. They do better mounted on a raft, preferably with some living moss, although they can be grown in shallow pots in a fine bark and sphagnum mixture. They need regular misting and should not be allowed to dry out.

Barbosella australis (Cogniaux) Schlechter

Plants creeping. Leaves oblong. Inflorescence erect. Flowers large, 5 cm long, translucent, pale yellow, lip oblong, forked at the tip.
Southern Brazil

Barbosella cucullata (Lindley) Schlechter

SYN. *Restrepia cucullata* Lindley
Leaves fleshy, narrowly linear. Inflorescence to 15 cm tall. Flowers 4 cm long, pale yellow or purple.

Epiphytic in dense bush, 1400–3450 m (4600–11,400 ft.)

Bolivia, Colombia, Venezuela

Barbosella dolichorhiza Schlechter

SYN. *Barbosella fuscata* Garay

Tufted plants with narrowly linear leaves to 6.5 cm long. Inflorescence ca. 9 cm tall. Flowers to 23 mm long; yellow, yellow-green, brown, or purple; lip yellow tinged with purple.

Epiphytic in rain forest, 1000–2000 m (3300–6600 ft.)

Costa Rica, Nicaragua, Colombia, Ecuador, Peru

Barkeria Knowles & Westcott

TRIBE: Epidendreae

SUBTRIBE: Laeliinae

ETYMOLOGY: Named for George Barker (1776–1845), a Birmingham solicitor who was the first to import the type species to England

DISTRIBUTION: 15 species from Mexico south to Panama

Epiphytic or lithophytic plants related to *Epidendrum*; pseudobulbs slender and canelike; roots numerous, silvery gray. Leaves distichous, linear-lanceolate to ovate. Inflorescences terminal, racemose, few- to many-flowered. Flowers showy, often long-lasting, white, pink, or magenta; sepals and petals subsimilar, spreading; lip entire, usually with a yellow or white keeled callus. Column long or short.

Since the late 1980s, the number of hybrids has increased to more than 60, leading to compact, free-flowering plants with long-lasting flowers. There are also a number of intergeneric hybrids with other genera in subtribe Laeliinae, including *Cattleya*, *Brassavola*, and *Sophronitis*, in which *Barkeria* is usually dominant.

CULTIVATION: Barkerias are grown in cool or intermediate conditions. In the growing season (midspring–midautumn) humidity should be high, plants should be sprayed daily, and the day temperature can rise to as much as 30°C (86°F). When plants become dormant they should be kept almost dry; the day temperature should not rise above 18°C (65°F) and the night temperature should be below 10°C (50°F). Most species flower during this dormant winter period. The roots rot readily if covered by compost so plants should be either mounted on rafts or slabs, with no moss around their roots, or planted in net pots, baskets, or clay pots with only a few pieces of coarse bark or charcoal at the base. In the wild, many species grow in areas where there is a long dry season.

Barkeria lindleyana Bateman ex Lindley

Plants up to 90 cm tall. Leaves distichous, up to 15 cm long, sometimes marked with purple. Inflorescence 30–40 cm long, few- to many-flowered. Flowers about 7.5 cm diameter, white, lilac, or purple; petals broader than sepals; lip suborbicular to oblong-quadrate, the edges undulate.

Usually epiphytic, in woodland and scrub, up to 2500 m (8250 ft.)

Mexico to Costa Rica

SIMILAR SPECIES: *Barkeria cyclotella* Reichenbach f., a Mexican endemic, is a smaller plant than *B. lindleyana*, with smaller, bright magenta flowers.

Barkeria melanocaulon A. Richard & Galeotti

Roots thick, numerous. Inflorescence long, few- to many-flowered. Flowers ca. 3 cm across, lilac-pink, opening in summer and lasting for about 2 months.

On rocks in open woodland in dry areas, sometimes epiphytic, 1600–1700 m (5300–5600 ft.)

Mexico

SIMILAR SPECIES: *Barkeria whartoniana* (C. Schweinfurth) Soto Arenas grows in dry forest at altitudes of about 250 m (825 ft.).

Barkeria skinneri Paxton

Plants to 50 cm high. Leaves distichous, elliptic or lanceolate. Inflorescence erect, 15–30 cm long, few- to many-flowered. Flowers long-lasting, 3–4 cm across, lilac-purple, rose-purple, or magenta, with yellow keels on lip.

Epiphytic in woodland, up to 1300 m (4300 ft.)

Guatemala, Mexico

Barkeria spectabilis Bateman ex Lindley

Erect plants up to 90 cm tall. Leaves up to 15 × 4 cm. Inflorescence laxly few- to many-flowered. Flowers large, 4–8 cm diameter, pale pink speckled with red.

Epiphytic, occasionally lithophytic, in oak forest, 1500–2200 m (5000–7260 ft.)

Southern Mexico, Guatemala, El Salvador, Nicaragua

Barkeria uniflora (Lexarza) Dressler & Halbinger

SYN. *Barkeria elegans* Knowles & Westcott

The type species of the genus and among the most beautiful. Inflorescence to 30 cm long, laxly 2- to 5-flowered. Flowers 5–6 cm across, deep pink, the lip white with a pink blush and a large, deep crimson blotch towards the apex.

Epiphytic in dry forest, often near the coast

Mexico

Batemannia Lindley

TRIBE: Maxillarieae

SUBTRIBE: Zygopetalinae

ETYMOLOGY: Named for James Bateman (1811–1897), an English orchid grower

DISTRIBUTION: 5 species in Trinidad and South America

Epiphytes related to *Galeottia*, with short, branching rhizomes; pseudobulbs clustered, 4-angled, with papery sheaths at the base, 1- to 3-leaved at the apex. Leaves elliptic, plicate. Inflorescences basal, unbranched; floral bracts large, concave. Flowers large, showy, scented (not always

Barbosella cucullata. S. Manning

Barkeria skinneri

Barkeria spectabilis

Barkeria lindleyana

pleasantly), facing one way; dorsal sepal elliptic to oblong; petals similar but slightly larger; lateral sepals linear, inrolled; lip trilobed, fleshy, erect, with a callus of 2 ridges, side lobes erect, the tips recurved and dentate, midlobe decurved, emarginate. Pollinia 4.

CULTIVATION: Plants are usually grown potted, in a standard to coarse epiphyte compost, in intermediate conditions, with good light and high humidity. They flower better if potbound and should not be repotted frequently. When growth is complete, plants should be kept dry, with occasional misting to prevent the pseudobulbs from wrinkling.

Batemannia colleyi Lindley

Pseudobulbs to 6 cm long. Leaves to 20 × 6 cm. Inflorescence arching or pendent, ca. 20 cm long, to about 10-flowered. Flowers to 7.5 cm across; sepals and petals greenish flushed with brown or maroon, often tipped with greenish white; lip yellowish cream, the base purple inside.

Epiphytic in heavy shade in wet forest, 50–400 m (165–1320 ft.)

Trinidad, Bolivia, Colombia, Ecuador, Peru, Venezuela

Beclardia A. Richard

TRIBE: Vandeae

SUBTRIBE: Aerangidinae

ETYMOLOGY: Named for Augustine Beclard, an anatomy professor in Paris

DISTRIBUTION: 2 species in Madagascar, Mauritius, and Réunion

Small to medium-sized plants with slightly flattened stems, rooting at the base. Leaves distichous. Inflorescences axillary, several-flowered. Flowers white and green; sepals and petals spreading, the petals broader than the sepals; lip large, papillose inside, 4-lobed, with a funnel-shaped spur at the base.

CULTIVATION: Plants can be slow to establish. They are usually grown potted in a standard epiphyte mixture, in intermediate conditions with moderate shade and high humidity.

Beclardia macrostachya

(Thouars) A. Richard

Erect plants 20–40 cm tall. Leaves narrowly oblong, to 15 × 2 cm. Inflorescence 20–40 cm long, 5- to 12-flowered. Flowers 3–4 cm across, white, the lip greenish inside; spur about 6 mm long.

Epiphytic on trunks and branches in various forest types, 0–2000 m (6600 ft.)

Madagascar, Mauritius, Réunion

SIMILAR SPECIES: *Beclardia grandiflora* Bosser from Madagascar has slightly larger flowers and a spur 15 mm long. It occurs in humid forests at 900–1000 m (3000–3300 ft.).

Bifrenaria Lindley

SYN. *Cydoniorchis* Senghas, *Stenocoryne* Lindley

TRIBE: Maxillarieae

SUBTRIBE: Zygopetalinae

ETYMOLOGY: From Latin *bi*, two, and *frenum*, rein or strap, referring to the 2 straplike stipites

DISTRIBUTION: About 20 species in Central and South America

Sympodial epiphytes or terrestrials with conical to ovoid pseudobulbs, 1- to 2-leaved at apex. Leaves thin-textured, pleated. Inflorescences arising at base of plant, short, erect or arching, unbranched, 1- to several-flowered. Flowers showy, scented, waxy; sepals and petals usually spreading, subsimilar; lateral sepals joined to column-foot forming a spurlike mentum; lip trilobed, clawed, with a fleshy, ridged callus.

CULTIVATION: Plants should be grown in intermediate conditions, with good light and high humidity. They flower better if pot-bound and should not be repotted frequently. When growth is complete, they should be kept dry, with occasional misting to prevent the pseudobulbs from wrinkling.

Bifrenaria atropurpurea

(Loddiges) Lindley

Pseudobulbs ovoid, to 8 cm long, 1-leafed. Leaves to 25 × 7 cm, lanceolate-oblong. Inflorescence 6–8 cm long, 3- to 5-flowered. Flowers 5–6 cm across, purple-brown, yellowish in center, the lip pink and white.

Epiphytic or lithophytic in open areas in forest, 200–2000 m (660–6600 ft.)

Brazil

Bifrenaria aureofulva Lindley

SYN. *Stenocoryne secunda* Hoehne, *Bifrenaria secunda* (Hoehne) Pabst

Pseudobulbs small, clustered, 4-angled at the base, 1-leafed. Inflorescence short, erect, arching or pendulous, 1- to 15-flowered. Flowers bright orange-yellow, fragrant, not opening wide, 2–3 cm long. Flowering summer.

Epiphytic in forest, 200–1500 m (660–5000 ft.)

Brazil

Bifrenaria harrisoniae (Hooker) Reichenbach f.

Pseudobulbs to 9 cm long, 4-angled, green, with a dark ring at apex, 1-leafed. Leaves to 30 × 12 cm, elliptic, dark green. Inflorescence to 7 cm long, 1- to 2-flowered. Flowers 7–8 cm across, waxy, strongly scented, creamy white; lip deep pink or red towards apex, deep yellow in the center. Flowering summer.

Epiphytic in open forest or woodland or lithophytic in rock cracks, 200–1150 m (660–3800 ft.)

Brazil

Bifrenaria tetragona (Lindley) Schlechter

SYN. *Cydoniorchis tetragona* (Lindley) Senghas, *Lycaste tetragona* (Lindley) Lindley

Leaf fleshy, pleated, elliptic. Inflorescence 3- or 4-flowered. Flowers ca. 5.5 cm across, waxy, long-

Batemannia colleyi

Beclardia macrostachya. J. Hermans

Bifrenaria aureofulva

Bifrenaria harrisoniae

lasting, yellow-green or yellow heavily striped with red-brown.

Montane forest at 300–1200 m (1000–4000 ft.), growing on rocks in open situations.

Southeast Brazil

SIMILAR SPECIES: *Bifrenaria wittigii* (Reichenbach f.) Hoehne (syn. *Lycaste wittigii* Reichenbach f., *Cydoniorchis wittigii* (Reichenbach f.) Senghas) has flowers that are similar in general appearance—yellow heavily striped with red-brown—but the lip when flattened is broader than long, whereas in *B. tetragona* it is longer than broad.

Bletia Ruíz & Pavón

TRIBE: Epidendreae
SUBTRIBE: Bletiinae
ETYMOLOGY: Named for Don Luis Blet (fl. 1794), a Spanish apothecary and botanist
DISTRIBUTION: About 30 species in Florida, West Indies, Central and South America, with most in Mexico

Terrestrial plants with subterranean corms, lying just below the surface. Leaves 1–5, deciduous, petiolate, lanceolate, acute, plicate. Inflorescences erect, occasionally branched, several- to many-flowered. Flowers often showy; sepals and petals free, subsimilar; lip entire or trilobed, the disc with lamellae, sometimes toothed.
CULTIVATION: Grow at intermediate to warm temperatures in good light in a free-draining compost based on bark, sharp sand, and leaf mold. Plants require plenty of water and fertilizer while growing but should be kept dry once the leaves die back. Plants are easily propagated by division.

Bletia campanulata Lexarza

A variable species but easily distinguished by the bell-shaped flowers that do not open wide. Flowers pink to magenta, lip white, the margins undulate, edged with pink.

Rocky hillsides, in grass under open forest, 1500–2100 m (5000–7000 ft.)

Mexico to Bolivia

Bletia catenulata Ruíz & Pavón

Robust plants; corms 6–8 cm long. Leaves to 90 × 8 cm. Inflorescence 50–150 cm, several- to many-flowered. Flowers large, ca. 8 cm across, bright pink to magenta, rarely white, with broad, almost round petals; lip darker, with white lamellae, the margins undulate.

In cultivation, *Bletia catenulata* does not require as long a dry rest period as most species.

Often in disturbed habitats, 400–2500 m (1320–8250 ft.)

Colombia to Bolivia

Bletia purpurea (Lamarck) De Candolle

Leaves 3–5, 80–90 × 4–6 cm. Inflorescence 50–150 cm long, sometimes branched, several- to many-flowered. Flowers 4–5 cm across, pink, white, mauve, or magenta, the lip darker with yellowish-white lamellae; sepals and petals ovate; lip deeply trilobed, midlobe ± rectangular.

Very varied habitat from dry, rocky places to swamps, to 2000 m (6600 ft.)

Florida to Brazil

Bletilla Reichenbach f.

TRIBE: Arethuseae
SUBTRIBE: Coelogyninae
ETYMOLOGY: Diminutive of *Bletia*
DISTRIBUTION: 5 species in East Asia

Terrestrial plants with cormlike pseudobulbs. Leaves apical, several, deciduous, pleated, linear to lanceolate. Inflorescences terminal, unbranched, loosely several-flowered. Sepals and petals similar, ± lanceolate. Lip trilobed, side lobes erect, midlobe recurved. Pollinia 4, in 2 pairs.
CULTIVATION: Bletillas are hardy except in severe frost. They prefer light shade and a humid but well-drained soil with plenty of organic material that does not become too wet in winter. They also do well in pots, and in wet climates this is probably a better option as they can be kept cool and dry in an alpine house or cold frame in winter, after the leaves have fallen.

Bletilla ochracea Schlechter

Plants to 50 cm tall. Leaves 3–4, to 35 × 2.5 cm, oblong-lanceolate. Inflorescence 3- to 8-flowered. Flowers 3.5 cm across; sepals and petals yellow, lip white mottled with yellow and purple, the disc with 5 lamellae extending for most of the length of the midlobe. Flowering summer.

Grassy and rocky places in open woodland, 900–2400 m (3000–7900 ft.)

China to Vietnam

Bletilla striata (Thunberg) Reichenbach f.

SYN. *Bletilla hyacinthina* (J. E. Smith) Reichenbach f.

Plants to 60 cm tall. Leaves to 45 × 4 cm, oblong-lanceolate. Inflorescence loosely 3- to 8-flowered. Flowers 5–5.5 cm across, pink, magenta, or white, the lip heavily marked with magenta and yellow, white in the throat, the disc with 5 frilly lamellae extending down the midlobe. Flowering in early summer.

This is by far the most widely grown species. Varieties with variegated leaves are particularly valued in Japan.

Among rocks on grassy slopes, 1100–3200 m (3600–10,500 ft.)

China, Japan, Tibet

Bolusiella Schlechter

TRIBE: Vandeae
SUBTRIBE: Aerangidinae
ETYMOLOGY: Named for South African botanist Sir Harry Bolus (1834–1911)
DISTRIBUTION: 6 species of epiphytes in tropical and South Africa

Small monopodial epiphytes, sometimes branching at the base to form clumps; stems very short; roots fine. Leaves fleshy, laterally flattened, distichous, arranged in a fan. Inflorescences axillary, few- to many-flowered, unbranched. Flowers very small, white; sepals and petals subequal; lip trilobed or entire, spurred at the base. Column very short.
CULTIVATION: With their fleshy leaves, these species are quick to rot and so should be mounted on a small slab of bark. They need intermediate to warm temperatures, high humidity throughout the year, and moderate shade.

Bifrenaria tetragona

Bletilla ochracea

Bletia catenulata

Bletia purpurea

Bletilla striata. E. la Croix

Bolusiella iridifolia (Rolfe) Schlechter

Leaves several, 1.5–4 cm long with a groove along the upper surface. Inflorescence 2–6 cm long, densely several- to many-flowered; bracts brown or black. Flowers tiny, sepals 1–3 mm long, lip 1–5 mm long, spur to 2 mm long.

Two subspecies are recognized. Subsp. *iridifolia* has brown bracts, shorter than the flowers, and a spur over 1 mm long. Subsp. *picea* P. J. Cribb has black bracts, longer than the flowers, and a spur less than 1 mm long.

Epiphytic in forest and high-rainfall woodland, 1350–2400 m (4450–7900 ft.)

Tropical and South Africa, Comoro Islands

Bolusiella maudiae (Bolus) Schlechter

SYN. *Bolusiella imbricata* (Rolfe) Schlechter

Leaves 5–10, 1–5 cm long, 1 cm deep, sword-shaped, the sides convex, with no groove on the upper surface. Inflorescence to 7 cm long, densely many-flowered. Flowers white, small; sepals and petals to 4 mm long, lip 2–3 mm long; spur 1–2 mm long, conical, pointing forwards.

Riverine forest and high-rainfall woodland, 550–1900 m (1800–6300 ft.)

Tropical Africa, South Africa

Bonatea Willdenow

TRIBE: Orchideae

SUBTRIBE: Orchidinae

ETYMOLOGY: Named for Guiseppe Antonio Bonat (1753–1856), a botany professor at the University of Padua

DISTRIBUTION: 17 species in mainland Africa with 1 extending to Yemen

Terrestrials with long fleshy, tuberous roots. Stems leafy, inflorescence terminal, 1- to many-flowered. Flowers green or yellowish and white; dorsal sepal forming a hood with the upper petal lobes, lateral sepals partly joined to lip, lower petal lobes and stigmatic arms; petals bilobed, the lower lobe deflexed; lip joined to column, lateral sepals and lower petal lobes at base; free part trilobed, spurred at the base, often with a tooth in the mouth of the spur; spur cylindrical, long or short. Anther erect with long anther-canals; pollinia 2, each with long caudicle and naked viscidium; stigmatic arms long, the basal part joined to the lip, the free part club-shaped.

CULTIVATION: *Bonatea* species are relatively easily grown in a standard, free-draining terrestrial mix in intermediate conditions. They should be kept dry while dormant, with just an occasional sprinkling of water to prevent the roots shriveling. In cultivation, *B. speciosa*, the most widely grown species, tends to remain evergreen, with new growths developing as the old flowering shoots die back, and so should be watered throughout the year, although less often in winter.

Bonatea speciosa (Linnaeus f.) Willdenow

SYN. *Habenaria bonatea* Linnaeus f.

Robust plants 40–100 cm tall. Leaves several, 7–10 × 2–3 cm, lanceolate or ovate, bright green, clasping the stem at the base. Inflorescence fairly densely to about 15-flowered. Flowers large, ca. 5 cm across, green, white in the center, with a faint, spicy scent; sepals to 22 mm long, the laterals rolled up lengthways; upper petal lobe linear, lower lobe to 25 mm long, linear or oblanceolate, slightly curved; lip 30 mm long including a claw 10 mm long, all lobes linear; spur 3–4 cm long; stigmatic arms to 16 mm long.

Coastal bush, open woodland, and forest edge, usually on sandy soil, 0–1200 m (4000 ft.)

South Africa, Zimbabwe

SIMILAR SPECIES: *Bonatea antennifera* Rolfe (syn. *B. speciosa* var. *antennifera* (Rolfe) Sommerville) from Botswana, Mozambique, northern South Africa, and Zimbabwe differs in having more numerous flowers and longer lip lobes (to 35 mm long). It tends to grow in drier areas and the leaves are usually withered at flowering time.

Bonatea steudneri (Reichenbach f.) Durand & Schinz

SYN. *Bonatea ugandae* Summerhayes

Robust plants to 100 cm tall or more. Leaves to 17 × 6 cm, ovate, clasping the stem at base. Inflorescence rather loosely few- to many-flowered. Flowers green, white in the center; sepals to 26 mm long, the laterals deflexed, lanceolate; upper petal lobes 20–25 mm long, lower lobes 55–60 mm long, all lobes less than 1 mm wide; lip 70–100 mm long, including a claw 20–30 mm long; all lobes linear; midlobe to 35 mm long, side lobes to 85 mm long; spur 10–21 cm long, slender but slightly swollen at the tip.

Dry woodland and scrub, 900–1100 m (3000–3600 ft.)

Widespread in East Africa from Zimbabwe to Ethiopia, also in Yemen and Saudi Arabia

Brachionidium Lindley

TRIBE: Epidendreae

SUBTRIBE: Pleurothallidinae

ETYMOLOGY: From Greek *brachion*, arm, and the Latin diminutive *-idium*, referring to the short "arms" of the rostellum

DISTRIBUTION: About 65 species in Central and South America and the West Indies

Small epiphytic, lithophytic, or terrestrial plants, erect or creeping; rhizome sometimes branched, covered in sheaths. Stems short, erect, 1-leafed at apex. Leaves leathery, petiolate, elliptical. Inflorescences 1-flowered. Flowers usually nonresupinate; sepals and petals thin-textured, often with tails; dorsal sepal free, lateral sepals joined into a synsepal; lip fleshy, entire or trilobed, hinged to column-foot. Pollinia 6 or 8.

CULTIVATION: These small plants are not easily grown. They require cool conditions, with high humidity and good ventilation at all times. Those with creeping stems need to

Bolusiella maudiae. E. la Croix

Bonatea speciosa

be mounted, while those with erect stems can be either mounted or grown in pots in a fine bark-based or a sphagnum/perlite mixture.

Brachionidium ballatrix Luer & Hirtz

Plants to 8 cm tall. Leaves to 3 × 1.2 cm, elliptical. Inflorescence 2.5–3 cm long. Flowers yellow; sepals and petals broadly ovate, 23–25 mm long including slender tails ca. 14 mm long, the petals with ciliate margins; lip very small.

Terrestrial in cloud forest, 1300 m (4300 ft.)

Southern Ecuador

Brachionidium rugosum Luer & Hirtz

Rhizome erect, 20–30 cm tall, sometimes branched. Leaves to 2 cm

Brachionidium ballatrix

Brachionidium rugosum

long, thick, wrinkled, purple below. Inflorescence ca. 1 cm long. Flowers nonresupinate, translucent green, flushed with brown, ca. 2 cm across, the sepals and petals lacking tails; lip broader than long.

Epiphytic in scrubby vegetation, ca. 3200 m (11,550 ft.)

Ecuador

Brachtia Reichenbach f.

TRIBE: Maxillarieae
SUBTRIBE: Oncidiinae
ETYMOLOGY: Named for Captain Albert Bracht, an Austro-Hungarian army officer
DISTRIBUTION: 7 species in the Andes from Venezuela to Ecuador

Small epiphytes with an ascending rhizome covered with papery sheaths; pseudobulbs compressed, narrowly oblong, 1- to 2-leaved at apex, enclosed in leaf-bearing sheaths. Leaves sometimes fleshy. Inflorescences lateral, many-flowered; bracts distichous, inflated, prominent. Flowers small, fleshy; sepals narrowly ovate, the laterals decurrent on the ovary; petals broader than the sepals; lip fleshy, saccate at base with a 2-ridged callus.

CULTIVATION: These cool-growing plants do best mounted and require shaded, humid conditions, like cool-growing masdevallias.

Brachtia andina Reichenbach f.

SYN. *Brachtia verruculitera* Schlechter

Pseudobulbs to 4 cm long, 1-leafed. Inflorescence to 20 cm long, erect, many-flowered; floral bracts inflated, about as long as the flowers. Flowers long-lasting, 10–15 mm across; sepals and petals orange-yellow, lip white, yellow in throat.

Epiphytic in wet cloud forest, 2000–2800 m (6600–9250 ft.)

Colombia, Ecuador

SIMILAR SPECIES: *Brachtia glumacea* Reichenbach f. from Colombia and Venezuela has bright yellow flowers.

Brachycorythis Lindley

TRIBE: Orchideae
SUBTRIBE: Orchidinae
ETYMOLOGY: From Greek *brachys*, short, and *korys*, helmet, referring to the hood formed by the dorsal sepal and petals
DISTRIBUTION: 36 species, most in Africa with about a dozen in tropical and subtropical Asia and 2 in Madagascar

Terrestrial, rarely epiphytic, plants with spindle-shaped or ellipsoid, hairy, tuberous roots. Stems leafy. Leaves usually numerous, sometimes hairy. Inflorescences terminal, unbranched, few- to many-flowered, with leafy floral bracts. Flowers often small, usually mauve, pink, or purple but sometimes white or yellow; sepals free, laterals spreading, dorsal forming a hood with the petals; petals entire, usually joined to the column at base; lip in 2 parts, the basal part (hypochile) boat-shaped and spurred or saccate at the base, the apical part (epichile) entire or lobed.

CULTIVATION: Although many species are showy, few are in cultivation. Plants should be grown in an open, free-draining mixture in intermediate conditions, in fairly heavy shade. They should be watered freely while in growth but kept almost dry when they die back after flowering, with only occasional sprinkling of water to stop the fleshy roots shriveling.

Brachycorythis helferi (Reichenbach f.) Summerhayes

Plants 15–60 cm tall. Leaves spreading, to 14 × 3.5 cm. Inflorescence several-flowered. Flowers ca. 3 cm across, mauve-pink, the lip with lines of brownish dots; lip epichile to 33 mm long, almost orbicular, the apex sometimes emarginate; spur 6.5–10.5 mm long.

Terrestrial in grassland, open deciduous forest, 10–1600 m (30–5300 ft.)

Northeastern India, Laos, Myanmar, Thailand

Brachycorythis kalbreyeri Reichenbach f.

Plants 15–40 cm tall. Leaves numerous, to 11 × 2.5 cm, lanceolate, acute. Inflorescence laxly several-flowered; floral bracts longer than basal flowers. Flowers showy, ca. 5 cm across, mauve-pink or lilac; dorsal sepal and petals to 15 mm long, lip to 30 mm long, trilobed, the midlobe triangular, much smaller than the broad side lobes; spur absent.

Although this species is usually epiphytic in the wild, in cultivation it can be grown as described elsewhere (see genus entry), in a similar way to species of *Stenoglottis*.

Epiphytic or lithophytic in evergreen and riverine forest in deep shade, often growing on mossy logs, 1800–2350 m (6000–7800 ft.)

Cameroon, DR Congo, Kenya, Liberia, Sierra Leone, Uganda

Brachycorythis macrantha (Lindley) Summerhayes

Robust plants to 40 cm tall. Leaves spreading, to 13 × 5 cm. Inflorescence densely to about 20-flowered. Flowers green with a mauve to lilac lip; sepals and petals ca. 10 mm long, lip ca. 20 mm long, the epichile fan-shaped; spur conical, 7–10 mm long.

Terrestrial in shade in forest, occasionally lithophytic on mossy rocks, 240–900 m (800–3000 ft.)

West and Central Africa

Brassavola R. Brown

TRIBE: Epidendreae
SUBTRIBE: Laeliinae
ETYMOLOGY: Named for Venetian botanist R. Brassavola (1500–1555)
DISTRIBUTION: About 20 species in Central and South America and the West Indies

Epiphytic or lithophytic plants with woody, creeping rhizome; pseudobulbs narrow, cylindrical,

Brachtia glumacea

Brachycorythis helferi. J. Hermans

1-leafed at the apex. Leaves narrowly terete, fleshy, usually pendent. Inflorescences arising either from rhizome or (usually) from apex of pseudobulb, 1- to several-flowered, often pendent. Flowers showy, white or green, night-scented; sepals and petals spreading, subsimilar, linear or narrowly lanceolate; lip unlobed, tubular at base, spreading towards apex. Pollinia 8.

CULTIVATION: Because of their pendent habit, brassavolas are usually grown mounted or in a basket in a fairly coarse epiphyte mixture. They require intermediate temperatures and good light. Water well while in growth but allow the compost to dry out between waterings.

Brachycorythis kalbreyeri. J. Stewart

Brassavola acaulis Lindley & Paxton

SYN. *Brassavola lineata* Hooker

Pseudobulbs clustered, to 15 cm long. Leaves to 60 cm, pendent, fleshy. Inflorescence arising from rhizome, 1- to 5-flowered. Flowers to 8 cm across, waxy, strongly scented; sepals and petals green or greenish white, lip white.

Epiphytic in wet forest in high rainfall areas, 1000–1300 m (3300–4300 ft.)

Costa Rica, Guatemala, Panama

Brassavola cucullata (Linnaeus) R. Brown

SYN. *Brassavola appendiculata* A. Richard

Pseudobulb very slender, to 12 cm long. Leaves to 25 cm long, pendent. Inflorescence arising at base of leaf, ca. 20 cm long, 1-flowered. Flowers scented, nodding, creamy white tipped with green; sepals and petals drooping, to 7 cm long and 7 mm wide; lip fringed at the base, sometimes with red marks.

Epiphytic in dryish, deciduous forest, 50–400 m (165–1320 ft.)

West Indies and Central America from Mexico to Venezuela.

Brassavola nodosa (Linnaeus) Lindley

LADY OF THE NIGHT

Pseudobulbs slender, to 15 cm long. Leaves to 30 × 2–3 cm, fleshy, curved. Inflorescence to 20 cm long, 3- to 5-flowered. Flowers to 8 cm across, pale green or creamy white with a white, heart-shaped lip, strongly scented at night. Flowers throughout year.

Epiphytic or lithophytic, often in rather dry areas, 0–500 m (1650 ft.)

Central America, West Indies

Brassavola subulifolia Lindley

SYN. *Brassavola cordata* Lindley

Pseudobulbs to 15 cm long, narrowly cylindrical. Leaves erect or arching, 12–15 cm long, narrowly cylindrical. Inflorescence 1- to few-flowered. Flowers 4.5 cm across, vanilla-scented at night, green or cream with a white lip. Flowering summer.

Epiphytic on large trees in woodland

West Indies, Brazil

Brassavola tuberculata Hooker

SYN. *Brassavola ceboletta* Reichenbach f., *B. fragrans* Lemaire, *B. perrinii* Lindley

Pseudobulbs very slender, to 15 cm long. Leaves terete, grooved above, to 25 cm long, pendulous. Inflorescence short, 3- to 6-flowered. Flowers to 7 cm across, very fragrant at night; sepals and petals linear, creamy yellow or lime green, sometimes red-spotted; lip elliptic, white, often green in the throat.

Epiphytic or lithophytic in forest

Brazil

Brassia R. Brown

SPIDER ORCHIDS

TRIBE: Maxillarieae

SUBTRIBE: Oncidiinae

ETYMOLOGY: Named for William Brass (d. 1783), an English botanist and illustrator

DISTRIBUTION: 33 species in tropical America

Small to large epiphytes, rarely terrestrial, with a stout rhizome; pseudobulbs usually well-spaced out, ovoid to cylindrical, 1- to 3-leaved at apex with several overlapping sheaths at the base. Leaves linear to oblong. Inflorescences arising from base of pseudobulbs, usually unbranched, few- to many-flowered. Sepals free, similar, linear-lanceolate, long acuminate. Petals similar but shorter. Lip shorter than sepals and petals with ridges or calli at the base. Column short, lacking a foot; pollinia 2, stipes and viscidium 1.

CULTIVATION: Plants can be potted in a free-draining mixture or mounted on a raft. They require cool or intermediate conditions with light shade and plenty of water while in growth. They should be kept fairly dry while resting.

Brassia arcuigera Reichenbach f.

SYN. *Brassia longissima* (Reichenbach f.) Nash

Pseudobulbs compressed with 2 sharp edges, 1-leafed. Inflorescence pendulous, to 80 cm long, loosely 4- to 15-flowered. Flowers large, yellow-green or orange with maroon or red-brown bars and blotches, lip white or cream with purple-brown spots at base; sepals 10–35 cm long, very slender and tapering.

Epiphytic in wet forest, 400–1500 m (1320–5000 ft.)

Costa Rica to Ecuador

SIMILAR SPECIES: *Brassia caudata* (Linnaeus) Lindley has 2-leaved pseudobulbs and shorter sepals (lateral sepals to 20 cm long). It is widely distributed from Florida to the West Indies, Central and South America. *Brassia verrucosa* Lindley, also from Central and South America, has prominent green warts on the lip.

Brassia cochleata Knowles & Westcott

SYN. *Brassia lawrenceana* Lindley

Pseudobulbs 10–12 cm long, laterally compressed, 2-leaved. Leaves 20–40 cm long. Inflorescence arching or pendent, longer than leaves, densely to 10-flowered. Flowers pale green or yellowish with red-brown spots at the base of the segments; sepals to 70 mm long, the lateral sepals twisted; lip fiddle-shaped, to 45 mm long, white or pale green.

Epiphytic in forest, 250–1200 m (825–4000 ft.)

Central and South America

Brassia lanceana Lindley

SYN. *Brassia pumila* Lindley

Pseudobulbs to 12 cm long, laterally compressed, 2-leaved. Leaves to 30 × 6 cm. Inflorescence to 35 cm tall, several-flowered. Flowers yellow,

Brassavola subulifolia

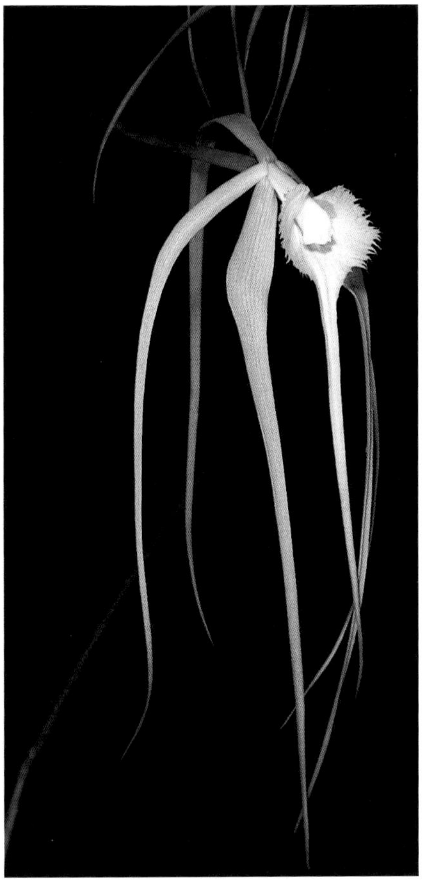

Brassavola cucullata

Brassavola nodosa

Brassavola tuberculata

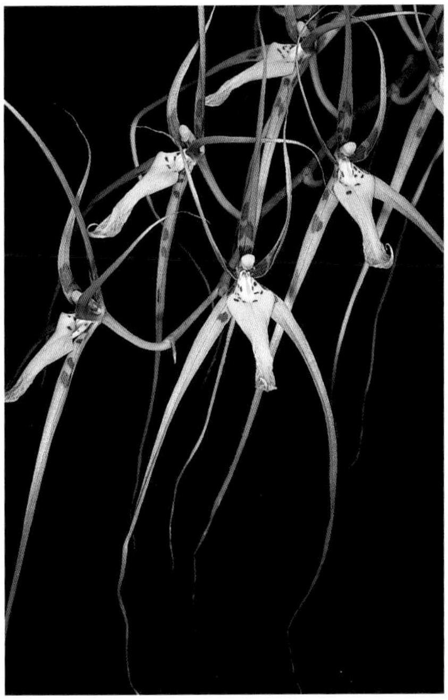

Brassia caudata

Brassia verrucosa

yellow-green, or yellowish brown with purple-brown marks; sepals to 65 mm long; lip to 35 mm long, cream spotted brown.

Epiphytic in wet forest, 500–1200 m (1650–4000 ft.)

Central and South America, Caribbean

Brassia maculata R. Brown
SYN. *Brassia guttata* Lindley
Pseudobulbs to 15 × 5 cm, laterally compressed, 1- to 2-leaved at apex. Leaves to 4 × 6 cm. Inflorescence 30–90 cm tall, loosely few- to many-flowered. Flowers showy, to 7 cm across, yellow-green marked with purple-brown; sepals to 65 mm long, linear-lanceolate, acuminate; lip to 32 × 25 mm, yellow spotted with purple.

Epiphytic or lithophytic on rocky slopes, 300–900 m (1000–3000 ft.)

Central America and the West Indies

SIMILAR SPECIES: *Brassia gireoudiana* Reichenbach f. & Warszewicz from Costa Rica and Panama has sepals up to 15 cm long and a yellow lip with brownish spots in the center only.

Broughtonia R. Brown

SYN. *Laeliopsis* Lindley, *Cattleyopsis* Lemaire
TRIBE: Epidendreae
SUBTRIBE: Laeliinae
ETYMOLOGY: Named for Arthur Broughton (d. 1796), an English botanist who worked in Jamaica
DISTRIBUTION: 6 species in the Greater Antilles (Caribbean)

Epiphytes, occasionally lithophytes, with clustered pseudobulbs, usually flattened, cylindrical to ovoid, enclosed by papery sheaths. Leaves 2, stiff, leathery or fleshy. Inflorescences terminal, the scape longer than the leaves, branched or unbranched, few- to several-flowered. Flowers showy; sepals subsimilar, petals much wider; lip entire or obscurely trilobed. Column winged towards the apex; pollinia 4 or 8.

Broughtonia has been used in intergeneric hybridization, almost all involving *B. sanguinea*.

CULTIVATION: Plants are most successful mounted on a slab or raft as good drainage is essential to prevent rot. They require warm conditions and bright light, and must not be overwatered.

Broughtonia sanguinea (Swartz) R. Brown
SYN. *Broughtonia coccinea* Hooker
Pseudobulbs to 5 cm long, round, flattened. Leaves to 18 cm, narrowly oblong. Inflorescence 20–50 cm tall, sometimes branched, to ca. 12-flowered. Flowers 2–5 cm across, ± flat, variable in color but usually brilliant red; lip yellow in throat, orbicular, the margins crisped or dentate.

Epiphytic in woodland, or lithophytic on exposed limestone rocks, 0–750 m (2460 ft.)

Jamaica

SIMILAR SPECIES: *Broughtonia negrilensis* Fowlie, also endemic to Jamaica, is a slightly larger plant with mauve-pink flowers and a tubular lip with an undulate margin, heavily veined with reddish purple.

Bryobium Lindley

TRIBE: Podochileae
SUBTRIBE: Eriinae
ETYMOLOGY: From Latin *bryos*, moss, and *bios*, life, referring to how the plants grow among moss
DISTRIBUTION: About 20 species from Sri Lanka through Asia to the Pacific Islands

Epiphytes with a creeping rhizome; roots branched; pseudobulbs ovoid to spindle-shaped, with 1–3 leaves at or near the apex, covered with sheaths at the base. Leaves leathery, folded, much longer than pseudobulbs. Inflorescences terminal or subterminal, unbranched. Flowers not opening wide, sometimes hairy; lateral sepals forming mentum with column-foot; petals free, smaller than sepals; lip recurved, simple or trilobed with a callus of 2 or 3 ridges. Pollinia 8, in 2 groups.

Bryobium has in the past been treated as a section of *Eria*.

CULTIVATION: As for *Eria*. Most species are easily grown in intermediate conditions with partial shade and high humidity. Plants with long, creeping rhizomes are better mounted. They should be kept drier in winter but their pseudobulbs not allowed to shrivel.

Bryobium hyacinthoides (Blume) Y. P. Ng & P. J. Cribb
SYN. *Eria hyacinthoides* (Blume) Lindley
Pseudobulbs conical, 6–10 cm long, 2-leaved at apex, the base covered with sheaths. Leaves to 40 × 5 cm, narrowly lanceolate. Inflorescence to 18 cm long, many-flowered. Flowers to 2 cm across, rather unpleasantly scented, white, the lip trilobed with purple side lobes.

Epiphytic, occasionally lithophytic, 450–1700 m (1500–5600 ft.)

Borneo, Bali, Java, Malaysia, Sumatra

Bulbophyllum Thouars

TRIBE: Dendrobieae
SUBTRIBE: Bulbophyllinae
ETYMOLOGY: From Greek *bulbos*, bulb, and *phyllon*, leaf, referring to the leafy pseudobulbs
DISTRIBUTION: More than 1000 species in Asia, Australasia, Africa, and tropical America

Very small to very large epiphytes, sometimes lithophytes, with pseudobulbs varying in shape, 1- or 2-leaved at apex, set close together or well apart on a long or short rhizome. Leaves thin-textured, leathery or fleshy. Inflorescences arising from base of pseudobulbs, unbranched, 1- to many-flowered, the rachis sometimes swollen or flattened. Dorsal sepal free, lateral sepals often larger, joined to the column-foot to form a mentum, sometimes joined to each other. Petals free, much smaller than sepals. Lip entire or trilobed, fleshy, often fringed or pubescent, hinged to column-foot.

One of the largest of all orchid genera. Some species are fragrant but others are very malodorous. Some authors (for example, Garay, Hamer, and Siegerist 1994; Siegerist 2001) have divided *Bulbophyllum* into several segregate genera, but here the genus is treated in the broad sense. Species that have been known as *Cirrhopetalum* have flowers in an umbel.

Bulbophyllum species have not been widely used in hybridization. The most widely grown hybrid is *B.* Elizabeth Ann (*B. longissimum* × *B. rothschildianum*).

CULTIVATION: Most species are easy to grow and will succeed in intermediate conditions although those from low altitudes will do better in warm. Species with clustered pseudobulbs do well in shallow pots in a fine to medium bark-based compost, but those with long rhizomes are better in baskets or mounted on a raft or vertical slab. Most require only light shade and should be given plenty of water while in growth, although care must be taken not to get water on the new growths as they rot easily. Plants should be kept dry while resting, but sprayed occasionally so that the pseudobulbs do not shrivel. Bulbophyllums are increasing in popularity and more are becoming available to growers.

Bulbophyllum ambrosia

(Hance) Schlechter

Pseudobulbs to 4 cm long, ovoid, 1-leafed, set well apart on the rhizome. Leaves ca. 12 cm long. Inflorescence 1-flowered. Flower scented, 20–30 mm across, white with red stripes on the sepals. It is a vigorous grower, best in a basket.

Epiphytic in forest, often on trunks, sometimes lithophytic, 300–1300 m (1000–4300 ft.)

Nepal to China and Vietnam

Bulbophyllum barbigerum

Lindley

Pseudobulbs ± orbicular, 2–3 cm across, flattened, 1-leafed. Leaves ca. 10 cm long. Inflorescence to 20 cm long, arching or erect, several-flowered. Flowers deep red, the sepals tinged with green, lip 10 mm long, the margins ciliate, with long, fine, clavate red-brown hairs near the apex.

Epiphytic on trunks and branches in forest, to 900 m (3000 ft.)

West and Central Africa

Bulbophyllum biflorum

Teijsmann & Binnendijk

SYN. *Cirrhopetalum biflorum* (Teijsmann & Binnendijk) J. J. Smith

Pseudobulbs ca. 4 cm tall, set close together, 1-leafed. Leaves to 13 × 3 cm. Inflorescence 9–10 cm long, 2-flowered. Flowers 8–10 cm long,

Broughtonia negrilensis

Bulbophyllum ambrosia

Bulbophyllum barbigerum

Bryobium hyacinthoides. J. Comber

greenish yellow lightly or heavily marked with dark red, the lateral sepals 7–8 cm long, linear, tapering, joined together to near the apex.

Epiphytic in woodland, often in good light, 700–1100 m (2300–3600 ft.)

Widespread in Southeast Asia

Bulbophyllum careyanum
(Hooker) Sprengel

Pseudobulbs oblong, 1-leafed, to 5 × 2.5 cm, set well apart on a stout rhizome. Leaves to 25 × 5 cm. Inflorescence 20–25 cm tall, the flowering head cylindrical, densely many-flowered. Flowers small, orange-yellow to greenish, spotted or flushed with red-brown or purple.

Epiphytic in evergreen and deciduous forest, 200–1500 m (660–5000 ft.)

Himalayas, Myanmar, Thailand, Vietnam

Bulbophyllum cocoinum
Lindley

Pseudobulbs ovoid, to 5 × 3 cm, 1-leafed, set 3–6 cm apart on rhizome. Leaves to 25 cm, lanceolate. Inflorescence 10–40 cm long, many-flowered, erect or pendent. Flowers white, sometimes pink-tipped, not opening wide; sepals to 12 mm long.

Epiphytic in lowland and submontane forest, to 2000 m (6600 ft.)

West and Central Africa

SIMILAR SPECIES: *Bulbophyllum schimperianum* Kraenzlin (syn. *B. acutisepalum* De Wildeman), also from West and Central Africa, is a smaller plant with slightly smaller flowers and pseudobulbs set close together.

Bulbophyllum dearei
(Reichenbach f.) Reichenbach f.

Pseudobulbs conical, to 3 cm long, 1-leafed. Leaves to 17 × 5 cm, oblong. Inflorescence 8–14 cm long, 1-flowered. Flowers large and showy, sometimes scented, to ca. 8 cm across, yellow, veined with orange and purple; dorsal sepal erect then arching forwards, lateral sepals curved, spreading.

Epiphytic in forest, occasionally lithophytic, 700–1200 m (2300–4000 ft.)

Borneo, Malaysia, Philippines

Bulbophyllum echinolabium
J. J. Smith

Pseudobulbs pear-shaped, 6–8 cm long, 1-leafed. Leaves to 35 × 10 cm. Inflorescence up to 70 cm long, the flowers open in succession. Flowers yellowish with red longitudinal stripes, to 40 cm long, the largest in the genus. The lip has short, sharp spines at the base and emits a smell of decay, which attracts blowflies.

Epiphytic in montane forest

Sulawesi

Bulbophyllum falcatum
(Lindley) Reichenbach f.

Pseudobulbs to 7 × 2 cm, 2-leaved, set up to 5 cm apart on the rhizome. Leaves lanceolate, to ca. 16 cm long. Inflorescence 3–40 cm long, several- to many-flowered. Rachis swollen or flattened, sometimes markedly so, sometimes hardly at all. Flowers distichous, greenish marked with brown, purple, yellow, or purple and yellow; dorsal sepal ca. 9 mm long.

Var. *bufo* (Lindley) J. J. Vermeulen (syn. *Bulbophyllum bufo* Lindley) has a rachis 30 cm long or more, with greenish-brown flowers opening over a long period.

Epiphytic in lowland and submontane forest, to 1800 m (6000 ft.)

West and Central Africa

Bulbophyllum graveolens
(Bailey) J. J. Smith

SYN. *Cirrhopetalum robustum* Rolfe

Pseudobulbs to 10 cm tall, 1-leafed, set ca. 4 cm apart on rhizome. Leaves to 60 × 10 cm. Inflorescence to 20 cm tall, umbellate, several- to many-flowered. Flowers 5 cm long, yellow, red in center, striking but with an unpleasant smell. In cultivation, requires warm temperatures, light shade, and high humidity.

Epiphytic in rain forest, 100–600 m (330–2000 ft.)

Papua New Guinea

Bulbophyllum lasiochilum
Parish & Reichenbach f.

SYN. *Cirrhopetalum breviscapum* Rolfe

Pseudobulbs 2–3 cm long, ovoid, 1-leafed, set ca. 3 cm apart on creeping rhizome. Leaves to 6 cm long. Inflorescence 1-flowered; dorsal sepals and petals purple, lateral sepals cream spotted red-brown, 2–3 cm long, incurved; lip purple with long marginal hairs.

Epiphytic in forest, to 1500 m (5000 ft.)

Malaysia, Thailand

Bulbophyllum lobbii Lindley

Pseudobulbs yellowish, 3–4 cm long, ovoid, 1-leafed, set ca. 4 cm apart on a stout, creeping rhizome. Leaves to 25 cm long. Inflorescence 10–15 cm long, 1-flowered. Flowers large, to 10 cm across, often with a spicy scent, variable in color but usually yellowish with red-brown marks and lines; dorsal sepal erect, lateral sepals curving under; lip strongly recurved.

Epiphytic in lowland and submontane forest, 100–2000 m (330–6600 ft.)

Widespread in Asia from northeastern India to Philippines

Bulbophyllum longiflorum
Thouars

SYN. *Cirrhopetalum umbellatum* (Forster f.) Hooker f. & Arnold

Pseudobulbs to 4 cm long, 1-leafed, set 3–6 cm apart on a creeping rhizome. Inflorescence to 20 cm long, umbellate, several-flowered. Flowers 4–5 cm long, variable in color, plain yellow, light purple mottled with darker purple, or mottled bronze.

Epiphytic in submontane and montane forest, 500–1700 m (1650–5600 ft.)

The most widespread species in the genus, occurring in tropical Africa, Madagascar, Asia, and Australasia

Bulbophyllum dearei

Bulbophyllum careyanum

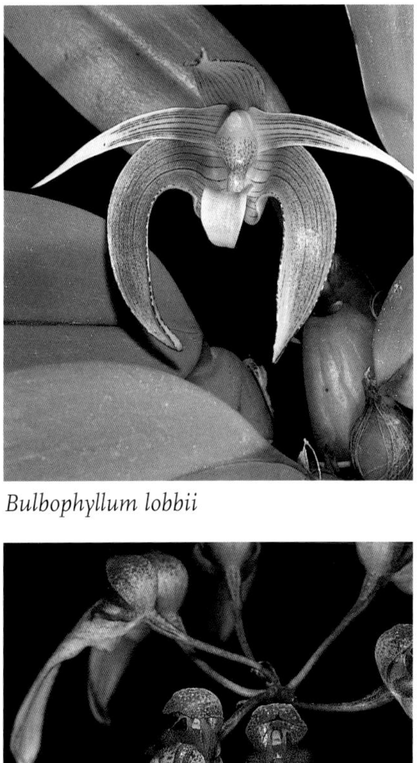

Bulbophyllum lobbii

Bulbophyllum echinolabium

Bulbophyllum falcatum. E. la Croix

Bulbophyllum longiflorum

Bulbophyllum longissimum (Ridley) J. J. Smith

SYN. *Cirrhopetalum longissimum* Ridley

Pseudobulbs to 4 cm long, 1-leafed, well-spaced out on rhizome. Leaves to 15 × 4.5 cm. Inflorescence arching or pendent, to 20 cm long, umbellate, 4- to 7-flowered. Flowers 20–30 cm long, white tinged with pink, the lateral sepals tapering to become filiform.

Epiphytic in lowland forest

Thailand

Bulbophyllum mastersianum (Rolfe) J. J. Smith

SYN. *Cirrhopetalum mastersianum* Rolfe

Pseudobulbs ovoid, 3–4 cm long, 1-leafed. Leaves to 13 × 2.5 cm. Inflorescence to 15 cm long, umbellate. Flowers ca. 5 cm long, yellow with a brownish tinge.

Epiphytic on tree trunks in hill forest, ca. 500 m (1650 ft.)

Borneo, Malaysia, Vietnam

Bulbophyllum maximum (Lindley) Reichenbach f.

SYN. *Bulbophyllum oxypterum* (Lindley) Reichenbach f., *B. platyrrhachis* (Rolfe) Schlechter

Pseudobulbs to 15 × 3 cm, yellow, ovoid, angled, 2-leaved, set 2–10 cm apart on a stout rhizome. Leaves to 20 × 6 cm, thick, leathery. Inflorescence to 80 cm long, many-flowered; rachis swollen and purple or orange-yellow and flattened. The latter form, where the rachis is almost leaflike, was known as *Bulbophyllum platyrrhachis*. Flowers small, yellow or green heavily mottled with purple, opening in succession.

Epiphytic in open woodland and riverine forest, occasionally lithophytic, to 1500 m (5000 ft.)

Widespread in tropical Africa

SIMILAR SPECIES: *Bulbophyllum sandersonii* (Hooker f.) Reichenbach f. (syn. *B. tentaculigerum*), also widespread in Africa, is a smaller plant with a swollen rachis, sometimes deep purple; the flowers are purplish, with narrow petals clubbed at the tip like a butterfly's antennae. *Bulbophyllum scaberulum* (Rolfe) Bolus is a variable species with greenish-brown flowers on a swollen rachis.

Bulbophyllum medusae (Lindley) Reichenbach f.

SYN. *Cirrhopetalum medusae* Lindley

Pseudobulbs to 4 cm long, set 5–6 cm apart on rhizome, 1-leafed. Leaves to 15 cm long. Inflorescence to 20 cm long, densely many-flowered, in an umbel. Flowers white or cream, the lateral sepals pendent, becoming filiform, ca. 15 cm long.

Epiphytic on trunks and large branches in lowland forest

Southeast Asia to Borneo and Sumatra

Bulbophyllum nymphopolitanum Kraenzlin

Pseudobulbs clustered, ovoid, ca. 3 × 2 cm, 1-leafed. Inflorescence erect, ca. 10 cm long (shorter than the leaves), 2- to 6-flowered, the flowers open in succession. Flowers large, to 8.5 cm long and 4 cm wide, glossy dark red, lip blackish red.

Epiphytic, occasionally lithophytic, in woodland, to 1000 m (3300 ft.)

Philippines

Bulbophyllum patens King ex Hooker f.

Pseudobulbs 1–2 cm long, set well apart, 1-leafed. Leaves ca. 15 × 5 cm. Inflorescence ca. 4 cm long, 1-flowered. Flowers opening almost flat, ca. 4.5 cm across, whitish or yellow heavily mottled with maroon.

Epiphytic on tree trunks in lowland forest, often in swampy areas, 0–100 m (330 ft.)

Southeast Asia to Borneo and Sumatra

Bulbophyllum plumatum Ames

SYN. *Bulbophyllum jacobsonii* J. J. Smith, *Rhytionanthos plumatum* (Ames) Garay, Hamer & Siegerist

Pseudobulbs ca. 2 × 1 cm, set 2–3 cm apart, 1-leafed. Leaves 7–10 cm long. Inflorescences slightly shorter, ± umbellate, 4-flowered. Flowers reddish purple or yellow, lateral sepals to 10 cm long, 7 mm wide, the inner margins joined at the base and the outer margins joined further up.

Epiphytic, ca. 1000 m (3300 ft.)

Malaysia, Philippines, Sumatra

Bulbophyllum purpureorhachis (De Wildeman) Schlechter

Pseudobulbs to 12 × 2 cm, 2-leaved, set 4–8 cm apart on the rachis. Leaves to 15 × 6 cm. Inflorescence to 90 cm long, erect, many-flowered, the rachis greenish brown flecked with purple, flattened and forming a spiral. Flowers small, purplish, set on either side of the rachis.

Epiphytic in lowland forest

West and Central Africa

Bulbophyllum putidum (Teijsmann & Binnendijk) J. J. Smith

SYN. *Cirrhopetalum fascinator* Rolfe, *C. putidum* Teijsmann & Binnendijk, *Mastigion putidum* (Teijsmann & Binnendijk) Garay, Hamer & Siegerist

Pseudobulbs to 2 cm high, ovoid, glossy green, clustered, 1-leafed. Leaves to 5 × 3 cm. Inflorescence to 10 cm tall, 1-flowered. Flower to 20 cm long, yellow-green marked with purple, the dorsal sepal fringed with fine purple hairs, the lateral sepals joined for most of their length, tapering to become filiform.

Epiphytic in wet submontane and montane forest, 1000–2500 m (3300–8250 ft.)

India to Borneo and the Philippines

SIMILAR SPECIES: *Bulbophyllum ornatissimum* (Reichenbach f.) J. J. Smith (syn. *Mastigion ornatissimum* (Reichenbach f.) Garay, Hamer & Siegerist) from India has an umbellate, 3- to 4-flowered inflorescence and slightly longer lateral sepals.

Bulbophyllum medusae

Bulbophyllum nymphopolitanum

Bulbophyllum sandersonii. E. la Croix

Bulbophyllum rothschildianum

(O'Brien) J. J. Smith
SYN. *Cirrhopetalum rothschildianum* O'Brien
Pseudobulbs ovoid, 1-leafed, to 4 cm long, set well apart on rhizome. Leaves to 15 × 2.5 cm. Inflorescence umbellate, 5- to 6-flowered. Flowers 9–15 cm long, smelling unpleasant, pinkish purple blotched with yellow, the lateral sepals tapering to become filiform, the dorsal sepal and petals with motile projections called palea round the margins.

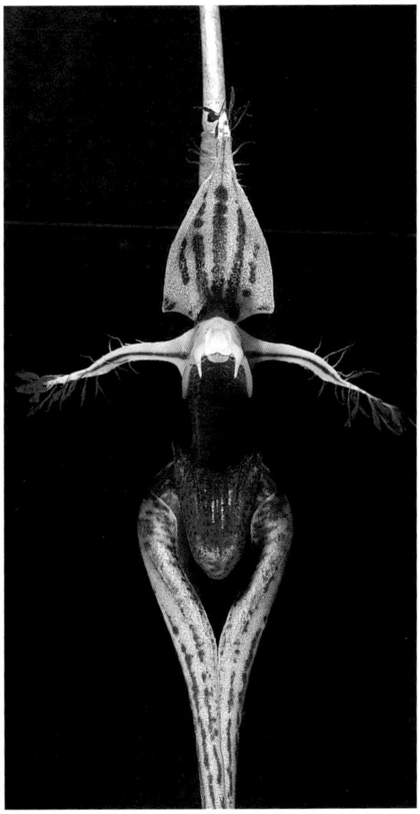

Bulbophyllum putidum

Bulbophyllum plumatum

Epiphytic in forest
India

SIMILAR SPECIES: *Bulbophyllum wendlandianum* (Kraenzlin) U. Dammer (syn. *Cirrhopetalum collettii* Hemsley, *C. wendlandianum* Kraenzlin) from Myanmar and Thailand is slightly smaller, with narrower and fewer flowers, which also have palea on the dorsal sepal and petals.

Bulbophyllum roxburghii (Lindley) Reichenbach f.

SYN. *Cirrhopetalum roxburghii* Lindley

Pseudobulbs subglobose, ca. 1 cm across, set 1–3 cm apart, 1-leafed. Leaves 3–5 cm long. Inflorescence slightly longer than leaves, umbellate, 5- to 12-flowered. Flowers 9–15 mm long, greenish yellow marked with reddish brown.

Epiphytic in low-lying, tropical woodland, 330 m (1100 ft.)

Northeastern India

Cadetia Gaudichaud

TRIBE: Dendrobieae
SUBTRIBE: Dendrobiinae
ETYMOLOGY: Named for Cadet de Gassicourt, a French chemist
DISTRIBUTION: About 60 species in Southeast Asia, the Pacific Islands, and Australia, with most in New Guinea

Small epiphytic plants related to *Dendrobium*; pseudobulbs slender and stemlike, occasionally ovoid, 1-leafed at apex. Flowers small, borne on slender pedicels singly or in small groups at the apex of the pseudobulb, subtended by a papery bract; sepals and petals free, the petals narrower than the sepals; lip trilobed, the side lobes joined at the base to the column-foot; midlobe hairy.

CULTIVATION: Clump-forming species can be grown in small pots in a standard, free-draining epiphyte mix, while those with a creeping rhizome do better on rafts. Most species need intermediate conditions with good light, high humidity, and good air movement.

Cadetia taylorii (F. Mueller) Schlechter

Stems to 10 cm tall, narrowly cylindrical, grooved, forming clumps. Leaves to 5 × 1 cm, oblong. Flowers ca. 12 mm across, borne 1 or 2 at a time, white, with a pink or yellow lip; lip midlobe recurved, fleshy, densely hairy.

Epiphytic or lithophytic in rain forest and open forest, 0–1200 m (4000 ft.)

Australia (northeastern Queensland), New Guinea

Caladenia R. Brown

TRIBE: Diurideae
SUBTRIBE: Caladeniinae
ETYMOLOGY: From Greek *kalos*, beautiful, and *adenos*, gland, referring to the prominent, often colored, calli on the lip
DISTRIBUTION: About 250 species, most in Australia but also in New Zealand, New Caledonia, and Indonesia (Bali, Java, Lombok, Timor, Sulawesi)

Deciduous terrestrials with paired, globose tubers enclosed in a fibrous tunic; new tubers formed on ends of short droppers. Leaf single, basal, usually linear to lanceolate, often hairy. Inflorescences erect, branched or unbranched, usually wiry, 1- to few-flowered. Flowers sometimes very brightly colored; sepals free (laterals rarely joined at the base), petals free, spreading; lip free, clawed, lacking a spur, usually trilobed, with 2 or more longitudinal rows of calli. Pollinia 4.

CULTIVATION: Grow in pans of standard terrestrial compost but with extra drainage material such as coarse sand, in light shade. The tubers rot easily, so it is essential that drainage is good and that the pans are not overwatered. Most species flower from late winter to late spring, and watering should start in midautumn and continue till mid or late spring, when the leaves start to turn yellow and die back. Many species are notoriously difficult to grow, but those that form colonies tend to be more successful in cultivation.

Caladenia catenata (Smith) Druce

Leaf linear, to 12 cm long, sparely hairy. Inflorescence to 30 cm tall, 1- or 2-flowered. Flowers ca. 3 cm across, white (rarely pinkish), lip midlobe orange; dorsal sepal erect, lateral sepals and petals deflexed; lip side lobes erect, midlobe recurved, the margins undulate.

Open woodland, often in sandy soil near coast

Australia (southern Queensland, New South Wales, eastern Victoria)

Caladenia latifolia R. Brown

PINK FAIRIES

Leaf linear, to 20 cm long, very hairy, often lying on the ground. Inflorescence to 40 cm tall, 1- to several-flowered. Flowers to 3.5 cm across, pale to deep pink; lip side lobes erect, with darker pink stripes, midlobe with several pairs of marginal, hairy, clublike calli.

Forms colonies in sandy coastal scrub and open woodland

South Australia, Tasmania

SIMILAR SPECIES: *Caladenia flava* R. Brown from Western Australia has bright yellow flowers and a different column shape. *Caladenia reptans* Lindley from Western Australia is like a small *C. latifolia* with the leaves purple-red on the underside. It sometimes hybridizes with *C. flava*.

Caladenia menziesii R. Brown

HARE ORCHID; RABBIT ORCHID

Leaf ca. 9 × 3 cm, ovate, glabrous, often lying on ground. Inflorescence to 25 cm tall, 1- to 3-flowered. Flowers pink and white, scented; dorsal sepal forming hood, lateral sepals deflexed, lanceolate, to 18 mm long; petals erect (like rabbit's or hare's ears), to 2 cm long; lip recurved, obscurely trilobed; calli stalked in 2–4 rows.

Bulbophyllum wendlandianum

Caladenia flava. H. Oakeley

Cadetia taylorii

Caladenia reptans. H. Oakeley

Caladenia latifolia. J. Stewart

This species is one of the easiest to grow but is reluctant to flower; in the wild, it flowers after fires. Storing dormant tubers with a ripe banana is said to promote flowering.

Forms colonies in open forest

Widespread in South Australia

Calanthe R. Brown

TRIBE: Collabieae

ETYMOLOGY: From Greek *kalos*, beautiful, and *anthos*, flower

DISTRIBUTION: Almost 200 species in Asia, Polynesia, Madagascar, and Africa

Mainly terrestrial, rarely epiphytic, plants with large or small pseudobulbs. Leaves 2 to several, pleated, petiolate, evergreen or deciduous. Flowers showy, white, pink, lilac, purple, or yellow; sepals and petals similar, usually spreading, lip trilobed, spurred, midlobe often deeply emarginate.

Calanthe Dominyi was the first recorded man-made orchid hybrid to flower, in 1856. In the late 19th century, deciduous hybrid calanthes were widely grown, then fell out of favor, but more recently have regained popularity.

CULTIVATION: Deciduous and evergreen species need different treatment. Pseudobulbs of deciduous species should be kept dry in a bright, cool (minimum 10°C (50°F)) place after the leaves have died back. In spring, pot the new pseudobulbs singly in a rich terrestrial compost and water and fertilize freely when the new growth starts to develop; while in growth, intermediate or even warm temperatures are suitable. Plants usually flower in autumn, then the leaves start to die back and the plants are dried off again. Some species, such as *Calanthe rosea*, *C. rubens*, and *C. vestita*, and hybrids derived from them flower in winter before the leaves appear. As far as I know, all Chinese and Japanese species are evergreen. Evergreen species should not be allowed to dry out completely, although they should be kept drier while resting. Many species are cool growing and do well in an alpine house or even in the open garden in temperate areas.

Calanthe alpina Hooker f.

SYN. *Calanthe schlechteri* Hara

Pseudobulbs ovoid, 2–2.5 cm long. Leaves evergreen, to 17 cm long. Inflorescence 20–25 cm long, few-flowered. Flowers ca. 2 cm across, white to lilac with a reddish-orange lip.

Terrestrial in shade in forest, 1300–1500 m (4300–5000 ft.)

China, Japan, Sikkim, Taiwan

Calanthe cardioglossa Schlechter

Pseudobulbs ovoid, to 6 cm long. Leaves deciduous, 20–25 × 4–5 cm, elliptic-lanceolate. Inflorescence 15–30 cm long. Flowers showy, ca. 2.5 cm across, white or pink, the lip white, striped purple. Intermediate to warm condition. Flowering in autumn.

Terrestrial in forest, ca. 1500 m (5000 ft.)

Vietnam, Laos, Thailand

Calanthe discolor Lindley

Pseudobulbs small. Leaves evergreen or semi-evergreen, to 25 × 9 cm, pubescent below. Inflorescence 18–30 cm tall, loosely 10- to 15-flowered. Flowers 4–5 cm across; sepals and petals purplish or bronze, lip pale pink, deeply trilobed, the midlobe emarginate. Flowering spring. One of the hardier and more easily grown species.

Terrestrial in forests, also in more open grassy places, 700–1500 m (2300–5000 ft.)

China, Japan, Ryukyu Islands, Korea

SIMILAR SPECIES: *Calanthe izu-insularis* from the Izu Islands off the coast of Japan has larger flowers with pink sepals and petals and a white lip with a yellow blotch at the base. This species is less hardy than *C. discolor*.

Calanthe reflexa Maximowicz

Leaves evergreen, broadly lanceolate, to 35 cm long. Inflorescence many-flowered, to 15 cm long. Flowers to 2.5 cm across, white, pink, or magenta; sepals and petals reflexed; lip deeply trilobed, yellowish at base, lacking a spur. Cool to intermediate conditions. Flowering in late summer.

Terrestrial in damp grassland or woodland, to 2700 m (8900 ft.)

Japan

Calanthe rosea (Lindley) Bentham

Pseudobulbs hourglass-shaped. Leaves deciduous, oblong-lanceolate. Inflorescence erect, 30–50 cm tall, appearing before leaves. Flowers pale pink, the lip even paler, turning white. Intermediate to warm conditions are preferred in cultivation. Flowering autumn–winter.

Terrestrial in forest

Myanmar

Calanthe striata (Banks) R. Brown

SYN. *Calanthe discolor* Lindley var. *flava* Yatabe, *C. sieboldii* Decaisne ex Regel

Leaves evergreen or semi-evergreen, 30–45 cm long, elliptic. Inflorescence to 50 cm tall, to about 20-flowered. Flowers 4–6.5 cm across, yellow or yellow and brown; sepals and petals spreading, lip trilobed, the midlobe wedge-shaped; spur slender. Cool conditions. Flowering spring.

Terrestrial in mountain forests, 1200–1500 m (4000–5000 ft.)

Taiwan, Japan

Calanthe sylvatica (Thouars) Lindley

SYN. *Calanthe masuca* (D. Don) Lindley, *C. natalensis* Reichenbach f., *C. volkensii* Rolfe

This variable species has many synonyms. Pseudobulbs small, rather obscure. Leaves evergreen, in a basal tuft, to 35 × 12 cm. Inflorescence 50–75 cm tall, densely many-flowered. Flowers 2.5–5 cm across, white

Calanthe cardioglossa

Calanthe striata

Calanthe tricarinata

or purple, orange in the throat. Flowering summer.

Deep shade in forest, 800–2700 m (2640–8900 ft.)

Africa, Madagascar, Mascarene Islands, India

Calanthe tricarinata Lindley
Pseudobulbs ovoid. Leaves evergreen, the new growth developing after flowering, elliptic, 15–30 cm long. Inflorescence 30–60 cm tall. Flowers yellow-green with a red-brown lip, undulate on the margin with several crests; spur absent.

Forest or grassy slopes, 1600–3500 m (5300–11,500 ft.)

China, India, Japan

Calanthe triplicata (Willemet) Ames
SYN. *Calanthe veratrifolia* (Willdenow) R. Brown
Robust, variable species. Leaves evergreen, 45–60 × 10–12 cm, dark green. Inflorescence to 1 m or more tall, densely many-flowered. Flowers white, pale green at the tips, with yellow or orange mark on lip. Intermediate conditions. Flowering summer.

Terrestrial in forest, 1000–1200 m (3300–4000 ft.)

From India through Southeast Asia to Australia

Calanthe vestita Wallich ex Lindley
Pseudobulbs large, 8–13 cm long, oblong. Leaves deciduous, 45–60 cm

long. Inflorescence arching, to 90 cm tall, densely many-flowered. Flowers 3–7 cm across, white to pink with a yellow blotch on the lip. Intermediate to warm conditions. Flowering in winter.

This species is a parent of numerous hybrids.

Terrestrial in forest on limestone, 600–900 m (2000–3000 ft.)

Myanmar, Southeast Asia to Sulawesi

Calochilus R. Brown

TRIBE: Diurideae

SUBTRIBE: Thelymitrinae

ETYMOLOGY: From Greek *kalos*, beautiful, and *cheilos*, lip, referring to the long, hairlike calli on the lip of most species

DISTRIBUTION: 16 species in Australia, New Zealand, New Guinea, and New Caledonia

Terrestrial herbs with paired ovoid tubers and a single, erect, narrow, fleshy basal leaf. Inflorescences erect, terminal, unbranched, 1- to many-flowered. Sepals and petals free, ovate, the dorsal sepal forming a hood with the petals, the lateral sepals larger, decurved. Lip large, lacking a spur, more or less triangular but covered with long, hairlike calli. Column short, often with 2 dark, shiny eye-spots at the base. Pollinia 4.

CULTIVATION: These striking orchids are notoriously difficult to grow, dwindling after 1 or 2 seasons. Most species occur as scattered plants, not reproducing vegetatively to form colonies. If attempted, they should be grown in a free-draining compost in an open, well-ventilated position, such as in an alpine house. All species die back after flowering and should then be kept dry until new growth starts, when careful watering can begin.

Calochilus campestris R. Brown

COPPER BEARD ORCHID

Leaf to 30 × 10 mm, dark green. Inflorescence to 60 cm tall, 5- to 15-flowered. Flowers 18–25 mm across, pale green, the lip with purple hairs, the basal part smooth, metallic blue.

Open forest, in well-drained areas

Australia

Calochilus paludosus R. Brown

RED BEARD ORCHID

Leaf 1–18 cm long, triangular in cross-section, ribbed. Inflorescence to 35 cm tall, 2- or 3-flowered. Flowers scented, not opening wide, ca. 25 mm across, greenish, the lip covered with long purplish or reddish-bronze hairs.

Moist, low-lying areas but also well-drained places in open forest

Australia, New Zealand

Calopogon R. Brown

TRIBE: Arethuseae

SUBTRIBE: Arethusinae

ETYMOLOGY: From Greek *kalos*, beautiful, and *pogon*, beard, referring to the tuft of hair on the lip

DISTRIBUTION: 5 species in North America and the Caribbean

Slender, terrestrial orchids with small, underground corms. Leaves 1 or 2, sometimes 3, grasslike. Inflorescences terminal, erect, loosely few-flowered. Flowers showy, nonresupinate, white, pink, or magenta; sepals and petals free, spreading, subsimilar; lip erect, obscurely trilobed at the base, midlobe with a tuft of beardlike hairs in the center. Column slender, apex winged; pollinia 4, in 2 pairs.

The 5 species are all rather similar.

CULTIVATION: *Calopogon tuberosus* (the commonest species in cultivation) can be grown in a pot in live sphagnum moss or in very sandy soil. It should be successful in damp areas in a garden in temperate areas, but I have not heard of it being grown like this.

Calopogon tuberosus (Linnaeus) Britton, Sterns & Poggenburg

SYN. *Calopogon pulchellus* (Salisbury) R. Brown

COMMON GRASS-PINK

Plants 25–115 cm tall. Leaves 1 or 2, rarely 3, shorter than the plant. Inflorescence 3- to 17-flowered. Flowers pale to deep pink with a yellow crest on the lip, 25–35 mm across. Flowering spring–summer.

Open wet areas with sandy soil; sphagnum bogs

Widespread in central and eastern United States and Canada, also in Cuba and the Bahamas.

SIMILAR SPECIES: *Calopogon barbatus* (Walter) Ames, BEARDED GRASS-PINK, from southeastern United States is a smaller plant which flowers earlier.

Calypso Salisbury

TRIBE: Calypsoeae

ETYMOLOGY: From Greek *Calypso*, an elusive nymph

DISTRIBUTION: 1 species with a circumpolar distribution, in northern Europe, North America, and northern Asia

Dwarf terrestrial plants with 1 pseudobulb, 1-leafed at apex. Leaves petiolate, pleated. Inflorescence arising from basal sheaths, erect, 1-flowered. Sepals and petals similar, spreading to ± erect. Lip slipper-shaped, the saccate base with 2 small hornlike spurs. Column broad, pink; pollinia in 2 pairs.

CULTIVATION: Plants start to grow in autumn and are better grown in a shaded alpine house or cold frame. They can be grown in living sphagnum moss or in a compost of leaf mold or composted bark mixed with coarse grit. Plants flower from early spring to summer. In summer, after flowering, plants should be kept drier but not allowed to dry out completely.

Calypso bulbosa (Linnaeus) Oakes

Stems 10–20 cm tall. Leaf with petiole 1–6 cm long; blade ovate, 3–6 × 1–2 cm. Sepals and petals linear-lanceolate, to 2 cm long, bright pink to magenta. Lip to 2.5 cm long, white to pale pink with a few purple spots and a crest of yellow or white hairs near the base.

Four varieties are recognized. Var. *bulbosa* occurs from Sweden to Korea and has a white tuft of hairs. Var.

Calochilus paludosus. J. Stewart

Calopogon tuberosus. J. Hermans

Calypso bulbosa. J. Hermans

americana (R. Brown) Luer from the eastern United States and Canada has yellow hairs and only a few spots on the front of the lip. Var. *occidentalis* (Holzinger) Cockerell from the western United States has duller-colored flowers and a small tuft of white hairs. Var. *speciosa* (Schlechter) Makino from Japan has a yellow crest and longer spurs.

Damp places and bogs in coniferous forest, usually in moss or leaf litter, 0–3000 m (9900 ft.)

Asia, Europe, North America

Calyptrochilum Kraenzlin

TRIBE: Vandeae

SUBTRIBE: Angraecinae

ETYMOLOGY: From Greek *kalyptra*, covering, and *cheilos*, lip

DISTRIBUTION: 2 species in tropical Africa

Epiphytic plants with long, leafy stems and numerous thick roots. Leaves in 2 rows, twisted to face the same way, oblong, fleshy. Inflorescences borne along stem, short, few-flowered. Flowers white; sepals and petals subsimilar, spreading; lip trilobed, spurred. Column short; pollinia 2, stipes and viscidium 1.

CULTIVATION: Because of the long stems, plants are better mounted on a slab. They require intermediate or warm conditions, shade, and high humidity. They grow in places where rainfall is seasonal and in winter should be kept drier but not allowed to remain dry for long periods.

Calyptrochilum christyanum (Reichenbach f.) Summerhayes

Stems woody, to ca. 50 cm long, usually pendent, with stout roots. Leaves numerous, 6–8 × 1.5–2.5 cm, oblong or strap-shaped, unequally bilobed at the apex, dull olive green. Inflorescence to 4 cm long, densely 6- to 9-flowered, borne on the underside of the stem. Flowers lemon-scented, white, yellow in the throat; sepals and petals to 10 mm long; lip trilobed near the base, side lobes erect, midlobe to 10 × 8 mm, oblong; spur green, ca. 10 mm long, geniculate, swollen at the tip.

Epiphytic or rarely lithophytic in riverine forest and woodland, 900–1400 m (3000–4600 ft.)

Widespread in tropical Africa

SIMILAR SPECIES: *Calyptrochilum emarginatum* (Afzelius ex Swartz) Schlechter from West Africa usually has longer leaves and has strongly scented white flowers with a yellowish or yellow-green lip; the spur is incurved but not geniculate and is slightly swollen at the tip.

Campylocentrum Bentham

TRIBE: Vandeae

SUBTRIBE: Angraecinae

ETYMOLOGY: From Greek *kampylos*, crooked, and *kentron*, spur

DISTRIBUTION: About 60 species from Florida, Central and South America, and the Caribbean

Monopodial epiphytes with long or short stems, with or without leaves, the leafless species with many long, chlorophyll-bearing roots. Inflorescences lateral, short, unbranched, loosely or densely few- to many-flowered. Flowers small, white, yellowish, or pinkish; sepals and petals free, subsimilar; lip entire or trilobed, spurred at the base, lacking a callus. Column short, rostellum short, bilobed; pollinia, stipites and viscidia 2.

Many species are similar and difficult to identify.

CULTIVATION: Most species can be grown in intermediate or warm conditions with shade and high humidity. Leafless species must be mounted, preferably on smooth-barked wood; species with leaves are also better mounted than potted.

Campylocentrum micranthum (Lindley) Rolfe

SYN. *Campylocentrum jamaicense* (Reichenbach f. ex Grisebach) Bentham ex Fawcett, *C. lansbergii* (Reichenbach f.) Reichenbach f.

Stem up to 90 cm long. Leaves distichous, 4–9 × 1–2 cm, narrowly elliptic. Inflorescence 3–4 cm long, densely several-flowered, the flowers in 2 rows. Flowers very small, white or yellowish white; lip 4–5 mm long, trilobed at base; spur 4–5 mm long, incurved, swollen at apex.

Epiphytic in humid forest, sometimes in *Citrus* plantations, 70–750 m (230–2460 ft.)

Central and South America, Caribbean

Campylocentrum pachyrrhizum (Reichenbach f.) Rolfe

Stem short; roots to more than 50 cm long, 4–5 mm across, flattened. Leaves absent. Inflorescence 3–4 cm long, densely many-flowered, the flowers in 2 rows; bracts reddish brown. Flowers tiny, yellowish pink; lip trilobed, to 3 mm long; spur saccate, 2–3 mm long.

Epiphytic in swamp forest and humid forest, 0–1400 m (4600 ft.)

Florida, Central and South America, Caribbean

SIMILAR SPECIES: *Campylocentrum fasciola* (Lindley) Cogniaux, from Central and South America and the Caribbean, is another leafless species with round, not flattened roots, and small whitish flowers.

Capanemia Barbosa Rodrigues

TRIBE: Maxillarieae

SUBTRIBE: Oncidiinae

ETYMOLOGY: Named for Guillermo Schuch de Capanema, a Brazilian naturalist

DISTRIBUTION: 16 species in South America

Dwarf epiphytes related to *Rodriguezia* and *Quekettia*; pseudobulbs small, enclosed in 2 or 3 sheaths, 1-leafed at apex. Leaves small, fleshy, flat or terete. Inflorescences arising from base of pseudobulb, unbranched, few- to many-flowered. Flowers small, white or greenish; sepals and petals subsimilar, free or with lateral sepals joined for a short way; lip entire with 1 or 2 fleshy calli. Column short, pollinia 2, waxy.

CULTIVATION: These little plants are twig epiphytes in the wild and are usually mounted on bark and suspended in a bright situation but not in direct sunlight. They require intermediate to cool conditions and high humidity.

Capanemia superflua (Reichenbach f.) Garay

Pseudobulbs slender. Leaves terete, to 7 cm long. Inflorescence to 7 cm long, erect or pendent, few to many-flowered. Flowers small (sepals to 5 mm long), glistening white with a maroon line on the sepals and petals, a maroon spot at the base of the lip and a yellow disc with 2 calli.

Epiphytic on mossy branches and twigs, ca. 500 m (1650 ft.)

Argentina, Southern Brazil

SIMILAR SPECIES: *Capanemia micromera* Barbosa Rodrigues (syn. *Quekettia micromera* Barbosa Rodrigues) Cogniaux is even smaller with leaves ca. 2.5 cm long and sepals 2 mm long.

Capanemia theresae Barbosa Rodrigues

SYN. *Quekettia theresae* (Barbosa Rodrigues) Cogniaux

Pseudobulbs ovoid, 1 × 0.3 cm. Leaves elliptical. Inflorescence 2–3 cm long, 3- to 5-flowered. Flowers very small, greenish yellow.

Epiphytic on small twigs of shrubs and small trees on exposed mountain ridges

Brazil

Catasetum Richard ex Kunth

TRIBE: Cymbidieae

SUBTRIBE: Catasetinae

ETYMOLOGY: From Greek *kata*, downwards, and *seta*, bristle, referring to the antennae on the column

Calyptrochilum christyanum. E. la Croix

Campylocentrum micranthum

Capanemia superflua. R. Parsons

Capanemia micromera

DISTRIBUTION: More than 150 species in Central and South America and the West Indies

Medium to large-sized sympodial plants, most epiphytic but some lithophytic or terrestrial; pseudobulbs ovoid, conical, or spindle-shaped, covered in leaf sheaths when young. Leaves in 2 ranks, large, pleated, deciduous. Inflorescences unbranched, erect, arching or pendent, arising from base of new or mature pseudobulbs. Flowers showy, almost always unisexual; male and female flowers different in appearance, occurring on the same inflorescence or on separate ones. Colors most often yellow or yellow-green, spotted and blotched with maroon or brownish, the male flowers usually more brightly colored and more numerous than female ones. In both, sepals and petals free, spreading, and the lip saccate. The pollinia are ejected violently by a trigger mechanism activated by pressure on 2 antennae at the base of the column.

CULTIVATION: Plants may be potted but are usually grown in baskets in a coarse bark-based compost, in bright, humid, well-ventilated intermediate or warm conditions. Female flowers are more likely to be produced when plants are stressed, for example, when conditions are too bright and dry. After the leaves have fallen, plants should be kept cooler and drier.

Catasetum barbatum (Lindley) Lindley

A variable, medium-sized species. Leaves 20–45 × 3–8 cm. Inflorescence arching to pendent, many-flowered, longer than leaves. Male flowers ca. 5 cm across, thin-textured; sepals and petals deep green flecked with maroon, lip pale green with pink or red marks, the margins deeply fringed. Female flowers smaller, fleshy. Warm conditions.

Epiphytic in wet forest, 50–1200 m (165–4000 ft.)

Brazil, Colombia, Ecuador, Guyana, Peru, Venezuela

Catasetum cernuum (Lindley) Reichenbach f.

Racemes arching, to 30 cm long, 10- to 15-flowered. Flowers nodding, ca. 4 cm across, green, mottled with chocolate or maroon, in late spring or summer. Intermediate to warm conditions but needs cool nights.

Epiphytic in forest on hillsides, 200–2500 m (660–8250 ft.)

Southern Brazil

Catasetum expansum Reichenbach f.

Pseudobulbs spindle-shaped. Inflorescence to 30 cm long, arching, several- to many-flowered. Flowers large, showy, ca. 7.5 cm across, yellow, green, or white, sometimes dotted with maroon. Warm conditions.

Dry forest, 20–1500 m (66–5000 ft.)

Northeastern Ecuador

Catasetum fimbriatum (Morren) Lindley

Raceme pendent, 45–90 cm long, loosely several- to many-flowered. Flowers resupinate, 4–5 cm across, yellow or green marked with maroon, with a spicy scent; lip saccate, yellow-green tinged with pink at base, the margins fringed. Female flowers yellow-green; sepals and petals recurved; lip margins entire.

Epiphytic on palm trunks in dry, lowland woodland, 400–500 m (1320–1650 ft.)

Tropical South America

Catasetum macrocarpum Richard ex Kunth

JUMPING ORCHID

The type species of the genus. Large plants; racemes erect or arching, to 45 cm long, up to 10-flowered. Flowers nonresupinate. Male flowers large, fleshy, 7–8 cm across, yellow-green marked with maroon-purple; lip deeply saccate with undulate or dentate margins. Flowers late summer–autumn.

Epiphytic in forest, 0–1200 m (4000 ft.)

Tropical South America, Trinidad

SIMILAR SPECIES: *Catasetum integerrimum* Hooker from Guatemala has flowers less heavily marked with maroon and with a more broadly conical lip.

Catasetum microglossum Rolfe

Medium-sized plants. Inflorescences arching to pendent, to 65 cm long, loosely several- to many-flowered. Flowers resupinate, ca. 4.5 cm across, maroon, the lip small, greenish yellow, covered with toothlike calli. Female flowers of similar color to male. Warm conditions.

Epiphytic in lowland forest

Colombia, Ecuador, Peru

Catasetum pileatum Reichenbach f.

Large plants; inflorescences usually pendent, 30–40 cm long, several- to many-flowered. Flowers resupinate. Male flowers large, 10–11 cm across, opening flat, scented, varying in color from greenish yellow to maroon-red and white; female flowers green and white. Warm conditions.

Epiphytic in lowland forest with a short dry season.

Brazil, Ecuador, Colombia, Trinidad, Venezuela

Catasetum saccatum Lindley

SYN. *Catasetum christyanum* Reichenbach f.

Large plants with pseudobulbs 8–20 cm long; leaves to 40 × 6 cm, erect or spreading. Inflorescence erect to pendent, to 40 cm long, loosely several-flowered. Male flowers to 10 cm across, greenish marked with purple-brown; female flowers smaller, yellow-green with red-brown dots. Warm conditions. Flowering summer–winter.

Epiphytic in open places in tropical forest, 200–1700 m (660–5600 ft.)

Brazil, Guyana, Peru

Catasetum barbatum, male flowers

Catasetum expansum, male flowers

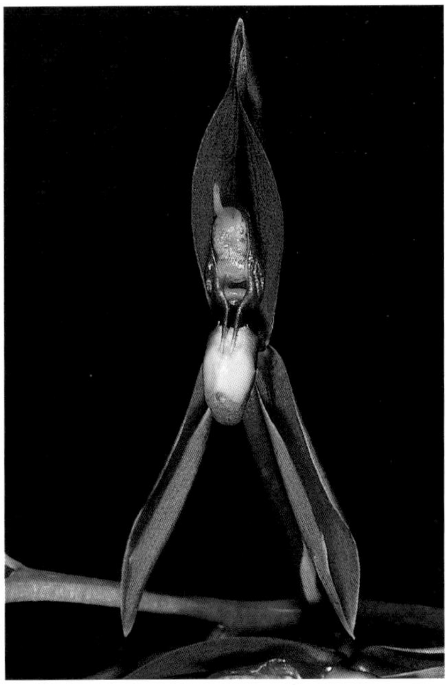

Catasetum microglossum, male flowers

Catasetum macrocarpum, male flowers

Catasetum pileatum, male flowers

Catasetum sanguineum Lindley
Medium-sized plants. Racemes to 30 cm long, erect to pendent, many-flowered. Flowers to 4 cm across, nonresupinate, scented, usually greenish white, spotted or banded with maroon; midlobe of lip dark red. Warm conditions.

Epiphytic in low-altitude woodland, less than 800 m (2640 ft.), with a long, dry season

Colombia, Venezuela

Catasetum tabulare Lindley
Inflorescence suberect, few- to many-flowered. Flowers fleshy, scented, opening wide, about 10 cm across, pale green with maroon blotches or solid maroon, lip with a conspicuous cream callus. Warm conditions. Flowering spring–autumn.

Tropical forest, including riverine forest, to 1000 m (3300 ft.)

Colombia

Catasetum tenebrosum Kraenzlin
Medium-sized plants; pseudobulbs to 15 cm long. Leaves 20–30 cm long. Inflorescences suberect, 20–25 cm long, densely several- to many-flowered. Male flowers 3–4 cm across, showy, maroon to brownish red, lip yellow. Female flowers yellow-green. Flowering spring–autumn.

Epiphytic in riverine forest or lithophytic on rocks or boulders in full sun, 500–1800 m (1650–6000 ft.)

Ecuador, Peru

Cattleya Lindley

TRIBE: Epidendreae
SUBTRIBE: Laeliinae
ETYMOLOGY: Named for William Cattley (1788–1832), who was the first to flower *Cattleya labiata* (which became the type species of the genus) in cultivation
DISTRIBUTION: Almost 50 species and numerous natural hybrids in South America with 1 species in Central America

Epiphytes or lithophytes with erect, cylindrical, spindle-shaped or club-shaped pseudobulbs, 1- or 2-leaved at apex, rarely 3-leaved. Leaves thick and leathery, usually oblong. Inflorescences terminal, unbranched, arising from a thick sheath, few- to several-flowered. Flowers usually large, showy, and scented; sepals spreading, free, similar; petals usually broader; lip usually trilobed, funnel-shaped, the mid-lobe often with an undulate margin. Column long, arched; pollinia 4.

Most *Cattleya* species occur in a range of color forms and many selected cultivars exist. They have been widely used in hybridization, both intrageneric and intergeneric with related genera such as *Brassia, Laelia, Rhyncholaelia,* and *Sophronitis.* Many hybrids involving the last genus are more compact plants than *Cattleya* species themselves. *Cattleya* species and hybrids are among the most spectacular of all orchids but are perhaps less widely grown now than in the past, when they were very popular, particularly in the United States, as cut flowers and corsages. This may be partly due to the size of the plants.
CULTIVATION: Cattleyas should be grown in pots or baskets in a coarse, free-draining compost, in good light (necessary if they are to flower well), with good air movement and with plenty of water and fertilizer while they are growing. Less water should be given while plants are resting as the roots rot easily at this time. Repotting or dividing should be carried out just as the new roots are starting to form. Most species do well in intermediate conditions, but a few like warmer temperatures; this is mentioned in the text.

Cattleya aclandiae Lindley
One of the smaller species. Pseudobulbs cylindrical, to 12 cm long, 2-leaved. Leaves to 10 × 2.5 cm. Inflorescence 1- or 2-flowered. Flowers long-lasting, strongly scented, 7–11 cm across; sepals and petals lime green, yellow, or buff, spotted and blotched with maroon and brown; lip bright purple, yellow at base.

Epiphytic in rather dry coastal areas, 100–400 m (330–1320 ft.)

Brazil

Cattleya amethystoglossa Linden & Reichenbach f. ex Warner
Pseudobulbs cylindrical, 50–100 cm long, 2-leaved. Inflorescence to 25 cm long, 5- to 10-flowered. Flowers 5–10 cm across; sepals and petals white or pale pink, spotted with deep purple; lip side lobes white, midlobe magenta.

Epiphytic or lithophytic at fairly low altitudes

Brazil

SIMILAR SPECIES: *Cattleya guttata* Lindley from Brazil has green or yellow-green sepals and petals spotted

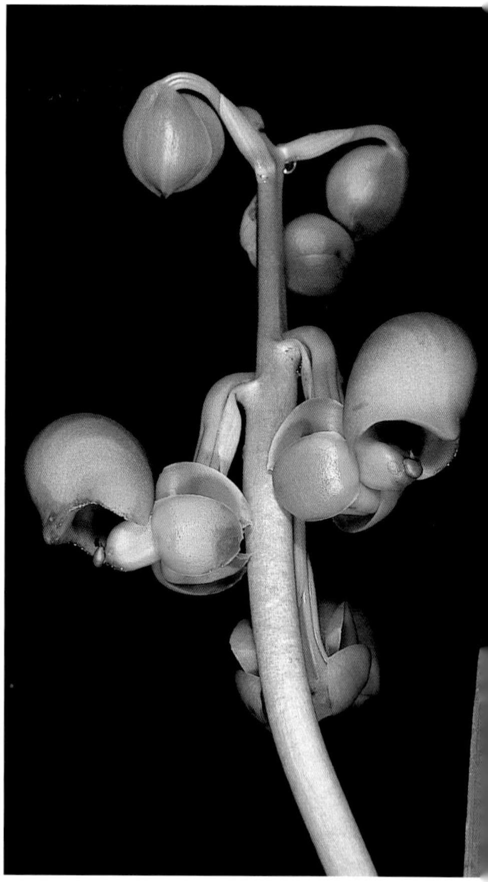

Catasetum tabulare, female flowers

Catasetum tenebrosum, male flowers

Cattleya guttata

Cattleya aclandiae

Cattleya amethystoglossa

and blotched with purple or brown. *Cattleya leopoldii* Verschaffelt ex Lemoine, again from Brazil, has bronze-green sepals and petals densely spotted with maroon and a lip with pale pink side lobes and a purple midlobe.

Cattleya bicolor Lindley

Pseudobulbs slender, cylindrical, to 30 cm tall, 2-leaved. Inflorescence to 20 cm long, 2- to 5-flowered. Flowers 10 cm across, long-lasting, scented; sepals and petals green flushed with bronze; lip entire, rich crimson-purple, oblong or wedge-shaped, clawed at the base.

Epiphytic in forest on coastal mountains

Brazil

Cattleya dowiana Bateman & Reichenbach f.

Pseudobulbs club-shaped, to 22 cm long, unifoliate. Inflorescence erect, few- to several-flowered. Flowers large, scented, to 18 cm across; sepals and petals yellow to pale bronze; lip rich purple-red, veined with yellow. Flowering summer. Needs warm conditions with a night minimum of 18°C (65°F). Should be kept almost dry from autumn to spring.

Epiphytic in rain forest, 250–800 m (825–2640 ft.)

Costa Rica, Colombia, Panama

Cattleya intermedia Graham ex Hooker

Pseudobulbs cylindrical, to 40 cm tall, 2-leaved. Inflorescence to 25 cm tall, 3- to 7-flowered. Flowers to 13 cm across, long-lasting, strongly scented; sepals and petals white to mauve, sometimes with purple spots; lip trilobed, side lobes white, midlobe purple, the margins crisped and undulate.

Epiphytic and lithophytic in Atlantic coastal forest

Brazil, Paraguay, Uruguay

Cattleya labiata Lindley

Pseudobulbs to 30 cm tall, club-shaped, unifoliate. Inflorescence erect, 4- to 5-flowered. Flowers 15–20 cm across; sepals and petals white to pink; lip large, obscurely trilobed, funnel-shaped, deep purple with a yellow blotch in the throat, the margins crisped and undulate. Many color forms exist. Flowers in autumn

Cattleya bicolor

as the days get shorter. Can be made to flower at any time of year by giving it a shorter day-length.
Brazil

SIMILAR SPECIES: *Cattleya warneri* Moore, also from Brazil, is a more compact plant and flowers in late spring rather than autumn.

Cattleya lawrenceana Reichenbach f.

Pseudobulbs club-shaped, often reddish, to 25 cm long, unifoliate. Leaves sometimes with purple spots. Inflorescence ca. 15 cm tall, 5- to 8-flowered. Flowers to 12.5 cm across; sepals and petals blush-white to rose-pink, lip entire with a long, slender tube, white at the base, purple towards the apex. Needs warm

Cattleya warneri

Cattleya lawrenceana

Cattleya dowiana

Cattleya labiata

conditions with a minimum temperature of about 18°C (65°F).

Epiphytic in rain forest or lithophytic in open rocky areas, 400–1900 m (1320–6300 ft.)

Brazil, Guyana, Venezuela

Cattleya loddigesii Lindley

Pseudobulbs slender, cylindrical, to 30 cm tall, 2-leaved. Flowers to 11 cm across, scented, long-lasting, blush-white to pink; lip trilobed, pale to deep lilac-pink, side lobes erect, midlobe almost square, the margins crisped.

Epiphytic or lithophytic

Northeastern Argentina, southeastern Brazil, Paraguay

Cattleya lueddemanniana

Reichenbach f.

Pseudobulbs cylindrical, to 25 cm long, unifoliate. Leaves gray-green, sometimes with purplish spots when young. Inflorescence 3- to 5-flowered. Flowers strongly scented, to 22 cm across; sepals and petals usually pale to deep lavender, sometimes purple; lip midlobe suborbicular, the margins crisped, deeper in color with 2 yellow blotches towards the base. Column winged at the tip. Flowering spring but needs a lot of sun to flower well.

Epiphytic in scrub woodland, 0–1500 m (5000 ft.)

Venezuela

Cattleya luteola Lindley

Pseudobulbs 9–15 cm long, compressed, ovoid or club-shaped, unifoliate. Inflorescence shorter than leaves, 2- to 6-flowered. Flowers to 5 cm across, yellow or yellow-green, the lip streaked with red inside.

Epiphytic in rain forest, 100–1200 m (330–4000 ft.), rarely to 2000 m (6600 ft.)

Bolivia, Brazil, Ecuador, Peru

Cattleya maxima Lindley

Pseudobulbs 18–35 cm tall, club-shaped, unifoliate. Inflorescence to 20 cm tall, 5- to 15-flowered. Flowers to 16 cm across, scented, long-lasting; sepals and petals pink to lilac; lip trilobed, pale pink with purple veins with a yellow streak down the center, the edges undulate. Flowering in early winter.

Epiphytic or lithophytic, in seasonally dry coastal forest, also inland, to 1800 m (6000 ft.)

Colombia, Ecuador, Peru, Venezuela

Cattleya mossiae Hooker

Pseudobulbs to 25 cm long, spindle-shaped, unifoliate. Inflorescence to 30 cm tall, 2- to 7-flowered. Flowers to 20 cm across, scented, long-lasting; sepals and petals white to pink or lilac, lip white or pink with a yellow blotch in the throat, veined with purple, midlobe suborbicular, deep purple, the edges undulate. Flowering spring.

Epiphytic in forest, 900–1500 m (3000–5000 ft.)

Venezuela (national flower)

Cattleya percivaliana

(Reichenbach f.) O'Brien

Pseudobulbs to 15 × 2 cm, cylindrical or club-shaped, compressed, unifoliate. Inflorescence to 25 cm tall, 2- to 5-flowered. Flowers to 12.5 cm across, short-lived, with a musty or spicy scent; sepals and petals lilac-

Cattleya loddigesii

Cattleya lueddemanniana

Cattleya luteola

Cattleya maxima

Cattleya mossiae

pink, lip midlobe purple, paler round the margins, orange in the throat. Flowering in winter.

Usually lithophytic, sometimes epiphytic, in full sun, 1300–2000 m (4300–6600 ft.)

Colombia, Venezuela

Cattleya trianae Linden & Reichenbach f.

Pseudobulbs to 30 cm long, becoming grooved, club-shaped, unifoliate. Inflorescence to 30 cm tall, 2- to 5-flowered. Flowers to 20 cm across, long-lasting, white, pink, or lilac to purple; lip obscurely trilobed, midlobe usually deep magenta-purple, disc usually orange-yellow. Flowering in winter.

Colombia (national flower)

SIMILAR SPECIES: *Cattleya schroderae* Reichenbach f., also from Colombia, has even larger flowers, usually white or lilac, very fragrant, and with the lip strongly crisped.

Cattleya violacea (Kunth) Rolfe

Pseudobulbs to 30 cm tall, cylindrical to club-shaped, often reddish, becoming grooved, 2-leaved. Leaves green flushed with purplish. Inflorescence to 30 cm tall, 3- to 7-flowered. Flowers scented, ca. 12 cm across, long-lasting; sepals and petals purple-pink; lip trilobed, deep violet with yellow markings, white at the base; midlobe transversely oblong, emarginate. Flowering late spring–early summer.

Epiphytic in rain forest, 0–600 m (2000 ft.)

Tropical South America

Cattleya walkeriana Gardner

A small species with pseudobulbs to 12 cm long, 1- or 2-leaved. Inflorescence to 20 cm tall, 1- or 2-flowered. Flowers to 12 cm across, scented, rose-pink to purple, the lip deeper purple with a white or yellow disc streaked purple. Flowers late winter–spring.

Epiphytic or lithophytic, to 2000 m (6600 ft.)

Brazil

Cattleya wallisii (Linden) Linden ex Reichenbach f.

SYN. *Cattleya eldorado* Linden

Pseudobulbs to 15 cm tall, unifoliate. Inflorescence 1- to few-flowered. Flowers 14–17 cm across.; sepals and petals pink, lip purple with an orange-yellow blotch bordered with white in the throat; apex emarginate. Flowering summer–autumn.

Like *Cattleya dowiana*, it needs warm temperatures and a dry rest after flowering. This species is better known by the later name of *C. eldorado*.

Epiphytic in lowland rain forest

Brazil

Cattleya warscewiczii Reichenbach f.

SYN. *Cattleya gigas* Linden & André

Pseudobulbs 20–40 cm long, ± cylindrical, becoming grooved, unifoliate. Inflorescence to 45 cm tall, 3- to 10-flowered. Flowers scented, 18–27 cm across, the largest in the genus; sepals and petals pink to lavender, lip purple-red with 2 yellow eyes towards the throat, the edges undulate, deeply emarginate at apex. Flowering summer.

Epiphytic in bright light, 500–1500 m (1650–5000 ft.)

Colombia

Cattleyella van den Berg & M. W. Chase

SYN. *Schluckebieria* Braem

TRIBE: Epidendreae

SUBTRIBE: Laeliinae

ETYMOLOGY: Diminutive of *Cattleya*

DISTRIBUTION: 1 species from Brazil

Epiphytic plants; pseudobulbs cylindrical with 3 internodes of different lengths, 1-leafed at apex. Inflorescence terminal, 1-, sometimes 2-flowered. Sepals and petals similar, linear, free, spreading. Lip free, obscurely trilobed, trumpet-shaped. Column club-shaped, pollinia 4.

CULTIVATION: Plants seem to be most successful in a small pot in intermediate to warm conditions, with moderate shade, high humidity, and good ventilation. They should be kept drier when not in growth.

Cattleyella araguaiensis (Pabst) van den Berg & M. W. Chase

SYN. *Cattleya araguaiensis* Pabst

Pseudobulbs 7–8 cm tall. Flowers ca. 10 cm across, long-lasting; sepals and petals mottled bronze; lip side lobes white, midlobe reddish brown.

Epiphytic in low-altitude forest, 400–600 m (1320–2000 ft.)

Brazil

Caucaea Schlechter

TRIBE: Maxillarieae

SUBTRIBE: Oncidiinae

ETYMOLOGY: From the department of Cauca, Colombia, where the type species of the genus (*C. radiata*) was originally collected

DISTRIBUTION: 18 species in northern and western South America

Pseudobulbs ovoid or oblong, compressed, 1-leafed, occasionally 2-leaved at the apex. Inflorescences axillary, branched or unbranched. Dorsal sepal and petals free, lateral sepals joined almost to apex; lip entire (in *Caucaea radiata*) or trilobed, much larger than the other floral parts. Column short, hooded.

Caucaea was established in 1920 and until 2001 was considered to be monospecific. However, DNA analysis has added some species previously considered to belong to *Oncidium* section *Cucullata* to the genus.

CULTIVATION: These are high-altitude, cloud forest plants and need to be grown in cool conditions, in shade with high humidity. They can be grown in pots in an open, free-draining compost.

Cattleya percivaliana

Cattleya trianae

Cattleya schroderae

Cattleya walkeriana

Cattleyella araguaiensis

Caucaea nubigena (Lindley) N. H. Williams & M. W. Chase

SYN. *Caucaea cucullata* (Lindley) N. H. Williams & M. W. Chase, *Oncidium cucullatum* Lindley, *O. nubigenum* Lindley

Pseudobulbs to 5 cm long, 1- or 2-leaved. Leaves to 20 × 3.5 cm. Inflorescence 50–60 cm long, branched or unbranched, few- to many-flowered. Flowers 3.5–4 cm across; sepals and petals dark brown or olive green, the margins sometimes yellow, the lip white or pink with a large purple blotch and purple spots towards the base and a yellow callus in the throat; lip obscurely trilobed, the midlobe broad, emarginate.

Epiphytic at 2500–4000 m (8250–13,200 ft.)

Colombia, Ecuador, Peru, Venezuela

Caucaea olivacea (Kunth) N. H. Williams & M. W. Chase

SYN. *Oncidium olivaceum* Kunth

Sepals and petals dull purple, yellow at the tip; lip pink, heavily blotched and spotted with purple, basal callus orange.

Epiphytic at 2300–2600 m (7600–8600 ft.)

Colombia to Ecuador

Caucaea phalaenopsis (Linden & Reichenbach f.) N. H. Williams & M. W. Chase

SYN. *Oncidium phalaenopsis* Linden & Reichenbach f.

Leaves to 18 × 2 cm, narrowly lanceolate. Inflorescence unbranched, few-flowered. Flowers 3–3.5 cm across; sepals and petals white to greenish yellow, heavily blotched and barred with purple; lip white to pale pink with large purple spots in the middle, callus yellow, the midlobe transversely oblong, emarginate.

Epiphytic at 2700–2800 m (8900–9250 ft.)

Ecuador

Caularthron Rafinesque

SYN. *Diacrium* Bentham

TRIBE: Epidendreae

SUBTRIBE: Laeliinae

ETYMOLOGY: From Greek *kaulos*, stem, and *arthron*, joint

DISTRIBUTION: 3 or 4 species in Central and South America and the West Indies

Epiphytes, occasionally lithophytes; pseudobulbs spindle-shaped, with several internodes, covered with papery sheaths, sometimes hollow and colonized by ants. Leaves up to 5, on upper nodes of pseudobulbs, lanceolate or strap-shaped. Inflorescences terminal, unbranched, several- to many-flowered. Flowers showy, white or pink; sepals and petals free, subsimilar; lip entire or trilobed, with 2 hollow yellow projections on the disc. Column winged; pollinia 4 in 2 pairs.

CULTIVATION: Plants should be grown in pots in a coarse, free-draining mixture in intermediate to warm temperatures and only light shade. They should not be allowed to dry out completely.

Caularthron bicornutum (Hooker) Rafinesque

SYN. *Diacrium bicornutum* (Bentham) Hooker, *D. amazonicum* Schlechter

Pseudobulbs spindle-shaped, hollow, 2- or 3-leaved. Inflorescence to 45 cm tall, to 20-flowered. Flowers ca. 7 cm across, white flushed with pink, with red spots on lip.

Epiphytic or lithophytic in moist forest, 100–300 m (330–1000 ft.)

Venezuela to Brazil, Trinidad, Tobago

Caularthron bilamellatum (Reichenbach f.) R. E. Schultes

SYN. *Diacrium bilamellatum* (Reichenbach f.) Hemsley, *D. venezuelanum* Schlechter

Pseudobulbs to 20 cm long, 3 cm diameter, hollow, 2- to 4-leaved. Leaves to 20 × 4 cm. Inflorescence to 45 cm long, several-flowered. Flowers ca. 3 cm across, scented, fleshy, often cleistogamous, white sometimes flushed with pink on the outside.

Epiphytic or lithophytic in open situations in rain forest, 150–400 m (500–1320 ft.)

Central and northern South America, Trinidad

Cephalanthera Richard

TRIBE: Neottieae

ETYMOLOGY: From Greek *kephale*, head, and *anthera*, stamen, presumably referring to the shape of the stamen

DISTRIBUTION: About 20 species in northern temperate regions from Europe and North Africa, through Asia to Japan

Terrestrial orchids with creeping rhizomes; stems erect, leafy. Inflorescences terminal, unbranched, several-flowered. Flowers often not opening wide; sepals and petals similar, forming hood; lip with a basal hypochile, saccate or shortly spurred, the apical epichile often ridged.

CULTIVATION: *Cephalanthera* species are not widely grown but can be naturalized in a garden on calcareous soil or grown in containers in a standard terrestrial compost with added limestone. In the wild, most grow in woodland or grassland. The rhizomes are very thin and can dry out rapidly if plants are being moved.

Caucaea nubigena

Caucaea olivacea

Caucaea phalaenopsis

Caularthron bicornutum

Cephalanthera damasonium (Miller) Druce

WHITE HELLEBORINE

Stems to 60 cm tall. Leaves several, to 10 cm long, ovate, merging into bracts at the top of the stem. Inflorescence laxly several-flowered. Flowers whitish, not opening wide; lip yellow at base, epichile with 5 yellow ridges. Flowering spring–summer.

Woodland, particularly beech, on chalk or limestone, occasionally on downland

Northern and central Europe, Russia, North Africa

SIMILAR SPECIES: *Cephalanthera falcata* (Thunberg) Blume from Japan has yellow flowers with a trilobed lip and a short spur.

Cephalanthera kurdica Bornmüller

Stems 50–70 cm tall, forming clumps. Flowers opening quite widely, rose-pink, rarely purple, lip with a white midlobe; sepals ca. 2 cm long.

In pine woods or in scrub on limestone soil, 800–2100 m (2640–7000 ft.)

Turkey to Iran

Cephalanthera longifolia (Linnaeus) Fritsch

SWORD-LEAVED HELLEBORINE

Erect, leafy terrestrial, 15–60 cm tall. Leaves dark green, ribbed, narrowly lanceolate, to 18 cm long. Inflorescence densely or loosely 10- to 20-flowered. Flowers spreading, clear white with orange-yellow ridges on lip, not opening wide. Flowering spring–summer.

Most often in relatively open areas in woodland on chalk or limestone soil

Europe, North Africa, Middle East

Ceratochilus Blume

TRIBE: Vandeae

SUBTRIBE: Aeridinae

ETYMOLOGY: From Greek *cerato*, horn, and *cheilos*, lip

DISTRIBUTION: 1 species in Java

Small, monopodial epiphyte with short stems. Leaves distichous, fleshy, V-shaped in cross-section. Inflorescence lateral, 1-flowered. Flowers large for the size of plant; sepals and petals free, spreading, the petals narrower and shorter than the sepals; lip with a large, saclike spur, hairy inside, and a short blade lying in front of the spur. Pollinia 4, in 2 pairs.

CULTIVATION: These dwarf plants are more successful when mounted. They require intermediate conditions, light shade, and high humidity throughout the year.

Ceratochilus biglandulosus Blume

Stems 2–10 cm long. Leaves 1 cm long, 2.5 mm thick. Inflorescences several. Flowers ca. 3 cm across; sepals, petals, and spur white, turning pink to red as they age; lip green.

Epiphytic on lichen-covered branches on isolated trees in montane grassland, 1000–2000 m (3300–6600 ft.)

Java

Ceratostylis Blume

TRIBE: Podochileae

SUBTRIBE: Eriinae

ETYMOLOGY: From Greek *cerato*, horn, and *stylis*, column, referring to the hornlike column

DISTRIBUTION: About 140 species from the Himalayas through China and Southeast Asia to New Guinea and the Pacific Islands

Small epiphytes, erect or pendent, creeping or forming clumps; stems not swollen, 1-leafed at apex. Leaves fleshy, narrow, linear or terete. Inflorescences terminal, 1- to few-flowered. Sepals and petals similar; lateral sepals joined to column-foot forming a mentum. Lip entire or trilobed, saccate at base, often thickened at apex.

CULTIVATION: Grow in intermediate conditions in moderate shade, with plenty of water while in growth. Pendent species should be mounted or grown in a shallow basket, while erect species can be grown in a pot. Plants should be kept drier while resting.

Ceratostylis retisquamata Reichenbach f.

SYN. *Ceratostylis rubra* Ames

Stems semi-pendent, branched, to 40 cm long, covered with brown, papery bracts. Leaves linear, to 12 × 1 cm. Inflorescence short, usually 1-flowered, occasionally with 2. Flowers 3–4 cm across (the largest in the genus), bright orange-red; sepals and petals spreading, lanceolate or oblanceolate; lip very small, ca. 3 mm long.

Epiphytic in forest to 500 m (1650 ft.)

Philippines

Chamaeangis Schlechter

TRIBE: Vandeae

SUBTRIBE: Aerangidinae

ETYMOLOGY: From Greek *chamai*, lowly, and *angos*, vessel

DISTRIBUTION: 10 species in tropical Africa

Stems short or long; roots usually slender. Leaves usually fleshy, narrow, slightly curved and unequally bilobed at the apex. Inflorescences racemose, erect or pendent, densely many-flowered with the flowers usually borne in opposite pairs or in whorls of 2 to 6. Flowers small, green, yellow, or dull orange-salmon; sepals and petals free; lip unlobed, spurred, the spur often swollen at the tip. Pollinia and stipites 2, viscidium 1.

CULTIVATION: Plants in the wild are usually found in humid, shady conditions. In cultivation, they grow well in an intermediate greenhouse and can either be potted in a medium bark mix or mounted. Good air movement is necessary as the fleshy leaves can easily rot.

Chamaeangis odoratissima (Reichenbach f.) Schlechter

Pendent plants with woody stems 20–50 cm long. Leaves fleshy, olive green, 10–25 × 2–3 cm, strap-shaped, unevenly and acutely bilobed at the

Cephalanthera damasonium. E. la Croix

Ceratochilus biglandulosus

Ceratostylis retisquamata. J. Hermans

Chamaeangis odoratissima. E. la Croix

apex. Inflorescence to 25 cm long, densely many-flowered. Flowers small, greenish white or yellow-green, turning more yellow as they age, scented, arranged in whorls of 2–6, usually 4; spur ca. 12 mm long, slender but slightly swollen at the tip.

Low-level epiphyte usually in riverine forest, 900–2100 m (3000–6900 ft.)

From West to East Africa, as far south as Malawi

Chamaeangis sarcophylla Schlechter

SYN. *Chamaeangis orientalis* Summerhayes

Short-stemmed, pendent plants. Leaves narrow, fleshy, curved, olive green often tinged with orange, to 25 × 1.5 cm. Inflorescence erect, 10–15 cm long, densely many-flowered. Flowers dull orange or pinkish orange, small, slightly scented; spur 2–3 cm long. Does better on the cool side of intermediate conditions.

High-level epiphyte in submontane and montane forest, 1500–2400 m (5000–7900 ft.)

East and Central Africa as far south as northern Malawi

Chamaeangis vesicata (Lindley) Schlechter

Short-stemmed plants with slender roots. Leaves several, pendent, fleshy, falcate, linear, unequally and acutely bilobed at the apex, to 40 × 3 cm. Inflorescence pendent, to 30 cm long, densely many-flowered. Flowers small, green or yellow-green, in opposite pairs or occasionally 3 at a node; spur 5–10 mm long, very swollen at the apex.

Riverine and submontane forest, 1100–1800 m (3600–6000 ft.)

West and East Africa

SIMILAR SPECIES: *Chamaeangis ichneumonea* (Lindley) Schlechter from West Africa has the flowers spirally arranged on the rachis.

Chaubardia Reichenbach f.

TRIBE: Maxillarieae

SUBTRIBE: Zygopetalinae

ETYMOLOGY: Named for French botanist L. A. Chaubard (1785–1854), a friend of Reichenbach

DISTRIBUTION: 5 species in tropical Central and South America

Sympodial epiphytes with small pseudobulbs, 1-leafed at apex and subtended by leaf-bearing sheaths. Inflorescences axillary, 1-flowered, erect or arching. Flowers small to medium-sized; sepals and petals subsimilar, spreading; lip attached to top of column-foot, entire or obscurely trilobed, lacking a spur. Column long, pubescent below, with a short foot; pollinia 4.

CULTIVATION: Plants can be grown mounted or in pots and require humid, shady conditions. Species from lower altitudes require temperatures on the warm side of intermediate, while those from higher altitudes need intermediate temperatures. They should not be allowed to dry out completely. Plants tend to flower off and on throughout the year.

Chaubardia heteroclita (Poeppig & Endlicher) Dodson & D. E. Bennett

SYN. *Huntleya heteroclita* (Poeppig & Endlicher) Garay, *Maxillaria heteroclita* Poeppig & Endlicher

Pseudobulbs small, hidden in leaf sheaths. Leaves to 44 × 6.5 cm, lanceolate or oblanceolate. Inflorescence to 15 cm long. Flowers 5–6 cm across; sepals and petals greenish yellow, flushed and streaked with reddish brown; lip pink, obscurely trilobed, with a prominent white callus.

Epiphytic in forest, 1500–2400 m (5000–7900 ft.)

Ecuador, Peru

Chaubardia surinamensis Reichenbach f.

Leaves to 15 × 1.5 cm long. Inflorescence to 7 cm long. Flowers 25 mm across; sepals and petals green, lip white.

Epiphytic in wet forest, 300–500 m (1000–1650 ft.)

Widely distributed in Central and South America

Chaubardiella Garay

TRIBE: Maxillarieae

SUBTRIBE: Zygopetalinae

ETYMOLOGY: Diminutive of *Chaubardia*

DISTRIBUTION: 8 species in tropical Central and South America

Sympodial epiphytes differing from *Chaubardia* in lacking pseudobulbs. Leaves several, forming a fan. Inflorescences axillary, 1-flowered, usually lying on surface of substrate. Flowers small to medium-sized, opening wide; sepals and petals subsimilar, ovate or lanceolate; lip entire, very concave, not spurred. Pollinia 4.

CULTIVATION: Plants require intermediate, shady conditions and should be watered throughout the year.

Chaubardiella dalessandroi Dodson & Dalström

Flowers ca. 20 mm across, green, heavily mottled with purple-brown, with an unpleasant smell. Flowering spring.

Epiphytic in wet submontane forest, 900–1800 m (3000–6000 ft.)

Ecuador, Peru

Chaubardiella tigrina (Garay & Dunsterville) Garay

SYN. *Chaubardia tigrina* Garay & Dunsterville

Leaves to 20 × 3 cm, strap-shaped, in a loose fan, Inflorescence ca. 5 cm long. Flowers to 45 mm across, pale greenish brown, heavily banded with maroon; lip with waxy, yellow-brown callus of about 10 radiating ridges.

Epiphytic in wet forest, 600–800 m (2000–2640 ft.)

Colombia, Ecuador

Chelonistele Pfitzer

TRIBE: Arethuseae

SUBTRIBE: Coelogyninae
ETYMOLOGY: From Greek *chelone*, turtle, and *stele*, column, referring to the shape of the column hood
DISTRIBUTION: 12 species, 11 only in Borneo, the other also in peninsular Malaya, Java, Sumatra, and the Philippines
Epiphytes or lithophytes with a creeping rhizome; pseudobulbs set close together, 1- or 2-leaved at apex. Inflorescences borne on a new shoot just before or with the leaves, unbranched, several-flowered. Flowers distichous or secund, wide open or bell-shaped; sepals subsimilar, broader than the linear petals; lip trilobed, saccate or concave at base, midlobe bilobed, with a callus of 2 or more parallel ridges.
CULTIVATION: Most species are intermediate growing. They require a well-drained compost and a shaded situation, and should not be allowed to dry out for long, but should be watered with care when new growth is developing.

Chelonistele sulphurea (Blume) Pfitzer
SYN. *Coelogyne sulphurea* (Blume) Reichenbach f.
Pseudobulbs to 8 cm long, 1- or 2-leaved. Leaves petiolate, 20–30 × 4–5 cm. Inflorescence to 30 cm long, arched, 4- to 18-flowered. Flowers ± secund, 20–22 mm across, white, yellow, buff, or pinkish, the lip with a yellow-brown blotch in the middle.

Epiphytic in wet forest, usually on trunks and large branches, 600–2700 m (2000–8900 ft.)

Borneo, Java, Malaya, Philippines, Sumatra

Chiloglottis R. Brown

BIRD ORCHIDS
TRIBE: Diurideae
SUBTRIBE: Drakaeinae
ETYMOLOGY: From Greek *cheilos*, lip, and *glottis*, glottis

Chaubardia heteroclita

Chaubardiella dalessandroi

Chelonistele sulphurea

DISTRIBUTION: About 22 species in eastern and southeastern Australia and New Zealand

Deciduous terrestrials with underground tubers, often forming colonies. Leaves basal, 2, usually elliptic. Inflorescences erect, terminal, 1-flowered. Flowers resupinate, dull-colored; dorsal sepal curving over the column, much broader than lateral sepals; lateral sepals narrowly linear; petals lanceolate; lip entire, joined by a short claw to the column-foot, sometimes motile; blade insectlike, heart-shaped or ovate, with a variety of dark, shiny calli.

Flowers are pollinated by male wasps trying to mate with the lip. After pollination, the pedicel elongates to about 20 cm.

CULTIVATION: Many species are easily grown in shallow pans in a coarse, free-draining terrestrial compost in cool conditions and moderate shade. Water freely while plants are in active growth; keep dry when dormant.

Chiloglottis formicifera Fitzgerald

ANT ORCHID

Leaves ovate-lanceolate, to 6 × 2.5 cm, dark green, the margins sometimes undulate. Inflorescence 10–12 cm tall. Flowers about 20 mm across, green marked with purple or brownish; dorsal sepal arched over column; lateral sepals and petals usually recurved or reflexed; lip rhomboid, to 12 mm long, with a shiny, antlike pink-and-black callus. Flowering in autumn.

Forms colonies in open forest, often near a stream

Southeastern Australia

Chiloglottis gunnii Lindley

Leaves ovate, to 10 × 3.5 cm, dark green. Inflorescence to 4 cm tall, rarely 2-flowered. Flowers to 40 mm across, maroon to purplish green; dorsal sepal arched over column, lateral sepals linear, projecting below lip; petals spreading or incurved; lip broadly ovate, motile, purple, with dark red to black calli and a prominent slender, stalked gland near the base. Flowers autumn–winter.

Forms colonies both in high-rainfall forest and drier, open forest at low to moderate altitudes

Southeastern Australia

Chiloschista Lindley

TRIBE: Vandeae

SUBTRIBE: Aeridinae

ETYMOLOGY: From Greek *cheilos*, lip, and *schistos*, cleft

DISTRIBUTION: About 20 species from India through Asia to the Pacific Islands and Australia

Small, leafless epiphytes with flattened, greenish-gray roots, rarely with a few small, ephemeral leaves. Inflorescences unbranched, several-flowered. Flowers small but showy, white or yellow, often with red spots; sepals and petals subequal; lip trilobed, spurred or saccate, with a fingerlike callus at the base.

CULTIVATION: Plants must be mounted and, like most leafless orchids, they seem to do better on smooth wood or bark. They can also be grown on the outside of a clay pot. They need intermediate temperatures and light shade, and should be sprayed throughout the year.

Chiloschista lunifera (Reichenbach f.) J. J. Smith

Roots long; stem very short. Inflorescence arching to pendent, to 20 cm long, 10- to 20-flowered. Flowers 12–20 mm across, yellow with a large brown blotch on each sepal and petal; lip saccate at base.

Epiphytic in forest

Laos, Myanmar, Thailand

SIMILAR SPECIES: *Chiloschista parishii* Seidenfaden, from Myanmar, Nepal, and northeastern India, where it grows in rain forest at 660–1800 m (2170–6000 ft.), differs in having yellow flowers spotted with red-brown, densely pubescent on the outside.

Chloraea Lindley

TRIBE: Chloraea

ETYMOLOGY: From Greek *chloros*, green, referring to the greenish flowers of the type species, *Chloraea virescens* (Willdenow) Lindley

DISTRIBUTION: Almost 50 species in South America, all but 2 endemic to the Andes.

Terrestrials with thick, fleshy cylindrical roots. Leaves several in a basal rosette. Inflorescences few- to many-flowered. Flowers white, green, yellow, orange, or reddish. Sepals free, the dorsal broader than the laterals; petals similar to dorsal sepal. Lip entire or trilobed, recurved, lacking a spur, often papillose, with a basal callus of crests.

Chiloschista lunifera

Chiloglottis formicifera. R. Parsons

Chiloschista parishii

Chiloglottis gunnii. R. Parsons

CULTIVATION: Few species are in cultivation, but this may be because of the difficulty in obtaining them. *Chloraea crispa* flowered at the Royal Botanic Gardens, Kew, in 1903. The long roots require deep pots and they should be successful in a standard free-draining terrestrial mix, in cool conditions or in an alpine house. All species grow in areas with a seasonal climate so require a resting season, but as they have fleshy roots rather than tubers, they should not be allowed to dry out completely.

Chloraea gavilu Lindley

Plants 50–80 cm tall. Inflorescence densely 10- to 18-flowered. Flowers opening wider than usual, 4–6 cm across, yellow with dark green markings.

Grassland, at medium altitudes

Chile

Chloraea magellanica Hooker f.

Plants 30–60 cm tall. Inflorescence 4- to 12-flowered. Flowers 5–8 cm across, fragrant, white, veined with green. Flowering spring. Requires cool or alpine house conditions.

Grassland and open scrub

Argentina (Patagonia), southern Chile

Chloraea membranacea Lindley

Plants 40–50 cm tall. Inflorescence several-flowered. Flowers white tinged with green.

Terrestrial in forest

Northeastern Argentina to southern Brazil

Chondrorhyncha Lindley

TRIBE: Maxillarieae
SUBTRIBE: Zygopetalinae
ETYMOLOGY: From Greek *chondros*, cartilage, and *rhynchos*, beak, referring to the beaklike rostellum
DISTRIBUTION: About 27 species from Mexico to Peru

Small sympodial epiphytes with pseudobulbs lacking or only rudimentary. Leaves in 2 rows, forming a fan, strap-shaped, keeled below, articulated to the leaf sheaths. Inflorescences basal, 1-flowered. Sepals subsimilar, the laterals often reflexed or hook-shaped. Lip unlobed, concave, surrounding the column, with a toothed callus at the base. Column not winged; pollinia 4.

CULTIVATION: Plants are grown in pots or baskets in a free-draining epiphyte mixture. They need intermediate conditions, shade, and high humidity and should not be allowed to dry out completely.

Chondrorhyncha andreettae Jenny

Inflorescence ca. 5 cm long. Flowers 3 cm across, white, the lip yellow towards the base with purple-red markings in front, the margins crisped.

Epiphytic in wet forest, 800–1500 m (2640–5000 ft.)

Ecuador

Chondrorhyncha rosea Lindley

Inflorescence 6–8 cm long. Flowers to 8.5 cm across. Sepals pale green, petals white; lip ± tubular, white, pale green at the base, with red spots.

Epiphytic in cloud forest, 1300–2000 m (4300–6600 ft.)

Colombia, Venezuela

Chondroscaphe (Dressler) Senghas & G. Gerlach

TRIBE: Maxillarieae
SUBTRIBE: Zygopetalinae
ETYMOLOGY: From Greek *chondros*, cartilage, and *scaphe*, bowl
DISTRIBUTION: About 13 species from Costa Rica to Peru

Small, sympodial epiphytes with no or only rudimentary pseudobulbs. Leaves in 2 rows, forming a fan. Inflorescences lateral, 1-flowered. Lateral sepals often reflexed; petals with a fringed margin. Lip entire, concave, surrounding the column, with a bilobed basal callus, the margins deeply fringed. Column not winged; pollinia 4.

Chondroscaphe is closely related to *Chondrorhyncha* and includes those species formerly assigned to *Chondrorhyncha* that have fringed petals and lip.

CULTIVATION: As for *Chondrorhyncha*. Plants are grown in pots or baskets in a free-draining epiphyte mixture. They need intermediate conditions, shade, and high humidity and should not be allowed to dry out completely.

Chondroscaphe chestertonii (Reichenbach f.) Senghas & G. Gerlach

SYN. *Chondrorhyncha chestertonii* Reichenbach f.

Inflorescence 7–8 cm long, pendulous. Flowers fleshy, to 7 cm across, strongly scented, pale green to cream, the lip usually lime green or yellow, the margins frilled and deeply fringed.

Epiphytic in wet forest, 1400–1500 m (4600–5000 ft.)

Colombia, Ecuador

Chondroscaphe endresii (Schlechter) Dressler

SYN. *Chondrorhyncha endresii* Schlechter

Leaves several, 20–50 cm long, strap-shaped. Inflorescence 5–8 cm long. Flowers 5–6 cm across, cream, the lip with dull purple marks, the margins toothed.

Chondroscaphe endresii has often been confused with *C. bicolor* (Rolfe) Dresser (syn. *Chondrorhyncha bicolor* Rolfe), a species known only from the type collection.

Epiphytic in wet forest, 950–1200 m (3100–4000 ft.)

Costa Rica

Chysis Lindley

TRIBE: Epidendreae
SUBTRIBE: Chysinae
ETYMOLOGY: From Greek *chysis*, melting, referring to the fused pollinia in self-pollinating forms
DISTRIBUTION: 9 species in Central and South America

Chloraea gavilu

Chloraea magellanica

Chondrorhyncha andreettae

Chondroscaphe chestertonii

Pseudobulbs large, club-shaped or spindle-shaped, pendent, covered with papery sheaths, several-leaved. Leaves plicate, lasting for 1 season. Inflorescences arising from base or a lower node of a new pseudobulb, arching, unbranched, several-flowered. Flowers waxy, scented; sepals and petals spreading, lateral sepals joined at base to column-foot to form a mentum. Lip trilobed, joined to column-foot, with a callus of 3–5 ridges between the side lobes.

CULTIVATION: Plants should be grown in baskets in a fairly coarse compost, or mounted, in intermediate conditions in light shade. Water and fertilize freely while in growth but keep dry and cooler after the new pseudobulbs have formed.

Chysis bractescens Lindley

Pseudobulbs to 40 cm long, 3 cm in diameter, pendent, often curved. Leaves to 35 × 7 cm, elliptic. Inflorescence to 20 cm long, 2- to 8-flowered; floral bracts green, to 3 cm long. Flowers fleshy, scented, 7–8 cm across; sepals and petals white, sometimes tinged with yellow at tips; lip yellow with red-brown markings, with a pubescent callus of 7–8 ridges.

Epiphytic in wet forest, 100–600 m (330–2000 ft.)

Belize, Guatemala, Mexico

SIMILAR SPECIES: *Chysis aurea* Lindley, from Panama, Venezuela, and Colombia, has slightly smaller yellow flowers with less conspicuous bracts and 5 yellow ridges on the lip. *Chysis laevis* Lindley has yellow flowers, orange toward the tips, 6–7 cm across, and a yellow lip marked with red-brown, with 3 prominent keels and 2–4 smaller ones on either side.

Cirrhaea Lindley

TRIBE: Maxillarieae

SUBTRIBE: Stanhopeinae

ETYMOLOGY: From Latin *cirrhus*, a tendril, referring to the long, slender rostellum

DISTRIBUTION: 7 species in eastern and central Brazil

Epiphytes with ribbed ovoid or angled pseudobulbs, 1-leafed at apex. Leaves plicate, petiolate. Inflorescences unbranched, basal, pendent, many-flowered. Flowers nonresupinate; sepals and petals free; lip clawed, trilobed, attached to the column-foot. Pollinia 2.

CULTIVATION: Because of their pendent inflorescences, plants of *Cirrhaea* are usually grown in baskets in an open compost. They need intermediate conditions, moderate to heavy shade, high humidity, and, while they need less water while resting, should not be kept dry for long periods.

Cirrhaea dependens (Loddiges) Loudon

SYN. *Cirrhaea warreana* Loddiges

Pseudobulbs ovoid, ridged, to 7 cm long. Leaves 20–50 × 3–5 cm. Inflorescence pendent, to 45 cm long, several- to many-flowered. Flowers 4–5 cm across, scented, not opening wide; sepals and petals greenish or yellowish, marked with purple; lip greenish cream marked with purple or all purple. Flowering spring–summer.

Epiphytic in deep shade in forest, to 1200 m (4000 ft.)

Brazil

SIMILAR SPECIES: *Cirrhaea loddigesii* Lindley, also from Brazil, may be synonymous.

Cischweinfia Dressler & N. H. Williams

TRIBE: Maxillarieae

SUBTRIBE: Oncidiinae

ETYMOLOGY: Named for American botanist Charles Schweinfurth (1890–1979)

DISTRIBUTION: About 10 species in Central and South America

Small epiphytes with small, laterally compressed pseudobulbs, 1-leafed at apex and subtended by leaf-bearing sheaths. Leaves thin-textured, strap-shaped. Inflorescences short, arising from basal leaf axils, unbranched, few-flowered. Sepals and petals free, spreading, subsimilar. Lip entire, funnel-shaped, joined to the column at the base. Column with a hooded extension over the anther; pollinia 2.

CULTIVATION: Plants require an open, free-draining compost in intermediate conditions with light shade, high humidity, and good ventilation. They should be watered and sprayed throughout the year.

Cischweinfia dasyandra (Reichenbach f.) Dressler & N. H. Williams

Pseudobulbs to 3.5 × 1 cm, ellipsoid. Leaves to 20 × 1. Inflorescence 4–5 cm long, 2- to 5-flowered. Flowers 20–30 mm across; sepals and petals green to yellow-green; lip cream, marked with pink, yellowish in throat.

Epiphytic in very wet woodland, 300–1300 m (1000–4300 ft.)

Costa Rica to Ecuador

Cleisostoma Blume

TRIBE: Vandeae

SUBTRIBE: Aeridinae

ETYMOLOGY: From Greek *kleistos*, closed, and *stoma*, mouth referring to the narrow mouth of the spur which is almost blocked by calli

DISTRIBUTION: About 90 species in tropical Asia

Small to medium-sized monopodial, erect or pendent epiphytes. Leaves flat or terete. Inflorescences often branched, erect or pendent, few- to many-flowered. Flowers small, fleshy; sepals and petals spreading, subsimilar; lip spurred or saccate, trilobed, with a conspicuous callus on the back wall of the spur. Pollinia 4, in 2 pairs.

CULTIVATION: Grow in pots or baskets in an open, free-draining compost at intermediate temperatures in shady, humid conditions. Plants should be kept drier when not actively growing but should not dry out completely.

Chysis bractescens

Chysis laevis

Cirrhaea dependens

Cischweinfia dasyandra

Cleisostoma racemiferum (Lindley) Garay

SYN. *Aerides racemifera* Lindley

Robust plants with thick roots. Leaves strap-shaped, to 36 × 3.5 cm. Inflorescence paniculate, longer than leaves, many-flowered. Flowers ca. 8 mm across; sepals and petals brownish black edged with yellow, lip yellow or white, column white.

Epiphytic in evergreen forest, 800–2150 m (2640–7100 ft.)

India to Vietnam

Cleisostoma simondii (Gagnepain) Seidenfaden

SYN. *Vanda simondii* Gagnepain

Stem erect. Leaves terete, fleshy, to 8.5 cm × 2 mm. Inflorescence pendent, branched or unbranched, laxly to 20-flowered. Flowers 7–9 mm across; sepals and petals yellow or buff with longitudinal purple stripes; lip midlobe mauve or pink; spur conical, ca. 2 mm long.

Epiphytic in forest, 100–1000 m (330–3300 ft.)

Northeastern India to Vietnam

Clowesia Lindley

TRIBE: Cymbidieae

SUBTRIBE: Catasetinae

ETYMOLOGY: Named for John Clowes of Broughton Hall, Manchester, who was the first to flower the type species (*C. rosea*)

DISTRIBUTION: 7 species from Mexico to Brazil and Ecuador

Epiphytes with stout fleshy, clustered, ovoid pseudobulbs. Leaves several, large, plicate, deciduous. Inflorescences basal, pendent, unbranched, few- to many-flowered. Flowers bisexual; sepals and petals free, petals usually broader and often fringed; lip fleshy, trilobed, spurred or saccate, midlobe often fringed or finely toothed at the apex. Pollinia 2, stipes 1, attached to a large viscidium which is released explosively when the stipes is touched, but less so than in catasetums—the bee is not knocked out of the flower.

CULTIVATION: Because of the pendent inflorescences, plants are usually grown in baskets or suspended pots in a coarse bark-based compost in light shade or bright light in intermediate to warm conditions. They should be given plenty of water and fertilizer while in active growth but kept cooler and drier while resting. In the wild, they are most often found growing on rotten wood. One grower gets excellent results growing them in horse manure with wood shavings and charcoal.

Clowesia rosea Lindley

Pseudobulbs to 6 cm tall, covered with gray sheaths, 4- or 5-leaved. Leaves elliptic, to 40 × 6 cm. Inflorescence to 12 cm long, several-flowered. Flowers scented of cinnamon in the afternoon, ca. 25 mm across, bell-shaped, pale to deep pink; lip fringed, saccate at base, callus 2-ridged. Flowering in early winter when leafless.

Epiphytic in oak forest, ca. 1000 m (3300 ft.)

Belize, Mexico

Clowesia russelliana (Hooker) Dodson

Pseudobulbs 12–15 × 3.5 cm, gray-green, several-leaved. Leaves to 40 × 7 cm. Inflorescence to 35 cm long, many-flowered. Flowers scented, to 6 cm across, green to greenish white with darker veining. Flowering summer.

Epiphytic in rather dry pine forest, ca. 600 m (2000 ft.)

Central America, Mexico

Clowesia thylaciochila (Lemaire) Dodson

Pseudobulbs 12–15 × 3 cm, covered with gray sheaths. Leaves elliptic, to 40 × 6 cm. Inflorescence to 35 cm long, many-flowered. Flowers scented, to 9 cm across, yellow-green with brownish veins; sepals and petals spreading; lip ovate, saccate at base, side lobes reflexed, callus 3-ridged. Flowering summer.

Epiphytic on palms, 1100–1700 m (3600–5600 ft.)

Mexico

SIMILAR SPECIES: *Clowesia dodsoniana* E. Aguirre was for many years confused with *C. thylaciochila*. It has paler green flowers with less prominent stripes and the lip side lobes are not reflexed. It comes from southern Mexico where it grows in rather dry forest at ca. 100 m (330 ft).

Clowesia warczewiczii (Lindley & Paxton) Dodson

Pseudobulbs to 9 × 4 cm, 4- to 6-leaved. Leaves to 40 × 8 cm. Inflorescence 10–15 cm long, several- to many-flowered. Flowers scented, 3–4 cm across, bell-shaped, green or greenish white with green veins; lip saccate at base, side lobes and midlobe fringed. Flowering in winter when leafless.

Epiphytic in wet forest, 200–900 m (660–3000 ft.)

Costa Rica south to Ecuador

Cochleanthes Rafinesque

TRIBE: Maxillarieae

SUBTRIBE: Zygopetalinae

ETYMOLOGY: From Greek *kochlos*, shell, and *anthos*, flower, referring to the shape of the lip

DISTRIBUTION: 2 species in Central America

Relatively large plants, lacking pseudobulbs or with very small pseudobulbs hidden in leaf sheaths. Inflorescences 1-flowered. Sepals and petals subsimilar, spreading. Lip flat or only slightly concave, not enfolding the column, with a rounded callus of adjacent ridges laterally fused with the lip. Column with a ventral keel.

Recent DNA work has resulted in most species previously treated in *Cochleanthes* being removed to other genera, mainly *Warczewiczella*.

CULTIVATION: Plants can be grown in shallow pots or baskets in a coarse, free-draining compost; if mounted, they must have high humidity. They require intermediate temperatures

Clowesia dodsoniana. G. Carr

Cleisostoma simondii

Clowesia rosea. M. Whitten

Clowesia russelliana

Clowesia thylaciochila. H. Hills

and fairly heavy shade and should not be allowed to dry out completely.

Cochleanthes aromatica

(Reichenbach f.) Schultes & Garay

SYN. *Zygopetalum aromaticum* Reichenbach f., *Warczewiczella aromatica* (Reichenbach f.) Reichenbach f., *Chondrorhyncha aromatica* (Reichenbach f.) P. H. Allen

Leaves 18–40 × 2–5 cm, oblanceolate, thin-textured. Inflorescence to 15 cm long. Flowers large, scented; sepals and petals pale green or greenish cream, sepals to 55 mm long, petals slightly smaller; lip trilobed, creamy white with a violet-purple median band, fiddle-shaped, to 45 × 38 mm, apical edge crisped, callus of 14–18 low ridges.

Epiphytic in wet tropical and submontane forest, 400–1200 m (1320–4000 ft.)

Costa Rica, Panama

Cochleanthes flabelliformis

(Swartz) Schultes & Garay

SYN. *Epidendrum flabelliforme* Swartz, *Zygopetalum flabelliforme* (Swartz) Reichenbach f., *Warczewiczella flabelliformis* (Swartz) Cogniaux, *Zygopetalum cochleare* Lindley, *Cochleanthes fragrans* Rafinesque

Leaves to 30 × 5 cm, oblanceolate, thin-textured. Inflorescence to 10 cm long. Flowers large, sometimes scented; sepals and petals pale green, sepals to 48 mm long, petals slightly shorter; lip obscurely trilobed, fan-shaped, creamy white veined with violet-purple at the base, the apex sometimes solid violet, the margin undulate; callus white spotted purple.

Epiphytic, rarely lithophytic, in wet tropical and submontane forest, 200–1000 m (660–3300 ft.)

Caribbean, Central and South America

Cochlioda Lindley

TRIBE: Maxillarieae

SUBTRIBE: Oncidiinae

ETYMOLOGY: From Greek *cochliodes*, a snail shell or spiral, referring to the shape of the lip callus

DISTRIBUTION: 8 species and 1 natural hybrid in western South America

Pseudobulbs laterally compressed, 1- or 2-leaved at apex. Leaves linear or strap-shaped. Inflorescences basal, usually unbranched. Flowers brightly colored; sepals and petals spreading, petals broader than sepals; lip lacking a spur, clawed at base, partly joined to the column, trilobed, midlobe entire or bilobed. Column winged at apex, pollinia 2, stigmatic cavities 2.

Species of *Cochlioda* have been widely used in hybridization with species in the *Oncidium* alliance, in hybrid genera such as ×*Odontioda* and ×*Vuylstekeara*, where they provide bright red colors.

CULTIVATION: Plants are usually grown in pots in a standard bark-based compost. They require cool, shady conditions with good air movement and moderate humidity. They should be given less water when they are resting.

Cochlioda noezliana (Masters) Rolfe

Pseudobulbs ca. 5 cm tall, 1-leafed. Leaves to 25 cm long, strap-shaped. Inflorescence arching, to 45 cm long, several-flowered. Flowers 4–5 cm across, bright scarlet or orange-red, the lip with a yellow disc with 4 keels. Flowering summer–autumn.

Epiphytic, sometimes lithophytic, in cloud forest, 2000–3500 m (6600–11,500 ft.)

Northern Peru

Cochlioda rosea (Lindley) Bentham

Pseudobulbs to 8 cm tall, 1-leafed. Leaves 15–20 cm long, strap-shaped. Inflorescence arching, to 45 cm long. Flowers 2–3.5 cm across, deep pink to crimson, lip with a white callus. Flowers late spring–summer.

Epiphytic in wet montane forest, 1500–2200 m (5000–7260 ft.)

Ecuador, Peru

Coelia Lindley

SYN. *Bothriochilus* Lemaire

TRIBE: Epidendreae

SUBTRIBE: Coeliinae

ETYMOLOGY: From Greek *koilos*, hollow, referring (mistakenly) to the pollinia

DISTRIBUTION: 5 species in Mexico, Central America, and the Caribbean

Epiphytic, lithophytic, or terrestrial plants with a short rhizome; pseudobulbs clustered, usually ovoid, with several sheaths at the base, several-leaved at the apex. Leaves petiolate, linear-lanceolate, pleated or ribbed. Inflorescences arising from basal sheaths, unbranched, almost covered by overlapping bracts. Flowers fleshy, scented, often not opening wide, white to pink; dorsal sepal and petals similar, lateral sepals oblique; lip entire, sometimes saccate at base. Pollinia 8.

CULTIVATION: Grow in pots in a free-draining compost, in intermediate conditions, in only light shade. Only very weak fertilizer should be given, preferably as a foliar feed, as the roots are sensitive to high concentrations of salt.

Coelia bella (Lemaire) Reichenbach f.

SYN. *Bothriochilus bellus* Lemaire

Pseudobulbs to 6 × 4 cm, almost globose, 3- to 5-leaved. Leaves linear-lanceolate, plicate, to 50 cm long. Inflorescence 2–6 cm tall, 3- to 6-flowered. Flowers 5–6 cm across, white, the sepals tipped with deep pink, the lip yellow.

Epiphytic, lithophytic, or terrestrial in wet broad-leaved forest, 600–1500 m (2000–5000 ft.)

Honduras to Mexico

Coelia triptera (Smith) G. Don ex Steudner

Pseudobulbs 3–5 cm long, narrowly ovate. Leaves several, 20–40 × 1–2 cm. Inflorescence 8–15 cm long, densely many-flowered. Flowers

Cochleanthes aromatica

Cochlioda noezliana

Cochlioda rosea

strongly scented, ca. 1.5 cm across, not opening wide, glistening white or pale yellow. This species does better in warm conditions.

Lithophytic on rocks in woodland, sometimes epiphytic, 500–1400 m (1650–4600 ft.)

Cuba, Guatemala, Jamaica, Mexico

Coeliopsis Reichenbach f.

TRIBE: Maxillarieae
SUBTRIBE: Stanhopeinae
ETYMOLOGY: From *Coelia* and Greek *opsis*, like, meaning resembling *Coelia*
DISTRIBUTION: 1 species in Costa Rica, Ecuador, and Panama

Pseudobulbs ovoid, to 10 cm long. Leaves 3 or 4, plicate, petiolate. Inflorescence basal, pendent, ± capitate, densely several-flowered. Flowers not opening wide; sepals subsimilar, the laterals fused at the base to form a mentum; petals narrower than sepals; lip trilobed, lacking a callus. Pollinia 2.

CULTIVATION: Because of the pendent inflorescences, plants should be mounted or grown in a basket. They require intermediate conditions and moderate shade, and should be watered throughout the year, letting the plants dry between waterings.

Coeliopsis hyacinthosma Reichenbach f.

Leaves to 60 × 8 cm. Inflorescence 5–15 cm long, to 15-flowered. Flowers waxy, scented like hyacinths, white with an orange spot in the throat; sepals and petals 13–15 mm long, lip 16–18 mm long.

Epiphytic in wet forest, 50–1150 m (165–3800 ft.)

Colombia, Costa Rica, Ecuador, Panama

Coelogyne Lindley

TRIBE: Arethuseae
SUBTRIBE: Coelogyninae
ETYMOLOGY: From Greek *koilos*, hollow, and *gyne*, woman, referring to the deep stigmatic cavity
DISTRIBUTION: About 200 species in tropical Asia and the Pacific Islands

Sympodial epiphytes, occasionally lithophytes or terrestrials, with a slender or stout rhizome; pseudobulbs ovoid, conical, globose, or cylindrical, 1- or 2-leaved at apex, set close together or far apart. Leaves elliptic to lanceolate, sometimes pleated. Inflorescences terminal or lateral, erect or pendent, unbranched, 1- to many-flowered. Sepals and petals free. Lip trilobed, lacking a spur, the disc variously keeled. Pollinia 4, in pairs.

Coelogyne has been divided into 22 sections. For further information, see Clayton (2002) in the "monographs" section of the bibliography.

Only about 30 *Coelogyne* hybrids have been registered. The 2 most frequently grown are Burfordiense (*C. asperata* × *C. pandurata*) and Memoria W. Micholitz (*C. lawrenceana* × *C. mooreana* 'Brockhurst').

CULTIVATION: Most species are grown in pots or baskets in a coarse bark-based compost; if grown in pots, species with pendent inflorescences need to be suspended. Smaller species can be mounted on bark. Most need good light and cool to intermediate temperatures, but species that grow at low altitudes and most of those from Borneo prefer warm conditions. All need plenty of water while growing, although the compost should be allowed to dry out between waterings. Plants should be kept dry while resting, although they should be sprayed occasionally to prevent the pseudobulbs from shriveling. A dry rest seems to be necessary to promote flowering.

Coelogyne corymbosa Lindley

Pseudobulbs ovoid, clustered, to 4 cm long, 2-leaved. Leaves to 20 × 3.5 cm. Inflorescence erect or pendent, 8–15 cm long, 2- to 4-flowered. Flowers to 7 cm across, scented, white with 4 yellow marks bordered with orange-red on the lip; lip midlobe ovate, callus of 3 keels.

Epiphytic on mossy branches and tree trunks in damp shade in montane forest, 1400–3000 m (4600–9900 ft.)

China to Nepal

Coelogyne cristata Lindley

Pseudobulbs globose to oblong, clustered or up to 6 cm apart, 2-leaved. Leaves lanceolate, to 30 × 3 cm. Inflorescence pendent, 3- to 10-flowered. Flowers to 8 cm across, white, the lip with yellow, fringed keels. Flowers winter–early spring.

Epiphytic or sometimes lithophytic in shady, montane forest, 1000–2600 m (3300–8600 ft.)

China to Tibet

Coelogyne cumingii Lindley

Pseudobulbs ovoid, to 7 cm long, set ca. 3 cm apart on a creeping rhizome. Leaves 2, to 20 × 4 cm. Inflorescence erect, to 25 cm long, developing with the new leaves, 3- to 5-flowered. Flowers scented, 6–7 cm across, white, the lip veined with yellow or orange, with 5 yellow or orange keels; midlobe margins crisped.

Epiphytic or lithophytic in hill forest, 900–2130 m (3000–7000 ft.)

Borneo, peninsular Malaysia, Thailand

Coelogyne fimbriata Lindley

Pseudobulbs ovoid, to 4 cm tall, set 3–4 cm apart on a creeping rhizome, 2-leaved. Leaves to 10 × 1.5 cm, oblong-elliptic. Inflorescence to 5 cm long, 1- to 3-flowered, the flowers open in succession. Flowers 3–3.5 cm across, pale yellow, the lip whitish with dark brown markings; lip midlobe orbicular, fringed with long hairs, disc with 3 keels.

Epiphytic in riverine forest, 640–1300 m (2100–4300 ft.), occasionally to 2290 m (7500 ft.)

Nepal to China and Southeast Asia

Coelogyne flaccida Lindley

Pseudobulbs conical, to 12 cm long, set close together, 2-leaved. Leaves to

Coelia triptera

Coeliopsis hyacinthosma. R. Parsons

Coelogyne cristata

Coelogyne corymbosa

Coelogyne fimbriata

20 × 3 cm, lanceolate, with a petiole 4 cm long. Inflorescence pendent, to 20 cm long, to 12-flowered, the flowers open together. Flowers 3–5 cm across, white; lip with a yellow central blotch and red spots at the base of the midlobe; side lobes with yellow and red stripes.

Epiphytic in submontane and montane forest, lithophytic in clearings, 900–2300 m (3000–7600 ft.)

Nepal to China and Southeast Asia

Coelogyne nitida (Wallich ex D. Don) Lindley

SYN. *Coelogyne ochracea* Lindley

Pseudobulbs to 10 × 2.5 cm, set 2–3 cm apart, 1- or 2-leaved. Leaves narrowly lanceolate, to 25 × 3 cm. Inflorescence erect or pendulous, to ca. 20 cm long, 3- to 6-flowered, the flowers open together. Flowers fragrant, 4 cm across, white, the lip with yellow spots edged with red on the side lobes and midlobe.

Epiphytic in submontane and montane forest, sometimes lithophytic on mossy rocks, 1300–2600 m (4300–8600 ft.)

Nepal to China and Southeast Asia

Coelogyne ovalis Lindley

Pseudobulbs 5–8 × 1.5 cm, set 5–7 cm apart, 2-leaved. Leaves to 17 × 4 cm, narrowly elliptic. Inflorescence 8–12 cm long, few-flowered, the flowers open in succession. Flowers to 3 cm across, pale yellow-green to brownish, the lip marked with darker brown; lip midlobe ovate, the margin fringed, with a callus of 3 keels at the base.

Epiphytic or lithophytic on boulders in hill forest, 800–1700 m (2640–5600 ft.)

Nepal to China and Thailand

Coelogyne pandurata Lindley

Pseudobulbs to 12.5 × 3 cm, oblong, set 3–10 cm apart, 2-leaved. Leaves 20–45 × 2–7 cm, elliptic-lanceolate. Inflorescence to 40 cm long, about 6-flowered, the flowers open together. Flowers fragrant, 7–13 cm across, clear green; lip with black markings, to 4 cm long, fiddle-shaped, the midlobe margins crisped and undulate. Intermediate to warm conditions.

Epiphytic, lithophytic, or terrestrial in lowland rain forest and submontane forest and in scrub, 0–1800 m (6000 ft.), rarely to 3700 m (12,200 ft.)

Borneo, Java, peninsular Malaysia, Sumatra

Coelogyne pulverula Teijsmann & Binnendijk

SYN. *Coelogyne dayana* Reichenbach f.

Pseudobulbs conical, 10–25 cm long, set close together, 2-leaved. Leaves to 65 × 11 cm. Inflorescence pendent, 25–110 cm long, to about 50–flowered. Flowers 5–6 cm across, cream to pale greenish brown, the lip mainly brown with a white margin, with 3 keels.

Epiphytic in lowland rain forest and submontane forest, 275–1900 m (900–6300 ft.)

Borneo, Java, peninsular Malaysia, Thailand, Sumatra

Coelogyne speciosa (Blume) Lindley

Pseudobulbs ovoid, to 7 cm long, set close together, 1- to 2-leaved.

Coelogyne speciosa

Leaves lanceolate, to 35 × 10 cm. Inflorescence erect, becoming pendulous, 1- to 8-flowered. Flowers to 7 cm across, greenish yellow to salmon-pink, the lip white or cream, red-brown at the base, the margins erose, the disc with 3 keels with warty projections.

Three subspecies are recognized: subsp. *speciosa*, subsp. *fimbriata* (J. J. Smith) Gravendeel with margins of the lip midlobe fringed, and subsp. *incarnata* Gravendeel with more or less salmon-pink flowers.

Epiphytic in forest, rarely terrestrial, 760–2000 m (2500–6600 ft.)

Java, Sumatra

Coelogyne stricta (D. Don) Schlechter

Pseudobulbs oblong, to 15 × 6 cm long, the base enclosed by bracts, 2-leaved. Leaves to 35 × 7 cm with a petiole to 7 cm long. Inflorescence erect, ca. 40 cm long, 10- to 15-flowered. Flowers 3 cm across, white, the midlobe with an orange-yellow patch near the base.

Epiphytic on broad-leaved trees on river banks in forest, 1100–2000 m (3600–6600 ft.)

Nepal, Bhutan, northeastern India, Myanmar, China

Coelogyne tomentosa Lindley

SYN. *Coelogyne massangeana* Reichenbach f., *C. dayana* Reichenbach f. var. *massangeana* Ridley

Pseudobulbs 4–15 cm long, ovoid, set close together, 2-leaved. Leaves 10–70 × 3–10 cm, ovate to elliptic. Inflorescence pendent, to 55 cm long, 10- to 30-flowered. Flowers to 6 cm across, cream, pale greenish yellow, or brown, the lip midlobe veined with brown and yellow, the disc warty with 3 lamellae.

Epiphytic in submontane and montane forest or lithophytic on limestone, 1500–2100 m (5000–6900 ft.)

Java, peninsular Malaysia, Sumatra

Coelogyne flaccida

Coelogyne nitida

Coelogyne pandurata

Coelogyne stricta

Coelogyne tomentosa

Comparettia Poeppig & Endlicher

TRIBE: Maxillarieae
SUBTRIBE: Oncidiinae
ETYMOLOGY: Named for Italian botanist Andrea Comparetti (1745–1801)
DISTRIBUTION: 5 species and 1 natural hybrid from Mexico, Central and South America, and the West Indies

Epiphytes or lithophytes with a short, creeping rhizome. Pseudobulbs small, 1-leafed at apex. Inflorescences basal, arching, simple or branched, loosely few- to many-flowered. Flowers brightly colored and showy; dorsal sepal and petals free, erect; lateral sepals joined at the base to form a spurlike mentum; lip much larger than other parts, clawed, with 2 "tails" at the base that are enclosed in the mentum; trilobed, side lobes small, midlobe usually broader than long.

CULTIVATION: Plants can be grown in pots in a fine bark-based compost but seem to do better mounted on bark or tree fern. They need shady, intermediate conditions with high humidity and good air movement throughout the year; they should not be allowed to dry out completely.

Comparettia falcata Poeppig & Endlicher

SYN. *Comparettia rosea* Lindley

Pseudobulbs 1–4 cm long, 1-leafed at apex, covered with sheaths, sometimes leaf-bearing. Leaf to 18 × 5 cm, elliptic. Inflorescence to 90 cm long, sometimes branched, loosely few- to many-flowered. Flowers ca. 2 cm across, pink to purple-red, whitish in middle; midlobe notched; spur 12–15 mm long.

Twig epiphyte in rain forest and cloud forest, 1000–2000 m (3300–6600 ft.)

The most widespread species, from Mexico to Bolivia and the West Indies

SIMILAR SPECIES: *Comparettia macroplectron* Reichenbach f. & Triana (syn. *C. splendens* Schlechter), from Colombia, has pale lilac flowers spotted with purple, 4 cm across, and a spur to 5 cm long.

Comparettia speciosa Reichenbach f.

Pseudobulbs small, ± cylindrical, covered with scarious sheaths. Leaf to 25 × 4 cm. Inflorescence to 50 cm long, branched or unbranched, several- to many-flowered. Flowers 3–5 cm across, bright orange-red; spur slender, to 3.5 cm long.

Twig epiphyte in montane forest and lower cloud forest, 700–2000 m (2300–6600 ft.)

Ecuador

Constantia Barbosa Rodrigues

TRIBE: Epidendreae
SUBTRIBE: Laeliinae
ETYMOLOGY: Named for Constantia Barbosa Rodrigues, wife of João Barbosa Rodrigues, the Brazilian botanist (1842–1909) and author of the genus
DISTRIBUTION: 5 species in southern and southeastern Brazil

Very small epiphytes with globose pseudobulbs 2-leaved at apex, set close together on branched, creeping rhizomes. Inflorescences 1-flowered, rarely 2-flowered. Flowers white, pinkish, or reddish; sepals and petals ovate, the petals smaller and pointing forwards; lip ± entire with a ridged callus. Pollinia 8.

CULTIVATION: These attractive little species are said to be difficult to grow, perhaps because of their specialized habitats. They have been successfully grown on slabs of tree fern or bark, at intermediate temperatures, in light shade, with frequent misting.

Constantia cipoensis Campos Porto & Brade

Pseudobulbs ca. 5 mm across. Leaves almost round, 5 × 5 mm. Flowers to 30 mm across, white, the lip with a yellow blotch at the base. Flowers autumn–early winter.

Epiphytic on branches of *Vellozia* species, 1000–1200 m (3300–4000 ft.)

Brazil (endemic to Serra do Cipo in Minas Gerais state)

Coryanthes Hooker

BUCKET ORCHIDS
TRIBE: Maxillarieae
SUBTRIBE: Stanhopeinae
ETYMOLOGY: From Greek *korys*, helmet, and *anthos*, flower, referring to the helmet-shaped lip
DISTRIBUTION: More than 40 species in Mexico, Central and South America, and Trinidad

Robust epiphytes, occasionally lithophytes, with large, ribbed pseudobulbs set close together on a stout rhizome, 2- or 3-leaved at apex. Leaves petiolate, pleated. Inflorescences arising from base of pseudobulb, pendent, few-flowered. Flowers large, fragrant, short-lived and complex; sepals free, spreading, twisted, the dorsal smaller than laterals; petals undulate, smaller than sepals; lip fleshy, clawed at the base, divided into 3 parts—a saccate hypochile, a long, slender mesochile, and a bucket-shaped epichile. Column long, winged, with 2 basal horns which exude fluid into the epichile.

Male euglossine bees are attracted to the scent given out by the hypochile and soon fall into the epichile. To escape, they crawl up the tubular mesochile and as they do, pick up pollinia. When they visit another flower the process is repeated and the pollinia are deposited on to the stigma. In the wild, *Coryanthes* plants are often associated with ant nests.

CULTIVATION: Because of their pendent inflorescences, *Coryanthes* species are grown in baskets, like *Stanhopea* species. They need intermediate to warm conditions, with moderate shade and plenty of water and fertilizer during the growing season. They should be given less water while resting but should not be kept completely dry.

Comparettia macroplectron

Comparettia falcata

Comparettia speciosa

Constantia cipoensis. R. Parsons

Coryanthes alborosea C. Schweinfurth

Pseudobulbs ovoid, 2-leaved. Inflorescence to 17 cm long, 1- or 2-flowered. Flowers ca. 6 cm long, white with red spots; the lip hypochile pink, heavily blotched with red.

Epiphytic in lowland forest, 100 m (330 ft.)

Peru

Coryanthes leucocorys Rolfe

Pseudobulbs conical to ovoid, ribbed, 2-leaved. Inflorescence to 30 cm long, 1- or 2-flowered. Flowers ca. 11 cm long, mint-scented; sepals and petals grayish red; lip hypochile inflated, white; epichile deep red.

Epiphytic in forest, 0–1600 m (5300 ft.)

Ecuador to Peru

Coryanthes macrantha (Hooker) Hooker

Pseudobulbs clustered, ovoid, 10–12 cm long, 2-leaved. Leaves to 45 × 8 cm. Inflorescence 13–18 cm long, 1- to 3-flowered. Flowers large, to 13 cm long, buff yellow to orange or red, spotted with purple-red.

Epiphytic in lowland rain forest, 50–500 m (165–1650 ft.)

Trinidad to South America

Coryanthes speciosa Hooker

Flowers to 6 cm long, variable in color, most often light bronze densely spotted with maroon, the lip cream, flushed with maroon.

Three varieties are recognized: var. *espritosantense* Ruschi and var. *sumneriana* (Lindley) G. Gerlach, both from Brazil, and var. *speciosa*.

Epiphytic in lowland forest, ca. 100 m (330 ft.)

Trinidad to Brazil

Corybas Salisbury

HELMET ORCHIDS

TRIBE: Diurideae

SUBTRIBE: Acianthinae

ETYMOLOGY: From Greek *korybas*, a dancing priest

DISTRIBUTION: About 125 species in Asia, the Pacific Islands, Australia, and New Zealand

Small, deciduous terrestrials, rarely epiphytes, with small, paired, globose tubers. Leaf single, basal, round or heart-shaped, lying flat on the ground. Flower 1, sessile or with a short pedicel, borne in leaf axil; dorsal sepal large, forming a hood; lateral sepals and petals free, subsimilar, much smaller than dorsal sepal; lip erect and tubular in basal part, then recurved, sometimes fringed.

CULTIVATION: Several of the colony-forming Australian species, including those mentioned below, do well in cultivation. These usually grow in damp areas and require an acid compost with extra leaf mold, a fairly humid atmosphere, and moderate shade. Buds may abort if the atmosphere is too dry and it may be necessary to cover the pot with a bell jar or plastic dome. Plants should be watered freely while in growth and sprinkled from time to time even while resting as the very small tubers are prone to desiccation.

Corybas aconitiflorus Salisbury

Leaf heart-shaped, to 3.5 × 3 cm, dark green above, purple below. Flower purple, erect, on pedicel 3 cm long; dorsal sepal to 30 × 12 mm, covering rest of flower; lip tubular in basal half, then broader and recurved, the surface smooth or with tiny hairs. Flowers late spring–summer.

Forms colonies in damp, sheltered places

Australia (southeastern Queensland, Tasmania)

Corybas diemenicus (Lindley) Rupp

SYN. *Corybas dilatatus* (Rupp & Nicholls) Rupp

Leaf heart-shaped to ovate, green above and below. Flowers dark red and white on a slender pedicel; dorsal sepal to 24 × 15 mm, spoon-shaped, forming a hood; lip orbicular with prominent veins, the margins toothed, with a smooth, white swelling in the center. Flowers midsummer–autumn.

Forms colonies in damp, shady gullies, sometimes on mossy logs

Southeastern Australia

Corybas fimbriatus (R. Brown) Reichenbach f.

Leaf heart-shaped to round, to 4 × 4 cm, green above and below. Flowers sessile, dark red-purple with lighter mottling; dorsal sepal to 25 × 18 mm, spoon-shaped, forming a hood; lip ca. 12 mm across, almost round, with coarse teeth and a round, purple dome in the center. Flowering spring–late summer.

Forms colonies in sandy soil in coastal scrub and in gullies in open woodland

Eastern and southeastern Australia

SIMILAR SPECIES: *Corybas hispidus* D. L. Jones from southeastern Australia differs in having the lip covered with stiff hairs and a white central dome, notched at the top.

Corybas incurvus D. Jones & M. Clements

Leaf heart-shaped to ovate, to 3 × 2 cm, green above and below. Flowers purple; dorsal sepal ca. 20 × 13 mm, forming a hood, sepals and petals filiform, lip ovate with a white domed patch in the center, the margins toothed and incurved. An easily grown species.

Forms colonies on moist slopes, in coastal scrub and in open forest

Eastern and southeastern Australia

Corybas pictus (Blume) Reichenbach f.

Leaf heart-shaped, ca. 2.5 × 2.5 cm, veined with white or pink. Dorsal sepal deep purple, ca. 16 mm long; lateral sepals and petals white, filiform, ca. 3 cm long. Lip decurved, apical third deep red with toothed margins, basal part white.

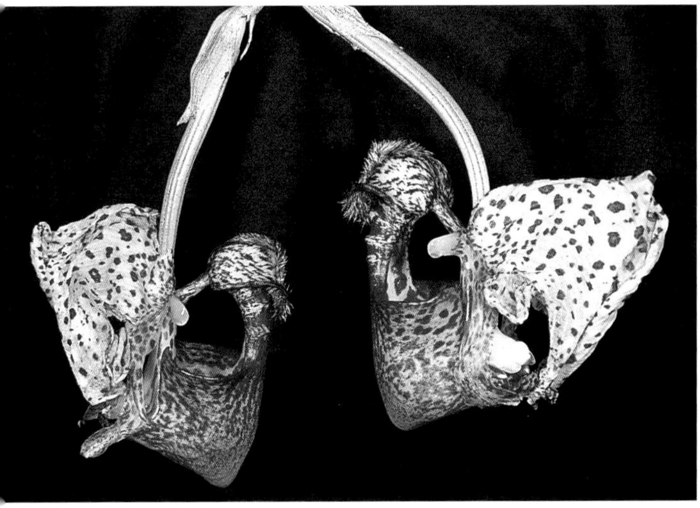

Coryanthes alborosea

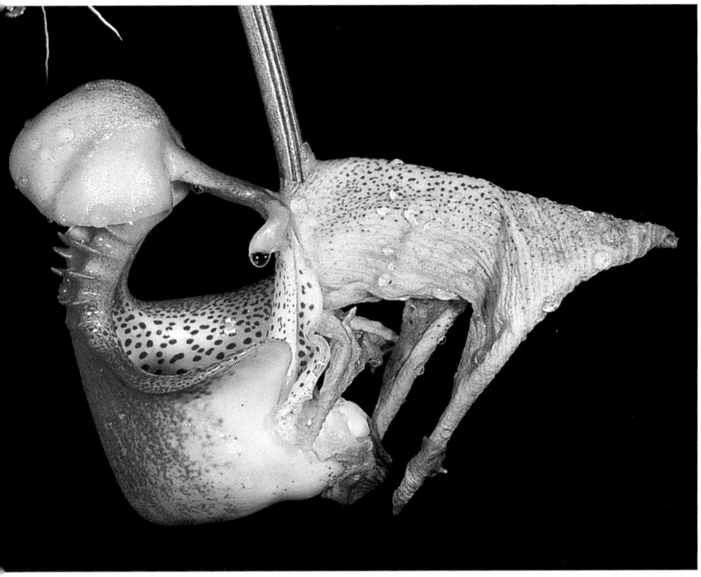

Coryanthes macrantha

Corybas pictus. P. O'Byrne

Corybas diemenicus. R. Parsons

Corybas incurvus. R. Parsons

On forest floor, 700–1800 m (2300–6000 ft.)

Borneo, Java, Sumatra

Corybas pruinosus

(R. Cunningham) Reichenbach f.

Leaf heart-shaped to ovate, ca. 3 × 2 cm, green above and below. Flower sessile or shortly stalked; dorsal sepal to 17 × 5 mm, grayish, blotched with purple; lateral sepals filiform, to 20 mm long; lip ca. 10 mm across, round, the margins coarsely toothed, the central dome with many small calli. Flowering spring–midsummer.

Forms colonies under bracken and scrub in open woodland

Australia (eastern New South Wales)

Corymborkis Thouars

TRIBE: Tropidieae

ETYMOLOGY: From Greek *corymbos*, corymb, and *orchis*, referring to the clustered inflorescence

DISTRIBUTION: 6 species occurring throughout the tropics

Terrestrial plants with a short, creeping rhizome, wiry roots and erect, unbranched, leafy, reedlike stems. Leaves pleated, usually ovate or elliptic. Inflorescences axillary, usually branched, few- to many-flowered. Flowers pale green, white, or yellowish, often scented; sepals and petals narrow, clawed, subsimilar but the petals often slightly broader; lip spoon-shaped—narrow at the base and clasping the column, wider at the apex. Column long and slender; pollinia 2, viscidium 1.

CULTIVATION: Species of *Corymborkis* are not widely grown. They require a well-drained terrestrial compost and humid, shady conditions. As most plants are fairly tall, they are better in a heavy clay pot.

Corymborkis veratrifolia

(Reinwardt) Blume

Plants 50–300 cm tall. Leaves pleated, to 50 × 15 cm, the edges somewhat undulate, the bases sheathing. Inflorescence branched, erect or nodding, few- to many-flowered. Flowers ca. 2.5 cm across, scented, green, the lip white, tubular, the apex ovate.

Deep shade in forest, 0–2000 m (6600 ft.)

Tropical Asia, from India to the Pacific Islands

SIMILAR SPECIES: *Corymborkis corymbis* Thouars (the type species of the genus), from tropical and South Africa, Madagascar, and the Mascarene Islands, is up to 150 cm tall and has larger flowers, the sepals ca. 85 mm long.

Cremastra Lindley

TRIBE: Calypsoeae

ETYMOLOGY: From Greek *cremastra*, pedicel, referring to the long pedicel and ovary

DISTRIBUTION: 2 or 3 species from the Russian Far East to Indochina

Terrestrials with clustered, ovoid corms. Leaves 1 or 2, plicate, petiolate. Inflorescences lateral, few- to many-flowered. Flowers pendent, tubular, scented; sepals and petals similar, free; lip trilobed, saccate at base. Pollinia 4, in 2 pairs.

CULTIVATION: *Cremastra* species are rare in cultivation but are grown in the Far East. They should grow in cool, shady conditions, in a free-draining terrestrial compost.

Cremastra appendiculata (D. Don) Makino

Plants 20–60 cm tall. Leaves 1 or 2, elliptic, to 50 cm long. Inflorescence to about 30-flowered. Flowers to 4 cm long, pink, purplish, or yellowish; sepals and petals linear, wider at the apex; disc of lip with a large warty callus.

Moist places in dense forest, 500–2900 m (1650–9600 ft.)

Nepal, India, China, Taiwan, Japan

Cribbia Senghas

TRIBE: Vandeae

SUBTRIBE: Aerangidinae

ETYMOLOGY: Named for Phillip Cribb, for many years head of the orchid herbarium at the Royal Botanic Gardens, Kew

DISTRIBUTION: 4 species in tropical Africa, 2 of which are endemic to São Tomé and Principé

Small monopodial epiphytes, occasionally lithophytes. Leaves distichous, strap-shaped. Inflorescences axillary, unbranched, peduncles very slender, rather loosely several-flowered. Flowers translucent, greenish, straw-colored, or white; sepals and petals free, ± lanceolate, the lateral sepals longer than the dorsal sepal; lip entire, spurred at the base, with no callus. Pollinia, stipites and viscidia 2.

CULTIVATION: Plants do well in pots in a standard bark compost, in intermediate or warm conditions, with fairly heavy shade and high humidity.

Cribbia brachyceras

(Summerhayes) Senghas

SYN. *Aerangis brachyceras* Summerhayes, *Rangaeris brachyceras* (Summerhayes) Summerhayes

Stem erect, to 20 cm long, sometimes branched at the base. Leaves several, to 13 × 1 cm, narrowly strap-shaped, unequally bilobed at the tips. Inflorescence erect, 4–17 cm long, to 15-flowered. Flowers ca. 10 mm across, greenish white or yellow-green tinged with orange; lip 5 × 3 mm; spur 5–6 mm long.

Epiphytic or lithophytic on mossy rocks, 1500–2200 m (5000–7260 ft.)

West and Central Africa

SIMILAR SPECIES: *Cribbia confusa* P. J. Cribb from West Africa and São Tomé is usually a slightly smaller plant, with larger greenish-yellow flowers tinged with orange, very strongly honey-scented.

Cryptocentrum Bentham

TRIBE: Maxillarieae

SUBTRIBE: Maxillariinae

ETYMOLOGY: From Greek *kryptos*, hidden, and *kentron*, spur

DISTRIBUTION: About 20 species in Central and South America

Corymborkis veratrifolia. P. O'Byrne

Corymborkis corymbis. E. la Croix

Cremastra appendiculata. H. Oakeley

Cribbia confusa

Epiphytes usually without pseudobulbs. Leaves distichous or in a rosette, cylindrical or folded. Inflorescences lateral, 1-flowered; peduncle with several sheaths. Flowers resupinate; sepals and petals spreading, narrow, the sepals longer than the petals; lip unlobed, similar to petals; spur usually hidden by the topmost bract.
CULTIVATION: Plants should be grown in intermediate conditions, in moderate shade and high humidity, but kept drier in winter, although not completely dry. They can be grown mounted or in small pots in a free-draining bark mix with some added sphagnum.

Cryptocentrum gracillimum Ames & C. Schweinfurth

Leaves distichous, to 15 × 2 cm, linear, semi-cylindrical. Inflorescence 3–6 cm tall, topmost bract to 2 cm long. Flowers to 2 cm across, olive green to tan; sepals 8–10 × 2–2.5 mm; spur 14 mm long. Flowers off and on throughout year but mostly in autumn.

Epiphytic in wet woodland, 750–900 m (2460–3000 ft.)

Costa Rica

SIMILAR SPECIES: *Cryptocentrum pergracile* Schlechter from Colombia has larger, paler flowers.

Cryptocentrum pergracile

Cryptochilus Wallich

TRIBE: Podochileae
SUBTRIBE: Eriinae
ETYMOLOGY: From Greek *kryptos*, hidden, and *cheilos*, lip, referring to the lip being concealed by the sepals
DISTRIBUTION: 4 species from the Himalayas to China

Epiphytes or lithophytes with clustered pseudobulbs. Leaves borne at apex of pseudobulb, leathery, petiolate. Inflorescences terminal, unbranched, secund, the floral bracts longer than the flowers. Sepals joined for three-quarters of their length to form a cylindrical or urn-shaped tube; petals free. Lip entire. Pollinia 8.
CULTIVATION: Plants require cool to intermediate conditions. They do best grown in pots as the fine roots should not be allowed to dry out completely. They need high humidity and moderate shade.

Cryptochilus sanguineus Wallich

Pseudobulbs ovoid to narrowly ellipsoid, to 4.5 × 1 cm. Leaves 2, to 20 × 4 cm, including a petiole 4–5 cm long. Inflorescence to 28 cm long, many-flowered. Flowers in 2 rows, pubescent on the outside, 10–15 mm long; sepaline tube urn-shaped, bright red with purple tips, petals and lip yellow, pedicel and ovary covered with white hairs.

Epiphytic in broad-leaved forest, 1940–2330 m (6400–7700 ft.)

Nepal to Thailand

Cryptopus Lindley

TRIBE: Vandeae
SUBTRIBE: Angraecinae
ETYMOLOGY: From Greek *kryptos*, hidden, and *pous*, foot
DISTRIBUTION: 4 species in Madagascar and the Mascarene Islands

Monopodial epiphytes or lithophytes with long, leafy stems, sometimes branched; roots arising along stem. Leaves distichous, leathery. Inflorescences lateral, longer than the leaves, simple or branched, few- to many-flowered. Flowers white or greenish white with red or yellow marks on lip; sepals and petals free; petals lobed or divided, rather similar to lip; lip 3-, 4-, or 5-lobed; spur short, conical or cylindrical.
CULTIVATION: In the wild, plants scramble over trees and rocks. The roots do not like to be confined so plants grow best mounted on a cork slab, or potted with a moss pole to climb. They require intermediate conditions with good to strong light and high humidity.

Cryptopus elatus (Thouars) Lindley

Stem 50–100 cm long with numerous roots. Leaves to 7 × 1.5 cm, oblong or elliptic. Inflorescence to 60 cm long, arching, usually unbranched, many-flowered. Flowers white or cream with a red mark at base of lip; sepals 20 mm long, spathulate; petals 25 mm long, clawed at the base, 4-lobed at apex; lip 4-lobed, 15 mm long.

Epiphytic or lithophytic in open forest, 0–700 m (2300 ft.)

Mauritius, Réunion

SIMILAR SPECIES: *Cryptopus dissectus* (Bosser) Bosser from Madagascar has smaller, yellow-green flowers with deeply dissected petals and lip. *Cryptopus paniculatus* H. Perrier from Madagascar has branched inflorescences to 30 cm long and yellow-green flowers with anchor-shaped petals.

Cryptostylis R. Brown

TRIBE: Diurideae
SUBTRIBE: Cryptostylidinae
ETYMOLOGY: From Greek *kryptos*, hidden, and *stylos*, column, referring to the very short column
DISTRIBUTION: About 23 species in Asia, the Pacific Islands, Australia, and New Zealand

Terrestrials with an underground rhizome and thick, fleshy roots; tubers absent. Leaves few per shoot, basal, petiolate, sometimes with contrasting spots and veins. Inflorescences erect, unbranched, several-flowered. Flowers nonresupinate; sepals and

Cryptochilus sanguineus

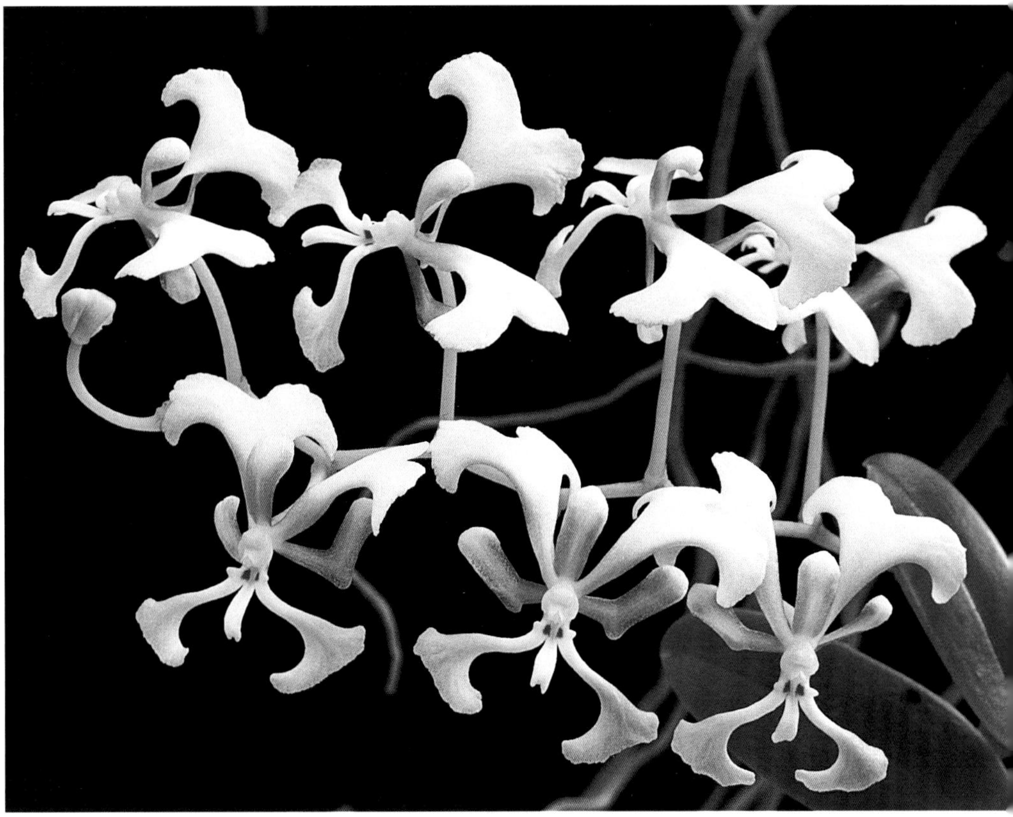

Cryptopus paniculatus. J. Hermans

Cryptopus elatus. H. Oakeley

petals small, narrow; lip much larger and more colorful, entire, clasping the column at the base, covered with glandular hairs, the margins reflexed, with a callus of several ridges and keels.

CULTIVATION: Plants can be grown in a standard terrestrial compost in a large container. They dislike disturbance and should only be repotted if the pot has become overcrowded or the compost has deteriorated. They should be watered freely while in active growth and should not be allowed to dry out completely even when resting.

Cryptostylis arachnites (Blume) Hasskarl

Leaves with petiole 4–16 cm long, blade to 16 × 6.5 cm. Inflorescence 20–60 cm long, many-flowered. Flowers ca. 4 cm across; sepals and petals linear, pale green, lip deep red-brown, obscurely dotted with red, the apex curved forwards.

Terrestrial in forest, often in moss at base of trees, 800–2200 m (2640–7260 ft.)

Widespread in Asia

SIMILAR SPECIES: *Cryptostylis conspicua* J. J. Smith from Java, Malaysia, and Sumatra has a lip without the apex curved forwards, with a red-brown streak but no spotting.

Cryptostylis subulata (Labillardière) Reichenbach f.

Leaves several, lanceolate, green on both surfaces, to 15 × 3 cm with a petiole to 8 cm long. Inflorescence 80–90 cm tall, 2- to 20-flowered. Sepals and petals 15–30 cm long, spreading or deflexed, yellowish to green, the margins inrolled. Lip projecting, to 30 mm long, oblong, the margins recurved, red-brown or purplish, callus of 2 glossy deep purple ridges ending in a bilobed projection.

Usually in swampy areas, occasionally in sandy soil

Eastern and southeastern Australia

Cuitlauzina Lexarza

TRIBE: Maxillarieae
SUBTRIBE: Oncidiinae
ETYMOLOGY: Named for Cuitlauhuatzin, horticulturist and governor of Itzapalapa in Mexico
DISTRIBUTION: 5 species in Central America and Mexico

Epiphytes or lithophytes, occasionally terrestrials, related to *Odontoglossum*; pseudobulbs ovoid, compressed, 2-leaved at the apex. Leaves strap-shaped. Inflorescences basal, unbranched, erect or pendent. Flowers scented; sepals and petals subsimilar but with the petals broader than the sepals; lip clawed at the base, the blade usually broader than long.

Except for *Cuitlauzina pendula*, the species in this small genus have been in and out of other genera at various times, in particular *Osmoglossum* and *Odontoglossum*.

CULTIVATION: Plants require cool to intermediate conditions, light to moderate shade, high humidity, and good ventilation. They are usually grown in pots or baskets (if the inflorescence is pendent) in a fine to standard bark-based compost. While resting, they need drier and cooler conditions.

Cuitlauzina convallarioides (Schlechter) Dressler & N. H. Williams

SYN. *Osmoglossum convallarioides* Schlechter

Pseudobulbs to 8 × 4 cm, leaves 25–35 × 1–1.5 cm. Inflorescence erect, 15–35 cm tall, several-flowered. Flowers fleshy, ca. 2 cm across, white or pinkish white; sepals and petals concave; lip with an orange callus.

Epiphytic in wet woodland, 1450–2000 m (4800–6600 ft.)

Costa Rica, Guyana, Mexico

SIMILAR SPECIES: *Cuitlauzina egertonii* (Lindley) Dressler & N. H. Williams (syn. *Osmoglossum egertonii* (Lindley) Schlechter), also from Mexico and Central America, has slightly larger flowers.

Cuitlauzina pendula Lexarza

Pseudobulbs to 15 × 7 cm, clustered, 2-leaved at apex. Leaves to 30 × 5 cm. Inflorescence pendent, 40–100 cm long. Flowers 5–7.5 cm across, lemon-scented, long-lasting; sepals and petals spreading, white, tinged pink or lilac at the base, lip emarginate, pale to bright lilac-pink with a yellow claw.

Epiphytic in montane forest, 1900–2000 m (6300–6600 ft.)

Mexico

Cyanicula S. D. Hopper & A. P. Brown

TRIBE: Diurideae
SUBTRIBE: Caladeniinae
ETYMOLOGY: From Greek *cyano*, blue, and the diminutive suffix *-ula*, referring to the small blue flowers
DISTRIBUTION: 10 species in Australia, most in Western Australia

Tubers globose, paired, enclosed in a persistent fibrous tunic; replacement tubers formed inside the tunic at the end of short droppers. Leaf single, basal, sessile, ovate to linear. Inflorescences erect, terminal, unbranched, 1- to few-flowered. Flowers blue, rarely white or yellow; sepals and petals free, subsimilar; lip free, clawed, lacking a spur, entire or trilobed, with several rows of variously shaped calli. Column winged.

CULTIVATION: As for *Caladenia*. Grow in pans of standard terrestrial compost but with extra drainage material such as coarse sand, in light shade. The tubers rot easily, so it is essential that drainage is good and that the pans are not overwatered. Most species flower from late winter to late spring, and watering should start in midautumn and continue till mid or late spring, when the leaves start to turn yellow and die back. Many species are notoriously difficult to grow, but those that form colonies tend to be more successful in cultivation.

Cryptostylis arachnites. P. O'Byrne

Cryptostylis conspicua. P. O'Byrne

Cuitlauzina convallarioides

Cuitlauzina pendula

Cyanicula caerulea (R. Brown) Hopper & A. P. Brown

SYN. *Caladenia caerulea* R. Brown

Leaf linear, to 7 cm long, with sparse hairs. Inflorescence to 15 cm tall, 1-flowered. Flowers to 2.5 cm across, clear blue to blue-mauve; dorsal sepal erect, lateral sepals and petals deflexed.

Terrestrial in open forest and woodland and in open scrub in well-drained soil

Western Australia

Cyanicula gemmata (Lindley) Hopper & A. P. Brown

SYN. *Caladenia gemmata* Lindley

Leaf to 4 × 2 cm, ovate, glossy dark green above, purple below, hairy. Inflorescence 10–20 cm tall, usually 1-flowered, occasionally with 2 or 3 flowers. Flowers to 7 cm across, deep blue; lip with rows of beadlike calli. In some areas plants only flower after a fire.

Terrestrial in open forest and scrub

Western Australia

Cyclopogon C. Presl

TRIBE: Cranichideae

SUBTRIBE: Spiranthinae

ETYMOLOGY: From Greek *cyclo*, circle, and *pogon*, beard, possibly referring to the pubescent sepals

DISTRIBUTION: About 80 species from Florida to South America

Small to medium-sized terrestrials, occasionally lithophytes or epiphytes, with fleshy roots. Leaves petiolate, in a basal rosette, green or brownish, often with white or silver stripes. Inflorescences erect, unbranched, sometimes pubescent, sometimes secund, loosely or densely many-flowered. Flowers often drooping, scented, fleshy, not opening wide, usually greenish or green and white, the sepals pubescent on the outside; lip clawed at the base, oblong or fiddle-shaped. Pollinia 4, in 2 pairs.

Cyclopogon species have in the past been included in *Spiranthes*.

CULTIVATION: Some species are grown for their attractively variegated leaves. Most are easily cultivated in intermediate conditions in a standard, humus-rich but free-draining, terrestrial mix. They need moderate shade and although they need less water while resting, should not be allowed to dry out completely.

Cyclopogon lindleyanus (Link, Klotzsch & Otto) Schlechter

Leaves ovate, green with white longitudinal streaks. Inflorescence 25–30 cm long, densely many-flowered. Flowers 1–1.5 cm long, pinkish brown to greenish.

Terrestrial in forest, 450–1600 m (1500–5300 ft.)

Bolivia, Colombia, Ecuador, Peru, Venezuela

Cycnoches Lindley

SWAN ORCHIDS

TRIBE: Cymbidieae

SUBTRIBE: Catasetinae

ETYMOLOGY: From Greek *kyknos*, swan, and *auchen*, neck, referring to the slender, arching column of the male flowers

DISTRIBUTION: About 32 species in Central and South America

Large, epiphytic, rarely terrestrial plants; pseudobulbs long, conical or spindle-shaped, covered with fibrous sheaths when young. Leaves thin-textured, pleated, deciduous. Inflorescences arising from apical nodes of pseudobulbs, erect, arching or pendent, unbranched, few- to many-flowered. Flowers unisexual, nonresupinate, often large and showy, with the male and female flowers rather similar in some species, differing in appearance in others; sepals and petals subsimilar; lip sometimes clawed. Male flowers usually have reflexed sepals and petals and a long, arched column; female flowers are fleshy with a short, thick column.

In the wild, the flowers are pollinated by euglossine bees.

CULTIVATION: Plants can be potted, but they are more successful in baskets, which should be hung up in a well-ventilated, humid position, in bright but not full sun, in intermediate to warm conditions. Male flowers tend to be produced at lower light levels and so are commoner in cultivation. When the plants are resting, they should be kept dry and given as much light as possible.

Cycnoches aureum Lindley & Paxton

Inflorescence 8- to 9-flowered. Flowers to 8 cm across, yellow or yellow-green often spotted with red; lip small, white.

Epiphytic in humid lowland forest, 0–600 m (0–2000 ft.)

Panama

Cycnoches barthiorum G. F. Carr & Christenson

Pseudobulbs to 18 × 1.7 cm. Leaves to 21 × 5 cm. Inflorescence pendent, to 17 cm long, densely to about 15-flowered. Male flowers to ca. 6 cm across; sepals and petals pale olive green, flushed with red-brown on the outside, with large maroon spots inside; lip white with purple spots, the mesochile with four pairs of lateral appendages.

Epiphytic near sea level

Colombia

SIMILAR SPECIES: *Cycnoches herrenhusanum* Jenny & G. A. Romero has bright green-gold, unspotted flowers and lip appendages of a different shape.

Cycnoches egertonianum Bateman

Pseudobulbs to 30 × 3 cm. Leaves to 25 × 8 cm. Male inflorescences pendent, to 80 cm long, to 16-flowered; flowers purple or pale green, spotted purple, to 6.5 cm across, the lip with fingerlike projections round the margin. Female inflorescences erect, to 15 cm long, 1- or 2-flowered; flowers fleshy, yellow-green with darker

Cyanicula gemmata. H. Oakeley

Cycnoches barthiorum, male flowers. J. C. Uribes

Cyclopogon lindleyanus

Cycnoches barthiorum, female flowers. J. C. Uribes

veins, smaller than and different from male flowers.

Epiphytic in wet forest, 100–750 m (330–2460 ft.)

Belize, Guatemala, Honduras, Mexico

Cycnoches loddigesii Lindley

SYN. *Cycnoches cucullata* Lindley

Large plants with cylindrical pseudobulbs to 25 cm long. Leaves several, to 40 × 7 cm. Inflorescence arching or pendent, to 10-flowered. Flowers large and showy, to 12 cm across, male and female subsimilar; sepals and petals brownish green, veined and marked with maroon; lip white or pale pink with brown spots, veined with green-maroon towards apex.

Epiphytic in wet forest, 200–1000 m (660–3300 ft.)

Brazil, Colombia, Guianas, Venezuela

Cycnoches pentadactylon Lindley

Pseudobulbs to 15 × 2.5 cm, cylindrical or conical. Leaves to 30 × 5 cm. Male inflorescence arching or pendent, 18–25 cm long, densely many-flowered; flowers to 10 cm across, pendent, scented, sepals and petals white or yellow-green with red-brown blotches, lip fleshy, white with purple or brown spots, the basal claw with an erect, fingerlike projection, the blade 4-lobed. Female inflorescences erect, short, 1- to few-flowered; flowers fleshy, pendent, pale yellow spotted with maroon near the base, lip white with a yellow claw.

Epiphytic in wet forest, 750–1000 m (2460–3300 ft.)

Amazon basin of Brazil and Peru

Cycnoches pentadactylon, male flowers

Cycnoches peruvianum Rolfe

Pseudobulbs long, cylindrical or conical. Male inflorescence arching to pendent, 45–70 cm long, many-flowered. Flowers green, the lip white, clawed, with fingerlike processes round the margin of the blade.

Epiphytic in warm, wet forest, 450–900 m (1500–3000 ft.)

Ecuador, Peru

SIMILAR SPECIES: *Cycnoches densiflorum* Rolfe from Colombia has a dense inflorescence of brown-and-white flowers.

Cycnoches ventricosum Bateman

Pseudobulbs to 30 × 3 cm, cylindrical but slightly compressed, with several leaves. Leaves to 35 × 8 cm. Inflorescence 15–30 cm long, several-flowered. Male flowers 9–12 cm across, scented, green, the lip white with a long claw and a black callus. Female flowers rather similar but slightly larger.

Epiphytic in moist forest and woodland, 50–150 m (165–500 ft.)

Mexico to Panama

SIMILAR SPECIES: *Cycnoches chlorochilon* Klotzsch (syn. *C. ventricosum* var. *chlorochilon* (Klotzsch) Allen) from Colombia, Panama, and Venezuela has flowers 15 cm across and the lip lacks a claw.

Cycnoches warszewiczii Reichenbach f.

Pseudobulbs 15–70 × 2.5–4 cm. Leaves to 45 × 10 cm. Flowers apple-green, sepals and petals spreading; lip with a short claw.

Epiphytic in wet forest and woodland, 0–1050 m (0–3500 ft.)

Costa Rica, Panama

Cymbidiella Rolfe

TRIBE: Cymbidieae

SUBTRIBE: Cymbidiinae

ETYMOLOGY: Diminutive of *Cymbidium*

DISTRIBUTION: 3 species in Madagascar

Large epiphytes or terrestrials with long pseudobulbs with many distichous leaves. Leaves linear or narrowly strap-shaped, plicate, ± covering the pseudobulb. Inflorescences arising from axils of lower leaves, near base of pseudobulb, branched or unbranched, many-flowered. Flowers large and showy; sepals and petals free or joined to column-foot; lip 3- or 4-lobed, without a spur, with a basal callus.

CULTIVATION: Species of *Cymbidiella* are not easy to grow but are so striking they are worth an effort. In the wild, they have very specialized habitats. *Cymbidiella pardalina* grows on an epiphytic stag-horn fern, *Platycerium madagascariense*, while *C. falcigera* grows on the trunks of palm trees. In a greenhouse, they can be grown in a very coarse, free-draining bark mix in intermediate to warm conditions, in a bright, humid situation. They should be watered freely while growing but kept much drier after the pseudobulbs have finished growing as they rot easily. *Cymbidiella flabellata* is terrestrial, growing in peaty soil and should be grown in a humus-rich terrestrial compost.

Cymbidiella pardalina (Reichenbach f.) Garay

SYN. *Cymbidiella rhodocheila* (Rolfe) Rolfe

Pseudobulbs conical, to 12 cm long, 5- to 10-leaved. Leaves to 100 cm long, narrowly strap-shaped. Inflorescence to 100 cm tall, many-flowered. Flowers fleshy, 10 cm across; sepals and petals green with

Cycnoches densiflorum, male flowers. G. Carr

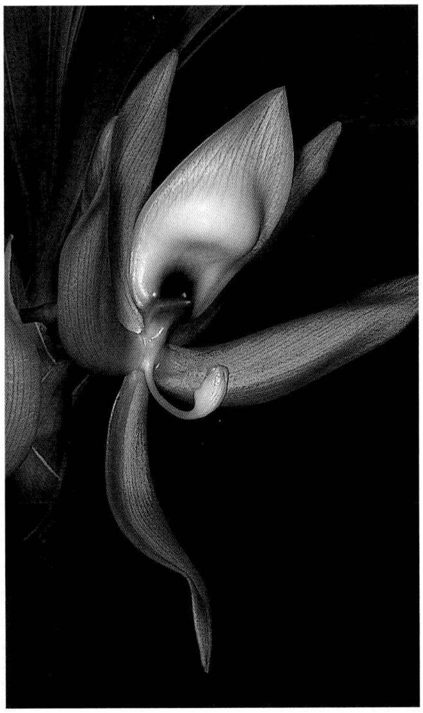

Cycnoches chlorochilon, male flower

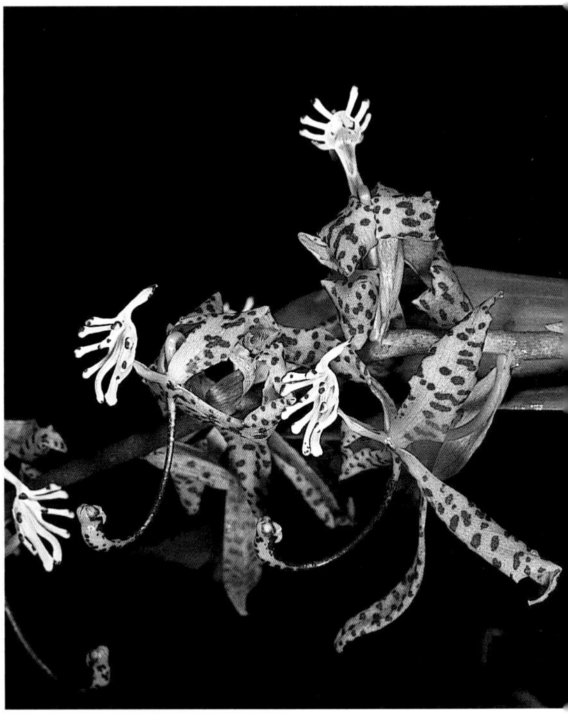

Cycnoches peruvianum, male flowers

Cycnoches warszewiczii, male flower. G. Carr

Cymbidiella pardalina

purplish blotches; lip red, yellow in the throat, recurved, 4-lobed.

Epiphytic on *Platycerium madagascariense*, 500–2000 m (1650–6600 ft.)

Madagascar

SIMILAR SPECIES: *Cymbidiella falcigera* (Reichenbach f.) Garay (syn. *C. humblotii* (Rolfe) Rolfe) has up to 40 leaves to 60 cm long and a branched inflorescence with many pale green flowers with purple-black markings on the lip. It grows at altitudes of 0–400 m (1320 ft.). *Cymbidiella flabellata* (Thouars) Rolfe has a long rhizome with pseudobulbs set well apart. The flowers are yellow-green, dotted with red. It grows in coastal forest and marshland and in sphagnum moss.

Cymbidium Swartz

TRIBE: Cymbidieae

SUBTRIBE: Cymbidiinae

ETYMOLOGY: From Greek *kymbes*, boat-shaped, referring to the shape of the lip

DISTRIBUTION: About 50 species in Asia and Australia

Epiphytes, lithophytes, or terrestrials with ovoid or elongate pseudobulbs. Leaves persistent, linear or strap-shaped. Inflorescences erect, arching or pendent, unbranched, basal, 1- to many-flowered; peduncle covered with sheaths. Flowers sometimes scented; sepals and petals free, usually subsimilar, spreading or pointing forwards; lip trilobed, side lobes erect, midlobe recurved, callus usually with parallel ridges.

Cymbidium hybrids are among the most widely grown orchids. In Australia, New Zealand, and parts of the United States, they are grown out of doors. The first hybrid, between *C. eburneum* and *C. lowianum*, flowered in 1889 and these species, with *C. insigne*, were for a long time the basis of most hybrids. In recent years, more species have been involved and miniature hybrids are available as well as ones with pendent inflorescences, these mainly derived from *C. devonianum*.

CULTIVATION: Most species of *Cymbidium* are easily grown, although it is not always so easy to get them to flower. They are usually grown in pots in a coarse, free-draining compost—clay pots are more stable for large plants; species with pendent inflorescences can be grown in suspended pots or baskets. Du Puy and Cribb (1988) divide cymbidiums into 3 groups as regards cultivation.

GROUP 1. *Large-flowered species* from the Himalayas, the mountains of China and Indo-China, and most hybrids require good light in summer and warm, humid conditions. The night temperature should not be over 12°C (54°F) and can fall as low as 5°C (41°F) without harm. The day temperature should not be more than 27°C (81°F) and ample water and fertilizer should be given then as this is when the flower buds are initiated. In winter, plants need cool, bright and dry conditions. Most of these flower in winter and early spring.

GROUP 2. *Small-flowered tropical and subtropical species* from India, southern China, Malaysia, and Australia grow and flower in summer and require temperatures of about 30°C (86°F) during the day and 18–20°C (65–68°F) at night, with ample water and fertilizer. In winter they need good light and less water.

GROUP 3. *Small-flowered temperate species* from Japan, China, and the Himalayas are mainly terrestrial and require cool, moist conditions. Some are hardy in sheltered, cool-temperate gardens, but they are better grown in a cool glasshouse or alpine house. They have fleshy roots and should be grown in a free-draining, epiphyte-type compost.

Cymbidium aloifolium

(Linnaeus) Swartz

Pseudobulbs ovoid, 4–6 cm long. Leaves to 80 × 4 cm, stiff, fleshy, strap-shaped. Inflorescence pendent, to 90 cm long, many-flowered. Flowers to 5.5 cm across, sepals and petals cream to pale yellow with a central maroon-brown stripe, lip cream or white with maroon veins and a yellow callus. Flowering spring–summer. (Group 2)

Epiphytic in forks of tree trunks and branches in open forest, 0–1500 m (5000 ft.)

India to southern China, Southeast Asia, Java

SIMILAR SPECIES: *Cymbidium bicolor* Lindley is a slightly smaller plant and the lip is mottled with brown rather than veined and streaked. It grows in similar habitats.

Cymbidium canaliculatum

R. Brown

Pseudobulbs to 10 × 4 cm. Leaves to 65 × 4 cm, rigid, gray-green, linear, grooved on the upper surface. Inflorescence 1–2 per pseudobulb, arching, several- to many-flowered. Flowers to 4 cm across; sepals and petals lanceolate, acute, greenish or brown on outside, green or yellow within; lip cream with purple or red spots, callus of 2 parallel ridges. Flowers autumn–winter. (Group 2)

Epiphytic in hollows formed by fallen branches, often in dry areas, 0–1000 m (3300 ft.)

Northern and northeastern Australia

SIMILAR SPECIES: *Cymbidium madidum* Lindley from northeastern Australia has less rigid leaves, broader and more rounded sepals, and the lip lacks callus ridges but has a tonguelike depression at the base. *Cymbidium suave* R. Brown from eastern Australia has a similar depression on the lip but is a smaller plant, lacking pseudobulbs.

Cymbidium aloifolium

Cymbidium devonianum

Cymbidium bicolor

Cymbidium devonianum Lindley & Paxton
Pseudobulbs small, hidden by sheaths. Leaves to 30 × 6 cm, oblong or elliptic, acute, dark green. Inflorescence pendent, to 50 cm long, densely many-flowered. Flowers to 3.5 cm across, bronze or green, marked with maroon; lip side lobes cream, midlobe maroon with 2 purple spots at the base. Flowering spring–early summer. (Group 3)

Lithophytic on mossy rocks or epiphytic on mossy trees, 1450–2200 m (4800–6600 ft.)

Eastern India to northern Thailand

Cymbidium eburneum Lindley
Pseudobulbs obscure. Leaves several, narrowly strap-shaped, to 60 × 2 cm, thin-textured. Inflorescence to 35 cm

Cymbidium eburneum

Cymbidium mastersii

Cymbidium parishii

long, 1- to 3-flowered. Flowers to 12 cm across, scented, waxy white, often pink-tinged, lip with a yellow, wedge-shaped ridge, midlobe sometimes purple-dotted, with a yellow blotch. Flowers winter–spring. (Group 1)

Epiphytic in shade in moist, warm forest, 300–1700 m (1000–5600 ft.)

Northern India, northern Myanmar, southern China

SIMILAR SPECIES: *Cymbidium mastersii* Griffith ex Lindley from northern India, Myanmar, and northern Thailand has an arching to pendent inflorescence and smaller flowers that do not open widely. *Cymbidium parishii* Reichenbach f. from Myanmar has flowers ca. 7 cm across with purple markings on the lip and a callus of 2 convergent ridges.

Cymbidium ensifolium

(Linnaeus) Swartz

Pseudobulbs small, often subterranean. Leaves to 95 cm long, arching, grasslike. Inflorescence to 70 cm long, several-flowered. Flowers 3–5 cm across, often scented; sepals and petals spreading, yellow or green with red or brown lines; lip green, pale yellow, or white, the midlobe marked with red, the side lobes with red streaks. This species has been cultivated in China and Japan for over 2000 years. Flowers winter–spring. (Group 3)

Terrestrial in broad-leaved forest

Sri Lanka and southern India to Philippines

SIMILAR SPECIES: *Cymbidium sinense* (Jackson) Willdenow (syn. *C. fragrans* Salisbury) has more flowers, strongly scented, with purple-brown sepals and petals, the petals pointing forwards close to the column. *Cymbidium faberi* Rolfe has more leaves and the lip midlobe is covered with papillae.

Cymbidium erythrostylum

Swartz

Pseudobulbs to 6 × 2 cm. Leaves linear, arching, to 50 cm long. Inflorescence erect or arching, to 60 cm long, 4- to 8-flowered. Flowers 6–11 cm across, sepals spreading, petals projecting; sepals white, petals white with pink marks near the base, lip yellow-white, midlobe yellow with red veins and blotches. Flowers autumn–winter. (Group 1).

Epiphytic, lithophytic, or terrestrial at ca. 1500 m (5000 ft.)

Vietnam

Cymbidium floribundum

Lindley

SYN. *Cymbidium pumilum* Rolfe

Pseudobulbs small. Leaves linear, leathery. Inflorescence erect, to 30 cm long, densely many-flowered. Flowers 3 cm across; sepals and petals purple or red-brown, lip white with red spots. This species has been used in hybridization to produce miniature cymbidiums. Flowering spring-summer. (Group 3)

Lithophytic on rocks in gorges or pine forest, in shade or full sun; occasionally epiphytic, 800–2800 m (2640–9250 ft.)

China

Cymbidium goeringii

(Reichenbach f.) Reichenbach f.

Dwarf plants with small pseudobulbs. Leaves grasslike, the margins usually serrated. Inflorescence 10–15 cm tall, 1-flowered. Flowers ca. 5 cm across, often scented; sepals and petals green, yellow-green, or brownish; lip white with purple marks. This species has been cultivated in China for more than 2500 years and in Japan for several hundred. It is a variable species and many selected forms are grown. Flowering spring. (Group 3).

Terrestrial in leaf litter in open forest, often on slopes, 500–3000 m (1650–9900 ft.)

China, Japan

Cymbidium kanran Makino

Pseudobulbs to 6 cm tall, narrowly ovoid. Leaves linear, arching, 30–90 cm long. Inflorescence to 60 cm tall, erect, 5- to 12-flowered. Flowers very fragrant, 5–7 cm across, rather spidery; sepals and petals linear, tapering, clear green or olive green; lip pale yellow or pale green, marked with red. This species has been cultivated for hundreds of years in Japan and China. (Group 3)

Terrestrial in shade in forest, 800–1800 m (2640–6000 ft.)

China, Japan, Korea

Cymbidium lowianum

(Reichenbach f.) Reichenbach f.

Pseudobulbs 10–15 cm long. Leaves

Cymbidium ensifolium

Cymbidium floribundum

Cymbidium erythrostylum

Cymbidium lowianum

linear, 50–90 cm long. Inflorescence to 150 cm tall, several- to many-flowered. Flowers 7.5–10 cm across, sepals and petals yellowish green veined with brown, lip yellow to white, the midlobe with a large V-shaped purple-red mark. Flowers late winter–early summer. (Group 1).

Epiphytic in shady forest

Myanmar, China, Thailand

Cymbidium tigrinum Parish ex Hooker

Pseudobulbs to 6 cm long, ovoid. Leaves arching, lanceolate, to 25 × 3.5 cm. Inflorescence usually longer than leaves, 3- to 6-flowered. Flowers 5–8.5 cm across, scented; sepals and petals yellowish green with faint purple lines and dots, lip white, lined and spotted with purple. Flowering spring–midsummer. (Group 1)

Lithophytic in open places, 1500–2700 m (5000–8900 ft.)

Myanmar, northeastern India

Cynorkis Thouars

TRIBE: Orchideae

SUBTRIBE: Orchidinae

ETYMOLOGY: From Greek *kyon*, dog, and *orchis*, testicle, referring to the shape of the tubers

DISTRIBUTION: About 125 species from Madagascar, Mascarene Islands, Comoro Islands, and mainland Africa

Small terrestrials or occasionally epiphytes with 1 or 2 globose tubers or clusters of fleshy roots. Leaves 1–several, mostly basal. Stem, ovary, and calyx often with glandular hairs. Inflorescences terminal, unbranched, 1- to many-flowered. Flowers pink, mauve, or purple, occasionally white, yellow, or orange; dorsal sepal forming hood with petals; lateral sepals spreading; lip entire or 3- or 5-lobed, spurred at the base, usually much larger than sepals and petals.

CULTIVATION: Species of *Cynorkis* should be grown in shallow pans in a humus-rich but free-draining terrestrial compost, in intermediate conditions with moderate shade. After flowering, plants die back and should be kept dry. There is a risk then of the tubers shriveling and one method of preventing that is to grow them in clay pots and plunge these in damp sand. Once new growth appears, careful watering can be resumed.

Cynorkis calanthoides Kraenzlin

SYN. *Cynorkis uncinata* H. Perrier

Leaf 1, 7–22 × 2.5–8 cm, ovate. Inflorescence subcapitate, densely many-flowered. Flowers 32 × 32 mm, lilac-purple, the lip 4-lobed, white in center; spur slender, to 25 mm long. In cultivation, the pot must be hung up or raised off the bench so that the large leaf does not touch the ground.

Epiphytic on *Pandanus* or terrestrial in rocky grassland

Madagascar

SIMILAR SPECIES: *Cynorkis guttata* Hermans & P. J. Cribb, also from Madagascar, was only described in 2007 but has been in cultivation for some time, usually under the name *C. uncinata*. It differs in the color of its flowers—creamy white strongly flushed with purple, with a carmine-purple blotch at the base of the lip—and in the proportions of the lip. It is one of the easier species to cultivate.

Cynorkis compacta (Reichenbach f.) Rolfe

Leaf 1, ovate, to 8 cm long. Inflorescence to 20 cm tall, glabrous, fairly densely to about 15-flowered. Flowers white, the lip with purple-red spots; lip ca. 9 mm long, 3- or 5-lobed, the lobes broader at the tips.

Terrestrial among rocks, ca. 700 m (2300 ft.)

South Africa (KwaZulu-Natal)

Cynorkis fastigiata Thouars

Leaves 1–2, narrowly lanceolate, to 20 × 4 cm. Inflorescence 10–30 cm tall, rachis short, densely few- to many-flowered. Flowers lilac-pink, the lip mostly creamy yellow; lip 10–15 mm long, 4-lobed, the lobes ± equal; spur slender, to 30 mm long. Several varieties of this species have been described. *Cynorkis fastigiata* usually sets seed in cultivation and seedlings often appear in pots of other orchids.

Terrestrial in woodland and at forest edge, 0–1400 m (4600 ft.)

Comoro Islands, Madagascar, Mascarene Islands, Seychelles

Cynorkis gibbosa Ridley

Roots elongate, tuberous, in a cluster. Leaf 1, rarely 2, to 20 × 5.5 cm, ovate, often purple-spotted. Inflorescence 25–50 cm tall, usually glandular hairy but sometimes glabrous, densely 10- to 40-flowered. Flowers large, ca. 35 mm long, salmon-pink or red; lip trilobed, the midlobe deeply emarginate; spur slender, slightly swollen at tip, 2–2.5 cm long.

Forest edge and on shaded, humid rocks, 600–1500 m (2000–5000 ft.)

Madagascar

Cynorkis lowiana Reichenbach f.

Leaf 1, linear-lanceolate, to 13 × 1.6 cm. Inflorescence 7–12 cm long, 1- or 2-flowered. Sepals and petals green tinged with pink. Lip trilobed, 22 × 27 mm, carmine-red with a darker spot in the center; side lobes oblong, midlobe bilobed; spur green, slender, 25–45 mm long.

Terrestrial in humid evergreen forest and on mossy rocks

Madagascar

RELATED PLANT: *Cynorkis* Kewensis is an old hybrid (1903) between *C. lowiana* and *C. calanthoides*.

Cypripedium Linnaeus

SUBFAMILY: Cypripedioideae

ETYMOLOGY: From Greek *cypros*, Cyprus, the island sacred to Venus, and *pedilon*, slipper

DISTRIBUTION: 45 species in northern temperate Asia, Europe, and America as far south as Guatemala.

Terrestrials with creeping rhizomes and erect stems. Leaves 2 to 4, basal or along the stem, paired or spirally arranged, glabrous or pubescent, plicate. Inflorescences usually 1-flowered, but sometimes several-flowered, unbranched. Dorsal sepal and petals free, lateral sepals almost always joined to form a synsepal. Lip inflated, pouchlike, the upper margin inrolled. Anthers 2, behind staminode.

CULTIVATION: Many species of *Cypripedium* are hardy in temperate gardens; others (for example, *C. formosanum* and *C. japonicum*) are better grown in pots in an alpine house for protection against severe frost or heavy winter rain. Most like shaded situations in humus-rich but well-drained soil, acid or calcareous depending on the natural habitat. In recent years, more species have become available to growers and many beautiful hybrids have been developed, particularly in Germany.

Cymbidium tigrinum

Cynorkis calanthoides. H. Oakeley

Cynorkis fastigiata. J. Hermans

Cynorkis gibbosa. J. Hermans

Cynorkis lowiana. J. Hermans

These tend to be more easily grown and are better garden plants. All plants should be left undisturbed for as long as possible.

Cypripedium acaule Aiton

MOCCASIN FLOWER

Leaves 2, 10–30 × 5–15 cm, elliptic, plicate. Inflorescence erect, to 40 cm tall, 1-flowered (rarely with 2). Flowers nodding, 6 cm across; sepals and petals yellow-green to maroon; lip pink, rarely white. Flowering spring–summer.

Cypripedium acaule needs very acidic conditions, with a pH of about 3.5. This may be achieved by watering plants with a dilute solution of vinegar.

Coniferous woodland and acid bogs

Canada, eastern United States

Cypripedium calceolus Linnaeus

LADY'S SLIPPER

Leaves 3–4, spread along stem, to 18 × 9 cm, pleated, broadly elliptic. Inflorescence usually 1-flowered, sometimes 2- or 3- flowered. Sepals and petals 4–6 cm long, maroon-brown, the petals twisted; lip bright yellow. Flowers late spring–midsummer.

Partial shade in open deciduous woodland on limestone, 0–2500 m (8250 ft.)

Northern and central Europe and Asia as far east as central China

SIMILAR SPECIES: *Cypripedium henryi* Rolfe from western China has a 2- or 3-flowered inflorescence and smaller flowers with untwisted petals.

Cypripedium californicum A. Gray

Clump-forming plants. Leaves 5–10, plicate, 5–15 × 2–6 cm. Raceme laxly 4- to 10-flowered, all flowers open together. Flowers scented, nodding, small, 3.5 cm across; sepals and petals pale yellow-green; lip globular, white, yellow at the base, with brownish marks inside. Flowers midspring–midsummer.

Coniferous woodland, often by rocky streams

Western United States (California, Oregon)

Cypripedium debile Reichenbach f.

Slender plants 10–30 cm tall. Leaves 2, opposite, at the top of the stem, to 7 × 7 cm, ovate or heart-shaped. Inflorescence 1-flowered. Flower nodding, 1–2 cm across, pale green or yellow-green

In leaf litter in forest, 2000–3000 m (6600–9900 ft.)

China, Japan

Cypripedium formosanum Hayata

SYN. *Cypripedium japonicum* Thunberg var. *formosanum* (Hayata) S. S. Ying

Plants 35–40 cm tall. Stem glabrous. Leaves 2, opposite, spreading, fan-shaped, plicate, to 13 × 11 cm. Inflorescence 1-flowered; peduncle glabrous or sparely hairy. Flowers nodding, 6–7 cm across, white to pink spotted with red. *Cypripedium formosanum* grows well in open sandy soil but is not frost hardy and needs to be kept in an alpine house or cool greenhouse in winter.

Open, damp places in forest, 2300–3000 m (7600–9900 ft.)

Taiwan

SIMILAR SPECIES: *Cypripedium japonicum* Thunberg from Japan differs in its densely woolly-hairy stem and peduncle and yellow or greenish-yellow sepals and petals.

Cypripedium macranthos Swartz

Plants 25–50 cm tall. Leaves 3–4, to 15 × 8 cm, elliptic. Inflorescence 1-flowered. Flowers red, purple, or pink, the sepals and petals with darker veins; dorsal sepal 4–5 cm long, petals to 6 cm long; lip to 5.5 cm long, subglobose or ellipsoid.

In rich, well-drained soil in forest or shady slopes, 500–2400 m (1650–7900 ft.)

China, Japan, Korea, Russia

SIMILAR SPECIES: *Cypripedium tibeticum* King ex Rolfe, from Sikkim, Bhutan, and China, has slightly larger, somewhat nodding, dark purple flowers, the lip with a white rim. Flowering summer.

Cypripedium margaritaceum Franchet

Small plants to 10 cm tall. Leaves 2, prostrate, to 15 × 13 cm, suborbicular or ovate, dark green spotted with maroon-black. Inflorescence 1-flowered. Flowers to 5 cm across, held just above leaves, yellow with maroon stripes on sepals and petals and maroon dots on lip; staminode maroon.

In leaf litter under coniferous woodland on limestone, 2500–3600 m (8250–12,000 ft.)

China

Cypripedium parviflorum Salisbury var. *parviflorum*

SYN. *Cypripedium calceolus* Linnaeus var. *parviflorum* (Salisbury) Fernald

Leaves 3–4, in 2 rows, pleated, 5–15 × 2–8 cm, blue-green. Inflorescence 1- or 2-flowered. Flowers scented, relatively small; sepals and petals to 5 cm long, glossy maroon-purple, the petals twisted; lip yellow. Flowering spring–summer.

Var. *pubescens* (Willdenow) O. W. Knight has flowers slightly larger than in var. *parviflorum*; sepals and petals yellow or greenish, sometimes flushed with brown; lip yellow.

Open areas in marshy areas, usually on calcareous soil. Var. *pubescens* grows in woodland, on rich but well-drained soils, usually in neutral or slightly acid areas but sometimes on limestone, 0–2000 m (6600 ft.)

Canada, United States (var. *pubescens* particularly in eastern areas)

Cypripedium acaule

Cypripedium formosanum

Cypripedium calceolus

Cypripedium tibeticum. E. la Croix

Cypripedium reginae Walter

Robust plants to 90 cm tall. Leaves 3–7, ovate or lanceolate, the edges undulate, to 25 cm long. Flowers to 9 cm across, white, the lip pink, rarely white. Flowering spring–summer.

Forms colonies in bogs or wet meadows, on neutral or calcareous soil, 0–500 m (1650 ft.)

Eastern Canada, eastern and central United States

Cyrtochilum Kunth

TRIBE: Maxillarieae

SUBTRIBE: Oncidiinae

ETYMOLOGY: From Greek, *kyrtos*, curved, and *chilus*, lip

DISTRIBUTION: More than 120 species in Central and South America

Large epiphytic or lithophytic sympodial orchids with large pseudobulbs, leafy at apex. Inflorescences long, erect or arching, sometimes scrambling, arising from base of pseudobulb, simple or branched, rather loosely many-flowered. Flowers large or small, often showy; sepals and petals often clawed, spreading, the petals usually slightly smaller; lip fleshy, smaller than the sepals and petals, entire or trilobed, with a basal, ridged callus.

CULTIVATION: Because of their size, plants are not widely grown in glasshouses but do well in clay pots in a standard epiphyte compost; water throughout the year, though less after growth is complete. Most require cool conditions and moderate shade and humidity. The long inflorescences need to be staked or trained.

Cyrtochilum falcipetalum (Lindley) Kraenzlin

SYN. *Oncidium falcipetalum* Lindley

Large plants with a scrambling habit. Pseudobulbs set 20–25 cm apart on an ascending rhizome, to 15 cm long, 1- or 2-leaved. Leaves to 60 × 5–6 cm. Inflorescence branched, to 6 m long. Flowers to 7.5 cm across, sepals dark brown with yellow apex, petals yellow and brown, lip greenish brown with a bright yellow callus.

Epiphytic, lithophytic, or occasionally terrestrial in montane forest, to 2700 m (8900 ft.)

Colombia, Ecuador, Peru, Venezuela

Cyrtochilum macranthum (Lindley) Kraenzlin

SYN. *Oncidium macranthum* Lindley

Pseudobulbs 7–15 cm long, ovoid, 2-leaved. Leaves to 55 × 5 cm, narrowly oblong to oblanceolate. Inflorescence branched, 60–300 cm long, each branch to 5-flowered. Flowers large and showy, to 10 cm across, yellowish, lip with purple side lobes.

Epiphytic in montane forest, to 3000 m (9900 ft.)

Colombia, Ecuador, Peru

Cyrtopodium R. Brown

TRIBE: Cymbidieae

SUBTRIBE: Cyrtopodiinae

ETYMOLOGY: From Greek *kyrtos*, curved, and *podion*, foot, referring to the shape of the lip

DISTRIBUTION: More than 40 species from Florida to tropical South America

Large terrestrials or epiphytes with canelike to long-ovoid pseudobulbs usually covered in sheaths and old leaf bases. Leaves several, distichous, linear-lanceolate, ribbed or plicate, deciduous. Inflorescences basal, long, branched or unbranched, many-flowered. Flowers large, mostly yellow, fleshy; sepals and petals free, spreading; lip trilobed.

CULTIVATION: Terrestrial species require large pots and a rich but free-draining terrestrial compost; epiphytes need large pots or baskets and a coarse, free-draining epiphyte mix. All need intermediate to warm conditions, good light, and plenty of water and fertilizer while actively growing. After the leaves have fallen, keep plants cooler and drier.

Cyrtopodium andersonii (Lambert ex Andrews) R. Brown

Pseudobulbs spindle-shaped, 60–100 cm long, 3–6 cm wide. Leaves 30–60 × 2–5 cm. Inflorescence branched, to 2 m tall, many-flowered. Flowers showy, to 5 cm across, sepals and petals yellow, tinged green, the edges undulate; lip bright yellow.

Terrestrial in sandy, rocky savanna, 300–1500 m (1000–5000 ft.)

Florida, West Indies, Central and South America

Cyrtopodium punctatum (Linnaeus) Lindley

Pseudobulbs canelike, to 40 cm tall. Leaves linear-lanceolate, to 65 × 5 cm. Inflorescence branched, many-flowered, to 1 m long. Flowers to 4 cm across, yellow, sepals heavily blotched with maroon, lip with a maroon margin.

Epiphytic, usually in forks of trees, or lithophytic, 0–300 m (1000 ft.)

Florida, West Indies, Central and South America

SIMILAR SPECIES: *Cyrtopodium aliciae* Linden & Rolfe from Brazil has smaller flowers with clawed petals

Cyrtorchis Schlechter

TRIBE: Vandeae

SUBTRIBE: Aerangidinae

ETYMOLOGY: From Greek *kyrtos*, curved, and *orchis*, orchid, probably referring to the curved petals or the spur

DISTRIBUTION: About 16 species in Africa and the Gulf of Guinea islands

Small to medium-sized monopodial epiphytes with long or short stems and usually thick roots. Leaves fleshy or leathery, usually strap-shaped, unequally bilobed at apex. Inflorescences unbranched, axillary, several- to many-flowered, with large, rather loose bracts. Flowers in 2 rows, waxy white or cream, turning apricot as they age, scented; sepals and petals free, subsimilar, curling back; lip spurred, the spur tapering from a wide mouth. Column short and stout; pollinia and stipites 2, viscidium 1.

CULTIVATION: Most species like intermediate to warm conditions. They

Cyrtochilum falcipetalum

Cyrtochilum macranthum

Cyrtopodium punctatum

Cyrtopodium aliciae

need a coarse bark-based compost and do better in baskets than pots, or can be mounted. Good air movement is essential as all species tend to rot easily in stagnant air. Plenty of water should be given in the growing season, but the leaves must be allowed to dry before night; less water should be given in winter but plants should not be kept dry for a long period.

Cyrtorchis arcuata (Lindley) Schlechter

SYN. *Cyrtorchis sedenii* (Reichenbach f.) Schlechter

Robust plants often forming large clumps. Stems woody, to ca. 30 cm long. Leaves several, 20–25 × 2–5 cm, oblong or strap-shaped. Inflorescence to 20 cm long, 5- to 15-flowered. Flowers white or cream; sepals and petals lanceolate, acute, spreading then recurved; sepals 20–50 × 6–8 mm, petals and lip similar but slightly smaller; spur 5–10 cm long, usually S-shaped.

Two subspecies are recognized. Subsp. *arcuata* is more widespread and usually grows at lower altitudes, although there is some overlap. Subsp. *whytei* (Rolfe) Summerhayes is larger, with leaves and flowers at the upper end of the size range.

Epiphytic in woodland and riverine forest, occasionally lithophytic, 600–2000 m (2000–6600 ft.)

Widespread in tropical and South Africa

SIMILAR SPECIES: *Cyrtorchis acuminata* Summerhayes, from São Tomé and Principé, has broader leaves and may just be a form of *C. arcuata*. *Cyrtorchis chailluana* (Hooker f.) Schlechter from West Africa has longer stems and larger but more spidery flowers with a spur to 16 cm long. *Cyrtorchis neglecta* Summerhayes may be synonymous with *C. arcuata*, but is smaller in all its parts.

Cyrtorchis crassifolia Schlechter

Stem very short; roots stout. Leaves several, distichous, succulent, gray-green, 3–6 × 1 cm, V-shaped in cross-section, recurved. Inflorescence ca. 4 cm long, densely 3- to 8-flowered. Flowers creamy white, sweetly scented in evening, rather bell-shaped; sepals and petals lanceolate, acute, recurved; sepals 7–14 mm long, petals and lip shorter; spur 2–3 cm long.

This attractive little species must be mounted, as when grown in a pot it rots very readily.

Epiphytic in high-rainfall woodland, usually in moss and lichen, 1200–2000 m (4000–6600 ft.)

East and Central Africa

Cyrtorchis praetermissa Summerhayes

Stem usually short but to 25 cm in old plants. Leaves distichous in 4–6 pairs, 6–9 × 1 cm, linear, recurved, thick-textured, V-shaped in cross-section. Inflorescences 2–4, arising below leaves, arching, to 10 cm long, densely 8- to 12-flowered. Flowers ca. 2 cm diameter, scented; sepals 8–12 mm long, petals and lip shorter; spur 3–4 cm long, slightly incurved.

Epiphytic in woodland, occasionally riverine forest, 450–1850 m (1500–6100 ft.)

East and Central Africa, South Africa

Cyrtostylis R. Brown

TRIBE: Diurideae

SUBTRIBE: Acianthinae

ETYMOLOGY: From Greek *kyrtos*, curved, and *stylos*, column

DISTRIBUTION: 3–6 species in Australia and New Zealand

Terrestrials with paired, globose tubers. Leaf single, basal. Inflorescences unbranched, erect, terminal, 1- to several-flowered. Flowers small, resupinate; sepals free, the dorsal sepal broader than the laterals; petals free, similar to lateral sepals; lip relatively large, entire, the margins sometimes toothed, with a raised central callus running down most of is length and 2 erect basal glands.

Flowers are pollinated by gnats.

CULTIVATION: *Cyrtostylis* species form colonies and grow well in cultivation. Grow in a terrestrial compost containing leaf mold, in a cool greenhouse or alpine house. Plants need ample water while in growth and should be kept dry while dormant in summer. As they multiply vegetatively, plants should be repotted when the pot becomes overcrowded.

Cyrtostylis reniformis R. Brown

GNAT ORCHID

Leaf kidney-shaped, to 4 × 3 cm, gray-green with lighter veins. Flowering stem to 8 cm tall, 1- to 4-flowered. Flowers small, greenish brown, reddish brown, or yellowish; sepals and petals ca. 8 mm long; lip to 10 × 4 mm, oblong, projecting forwards.

Forms colonies in open woodland and heath, often near the coast

Southern and eastern Australia, New Zealand

SIMILAR SPECIES: *Cyrtostylis robusta* D. Jones & M. Clements, from South Australia, is a more robust plant with larger flowers and a bright green leaf.

Dactylorhiza Necker ex Nevski

TRIBE: Orchideae

SUBTRIBE: Orchidinae

ETYMOLOGY: From Greek *dactylos*, finger, and *rhiza*, root, referring to the deeply lobed tubers

DISTRIBUTION: About 50 species (and many subspecies and natural hybrids) in Europe, North Africa, Himalayas, Japan, and Aleutian Islands

Terrestrial herbs with tubers deeply 2- to 5-lobed. Leaves deciduous, basal and/or along the stem, linear to lanceolate, sometimes spotted purple. Inflorescences usually cylindrical, densely several- to many-flowered; bracts leafy. Flowers small but showy,

Cyrtorchis arcuata. E. la Croix

Cyrtorchis chailluana. E. la Croix

Cyrtorchis crassifolia. E. la Croix

Cyrtorchis praetermissa. E. la Croix

Cyrtostylis reniformis R. Parsons

mauve-pink, purple, yellow, or white, often spotted; dorsal sepal forming hood with petals, lateral sepals spreading; lip entire or trilobed, spurred, marked with lines, whorls, and dots.

Many species are very similar and interbreed freely.

CULTIVATION: These species are among the easiest terrestrial orchids to grow. Many become naturalized in temperate gardens and increase by seed. The conditions preferred can be inferred from their natural habitats; those known as marsh orchids prefer damp, often acid, soil. Species with a more southern distribution can be grown in an alpine house or cold frame in a standard terrestrial compost.

Dactylorhiza elata (Poiret) Soó

Leaves 5–10, to 25 × 4.5 cm or more, usually unspotted. Inflorescence 30–120 cm tall, densely many-flowered, the bracts longer than the flowers. Flowers rich magenta-purple, in a cylindrical head; lip with dark purple streaks, side lobes reflexed.

Marshes and wet meadows, usually in full sun, to 2200 m (7260 ft.)

Atlas Mountains, southwestern Europe, North Africa

SIMILAR SPECIES: *Dactylorhiza foliosa* (Reichenbach f.) Soó, MADEIRA ORCHID, has larger and broader, unspotted, glossy green leaves and a broader lip with only faint markings. Although endemic to Madeira, it is hardy in Britain as is *Dactylorhiza elata*.

Dactylorhiza fuchsii (Druce) Soó

COMMON SPOTTED ORCHID

Leaves several, narrowly lanceolate, heavily blotched and spotted. Inflorescence 15–50 cm tall, flowering head pyramidal at first then becoming cylindrical, densely many-flowered. Flowers pink to mauve, occasionally white, with purple dots and lines on the lip; lip trilobed, the midlobe pointed and longer than the side lobes. Flowering summer.

Grassland and scrub, usually on calcareous or neutral soil

West and central Europe

SIMILAR SPECIES: *Dactylorhiza maculata* (Linnaeus) Soó is a smaller plant with narrower leaves, a shorter inflorescence, and a broader lip with the midlobe shorter and much narrower than the side lobes. It grows in grassland and moorland on acid soil.

Dactylorhiza majalis (Reichenbach f.) P. F. Hunt & Summerhayes

BROAD-LEAVED MARSH ORCHID

Leaves 4–8, to 15 × 5 cm, usually with maroon spots on the upper surface. Inflorescence 20–75 cm tall, densely many-flowered, the bracts sometimes longer than the flowers, flowering head ovoid to cylindrical. Flowers lilac to magenta-purple; lip paler in the throat with darker streaks and whorls, trilobed, the side lobes broader than the midlobe; spur curving downwards. Flowers late spring–midsummer.

Swamps and marshes, to 2000 m (6600 ft.)

Continental Europe, western Russia

Dactylorhiza praetermissa (Druce) Soó

SYN. *Dactylorhiza majalis* subsp. *praetermissa* (Druce) D. M. Moore & Soó

SOUTHERN MARSH ORCHID

Leaves 4–9, suberect, to 25 × 4.5 cm, spotted or unspotted. Inflorescence 20–70 cm tall, densely many-flowered, flowering head cylindrical. Flowers pinkish purple to red-purple; lip spotted, with 3 shallow, equal lobes; spur conical, curving down. Flowering summer.

Marshes and water meadows, usually on calcareous soil

Western Europe

Dactylorhiza sambucina (Linnaeus) Soó

ELDERFLOWER ORCHID

Leaves 3–7, sometimes in a basal rosette, unspotted, to 25 × 3 cm. Inflorescence 10–30 cm tall, the spike cylindrical, densely many-flowered. Flowers scented like elder flowers, yellow or magenta, rarely bicolored; lip with 3 shallow lobes of equal length, marked with brownish dots in a horseshoe pattern; spur to 15 mm long, downcurved. Flowering spring–midsummer.

Meadows and open woodland, to 2000 m (6600 ft.)

Widespread in Europe

SIMILAR SPECIES: *Dactylorhiza romana* (Sebastiani) Soó, from southern Europe, also has 2 color forms; it has a laxer inflorescence and the midlobe of the lip is shorter than the side lobes.

Dendrobium Swartz

TRIBE: Dendrobieae

SUBTRIBE: Dendrobiinae

ETYMOLOGY: From Greek *dendron*, tree, and *bios*, life, referring to the epiphytic habit of many of the species

DISTRIBUTION: 1000 to 1400 species, widespread from the Himalayan region to Japan and southwards to Fiji but many have a rather restricted distribution within this wide range

Epiphytic, lithophytic, or (rarely) terrestrial plants with sympodial habit of growth; stems long or short, swollen to form pseudobulbs that are variously elongated, often canelike, each 1 arising from near the base of the preceding so that the plant has a tufted habit, rooting from the base. Leaves few to many, alternate along the stem, thin, and referred to as deciduous though often shed after a few months, or thick and leathery and lasting for several seasons or throughout the life of the plant, usually strap-shaped or lanceolate, always longer than wide, or very narrow, bright or dark green. Flowers large or small, borne singly or on short or long inflorescences near the apex of the stem or at some or all of the nodes; dorsal sepal free, held on the upper side of the flower, lateral sepals adnate to the foot of the column forming a mentum or spur between the column and base of the lip; petals free, spreading; lip larger than sepals and petals, variously marked. Column short and stout with 1 apical stamen; pollinia 4, waxy.

CULTIVATION: Dendrobiums grow in a wide range of habitats, and the various species tolerate different growing conditions. All require frost-free conditions and some need warm and humid, tropical conditions. Many need a dry rest in somewhat cooler temperatures, sometimes of several months duration, once the new growth is complete and before flowering. Most species are potted in bark or a bark mix in plastic pots or slatted baskets, but some species do better mounted on a piece of wood or bark and suspended in a well-lit part of the glasshouse. Knowledge of the habitat and altitudinal range of each species is the best guide to choosing the right growing conditions to achieve success in cultivation.

Dendrobium aberrans Schlechter

Pseudobulbs very narrow at the base, club-shaped above, to 20 × 1 cm with 2 or 3 leaves at the apex. Leaves dark green, oval, long-lasting, 4–10 cm long, 1.5–3 cm wide. Inflorescence upright or pendulous, from the apical nodes, each 2- to 6-flowered. Flowers lasting 3–4 weeks, white, flushed pink around the column; lip trilobed, the central lobe narrower and with 2 apical lobes and a prominent crest on the surface near the base.

Epiphytic in shade in mossy forests in areas with high rainfall and high humidity all year, 300–1900 m (1000–6300 ft.)

Eastern Papua New Guinea

Dendrobium aduncum Wallich ex Lindley

Pseudobulbs slender, cylindrical and pendulous, 40–60 cm long with 4–6 leaves toward the apex. Leaves deciduous, elliptic-lanceolate, 5–9 cm long, thin. Inflorescence short, borne

Dactylorhiza foliosa. E. la Croix

Dactylorhiza maculata subsp. *ericetorum*. E. la Croix

Dactylorhiza fuchsii. E. la Croix

Dendrobium aberrans

Dendrobium aduncum

from the apical third of the leafless stems, each 3- to 5-flowered. Flowers fragrant, 1–2.5 cm across, lasting 3–4 weeks, white flushed pink with a bright purple anther-cap; lip small, bulbous, hairy within, apex with a short hook.

Epiphytic in open montane forests in areas with a seasonal climate, dry in winter, 300–1300 m (1000–4300 ft.)

Widespread in Southeast Asia, India, Myanmar, Thailand, Vietnam, southwestern China

Dendrobium alexandrae Schlechter

Pseudobulbs narrow below, widened above, 50–70 × 1 cm, with 3 or 4 leaves near the apex. Leaves dark green, glaucous below, elliptic, 11–16 × 3–5 cm. Inflorescence erect, arising above the leaves from the apical nodes, to 25 cm long, 3- to 7-flowered. Flowers long-lasting, 5–8 cm in diameter; sepals and petals narrow, cream, dotted with dull red on the outside; lip trilobed, striped red on the inner surface.

Epiphytic in cool, shady conditions on moss-covered branches in rain forest, 900–1100 m (3000–3600 ft.)

Papua New Guinea, restricted to a few areas

Dendrobium amabile (Loureiro) O'Brien

Pseudobulbs widening towards the apex, somewhat ribbed longitudinally, to 70 × 1.5 cm, with 4–6 leaves toward the apex. Leaves ovate, acute, 12 × 5 cm, shiny, green. Inflorescence 1 or 2, pendulous, from near the apex of older pseudobulbs, many-flowered. Flowers ca. 30, up to 4.5 cm in diameter, lasting up to 10 days; sepals and petals pale pink or white; lip white with a bright orange patch towards the base, the margin minutely fringed.

Epiphytic in lowland and submontane evergreen forest, up to 2500 m (8250 ft.)

Vietnam

SIMILAR SPECIES: *Dendrobium farmeri* Paxton from the Himalayas also has pink or white flowers and is warmer-growing. *Dendrobium furcatum* Reinwardt (syn. *D. amabile* Schlechter) from Sulawesi has white flowers with a long spur.

Dendrobium amethystoglossum Reichenbach f.

Pseudobulbs usually upright, slender, 50–100 cm long, few-leaved near the apex. Leaves deciduous, light green, elliptic, acute, 12 × 1.2 cm, thin. Inflorescence pendent, usually arising on leafless canes, with up to 20 flowers in a dense cluster. Flowers 3–4 cm in diameter, white, the apical half of the pointed lip amethyst purple, long-lasting.

Epiphytic on trees growing on limestone cliffs, in moist, montane forests with a dry winter, 1400 m (4600 ft.)

Philippines (northern Luzon Island, Mindoro Island)

Dendrobium antennatum Lindley

Pseudobulbs yellow, 4-angled, becoming narrow and cylindrical above, 15–80 cm tall, many-leaved. Leaves in 2 rows, long-lasting, becoming leathery, variable in size. Inflorescence erect, often several from the upper nodes, to 50 cm long, 3- to 15-flowered. Flowers white with twisted green, upright petals; lip strongly veined in red or purple.

Epiphytic on trees in coastal areas including swamps and mangroves, 0–1200 m (4000 ft.)

New Guinea, Solomon Islands, Australia (Cape York Peninsula)

SIMILAR SPECIES: *Dendrobium stratiotes* Reichenbach f. from the Moluccas resembles *D. antennatum* but is larger and finer in all respects.

Dendrobium aphyllum (Roxburgh) Fischer

Pseudobulbs long and slender, pendulous, 30–90 cm long, 8 mm in diameter, bearing short-lived, thin leaves in 2 rows along the whole stem. Leaves linear to ovate, 10–13 cm long. Flowers borne singly or in pairs throughout the leafless stem, 3–5 cm in diameter, thin, lasting 10–20 days; sepals and petals pale pink; lip broad, tubular at the base, pale yellow or greenish white.

Epiphytic or lithophytic in warm forests with a seasonal climate, 200–1800 m (660–6000 ft.)

India, Myanmar, Thailand, Indochina, southwestern China

SIMILAR SPECIES: The larger-flowered *Dendrobium anosmum* Lindley is more widespread, from India to the Philippines and New Guinea, and similar in habit but with even longer pendulous pseudobulbs and rose-pink or white flowers.

Dendrobium bellatulum Rolfe

Pseudobulbs clustered, usually erect, widest at the middle, tapering above and below, 5–8 × 1.5 cm, covered with black hairs and bearing few grayish-

Dendrobium alexandrae

Dendrobium amabile

Dendrobium aphyllum

Dendrobium antennatum

Dendrobium amethystoglossum

Dendrobium bellatulum

Dendrobium scabrilingue

green leaves near the apex. Leaves 2–4, ovate, 3–6 × 1.5 cm. Inflorescence short, single, on mature growths, 1- to 3-flowered. Flowers 4–4.5 cm in diameter, long-lasting; sepals and petals creamy white; lip broad, bright orange, becoming red in throat.

Epiphytic in montane forest, often growing on bare bark, 1000–2100 m (3300–6900 ft.)

Widespread from India, Myanmar, Thailand, Vietnam, Laos, China (Yunnan)

SIMILAR SPECIES: *Dendrobium scabrilingue* Lindley is a taller plant with pure white sepals and petals and an orange, narrower lip. *Dendrobium christyanum* Reichenbach f. is also taller and the flower has a narrower lip with a splash of red in the center.

Dendrobium bracteosum Reichenbach f.

Pseudobulbs slender, clustered, leafy, up to 40 × 0.5–1 cm. Leaves narrow, 5–8 cm long, deciduous after 2 years. Inflorescence borne at the nodes, with 5–15 densely spaced flowers. Flowers white to deep pink, usually with yellow-orange lip, lasting up to 6 months.

Epiphytic in hot humid forests and mangroves, 0–600 m (2000 ft.)

Papua New Guinea

Dendrobium brymerianum Reichenbach f.

Pseudobulbs narrow at base and above, thickened in the middle, 30–50 × 1–1.5 cm, leafy near the apex. Leaves 3–6, lanceolate, acuminate, 10–15 × 1.2–2.6 cm. Inflorescence arising near the apex, to 11 cm long, 1- to 7-flowered. Flowers bright yellow, 5–6 cm across; sepals and petals similar; lip cordate, strongly fringed.

Var. *histrionicum* Reichenbach f. has a similar flower but with a smaller fringe on the lip, only at the apex, and is often self-pollinating

Epiphytic in montane forest, up to 1700 m (5600 ft.)

Myanmar, Laos, Thailand

SIMILAR SPECIES: *Dendrobium harveyanum* Reichenbach f. has petals wider than sepals and deeply fringed; the fringe on the lip is very short.

Dendrobium bullenianum Reichenbach f.

Pseudobulbs erect at first, then pendulous, 60 × 0.5–0.8 cm, longitudinally grooved with leaves in 2 rows on the apical half. Leaves 7–14 × 2 cm, deciduous after 2 years. Inflorescence short, densely flowered, on the apical half of the stems. Flowers narrow, yellow or orange with red or purple stripes on the inner surface.

Epiphytic in mangroves and coastal forests with year-round rainfall, below 100 m (330 ft.)

Philippines

Dendrobium cariniferum Reichenbach f.

Pseudobulbs clustered together, covered with soft black hairs, bearing leaves near the stem apex, 15–25 cm long. Leaves 5–8 × 2 cm. Inflorescence near the stem apex bearing 1–3 flowers, each 2–3 cm across. Flowers fleshy, white with orange on the lip; sepals strongly keeled on the back.

Epiphytic in montane forests in light shade, 700–1000 m (2300–3300 ft.)

India, Myanmar, Thailand, Laos, Cambodia, Vietnam, southern China

SIMILAR SPECIES: *Dendrobium williamsonii* Day & Reichenbach f. has thinner flowers and lacks the keel on the ovary and back of the sepals.

Dendrobium chrysotoxum Lindley

Pseudobulbs upright, variable in size and shape, usually narrower towards the base and distinctly grooved, 10–30 × 2–3 cm, with 2–8 leathery, persistent leaves near the apex. Leaves 12–20 × 3–4 cm. Inflorescence arching, from the upper nodes with 10–25 well-spaced flowers. Flowers bright yellow, shiny, to 5 cm in diameter, sepals and petals waxy; lip softly hairy and shortly fringed.

Epiphytic in deciduous forests, 400–1600 m (1320–5300 ft.)

India, Myanmar, Thailand, Laos, China (Yunnan)

Dendrobium compactum Rolfe ex W. Hackett

Pseudobulbs very small, 4 × 0.6 cm. Leaves 3–5, thin, 4 × 0.6 cm. Inflorescences 1–3 from terminal nodes after leaves have fallen. Flowers cream or pale green, 1 cm in diameter, lasting 2 weeks.

Epiphytic in montane forests, 1000–1800 m (3300–6000 ft.)

Myanmar, Thailand, China

Dendrobium bracteosum

Dendrobium brymerianum

Dendrobium bullenianum

Dendrobium cariniferum

Dendrobium harveyanum

Dendrobium chrysotoxum

Dendrobium crepidatum Lindley & Paxton

Pseudobulbs pendulous, to 45 cm long, often shorter, 1–1.5 cm wide. Leaves few, thin, deciduous, linear-lanceolate, 5–13 cm long, on the apical half of the stem. Inflorescences along the stem in groups of 2–3 flowers at the nodes. Flowers 3–4 cm in diameter, lasting 1–3 weeks; sepals and petals pale to deep pink;

Dendrobium crepidatum

lip round, margined pink, yellowish green in the basal half; some forms not opening fully.

Epiphytic in deciduous montane forests with a seasonal climate, 600–2100 m (2000–6930 ft.)

Widespread from India, Nepal, Bhutan, Myanmar, Thailand, Laos, Vietnam, China (Yunnan)

Dendrobium cruentum

Reichenbach f.

Pseudobulbs upright, swollen at the base, narrowing above, to 50 cm, with soft black hairs on the leaf sheaths. Leaves on the upper part of the stem, elliptic-oblong, 5–13 cm long. Inflorescence short, borne among or after the leaves, bearing 1–3 flowers. Flowers lasting 1 month or more; sepals and petals cream or pale green; lip with bright red crest and margin.

Epiphytic in warm, rather open forests, below 1000 m (3300 ft.)

Thailand

Dendrobium crystallinum

Reichenbach f.

Pseudobulbs pendulous, slender, to 60 × 0.8 cm with leaves on the apical third. Leaves linear-lanceolate, 10 cm long, thin and soon deciduous. Inflorescence lateral at the nodes, short, bearing 1–3 flowers. Flowers creamy white; petals with deep pink tip; lip with basal part greenish orange, then a white ring before bright pink tip.

Epiphytic in montane forests with a seasonal climate, 900–1500 m (3000–5000 ft.)

Myanmar, Thailand, Laos, Cambodia, Vietnam, China

Dendrobium cuthbertsonii

F. von Mueller

Pseudobulbs small, cylindrical or round, 1.8 × 1 cm, usually in clusters. Leaves 1–5, borne near the apex of the stems, dark green

Dendrobium cruentum

Dendrobium crystallinum

with black or silvery warts, to 4 × 1 cm. Inflorescence single-flowered. Flowers very long lasting (to 10 months), 3 × 5 cm, variable in color, pink, white, yellow, or orange combinations, commonly red.

Epiphytic, lithophytic, or terrestrial in cool areas with high humidity and rainfall, 750–3400 m (2,460–11,200 ft.)

New Guinea

Dendrobium cyanocentrum

Schlechter

Plants tufted, erect, to 3 cm high. Pseudobulbs 0.4–1.6 cm high, bearing 2–3 linear leaves to 3 cm long. Inflorescence from the apex of the stems with 2 flowers. Flowers 1 × 3 cm across, white or pale blue, darker in the center, often striped with dark pink; sepals and petals reflexed.

Dendrobium cuthbertsonii

Dendrobium cyanocentrum

Epiphytic, sometimes on twigs, in primary and secondary forests, 0–1600 m (5300 ft.), mostly at the higher elevations.

New Guinea

Dendrobium densiflorum

Lindley

Pseudobulbs narrow at the base, widening above, 4- or 5-angled, 30–45 × 2 cm. Leaves at the apex of the stems, 3–5, persistent for several years, ovate, 15 × 5 cm. Inflorescence arising below or among the leaves, pendent, with many golden flowers arranged like a bunch of grapes. Flowers numerous, 3–5 cm across, fragrant, lasting 1–2 weeks.

Epiphytic or lithophytic in montane forests with a seasonal climate, 1000–1900 m (3300–6300 ft.)

Widespread from Nepal, Bhutan, northeastern India, Myanmar, Thailand, southwestern China

SIMILAR SPECIES: *Dendrobium griffithianum* Lindley is more slender and the flowers more widely spaced. *Dendrobium thyrsiflorum* Reichenbach f. has flowers with white sepals and petals.

Dendrobium devonianum

Paxton

Pseudobulbs long and very slender, 150 × 0.3 cm, leafy throughout. Leaves thin, soon deciduous, 10 × 0.8 cm. Flowers borne singly or in pairs along upper part of stem, 5–6 cm across; petals wider than sepals and both white tipped with purple; lip fringed at the margin, segments of fringe branched, with 2 orange blotches in the throat.

Epiphytic in deciduous forests with a seasonal climate, dry in winter, 550–2000 m (1800–6600 ft.), mostly above 1000 m (3300 ft.)

Widespread from northeastern India, Myanmar, Thailand Laos, Vietnam, China (Yunnan), Taiwan

Dendrobium discolor Lindley

Plants large with canelike pseudobulbs, to 5 m × 8 cm. Leaves leathery, ovate, 5–20 cm long, persistent. Inflorescence erect from near the apex of the stems, many-flowered. Flowers yellowish brown or golden yellow, all tepals shiny, with undulate margins.

Lithophytic or epiphytic in warm forests and near the coast, 0–700 m (2300 ft.)

Northeastern Australia, Torres Strait Islands, New Guinea

Dendrobium draconis

Reichenbach f.

Pseudobulbs in clusters, 20–60 cm tall, leaf sheaths covered with black hairs. Leaves hairy, persistent, lanceolate-ovate, 3–5 cm long. Inflorescences at the upper nodes, each bearing 2–5 flowers. Flowers shiny, creamy white, to 6 cm across; lip with wavy margins and bright orange blotch in the throat; spur ca. 2.5 cm long at the base.

Epiphytic in warm forests, 200–1300 m (660–4300 ft.)

Myanmar, Thailand, Laos, Cambodia, Vietnam

Dendrobium findlayanum

Parish & Reichenbach f.

Pseudobulbs upright or pendent, 30–60 cm long, curiously swollen at the nodes to resemble a string of beads on a very slender stem. Leaves 7.5 × 1.5 cm, soon deciduous. Inflorescences few, near the stem apex, with 2 or 3 flowers. Flowers pale lilac, 5–7 cm across; petals

Dendrobium densiflorum

Dendrobium devonianum

Dendrobium draconis

Dendrobium discolor

much wider than sepals; lip ochre-yellow with white margin, sometimes with a dark brown blotch in the throat.

Epiphytic or lithophytic in montane forests, 1000–1700 m (3300–5600 ft.)

Laos, Myanmar, Thailand

Dendrobium forbesii Ridley

Plants robust with upright pseudobulbous stems, 30 × 2.5 cm. Leaves 2, large, leathery, 19 × 10 cm, at the apex of the stem. Inflorescences arise between the leaves, short, erect, with 8–20 fragrant flowers, each 5–7 cm across. Flowers white, cream, or pale green, long-lasting, slightly hairy on the back of the sepals; ovary densely hairy.

Epiphytic in montane rain forest, usually high up in the trees, 900–1700 m (3000–5600 ft.)

New Guinea

Dendrobium formosum Roxburgh ex Lindley

Pseudobulbs robust, upright, to 45 cm long, with leaves in the upper two-thirds, leaf sheaths covered with fine black hairs. Leaves in 2 rows, persistent, 9–15 × 2–3 cm. Inflorescences 1 or 2 from the apical nodes with up to 5 flowers. Flowers white, papery but lasting several weeks, to 12 cm across; petals much wider than sepals; lip bright orange in the throat.

Epiphytic in warm forests, 0–500 m (1650 ft.)

Bhutan, Nepal, northeastern India, Myanmar, Thailand, Vietnam

SIMILAR SPECIES: *Dendrobium infundibulum* Lindley grows at higher altitudes, above 1000 m (3300 ft.), and has somewhat smaller flowers, to 10 cm across.

Dendrobium goldschmidtianum Kraenzlin

SYN. *Dendrobium miyakei* Schlechter

Pseudobulbs erect or pendulous, robust, 60–90 × 1 cm, somewhat thickened at the nodes. Leaves in 2 rows, deciduous, thin, oblong-lanceolate, 5–10 × 1–2 cm. Inflorescences form tight clusters at the nodes, with up to 10 bright purple flowers each; column bright yellow.

Epiphytic at low altitudes, in semi-shade, 0–300 m (1000 ft.)

Northern Philippines, Taiwan

Dendrobium gracilicaule F. von Mueller

Pseudobulbs slender, usually upright, covered with brown papery sheaths when young, 80–90 cm long. Leaves 3–6 near the stem apex, persistent, ovate-lanceolate, 5–13 cm long. Inflorescence 10–12 cm long, spreading or pendent, with 5–30 flowers each 1–1.5 cm across. Flowers green, yellow, or orange inside, blotched with red on the outside.

Epiphytic and lithophytic in rain forest and open woodland, 0–1000 m (3300 ft.)

Eastern Australia and adjacent islands

Dendrobium hercoglossum Reichenbach f.

Pseudobulbs club-shaped, very narrow at the base, much wider in the upper half narrowing again towards the apex, 20 × 1 cm. Leaves lanceolate, 5–10 cm long, in 2 rows on the swollen part of the stem, deciduous. Inflorescence short, usually from the leafless stems, with 5–7 waxy flowers. Flowers 2.5 cm across, deep pink with a small white lip and purple anther-cap.

Epiphytic in rain forest with a seasonal climate, at low altitudes

Thailand, Indochina, China, Hong Kong; also reported from the Philippines and Sumatra

SIMILAR SPECIES: Often confused with *Dendrobium aduncum* (see description elsewhere) and *D. linguella* Reichenbach f.; both have narrow pseudobulbs but the details of the interior of the lip are different.

Dendrobium findlayanum

Dendrobium heterocarpum Wallich ex Lindley

SYN. *Dendrobium aureum* Lindley

Pseudobulbs erect at first, becoming pendulous, up to 60 cm long, usually shorter. Leaves in 2 rows, light green, oblong to linear-lanceolate, 9–10 × 2 cm. Inflorescences borne along the upper part of the stems, each with 2–3 light yellow flowers. Flowers 4–7 cm across; sepals and petals similar; lip narrow, bright orange with reddish veins especially on the side lobes.

Epiphytic in a range of habitats, usually in strong light and with a cooler dry season, 600–1800 m (2000–6000 ft.)

Widespread from Sri Lanka, India, Nepal, Bhutan, Myanmar, Malaysia, Thailand, Laos, Vietnam, southern China, Sumatra, Java, Borneo, Philippines, Sulawesi

Dendrobium forbesii

Dendrobium gracilicaule

Dendrobium formosum

Dendrobium hercoglossum

Dendrobium heterocarpum

Dendrobium infundibulum

Dendrobium kingianum Bidwill ex Lindley.

Size variable, depending on habitat and growing conditions. Pseudobulbs tapering from the base upwards, 4–50 cm long. Leaves 2–7, ovate-obovate, persistent, 5–8 × 1–1.5 cm. Inflorescences 1 or more from near the apex of stem, erect, to 20 cm long with up to 15 flowers. Flowers light to dark pink, up to 2.5 cm across, lasting 2 weeks.

Usually lithophytic, often in full sun, 0–1200 m (4000 ft.)

Australia (New South Wales to southeastern Queensland)

Dendrobium kingianum

Dendrobium lawesii

Dendrobium lawesii F. von Mueller

Pseudobulbs pendulous in untidy masses, each to 60 cm long with leaves in 2 rows. Leaves dark green, often tinged purple, lanceolate, 5–6 × 1–2 cm, deciduous. Inflorescence usually borne on a leafless stem, bearing 1–8 (usually 4) waxy, bell-shaped flowers. Flowers 2.5 cm long, pink, red, purple, orange, or yellow, sometimes bicolored, long-lasting.

Epiphytic in rain forests among mosses on larger tree branches and trunks, 500–1500 m (1650–5000 ft.)

Irian Jaya, Papua New Guinea, Bougainville Island, Solomon Islands

Dendrobium lindleyi Steudel

SYN. *Dendrobium aggregatum* Roxburgh

Pseudobulbs short and clustered, appressed to the substrate or erect, strongly ridged, 4–10 cm long. Leaf single, leathery, strap-shaped, to 10 × 3 cm. Inflorescence arising near the apex of the stem, erect or spreading, with up to 15 flowers on slender pedicels. Flowers yellow or bright orange to 4 cm across; lip darker in the throat.

Epiphytic in seasonal climates, often on deciduous trees in strong winter light, 500–2000 m (1650–6600 ft.)

India, Myanmar, Thailand, Laos, Vietnam, China (Hainan and Yunnan)

SIMILAR SPECIES: *Dendrobium jenkinsii* Wallich ex Lindley differs in its smaller, laterally compressed pseudobulbs, and larger flowers, only 1–3 per inflorescence.

Dendrobium linguiforme Swartz

Rhizome and stem prostrate and inconspicuous. Leaf single, arising alternately along the stem, oblong to obovate, 4.5 × 1.5 cm, prostrate, fleshy, dark green, surface furrowed. Inflorescence erect, to 15 cm long, bearing 6–20 flowers. Flowers white or cream, 2 cm across.

Lithophytic or epiphytic forming matlike colonies, 0–1000 m (3300 ft.)

Australia (southeastern New South Wales to northeastern Queensland)

SIMILAR SPECIES: *Dendrobium nugentii* (Bailey) M. A. Clements & D. L. Jones differs by its rugose leaves and longer inflorescences with more, smaller flowers that have reddish-purple veins on the lateral lobes of the lip.

Dendrobium loddigesii Rolfe

Stems slender, erect or prostrate, 7–10 × 0.5 cm, new stems arising half way along length of mature stem. Leaves small, fleshy, light green, deciduous, 4–6 cm long. Flowers solitary at nodes, 4–5 cm across; sepals and petals rosy lilac; lip broad, deep orange with a pale lilac, fringed margin.

Epiphytic or lithophytic, branching stems forming matlike colonies in areas with distinct dry season, 400–1500 m (1320–5000 ft.)

Vietnam, Laos, China (including Hainan, Hong Kong)

Dendrobium longicornu Lindley

Pseudobulbs erect, sometimes becoming pendent, narrow, 20–40 cm long. Leaves dull yellow green, deciduous, 7 × 3 cm, black hairs on the leaf sheaths. Inflorescence near the apex, 1- to 3-flowered. Flowers white, nodding, not opening fully, 6.5 cm across; sepals and petals narrow; lip with fringed margin at the front and long spur at the base.

Epiphytic on forest trees and also lithophytic on rocks in valleys, 1150–2300 m (3800–7600 ft.)

Dendrobium lindleyi

Dendrobium loddigesii

Dendrobium linguiforme

Dendrobium longicornu

Dendrobium macrophyllum

Widespread from India and Nepal to Sikkim, Bhutan, Myanmar, and China

Dendrobium macrophyllum A. Richard

Pseudobulbs narrow at the base, grooved above, to 60 cm long with 3 large leaves at the apex. Leaves leathery, oblong-elliptic, 30 × 4 cm, persistent. Inflorescence erect, above the leaves, with 25 hairy or bristly flowers. Flowers 3–5 cm across, pale green or yellowish; lip variously striped with purple.

Epiphytic in rain forests forming large clumps in the canopy, sea level (in Fiji) to 500 m (1650 ft.), recorded up to 1700 m (5600 ft.) in New Guinea

Widespread from Java, Philippines, New Guinea, eastwards and southwards to Fiji

SIMILAR SPECIES: *Dendrobium polysema* Schlechter is similar but bears only 2 leaves on each pseudobulb and has spots, not stripes on the lip.

Dendrobium moniliforme (Linnaeus) Swartz

Pseudobulbs erect or spreading, slender, 10–40 × 0.5–1 cm with deciduous leaves in 2 rows along the upper half. Leaves linear-lanceolate, 3–5 ×

1 cm. Inflorescences short, borne on the apical third of the leafless pseudobulbs, bearing 1–3 flowers. Flowers white or pale pink, fragrant, lasting 2 weeks, 2–5 cm across; lip narrow, dark green or brown in the throat.

Epiphytic or lithophytic in cool-temperate forests, 600–3000 m (2000–9900 ft.)

Japan, Ryukyu Islands, Korea, China, Taiwan

Dendrobium moschatum

(Buchanan-Hamilton) Swartz

Large, robust plants with erect or pendent pseudobulbs 50–200 cm long. Leaves oblong-lanceolate, green tinged purple, deciduous after 2 years, 8–15 × 4.5 cm. Inflorescences arise from upper nodes of old stems, pendulous, with 7–15 flowers each. Flowers short-lived, pink, white, or coppery yellow, 5–8 cm across; lip slipper-shaped, shortly hairy.

Epiphytic in deciduous forests with a seasonal climate, 300–2000 m (1000–6600 ft.)

Sikkim, Nepal, Bhutan, India, Myanmar, Thailand, Laos, Vietnam

Dendrobium nobile Lindley

Pseudobulbs erect at first, sometimes pendulous later, 60 × 1.5–2 cm, swollen at the nodes. Leaves strap-shaped to lanceolate, 7–10 cm long, deciduous. Inflorescence short, with 2–4 flowers from leafless nodes. Flowers 6–8 cm across, lasting 3–6 weeks; usually white, all parts tipped deep pink-lilac; lip dark purple in throat.

Many different forms have been described including the pure white var. *virginale*.

Epiphytic or lithophytic, forming dense clumps in seasonally deciduous forests, often in full sun, 200–2000 m (660–6600 ft.)

Bhutan, Nepal, India, Myanmar, Thailand, Laos, Vietnam, China

Dendrobium parishii

Reichenbach f.

Pseudobulbs short and thick, often curved or misshapen, 20–30 × 1–2 cm, clothed in white leaf sheaths when old. Leaves oblong-lanceolate, 5–15 cm long, soon deciduous. Inflorescences at the leafless nodes, each with 2–3 flowers. Flowers pale or bright rosy lilac; lip darker, softly hairy.

Epiphytic in deciduous forests with a strongly seasonal climate, 250–1500 m (825–5000 ft.)

India, Myanmar, Thailand, Laos, Vietnam, China (Yunnan)

Dendrobium pendulum

Roxburgh

Pseudobulbs 30–60 cm long, curiously thickened with rounded swellings just below each node (like beads on a rosary), curved or pendent. Leaves narrow, light green, 15 × 0.5 cm, deciduous. Inflorescences at the leafless nodes, each with 1–3 flowers. Flowers white; petals wider than sepals, both tipped with mauve-purple; lip rounded-cordate, with a deep yellow blotch in basal half, mauve-purple apex.

Epiphytic in treetops of deciduous forests, 750–1500 m (2460–5000 ft.)

India, Myanmar, Thailand, Laos, China

Dendrobium primulinum

Lindley

Pseudobulbs erect or pendulous, 30–45 cm long. Leaves in 2 rows but soon deciduous, lanceolate, 8–13 cm long. Inflorescences at the leafless nodes, usually 1- or 2-flowered. Flowers fragrant, 4–8 cm across; sepals and petals narrow, pink, mauve, purple, or white; lip wider than long, pale yellow with reddish veins.

Epiphytic in deciduous forests with a distinct dry season, 300–1600 m (1000–5300 ft.)

Nepal, India, Myanmar, Thailand, Laos, Vietnam, China (Yunnan)

SIMILAR SPECIES: *Dendrobium polyanthum* Lindley is also somewhat similar with white flowers.

Dendrobium rhodostictum

F. von Mueller & Kraenzlin

Stems erect and characteristic, pseudobulbs very narrow below, with a fusiform or ovoid swelling in the apical third, somewhat variable, up to 25 cm long. Leaves 2–4, arising above the swollen part of the pseudobulb, persistent, leathery, 5–11 × 1–2.5 cm. Inflorescence erect from near the apex, bearing 2–6 large flowers. Flowers 6–9 cm across, lasting 6 weeks, white; lip with conspicuous purple margin or spots along the margin.

Epiphytic in montane rain forests or terrestrial on steep mossy slopes of limestone, 800–2000 m (2640–6600 ft.)

Papua New Guinea, Bougainville Island, Solomon Islands

Dendrobium sanderae Rolfe

Pseudobulbs erect, in large clumps, 30–100 × 1 cm. Leaves dark green, leathery, 10 × 3 cm. Inflorescence slender, arising among the leaves near the top of the stem, bearing

Dendrobium moschatum

Dendrobium pendulum

Dendrobium nobile

Dendrobium rhodostictum

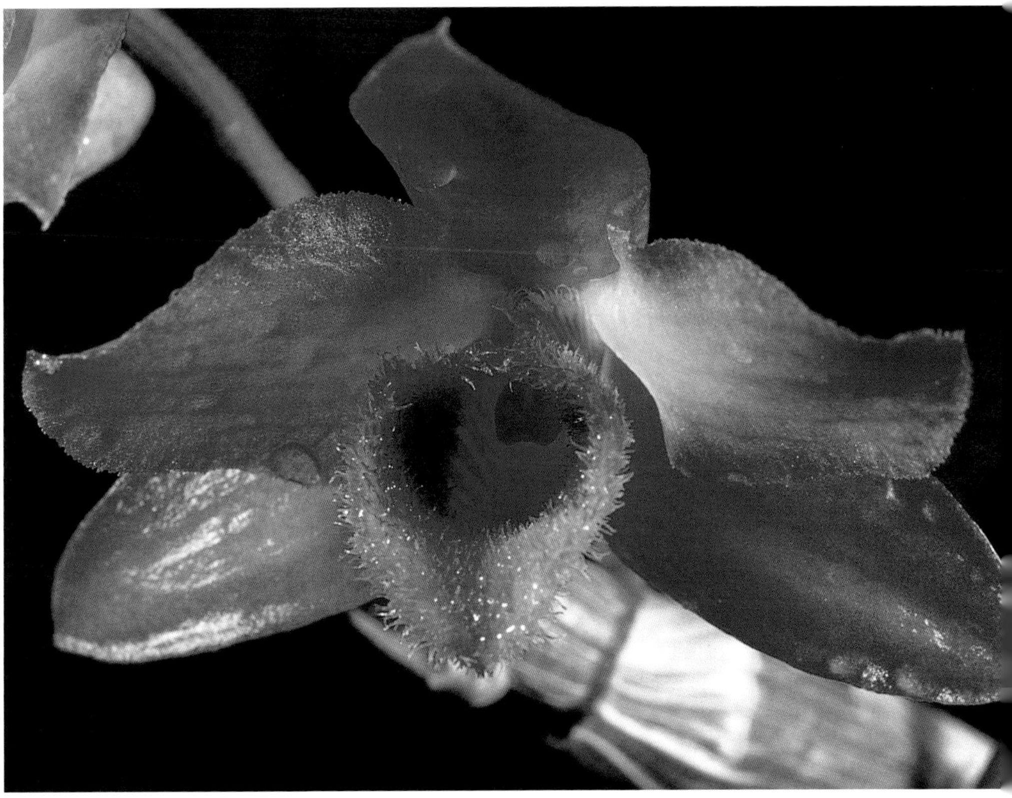

Dendrobium parishii

8–10 flowers. Flowers pure white, papery, lip with purple lines at the base and on the side lobes.

A larger variety with larger flowers, usually called var. *major* Hort., flowers in spring while a smaller one, var. *parviflorum* Anschutz ex Quisumbing, flowers in autumn.

Epiphytic in montane rain forests, 1100–1650 m (3630–5410 ft.)

Philippines (Luzon Island)

Dendrobium senile Parish & Reichenbach f.

Pseudobulbs and leaves covered with dense layer of white hairs. Pseudobulbs short and thick, 5–20 × 1 cm. Leaves 5–6, grayish green, lanceolate, 5 cm long, deciduous. Flowers 3–5, borne singly from the upper nodes on old stems; shiny, bright yellow; lip green on inner surface in throat and on side lobes.

Epiphytic in montane forests with a distinct dry season and bright light, 500–1500 m (1650–5000 ft.)

Laos, Myanmar, Thailand

Dendrobium smillieae F. von Mueller

Pseudobulbs erect at first, becoming pendulous with age, to 100 cm long, forming large clumps. Leaves lanceolate, acuminate, lasting 1 year, 15 × 4 cm. Inflorescences 1–3 per leafless stem, bearing many flowers in a short dense "bottlebrush." Flowers white or pink; lip apex bright green; bird-pollinated.

Epiphytic in coastal rain forests and on rocks in open forests, 0–500 m (1650 ft.)

Australia, New Guinea, Moluccas, Sulawesi

Dendrobium speciosum J. E. Smith

Pseudobulbs large, 30–60 × 2–6 cm, forming large clumps. Leaves 2–6, leathery, persistent, 4–25 × 2–4 cm. Inflorescence apical, erect or horizontal, to 60 cm long with up to 100 flowers. Flowers white cream or yellow, 2.5–5 cm across. Very variable throughout its wide range and several varieties have been recognized.

Lithophytic, occasionally epiphytic, in areas with rainfall throughout the year, 0–1200 m (4000 ft.)

Australia (eastern Victoria to southeastern Queensland)

Dendrobium spectabile (Blume) Miquel

Pseudobulbs cylindrical, gradually widening from a narrow base, 60 × 2–3 cm forming large clumps. Leaves 4–6, in clusters at the apex of the stems, leathery, persistent, 18 × 5 cm. Inflorescence erect, up to 20-flowered. Flowers 4–8 cm across, distinctively convoluted and twisted in all parts, yellowish green, heavily spotted and striped with maroon.

Epiphytic in the forest canopy or sometimes lithophytic, in hot humid lowland forests, coconut plantations, and lower montane forests, 0–1000 m (3300 ft.)

New Guinea, Bougainville Island, Solomon Islands, Vanuatu

Dendrobium subclausum Rolfe

SYN. *Dendrobium phlox* Schlechter

Pseudobulbs branched, erect or pendulous, commonly 25–40 cm long, slender, leafy in the upper part. Leaves deciduous, thin, 3.5–7.5 × 0.4–1.5 cm. Inflorescence short, bearing 3–8 flowers laterally on the leafless stems. Flowers tubular, 1–4 cm long, pale yellow, gold, or orange, sometimes with an orange mentum, sometimes paler on the inner surface.

Epiphytic in montane rain forest and cloud forest or terrestrial in alpine grasslands and on cliffs, 1200–3300 m (4000–10,900 ft.)

New Guinea

Dendrobium tangerinum P. J. Cribb

Pseudobulbs erect to 75 × 3 cm, leafy in the upper half. Leaves oblong or elliptical, 7–11 × 3–5 cm. Inflorescence erect from near the apex of the stem, to 30 cm long, bearing ca. 15 large flowers. Flowers orange, greenish, or reddish brown; sepals broader and shorter than petals which are lightly twisted; lip narrow with lilac-purple ridges.

Epiphytic in coastal and montane forests and on rocks, 0–400 m (1320) and at 1600 m (5300 ft.)

Papua New Guinea

Dendrobium senile

Dendrobium smillieae

Dendrobium speciosum

Dendrobium subclausum

Dendrobium spectabile

Dendrobium tangerinum

Dendrobium teretifolium

Dendrobium tetragonum

Dendrobium teretifolium

R. Brown

Stems long and branching, not differentiated into pseudobulbs, forming large pendulous clumps to 3 m long, rooting only at the base. Leaf single, terete, to 60 cm long. Inflorescence slender, erect or arching, 1–2 per stem and bearing 4–15 flowers. Flowers white, cream, or yellow, spidery, up to 3.5 cm across; midlobe of lip with frilled margins.

Epiphytic in mangroves and montane forest in bright situations, also on rocks, 0–1000 m (3300 ft.)

Australia (southeastern New South Wales to eastern Queensland)

Dendrobium tetragonum

A. Cunningham

Pseudobulbs erect or pendent in tufts, very narrow at the base, swollen above, 4-angled, to 45 × 1–1.5 cm. Leaves 2–5 at the apex of stem, dark green, thin but stiff, 3–8 × 1.5–2.5 cm. Inflorescence terminal, with 3–8 flowers each 3–8 cm long. Flowers pale green, cream, or brownish; sepals wider at the base and usually longer than petals; lip shorter and broader than other parts, white with brown markings. Very variable throughout its range; several varieties are recognized, sometimes as distinct species.

Epiphytic, usually in forests, in lowlands and up to 1000 m (3300 ft.)

Eastern Australia

Dendrobium transparens

Wallich ex Lindley

Pseudobulbs slender and usually pendulous, 30–50 cm long. Leaves light green, deciduous. Inflorescence at the upper nodes on leafless stems, 2- or 3-flowered. Flowers 3–4 cm across; petals wider than sepals, both white, tinted with pale rosy mauve towards the tips; lip ovate-oblong, enclosing the column at its base, with 2 deep purple blotches near the base, tipped with mauve purple.

Epiphytic in forests on lower slopes of Himalayas, 1000–1500 m (3300–5000 ft.)

Northeastern India, Myanmar

Dendrobium trigonopus

Reichenbach f.

Pseudobulbs clustered, erect, short, 10–25 × 1 cm, grooved and somewhat hairy, leafy near the tip. Leaves narrowly oblong, 10 × 2.5 cm, hairy beneath and on the leaf sheaths. Inflorescence short, borne near the stem apex, with 2 or 3 flowers.

Dendrobium trigonopus

Dendrobium unicum

Dendrobium transparens

Flowers fragrant, 5 cm across, waxy, bright yellow; lip green and hairy on the inner surface.

Epiphytic in montane forests with a distinct dry season, 1500–1800 m (5000–6000 ft.)

Myanmar, Thailand, Laos, China (Yunnan)

Dendrobium unicum Seidenfaden

Pseudobulbs erect or becoming pendulous with age, slender, darkening to brown or black, 25 × 1 cm. Leaves few, narrow, 4.5 × 1.5 cm, near the apex of the stem. Inflorescence lateral from the upper nodes, bearing 2–4 bright orange flowers. Flowers 4–5 cm across; sepals and petals narrow, strongly reflexed; lip entire, held on the upper side of the flower, paler orange with darker veins and a white longitudinal crest.

Epiphytic on low shrubs and trees and lithophytic in areas with strong light and a seasonal climate, 800–1500 m (2640–5000 ft.)

Thailand, Laos, Vietnam

Dendrobium vexillarius J. J. Smith

Pseudobulbs growing in tufts, 3–15 cm high. Leaves 2–10, narrow, towards the apex of each stem. Flowers borne in clusters of 2–5 near the tips of stems, 2–4 cm long and very long-lasting; ovary 3-winged.

Seven varieties have been recognized based on plant habit and flower color. Var. *vexillarius* has yellow to greenish yellow flowers; lip dark green or blackish with a bright orange or red apex. Other varieties are orange-red, pink, yellow, white, or bluish gray.

Dendrobium vexillarius

Epiphytic on trees in cool rain forest and terrestrial in grassland, 1000–4000 m (3300–13,200 ft.)

New Guinea, Moluccas, Bismarck archipelago

Dendrobium victoriae-reginae Loher

Pseudobulbs long, slender, branching, forming tangled masses, 30–40 cm long or up to 100 cm, leafy in the apical third. Leaves deciduous, narrow, 7 × 1.3 cm. Inflorescence lateral on the leafless stems, bearing 2–5(–12) waxy flowers, 3–4 cm across. Flowers various shades of violet-blue, usually with darker venation; column white.

Epiphytic in cloud forest, shady and very wet conditions, 1300–2600 m (4300–8600 ft.)

Philippines

Dendrobium violaceum Kraenzlin

Pseudobulbs erect and close together, forming tufts of fusiform or ovoid stems, 1–5 cm tall. Leaves usually 3, near the apex of young stems, very narrow, erect, 5–30 cm long. Inflorescence arising near the apex of leafless stems, 1- to 4-flowered. Flowers opening wide, to 3 cm long but with flattened appearance; sepals and petals pink to deep violet, sometimes with blue tips; lip dark purple with orange or red apex.

Epiphytic on branches of shrubs and small trees in exposed situations in montane forests, 750–2000 m (2460–6600 ft.)

New Guinea

Dendrochilum Blume

SYN. *Acoridium* Nees, *Platyclinis* Bentham

GOLDEN CHAIN ORCHIDS

TRIBE: Arethuseae

SUBTRIBE: Coelogyninae

ETYMOLOGY: From Greek *dendron*, tree, and *cheilos*, lip

DISTRIBUTION: More than 120 species in Southeast Asia, Indonesia, Philippines, and New Guinea

Dendrobium victoriae-reginae

Dendrobium violaceum

Small to medium-sized sympodial epiphytes, occasionally lithophytes, with creeping rhizomes; pseudobulbs clustered or spaced out on rhizome, narrowly cylindrical or ovoid, 1-leafed. Leaves linear to elliptic. Inflorescences lateral or terminal, slender, unbranched, erect at first then arching over and pendent, densely many-flowered. Flowers small, often scented; bracts often prominent; sepals spreading, the laterals joined to the base of the column; petals smaller; lip mobile, oblong, simple or trilobed, fleshy at the base, not spurred. Column winged at apex; pollinia 4.

CULTIVATION: Most species grow well potted in a medium to fine compost, in intermediate conditions in light shade. They should not be repotted too often as they do better when slightly pot-bound. Only a short rest in winter is required.

Dendrochilum arachnites

Reichenbach f.

Pseudobulbs to 5 cm tall, ovoid, set about 5 cm apart. Leaves to 16 × 2.5 cm. Inflorescence arching, to about 30-flowered. Flowers pale yellow, to 2 cm across, among the largest in the genus.

Epiphytic, often in bright light, 660–2300 m (2170–7600 ft.)

Philippines

Dendrochilum cobbianum

Reichenbach f.

Pseudobulbs clustered, 4–8 cm tall, narrowly conical. Leaves 6–18 × 2.5–5.5 cm, narrowly oblong, the midrib prominent. Inflorescence to 80 cm long, densely many-flowered, with papery bracts. Flowers to 12 mm across, orange, green, or whitish with an orange lip. Flowering in autumn.

Epiphytic on mossy trunks, occasionally on rocks in full sun, over 1200 m (4000 ft.)

Philippines

Dendrochilum filiforme Lindley

Pseudobulbs clustered, to 3 cm long, ovoid. Leaves to 18 × 1.5 cm, narrowly strap-shaped. Inflorescence very slender, 35–45 cm long, densely many-flowered. Flowers small, scented, pale yellow, lip often golden yellow.

Epiphytic, 660–2250 m (2170–7350 ft.)

Philippines

Dendrochilum glumaceum Lindley

Pseudobulbs to 4 × 2 cm, ovoid, clustered. Leaves to 45 × 4 cm, narrowly elliptic. Inflorescence very slender, to 50 cm long, densely many-flowered; floral bracts large, whitish. Flowers ca. 2 cm across, white, the lip yellow, orange, or brown. Flowering spring.

Epiphytic, up to 2300 m (7600 ft.)

Borneo, Philippines

Dendrochilum wenzelii Ames

Pseudobulbs clustered, narrow, ca. 2.5 cm long. Leaves to 30 × 0.5 cm, linear, leathery. Inflorescence arching, densely many-flowered. Flowers ca. 1 cm across, red, brown, orange, or yellow-green.

Epiphytic, over 1000 m (3300 ft.)

Philippines

Dendrophylax Reichenbach f.

SYN. *Polyrrhiza* Pfitzer, *Harrisella* Fawcett & Rendle, *Polyradicion* Garay

TRIBE: Vandeae

SUBTRIBE: Angraecinae

ETYMOLOGY: From Greek *dendron*, tree, and *phylax*, guard, a reference to the epiphytic habit

DISTRIBUTION: 14 species in Florida, Mexico, Central America, and the West Indies

Short-stemmed, leafless monopodial epiphytes with photosynthetic roots. Inflorescences sometimes branched, loosely few-flowered; flowers not all open together. Flowers large or small, white, greenish or yellowish; sepals and petals subsimilar, spreading; lip entire or lobed.

CULTIVATION: Because of their photosynthetic roots, plants must be mounted on bark, preferably smooth, or they can be grown on the outside of a suspended clay pot. They require warm conditions, heavy shade, high humidity, and good air movement. They should not be allowed to become dry for long periods. *Dendrophylax lindenii* is notoriously difficult to cultivate.

Dendrophylax funalis (Swartz) Bentham ex Rolfe

SYN. *Polyrrhiza funalis* Lindley

Roots slender, to 30 cm long. Stem to 2 cm long, forming woody stolons. Inflorescence erect, unbranched, to 10 cm long, loosely few-flowered. Flowers to 6 cm across, scented, sepals and petals greenish, lip white, bilobed; spur to 5.5 cm long, tapering from a wide mouth.

Epiphytic in open woodland or lithophytic on limestone rocks, 250–500 m (825–1650 ft.)

Jamaica

Dendrophylax lindenii (Lindley) Bentham ex Rolfe

SYN. *Polyrrhiza lindenii* (Lindley) Cogniaux, *Polyradicion lindenii* (Lindley) Garay

GHOST ORCHID, FROG ORCHID

Roots to 50 cm long. Stem short. Inflorescence to 50 cm long, 1- to 5-flowered, the flowers open in succession. Flowers to 12 cm long, 3–4 cm across, scented; sepals and petals pale green or white, lip white, with small, rounded side lobes, midlobe to 8 cm long, deeply bifid with a small apiculus in the sinus; spur 12–15 cm long, slender from a wide mouth.

In Florida, epiphytic on trees on hammocks in the Everglades in deep shade; in Cuba in thicket and coastal scrub.

Dendrochilum cobbianum

Dendrochilum filiforme

Dendrochilum glumaceum

Dendrochilum wenzelii

Dendrophylax funalis

Dendrophylax lindenii. C. McCartney

Cuba, United States (Florida)
SIMILAR SPECIES: *Dendrophylax sallei* (Reichenbach f.) Bentham ex Rolfe from Hispaniola has a lip with triangular side lobes and the lateral segments of the midlobe to 22 cm long.

Diaphananthe Schlechter

SYN. *Sarcorhynchus* Schlechter
TRIBE: Vandeae
SUBTRIBE: Aerangidinae
ETYMOLOGY: From Greek *diaphanes*, transparent, and *anthos*, flower, referring to the translucent flowers
DISTRIBUTION: About 24 species from mainland Africa and the Gulf of Guinea islands
Epiphytes with long or short stems; roots numerous, often with white streaks noticeable when wet. Inflorescences racemose. Flowers small or medium-sized, translucent, white, green, yellow, straw-colored, or pinkish; sepals and petals free, spreading, the petals often shorter and broader than the sepals; lip spurred, usually as broad as or broader than long, with a peglike callus in the throat. Pollinia and stipites 2, viscidium 1.

Many species previously in *Diaphananthe* are now placed in *Rhipidoglossum*.
CULTIVATION: Most species require intermediate to warm conditions with fairly heavy shade and high humidity. Those with short stems can be grown in pots in a medium bark-based compost, but those with long stems and numerous roots do better mounted on bark or a moss pole. While not actively growing, they should be kept drier but not allowed to dry out completely.

Diaphananthe bidens (Swartz ex Persoon) Schlechter

Stems pendent or scandent, 50–100 cm long. Leaves numerous, distichous, facing the same way, 5–15 cm long, 2–4 cm wide, ovate or oblong, unequally and acutely bilobed at the apex. Racemes arising along the stem, pendent, to ca. 20 cm long, densely many-flowered. Flowers smallish, salmon-pink to white; lip almost square, apiculate; spur to 7 mm long, slightly swollen in the middle.

Epiphytic in rain forest, 1100–1300 m (3600–4300 ft.)

Widespread in West and Central Africa

Diaphananthe fragrantissima (Reichenbach f.) Schlechter

Stems pendent, to 50 cm long. Leaves narrow, pendent, fleshy, dull green, 10–40 × 1–3 cm, the apex very unequally and acutely bilobed. Inflorescence pendent, 20–60 cm long, densely or occasionally loosely many-flowered. Flowers translucent cream or yellow-green, scented, ca. 2 cm in diameter; lip almost square but apiculate at tip; spur 10 mm long.

Epiphytic in low altitude woodland or riverine forest, 150–1400 m (500–4600 ft.)

Widespread in tropical Africa, South Africa (KwaZulu-Natal)

Diaphananthe pellucida (Lindley) Schlechter

Stems short. Leaves numerous, pendent, 18–40 cm long, 2–9 cm across, oblanceolate, pale or dark green. Inflorescence arising below leaves, pendent, to 50 cm long, densely many-flowered. Flowers translucent creamy yellow or pale green, 15–20 mm across; lip deflexed, almost square, the margins fringed; spur 9–10 mm long.

Low-level epiphyte in dense shade in evergreen forest, 600–1500 m (2000–5000 ft.)

West and Central Africa

Dichaea Lindley

TRIBE: Maxillarieae
SUBTRIBE: Zygopetalinae
ETYMOLOGY: From Greek *diche*, in 2 parts, referring to the distichous leaf arrangement
DISTRIBUTION: About 112 species in Mexico and tropical Central and South America
Epiphytes or lithophytes lacking pseudobulbs, with long, leafy stems, pendent or sprawling, rooting at the nodes, sometimes branched, covered with old leaf bases below the leaves. Leaves distichous, alternate or opposite, evergreen or deciduous, spreading or reflexed. Inflorescences 1-flowered, arising opposite leaf axils. Flowers fleshy, relatively large, often scented; sepals and petals free, spreading, subsimilar; lip joined to column-foot, sometimes clawed, usually trilobed, elliptic to arrow-shaped; ovary smooth or spiny. Pollinia 4.
CULTIVATION: Because of their pendent or sprawling habit, *Dichaea* species are best planted in baskets or mounted on slabs. They require intermediate conditions, shade, and high humidity and need to be watered throughout the year.

Dichaea glauca (Swartz) Lindley

Stems to 60 cm long, erect or pendent. Leaves overlapping, to 4 cm long, oblong, gray-green. Inflorescence borne near top of stem, to 2.5 cm long, 1-flowered. Flowers scented, 1.5–2 cm across, grayish white with mauve or lavender marks.

Epiphytic in rain forest, 950–1700 m (3100–5600 ft.)

Caribbean, Mexico, Central America

Dichaea hystricina Reichenbach f.

Stems suberect, to 15 cm long, with a few branches. Leaves persistent, to 1 cm long, 2 mm wide, the margins ciliate. Flowers small, sepals to 7 mm long, rather bell-shaped, white or greenish white spotted with mauve, lip clawed, the blade anchor-shaped.

Epiphytic in woodland and cloud forest, 500–1700 m (1650–5600 ft.)

Caribbean, Central and South America

Diaphananthe bidens. E. la Croix

Dichaea morrisii Fawcett & Rendle

Stem 15–20 cm long, erect or pendent. Leaves to 6 × 1.5 cm. Inflorescence ca. 1 cm long. Flowers fleshy, white or greenish white marked with lilac; sepals to 16 mm long; lip clawed, the blade arrow-shaped.

Epiphytic on mossy tree trunks in forest, 200–1400 m (660–4600 ft.)

Caribbean, Central and South America

Dichaea muricata (Swartz) Lindley

Stems pendent or sprawling, to 50 cm long, somewhat flattened, covered with leaf sheaths and leaves. Leaves fleshy, persistent, to 1.5 cm long, oblong, ± reflexed. Inflorescence ca. 2.5 cm long. Flowers scented, greenish white flushed with bronze, often spotted with violet, ca. 2.5 cm across.

Diaphananthe pellucida. E. la Croix

Dichaea morrisii

Epiphytic in wet forest or lithophytic on rocks near streams, 780–1200 m (2600–4000 ft.)

Caribbean, Colombia, Peru, Brazil

Dichaea pendula (Aublet) Cogniaux

Stems to 50 cm long, pendent, branched. Leaves overlapping, to 4 × 1 cm. Flowers ca. 2 cm across, fleshy, yellowish with lilac markings or pinkish buff; lip lilac.

Epiphytic on trees and tree ferns or lithophytic on mossy banks, 830–2000 m (2750–6600 ft.)

Caribbean, Central and South America

Dichaea picta Reichenbach f.

Stems 5–20 cm long, erect, arching or pendent, unbranched or branched at base. Leaves to 15 × 5 mm. Flowers small, rather bell-shaped, 10–12 mm across, white or greenish with red or mauve dots.

Epiphytic in rain forest, 50–1000 m (165–3300 ft.)

Ecuador, Guyana, Trinidad, Venezuela

Dimerandra Schlechter

TRIBE: Epidendreae

SUBTRIBE: Laeliinae

ETYMOLOGY: From Greek *dimeres*, bipartite, and *andra*, stamens

DISTRIBUTION: 4 species in Mexico, Central and South America

Sympodial epiphytes with short, creeping rhizomes and canelike pseudobulbs. Leaves distichous with sheathing bases. Inflorescences terminal, unbranched, the flowers open in succession 1–3 at a time. Flowers showy but short-lived; sepals and petals spreading, sepals free, similar, petals broader; lip joined to the column at base, wedge-shaped or fan-shaped with a complex callus at the base. Column with winglike projections on either side of the anther; pollinia 4.

CULTIVATION: Plants should be potted in a free-draining bark compost in intermediate to warm conditions with light shade and plenty of water while in growth. They should be kept cooler and drier while resting.

Dimerandra emarginata (G. Meyer) Hoehne

SYN. *Dimerandra elegans* (Focke) Siegerist

Pseudobulbs to 35 cm long, leafy in the upper third. Leaves to 12 × 1 cm, strap-shaped to lanceolate. Flowers to 3 cm across, pink to magenta, the lip with a white patch near the base; column pink.

Epiphytic in semi-deciduous forest and rain forest, 0–300 m (1000 ft.)

Mexico, Central and South America, Caribbean

Dimorphorchis Rolfe

TRIBE: Vandeae

SUBTRIBE: Aeridinae

ETYMOLOGY: From Greek *di*, two, *morphe*, shape, and *orchis*, orchid, referring to the 2 types of flowers

DISTRIBUTION: 2 species in Borneo

Large monopodial epiphytes with erect or more often pendent stems, leafy towards the apex, covered with old leaf sheaths towards the base. Leaves large, arching, leathery, strap-shaped, bilobed at the apex. Inflorescences long, pendent, with the basal flowers markedly different in appearance from the apical flowers although both types are fully fertile.

CULTIVATION: Because of their size, plants should be grown in pots, preferably heavy clay pots, in a coarse bark mix. They do best in warm conditions in medium to light shade with high humidity and should be watered throughout the year.

Dimorphorchis lowii (Lindley) Rolfe

Stems 75–150 cm long, Leaves 50–90 × 4–5 cm. Inflorescence pendent, to 300 cm long, laxly many-flowered. Lower flowers 2–5, to 7.5 cm across, yellow spotted with purple or red-brown, strongly scented. Apical flowers of similar size, not scented, yellow or cream with large, irregular purple or red-brown blotches, the edges of the sepals and petals undulate. Lip 10–15 mm long, very fleshy, trilobed.

Riverine or swamp forest, often overhanging water, 0–1300 m (4300 ft.)

Borneo

SIMILAR SPECIES: *Dimorphorchis rossii*, also from Borneo, is more slender with shorter inflorescences (50–80 cm) and smaller flowers, to 5 cm across.

Dinema Lindley

TRIBE: Epidendreae

SUBTRIBE: Laeliinae

ETYMOLOGY: From Greek *di*, two and *nema*, thread, referring to the slender column appendages

DISTRIBUTION: 1 species in Mexico, Central America, and the Caribbean

Epiphytes, rarely lithophytes, with a creeping rhizome; pseudobulbs ovoid, well-spaced out on rhizome, 2-leaved at apex. Inflorescence terminal, subtended by a spathe, 1-flowered; sepals and petals free, spreading; lip clawed, with 2 oblong calli near the margins of the claw, blade suborbicular. Pollinia 4.

CULTIVATION: Plants grow well potted in a free-draining fine to medium bark mix in intermediate conditions, in light shade, and with plenty of water while in growth. However, they soon straggle out of a pot and are better accommodated in a shallow basket or on a raft of bark.

Dinema polybulbon (Swartz) Lindley

SYN. *Epidendrum polybulbon* Swartz, *Encyclia polybulbon* (Swartz) Dressler

Dichaea muricata

Dichaea picta

Dimerandra emarginata

Dimorphorchis lowii. J. Stewart

Pseudobulbs to 20 × 8 mm, set 1–4 cm apart. Leaves to 8 × 1 cm, elliptic to oblong. Inflorescence 1–3 cm tall. Flowers to 3 cm across; sepals and petals yellowish flushed with brown, the petals narrower than the sepals; lip white.

Epiphytic in humid forest, 600–2000 m (2000–6600 ft.)

Mexico, Central America, Caribbean

Diplocaulobium (Reichenbach f.) Kraenzlin

TRIBE: Dendrobieae

SUBTRIBE: Dendrobiinae

ETYMOLOGY: From Greek *diplous*, folded, *caulos*, stem, and *bios*, life, believed to refer to the creeping stems and swollen pseudobulbs

DISTRIBUTION: About 100 species in Malaysia, New Guinea, the Pacific Islands, and northeastern Australia

Small to medium-sized epiphytes or sometimes lithophytes; pseudobulbs 1-leafed, either swollen at the base and cylindrical above, set closely on the rhizome, or rather flattened and set apart. Inflorescences axillary, 1-flowered, appearing in succession. Flowers small to medium-sized, dull-colored or showy, ephemeral; sepals and petals subsimilar; lip entire or trilobed. Pollinia 4.

CULTIVATION: Diplocaulobiums can be grown in pots or baskets in a standard bark mixture, or mounted. They do best in light shade in intermediate to cool conditions.

Diplocaulobium aratriferum (J. J. Smith) P. F. Hunt & Summerhayes

SYN. *Dendrobium aratriferum* J. J. Smith

Plants 12–15 cm high. Flowers ca. 10 cm across, white or cream, the lip and tips of sepals and petals marked with yellow and maroon, opening off and on throughout year but each lasting for less than a day; sepals and petals spidery, the lateral sepals 7 cm long; lip small.

Epiphytic in forest

New Guinea

Diplocaulobium chrysotropis (Schlechter) A. D. Hawkes

SYN. *Dendrobium chrysotropis* Schlechter

Pseudobulbs 1.5–2.5 cm long. Leaves to 5 × 1 cm. Flowers white, the parts tipped with yellow; lip ca. 5.5 cm long, sometimes with red marks towards the base, with yellow crests; ovary 4-winged.

Epiphytic on tall forest trees, 1000–1300 m (3300–4300 ft.)

New Guinea

Diplocaulobium regale (Schlechter) A. D. Hawkes

SYN. *Dendrobium regale* Schlechter

Pseudobulbs cylindrical, swollen at base, 15–60 cm tall. Leaves oblong, to 20 cm long. Flowers showy, white, pink, or red, 7–8 cm across, lasting for 1–3 days.

Epiphytic in forest, 700–2100 m (2300–6900 ft.)

New Guinea

Dipodium R. Brown

TRIBE: Cymbidieae

SUBTRIBE: Cyrtopodiinae

ETYMOLOGY: From Greek *di*, two, and *podion*, foot, referring to the 2 prominent stipites

DISTRIBUTION: More than 20 species from Southeast Asia to the Pacific Islands and Australia

Terrestrial or climbing plants, some of the terrestrials saprophytic. Climbers with leafy stems, rooting at the nodes. Inflorescences axillary, laxly few- to many-flowered. Sepals and petals free, spreading, subsimilar. Lip fleshy, lacking a spur, trilobed, the callus and midlobe hairy. Pollinia 2.

CULTIVATION: The saprophytic species cannot be cultivated. The scandent species can be grown in a pot in a coarse, free-draining epiphyte mixture with a support such as a moss pole to climb on. They require intermediate temperatures and good light and should be watered throughout the year, although less water should be given when temperatures are low.

Dipodium ensifolium F. Mueller

Terrestrial plant with leafy stems to 1 m tall, erect at first but becoming straggling. Leaves to 20 × 1.5 cm, linear, channeled, ribbed. Inflorescence erect, to 55 cm long, 2- to 20-flowered. Flowers 3–4 cm across, pink or mauve, spotted and blotched with deep purple.

Terrestrial in open forest and woodland, ca. 800 m (2640 ft.)

Australia (northeastern Queensland)

Dipodium pictum (Lindley) Reichenbach f.

Scandent plant with leafy stems 1–10 m long, rooting at nodes. Leaves in 2 rows, linear to strap-shaped, to 55 × 4 cm. Racemes erect, 30–60 cm long, several- to many-flowered. Flowers 3–4 cm across, creamy white with dark red blotches on the outside showing through on the inside; lip with several red stripes and a hairy ridge on the midlobe.

Climbing up tree trunks in lowland rain forest

Malesia to Philippines and Australia

SIMILAR SPECIES: *Dipodium scandens* (Blume) J. J. Smith, with a similar distribution, is sometimes considered synonymous.

Disa Bergius

TRIBE: Diseae

SUBTRIBE: Disinae

ETYMOLOGY: Probably named for Queen Disa, who in Swedish folklore appeared before the king wrapped in a fishing net (presumably referring to the net veins on the sepals of *Disa uniflora*)

DISTRIBUTION: About 160 species in tropical and South Africa with 1 extending into Arabia and 4 in Madagascar and the Mascarene Islands

Terrestrial herbs with globose, ovoid, or ellipsoid tubers. Leaves either on flowering stem or on a separate sterile shoot. Inflorescences unbranched, 1- to many-flowered, often showy.

Dinema polybulbon

Diplocaulobium chrysotropis. J. Hermans

Dipodium ensifolium. J. Stewart

Dipodium scandens. J. Hermans

Sepals free, the dorsal spurred, often forming a hood, the laterals spreading. Petals smaller, sometimes lobed, often lying inside the hood. Lip usually strap-shaped but sometimes deeply fringed. Column short, anther erect, transverse or reflexed, with the stigma lying below it; pollinia 2.

Several previously independent genera, such as *Monadenia* and *Herschelianthe* (syn. *Herschelia*) are now included in *Disa* as a result of DNA analysis.

CULTIVATION: *Disa* includes some lovely plants, but the only species in common cultivation are evergreen species from the Cape related to *D. uniflora*. These are cool-growing plants which require an open position but not too much direct sun. They need to be kept moist all year round, although more so while in active growth; some growers stand the pots in slowly moving water. Disas can be grown successfully in sphagnum moss, with or without perlite, and various very free-draining composts often containing river sand. They are intolerant of all but the weakest fertilizers. Hybrids derived from *D. uniflora* are grown in the same way.

Winter-dormant species from the summer rainfall areas of South Africa, such as *Disa sagittalis*, can be grown in a shallow pan with free-draining compost. Careful watering should start when green shoots appear. After flowering, when the plants die back, they are kept dry until new growth starts again, with only an occasional sprinkling of water to prevent the tubers shriveling.

The tropical, deciduous species are rarely grown, partly because they are reputed to be hard to grow and partly because they are difficult to obtain. Species that used to be included in *Herschelianthe* (for example, *Disa baueri*) are beautiful plants often with blue flowers and a deeply fringed lip. They are grown to some extent in South Africa but with little success elsewhere. For further information on growing *Disa*, see Wodrich (1997) in the "cultural" section of the Bibliography.

Disa cardinalis Linder

Evergreen plants, sometimes spreading by stolons. Leaves in basal rosette, 5–10 cm long. Raceme 30–70 cm tall, fairly densely to 25-flowered. Flowers bright red, ca. 5 cm across, the dorsal sepal forming a hood bearing a conical spur. Flowering spring–summer.

Forms groups beside streams, ca. 600 m (2000 ft.)

South Africa (Cape Province)

Disa crassicornis Lindley

Robust, deciduous plants to 100 cm tall. Inflorescence cylindrical, 5- to 25-flowered. Flowers ca. 5 cm across, fragrant, creamy white heavily mottled with pink or purple; dorsal sepal forming a funnel-shaped hood 20–40 mm long, tapering to a decurved, cylindrical spur 30–40 mm long.

Damp grassland, 1000–2700 m (3300–8900 ft.)

South Africa (Eastern Cape, KwaZulu-Natal), Lesotho

Disa racemosa Linnaeus f.

Evergreen plants with basal leaves in rosette, to 9 cm long. Raceme 7–100 cm tall, laxly or densely several-flowered. Flowers white or mauve-pink; dorsal sepal concave with a vestigial spur; lateral sepals spreading, 15–25 mm long. Flowering summer.

Often in swampy areas, flowering freely after fires, 0–1200 m (4000 ft.)

South Africa (Western and Southern Cape)

SIMILAR SPECIES: *Disa venosa* Swartz, also from Western Cape, has deeper pink flowers and a differently shaped dorsal sepal.

Disa sagittalis (Linnaeus f.) Swartz

Deciduous plants to 30 cm tall with basal leaves in a rosette, sheathing leaves along stem. Inflorescence laxly to densely few- to many-flowered. Flowers small, white or mauve, the petals usually darker; sepals to 10 mm long.

Grows on rocks or in rock crevices, often near streams, 0–1000 m (3300 ft.)

South Africa (Southern and Eastern Cape, KwaZulu-Natal)

Disa tripetaloides (Linnaeus f.) N. E. Brown

Slender evergreen plants, spreading by stolons. Leaves in basal rosette, to 15 cm long. Raceme 10–60 cm tall, to 25-flowered. Flowers to 2.5 cm across, white, fading to pink. Plants from Cape flower in summer but those from KwaZulu-Natal flower in winter.

Stream banks and damp hillsides, 0–1000 m (3300 ft.)

South Africa (Cape Province, KwaZulu-Natal)

SIMILAR SPECIES: *Disa aurata* (Bolus) L. T. Parker & Koopowitz (syn. *D. tripetaloides* var. *aurata* Bolus) has slightly larger, bright yellow flowers.

Disa uniflora Bergius

SYN. *Disa grandiflora* Linnaeus f.

Evergreen plants to 60 cm tall. Leaves along stem, to 25 cm long, the longest near the base. Inflorescence 1- to several-flowered. Flowers large and showy, 8–12 cm across, usually bright red, the inside of the hood orange with red veining, but sometimes yellow or pink. Dorsal sepal erect, concave, 20–60 × 15–20 mm; spur 10–15 mm long; lateral sepals spreading forward, to 65 mm long.

This beautiful species has been much used in hybridization, mainly with the related species *Disa cardinalis*, *D. racemosa*, and *D. tripetaloides*. Of the ca. 85 registered hybrids of *Disa*, almost all have *D. uniflora* in the ancestry.

Along streams and in seepages over rock, in shade to full sunlight, 100–1200 m (330–4000 ft.)

South Africa (West and Southwest Cape)

Disperis Swartz

TRIBE: Diseae

SUBTRIBE: Coryciinae

ETYMOLOGY: From Greek *dis*, double, and *pera*, pouch, referring to the saclike spur on each lateral sepal

DISTRIBUTION: About 100 species in South Africa, tropical Africa, Madagascar, and the Mascarene Islands with 1 species in Asia

Slender terrestrial herbs, occasionally epiphytic. Tubers small, ovoid. Leaves 1 to few, opposite or alternate, sometimes reduced to sheaths, lanceolate to ovate, the upper surface sometimes attractively marked with silver or pinkish net veining, the underside sometimes purple. Inflorescences unbranched, 1- to several-flowered; floral bracts leafy. Flowers small, usually less than 2 cm across, greenish, white, yellow, or mauve-pink; dorsal sepal joined to petals to form a shallow or deep hood, saccate or spurred, lateral sepals spreading or reflexed with a saclike spur; lip very complex with the base joined to the column, the limb bearing a simple or lobed appendage. Anther erect; pollinia granular, arranged in 2 rows.

CULTIVATION: Few species are in cultivation, but several are worth the attempt if they could be obtained. Many species grow in leaf litter in forest, while others are found in grassland, often montane grassland. The forest species can be grown like *Stenoglottis*, in a free-draining but humus-rich soil in cool to intermediate conditions. Plants should be kept dry while dormant, with careful watering starting when new growth appears.

Disa cardinalis

Disa tripetaloides

Disa uniflora

Disperis capensis (Linnaeus f.) Swartz

Slender plants to 40 cm tall. Leaves 2, alternate, on lower half of stem, to 9 × 1 cm. Inflorescence 1- or 2-flowered. Sepals green, the petals either yellow-green or magenta-purple; dorsal sepal to 3 cm long, forming an open hood with a long, erect or reflexed point at the apex; lateral sepals to 3 cm long, reflexed, acuminate, with sacs 2–3 mm long. Flowering in winter.

Terrestrial in grass and scrubland, often on seepage areas, 0–900 m (3000 ft.)

South Africa (Cape Province)

Disperis fanniniae Harvey

GRANNY'S BONNET

Plants 15–45 cm tall, Leaves 3–4, alternate, to 8 × 3 cm, lanceolate or ovate, clasping the stem. Inflorescence several-flowered. Flowers white flushed with pink or green; dorsal sepal forming a deep, blunt hood 1–2 cm long, lateral sepals deflexed, ca. 1 cm long, each with a saccate spur about the middle. Flowering in early spring.

Terrestrial in leaf litter in forest (including pine plantations), 700–2100 m (2300–6900 ft.)

South Africa (Eastern Cape to Northern Province), Lesotho, Swaziland

Diuris J. E. Smith

DONKEY ORCHIDS; DOUBLE TAILS

TRIBE: Diurideae

SUBTRIBE: Diuridinae

ETYMOLOGY: From Greek *dis*, double, and *oura*, tail, referring to the lateral sepals projecting below the lip

DISTRIBUTION: About 60 species, mainly in Australia, with 1 endemic in Timor

Deciduous terrestrials with paired underground tubers, sometimes forming stolons. Stem short, unbranched, with overlapping scales at the base. Leaves basal, 1 to several, narrow, often grasslike. Inflorescences unbranched, erect, terminal, 1- to many-flowered. Flowers showy, brightly colored; dorsal sepal forming a hood over the column, shorter than lateral sepals; lateral sepals long, narrow, decurved; petals usually erect, with a basal claw then a broad lamina; lip trilobed, the midlobe keeled.

CULTIVATION: Plants should be potted in a very free-draining terrestrial mix containing about 50 percent coarse sand and left undisturbed for several years. They should be kept constantly moist while actively growing and dry while dormant. Many species increase vegetatively. They require bright light and cool conditions.

Diuris lanceolata Lindley

SYN. *Diuris pedunculata* R. Brown var. *lanceolata* (Lindley) Domin

Leaves several, narrowly linear, to 15 cm × 2 mm. Inflorescence to 40 cm tall, 1- to 4-flowered. Flowers nodding, to 25 mm across, lemon-yellow with darker marks on the outside; petals with red-brown basal claw 5 mm long; lip midlobe ovate with a callus of 2 fleshy ridges.

Forms colonies in grassland, particularly where wet

Southeastern Australia

Diuris longifolia R. Brown

Leaves to 20 × 1.8 cm. Inflorescence to 30 cm tall, 1- to 6-flowered. Flowers 3 cm across, purple and mauve with yellow marks on the dorsal sepal and lip; lip midlobe wedge-shaped, the apex curved down, with a callus of 1 ridge.

Forms colonies in forest and woodland and around boulders

Southwestern Australia

Diuris maculata J. E. Smith

Leaves 2–3, linear, to 20 cm × 4 mm. Inflorescence to 30 cm tall, 2- to 8-flowered. Flowers to 30 mm across, yellow, heavily blotched with dark brown; petals with a dark red-brown basal claw 8 mm long; lip midlobe wedge-shaped with a callus of 2 fleshy ridges. One of the most widespread species.

Variable but usually forming colonies in open woodland

Southeastern Australia

Diuris punctata J. E. Smith

One of the most beautiful species. Leaves 2–4, linear, channeled, to 25 cm × 4 mm. Inflorescence to 60 cm tall, 2- to 10-flowered. Flowers ca. 6 cm across, purple, rarely white or yellow, sometimes scented; petals with a darker purple basal claw to 8 mm long; lip midlobe fan- or wedge-shaped, often folded, with a callus of 2 ridges.

Var. *sulphurea* Rupp, endemic to New South Wales, differs in having yellow flowers.

Forms colonies in open woodland and moist grassland

Southeastern Australia

Domingoa Schlechter

SYN. *Nageliella* L. O. Williams

TRIBE: Epidendreae

SUBTRIBE: Laeliinae

ETYMOLOGY: For Santo Domingo, a name that once referred to the whole island of Hispaniola

DISTRIBUTION: 5 species from Mexico, Central America, and the Caribbean

Small creeping or tufted epiphytes or lithophytes; pseudobulbs either slender and spindle-shaped or narrowly cylindrical, hidden in fibrous sheaths, 1-leafed. Leaves fleshy, sometimes purplish or mottled with white. Inflorescences apical, few-flowered, the flowers open either together or in succession. Sepals free, projecting forwards, spreading or reflexed, forming a mentum with the column-foot; petals free, usually broader than sepals. Lip sessile or clawed, sometimes saccate at base.

CULTIVATION: Most species grow well in intermediate conditions, either in a pot or mounted, in light shade. Plants need plenty of water while in

Diuris longifolia. J. Stewart

Disperis fanniniae. E. la Croix

Domingoa haematochila

active growth but should be allowed to dry out between waterings.

Domingoa gemma (Reichenbach f.) van den Berg & Soto Arenas

SYN. *Nageliella angustifolia* (Booth ex Lindley) Ames & Correll, *N. gemma* (Reichenbach f.) Ames & Correll

Pseudobulbs narrowly cylindrical, to 7 cm long. Leaves erect, to 10 × 2 cm, marked with reddish brown. Inflorescence wiry, to 30 cm tall, the flowers open in succession. Flowers bell-shaped, bright magenta, ca. 9 mm long.

Epiphytic in oak forests, 500–2200 m (1650–7260 ft.)

Mexico to El Salvador

SIMILAR SPECIES: *Domingoa purpurea* (Lindley) van den Berg & Soto Arenas (syn. *Nageliella purpurea* (Lindley) L. O. Williams) from Mexico and Central America has slightly larger red-purple flowers and a saclike spur.

Domingoa haematochila (Reichenbach f.) Carabia

SYN. *Domingoa hymenodes* Schlechter

Pseudobulbs ca. 3 cm long, cylindrical. Leaves to 7 × 1 cm, elliptic, dark green. Inflorescence to 20 cm long, 1- to 5-flowered. Flowers scented, 25 mm across; sepals and petals translucent greenish yellow, usually with purplish lines; lip maroon, oblong, emarginate, the disc with 2 ridges.

Humid, shady spots in coastal forest, also in more exposed places in wet forest, 0–600 m (2000 ft.), rarely to 1100 m (3600 ft.)

Cuba to Puerto Rico

Dossinia E. Morren

TRIBE: Cranichideae

SUBTRIBE: Goodyerinae

ETYMOLOGY: Named for Belgian botanist E. P. Dossin (1777–1852)

DISTRIBUTION: 1 species in Borneo

Domingoa gemma

Small terrestrial or lithophyte. Leaves few, in a loose rosette. Inflorescence erect, pubescent, many-flowered. Flowers resupinate; sepals pubescent outside, spreading; petals adnate to dorsal sepal; lip saccate at base, bilobed at apex, the lobes truncate.

One of the "jewel orchids" grown for its beautifully marked leaves.

CULTIVATION: Plants should be grown in a shallow pan in a free-draining terrestrial compost, preferably with added leaf mold and dolomite, in shaded, humid intermediate to warm conditions. They should be watered freely while in active growth and, although they need less water in winter, should not be allowed to dry out completely.

Dossinia marmorata E. Morren

Leaves to 7 cm long, broadly elliptic to almost round, deep velvety green with a dense network of gold, reticulate veins; petiole short. Inflorescence to 45 cm tall. Flowers ca. 2 cm long, brownish pink, the lip white.

Terrestrial in lowland rain forest; in shaded places in leaf litter in crevices of limestone boulders, 0–400 m (1320 ft.)

Borneo

Dracula Luer

TRIBE: Epidendreae

SUBTRIBE: Pleurothallidinae

ETYMOLOGY: From Latin *draco*, dragon, and the diminutive suffix *-ula*, referring to the appearance of the flowers

DISTRIBUTION: More than 100 species from southern Mexico to Colombia, Ecuador, and Peru, with most in the Colombian and Ecuadorean Andes

Tufted or creeping epiphytes, rarely terrestrial, many originally described in *Masdevallia*. Stems enclosed in sheaths, 1-leafed at apex. Leaves linear to elliptical or oblanceolate, rather thin-textured, with a short stalk. Inflorescences unbranched, 1-flowered or more often with several flowers opening in succession, almost always pendent; if erect, the flowers are pendent. Sepals ovate, usually with long tails, partly joined at the base to form either a flat or cup-shaped flower; petals small. Lip fleshy, divided into a hypochile (claw), hinged to the column-foot and an epichile (blade), rounded and often concave, usually with various ridges or lamellae. Column short and stout, pollinia 2.

Most species are rather similar vegetatively, differing mainly in size.

A number of interspecific hybrids have been made in *Dracula*, also some hybrids with *Masdevallia*, which are known as ×*Dracuvallia*.

CULTIVATION: Because of their pendent inflorescences, draculas should be planted in baskets or net pots. They seem to be most successful in a sphagnum-perlite mixture but can also be grown in a compost based on fine bark. They require cool to intermediate temperatures, shade, high humidity, and good ventilation. If the humidity is low, the flowers shrivel up.

Dracula bella (Reichenbach f.) Luer

Inflorescence pendent, to 20 cm long, 1-flowered. Sepals yellow, spotted and marked with red-brown, the sepaline cup ca. 5 cm across, with slender, dark red-brown tails ca. 13 cm long. Lip white, yellow at the base; epichile kidney-shaped.

Epiphytic in forest, 2400 m (7900 ft.)

Colombia, western Cordillera

SIMILAR SPECIES: *Dracula nycterina* (Reichenbach f.) Luer, also from Colombia, has smaller flowers with more divergent tails.

Dracula chimaera (Reichenbach f.) Luer

One of the larger species. Inflorescence erect or spreading, 15–60 cm long, up to 6-flowered. Flowers almost flat, white, yellow, green, purple, or brown, blotched with purple or brown, hairy within; sepals to 5.5 cm long, tails dark purple, 12–25 cm long; lip epichile very concave, inflated at apex, 2 cm long.

Epiphytic in cloud forest, 1500–2200 m (5000–7260 ft.)

Colombia

SIMILAR SPECIES: *Dracula wallisii* (Reichenbach f.) Luer, also from Colombia, differs in the shape of the lip.

Dracula cordobae Luer

Inflorescence pendent, several-flowered. Flowers open and flat, creamy white, spotted with reddish brown along the margins and with long hairs inside; sepals to 25 mm long, tails dark brown, 4–7 cm long; lip epichile round, concave, white.

Epiphytic in cloud forest, 800–1000 m (2640–3300 ft.)

Ecuador

Dracula erythrochaete

Dossinia marmorata. P. O'Byrne

Dracula erythrochaete (Reichenbach f.) Luer

Inflorescence usually pendent, to 20 cm long, 1- to 4-flowered. Sepals forming a shallow cup, white to pale yellow, dotted with brown or purple, often flushed with red or purple, to 17 mm long, tails dark red, 3–7 cm long. Lip epichile concave, suborbicular.

Epiphytic in cloud forest, 1100–2000 m (3600–6600 ft.)

Costa Rica, Panama

Dracula gigas (Luer & Andreetta) Luer

Inflorescence erect or horizontal, to 65 cm long, few-flowered. Sepals light pinkish brown, forming an open cup, sepals to 4 cm long, tails red-brown, to 6 cm long. Lip epichile pink, concave, suborbicular with several radiating lamellae.

Epiphytic, sometimes terrestrial, in cloud forest, 1800–2550 m (6000–8400 ft.)

Colombia, Ecuador

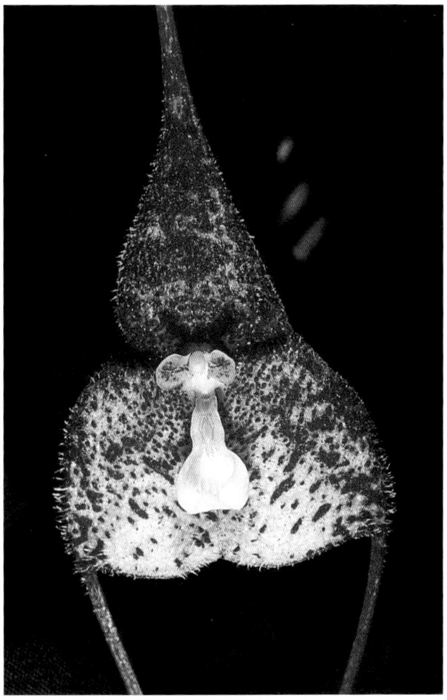

Dracula nycterina

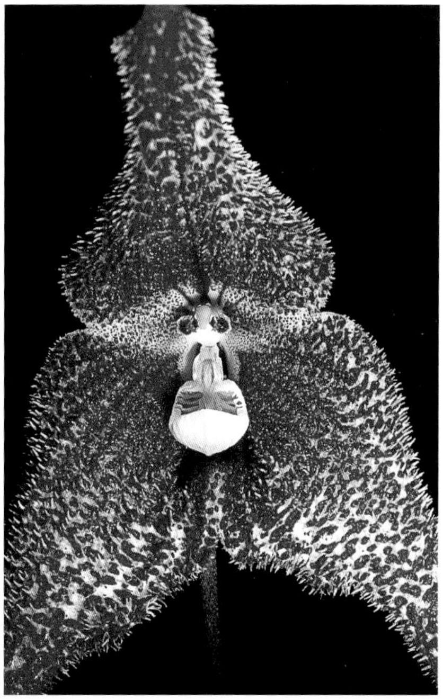

Dracula chimaera

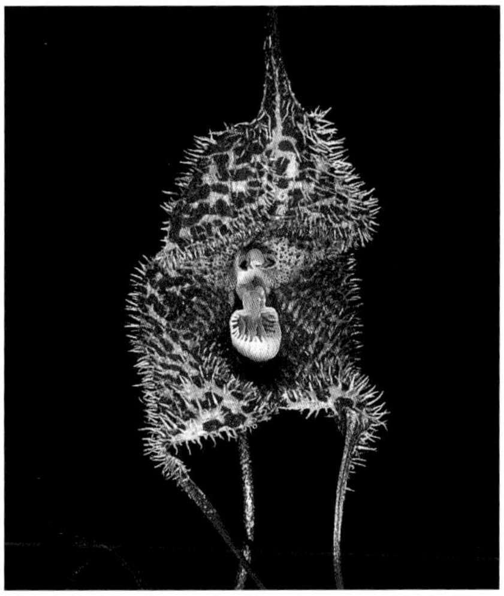

Dracula wallisii

Dracula cordobae

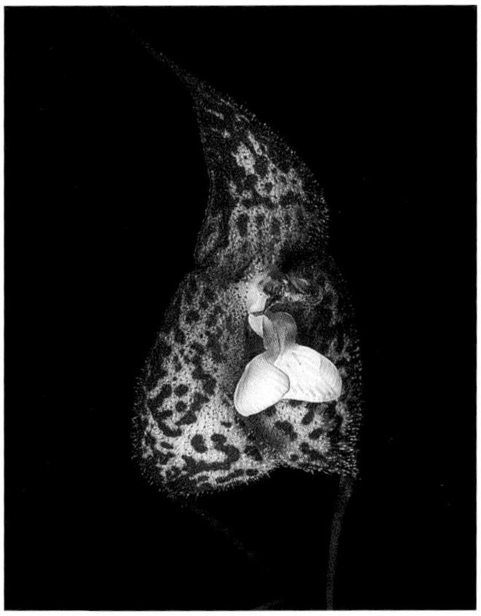

Dracula bella

Dracula gigas

Dracula gorgona (Veitch) Luer & R. Escobar
Relatively large plants. Inflorescence pendent, several-flowered. Flowers flat, greenish or yellowish white, flushed or dotted with brown or purple, hairy inside; sepals to 4 cm long with purple-brown tails 6–11 cm long; lip epichile pink or orange, transversely oblong, concave.

Epiphytic in cloud forest, 1800–2200 m (6000–7260 ft.)

Colombia

SIMILAR SPECIES: *Dracula gorgonella* Luer & R. Escobar is a rarer plant from Colombia with smaller flowers with shorter tails.

Dracula inaequalis (Reichenbach f.) Luer & R. Escobar
SYN. *Dracula carderi* (Reichenbach f.) Luer
Inflorescence pendent, few-flowered. Sepals to 25 mm long, forming a broadly cylindrical cup, white or cream with purple-brown spots and bands, tails yellowish with purple dots, to 3 cm long. Lip epichile white with pink dots, concave.

Epiphytic in cloud forest, 1000–1500 m (3300–5000 ft.)

Colombia

Dracula platycrater (Reichenbach f.) Luer
Inflorescence pendent, to 50 cm long, few-flowered. Flowers flat, white or greenish white with purple dots; sepals narrowly oblong, to 4 cm long, with short tails 1.5–3.5 cm long. Lip epichile pink, convex, deflexed.

Epiphytic in cloud forest, 1500–2000 m (5000–6600 ft.)

Colombia

Dracula robledorum (P. Ortiz) Luer
Inflorescence erect to horizontal, few-flowered, to 28 cm long. Flowers large, open, nodding, yellow, orange, or green with purple spots turning to lines at the base of the dorsal sepal; sepals to 33 mm long, tails red-brown, to 35 mm long; lip white flushed with pink.

Epiphytic in cloud forest, 2000–2200 m (6600–7260 ft.)

Colombia

Dracula simia (Luer) Luer
Inflorescence few-flowered. Flowers flat, reddish purple, white towards the base, hairy inside, thought to resemble a monkey's face; sepals 2 cm long with maroon tails 7 cm long; petals white with brown marks; lip white.

Epiphytic in cloud forest, 1550–2000 m (5100–6600 ft.)

Ecuador

Dracula sodiroi (Schlechter) Luer
Inflorescence erect, to 25 cm long, with 1–3 flowers open together—the only species of *Dracula* with an erect raceme with more than 1 flower open at a time. Flowers nodding, bell-shaped, orange; sepals 16 mm long, tails purple-brown, pointing down, 15–20 mm long.

Epiphytic in cloud forest or terrestrial on road embankments, 1800–2430 m (6000–8000 ft.)

Ecuador

Dracula vampira (Luer) Luer
Inflorescence horizontal or pendent, to 50 cm long, several-flowered. Flowers large, open, flat, greenish but densely covered with purple-black veins and flushed with purple-black, with a yellow blotch above the column; sepals 5–6 cm long with slender, blackish tails 5–11 cm long; lip concave, white with pink or yellow veins.

Epiphytic in cloud forest, 1800–2200 m (6000–7260 ft.)

Ecuador

Dracula velutina (Reichenbach f.) Luer
Inflorescence pendent, 1- to few-flowered. Flowers small, cup-shaped, white flushed with purple, densely hairy within; sepals 9 mm long, tails dark purple, 2–5 cm long.

Epiphytic in forest, ca. 1200 m (4000 ft.)

Colombia

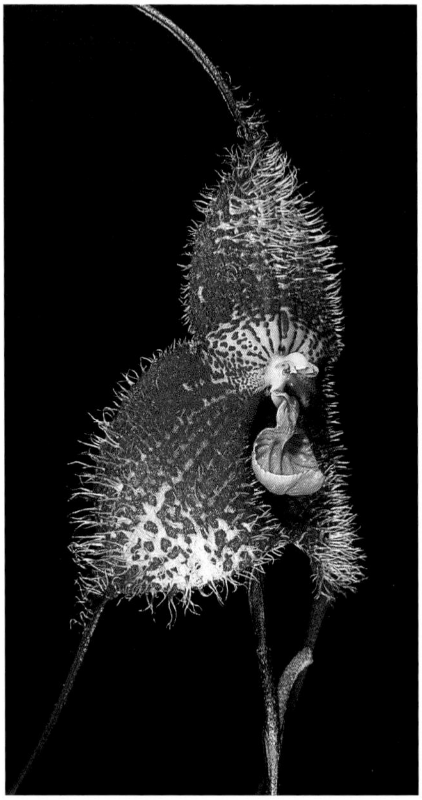

Dracula gorgona

Drakaea Lindley

HAMMER ORCHIDS

TRIBE: Diurideae

SUBTRIBE: Drakaeinae

ETYMOLOGY: Named for Sarah Anne Drake (1803–1857), the artist who illustrated many of John Lindley's works

DISTRIBUTION: About 4 species endemic in southwestern Australia

Deciduous terrestrials with underground tubers. Leaf single, basal, ovate or orbicular, fleshy. Inflorescences terminal, erect, 1-flowered. Flowers bizarre, resupinate; sepals and petals subsimilar, recurved; lip free, projecting, the claw hinged to the top of the column-foot, the blade unlobed, resembling an insect, with a variety of calli and clavate hairs. Pollinia 4.

Dracula inaequalis

Dracula platycrater

Dracula sodiroi

Dracula robledorum

Dracula simia

Dracula vampira

Pollination is carried out by male wasps trying to mate with the lip.
CULTIVATION: Plants are difficult to keep in cultivation. They are likely to do best in a very free-draining terrestrial mixture containing leaf mold, kept moist while actively growing from autumn to spring, and kept dry while dormant in summer. They seem to dislike high humidity.

Drakaea glyptodon Fitzgerald

Leaf ovate to heart-shaped, to 20 × 20 mm. Flowering stem wiry, to 30 cm tall. Flowers dull red, ca. 25 mm long; sepals and petals ca. 12 mm long; lip claw 5 mm long; lip blade ovoid, dark red, covered with bristly hairs.

Usually in sandy soil in coastal scrub but also in gravelly soil on hills

Southwestern Western Australia

SIMILAR SPECIES: *Drakaea livida* J. Drummond has straw-colored flowers ca. 35 mm long; blade of lip blackish red.

Dresslerella Luer

TRIBE: Epidendreae
SUBTRIBE: Pleurothallidinae
ETYMOLOGY: Named for American orchid taxonomist Robert Dressler, with the diminutive *-ella*
DISTRIBUTION: About 11 species in Central and South America

Small, tufted epiphytes, occasionally lithophytes, with erect or pendent stems, 1-leafed. Leaves petiolate, leathery, pubescent, elliptic to ovate. Flowers borne singly, often resting on leaf surface; sepals pubescent, dorsal sepal free, lateral sepals joined almost to the apex forming a concave synsepal; petals membranous; lip trilobed, clawed, hinged to the column-foot. Pollinia 4, in 2 unequal pairs.

CULTIVATION: Plants can be grown mounted or potted in a fine bark mixture. They require intermediate conditions, shade, good air movement, and high humidity. They should not be allowed to dry out for long but also must not be kept too wet, as they tend to rot.

Dresslerella pilosissima (Schlechter) Luer

Stem horizontal or suberect, 1–3 cm long. Leaves to 4 × 1.5 cm, fleshy, elliptic, papillose, densely covered on both sides with long, white hairs. Flowers hairy, greenish white, heavily striped with purple; sepals 10–11 mm long.

Epiphytic in very wet forest, 1000–1200 m (3300–4000 ft.)

Costa Rica

SIMILAR SPECIES: *Dresslerella hirsutissima* (C. Schweinfurth) Luer from Ecuador and Peru has spotted, not striped sepals and petals.

Dresslerella stellaris Luer & R. Escobar

One of the largest species. Stems 8–10 cm long. Leaves to 12 × 4 cm. Flowers large, fleshy, the sepals covered with stellate hairs; synsepal to 3 cm long, deep purple-red but not opening wide.

Epiphytic in rain forest, 1300–1800 m (4300–6000 ft.)

Costa Rica, Colombia

Dressleria Dodson

TRIBE: Cymbidieae
SUBTRIBE: Catasetinae
ETYMOLOGY: Named for American orchid taxonomist Robert Dressler
DISTRIBUTION: 10 species in Central America, Colombia, Ecuador, and Peru

Robust epiphytes with clustered, cylindrical to spindle-shaped pseudobulbs, covered in their first year by sheathing leaf bases which later become papery. Leaves plicate, up to 8 in 2 rows, usually remaining on plant for 2 to 3 years, unlike in other members of the Catasetinae. Inflorescences arising from basal nodes of pseudobulbs, erect, unbranched. Flowers fleshy, nonresupinate, bisexual; sepals similar, reflexed or spreading, narrowly lanceolate, apiculate; petals broader, also reflexed or spreading; lip entire, saccate, joined at base to the column, with or without a callus. Column short and stout, lacking a foot; pollinia 2.

CULTIVATION: Plants should be grown in clay pots or baskets in sphagnum moss, in intermediate conditions as for *Phalaenopsis*. They require light to moderate shade, good ventilation, and high humidity and unlike other Catasetinae, should not be allowed to dry out completely.

Dressleria dilecta (Reichenbach f.) Dodson

Pseudobulbs to 10 × 2.5 cm. Leaves persistent, to 40 × 7 cm. Inflorescence 20–25 cm long, 10- to 20-flowered, the flowers densely packed towards the apex. Flowers scented, ivory white, the lip yellow with red markings inside; sepals to 18 mm long; lip to 17 mm long.

Epiphytic in rain forest, 300–1200 m (1000–1400 ft.)

Costa Rica

Dressleria dodsoniana H. G. Hills

Pseudobulbs spindle-shaped, to 12 × 4 cm. Leaves 30–35 × 5–6 cm. Inflorescence arching, 25–35 cm long. Flowers fleshy, strongly scented, white to greenish white; sepals 23–26 mm long; lip 18–20 mm long, 12–14 mm wide; sac transverse, obscurely bilobed with an X-shaped opening.

Epiphytic in wet places

Colombia, Ecuador, Peru

Dressleria eburnea (Rolfe) Dodson

Pseudobulbs to 12 × 2.5 cm. Leaves 5 or 6, persistent, to 40 × 6 cm. Inflorescence 20–30 cm long, loosely several-flowered. Flowers ivory white, the lip orange-yellow with red dots inside; sepals to 26 mm long, lip to 20 mm long; sepals and petals reflexed, lying beside the ovary.

Epiphytic in rain forest, 500–1200 m (1650–4000 ft.)

Costa Rica, Nicaragua

SIMILAR SPECIES: *Dressleria allenii* H. G. Hills from Panama has smaller flowers with the sepals fully reflexed and the petals spreading.

Drakaea livida. R. Parsons

Dresslerella pilosissima

Dressleria allenii. G. Carr

Dresslerella hirsutissima

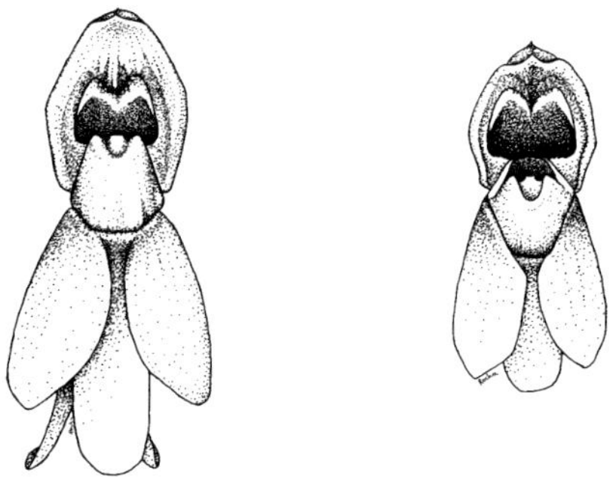

Dressleria eburnea

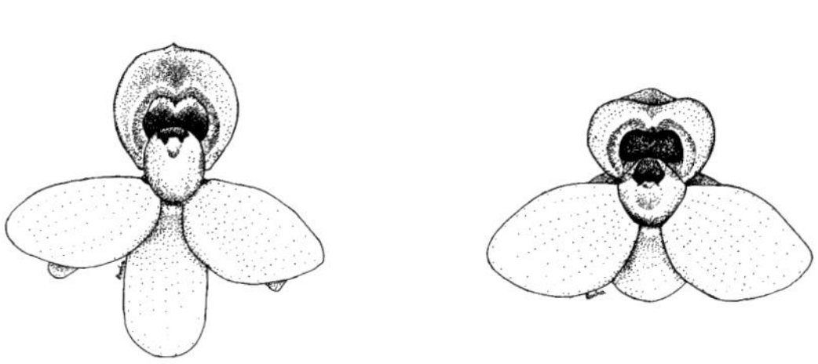

Dressleria allenii

Dryadella Luer

TRIBE: Epidendreae
SUBTRIBE: Pleurothallidinae
ETYMOLOGY: From Greek *dryas*, a wood nymph, and the diminutive suffix *-ella*
DISTRIBUTION: About 50 species from Mexico south through Central America to South America

Dwarf epiphytes or lithophytes forming clumps. Stems short, erect, unifoliate. Leaves leathery, petiolate, narrowly elliptic to obovate. Inflorescences 1- to several-flowered, the floral bracts overlapping. Flowers borne near the base of the plant, white, cream, greenish, or brownish, spotted and banded with maroon or purple, rather similar in most species; sepals fleshy, ovate or triangular, joined at the base and forming a cup, the lateral sepals with a transverse callus at the base; petals small, angled; lip hinged to the column-foot by a basal claw with 2 auricles, the blade usually oblong, obtuse. Pollinia 2.

Dryadella was split from *Masdevallia* by Carlyle Luer in 1978.

CULTIVATION: Plants are cool-growing and require high humidity, shade, and good ventilation. They are usually grown potted in fine bark or in a sphagnum/perlite mixture. They should not be allowed to dry out completely.

Dryadella aviceps (Reichenbach f.) Luer

SYN. *Dryadella obrieniana* Rolfe

One of the larger species. Leaves relatively broad, purple tinged. Flowers whitish or yellow-green with purple spots; sepal tails short.

Epiphytic in wet forest, 310–1500 m (1020–5000 ft.)

Brazil, Paraguay

Dryadella edwallii (Cogniaux) Luer

PARTRIDGE-IN-THE-GRASS

Leaves to 4.5 × 0.5 cm. Inflorescence ca. 2 cm long, few-flowered. Flowers relatively large, 25–30 mm across, yellow spotted and banded with dark red; sepal tails 1 cm long.

Epiphytic in wet forest, 350–1800 m (1150–6000 ft.)

Brazil

Dryadella lilliputiana (Cogniaux) Luer

Leaves 12–16 mm long, 2 mm wide. Flowers ca. 10 mm across; sepals cream, spotted dark red, tails yellow; lip yellow with red spots.

Epiphytic in wet forest, 700–1700 m (2300—5600 ft.)

Bolivia, Brazil

Dryadella simula (Reichenbach f.) Luer

Leaves linear, to 10 cm long. Inflorescence ca. 2 cm long, 1-flowered. Flowers fleshy, ca. 15 mm across, white or yellow, densely marked with deep purple.

Epiphytic in cloud forest, 2000–3100 m (6600–10,200 ft.)

Central and South America, Mexico

SIMILAR SPECIES: *Dryadella guatemalensis* (Schlechter) Luer, from Mexico, Guatemala, and Costa Rica, where it is epiphytic in very wet forest often at low altitudes of 50–1200 m (165–4000 ft.), has much longer and narrower leaves than *D. simula*.

Dryadella zebrina (Porsch) Luer

Leaves dark green, tinged with purple, ca. 5 cm long, 5 mm wide. Inflorescence ca. 1 cm long, 1-flowered. Flowers yellowish, densely spotted with purple.

Epiphytic in montane forest, 600–2550 m (2000–8400 ft.)

Bolivia, Brazil, Colombia, Peru

Dyakia E. A. Christenson

TRIBE: Vandeae
SUBTRIBE: Aeridinae
ETYMOLOGY: Named for the Dyak aboriginal people of Borneo
DISTRIBUTION: 1 species in Borneo

Small, short-stemmed monopodial epiphyte related to *Ascocentrum*. Leaves distichous, flat, obtusely bilobed at the apex. Inflorescence erect, unbranched, densely many-flowered. Sepals and petals subsimilar, spreading. Lip short, trilobed with very small side lobes, spurred, the spur with a large callus on the back wall. Column short; pollinia 2.

CULTIVATION: Plants can be mounted on bark or grown in small pots in humid, intermediate to warm conditions. They need good light and plenty of water while growing but should not be allowed to dry out completely even while resting.

Dyakia hendersonianum (Reichenbach f.) E. A. Christenson

SYN. *Saccolabium hendersonianum* Reichenbach f., *Ascocentrum hendersonianum* (Reichenbach f.) Schlechter

Leaves to 15 × 3 cm, light green. Inflorescence to 15 cm long. Flowers showy, scented, 10–25 mm across, bright pink to magenta with a white lip and spur; spur pendent, to 10 mm long.

Epiphytic in lowland forest

Borneo

Elleanthus Presl

TRIBE: Sobralieae
ETYMOLOGY: From Greek *elle*, Helen, and *anthos*, flower
DISTRIBUTION: About 100 species from Mexico through Central and South America and the West Indies, with most in the Andes

Epiphytes, sometimes lithophytes or terrestrials, with fleshy roots. Stems canelike, branched or unbranched, erect, leafy, usually in clumps. Leaves distichous, plicate or folded. Inflorescences terminal, unbranched, the flowers sometimes in a dense head; floral bracts conspicuous, often colored. Flowers usually brightly colored, often bell-shaped; sepals and petals free, subsimilar; lip saccate, enfolding column, with 2 oval basal

Dryadella lilliputiana

Dyakia hendersonianum

calli, the margins entire, ciliate or finely toothed. Column winged, lacking a foot; pollinia 8.

CULTIVATION: Probably because of their size, *Elleanthus* species are not widely cultivated. They should be grown like *Sobralia*, in large pots in a free-draining, coarse bark mixture with some added humus at intermediate temperatures in light shade. Keep them moist all year round.

Elleanthus aurantiacus (Lindley) Reichenbach f.

Stems to 3 m tall, often branched. Leaves to 17 × 3 cm. Inflorescence to 10 cm tall; floral bracts to 15 mm long. Flowers bright orange to yellow, ca. 12 mm long.

Epiphytic, lithophytic, or terrestrial on steep rocks in cloud forest and on roadside banks, 1200–2650 m (4000–8750 ft.)

Central America to Peru

Elleanthus aurantiacus

Dryadella zebrina

Elleanthus capitatus (Poeppig & Endlicher) Reichenbach f.

SYN. *Elleanthus cephalotus* Garay & H. R. Sweet

Stems to 1.5 m tall. Leaves to 23 × 7 cm. Inflorescence in a dense head 8–9 cm across, mucilaginous; bracts large, usually purplish. Flowers ca. 15 mm long, pink, petals paler than sepals.

Epiphytic in wet woodland, sometimes lithophytic or terrestrial, 900–1480 m (3000–4900 ft.)

Mexico, Central and South America, West Indies

Elythranthera (Endlicher) A. S. George

ENAMEL ORCHIDS

TRIBE: Diurideae

SUBTRIBE: Caladeniinae

ETYMOLOGY: From Greek *elytron*, cover, and *anthera*, anther

DISTRIBUTION: 2 species in southwestern Western Australia

Terrestrials with paired, globose tubers covered in a fibrous tunic. Leaf single, basal, lanceolate, glandular-hairy. Inflorescence erect, 1- to 3-flowered. Flowers showy, bright pink or purple, glossy; sepals and petals subsimilar, spreading, glandular on the outer side; lip unlobed, lacking a spur, much smaller than the sepals and petals, with 2 prominent basal calli.

CULTIVATION: Plants are not easy to grow and tend not to persist for long in cultivation. They are winter-growing and need to be carefully watered then and kept dry after the leaves die back. They require a free-draining, gritty terrestrial mixture; it is sometimes recommended that this should contain chopped *Eucalyptus* leaf litter.

Elythranthera brunonis (Endlicher) A. S. George

Leaf to 8 × 0.7 cm, dark green, purple-tinged at the base. Scape to 30 cm tall, wiry, glandular-hairy, 1- to 3-flowered. Flowers ca. 3 cm across, glossy purple, blotched with darker purple on the reverse; sepals and petals to 20 mm long; lip 5 mm long, linear, whitish, the tip recurved. Flowering spring.

Terrestrial in open woodland and heathland

Southwestern Western Australia

SIMILAR SPECIES: *Elythranthera emarginata* (Lindley) A. S. George is a slightly shorter plant with pink flowers and the lip folded in an S-bend at the tip. It tends to grow in wetter situations.

Embreea Dodson

TRIBE: Maxillarieae

SUBTRIBE: Stanhopeinae

ETYMOLOGY: Named for orchidologist Alvin Embree

DISTRIBUTION: 1 species in Colombia and Ecuador

Pseudobulbs 4-angled, 1-leafed at apex. Leaves gray-green, plicate. Inflorescence pendent, 1-flowered. Flowers large; sepals and petals spreading; lip complex, divided into a hypochile, mesochile, and epichile, the mesochile with T-shaped erect horns at the margins.

CULTIVATION: With the pendent inflorescences, plants must be grown in baskets like *Stanhopea*, in a coarse, free-draining bark-based mixture. They require intermediate temperatures, light to moderate shade, good ventilation, high humidity, and ample water throughout the year.

Embreea rodigasiana (Claes ex Cogniaux) Dodson

SYN. *Stanhopea rodigasiana* Claes ex Cogniaux

Pseudobulbs clustered, 4–6 × 3–4 cm. Leaf erect, to 50 × 10 cm, elliptic to oblong. Inflorescence 8–25 cm long. Flowers to 16 cm across, fleshy, short-lived, greenish white spotted with chestnut; lip grayish white spotted with red or chestnut.

Var. *herrenhusana* Jenny is confined to northwestern Colombia.

Epiphytic in wet submontane and cloud forest, 500–1500 m (1650–5000 ft.)

Colombia, Ecuador

Encyclia Hooker

TRIBE: Epidendreae

SUBTRIBE: Laeliinae

ETYMOLOGY: From Greek *enkyklo*, encircle, referring to how the lip side lobes clasp the column

DISTRIBUTION: About 120 species in Mexico, Central and South America, and the West Indies

Epiphytic, occasionally lithophytic or terrestrial, plants with round, ovoid, or spindle-shaped pseudobulbs, 1- to 3-leaved at apex. Inflorescences terminal, usually branched, 1- to many-flowered, without a spathe. Flowers resupinate, often scented; sepals and petals usually subsimilar; lip free or partly joined to the column at base, trilobed, side lobes usually clasping the column, midlobe with a callus usually of 2 ridges. Column winged, pollinia 4, equal in size. Capsule ± ellipsoid, sometimes warty.

Most species of *Encyclia* were originally described under *Epidendrum*, so there seems little point in giving these names as synonyms. Many species previously treated as *Encyclia*, and often well-known under that name, are now included in *Prosthechea*.

CULTIVATION: Encyclias grow in a range of habitats in the wild. Many species grow in hot, dry situations, while others grow in rain forest. Relatively few grow at high altitudes. Most species will grow in intermediate conditions, either potted in a standard epiphyte mixture, preferably in a rather small pot, or mounted on bark or a tree fern block. Most need only light shade and should be given a dry rest in winter.

Encyclia adenocaula (Lexarza) Schlechter

Pseudobulbs to 8 × 6 cm, 1- to 3-leaved. Leaves strap-shaped, to 35 × 3 cm. Inflorescence to 1 m tall, branched, many-flowered. Flowers 10 cm across, pink to mauve, sometimes streaked with red-purple; sepals and petals spreading; lip suborbicular.

Elythranthera brunonis. H. Oakeley

Encyclia adenocaula

Elythranthera emarginata. H. Oakeley

Embreea rodigasiana

Epiphytic in open rather dry forest, 1000–2000 m (3300–6600 ft.)
Mexico

Encyclia alata (Bateman) Schlechter

Pseudobulbs to 12 × 6 cm, 1- to 3-leaved. Leaves to 60 × 6 cm, linear, dark green. Inflorescence to 1.5 m long, usually branched, many-flowered. Flowers 5–6 cm across, strongly scented, pale yellow-green marked with purple and brown, lip white or yellowish, veined maroon. Column with an oblong incurved wing on either side of the apex.

Epiphytic in wet broad-leaved forest, 0–600 m (2000 ft.)
Mexico, Central America

Encyclia ambigua (Lindley) Schlechter

Pseudobulbs to 8 × 4 cm, 2- or 3-leaved. Leaves to 37 × 3 cm, narrowly strap-shaped. Inflorescence to 80 cm long, usually branched, several- to many-flowered. Flowers to 3.5 cm across, scented; sepals and petals cream to greenish yellow, lip cream to yellow, streaked and spotted with red along the veins.

Epiphytic in rather dry forest, 1500–2200 m (5000–7260 ft.)
Mexico, Central America

Encyclia cordigera (Kunth) Dressler

Pseudobulbs to 6 × 4 cm, 1- to 3-leaved. Leaves to 30 × 3 cm. Inflorescence to 60 cm long, usually unbranched, 3- to 20-flowered. Flowers to 7 cm across, scented; sepals and petals purple-brown or purple-green; lip cream to magenta with 3 purple lines at the base.

Epiphytic in moist broad-leaved forest, 0–500 m (1650 ft.)
Mexico, Central and South America

Encyclia guatemalensis (Klotzsch) Dressler

Pseudobulbs rounded, 4–5 cm tall, Leaves to 35 × 2 cm, narrowly strap-shaped. Inflorescence to 90 cm tall, branched or unbranched, many-flowered. Flowers 3–4 cm across, slightly scented; sepals and petals dark red-brown; lip with erect, greenish-yellow side lobes, midlobe purple-veined, margins yellow and undulate.

Epiphytic in open forest, 100–700 m (330–2300 ft.)
Mexico, Central America

Encyclia hanburyi (Lindley) Schlechter

Pseudobulbs to 8 × 4 cm, 1- or 2-leaved. Leaves to 23 × 3 cm, elliptic. Inflorescence to 1 m tall, sometimes branched, many-flowered. Flowers 5 cm across, purple-brown to yellow-brown streaked with purple; lip white to pink, veined with red-purple, midlobe suborbicular, margins undulate.

Lithophytic or terrestrial in dry forest, 1200–1800 m (4000–6000 ft.)
Guatemala, Mexico

Encyclia microbulbon (Hooker) Schlechter

Pseudobulbs to 4 × 2.5 cm, 1- or 2-leaved. Leaves to 12 × 1 cm, linear. Inflorescence to 45 cm long, sometimes branched, few- to many-flowered. Flowers 2–3 cm across, green with red-brown veining; lip white, sometimes with red spots.

Epiphytic in forest, 1400–2400 m (4600–7900 ft.)
Mexico

Encyclia selligera (Lindley) Schlechter

Pseudobulbs to 10 × 5 cm, 1- or 2-leaved. Leaves to 30 × 4 cm. Inflorescence to 1 m tall, usually branched, many-flowered. Flowers 3–4 cm across, scented; sepals and petals spreading, spathulate, dark purple-brown; lip white or pink, purple-veined.

Epiphytic and lithophytic in forest, 0–2200 m (7260 m)
Mexico, Guatemala, Bahamas

Encyclia tampensis (Lindley) Small

Pseudobulbs to 8 cm tall, 1- to 3-leaved. Leaves to 40 × 2 cm. Inflorescence to 80 cm tall, sometimes branched, few- to many-flowered. Flowers 4 cm across, scented, yellowish or greenish brown, often flushed with purple; lip white veined with purple and with a purple blotch on the midlobe.

Forma *albolabia* (A. D. Hawkes) Christenson has light green flowers with a pure white lip.

Epiphytic in moist forest at low altitudes
Bahamas, Florida

Epidendrum Linnaeus

TRIBE: Epidendreae
SUBTRIBE: Laeliinae
ETYMOLOGY: From Greek *epi-*, upon, and *dendron*, tree, referring to the epiphytic habit of most species
DISTRIBUTION: About 1500 species in America, from North Carolina south to northern Argentina

Epiphytic, lithophytic, or terrestrial plants. Stems usually canelike, sometimes thickened and spindle-shaped, rarely with pseudobulbs. Leaves distichous, sheathing at the base, flattened or terete, of various shapes. Inflorescences apical or lateral, rarely basal, branched or unbranched, 1- to many-flowered. Flowers small to large; sepals subequal, usually free, generally spreading or reflexed; petals often narrower than sepals; lip usually joined to the sides of the column along the length of the latter forming a nectar tube, the blade free, entire or trilobed, often complex. Pollinia 2 or 4.

Many species originally described as *Epidendrum* are now placed in other genera, such as *Encyclia* and *Prosthechea*, while others, such as *Oerstedella*, are now included in *Epidendrum*.

Epidendrum has been widely used in hybridization with other genera in the Laeliinae, such as *Cattleya* (giving

Encyclia cordigera

Encyclia microbulbon

Encyclia tampensis

Encyclia ambigua

Encyclia selligera

×*Epicattleya*), and many intrageneric hybrids also exist.

CULTIVATION: Epidendrums grow in a wide range of habitats and at altitudes from sea level to ca. 4000 m (13,200 ft.), so it is impossible to give cultural information that suits all. Most species are easily grown in intermediate conditions in light shade, either potted in a bark mix or mounted, but some require warm or cool conditions. The altitudes at which they grow provide a clue to the preferred temperature range. The species with reedlike stems, such as *Epidendrum radicans* and *E. ibaguense*, and the hybrid *E.* ×*obrienianum* (*E. ibaguense* × *E. secundum*), like warm, sunny situations and are widely grown in tropical and subtropical gardens.

Epidendrum amethystinum Reichenbach f.

Stems short, tufted, canelike. Inflorescence arching or pendent, densely several- to many-flowered. Flowers not opening wide, ca. 15 mm across, deep magenta to rose-mauve, lip paler than sepals and petals. Cool conditions.

Epiphytic at high altitudes

Ecuador

Epidendrum anceps Jacquin

Stems 30–60 cm tall, compressed, forming clumps. Leaves several, to 20 × 4 cm. Inflorescence terminal, to 50 cm long, flowers in a dense head. Flowers to 15 mm across; sepals and petals green-brown to chocolate; lip green tinged with pink.

Epiphytic in rain forest, ca. 100 m (330 ft.)

Mexico, Central and South America, West Indies

Epidendrum avicula Lindley

SYN. *Lanium avicula* (Lindley) Bentham

Rhizome creeping; stems short, pseudobulbous, ca. 3 cm long. Leaves to 3 × 1.5 cm. Inflorescence to 16 cm long, several- to many-flowered. Flowers 7–8 mm across, cream-yellow to yellow-green, densely hairy outside. With its creeping habit, this species should be mounted on a raft.

Epiphytic in very humid forest, to 1200 m (4000 ft.)

Brazil, Ecuador, Peru

Epidendrum centradenia (Reichenbach f.) Reichenbach f.

SYN. *Oerstedella centradenia* Reichenbach f.

Stems slender, canelike, to 40 cm tall. Leaves distichous, linear, to 6 × 0.5 cm. Inflorescence apical, usually unbranched, several- to many-flowered. Flowers bright magenta-pink, ca. 1 cm across; lip trilobed, the midlobe deeply bilobed.

Epiphytic in rain forest and cloud forest, 800–1800 m (2640–6000 ft.)

Mexico, Central America

Epidendrum ciliare Linnaeus

Pseudobulbs to 16 × 2 cm, 1- or 2-leaved. Leaves to 28 × 8 cm, oblong, leathery, glossy green. Inflorescence to 30 cm long, few to several-flowered; peduncle covered in large, purple-spotted sheaths. Flowers large, 8–15 cm across; sepals and petals greenish; lip white, deeply trilobed, midlobe linear, side lobes deeply fringed.

Epiphytic or lithophytic in rain forest and humid ravines, 700–1900 m (2300–6300 ft.)

Mexico, Central and South America, West Indies

SIMILAR SPECIES: *Epidendrum oerstedii* Reichenbach f. from Central America has slightly smaller flowers and the lip side lobes are not fringed.

Epidendrum cinnabarinum Salzmann

Stems canelike, leafy, to 1.3 m tall. Leaves oblong. Inflorescence terminal, branched or unbranched, few- to many-flowered, the flowers open in succession over a long period. Flowers to 6 cm across, bright red to orange; lip trilobed, the margins deeply cut. Warm sunny conditions.

Epiphytic, lithophytic, or terrestrial in open woodland, 50–850 m (165–2800 ft.)

Brazil, Venezuela

Epidendrum coriifolium Lindley

Stems 20–35 cm long, leafy towards the top, forming clumps. Leaves to 17 × 1.5 cm, stiff, semi-cylindrical. Inflorescence apical, few- to many-flowered. Flowers green or yellow-green, sometimes tinged with purple, with conspicuous fleshy bracts; sepals 12–20 mm long; lip entire, heart-shaped.

Epiphytic or lithophytic in rain forest, 900–1500 m (3000–5000 ft.)

Costa Rica, Mexico, Panama

Epidendrum coronatum Ruíz & Pavón

Stems 50–100 cm tall, leafy towards the top. Leaves to 17 × 4 cm. Inflorescence apical, arching or pendent, 7–20 cm long, few- to many-flowered. Flowers 3–4 cm across, ivory white to yellowish green; sepals and petals spreading; lip trilobed, side lobes large, rounded, midlobe bilobed at the apex.

Epiphytic, rarely lithophytic, in moist forest, 350–1300 m (1150–4300 ft.)

Mexico, Central and South America, Trinidad

Epidendrum cristatum Ruíz & Pavón

SYN. *Epidendrum raniferum* Lindley

A variable species, erect with reedlike stems to 1.3 m tall. Leaves deciduous, to 25 × 5 cm. Inflorescence terminal, to 30 cm long, several-flowered. Flowers usually scented, to 3 cm across; sepals and petals yellow or green, spotted with purple; lip mostly white, obscurely trilobed, with 2 basal calli and a central ridge, the side lobes toothed or fringed, midlobe bilobed at apex.

Epiphytic or terrestrial in rain forest, 200–600 m (660–2000 ft.)

Mexico, Central and South America, Trinidad

Epidendrum avicula

Epidendrum ciliare

Epidendrum centradenia

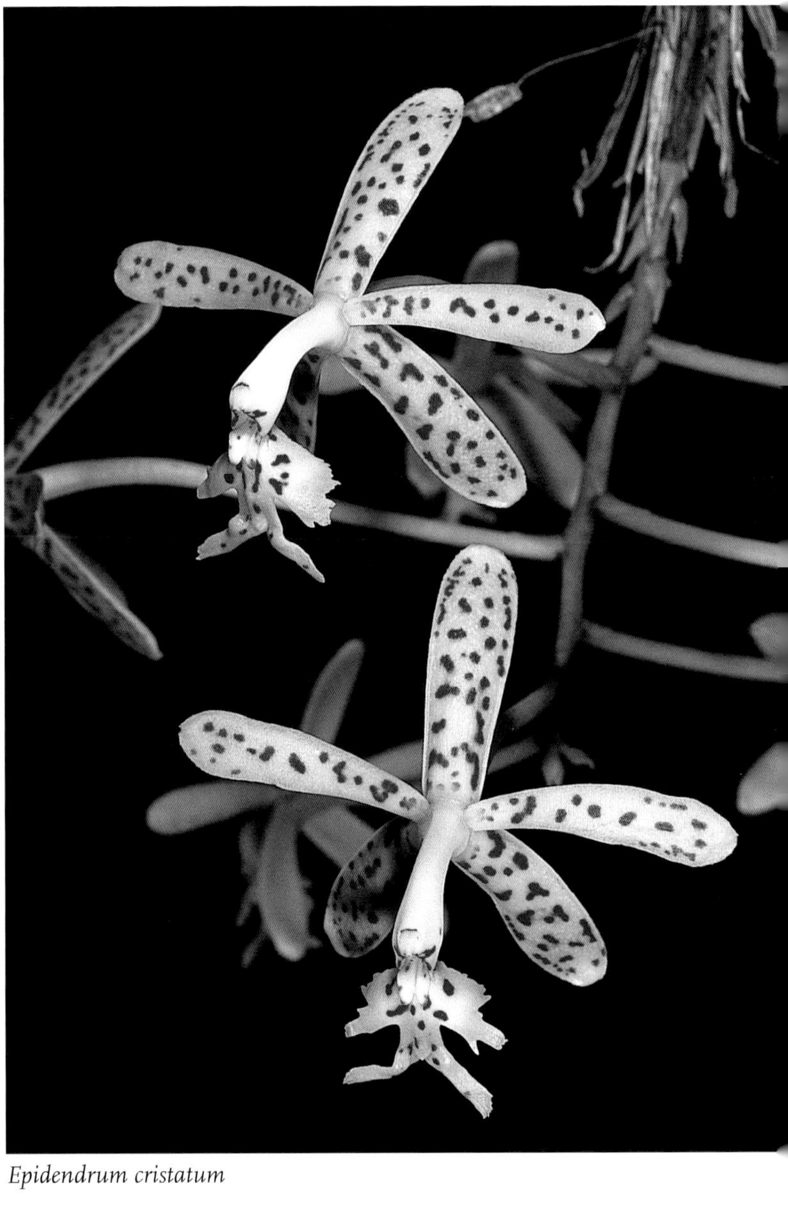
Epidendrum cristatum

Epidendrum difforme Jacquin

Stems erect or arching, canelike, to 40 cm long but often less. Leaves to 11 × 4 cm. Inflorescence terminal, umbel-like, few- to many-flowered. Flowers to 5 cm across, pale green, yellow-green, or white; lip kidney-shaped.

Plants under this name are probably a complex of several closely related species.

Epiphytic in open forest

Lesser Antilles

Epidendrum flexuosum G. Meyer

SYN. *Epidendrum imatophyllum* Lindley

Stems reedlike, to 1 m tall. Leaves light green, to 20 × 3 cm. Inflorescence terminal, to 25 cm long, sometimes branched, densely many-flowered. Flowers nonresupinate, 2–3 cm across, pink to purple; lip obscurely trilobed, the margins toothed or fringed.

Epiphytic in riverine forest and rain forest, 0–900 m (3000 ft.)

Mexico, Central and South America, Trinidad

Epidendrum gastropodium Reichenbach f.

A small species. Stems canelike. Leaves ovate. Flowers in a dense head, small, bright purple with an orange callus and a black column. Requires cool conditions, good air movement, and high humidity.

Epiphytic, rarely terrestrial, in cloud forest, 1500–3400 m (5000–11,200 ft.)

Colombia, Ecuador

Epidendrum ibaguense Kunth

Stems reedlike, slender, covered with sheaths, scrambling, to 2 m tall, branching and rooting at nodes. Leaves to 12 × 4 cm. Inflorescence terminal, erect, to 70 cm long, sometimes branched, many-flowered, the flowers open in succession several at a time over a long period. Flowers showy, 3–3.5 cm across, orange to bright red; lip deeply trilobed, side lobes rounded, irregularly toothed or fringed, midlobe bilobed at apex, the lobes fringed.

Terrestrial or lithophytic, occasionally epiphytic, in open scrub, 50–1500 m (165–5000 ft.)

Central and South America, Trinidad

SIMILAR SPECIES: *Epidendrum secundum* Jacquin has nonresupinate flowers and a complex callus of several tubercles. *Epidendrum xanthinum* Lindley from Colombia and Brazil has yellow flowers turning orange with age.

Epidendrum ilense Dodson

Stems slender, leafy, ca. 1 m tall. Inflorescence pendent, several-flowered, continuing throughout the year. Flowers ca. 5 cm across, showy, scented at night; sepals and petals green; lip large, white, very deeply fringed. This beautiful species comes from coastal areas and is severely endangered, perhaps extinct in the wild. It needs warm conditions with high humidity all year round.

Epiphytic or terrestrial in rain forest on coastal plains (most of which has now been cleared)

Ecuador

Epidendrum incomptum Reichenbach f.

Stems 30–70 cm tall, the new growths emerging from intermediate nodes on the previous year's stems, often rooting. Leaves 3–4 near apex, to 13 × 4 cm. Inflorescence apical, unbranched, arching, several-flowered. Flowers green, fleshy; sepals 11–16 mm long; lip trilobed, without a callus, midlobe longer than side lobes. This species needs cool conditions and is better mounted.

Epiphytic in rain forest, 1200–1800 m (4000–6000 ft.)

Costa Rica, Guyana, Mexico, Panama

Epidendrum lacustre Lindley

Stems 20–50 cm long, erect, leafy, laterally compressed. Leaves to 16 × 7 cm. Inflorescence apical, unbranched, 30–40 cm long, 4- to 10-flowered. Flowers 7–8 cm across; sepals and petals green, linear; lip white, trilobed, side lobes rounded, midlobe narrowly triangular.

Epiphytic or lithophytic in rain forest and cloud forest, 1200–1450 m (4000–4850 ft.)

Central and South America

Epidendrum laucheanum Bonhof ex Rolfe

Stems erect, unbranched, 20–30 cm tall. Leaves to 17 × 1.5 cm, linear-lanceolate. Inflorescence apical, unbranched, arching or pendent, 25–70 cm long, many-flowered. Flowers fleshy, long-lasting, ca. 2.5 cm across, sepals and petals yellow-brown, lip green, orange, or purple, concave with a thick central keel. Needs cool, humid conditions.

Epiphytic in rain forest and cloud forest, 1000–2100 m (3300–6900 ft.)

Mexico, Central and South America

Epidendrum longipetalum A. Richard & Galeotti

Stems short. Leaves 2–3, near apex. Inflorescence apical, unbranched, 50–75 cm long, the flowers open in succession over a long period. Flowers 4–5 cm long, green or bronze; petals long and slender; lip almost round, obscurely trilobed.

Epiphytic, sometimes lithophytic, in cloud forest, 1700–2600 m (5600–8600 ft.)

Mexico

Epidendrum macroclinium Hágsater

Stems cylindrical, 7–28 cm tall. Leaves to 11 × 1 cm, twisted at the base so that they lie in one plane parallel to the stem. Inflorescence apical, unbranched, several-flowered, the flowers open in succession over

Epidendrum difforme

Epidendrum lacustre

Epidendrum gastropodium

Epidendrum ilense

a long period. Flowers small, translucent yellowish pink; lip yellow, tinged with pink and red; anther-bed much longer than the rest of the column. Requires warm, humid, shady conditions.

Low-level epiphyte in tropical rain forest, 150–1000 m (500–3300 ft.)

Mexico, Central America

Epidendrum magnoliae Muhlenberg

SYN. *Epidendrum conopseum* R. Brown

GREEN-FLY ORCHID

Plants to 30 cm tall, forming large clumps. Leaves 2–3, to 10 × 1.5 cm. Inflorescence an apical raceme, loosely to about 20-flowered. Flowers to 25 mm across, scented, yellow-green sometimes purple-tinged; sepals and petals similar, spreading; lip trilobed. This is the only epiphytic orchid found in the United States outside Florida, growing as far north as North Carolina.

Epiphytic on large branches of evergreen and deciduous trees, to ca. 1500 m (5000 ft.)

Eastern United States, Mexico

Epidendrum marmoratum Reichenbach f.

Stems pseudobulbous, cigar-shaped, 2-leaved at apex. Leaves broad, leathery. Inflorescence terminal, arching, many-flowered. Flowers 3 cm across, mottled and striped white and maroon; lip broad with several longitudinal ridges.

Epiphytic in oak and pine forest, 1000–1500 m (3300–5000 ft.)

Mexico

Epidendrum nocturnum Jacquin

A widespread and variable species. Stems reedlike, to 1 m tall. Leaves leathery, to 11 × 4 cm. Inflorescence terminal, sometimes branched, 1- to few-flowered. Flowers large, scented; sepals and petals 80–90 mm long, narrowly linear, white to yellow-green, often tinged with purple; lip white, yellow at base, deeply trilobed, side lobes ovate, midlobe to 55 mm long, narrow, acuminate.

Epiphytic in rain forest and plantations, sometimes lithophytic or terrestrial, 0–1000 m (3300 ft.)

United States (Florida), Mexico, Central and South America

Epidendrum paniculatum Ruíz & Pavón

SYN. *Epidendrum floribundum* Kunth

Stems canelike, to 2 m tall. Leaves purple tinged, to 18 × 5 cm, deciduous. Inflorescence terminal, to 30 cm long, branched, several- to many-flowered. Flowers slightly scented, to 2.5 cm across; sepals and petals greenish white to purplish, sepals often reflexed, petals filiform; lip white blotched with purple, trilobed, side lobes rounded, midlobe bilobed.

Epiphytic or terrestrial in moist forest, to 2000 m (6600 ft.)

Central and South America

SIMILAR SPECIES: *Epidendrum veroscriptum* Hágsater from Mexico has lime-green sepals and petals and a white lip with the callus surrounded by maroon spots.

Epidendrum parkinsonianum Hooker

SYN. *Epidendrum pugioniforme* Regel

Stems short, 1-leafed, arising from a stout, creeping, sometimes branched rhizome. Leaves very fleshy, to 50 × 3 cm, curved, pendent. Inflorescence terminal, short, pendent, 2- to 5-flowered. Flowers large, showy, scented, to 15 cm across; sepals and petals linear-lanceolate, pale green or yellow-green; lip white with a yellow mark in throat, deeply trilobed, side lobes obliquely ovate, midlobe linear, to 55 mm long.

Epiphytic in rain forest and cloud forest, 1500–1600 m (5000–5300 ft.)

Mexico, Central America

SIMILAR SPECIES: *Epidendrum falcatum* Lindley from Mexico has pink-tinged flowers.

Epidendrum peperomia Reichenbach f.

SYN. *Epidendrum porpax* Reichenbach f.

Dwarf, creeping plant to 8 cm tall, forming mats. Leaves to 8 × 1 cm. Inflorescence terminal, 1-flowered. Flowers ca. 2.5 cm across; sepals and petals spreading, slender, pale green; lip orbicular, glossy red-brown.

Epiphytic in rain forest, 1300–1500 m (4300–5000 ft.)

Mexico, Central and South America

Epidendrum peraltum Schlechter

SYN. *Epidendrum altissimum* Lehmann & Kraenzlin

Stem reedlike. Inflorescence terminal, branched, to 12 cm long, several- to many-flowered. Flowers ca. 2.5 cm across, light purple.

Epiphytic in cloud forest, 1850–3100 m (6100–10,200 ft.)

Colombia, Ecuador

Epidendrum porphyreum Lindley

Stems slender, canelike. Leaves linear. Inflorescence terminal, several arising together, arching, densely several- to many-flowered. Flowers ca. 1 cm across, purple or magenta-purple with a white blotch on the lip. Lip trilobed, the midlobe bilobed.

Epiphytic in wet forest, sometimes lithophytic or terrestrial on embankments, 1800–3900 m (6000–12,870 ft.)

Colombia, Ecuador

Epidendrum pseudepidendrum (Reichenbach f.) Reichenbach f.

Stems canelike, unbranched, to 1 m tall or more, leafy in the upper half. Leaves to 20 × 6 cm. Inflorescence arising at or near the stem apices, arching, few-flowered. Flowers showy, 6–7 cm across; sepals and petals apple-green, spreading, narrowly oblanceolate; lip bright orange or reddish orange, suborbicular, convex, the margins fringed.

Epidendrum marmoratum

Epidendrum nocturnum

Epidendrum parkinsonianum

Epidendrum paniculatum

Epidendrum porphyreum

Epiphytic in wet woodland and rain forest, 200–1700 m (660–5600 ft.)
Costa Rica, Panama

Epidendrum purum Lindley

Stem erect, to 60 cm tall. Leaves to 20 × 1 cm, narrowly linear. Inflorescence terminal with spreading branches, many-flowered. Flowers rather bell-shaped, white or pale yellow-green, anther-cap pink; sepals ca. 1 cm long, lip deeply trilobed.

Epiphytic in forest, 500–2800 m (1650–9250 ft.)
Colombia, Ecuador, Peru, Venezuela

Epidendrum radicans Pavón ex Lindley

Stems straggling, 30–150 cm tall. Leaves numerous, to 9 × 2.5 cm. Inflorescence terminal, many-flowered, the flowers set close together and opening over a long period. Flowers ca. 2.5 cm across, yellow, orange, or red; sepals and petals spreading, lip trilobed, the margins fringed; column arched.

This widespread species is common in cultivation and has become naturalized in many parts of the world. It is easily grown in warm to intermediate conditions.

Terrestrial or lithophytic in rain forest and cloud forest, 400–1900 m (1320–6300 ft.)
Mexico, Central and South America, Caribbean

Epidendrum ramosum Jacquin

Stems branched, to 60 cm long, arising from a stout rhizome. Leaves numerous, to 9 × 1 cm. Inflorescence terminal, short, 3- to 6-flowered; floral bracts large, keeled. Flowers not opening wide, ca. 6 mm long, greenish yellow.

Epiphytic in rain forest and in exposed situations on mountain ridges, 450–1600 m (1500–5300 ft.)
Mexico, Central and South America, West Indies

Epidendrum rigidum Jacquin

Stems erect, to 25 cm long, from a creeping rhizome. Leaves several, strap-shaped, to 9 × 2.5 cm. Inflorescence terminal, unbranched, to 15 cm long, with several flowers set alternately. Flowers small, non-resupinate, scented, greenish, partly hidden by bracts. A common and widespread species.

Epiphytic in riverine forest and rain forest, 50–1500 m (165–5000 ft.)
Florida, Mexico, Central and South America

Epidendrum sophronitoides Lehmann & Kraenzlin

Dwarf plants forming clumps. Inflorescence arising from lower half of stem, the flowers produced 1 at a time in succession. Flowers large for size of plant, bronze-pink to red. Likes cool conditions with plenty of air movement and high humidity year-round.

Epiphytic in cloud forest, 1400–3300 m (4600–10,900 ft.)
Ecuador

Epidendrum stamfordianum Bateman

Pseudobulbs spindle-shaped, to 25 × 2 cm, covered in brownish sheaths, 2- to 4-leaved. Leaves to 24 × 6 cm. Inflorescence arising from base of newly mature pseudobulb, to 45 cm long, branched or unbranched, erect to arching, several- to many-flowered. Flowers ca. 4 cm across, scented; sepals and petals spreading, yellow-green to light bronze spotted with purple; lip white, sometimes pink-tinged, trilobed, the midlobe bilobed.

Epiphytic in dry woodland and rain forest, 100–1050 m (330–3500 ft.)
Mexico, Central and South America

Epigeneium Gagnepain

TRIBE: Dendrobieae
SUBTRIBE: Dendrobiinae
ETYMOLOGY: From Greek *epi*, upon, and *geneion*, chin, referring to the position of the lateral sepals and petals in relation to the column-foot
DISTRIBUTION: About 35 species occurring from India and Nepal across Asia to the Philippines.

Small to medium sympodial, epiphytic or lithophytic plants; pseudobulbs ovoid or conical, 2-leaved, well-spaced on a creeping rhizome. Inflorescence racemose, terminal on the pseudobulb, 1- to several-flowered. Flowers medium to large, often showy, white, greenish white, or bronze-pink, often striped or spotted with red; sepals and petals spreading, lip trilobed, motile.

CULTIVATION: With their creeping habit, species should be mounted on rafts of bark or tree fern or grown in shallow baskets in a medium bark compost. Plants need high humidity while in growth; they should be kept drier while resting but the pseudobulbs should not be allowed to shrivel.

Epigeneium amplum (Lindley) Summerhayes

SYN. *Dendrobium coelogyne* Reichenbach f., *Epigeneium coelogyne* (Reichenbach f.) Summerhayes

Pseudobulbs 4–7 cm long, 4-angled, set 5–12 cm apart on the rhizome. Leaves 10–15 × 3–5 cm. Inflorescence 1-flowered. Flowers 7–9 cm across, scented, waxy, cream to yellow, mottled with maroon, lip deep maroon-purple.

Epiphytic in broad-leaved forest or lithophytic on rocks, 1000–2000 m (3300–6600 ft.)
Bhutan, Nepal, northeastern India, Myanmar, Thailand

Epigeneium lyonii (Ames) Summerhayes

SYN. *Dendrobium lyonii* Ames

Pseudobulbs 6 cm long, 4-angled, with an apical tooth remaining after the leaves fall. Leaves to 15 × 4 cm, falling after 2 years. Inflorescence to 15-flowered. Flowers 8–12 cm across,

Epidendrum pseudepidendrum

Epidendrum purum

Epidendrum radicans

Epidendrum sophronitoides

Epidendrum stamfordianum

Epigeneium amplum

white, yellow or green, flushed with maroon, the lip dark purple-red.

Epiphytic and lithophytic at altitudes up to 1000 m (3300 ft.)

Philippines

SIMILAR SPECIES: *Epigeneium treacherianum* (Reichenbach f. ex Hooker f.) Summerhayes, also from the Philippines, may be synonymous with *E. lyonii,* in which case *E. treacherianum* would be the correct name.

Epigeneium triflorum (Blume) Summerhayes

SYN. *Dendrobium triflorum* (Blume) Lindley

Pseudobulbs 2–3 cm long, 4- or 5-angled. Leaves narrow, to 12 × 2 cm. Inflorescence to 6 cm long, several-flowered. Flowers 3 cm in diameter, yellow, lip deeper yellow, bordered with white and mottled with red. Rather variable; 3 varieties have been described.

Epiphytic in forest, usually on high branches, 1000–1800 m (3300–6000 ft.)

Java

Epipactis Zinn

TRIBE: Neottieae

ETYMOLOGY: From Greek *epipaktis*, a name used by the ancient Greeks for a medicinal plant

DISTRIBUTION: About 25 species in temperate areas of Europe, Asia, and

North America, with 3 species in tropical Africa.

Terrestrial plants with a creeping rhizome, fleshy roots, and erect, leafy stems. Leaves distichous or spirally arranged, usually pleated. Inflorescences terminal, unbranched, few- to many-flowered, often with prominent, leafy bracts. Flowers usually green, greenish purple, or red-purple; sepals and petals free, subsimilar, spreading or curving forwards; lip not spurred but saccate at the base, constricted in the middle, the apical part spreading, ridged.

CULTIVATION: Many species are frost hardy and can be grown in the open garden in temperate areas, where they may spread to form colonies. Nonhardy species can be grown in an alpine house, in pots in a standard terrestrial compost.

Epipactis gigantea Douglas ex Hooker

CHATTERBOX; STREAM ORCHID

Stem erect, 30–100 cm tall (seldom more than 50 cm in cultivation), leafy, the leaves grading into bracts. Leaves 5–20 × 2–7 cm, ovate or lanceolate, pleated. Inflorescence rather loosely 2- to 30-flowered. Flowers 3–5 cm across, sepals and petals spreading; sepals greenish, veined with purple, petals pinkish with purple veins; lip purple at base, the midlobe mainly yellow. Flowering summer.

This species naturalizes well in gardens.

Damp areas

Western United States

SIMILAR SPECIES: *Epipactis royleana* Lindley from Afghanistan, Bhutan, China, India, and Pakistan has smaller, more pink-tinged flowers. *Epipactis veratrifolia* Boissier & Hohenacker from southeastern Europe, Arabia, Ethiopia, and Asia has greenish-yellow flowers tinged with purple, 1.5–3.5 cm in diameter.

Epipactis helleborine (Linnaeus) Crantz

BROAD-LEAVED HELLEBORINE

Stem erect, 20–100 cm tall. Leaves 4–10, spirally arranged up the stem, to 15 × 10 cm, ovate. Inflorescence loosely or densely many-flowered, the flowers facing one way. Flowers rather small, greenish to dull purple. Flowering summer.

Woodland, usually at the edge, sometimes appearing in town gardens

Widespread in Europe, naturalized in parts of North America

Epipactis palustris (Linnaeus) Crantz

MARSH HELLEBORINE

Plants 15–60 cm tall. Leaves several, spirally arranged, to 15 × 4 cm, lanceolate. Inflorescence rather loosely 4- to 20-flowered, ± secund. Flowers ca. 2 cm across; sepals purplish brown, petals white, flushed with pink at base; lip white, the side lobes red-veined; the midlobe frilly-edged with a yellow callus at the base. Flowering summer–early autumn.

Damp grassland and marshes

Europe, Middle East, central Asia, Japan

Epipactis purpurata J. E. Smith

VIOLET HELLEBORINE

Plants 20–90 cm tall. Leaves 4–10, spirally arranged up the stem, to 10 × 3 cm, ovate, gray-green, purplish tinged. Inflorescence secund, pubescent, densely many-flowered. Sepals and petals greenish, often violet-tinged, the lip white or pale pink. Flowers late summer–early autumn.

Deciduous woodland at low altitudes

Northwestern and central Europe, reaching as far east as Siberia

Erasanthe P. J. Cribb, Hermans & D. L.Roberts

TRIBE: Vandeae

SUBTRIBE: Aerangidinae

ETYMOLOGY: An anagram of *Aeranthes*

DISTRIBUTION: 1 species, with 2 subspecies, in Madagascar

Monopodial epiphyte with stout roots. Leaves strap-shaped to oblanceolate, the margins often undulate. Inflorescence axis stout, several-flowered. Flowers large, green and white; sepals and petals lanceolate, acuminate; lip fringed, spur slender.

The genus *Erasanthe* was established in 2007 to accommodate *Aeranthes henrici*, which differs in many ways from other species of *Aeranthes*; recent DNA work has indicated that it is more closely related to *Beclardia*, *Cryptopus*, and *Oeonia* than to *Aeranthes*.

CULTIVATION: Like species of *Aeranthes*, *Erasanthe henrici* requires intermediate to warm temperatures, shade, high humidity, and good ventilation. Plants rot very readily in pots, so because of that and the long, pendent inflorescences, they are more successful when mounted. They can be difficult to flower in cultivation.

Erasanthe henrici (Schlechter) P.J.Cribb, Hermans & D. L. Roberts

SYN. *Aeranthes henrici* Schlechter

Large plants with stem to 15 cm long, but usually less. Leaves several, to 25 × 5 cm, strap-shaped or oblanceolate, often undulate, dark green. Inflorescences pendent, to 40 cm long, 5- or 6-flowered. Flowers white, the lip green; sepals lanceolate, long acuminate, to 11 cm long; petals to 9 cm long; lip to 10 cm long, fringed, the apex truncate with a filiform acumen at the tip, spur 16 cm long, very slender.

Two subspecies are recognized. Subsp. *isaloensis* H. Perrier ex P. J. Cribb, Hermans & D. L. Roberts has smaller flowers with a shorter acuminate apex, a shorter spur, shorter ovary and pedicel, and a longer column. It is a low-level epiphyte on small trees and shrubs in dry and wet forest, ca. 750 m (2460 ft.), on Isalo Massif and further west in southern

Epipactis gigantea. E. la Croix

Erasanthe henrici

Madagascar. Subsp. *henrici* is epiphytic in humid evergreen forest of north and northeastern Madagascar at elevations between 800 and 1000 m (2640–3300 t.).

Epiphyte in humid evergreen or dry and wet forest, 750–1000 m (2460–3300 ft.)

Madagascar

Eria Lindley

TRIBE: Podochileae

SUBTRIBE: Eriinae

ETYMOLOGY: From Greek *erion*, wool, referring to the woolly hairs on the flowers of many species

DISTRIBUTION: About 370 species in tropical and subtropical Asia to the Pacific Islands.

Epiphytes or lithophytes, rarely terrestrial, with a creeping rhizome; pseudobulbs cylindrical to ovoid, 2- to 4-leaved at apex, the base covered with loose leaf sheaths. Inflorescences terminal or axillary, erect or arching. Flowers usually opening wide, often cream or yellow, sometimes with purple markings, the sepals hairy on the outside; sepals and petals subsimilar, the lateral sepals forming a mentum with the column-foot; lip entire or trilobed, often with calli or ridges. Pollinia 8, in 2 groups of 4.

Several sections of *Eria*, for example, section *Bryobium*, have recently been elevated to genera in their own right.

CULTIVATION: Most species are easily grown in intermediate conditions with partial shade and high humidity. Plants that form clumps, such as *Eria coronaria*, can be grown in pots in a bark-based compost, but those

Epipactis veratrifolia

with long, creeping rhizomes are better mounted. Plants should be kept drier in winter, but the pseudobulbs should not be allowed to shrivel.

Eria coronaria (Lindley) Reichenbach f.

Pseudobulbs clustered, cylindrical, 5–18 cm tall, green turning gray and then blackish with age. Leaves 2, to 18 × 5 cm, broadly lanceolate. Inflorescence arising at apex of new pseudobulb, 4- to 7-flowered. Flowers to 25 mm across, waxy, white; lip trilobed, with purple markings, midlobe yellow with 5 ridges. This species likes cooler conditions than most in cultivation.

Epiphytic in hill forest or lithophytic on rocky banks, 300–2300 m (1000–7600 ft.)

Himalayas, Malaysia, Myanmar, Thailand

Eria floribunda Lindley

Pseudobulbs clustered, stemlike, to 35 × 1 cm. Leaves 2–5, to 25 × 2 cm. Inflorescences several, borne near apex of pseudobulb, arching, to 20 cm long, many-flowered. Flowers 6 mm across, white, usually tinged with pink; anther-cap maroon.

Epiphytic in lowland and montane forest, 200–2400 m (660–7900 ft.)

Borneo, Malaysia, Philippines, Sumatra

Eria javanica (Swartz) Blume

Pseudobulbs to 7 × 2 cm, narrowly ovoid, set well apart on rhizome. Leaves 2–5, to 30 × 8 cm, lanceolate. Inflorescence 20–35 cm long, densely many-flowered. Flowers 3–4 cm across, starry, scented, white or cream, sometimes marked with maroon; lip trilobed, the midlobe with 3–5 ridges, the central ridge yellow. With its long rhizome, this showy species should be mounted.

Epiphytic in swamp forest and submontane forest, occasionally terrestrial in humus-rich soil and on limestone screes, 0–2400 m (7900 ft.)

Northeastern India through Asia to the Pacific Islands

Eria ornata (Blume) Lindley

Pseudobulbs to 11 × 5 cm, rather flattened, set well apart on a long, stout rhizome. Leaves 3–4, to 20 × 3 cm. Inflorescence erect or arching, to 40 cm long, densely many-flowered, the peduncle covered with brown hairs, the floral bracts orange. Flowers 2–3 cm across, sepals and petals greenish brown, lip white with red or purple marks and margins.

Epiphytic in hill and submontane forest, 300–1500 m (1000–5000 ft.)

Widespread in Southeast Asia

Eria spicata (D. Don) Handel-Mazzetti

SYN. *Eria convallarioides* Lindley

Pseudobulbs clustered, to 16 cm long, 2- to 4-leaved. Leaves 5–22 × 1–4 cm, narrowly elliptical. Inflorescence 5–8 cm long, ovoid, densely many-flowered. Flowers small, white or straw yellow, with brown marks on lip. Flowering summer–autumn.

Epiphytic on trunks of old trees in forest, 330–2330 m (1100–7700 ft.)

China, Himalayas, Myanmar, Thailand

Eriopsis Lindley

TRIBE: Maxillarieae

SUBTRIBE: Eriopsidinae

ETYMOLOGY: From *Eria* and Greek *opsis*, like, meaning resembling *Eria*

DISTRIBUTION: 5 species in Central and South America

Medium-sized to large epiphytic, lithophytic, or terrestrial plants with conical or cylindrical pseudobulbs with sheathing bracts at the base, 2- or 3-leaved at apex. Leaves plicate. Inflorescences basal, erect or arching, unbranched, several- to many-flowered. Sepals and petals spreading, subsimilar, petals slightly narrower than sepals. Lip trilobed, shorter and broader than the other parts with crests or calli on the disc.

CULTIVATION: Grow plants in pots in a free-draining epiphyte mixture at intermediate temperatures, in moderate shade, and with plenty of water while in growth. Keep them drier while resting.

Eriopsis biloba Lindley

Pseudobulbs clustered, pear-shaped to cylindrical, 10–45 cm long. Leaves to 40 × 8 cm, lanceolate, dark green. Inflorescence to 1 m long, many-flowered. Flowers 3–4 cm across; sepals and petals yellow flushed with maroon at the margins; lip side lobes yellow with purple veins, midlobe emarginate, white spotted with purple.

Epiphytic in humid woodland or terrestrial or lithophytic on sandy soil or on rocks, 100–2300 m (330–7600 ft.)

Central and South America

Erycina Lindley

SYN. *Psygmorchis* Dodson & Dressler

TRIBE: Maxillarieae

SUBTRIBE: Oncidiinae

ETYMOLOGY: Named for the Aphrodite of Mount Eryx in Sicily

DISTRIBUTION: 7 species from Mexico to Central and South America and Trinidad

Small epiphytes with or without pseudobulbs; if present, 1- to 2-leaved at apex; if absent, the leaves bilaterally flattened and forming a fan. Inflorescences axillary, branched or unbranched, few to many-flowered. Flowers large for the size of plant; dorsal sepal forming hood over column, lateral sepals much smaller; petals similar to dorsal sepal; lip much larger than sepals and petals, trilobed, midlobe sometimes 2- to 4-lobed.

CULTIVATION: Many species are twig epiphytes and are short-lived. They are best grown mounted, in intermediate conditions, in shade with high humidity and should not be allowed to dry out.

Eria coronaria

Eria javanica

Eriopsis biloba. H. Oakeley

Erycina crista-galli (Reichenbach f.) N. H. Williams & M. W. Chase
SYN. *Oncidium crista-galli* Reichenbach f., *Psygmorchis crista-galli* (Reichenbach f.) Dodson, *Oncidium iridifolium* Lindley, *O. decipiens* Lindley
Pseudobulbs clustered, to 1.5 × 1 cm, covered by leafy bracts, with a rudimentary leaf at the apex. Inflorescence slender, short, to few-flowered. Flowers to 2 cm across, yellow-green, lip bright yellow with red-brown markings, to 2 cm long, 3- to 5-lobed, the midlobe 4-lobed.

Epiphytic in rain forest, 300–1200 m (1000–4000 ft)

Mexico to Peru

Erycina echinata (Kunth) Lindley
Pseudobulbs clustered, to 5 cm long, stalked at the base. Leaves several, to 10 cm long, 1 terminal, the others sheathing and distichous. Inflorescence unbranched, to 15 cm long, to 10-flowered. Flowers ca. 2 cm across, cup-shaped, yellow-green, the lip golden yellow; lip side lobes rounded, incurved, midlobe round to kidney-shaped, apiculate.

Epiphytic in tropical deciduous forest, 30–800 m (100–2640 ft.)

Mexico

SIMILAR SPECIES: *Erycina hyalinobulbon* (Lexarza) N. H. Williams & M. W. Chase (syn. *E. diaphana* (Reichenbach f.) Schlechter), also from Mexico, where it grows in pine forest at ca. 2000 m (6600 ft.), has a smaller lip with a squarish, emarginate midlobe and spreading side lobes.

Erycina pusilla (Linnaeus) N. H. Williams & M. W. Chase
SYN. *Psygmorchis pusilla* (Linnaeus) Dodson & Dressler
Leaves bilaterally flattened, forming a fan, 4–7 cm long. Inflorescence 1- to 6-flowered. Flowers ca. 15 mm across, 30 mm high, yellow, with red-brown markings towards the center; lip midlobe 4-lobed.

Twig epiphyte in forest and plantations, 0–800 m (2640 ft.)

Mexico, Central and South America, Trinidad

Esmeralda Reichenbach f.

TRIBE: Vandeae
SUBTRIBE: Aeridinae
ETYMOLOGY: From Greek *smaragdus*, emerald green, probably referring to either the beauty of the flowers or the rich green foliage
DISTRIBUTION: 2 species from the Himalayas and Southeast Asia
Large, scrambling and scandent species related to *Vanda*. Leaves leathery, strap-shaped, in 2 rows, twisted at the base to face one way. Inflorescences unbranched, axillary. Flowers showy, yellow marked with brown; sepals and petals subsimilar, spreading; lip mobile, trilobed, saccate at base but with no spur.
CULTIVATION: Warm-growing plants that should be grown in heavy pots or in baskets in a coarse bark-based compost, with canes or wires to support the long stems. These plants need plenty of water and, in a glasshouse in temperate regions, as much light as possible.

Esmeralda cathcartii (Lindley) Reichenbach f.
Stems usually pendent, 100–200 cm long. Leaves to 20 × 5 cm, oblong. Inflorescence to 35 cm long, 3- to 6-flowered. Flowers fleshy, 6–9 cm across; sepals and petals spreading, almost round, the outside white, the inside yellow with dense, horizontal brown stripes; lip white in center with 2 or 3 red stripes and a broad yellow margin. Flowering spring–summer.

Epiphytic in shade in tropical broad-leaved forest, 660–2000 m (2170–6600 ft.)

Bhutan, northeastern India, Sikkim

Esmeralda clarkei Reichenbach f.
SYN. *Esmeralda bella* Reichenbach f.
Plants 20–100 cm tall. Leaves to 23 × 3.5 cm. Inflorescence erect, 3- to 4-flowered. Flowers 5–7.5 cm across, slightly scented; sepals and petals yellow with transverse streaks of reddish brown; lip midlobe kidney-shaped, reddish brown with 7–9 white keels.

Epiphytic on tree trunks in open woodland, 1700–1800 m (5600–6000 ft.)

China, Himalayas, northeastern India, Myanmar

Euanthe Schlechter

TRIBE: Vandeae
SUBTRIBE: Aeridinae
ETYMOLOGY: From Greek *euanthes*, blooming, referring to the showy flowers
DISTRIBUTION: 1 species in the Philippines
Large, monopodial epiphyte with many aerial roots. Leaves in 2 rows. Inflorescence axillary, unbranched. Sepals and petals free, spreading, subsimilar but the petals slightly smaller. Lip much smaller than sepals and petals, in 2 parts, with a saccate hypochile and a deflexed epichile with 3 central ridges.

Euanthe sanderiana has been much used in hybridization; for registration purposes it is still known as *Vanda*. In particular, many ×*Ascocenda* (*Ascocentrum* × *Vanda*) hybrids have *E. sanderiana* in their ancestry.
CULTIVATION: Plants require intermediate to warm temperatures (minimum 15°C (59°F)), bright light, and plenty of water and fertilizer while growing, less in winter. They are usually potted in a coarse bark mixture but most of the roots are aerial, so humidity must be high.

Euanthe sanderiana (Reichenbach f.) Schlechter
SYN. *Esmeralda sanderiana* (Reichenbach f.) Reichenbach f., *Vanda sanderiana* Reichenbach f.
Erect plants to 1 m tall. Leaves strap-shaped, to 40 × 3 cm. Inflorescence erect, 7- to 10-flowered. Flowers showy, to 10 cm across; dorsal sepal and petals broadly elliptic, pink with brown spots towards the base; lateral sepals

Erycina crista-galli

Erycina pusilla

Esmeralda clarkei

tawny yellow, flushed and veined with red-brown; lip purple-brown.

Various alba forms are available in cultivation, with the dorsal sepal and petals white and the lateral sepals and lip greenish yellow.

Epiphytic in woodland, 0–500 m (1650 ft.)

Philippines (Mindanao)

Eulophia R. Brown ex Lindley

SYN. *Lissochilus* Lindley, *Cyrtopera* Lindley

TRIBE: Cymbidieae

SUBTRIBE: Cyrtopodiinae

ETYMOLOGY: From Greek *eu*, well, and *lophos*, plume, thought to refer to the crests on the lip

DISTRIBUTION: More than 200 species throughout the tropics and subtropics, with most in Africa

Terrestrial plants with pseudobulbs, tubers, or fleshy roots. Leaves usually deciduous, appearing with or after the flowers, linear to lanceolate, pleated or fleshy. Inflorescences arising beside leafy growth, usually unbranched. Flowers sometimes showy; sepals and petals similar or dissimilar; lip almost always spurred, usually trilobed but occasionally entire, often with lamellae or papillae inside. Column long or short, sometimes winged; anther terminal with an anther-cap; pollinia 2.

CULTIVATION: Only a few species of this large genus are in general cultivation, but with increasing interest in tropical terrestrials, more may become available. The easiest species to grow are those with aboveground pseudobulbs such as *Eulophia guineensis* and *E. streptopetala*. Most species will grow in a compost of fine bark, loam, sharp sand, or fine gravel and perlag or coarse perlite. When dormant, they should be kept dry, with only an occasional sprinkling of water to stop the tubers shriveling. When new growth appears, careful watering can begin, and when plants are growing vigorously, plenty of water and fertilizer can be given. Intermediate temperatures and good light suit most species; good air movement is essential as the leaves easily develop black patches and may rot.

Eulophia alta (Linnaeus) Fawcett & Rendle

Robust plants with fleshy corms to 8 cm long. Leaves 4–6, to 120 × 10 cm, lanceolate, plicate, appearing with the flowers. Inflorescence 1–2 m tall, loosely many-flowered. Sepals green, petals and lip reddish purple, sepals 18–22 mm long, petals shorter and broader; lip to 20 × 12 mm, saccate at the base, trilobed; side lobes erect, midlobe ± round with 2–5 papillose crests, the edges undulate. This is one of the most widespread species in the genus.

Swamps and wet grassland, 15–1300 m (50–4300 ft.)

Tropical Africa, United States, Caribbean, Mexico, South America

Eulophia andamanensis Reichenbach f.

SYN. *Eulophia keithii* Ridley

Pseudobulbs conical, to 7 cm long. Leaves several, to 18 × 1.5 cm, linear. Inflorescence 20–35 cm long, 10- to 15-flowered. Flowers ca. 18 mm across; sepals and petals greenish brown, lip white veined with brown, the margins green.

Grassland or waste land

Indochina to Sumatra

Eulophia cucullata (Swartz) Steudel

Plants with a chain of white, knobby, underground tubers. Leaves to 70 × 1.5 cm, linear, plicate, just starting to develop at flowering time. Inflorescence to 1 m tall, rather loosely 2- to 9-flowered. Flowers large and showy, sepals greenish purple, petals and lip pale pink to deep purple-pink; sepals reflexed, to 30 mm long, petals to 25 × 25 mm, ovate to orbicular, lying over the column; lip 30 × 40 mm, with 2 projections in throat, the base saccate.

Woodland, rough grassland, 200–2300 m (660–7600 ft.)

Throughout tropical Africa, South Africa

Eulophia euglossa (Reichenbach f.) Reichenbach f.

Pseudobulbs to 25 × 1.5 cm, narrowly conical, above ground. Leaves several, 20–40 × 2–6 cm, ovate or lanceolate, pleated. Inflorescence 60–150 cm tall, laxly many-flowered. Flowers nodding, greenish, the lip white with purplish marks; sepals and petals subsimilar, sepals to 24 × 3 mm, petals shorter; lip trilobed, to 14 mm long, spur 5–7 mm long, club-shaped, decurved.

This species requires more shade than most *Eulophia* species.

Evergreen forest, 1200–1300 m (4000–4300 ft.)

West and Central Africa

Eulophia graminea Lindley

Pseudobulbs mostly subterranean, to 15 cm long. Leaves 3–5, to 35 × 1.5 cm, linear, appearing after the flowers. Inflorescence to 80 cm tall, usually with 1 or 2 branches, loosely many-flowered. Flowers ca. 3 cm across; sepals and petals olive green sometimes tinged with red; lip white, trilobed, midlobe ovate, the center covered with purple lamellae or papillae; spur 2–3 mm long.

Grassland and waste land, open woodland, 900–1200 m (3000–4000 ft.)

Widespread in tropical Asia

Eulophia guineensis Lindley

SYN. *Eulophia guineensis* var. *purpurata* Reichenbach f. ex Kotschy, *E. quartiniana* A. Richard

Pseudobulbs 3 × 2 cm, conical, above ground. Leaves 3 or 4, to 35 × 10 cm, ovate, pleated. Inflorescence 30–65 cm tall, rather loosely several-flowered. Flowers large, showy; sepals and petals similar, purple or

Euanthe sanderiana

Eulophia graminea. H. Oakeley

Eulophia cucullata. E. la Croix

Eulophia guineensis

greenish, erect, to 30 × 7 mm; lip trilobed near the base, purple-pink with a magenta blotch in the throat, to 35 × 32 mm, midlobe ± orbicular, the edge undulate; spur 10–25 mm long, tapering from a wide mouth, straight.

Scrub and woodland, in shade of rocks, occasionally in forest, 600–2000 m (2000–6600 ft.)

Widespread in tropical Africa, Arabia

Eulophia petersii (Reichenbach f.) Reichenbach f.

Pseudobulbs 6–30 × 2–5 cm, ovoid to cylindrical, above ground. Leaves 2 or 3, to 80 × 6 cm, evergreen, stiff, succulent, gray-green, the margins finely toothed. Inflorescence 1–3 m tall, branched, loosely many-flowered. Flowers green tinged with purple-brown, lip white with purple crests; sepals to 30 × 6 mm, erect, the tips curling back; petals shorter and broader, lying over the column; lip to 27 mm long, trilobed, the midlobe with 3 lamellae; spur cylindrical, 4–6 mm long.

In cultivation, this species requires a sandy, very free-draining soil and must be kept dry in the resting period. It will grow at intermediate temperatures but is better in warm.

Sandy soil in thicket, usually among rocks, in hot, dry areas, 0–1800 m (6000 ft.)

East Africa from Eritrea to South Africa, Arabia

SIMILAR SPECIES: *Eulophia taitensis* Cribb & Pfennig from Kenya is a smaller plant that grows in similar situations.

Eulophia pulchra (Thouars) Lindley

SYN. *Oeceoclades pulchra* (Thouars) P. J. Cribb & M. A. Clements

Pseudobulbs 10–14 × 1 cm, cylindrical, above ground. Leaves several, 30–80 × 1–9 cm, lanceolate, plicate, with a long petiole. Inflorescence 60–70 cm tall, densely many-flowered. Flowers yellow or pale green; sepals 12–15 × 3 mm, petals shorter and broader; lip 7 × 15 mm, trilobed, with an orange, bilobed callus in the throat; midlobe transversely oblong, emarginate; spur globose, 3–4 mm long.

In deep shade in submontane and riverine forest, 700–1400 m (2300–4600 ft.)

Madagascar, Mascarene Islands, Mozambique, Tanzania, Zimbabwe, Australia, western Pacific

Eulophia speciosa (R. Brown ex Lindley)

Plants with a chain of underground tubers. Leaves to 50 × 2 cm, fleshy, stiff, developing after flowering. Inflorescence 1–1.5 m tall, loosely many-flowered. Sepals green, reflexed; petals bright yellow, to 20 × 22 mm, spreading, orbicular. Lip trilobed, to 25 mm long, with some red lines spreading from mouth of spur; spur conical, to 8 mm long.

Usually rough grassland or open woodland, to 2000 m (6600 ft.)

Widespread in eastern and central tropical Africa, South Africa, Arabia

Eulophia spectabilis (Dennstaedt) Suresh

SYN. *Eulophia nuda* Lindley, *E. squalida* Lindley

Pseudobulbs subterranean, 3–4 cm diameter. Leaves to 50 × 5 cm, pleated, narrowly lanceolate. Inflorescence to 1 m tall, 10- to 25-flowered. Flowers not opening wide, 2–3 cm across, sepals ca. 20 mm long, scarlet, yellow, or reddish green with white petals; spur conical, 4–5 mm long.

Forest or grassland, 0–1500 m (5000 ft.)

China, tropical Asia, Pacific Islands

Eulophia streptopetala Lindley

Pseudobulbs to 10 × 3 cm, conical to ovoid, above ground. Leaves several, to 50 × 8 cm, lanceolate, plicate. Inflorescence to 1.5 m tall, laxly many-flowered. Sepals green blotched with purple-brown, to 18 × 9 mm, spreading or reflexed; petals bright yellow outside, pale inside, 18 × 20 mm, ± orbicular. Lip trilobed, to 20 mm long, with 3–5 fleshy ridges; spur conical, 2–4 mm long.

Var. *stenophylla* (Summerhayes) P. J. Cribb (syn. *Eulophia stenophylla* Summerhayes), from Kenya and Uganda, has narrower leaves and smaller flowers lacking the ridges on the lip.

Woodland, rough grassland, 1100–2550 m (3600–8400 ft.)

Widespread in eastern and central tropical Africa, South Africa, Arabia

Eulophiella Rolfe

TRIBE: Cymbidieae
SUBTRIBE: Cyrtopodiinae
ETYMOLOGY: Diminutive of *Eulophia*
DISTRIBUTION: 5 species in Madagascar

Large epiphytes, rarely terrestrials, with big pseudobulbs borne on a creeping rhizome. Leaves several, plicate, thin-textured. Inflorescences basal, unbranched, many-flowered. Flowers large; sepals and petals free, subsimilar, the lateral sepals joined to

Eulophia pulchra

Eulophia speciosa. E. la Croix

Eulophia streptopetala. E. la Croix

the column-foot to form a short mentum; lip trilobed, not spurred, with crests or lamellae inside. Column arched, slender; rostellum trilobed.

A hybrid between *Eulophiella elisabethae* and *E. roempleriana* is known as *E.* ×*rolfei*.

CULTIVATION: Species of *Eulophiella* do best in baskets or large pans in a coarse bark mix, in intermediate to warm conditions, with high humidity and moderate shade. Plants need plenty of water while growing but should be kept almost dry while resting.

Eulophiella elisabethae Linden & Rolfe

SYN. *Eulophiella perrieri* Schlechter

Pseudobulbs to 15 × 2.5 cm, ovoid, 4- or 5-leaved. Leaves 45–60 × 3–5 cm, narrowly lanceolate. Inflorescence arching, to 90 cm long, several- to many-flowered. Flowers showy, 4 cm across; sepals and petals white or pale pink inside, purple-pink outside; lip white with a yellow callus, side lobes rounded, midlobe broadly obovate, emarginate.

Epiphytic on the palm *Dypsis fibrosa* in coastal forest

Madagascar

Eulophiella roempleriana

(Reichenbach f.) Schlechter

SYN. *Eulophiella peetersiana* Kraenzlin

Rhizome to 6 cm diameter, pseudobulbs to 30 × 4 cm, set 10–30 cm apart. Leaves to 120 × 10 cm. Inflorescence erect, to 120 cm tall, several- to many-flowered. Flowers pink, sepals and petals 35–45 mm long, lip 40–45 mm long and wide with 3 lamellae towards base, midlobe emarginate.

Epiphytic in coastal and mid-altitude forest, 0–1000 m (3300 ft.)

Madagascar

Eurychone Schlechter

TRIBE: Vandeae

SUBTRIBE: Aerangidinae

ETYMOLOGY: From Greek *eury*, broad, and *chone*, funnel, referring to the shape of the spur

DISTRIBUTION: 2 species in West and Central Africa

Monopodial epiphytes with short stems. Leaves several. Inflorescences pendent, flowers large, scented; sepals and petals subsimilar, free; lip broadly funnel-shaped, obscurely trilobed, gradually tapering into a spur. Column short and stout.

The 2 species of *Eurychone* are among the most beautiful of African orchids. An intrageneric hybrid exists, *Eurychone* Virginie Moulin, which is intermediate between the parents, and *E. rothschildiana* has been crossed with several species of *Aerangis* and *Angraecum*.

CULTIVATION: Because of the pendent inflorescences, both species are better mounted rather than grown in pots. They require intermediate to warm temperatures—warm is better—fairly heavy shade, and high humidity throughout the year. As always, ventilation should be good.

Eurychone galeandrae

(Reichenbach f.) Schlechter

Leaves 6–20 × 1–2 cm, strap-shaped or narrowly oblanceolate, bilobed at the tips, dark olive green. Inflorescence to 15 cm long, 3- to 12-flowered. Flowers translucent salmon-pink, the spur with darker veins; sepals and petals to 18 × 5 mm, lanceolate, acute; lip to 25 mm long, funnel-shaped, tapering into a spur 25 mm long, the last 10 mm much narrower, the apical 5 mm reflexed and inflated at the tip.

Epiphytic in forest and woodland

Angola, Central African Republic, DR Congo, Gabon, Ivory Coast

Eurychone rothschildiana

(O'Brien) Schlechter

Leaves to 20 × 7 cm, broadly ovate or obovate, bilobed at the apex, the edges undulate, dark green. Inflorescence pendent, to 10 cm long, few- to several-flowered. Flowers white, lip white with a green band inside and below that a purple blotch; sepals and petals to 25 × 7 mm, lip to 27 × 25 mm, very concave, the edge undulate, tapering to a conical spur 15–25 mm long, narrowed in the middle then the apex swollen and recurved.

Epiphytic usually at a low level in forest and thicket, 300–1200 m (1000–4000 ft.)

West and Central Africa

Eurychone rothschildiana. E. la Croix

Fernandezia Ruíz & Pavón

SYN. *Centropetalum* Lindley, *Nasonia* Lindley

TRIBE: Maxillarieae

SUBTRIBE: Oncidiinae

ETYMOLOGY: Named for Spanish botanist Gregorio García Fernández

DISTRIBUTION: 10 species in Costa Rica, Colombia, Ecuador, Peru, and Venezuela

Dwarf epiphytes lacking pseudobulbs. Leaves distichous, dark green. Inflorescences axillary, unbranched, short, few-flowered. Flowers small, but large for the size of plant, brightly colored—red, orange, pink, or yellow; sepals and petals similar, lip much larger, concave at base. Column short with small wings; pollinia 2.

CULTIVATION: These small plants grow at high altitudes, usually in cloud forest. Although attractive, they are not widely cultivated. They require cool conditions, with day temperatures not rising above 24°C (75°F), and with high humidity all year round. They can be grown potted in a fine epiphyte compost or mounted with a pad of moss.

Fernandezia ionanthera

(Reichenbach f. & Warszewicz) Schlechter

Flowers ca. 2 cm long, bright scarlet with a violet column.

Epiphytic or lithophytic in cloud forest, 2800–3150 m (9250–10,400 ft.)

Ecuador, Peru

Fernandezia subbiflora Ruíz & Pavón

Stem erect, sometimes branched at base. Inflorescence 1- or 2-flowered. Flowers ca. 3 cm long, bright scarlet, with a yellow band on the column.

Epiphytic in cloud forest, 2100–3100 m (6900–10,200 ft.)

Ecuador, Peru

Fernandezia tica D. E. Mora & J. B. Garcia

Slender plants 4–8 cm tall. Leaves distichous, ca. 2 × 0.8 cm, succulent, reddish green. Inflorescence 2- or 3-

Eulophiella roempleriana. H. Oakeley

Fernandezia ionanthera

Eurychone galeandrae. E. la Croix

Fernandezia subbiflora

flowered. Flowers bell-shaped, ca. 10 mm long, bright purple-red.

Epiphytic in oak woodland, 1700–2000 m (5600–6600 ft.)

Costa Rica

Flickingeria A. D. Hawkes

SYN. *Desmotrichum* Blume, *Ephemerantha* P. F. Hunt & Summerhayes

TRIBE: Dendrobieae

SUBTRIBE: Dendrobiinae

ETYMOLOGY: Named for Edward A. Flickinger, a friend of A. D. Hawkes

DISTRIBUTION: About 75 species in tropical Asia and Australasia

Epiphytes with a creeping rhizome or with branched aerial stems ending in a pseudobulb of 1 node, 1-leafed at apex. The aerial stems lack roots and the pseudobulbs and leaves become smaller the further away they are from the root system. Inflorescences arising from papery bracts around the leaf base. Flowers single or clustered, lasting for less than a day; lateral sepals joined to column-foot forming a mentum; petals smaller than sepals; lip trilobed with 2 or 3 keels, side lobes erect, midlobe of various shapes, usually fringed with hairs. Pollinia 4.

CULTIVATION: Some species are stimulated to flower by a sudden drop of temperature. Most species require intermediate to warm temperatures, bright light, and high humidity. They are usually grown mounted on a slab.

Flickingeria comata (Blume) A. D. Hawkes

SYN. *Dendrobium comatum* (Blume) Lindley

Stems to ca. 1 m long; pseudobulbs to 15 × 2.5 cm. Leaves to 12 × 8 cm. Flowers opening wide, 2.5 cm across, sepals and petals creamy white or pale yellow, sometimes with red spots; lip light purple, midlobe long and narrow, fringed with many hairs ca. 8 mm long near the apex.

Epiphytic or lithophytic in rain forest, to 600 m (2000 ft.)

Taiwan, Malesia, western Pacific, Australia

Flickingeria fimbriata (Blume) A. D. Hawkes

Stems usually pendent; pseudobulbs to 8 × 4 cm. Flowers scented, 3.5 cm across, sepals and petals recurved, pale yellow with red spots, lip cream, midlobe pleated and divided.

Epiphytic in forest, usually on limestone, 0–1000 m (3300 ft.)

Tropical Asia

Flickingeria xantholeuca (Reichenbach f.) A. D. Hawkes

SYN. *Dendrobium xantholeucum* Reichenbach f.

Stems branched, ca. 15 cm long; pseudobulbs to 5 × 1 cm. Flowers with sepals and petals curling back, 1.5 cm across when flattened, cream, lip apex yellow, bilobed, the lobes rounded.

Epiphytic in wet lowland forest, 0–1100 m (3600 ft.)

Borneo, Java, Malaysia, Thailand, Sumatra

Galeandra Lindley

TRIBE: Cymbidieae

SUBTRIBE: Cyrtopodiinae

ETYMOLOGY: From Greek *galea*, helmet, and *andra*, stamens, referring to the anther-cap of some species

DISTRIBUTION: Almost 40 species in Central and South America and Indochina

Epiphytes and terrestrials with short to long, spindle-shaped pseudobulbs covered with gray sheaths, or small, round ones if terrestrial. Leaves plicate, grasslike, distichous. Inflorescences terminal, branched or unbranched, erect or nodding, usually few-flowered. Flowers showy; sepals and petals free, subsimilar, erect or spreading; lip large, entire or obscurely trilobed, ± tubular, flared at the end and spurred at the base. Pollinia 4.

CULTIVATION: Plants should be potted in a free-draining bark mix, in intermediate conditions with moderate shade, and plenty of water while in growth. After flowering, they need a cooler, drier rest in a brighter position.

Galeandra batemanii Rolfe

Pseudobulbs to 25 cm long. Leaves to 30 × 2 cm. Inflorescence to 30 cm long, often branched, to 8-flowered. Flowers 4–5 cm long, sepals and petals yellowish brown, lip purple inside, white and yellow outside, brownish at the base; spur slender, curved, to 2.5 cm long.

Epiphytic in wet forest, sometimes on palms, ca. 700 m (2300 ft.)

Central America, Mexico

SIMILAR SPECIES: *Galeandra baueri* Lindley, from South America, has been confused with this species and is sometimes considered synonymous, but differs in the shape and color of the lip.

Galeandra beyrichii Reichenbach f.

Terrestrial with small, round underground pseudobulbs. Stems to 90 cm tall. Leaves reduced to sheaths. Raceme many-flowered. Flowers pale green or greenish white, the lip striped with purple.

Wet, open forest, 1100–1300 m (3600–4300 ft.)

Central and South America, West Indies

SIMILAR SPECIES: *Galeandra bicarinata* P. M. Brown has recently been described from Florida.

Galeandra lacustris Barbosa Rodrigues

Pseudobulbs to 13 cm long. Leaves to 14 cm long. Inflorescence 1- to 3-flowered. Sepals and petals green flushed with maroon, lip pink and white.

Epiphytic in riverine forest at low altitudes

Brazil, Venezuela

Flickingeria fimbriata

Flickingeria xantholeuca

Galeottia A. Richard

SYN. *Mendoncella* A. D. Hawkes
TRIBE: Maxillarieae
SUBTRIBE: Zygopetalinae
ETYMOLOGY: Named for Henri Galeotti (1814–1858), an Italian botanist
DISTRIBUTION: 12 species in Mexico, Central and South America

Epiphytes or terrestrials with oblong pseudobulbs set close together or far apart on a rhizome, covered with papery sheaths when young. Leaves 2 or 3, plicate. Inflorescences basal, erect to arching, unbranched, few-flowered. Flowers showy, resupinate; sepals and petals spreading, the lateral sepals saccate at the base; lip fleshy, clawed, with a cup-shaped

Galeandra baueri

hypochile and an ovate epichile, or trilobed with toothed side lobes and a ridged callus. Pollinia 4.
CULTIVATION: Most species do well in intermediate conditions in moderate shade. They need a well-drained compost with plenty of water while in active growth, but then need a drier rest until new growth appears.

Galeottia burkei (Reichenbach f.) Dressler & Christenson

SYN. *Zygopetalum burkei* Reichenbach f.
Pseudobulbs 2- or 3-leaved. Inflorescence erect. Sepals and petals yellow-green mottled with purple-brown. Lip white with a purple crest. Column yellow, streaked with purple.

Terrestrial, rarely epiphytic, in swamp forest, 1000–2200 m (3300–7260 ft.)

Brazil, Guyana, Peru, Venezuela

Galeottia grandiflora A. Richard

SYN. *Zygopetalum grandiflorum* (A. Richard) Bentham & Hooker f.
Pseudobulbs to 10 × 4 cm. Leaves 2–3, to 40 × 8 cm. Inflorescence to 26 cm long, to 10-flowered. Flowers to 10 cm across; sepals and petals yellowish tinged and striped with red-brown; lip hinged to column-foot, trilobed, white with purple veins.

Epiphytic in rain forest, 150–1100 m (500–3600 ft.)

Belize, Colombia, Costa Rica, Guyana, Mexico

Galeottia jorisiana (Rolfe) Schlechter

SYN. *Zygopetalum jorisiana* Rolfe
Pseudobulbs ovoid, 2-leaved. Inflorescence erect or arching, arising from new growth, to 15 cm tall, 2-flowered. Flowers 5 cm across; sepals and petals pale green blotched with darker green and brown, lip white, deeply fringed, with a yellow callus.

Epiphytic in tall or dwarf forest, 1000–2000 m (3300–6600 ft.)

Brazil, Guyana, Venezuela

Gastrochilus D. Don

TRIBE: Vandeae
SUBTRIBE: Aeridinae
ETYMOLOGY: From Greek *gaster*, belly, and *cheilos*, lip, referring to the saccate lip
DISTRIBUTION: More than 50 species in Asia from India to Malaysia
Small to medium-sized, monopodial epiphytes with long or short stems. Leaves leathery, in 2 rows, strap-shaped, lanceolate or oblong. Inflorescences short, unbranched. Sepals and petals similar, spreading. Lip saccate, joined at the base to the column wings, the epichile projecting, entire or fringed.
CULTIVATION: Species of *Gastrochilus* can be grown in pots, but because the flowers are often held below the leaves, they look better when mounted. They require intermediate conditions, light or moderate shade, high humidity, and good ventilation. They should be kept drier in winter but should not be allowed to dry out so much that the leaves become wrinkled.

Gastrochilus bellinus (Reichenbach f.) O. Kuntze

SYN. *Saccolabium bellinum* Reichenbach f.
Stems to ca. 10 cm long. Leaves 15–30 × 2 cm, narrowly lanceolate. Inflorescence short, erect, 2- to 7-flowered. Flowers scented, thick-textured, to 4 cm across; sepals and petals greenish or yellowish, heavily blotched with brown or purple; lip papillose, the margins deeply fringed, white spotted purple, disc yellow. Flowers late winter–spring.

Epiphytic on tree trunks in forest, 1600–1900 m (5300–6300 ft.)

China, Myanmar, Thailand, Laos

Gastrochilus calceolaris (J. E. Smith) D. Don

SYN. *Aerides calceolaris* J. E. Smith, *Saccolabium calceolaris* (D. Don) Lindley
Stems 5–30 cm long. Leaves numerous, distichous, to 25 × 2.5 cm. Inflorescence pendent, 1–5 cm long, densely many-flowered. Flowers 1–2 cm across; sepals and petals yellow or greenish with red-brown markings, lip white or yellow with red blotches, deeply fringed. Flowers autumn–winter.

Epiphytic on tree trunks in submontane and montane forest, 1000–2100 m (3300–6900 ft.)

Nepal to China and Malaysia

Gastrochilus dasypogon (J. E. Smith) O. Kuntze

SYN. *Aerides dasypogon* J. E. Smith, *Saccolabium dasypogon* Lindley
Stems 1–3 cm long, pendent. Leaves to 20 × 4 cm. Inflorescence 2 cm long, densely 5- to 10-flowered. Flowers ca. 2.5 cm across, fleshy; sepals and petals red inside, green marked with purple outside; lip fringed, white or yellow spotted with red or purple.

Epiphytic in forest, 300–1000 m (1000–3300 ft.)

Nepal to Indochina

SIMILAR SPECIES: *Gastrochilus obliquus* (Lindley) O. Kuntze has yellow flowers with red spots and may be a color variant of *G. dasypogon*. The 2 species have often been confused.

Gastrochilus japonicus (Makino) Schlechter

SYN. *Gastrochilus somai* (Hayata) Hayata, *Saccolabium japonicum* Makino
Inflorescence 2–3 cm long, densely flowered. Flowers ca. 2 cm across, scented; sepals and petals spathulate, greenish yellow; lip fringed, white with a yellow blotch spotted with red in the center. Flowering in autumn.

Epiphytic in submontane and montane forest, 500–2000 m (1650–6600 ft.)

China, Japan

Gastrorchis Schlechter

TRIBE: Collabieae
ETYMOLOGY: From Greek *gaster*, belly, and *orchis*, orchid, referring to the saccate lip
DISTRIBUTION: 8 species from Madagascar

Galeottia grandiflora. R. Parsons

Gastrochilus bellinus

Gastrochilus calceolaris

Gastrochilus japonicus

Gastrochilus obliquus

Terrestrial, rarely epiphytic plants with small pseudobulbs, 2- to 4-leaved. Leaves petiolate, thin-textured, plicate. Inflorescences arising from base of pseudobulb, unbranched. Flowers showy, turning blue-black if damaged; sepals and petals free, similar, usually ovate, often spreading; lip obscurely trilobed, saccate at base, with a keeled callus. Pollinia 8, in 2 groups of 4.

Species of *Gastrorchis* have sometimes been included in *Phaius*, but differ in having a saccate rather than a spurred lip and a raised, often hairy, callus.

CULTIVATION: *Gastrorchis* species require intermediate to warm conditions and heavy shade. They should be potted in a humus-rich but free-draining compost and given plenty of water while growing, although it is better not to get water on the leaves as they damage readily. When resting, keep much drier.

Gastrorchis humblotii (Reichenbach f.) Schlechter

SYN. *Phaius humblotii* Reichenbach f.

Pseudobulbs ± globose. Leaves elliptic, to 40 × 10 cm. Inflorescence 60–90 cm tall, several-flowered. Flowers 6–8 cm across, rose-pink, the lip darker.

Var. *schlechteri* (H. Perrier) Bosser has white sepals and petals and white rather than green floral bracts. Var. *rubra* Bosser has more richly colored flowers.

Terrestrial on floor of humid evergreen forest and moss forest, 1000–2000 m (3300–6600 ft.)

Madagascar

Gastrorchis pulchra Humbert & H. Perrier

SYN. *Phaius pulcher* (Humbert & H. Perrier) Summerhayes

Flowers 4–5 cm across; sepals and petals white; lip broad, violet or bright pink round the edge, mottled with white in the center.

Var. *perrieri* Bosser has narrower leaves and a differently shaped lip.

Terrestrial in humid evergreen forest and moss forest, or lithophytic on shaded, humid rocks, 500–2000 m (1650–6600 ft.)

Madagascar

Geodorum G. Jackson

TRIBE: Cymbidieae

SUBTRIBE: Cyrtopodiinae

ETYMOLOGY: From Greek *geo*, earth, and *doron*, gift, referring to the terrestrial habit

DISTRIBUTION: 12 species from India through Asia to the Pacific Islands and Australia

Terrestrials with ovoid or globose pseudobulbs covered in leaf sheaths when young, arising at or just below ground level. Leaves few, petiolate, plicate, deciduous. Inflorescences lateral, unbranched, erect but curved down in a U-bend at the tip, becoming straight in fruit. Flowers small, waxy, bell-shaped, scented, white, yellow, or pink; sepals and petals subsimilar, free; lip entire or obscurely trilobed, saccate at the base. Pollinia 2.

CULTIVATION: Grow in a rich but free-draining terrestrial mixture in shady, intermediate conditions. Plants need plenty of water while growing but should be dried off when the leaves die back after flowering, and be kept dry until new growth starts to appear. In the wild, most species grow in the shade of forest or woodland.

Geodorum citrinum G. Jackson

Leaves to 35 cm long, including petiole. Inflorescence to 30 cm long, 5- to 10-flowered. Flowers to 4 cm across, pale yellow, the lip veined and streaked with purple-red.

Malaysia, Myanmar, Thailand

Geodorum densiflorum (Lamarck) Schlechter

SYN. *Geodorum pictum* (R. Brown) Schlechter

Leaves to 35 × 9 cm. Inflorescence 10–40 cm long, densely and compactly several- to many-flowered. Flowers ca. 1 cm long, white, the lip with yellow and red markings in the throat.

Terrestrial in woodland and forest and on grassy slopes, 0–1800 m (6000 ft.)

Widespread in tropical Asia

Gomesa R. Brown

TRIBE: Maxillarieae

SUBTRIBE: Oncidiinae

ETYMOLOGY: Named for Bernardino António Gomes (1769–1823), a naval physician and botanist

DISTRIBUTION: 12 species in Brazil and Argentina

Epiphytes or lithophytes, occasionally terrestrial, with slightly flattened pseudobulbs, 1- or 2-leaved at apex, with 2 or 3 small basal sheathing leaves. Inflorescences axillary, from near base of pseudobulb, arching or pendent, many-flowered. Flowers small, scented, usually white, yellowish, or green; sepals and petals subsimilar, dorsal sepal and petals free, spreading, lateral sepals sometimes joined at the base; lip entire or trilobed, midlobe spreading or reflexed, disc with 2 calli.

CULTIVATION: Plants are usually potted in a free-draining, medium-grade bark compost. They require cool to intermediate conditions, light shade, and high humidity while growing. When growth is finished, they should be given cooler and brighter conditions and less water, although the pseudobulbs should not be allowed to shrivel.

Gomesa crispa (Lindley) Klotzsch ex Reichenbach f.

Pseudobulbs ca. 8 cm long, ovate, somewhat flattened, pale green, 2-leaved at apex. Leaves to 20 cm long. Inflorescence sometimes branched, to 30 cm long, many-flowered. Flowers to 2 cm across, yellow or green; margins of sepals, petals, and lip undulate; lip entire, oblong, recurved.

Low-level epiphyte or sometimes terrestrial in dense forest, 1000–1400 m (3300–4600 ft.)

Brazil

Gomesa recurva R. Brown

Pseudobulbs to 7 × 3.5 cm, 2-leaved at apex. Leaves to 15 × 3 cm. Inflorescences often several per plant, pendent, unbranched, to 20 cm long, many-flowered. Flowers green or yellow, ca. 2 cm across; lateral sepals partly joined; lip obscurely trilobed, the apical half recurved, with 2 keels.

Epiphytic in open forest, sometimes terrestrial on roadside banks, 1000–1400 m (3300–4600 ft.)

Brazil

SIMILAR SPECIES: *Gomesa planifolia* (Lindley) Klotzsch & Reichenbach f., also from Brazil, has the edges of the sepals, petals, and lip crisped.

Gastrorchis humblotii

Gomesa crispa

Geodorum citrinum

Gomesa planifolia

Gongora Ruíz & Pavón

TRIBE: Maxillarieae
SUBTRIBE: Stanhopeinae
ETYMOLOGY: Named for Don Antonio Caballero y Gongora, Bishop of Cordoba
DISTRIBUTION: Almost 70 species in Mexico, Central and South America, and Trinidad

Epiphytes with ovoid to conical pseudobulbs, becoming ribbed with age, 2- or 3-leaved. Leaves large, plicate, petiolate. Inflorescences basal, long, arching or pendent, unbranched, loosely few- to many-flowered. Flowers scented, often rather dull-colored, arranged in 2 rows; dorsal sepal erect, lateral sepals joined to column-foot, reflexed; petals smaller than sepals, joined to side of column; lip fleshy, complex; side lobes erect, with horns or bristles, midlobe flattened or saccate, bilobed, the apex acute or acuminate. Column slender, arched, ± winged towards the apex; pollinia 2.

In the wild, plants are often associated with ant nests. Many species are rather similar and difficult to identify.

CULTIVATION: Because of their long, pendent inflorescences, species must be suspended in baskets or pots. They need intermediate conditions, moderate shade, high humidity, and plenty of water and fertilizer while actively growing. When growth has finished, plants should be kept drier but not allowed to dry out completely.

Gongora armeniaca (Lindley & Paxton) Reichenbach f.

Pseudobulbs to 7 × 4 cm, 2-leaved. Leaves elliptic, to 30 × 8 cm, with a petiole to 6 cm long. Inflorescence 15–40 cm long, few- to many-flowered. Flowers to 5 cm long, orange to apricot, spotted and streaked with red; lip shortly clawed, 10–11 mm long, 7–8 mm wide.

Epiphytic in rain forest, 700–1350 m (2300–4500 ft.)

Central America

Gongora horichiana

SIMILAR SPECIES: *Gongora horichiana* Fowlie from Costa Rica and Panama has red flowers and a much narrower lip.

Gongora atropurpurea Hooker

Inflorescence to 40 cm long, many-flowered. Flowers deep purple or reddish.

Epiphytic in wet forest, 50–2000 m (165–6600 ft.)

South America, Trinidad, Tobago

Gongora cassidea Reichenbach f.

Pseudobulbs to 4 × 3 cm, 2-leaved. Leaves to 25 × 6 cm, with petiole to 5 cm long. Inflorescence 10–25 cm long. Flowers clear green, densely spotted with maroon-violet, lip orange.

Epiphytic in rain forest and cloud forest, 850–1600 m (2800–5300 ft.)

Mexico, Central America

SIMILAR SPECIES: *Gongora amparoana* Schlechter from Costa Rica is very similar and may be synonymous.

Gongora galeata (Lindley) Reichenbach f.

Pseudobulbs to 4.5 × 2.5 cm, 1- or 2-leaved. Leaves to 32 × 5 cm. Inflorescence arching to pendent, to 28 cm long, many-flowered. Flowers

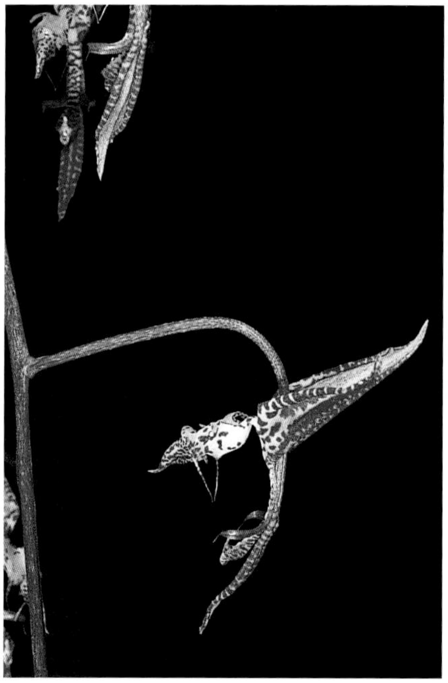

Gongora atropurpurea

to 5 cm long, yellow-brown or pale green, faintly flushed with orange.

Epiphytic (rarely terrestrial or lithophytic) in rain forest and cloud forest, 600–1800 m (2000–6000 ft.)

Mexico, Guatemala

Gongora quinquenervis Ruíz & Pavón

Pseudobulbs to 11 × 5 cm, 2-leaved. Leaves to 50 × 16 cm. Inflorescence to 75 cm long, loosely many-flowered. Flowers ca. 5 cm long, nonresupinate, scented, usually yellowish blotched and banded with red-brown.

Epiphytic on trees and rotten logs in rain forest, 50–900 m (165–3000 ft.)

Mexico, Central and South America, Trinidad

SIMILAR SPECIES: *Gongora unicolor* Schlechter has uniformly pink flowers.

Gongora truncata Lindley

Pseudobulbs to 8 × 3.5 cm, 2-leaved. Leaves to 45 × 10 cm. Inflorescence to 55 cm long, loosely many-flowered. Flowers 5 cm long, nonresupinate, strongly scented, creamy pink with purple-brown blotches, lip white, usually with purple-brown marks and a yellow base.

Gongora amparoana

Gongora quinquenervis

Gongora unicolor

Gongora galeata

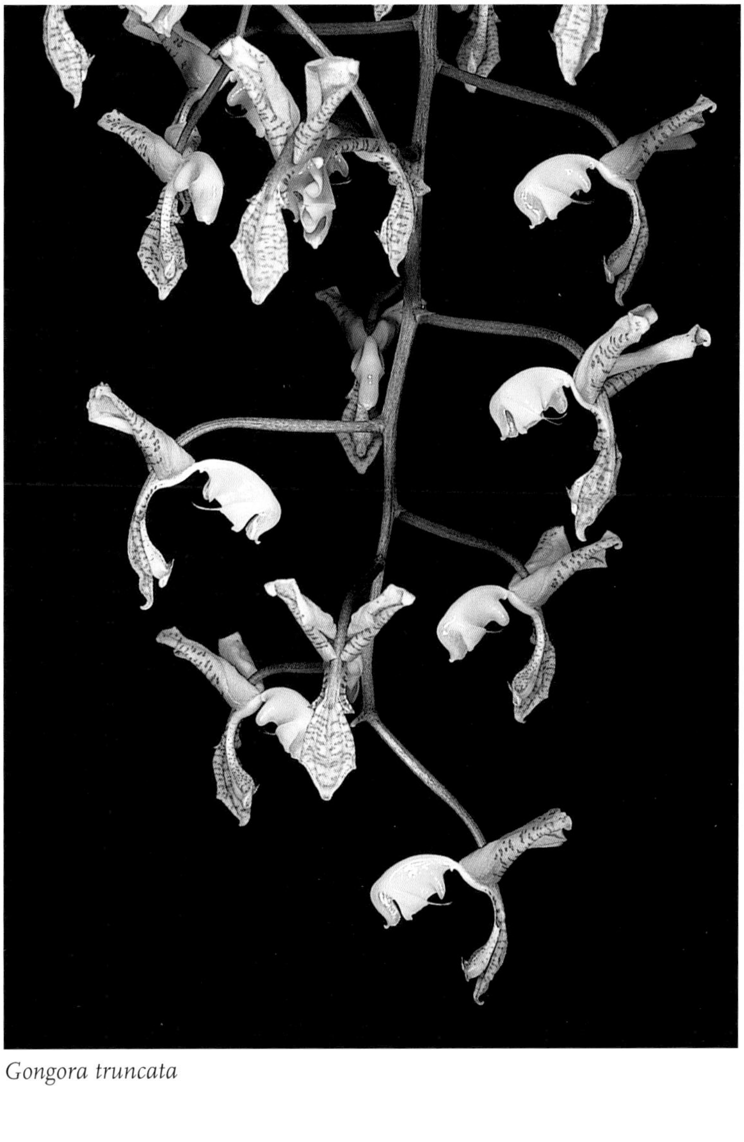
Gongora truncata

Epiphytic in rain forest, 200–850 m (660–2800 ft.)

Mexico, Central America

Goodyera R. Brown

TRIBE: Cranichideae

SUBTRIBE: Goodyerinae

ETYMOLOGY: Named for John Goodyer (1592–1664), an English botanist

DISTRIBUTION: Almost 100 species in Europe, North and Central America, Madagascar, Mozambique, Asia, and Australia

Terrestrial plants, rarely lithophytic or epiphytic, with creeping rhizomes rooting at the nodes. Leaves usually evergreen, in a basal rosette or along the stem, oblong to ovate with a sheathing, petiolate base, light to dark green often with colored veins. Inflorescences narrow spikes, few- to many-flowered with the flowers secund or spirally arranged. Flowers glabrous or hairy, small, white, greenish or brownish; sepals spreading or incurved, petals usually pointing forwards; lip saccate or spurred at base, entire, usually pubescent inside.

CULTIVATION: Several species are in cultivation, grown not for their flowers but as "jewel orchids," for their patterned leaves. Some, such as *Goodyera oblongifolia*, *G. pubescens*, and *G. repens*, can be grown outside in temperate areas in woodland or a shaded place. Others can be grown in pans or shallow pots in humus-rich compost or sphagnum moss in cool to intermediate, shady, humid but well-ventilated conditions. They should not be allowed to dry out completely.

Goodyera hemsleyana King & Pantling

Plants 12–25 cm tall. Leaves 3–5, along stem, to 5 × 2 cm with a petiole 1–1.5 cm long, ovate, dark green with white reticulate veining. Inflorescence 2- to 7-flowered. Flowers to 1 cm long, pinkish white, brownish and hairy outside.

Terrestrial in forest, 2100–2200 m (6900–7260 ft.)

Bhutan, Nepal, northeastern India

Goodyera oblongifolia Rafinesque

RATTLESNAKE PLANTAIN

Leaves evergreen, in basal rosette, to 8 × 3.5 cm, oblong, green with a white midvein and sometimes also with white reticulate veining. Inflorescence 20–50 cm tall, pubescent, secund, many-flowered. Flowers ca. 1 cm long, white tinged with green to greenish brown. Flowering summer–autumn.

Terrestrial usually in coniferous forest, in light to heavy shade, sometimes on rotting logs, 1750–3050 m (5800–10,050 ft.)

Canada, Mexico, United States

Goodyera repens (Linnaeus) R. Brown

CREEPING LADY'S TRESSES, LESSER RATTLESNAKE PLANTAIN

Leaves several, in basal rosette, to 4 × 2 cm, ovate, dark green, sometimes with white reticulate veining. Inflorescence to 35 cm tall, few- to many-flowered, most facing in the same direction. Flowers small, creamy white, densely glandular hairy.

Plants with plain green leaves seem commoner in Europe, while North American plants usually have well-marked leaves and have been known as var. *ophioides* Fernald.

Terrestrial in leaf litter of pine forest

Circumpolar; Europe (including Britain), Asia, North America

SIMILAR SPECIES: *Goodyera pubescens* (Willdenow) R. Brown, from Canada and the United States, is a bigger plant with slightly larger flowers and consistently white-veined leaves.

Goodyera schlechtendaliana Reichenbach f.

Plants 10–25 cm tall. Leaves 2–5, towards base of stem, to 4 × 2.5 cm with a petiole 1.5–3 cm long, ovate-lanceolate, green with white or yellowish spots or mottling. Inflorescence with dense glandular hairs, several- to many-flowered. Flowers to 1 cm long, sepals yellowish pink, petals white, lip green and white.

Terrestrial in forest or on mossy banks, 1500–2270 m (5000–7400 ft.)

Bhutan, China, Japan, Southeast Asia, Sumatra, Thailand

Govenia Lindley

TRIBE: Calypsoeae

ETYMOLOGY: Named for James R. Gowen, a 19th-century English horticulturist

DISTRIBUTION: About 20 species in Florida, Mexico, Central and South America, and the West Indies

Terrestrials with underground corms or rhizomes. Leaves 1–3, plicate, deciduous. Inflorescences lateral, with basal sheaths, few- to many-flowered. Flowers fleshy; sepals and petals free, dorsal sepal and petals forming hood over column, lateral sepals deflexed; lip entire, shorter than other parts. Pollinia 4.

CULTIVATION: Plants should be grown in a very free-draining terrestrial compost, in cool to intermediate conditions, in light shade. They need plenty of water while growing but should be kept dry after the leaves fall. Careful watering should be resumed when the new growth appears.

Govenia liliacea (Lexarza) Lindley

Corms ca. 4.5 cm across. Leaves to 45 × 12 cm, elliptic. Inflorescence to 90 cm tall. Flowers cream or white, the petals with light magenta stripes, the lip with dark blotches near the apex on the underside; sepals 20–30 mm long; lip ovate, 12 × 10 mm.

Terrestrial in wet woodland, 1000–1200 m (3300–4000 ft.)

Mexico, Central America

Govenia utriculata (Swartz) Lindley

SYN. *Govenia capitata* Lindley

Corms ca. 3 cm across. Leaves 2, to 28 × 10 cm, broadly ovate.

Goodyera repens. E. la Croix

Goodyera schlechtendaliana. E. la Croix

Govenia liliacea. R. Parsons

Govenia utriculata. J. Stewart

Inflorescence to 50 cm tall, many-flowered. Flowers 3 cm across, creamy white, the sepals and petals finely dotted with maroon, lip with 3 maroon spots near the tip.

Mexico, Central and South America, West Indies

Terrestrial in moist ground, often in forest, to 2000 m (6600 ft.). In Mexico, grows in fir forest, 3000–3200 m (9900–10,500 ft.)

Grammangis Reichenbach f.

TRIBE: Cymbidieae
SUBTRIBE: Cyrtopodiinae
ETYMOLOGY: From Greek *gramma*, marking or letter, and *angos*, a vessel, probably referring to the markings on the flowers
DISTRIBUTION: 2 species in Madagascar

Robust, sympodial epiphytes with large pseudobulbs, 3- to 5-leaved at the apex. Leaves flat, fleshy, articulated to the sheath. Inflorescences racemose, arising from the base of a new pseudobulb. Flowers large, fleshy and showy; sepals spreading, petals joined to lateral sepals at base, forming a mentum with the column-foot; lip attached to the apex of the column-foot, trilobed with crests and calli inside, lacking a spur. Column stout.

CULTIVATION: Plants should be grown in heavy, shallow clay pots or in baskets in a coarse bark mixture. They need plenty of water and fertilizer, high humidity, and moderate shade while in growth. In winter when plants are resting, watering should be reduced and light increased.

Grammangis ellisii (Lindley) Reichenbach f.

SYN. *Grammangis fallax* Schlechter

Pseudobulbs to 20 × 6 cm, 4-angled, with 3–5 leaves at the apex. Leaves to 40 × 4 cm, oblong, fleshy, flat but folded at base. Inflorescence arching, 50–65 cm long, 15- to 20-flowered. Flowers 8 cm across, thick; sepals glossy yellow with large brown blotches, petals smaller, yellow and brown; lip striped red and yellow, trilobed with a large, forked callus and keels and more calli at the junction of the lobes.

Coastal forest; humid evergreen forest, 0–1300 m (4300 ft.)

Madagascar

SIMILAR SPECIES: *Grammangis spectabilis* Bosser & Morat has smaller, less heavily blotched flowers and grows in dry, deciduous forest.

Grammatophyllum Blume

TRIBE: Cymbidieae
SUBTRIBE: Cyrtopodiinae
ETYMOLOGY: From Greek *gramma*, letter, and *phyllon*, leaf
DISTRIBUTION: 11 species from Indochina to the southwest Pacific

Very large plants with clusters of stout, canelike pseudobulbs. Leaves distichous, linear or strap-shaped. Inflorescences basal, erect or pendent, many-flowered. Flowers usually large, showy; sepals and petals spreading, subsimilar; lip smaller, trilobed, concave. Pollinia 2.

CULTIVATION: Species of *Grammatophyllum* are not widely grown in glasshouses because of their large size. If room can be found, they should be planted in a coarse bark mixture in intermediate to warm conditions, with little shade, high humidity, and plenty of water and fertilizer while in active growth. Plants should dry out between watering. In tropical gardens, they can be grown in a fork of a tree or as terrestrials.

Grammatophyllum speciosum Blume

Pseudobulbs to 3 m long or more. Leaves numerous, to 60 × 3 cm. Inflorescence erect, to 2 m tall, many-flowered. Flowers 7–12 cm across, cream, yellow, or yellow-green blotched with maroon or brown, lip whitish striped with yellow and red-brown. The first few flowers at the base of the inflorescence are often malformed. This species is often said to be the world's largest orchid.

Grammatophyllum elegans. H. Oakeley

High-level epiphyte in large trees, 0–900 m (3000 ft.)

Widespread from Southeast Asia to the Pacific Islands

SIMILAR SPECIES: *Grammatophyllum elegans* from Fiji is not quite such a large plant and has chestnut-brown flowers.

Graphorkis Thouars

TRIBE: Cymbidieae
SUBTRIBE: Cyrtopodiinae
ETYMOLOGY: From Greek *graphe*, writing, and *orchis*, orchid, probably referring to markings on the flowers
DISTRIBUTION: 4 species in tropical Africa, Madagascar, Mascarene Islands, Comoro Islands, and Seychelles

Epiphytes with large pseudobulbs, related to *Eulophia*. Leaves deciduous, appearing after flowering. Inflorescences branched, many-flowered. Flowers brownish, yellow-green, or dull purple; sepals and petals similar; lip trilobed, usually spurred.

Although only 4 species are currently recognized, 1 with 2 varieties, no fewer than 110 names have been applied.

CULTIVATION: Plants seem to do best in baskets in a coarse, free-draining mix, in intermediate to warm

Grammangis ellisii. J. Hermans

Grammatophyllum speciosum. H. Oakeley

Grammangis spectabilis. J. Hermans

conditions in fairly good light. They need plenty of water while growing, but care must be taken as the new growths tend to rot. After the leaves fall, plants should be kept almost dry.

Graphorkis concolor (Thouars) Kuntze var. ***alphabetica*** F. N. Rasmussen

SYN. *Graphorkis scripta* (Thouars) Kuntze

Pseudobulbs clustered, to 14 × 4 cm. Leaves several, grasslike, to 11 cm long, appearing after the flowers. Inflorescence 20–65 cm tall with 3–9 branches, loosely many-flowered. Flowers yellow marked with red; sepals and petals to 15 mm long; lip side lobes clasping column, midlobe wavy, emarginate; spur straight, 3 mm long.

Var. *concolor* from Réunion has no markings on the flowers.

Epiphytic in humid, low altitude forest

Madagascar, Mascarene Islands, Comoro Islands

Graphorkis lurida (Swartz) Kuntze

Pseudobulbs ovoid, 3–9 cm tall, yellowish, forming large clumps. Leaves several, to 40 × 4 cm, lanceolate, ribbed, appearing after flowering. Inflorescence 15–50 cm tall, branched, many-flowered. Flowers 10–15 mm across, yellowish, flushed with brown or purple; lip with 2 fleshy keels at the base; spur 4–6 mm long, bent forwards, sometimes notched at the tip.

Low- to mid-altitude forest, 300–1300 m (1000–4300 ft.), often growing in forks of *Hyphaene* palms

West and Central Africa

Grobya Lindley

TRIBE: Cymbidieae

SUBTRIBE: Cyrtopodiinae

ETYMOLOGY: Named for Lord Grey of Groby (d. 1836), a noted orchid grower

DISTRIBUTION: 5 species in Brazil

Epiphytes with small, round to ovoid pseudobulbs, several-leaved. Leaves plicate, grasslike. Inflorescences erect, arching or pendent, unbranched, arising from base of older pseudobulbs, several-flowered. Flowers quite showy, yellowish or greenish, flushed and marked with purple; dorsal sepal forming hood with petals, lateral sepals joined shortly at the base, spreading or deflexed, much longer and narrower than the dorsal sepal, twisted and often incurved. Lip small, trilobed, hinged to column-foot. Pollinia 2.

CULTIVATION: Plants require intermediate conditions with moderate shade, plenty of water, and good ventilation while growing. They can be grown in pots or baskets in a standard epiphyte compost and need a cooler, drier rest after the new pseudobulbs are formed.

Grobya amherstiae Lindley

Pseudobulbs round, 3–4 cm high, to 6-leaved. Leaves to 40 × 1.5 cm. Inflorescence arching or pendent, ca. 15 cm long, to about 16-flowered. Flowers ca. 3 cm across; sepals pale yellowish or greenish, flushed or spotted with purple, petals translucent yellow with darker veins, blotched with maroon-purple; lip yellow, tipped with red, orange in throat. Flowers late summer–autumn.

Epiphytic in Atlantic rain forest, often on dead wood, 200–1200 m (660–4000 ft.)

Eastern and southern Brazil

Grobya galeata Lindley

Inflorescence arching to pendent, densely many-flowered. Flowers yellow, the petals with brown marks at the base; lip side lobes large, ± quadrate, barred with brown; midlobe broadly fan-shaped. Flowering in autumn.

Epiphytic in Atlantic rain forest

Southern and southeastern Brazil

SIMILAR SPECIES: *Grobya fascifera* Reichenbach f. has more densely spotted petals and the lip midlobe is a different shape.

Grosourdya Reichenbach f.

TRIBE: Vandeae

SUBTRIBE: Aeridinae

ETYMOLOGY: Named for Dr. Grosourdy, a 19th-century expert on medicinal plants

DISTRIBUTION: 9 species from Indochina to Malesia

Short-stemmed monopodial epiphytes related to *Sarcochilus*. Inflorescences usually several, peduncle longer than rachis. Flowers short-lived; sepals and petals spreading, subsimilar but petals narrower, lip hinged to column-foot, trilobed, spurred. Pollinia 2.

CULTIVATION: Plants can be mounted or grown in small pots, in intermediate conditions with light shade and high humidity.

Grosourdya appendiculata (Blume) Reichenbach f.

Stem short with 5–8 leaves set close together. Leaves distichous, to 15 × 2 cm. Inflorescence numerous, from lower part of stem, ca. 3 cm long, several-flowered, the flowers open one at a time. Flowers 8–15 mm across; sepals and petals pale yellow, spotted or barred with red; lip white, the side lobes light red-brown, erect; midlobe also trilobed, side lobes spreading, midlobe short and obtuse.

Twig epiphyte, usually in lowland forest but sometimes up to 1200 m (4000 ft.)

Southeast Asia to Philippines

Guarianthe Dressler & W. E. Higgins

TRIBE: Epidendreae

SUBTRIBE: Laeliinae

ETYMOLOGY: From Costa Rican *guaria*, epiphyte, and Greek *anthe*, flower

DISTRIBUTION: 4 species and 1 natural hybrid in Mexico, Central America, Trinidad, and northern South America

Graphorkis lurida. J. Hermans

Graphorkis concolor var. *alphabetica*. J. Hermans

Grobya galeata

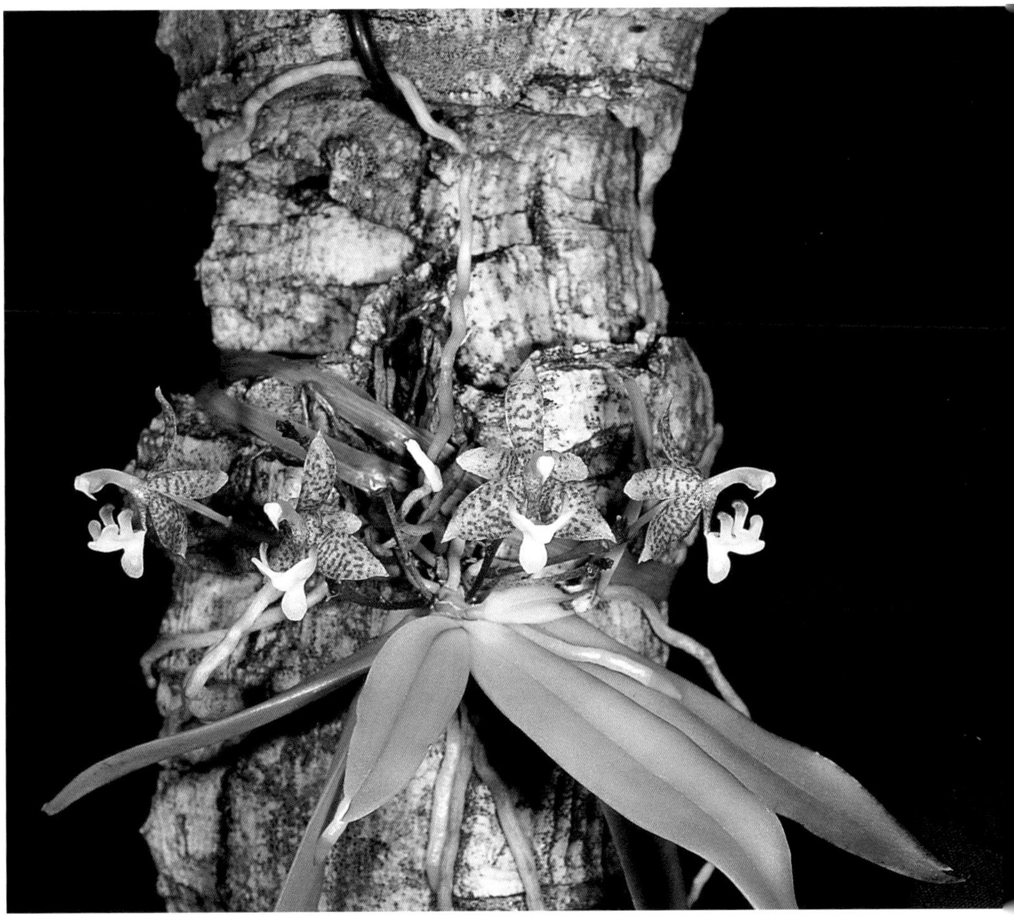

Grosourdya appendiculata

Epiphytes with club-shaped pseudobulbs, 2- or 3-leaved at apex. Infloarescences terminal, unbranched, arising from a papery sheath. Flowers large and showy; sepals and petals free, spreading, the petals broader than the sepals; lip entire, trumpet-shaped, enclosing the column. Column club-shaped with a fleshy tooth holding the anther; pollinia 4.

These beautiful species were separated from *Cattleya* by Robert Dressler and W. E. Higgins in 2003.

CULTIVATION: Species of *Guarianthe* are grown like cattleyas, in intermediate to warm temperatures and good light although not direct sun. They are usually grown in pots or baskets in a coarse, free-draining compost and require plenty of water and fertilizer while in growth. They should be kept dry while dormant but not allowed to shrivel.

Guarianthe aurantiaca (Bateman ex Lindley) Dressler & W. E. Higgins

SYN. *Cattleya aurantiaca* (Bateman ex Lindley) P. N. Don

A variable species. Pseudobulbs 12–35 cm tall, cylindrical, 2- or 3-leaved at apex. Leaves to 18 × 5 cm. Inflorescence 6–10 cm tall, few- to many-flowered. Flowers 2–4 cm across, orange-yellow to bright vermilion red, sometimes with darker spots and streaks on the lip.

This species is a parent of the natural hybrid *Guarianthe* ×*guatemalensis* (T. Moore) W. E. Higgins, which occurs in Mexico and Central America. The other parent is *G. skinneri*.

Epiphytic or lithophytic in low-altitude and submontane forest, 300–1600 m (1000–5300 ft.)

Central America

Guarianthe bowringiana (O'Brien) Dressler & W. E. Higgins

SYN. *Cattleya bowringiana* O'Brien

Pseudobulbs to 45 cm long, swollen at the base, 2- or 3-leaved at apex. Leaves oblong, to 22 × 7.5 cm. Inflorescence to 27 cm long, 4- to 13-flowered. Flowers slightly scented, 7–8 cm across; sepals and petals mauve, lip purple with a white center edged with deep purple and with yellow marks.

Lithophytic on rocks and cliffs near streams, rarely epiphytic, 100–1000 m (330–3300 ft.)

Belize, Guatemala

Guarianthe skinneri (Bateman) Dressler & W. E. Higgins

SYN. *Cattleya skinneri* Bateman

Pseudobulbs 15–35 × 2–3 cm. Leaves to 20 × 6 cm. Inflorescence to 13 cm tall, few- to many-flowered. Flowers 8–9 cm across, slightly scented, pink to purple, white or cream in the throat. Flowering in autumn.

Epiphytic in tropical semi-deciduous forest, 300–1400 m (1000–4600 ft.)

Costa Rica (national flower), Mexico

SIMILAR SPECIES: *Guarianthe patinii* (Cogniaux) Dressler & W. E. Higgins (syn. *Cattleya patinii* Cogniaux, *C. skinneri* var. *parviflora* Lindley) from Central and South America, has a self-colored lip, lacking a pale throat, and flowers in spring.

Gymnadenia R. Brown

SYN. *Nigritella* Richard

TRIBE: Orchideae

SUBTRIBE: Orchidinae

ETYMOLOGY: From Greek *gymnos*, naked, and *aden*, gland, referring to the viscidia

DISTRIBUTION: About 16 species in Europe and temperate parts of central and East Asia as far east as Japan

Terrestrial plants with lobed tubers and erect, leafy stems. Inflorescences cylindrical or conical, densely many-flowered. Flowers small, scented; sepals and petals free, either all spreading or with the dorsal sepal forming a hood with the petals; lip entire or trilobed with a long or short spur.

CULTIVATION: Plants are hardy in temperate gardens. If potted, they need a well-drained terrestrial compost with added lime, as most species grow on calcareous soil. Keep dry after the leaves have died back.

Gymnadenia conopsea (Linnaeus) R. Brown

CHALK FRAGRANT ORCHID

Stems 15–65 cm tall. Leaves 3–9, 5–25 cm long, linear or linear-lanceolate. Spike cylindrical, densely many-flowered. Flowers 9–12 mm across, lilac to pink, sweetly scented; lip with 3 more or less equal lobes, spur 12–14 mm long, slender, curving down. Flowers late spring–summer.

Dry calcareous pasture, chalk downland

Europe, including Britain (mainly southern Europe)

SIMILAR SPECIES: *Gymnadenia borealis* (Druce) R. M. Bateman, Pridgeon & M. W. Chase (syn. *G. conopsea* subsp. *borealis* (Druce) F. Rose), HEATH FRAGRANT ORCHID, has flowers 8–10 mm across and occurs in hill pasture and heaths. It is more common in northern Britain. *Gymnadenia densiflora* (Wahlenberg) A. Dietrich (syn. *G. conopsea* subsp. *densiflora* (Wahlenberg) E. G. Camus), MARSH FRAGRANT ORCHID, is more robust, with denser inflorescences with flowers 11–14 mm across and a spur 14–16 mm long. It occurs mainly in damp, calcareous places. *Gymnadenia odoratissima* (Linnaeus) Richard, SHORT-SPURRED FRAGRANT ORCHID, from Europe and Russia, is a shorter plant with smaller flowers.

Gymnadenia nigra (Linnaeus) Reichenbach f.

SYN. *Nigritella nigra* (Linnaeus) Reichenbach f.

BLACK VANILLA ORCHID

Plants 8–25 cm tall. Leaves several, suberect, narrow, channeled. Spike conical, 10–25 cm long, densely many-flowered. Flowers strongly vanilla-scented, usually blackish crimson but occasionally red, yellow, or white; sepals and petals spreading,

Guarianthe aurantiaca

Guarianthe skinneri

Guarianthe bowringiana

Gymnadenia conopsea

spur short and saccate. Flowering summer.

Mountain pastures and woodland edges. 1000–2800 m (3300–9250 ft.) but lower in Scandinavia

Upland Europe, from Scandinavia to the Balkans

Habenaria Willdenow

TRIBE: Orchideae

SUBTRIBE: Orchidinae

ETYMOLOGY: From Latin *habena*, strap or rein, referring to the long, slender petals and lip lobes of many species

DISTRIBUTION: More than 600 species in tropical and subtropical areas of all continents

Terrestrial, rarely epiphytic, herbs with ovoid, ellipsoid, or globose tubers or long, fleshy roots. Leaves either appressed to ground with a few sheaths on the flowering stem or arranged along stem. Inflorescences terminal, 1- to many-flowered. Flowers usually green or white, occasionally with a red, yellow, or pink lip; sepals usually free, the dorsal often forming a hood with petals, the laterals spreading or reflexed; petals entire or bilobed; lip entire or trilobed, the side lobes sometimes divided, spurred at the base; spur long or short, often inflated at apex. Column long or short, stigmatic arms 2, long and slender or short and thick.

CULTIVATION: Although many species have small, green flowers, others are large and showy and well worth growing. However, as with many tropical terrestrials, they are not easy to obtain and few species are in general cultivation. With such a large genus, only general information can be given. Plants should be grown in pots in a standard, free-draining terrestrial compost and most do well in intermediate conditions. Many species grow in seasonal climates where there is a long dry season; these should be kept dry while resting. When the new growth starts to appear, water with care, avoiding getting moisture on the young leaves. As the plants grow, give plenty of water and weak fertilizer until flowering is over and they start to die back.

Habenaria carnea Weathers

Leaves 3–6, to 12 × 3 cm, olive green irregularly blotched with white. Inflorescence 10–20 cm tall, 5- to 15-flowered. Flowers 35 mm long, 25 mm across, very pale pink; dorsal sepals and petals forming a hood, lateral sepals spreading; lip trilobed, side lobes spreading, midlobe bilobed; spur 5–6 cm long.

Terrestrial on rocky escarpments at low altitudes

Thailand

Habenaria macrandra Lindley

Plants with fleshy, woolly, cylindrical roots. Leaves mainly in a tuft at the base, petiolate, to 24 × 6 cm. Inflorescence to 20 cm long, rather loosely several-flowered. Flowers white or green and white; sepals 15–30 cm long, lanceolate, the dorsal erect, the laterals deflexed; petals 15–35 mm long, erect, linear; lip trilobed, midlobe to 45 mm long, side lobes to 55 mm long, all linear; spur 5–7.5 cm long, slightly curved, swollen towards the tip.

Terrestrial in leaf litter in forest, in deep shade, 900–1500 m (3000–5000 ft.)

Widespread in tropical Africa

Habenaria procera (Afzelius ex Swartz) Lindley

SYN. *Habenaria gabonensis* Reichenbach f.

Erect plants with long, woolly tubers and leafy stems. Leaves to 30 × 5.5 cm. Inflorescence loosely to fairly densely several- to many-flowered. Flowers white; sepals and petals to 12 mm long; lip trilobed, 15–30 mm long, midlobe to 18 mm long, side lobes to 27 mm long, narrowly linear; spur 6–11 cm long. This species is unusual in the genus in being mainly epiphytic but in cultivation, it is usually grown as a terrestrial. Flowering spring–summer.

Epiphytic, usually on tree trunks in forest, sometimes terrestrial in humus or in grassy places among rocks, to 1250 m (4100 ft.)

West and Central Africa

Habenaria radiata (Thunberg) Sprengel

SYN. *Pecteilis radiata* (Thunberg) Rafinesque

WHITE EGRET FLOWER

Leaves several, along stem, to 10 × 0.7 cm. Inflorescence to 45 cm tall, 1- to 3-flowered. Flowers ca. 3 cm across; sepals green, petals white, finely toothed; lip trilobed, midlobe narrowly strap-shaped, acute, side lobes spreading, triangular, the rear and side margins deeply fringed; spur green, pendent, 3.5–5 cm long. Flowering summer.

Terrestrial in wet places

Japan, Korea, Russia

Habenaria rhodocheila Hance

Leaves mainly towards base of stem, to ca. 12 × 2 cm. Inflorescence about 10-flowered. Sepals and petals green, ca. 10 mm long, the dorsal sepal forming a hood with the petals. Lip ca. 30 × 20 mm, usually red, sometimes orange, yellow, or pink, deeply trilobed, the midlobe bilobed; spur slender, pendent, 5 cm long.

Terrestrial or lithophytic on mossy rocks in lowland, evergreen forest

South China to peninsular Malaysia, Philippines

SIMILAR SPECIES: *Habenaria erichmichelii* Christenson from Thailand is a smaller plant with silvery markings on the leaves.

Hagsatera R. Gonzales

TRIBE: Epidendreae

SUBTRIBE: Laeliinae

ETYMOLOGY: Named for Mexican orchidologist Eric Hágsater

DISTRIBUTION: 2 species in Mexico and Guatemala

Habenaria carnea. W. Cavestro

Habenaria radiata. J. Stewart

Habenaria procera. E. la Croix

Habenaria rhodocheila. J. Stewart

Scandent epiphytes, rarely lithophytes; rhizome ascending, with pseudobulbs at intervals, separated by a length of erect rhizome, the roots arising only at the base of the plant; pseudobulbs 1- to 2-leaved at apex. Inflorescences apical, unbranched, few-flowered. Flowers nodding; sepals and petals free, subsimilar, the sepals slightly larger, spreading; petals projecting forwards; lip fleshy, obscurely trilobed. Column short, pollinia 8.

CULTIVATION: Plants are usually grown mounted on a slab of cork or tree fern. They need intermediate conditions, good light, and ventilation. Because plants rarely form roots along the stem, the basal roots must be kept moist—a pad of sphagnum is sometimes placed around them.

Hagsatera brachycolumna (L. O. Williams) R. Gonzales

Stem to 1 m tall. Pseudobulbs narrowly conical, to 4 cm long, set 1–6.5 cm apart on the rhizome. Leaf 1, to 15 cm long. Flowers 2–5, to 4 cm across, sepals and petals yellow or greenish yellow, lip purple with a yellow disc.

Epiphytic on oak trees (*Quercus elliptica*), 1200–1900 m (4000–6300 ft.)

Mexico

Haraella Kudô

TRIBE: Vandeae

SUBTRIBE: Aeridinae

ETYMOLOGY: Named for Yashi Hara, who discovered the type species

DISTRIBUTION: 1 or 2 species in Taiwan

Small, short-stemmed epiphytes with fleshy leaves. Flowers medium-sized; sepals and petals free, spreading, subsimilar; lip not spurred or saccate, constricted in middle, margin fringed. Column short and broad; pollinia 2, stipes 1, viscidium relatively large.

CULTIVATION: Plants do best mounted, in light to moderate shade in intermediate conditions with high humidity. They should not be allowed to dry out completely, although less watering should be given in winter.

Haraella retrocalla (Hayata) Kudô

Leaves 4–6, 3–7 cm long, narrowly oblong. Racemes 2–8 cm long, 1- to 4-flowered, the flowers open in succession. Flowers scented, fleshy, about 2 cm across; sepals and petals oblong, pale yellow, lip oblong, the edges wavy, whitish yellow with a deep purple blotch in the center. Flowering summer–autumn.

On tree trunks in evergreen forest, 500–1500 m (1650–5000 ft.)

Taiwan

SIMILAR SPECIES: *Haraella odorata* Kudô is probably synonymous with *H. retrocalla.*

Helcia Lindley

TRIBE: Maxillarieae

SUBTRIBE: Oncidiinae

ETYMOLOGY: From Latin *helcium*, horse-collar, referring to the appearance of the base of the lip

DISTRIBUTION: 4 species in western South America

Pseudobulbs oblong to ovoid. Leaves shortly petiolate. Flowers showy; sepals and petals subsimilar, spreading; lip entire. Column terete, with a fringed hood.

Differs from *Trichopilia* in the column being free from the base of the lip.

CULTIVATION: Grow plants in a rather small pot in a medium bark mix, in intermediate to cool conditions, moderate shade, and high humidity, with plenty of water while growing actively. They should be kept almost dry after the pseudobulbs are fully formed, until new growth appears.

Helcia sanguinolenta Lindley

SYN. *Trichopilia sanguinolenta* (Lindley) Reichenbach f.

Pseudobulbs ovate, to 8 cm long, 1-leafed at apex. Leaves to 20 × 5 cm. Inflorescence to 20 cm long, 1-flowered. Flowers 6–8 cm across, showy; sepals and petals yellow or yellow-green, heavily spotted with brown; lip hairy at the base, white with red veining, obovate, emarginate, the edges undulate, callus yellow dotted with red.

Epiphytic in submontane and montane forest, 600–3000 m (2000–9900 ft.)

Ecuador, Peru

Himantoglossum Koch

SYN. *Barlia* Parlatore, *Comperia* K. Koch

TRIBE: Orchideae

SUBTRIBE: Orchidinae

ETYMOLOGY: From Greek *himas*, strap, and *glossa*, tongue, referring to the lip

DISTRIBUTION: 8 species in Europe and the Middle East

Large terrestrials with 2 ovoid underground tubers. Leaves several, on lower half of stem, large, often withered by flowering time. Inflorescences narrowly cylindrical racemes, many-flowered. Flowers gray-green, yellow-green, or purple. Sepals and petals forming a hood; lip spurred, trilobed, midlobe relatively short and bilobed or very long and narrow, deeply cut.

CULTIVATION: Most species are frost hardy but do not like to be wet in winter, and so are usually grown in an alpine house or cold frame in a free-draining, calcareous terrestrial mixture.

Himantoglossum caprinum (M. Bieberstein) Sprengel

BALKAN LIZARD ORCHID

Plants 30–100 cm tall. Leaves numerous, to 17 × 3.5 cm, ovate near base, becoming narrower up the stem. Spike cylindrical, rather loosely 10- to 45-flowered. Flowers purplish; lip side lobes to 2.5 cm long, midlobe 5–8 cm long, deeply divided into 2, twisted in a spiral; spur conical. Flowering summer.

Rough pasture and light woodland on calcareous soil, to 1500 m (5000 ft.)

Eastern Europe

Hagsatera brachycolumna. R. Parsons

Haraella odorata

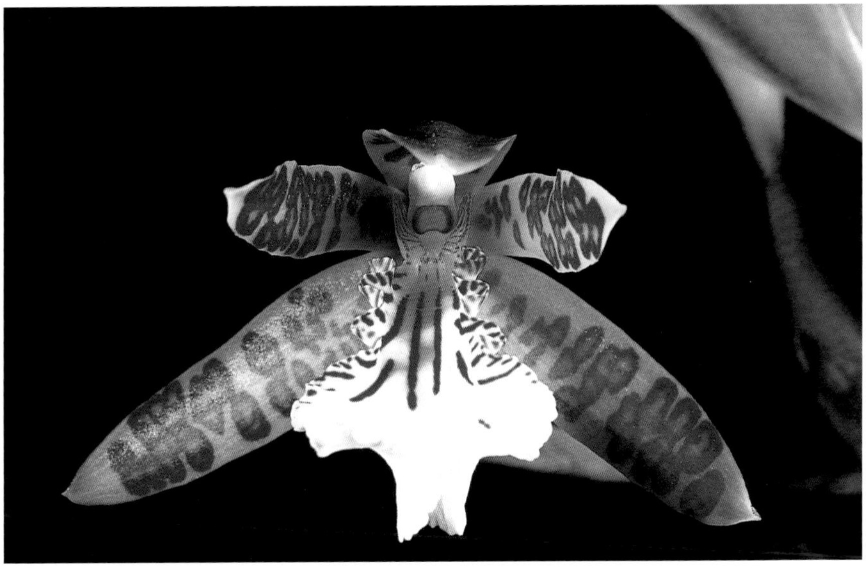

Helcia sanguinolenta

Himantoglossum comperianum

(Steven) P. Delforge

SYN. *Comperia comperiana* (Steven) Ascherson & Graebner

Leaves 2–4, to 15 × 4 cm. Flowering stem 25–60 cm tall; inflorescence cylindrical, loosely or densely many-flowered. Flowers greenish purple with a lilac lip or brownish purple with a pink lip; lip trilobed, the midlobe further divided into 2; all lobes are drawn out into threadlike processes 3–8 cm long; spur short, curving down. Flowering summer.

Dry, wooded upland areas.

Greek islands, Iran, Lebanon, Turkey

Himantoglossum hircinum

(Linnaeus) Sprengel

LIZARD ORCHID

Robust plants 25–90 cm tall. Leaves several, more or less in a basal rosette, starting to wither by flowering time. Flowers gray-green and purple, with an unpleasant, goatlike smell; lip hairy in the center, midlobe 3–7 cm long, narrow, twisted, notched at the tip; spur conical. Flowering summer.

Grassland on calcareous soil, to 1800 m (6000 ft.)

Southern Europe, northern Turkey, northwestern Africa

Himantoglossum hircinum

Himantoglossum robertianum

(Loiseleur) P. Delforge

SYN. *Barlia robertiana* (Loiseleur) Greuter

GIANT ORCHID

Robust terrestrial plants 30–80 cm tall. Leaves to 30 × 10 cm, shiny light green. Flowers 12–14 cm long, purple or greenish, fragrant; lip trilobed, the midlobe bilobed; spur conical. Spring flowering.

Open grassland and scrubland, on neutral or alkaline soil, often on poor chalky soil

Spain, Portugal, around Mediterranean; commonest in western Mediterranean area

SIMILAR SPECIES: *Himantoglossum metlesicsianum* (Teschner) P. Delforge (syn. *Barlia metlesicsiana* Teschner) is endemic to Tenerife in the Canary Islands.

Holcoglossum Schlechter

TRIBE: Vandeae

SUBTRIBE: Aeridinae

ETYMOLOGY: From Greek *holkos*, furrow, and *glossa*, tongue

DISTRIBUTION: 14 species from Assam to Taiwan

Monopodial epiphytes related to *Vanda* and previously included there. Stems long to short, covered with old leaf bases. Leaves terete, fleshy. Inflorescences axillary, pendent, few to many-flowered. Flowers showy; sepals and petals free, spreading, subsimilar; lip spurred, trilobed, side lobes clasping the column, disc with a callus of parallel ridges.

CULTIVATION: As these plants are often pendent, they are best mounted, in intermediate conditions with moderate shade and high humidity. They need a cooler, drier rest in winter.

Holcoglossum amesianum (Reichenbach f.) Christenson

SYN. *Vanda amesiana* Reichenbach f.

Stem to ca. 8 cm long. Leaves several, slender, 9–30 cm long. Inflorescence to 25 cm long, usually unbranched, several-flowered. Flowers 2–4 cm across, white to pale pink; lip with red-purple veins and keels; spur conical, 6 mm long.

Epiphytic in evergreen forest, 1200–2000 m (4000–6600 ft.)

Southeast Asia

Holcoglossum kimballianum (Reichenbach f.) Garay

SYN. *Vanda kimballiana* Reichenbach f.

Stem to 30 cm long, pendent. Leaves 4–5, slender, 30–60 cm long. Inflorescence arching, unbranched, to 28 cm long, loosely several-flowered. Flowers 4–5 cm across, scented, white; sepals and petals pink-tinged, lip heavily striped with red-purple; spur 1.5 cm long, decurved.

Epiphytic in submontane and montane forest, 1000–1600 m (3300–5300 ft.)

China, Myanmar, Thailand

Homalopetalum Rolfe

TRIBE: Epidendreae

SUBTRIBE: Laeliinae

ETYMOLOGY: From Greek *homalos*, equal, and *petalon*, petal, referring to the similar perianth parts of the type species, *H. vomeriforme* (Swartz) Fawcett & Rendle

DISTRIBUTION: 7 species in Mexico, Central and South America, and the West Indies

Dwarf, creeping or pendent epiphytes or lithophytes with small round to spindle-shaped pseudobulbs, 1-leafed at apex. Leaves linear, fleshy. Inflorescences terminal; peduncle threadlike, usually 1-flowered. Flowers bell-shaped or spreading, small to large, white or greenish white sometimes marked or flushed with maroon or purple; sepals and petals subsimilar, narrowly triangular; lip unlobed, sometimes clawed. Column broader at the apex, pollinia 4.

CULTIVATION: Plants are most successful mounted on a raft or slab, in only light shade, with high humidity and good air movement. They require cool conditions, except for *Homalopetalum pumilio*, the most widespread species and most often cultivated, which grows well in intermediate conditions. *Homalopetalum pumilio* can also be grown potted in a fine epiphyte compost.

Homalopetalum pumilio (Reichenbach f.) Schlechter

Pseudobulbs ovoid, ca. 5 mm long. Leaf 10–15 × 3 mm. Inflorescence 10–15 cm long. Flowers 5–6 cm across, spidery, translucent pale green or greenish white marked with purple; sepals and petals spreading, narrow, lip broader.

Epiphytic in wet forest, often oak forest, 700–1500 m (2300–5000 ft.)

Mexico, Central America, Ecuador

Houlletia Brongniart

TRIBE: Maxillarieae

SUBTRIBE: Stanhopeinae

ETYMOLOGY: Named for Jean-Baptiste Houllet (1815–1890), who collected the type species, *H. stapeliiflora* Brongniart, in Brazil

DISTRIBUTION: 9 species in Central and South America

Epiphytic or terrestrial plants related to *Stanhopea*; pseudobulbs ovoid, 1-leafed at apex. Leaves large, plicate, petiolate. Inflorescences lateral, erect, arching or pendent, laxly 1- to several-flowered. Flowers large, showy; sepals and petals free, spreading, subsimilar but the petals narrower; lip trilobed, hypochile with 2 horn-like lobes, epichile simple or lobed. Pollinia 2.

CULTIVATION: Epiphytic species should be grown in baskets like *Stanhopea* as the inflorescences are usually pendent. Species with erect inflorescences can be grown in pots in a coarse, free-draining compost. They need cool to intermediate conditions, with moderate shade and plenty of water while growing. They should be kept drier while resting but not allowed to dry out completely.

Houlletia odoratissima Linden ex Lindley & Paxton

SYN. *Houlletia picta* Linden & Reichenbach f., *H. boliviana* Schlechter

Pseudobulbs to 8 cm long. Leaves elliptic, to 50 cm long including a petiole to 20 cm long. Inflorescence erect, to 45 cm long, loosely several-flowered. Flowers ca. 7 cm across, nodding, long-lasting, scented; sepals and petals deep maroon-brown edged with pale brown; lip white marked with red, epichile clawed, trilobed.

Holcoglossum amesianum

Homalopetalum pumilio

Holcoglossum kimballianum

Houlletia odoratissima

Terrestrial in dense thickets, 1000–2000 m (3300–6600 ft.)

Bolivia, Brazil, Colombia, Ecuador, Peru, Venezuela

Houlletia tigrina Linden ex Lindley

SYN. *Houlletia landsbergii* Linden & Reichenbach f.

Pseudobulbs 3–5 cm long. Leaves to 50 cm long, including a long petiole. Inflorescence pendent, 1- to 4-flowered. Flowers ca. 6 cm across, reddish with yellowish reticulations; lip creamy white, the epichile barred with red.

Epiphytic in rain forest and cloud forest, 1000–1500 m (3300–5000 ft.)

Central and South America

Huntleya Bateman ex Lindley

TRIBE: Maxillarieae

SUBTRIBE: Zygopetalinae

ETYMOLOGY: Named for J. T. Huntley, a 19th-century orchid grower

DISTRIBUTION: 14 species in Central and South America and Trinidad

Sympodial plants lacking pseudobulbs. Leaves distichous, forming a fan, plicate, thin-textured or leathery, pale green. Inflorescences axillary, 1-flowered, shorter than leaves. Flowers large, showy, fleshy, starry, often glossy; sepals and petals subsimilar, spreading; lip articulated to apex of column-foot, with a transverse, fringed basal callus. Pollinia 4, flattened, superposed.

CULTIVATION: Plants can be grown in a pot or basket or mounted on a raft in intermediate conditions, in moderate shade with high humidity and good ventilation throughout the year.

Huntleya burtii (Endres & Reichenbach f.) Pfitzer

Leaves 8–10, to 40 × 4 cm. Inflorescence to 16 cm tall. Flowers to 12 cm across, waxy, long-lasting, cream to pale yellow, whitish in the center, the petals with a red blotch near the base, the tips of the sepals and petals glossy chocolate brown; lip brown, white at the base.

Epiphytic in rain forest, 400–900 m (1320–3000 ft.)

Central America

SIMILAR SPECIES: *Huntleya meleagris* Lindley from South America and Trinidad is sometimes considered synonymous. *Huntleya wallisii* (Reichenbach f.) Rolfe from Ecuador has larger flowers with the apical two-thirds of the sepals, petals, and lip deep red-brown.

Huntleya citrina Rolfe

Flowers small, 3–5 cm across, lemon yellow, the hairs on the callus purple.

Epiphytic in forest, ca. 250 m (825 ft.)

Colombia, Ecuador

Huntleya lucida (Rolfe) Rolfe

Flowers to 8 cm across; sepals and petals purple-brown with a green central band, white at the base; lip entire or obscurely trilobed, dark red, white at the base and apex; column white with purple lines.

Epiphytic in forest, 500–800 m (1650–2640 ft)

Venezuela

Hymenorchis Schlechter

TRIBE: Vandeae

SUBTRIBE: Aeridinae

ETYMOLOGY: From Greek *hymen*, membranous, and *orchis*, orchid, referring to the texture of the flowers

DISTRIBUTION: 10 species in Java, Philippines, New Guinea, and New Caledonia

Dwarf epiphytes with short stems and fine roots. Leaves fleshy, the margins finely serrated. Inflorescences short, unbranched, few- to several-flowered. Flowers very thin-textured; sepals and petals subsimilar, spreading or almost bell-shaped, the margins finely serrate; lip entire, concave, small, spurred at the base. Column short and stout, pollinia 2.

CULTIVATION: Species of *Hymenorchis* grow on tall trees in mist forest. They should be mounted and given light shade, intermediate conditions, and high humidity throughout the year.

Hymenorchis javanica (Teijsmann & Binnendijk) Schlechter

SYN. *Saccolabium javanicum* (Teijsmann & Binnendijk) J. J. Smith

Stems very short, 4- to 10-leaved. Leaves ca. 2 × 1 cm, oblong, fleshy, the margins serrated and with some short hairs. Inflorescence pendent, less than 2 cm long, 4- to 12-flowered. Flowers rather bell-shaped, ca. 1 cm long; sepals and petals translucent white, lip small, fleshy, green; spur 3–4 mm long, parallel to the ovary, swollen on the lower side.

Epiphytic in open forest, 900–1000 m (3000–3300 ft.)

Java

Ida A. Ryan & Oakeley

TRIBE: Maxillarieae

SUBTRIBE: Maxillariinae

ETYMOLOGY: Named for a mythical huntress from Crete, whose companion was called Lycaste

DISTRIBUTION: About 37 species and several natural hybrids in the West Indies and South America

Robust epiphytes, lithophytes, or terrestrials with ovoid to tall, tapering, cylindrical pseudobulbs, without spines, 2- to 4-leaved at apex. Leaves ovate-lanceolate, plicate. Inflorescences basal, erect to pendent, 1-flowered, occasionally 2-flowered. Flowers campanulate or semi-campanulate to pendulous, green, green-yellow, white, orange, or brown; lateral sepals usually falcate; lip usually trilobed, side lobes erect, not extending to base of flower; midlobe large, the margins usually fringed or toothed. Often fragrant at dusk or at night. Pollinia in 2 unequal pairs on long, S-shaped stipes.

CULTIVATION: These plants should be grown in pots or baskets in a

Huntleya meleagris

Huntleya wallisii

Hymenorchis javanica

Houlletia tigrina

Huntleya lucida

compost of 2 parts perlite or bark and 1 part chopped sphagnum moss. They require intermediate or cool conditions depending on their origin, plenty of water while in growth, and light shade. Leaves may become scorched in direct sunlight and are also easily damaged by water when young. Plants should be kept drier in the resting period.

Ida barringtoniae (J. E. Smith) A. Ryan & Oakeley

SYN. *Lycaste barringtoniae* (J. E. Smith) Lindley

Pseudobulbs 8 × 5 cm. Leaves 50 × 7 cm long. Scapes 6 cm long. Flowers nodding, 3.5 cm wide, not opening wide, greenish yellow to tawny-brown, midlobe yellow or orange, fringed; callus with 5 keels.

There are 2 geographically separated subspecies. Subsp. *barringtoniae* comes from the Caribbean. Subsp. *rossyi* (Hoehne) Oakeley is a rare coastal plant from southeastern Brazil and is probably extinct in the wild.

Epiphytic in woodland or thicket or lithophytic on cliffs and rocks, 750–1150 m (2460–3800 ft.)

Caribbean, southeastern Brazil

Ida cinnabarina (Lindley) Oakeley

SYN. *Lycaste denningiana* Reichenbach f., *L. cinnabarina* Lindley

Large plants. Pseudobulbs 8.5 × 6 cm. Leaves 75 × 10 cm. Scapes erect, 15–50 cm long. Flowers semi-campanulate, 7 cm wide, fragrant at dusk; sepals olive green, petals pale green to yellow, lip dark orange, indistinctly trilobed, callus wide, fleshy with 5 keels. Prefers full sun in cultivation.

Terrestrial in grassland and lithophytic or epiphytic in light woodland, 1500–2600 m (5000–8600 ft.)

Colombia, Ecuador, Peru (possibly Venezuela)

Ida fimbriata (Poeppig & Endlicher) A. Ryan & Oakeley

SYN. *Lycaste fimbriata* Poeppig & Endlicher

Long confused with *Ida ciliata*. Pseudobulbs ovoid, to 15 × 6.5 cm. Leaves to 120 × 15 cm. Scapes to 35 cm long. Flowers 7.5 cm across, semi-campanulate, night-scented, green or greenish white; lip cream to yellow with an orange or yellow callus, midlobe with a few fringes, callus flat with 5 large equal keels, apex expanded and fleshy.

Lithophytic and epiphytic, 1000–2800 m (3300–9250 ft.); terrestrial in full sun at higher altitudes

Bolivia, Colombia, Ecuador, Peru, Venezuela (doubtful)

SIMILAR SPECIES: *Ida ciliata* (Ruiz & Pavón) A. Ryan & Oakeley, from Peru, differs in having pale cream-yellow flowers, a grooved callus, and a finely laciniate margin to the midlobe. It more closely resembles *I. fragrans* than *I. fimbriata*.

Ida fragrans (Oakeley) Oakeley

SYN. *Lycaste fragrans* Oakeley

Pseudobulbs 10 × 6 cm. Leaves to 100 × 15 cm. Scape to 17 cm. Flowers pale green, to 6.5 cm wide, night-scented; lip side lobes erect, incurved, midlobe flat, margins finely fringed (laciniate); callus of 3 fine keels flanked by 2 large keels.

Terrestrial and epiphytic in forest margins or light woodland, 1400–1900 m (4600–6300)

Colombia, Ecuador, Peru

Ida locusta (Reichenbach f.) A. Ryan & Oakeley

SYN. *Lycaste locusta* Reichenbach f.

Pseudobulbs 8.5 × 5 cm. Leaves 75 × 8 cm. Inflorescence erect, to 40 cm. Flowers nodding, night-scented, 7 cm across, dark green; lip with a white fringe, callus fleshy with a deep groove between 2 keels.

Terrestrial or lithophytic in full sun on grassy slopes, epiphytic on woodland margins at lower altitudes, 2200–2700 m (7260–8900 ft.)

Peru

Ionopsis Kunth

TRIBE: Maxillarieae

SUBTRIBE: Oncidiinae

ETYMOLOGY: From Greek *ion*, violet, and *opsis*, like, meaning resembling violets

DISTRIBUTION: 6 species from Florida to South America

Pseudobulbs small, with or without an apical leaf, but with several distichous subtending leaves. Inflorescences branched, many-flowered. Flowers showy; sepals and petals similar, erect or spreading, the lateral sepals joined at the base forming a pouch or sac below the lip; lip much larger than other parts, clawed, with 2 calli. Pollinia 2.

CULTIVATION: Plants can be grown in small pots but are better mounted. They require intermediate temperatures, moderate shade, high humidity, and good ventilation and should not be allowed to dry out completely.

Ionopsis utricularioides (Swartz) Lindley

Pseudobulbs to 2 × 0.5 cm, hidden in leaf bases. Leaves several, lanceolate, to 20 × 3 cm. Inflorescence basal, much-branched, to 80 cm long, many-flowered. Flowers white, pink, or magenta, the lip with darker veining and darker at the base; sepals and

Ionopsis utricularioides

petals 6–7 mm long, lip to 16 mm long, fan-shaped, usually bilobed at the apex.

Twig epiphyte in woodland and forest, sometimes in citrus plantations, 0–800 m (2640 ft.)

United States (Florida), West Indies, Central and South America

Isabelia Barbosa Rodrigues

SYN. *Neolauchea* Kraenzlin, *Sophronitella* Schlechter

TRIBE: Epidendreae

SUBTRIBE: Laeliinae

ETYMOLOGY: Named for Brazilian princess Isabel de Alcantara (1911–2003), Countess of Eu

DISTRIBUTION: 3 species and 1 natural hybrid in Brazil and northeastern Argentina

Small epiphytes with short rhizome; pseudobulbs clustered, ovoid, covered with fibrous bracts, 1-leafed at apex. Leaves linear or needle-shaped. Inflorescence terminal, 1- or 2-flowered. Flowers white, pink, or magenta; sepals similar; petals either narrower or broader; lip entire.

CULTIVATION: Plants do well mounted on bark in intermediate, humid, moderately shady conditions, but can also be grown in pans. They should be allowed to dry out between waterings but not to remain dry for long periods.

Isabelia violacea (Lindley) van den Berg & M. W. Chase

SYN. *Sophronitella violacea* Schlechter

Pseudobulbs ca. 25 × 7 mm, sheathed, 1-leafed at apex. Leaves to 8 × 0.5 cm, linear. Inflorescence ca. 5 cm long, 1- or 2-flowered. Flowers ca. 4 cm across, violet-purple.

Epiphytic in forest, often in dryish areas, ca. 1000 m (3300 ft.)

Brazil

Isabelia virginalis Barbosa Rodrigues

Pseudobulbs covered with an open net of fibrous bracts. Leaves dark green, to 6 cm long. Flowers 10–12 mm across, long-lasting, white, the sepals tinged with pink or violet; sepals spreading, the lateral sepals joined at the base and forming a small sac with the lip; lip unlobed, recurved in the middle. Column fleshy, tipped with purple. Flowers autumn–winter.

Ida fimbriata

Ida locusta

Isabelia pulchella

Epiphytic in humid forest or in debris in rock crevices, 200–1500 m (660–5000 ft.)

Eastern Brazil, northeastern Argentina

SIMILAR SPECIES: *Isabelia pulchella* (syn. *Neolauchea pulchella* Kraenzlin, *Meiracyllium wettsteinii* Porsch), which grows as an epiphyte in Atlantic rain forest in Brazil, has rosy red to magenta flowers.

Isochilus R. Brown

TRIBE: Epidendreae

SUBTRIBE: Ponerinae

ETYMOLOGY: From Greek *iso*, equal, and *cheilos*, lip, probably referring to the lip's resemblance to the sepals and petals

DISTRIBUTION: About 15 species in Mexico, the West Indies, Central and South America

Epiphytes or lithophytes with a rhizome covered with dark brown sheaths and fleshy roots. Stems reed-like, covered in leaf sheaths. Leaves numerous, distichous, linear to narrowly elliptical, erect or spreading. Inflorescences terminal, unbranched, usually several-flowered. Flowers distichous, small, tubular to bell-shaped; sepals joined for part of their length, recurved near the apices, petals free, recurved at apex; lip with a short claw, simple, rather similar to sepals and petals. Pollinia 4.

CULTIVATION: Plants are usually grown in pots, which need to be big enough to accommodate their numerous roots, in a free-draining, bark-based mixture. Most species require intermediate conditions, light shade, and good ventilation with plenty of water while growing. In winter, they should be kept drier and given more light.

Isochilus linearis Jacquin

Stems to 80 cm long. Leaves linear, to 6 × 0.4 cm, set close together. Inflorescence 2–6 cm long, several-flowered. Flowers ca. 1 cm long, deep rose-pink to magenta, tubular, the sepals joined at the base.

Epiphytic in humid forest or lithophytic on mossy rocks, 600–1660 m (2000–5450 ft.)

Mexico, West Indies, Central and South America

Jacquiniella Schlechter

TRIBE: Epidendreae

SUBTRIBE: Laeliinae

ETYMOLOGY: Named for Nicholas Joseph von Jacquin (1727–1817), a professor of botany at Leiden

DISTRIBUTION: 11 species in Mexico, the West Indies, Central and South America

Small epiphytes with tufted, cane-like, leafy stems. Leaves distichous, fleshy, linear. Inflorescences terminal, 1- to several-flowered. Flowers small; sepals and petals subsimilar; sepals joined at the base; lip shortly joined at base to column-foot, entire or trilobed. Column short; pollinia 4, waxy.

CULTIVATION: Grow mounted or potted in an open bark mix in intermediate, humid, well-ventilated conditions in partial shade. Give ample water while growing; keep drier and brighter in winter.

Jacquiniella equitantifolia (Ames) Dressler

SYN. *Epidendrum equitantifolium* Ames

Stem leafy, to 40 cm long, usually pendent. Leaves laterally flattened, overlapping, to 20 × 1 cm. Inflorescence to 15 cm long, 1- to 3-flowered. Flowers ca. 13 mm long, greenish brown to reddish brown, scented at night; lip trilobed in the middle, the midlobe fleshy.

This species is easily grown and flowers for most of the year, though mainly in autumn and winter.

Epiphytic in wet montane forest and cloud forest, 1000–1600 m (3300–5300 ft.)

Mexico to Nicaragua

Jacquiniella globosa (Jacquin) Schlechter

SYN. *Epidendrum globosum* Jacquin, *Isochilus globosus* (Jacquin) Lindley

Stem to 15 cm long. Leaves linear, to 2 cm long, dark green, sometimes with purple marks. Flowers usually several in a terminal cluster, 3–5 mm long, not opening widely, yellow-brown or yellow-green, often tinged with red or purple; lip saccate at base.

Epiphytic in wet woodland, 330–1400 m (1100–4600 ft.)

Mexico, Central and South America, West Indies

Jumellea Schlechter

TRIBE: Vandeae

SUBTRIBE: Angraecinae

ETYMOLOGY: Named for Henri Jumelle (1866–1935), a French botanist who worked on the Madagascar flora

DISTRIBUTION: About 60 species in Madagascar, Comoro Islands, and the Mascarene Islands with 2 on mainland Africa

Monopodial epiphytes or lithophytes with long or short stems. Leaves distichous or forming a fan, usually strap-shaped, obtusely and unequally bilobed at the apex. Inflorescences always 1-flowered, but often numerous. Flowers scented, white or greenish white, often turning yellow

Isabelia virginalis

Isochilus linearis

Jacquiniella equitantifolia, flowers. M. MacConaill

Jacquiniella equitantifolia, leaves. M. MacConaill

or apricot as they age; dorsal sepal somewhat reflexed, lateral sepals joined at the base below the spur; sepals and petals usually deflexed; lip entire, narrow or clawed at the base and never encircling the column as in *Angraecum*, with a slender spur, long or short, at the base. Column with 2 arms at the base joined on the inner side to the edge of the mouth of the spur and on the outer side to the outer margin of the lateral sepals and petals, so that these are slightly twisted.
CULTIVATION: Most species do well in intermediate conditions and moderate shade. They are usually grown in pots in a bark-based compost, but smaller species and those with a pendent habit can be mounted.

Jumellea arborescens H. Perrier de la Bâthie
Robust plants with woody stems up to 1 m high, the lower part covered in old leaf bases, the upper part leafy, with up to 20 leaves. Leaves distichous, to 15 × 2.5 cm, folded towards the base. Sepals and petals to 30 mm long, linear-lanceolate. Lip 24–29 × 4–5.5 mm with a channeled claw and a thick keel in the mouth of the spur, the blade narrowly rhomboid; spur to 14 cm long, the basal 1.5–2 cm thickened and parallel to the ovary, then bent down and very slender.

Flowers of this species seem to self-fertilize as capsules almost always form.

Epiphytic on tree trunks, or lithophytic, ca. 1400 m (4600 ft.)

Madagascar

Jumellea comorensis (Reichenbach f.) Schlechter
Stem erect or pendent, branched, to 30 cm long, leafy along its length. Leaves distichous, to 10 × 1 cm, linear to strap-shaped, dark green. Inflorescences arising along stem. Sepals and petals ca. 30 mm long. Lip 33 mm long with a claw 13 mm long, blade rhomboid or ovate; spur 15 cm long.

Humid, low-elevation forest, 0–600 m (2000 ft.)

Comoro Islands

Jumellea confusa (Schlechter) Schlechter
Stems erect or pendent, woody, 12–60 cm long. Leaves numerous, narrowly strap-shaped but folded at the base, to 12 × 2.5 cm. Sepals, petals, and lip 2–3 cm long; spur 12–13 cm long.

Lithophytic or epiphytic in forest, 600–2000 m (2000–6600 ft.)

Madagascar

Jumellea densefoliata Senghas
Stem short. Leaves numerous, set close together in 2 rows, 5–7 cm long, oblong. Sepals and petals greenish white, 17–18 mm long. Lip white, of similar length, clawed at the base, the blade broadly ovate; spur slender, 11–13 cm long.

Lithophytic in woodland

Madagascar

Jumellea fragrans (Thouars) Schlechter
Erect plants from the Mascarene Islands, forming dense clumps. Stem woody, 24–60 cm tall, leafy near apex. Leaves 10–15 cm long, narrowly strap-shaped. Flowers medium-sized; sepals and petals ca. 20 mm long; lip 20 mm long, oblong-spathulate; spur 2.5–3.5 cm long. The leaves are aromatic and are infused in water to make a sort of tea, known as "fahan," and are also used to flavor rum.

Epiphytic in rain forest at medium altitudes

Mauritius, Réunion

Jumellea sagittata H. Perrier
Large plants, branching at the base. Stem short. Leaves forming a fan, 30–60 × 3–5 cm, strap-shaped, folded at the base. Flowers white, strongly scented at night; sepals, petals, and lip ca. 3.5 cm long; lip diamond-shaped, clawed at the base; spur ca. 7 cm long.

Epiphytic on tree trunks in mossy forest, ca. 1400 m (4600 ft.)

Madagascar

Jumellea walleri (Rolfe) la Croix
SYN. *Jumellea filicornoides* (De Wildeman) Schlechter
Stem 20–40 cm long, erect when young, leafy towards the apex, forming large clumps. Leaves several, distichous, to 12 cm long, strap-shaped, dark green. Flowers ca. 5 cm in diameter, glistening white turning apricot as they age, sweetly scented; lip to 25 mm long, rhomboid from a narrow base; spur 2–3 cm long.

Riverine forest and high rainfall woodland, 350–1700 m (1150–5600 ft.)

Kenya, Malawi, Mozambique, South Africa, Tanzania, Zimbabwe

Kefersteinia Reichenbach f.

TRIBE: Maxillarieae
SUBTRIBE: Zygopetalinae
ETYMOLOGY: Named for Mr. Keferstein, a 19th-century German orchid grower
DISTRIBUTION: 60–70 species in Central and South America
Small to medium-sized sympodial plants related to *Chondrorhyncha* with a long or short rhizome, lacking pseudobulbs. Leaves forming a fan, linear to lanceolate or oblanceolate, articulated to a sheath at the base. Inflorescences usually 1-flowered, arising from base of plant or between the leaves, several often borne at a time. Flowers thin-textured; sepals and petals subsimilar, spreading; lip broad, articulated to column-foot, entire or obscurely trilobed, with a basal fleshy callus, sometimes with the margins fringed. Column stout, keeled on the underside; pollinia 4, waxy, laterally compressed.
CULTIVATION: Many species grow in the Andes of Colombia and Ecuador and almost all require intermediate conditions and a humid but well-ventilated situation in heavy shade. Most are epiphytic but some also grow terrestrially in humus or moss. They are usually

grown in pots in a medium bark mix, but species with creeping rhizomes can be mounted. Plants should be watered carefully in spring to avoid getting water on the new growths, which are liable to rot. In winter, plants should be watered less but should not be allowed to remain dry.

Kefersteinia costaricensis Schlechter

SYN. *Chondrorhyncha costaricensis* (Schlechter) P. Allen

Leaves 12–18 cm long; inflorescence to 4 cm long, arching or pendent, 1-flowered. Flowers small, creamy-white, usually spotted with pink or red-brown; lip ca. 1 cm long, suborbicular, entire.

Epiphytic in rain forest and cloud forest, 50–1650 m (165–5410 ft.)

Costa Rica, Nicaragua, Panama

Kefersteinia graminea (Lindley) Reichenbach f.

SYN. *Zygopetalum gramineum* Lindley

Leaves 18–36 cm long, linear-lanceolate. Inflorescence to 7.5 cm long, 1- to 3-flowered. Flowers 5 cm across, sepals and petals pale green or yellow-green, lip white, all heavily spotted and blotched with maroon; lip

Jumellea comorensis. E. la Croix

Kefersteinia graminea

Jumellea sagittata. E. la Croix

orbicular, 2.4 cm across, concave, the margins undulate, the apex deflexed; callus of 2 lamellae.

Epiphytic on tree trunks in dense forest

Colombia, Ecuador, Venezuela

Kefersteinia lactea (Reichenbach f.) Schlechter

SYN. *Chondrorhyncha lactea* (Reichenbach f.) L. O. Williams, *Zygopetalum lacteum* Reichenbach f.

Leaves 8–12 cm long, elliptic, acute. Inflorescence 2 cm long, 1-flowered. Flowers small, white, the base of the petals and lip dotted with red-brown; lip suborbicular, ca. 1 × 1 cm.

Epiphytic in rain forest, 500–1300 m (1650–4300 ft.)

Costa Rica, Mexico, Panama

Kefersteinia laminata (Reichenbach f.) Schlechter

Leaves ca. 10 cm long. Inflorescences 1-flowered, numerous, arising between the leaves. Flowers ca. 2 cm across, white, lightly or heavily spotted with pink; lip recurved, with a pink to purple blotch in the center and a white apex.

Epiphytic in rain forest, 1000–1300 m (3300–4300 ft.)

Colombia, Ecuador

Kefersteinia laminata

Kefersteinia mystacina (Reichenbach f.) Reichenbach f.

Leaves gray-green. Inflorescence erect, to 30 cm long; flowers ca. 4 cm across, yellow-green, the lip white, deeply fringed, with erect, pink side lobes forming a horse-shoe shape below the column.

Epiphytic in rain forest, 1100–1400 m (3600–4600 ft.)

Panama to Peru

Kefersteinia ocellata Garay

Leaves broad, 8–12 cm long. Flowers 2.5 cm across, pale yellow striped with purple. This species grows quickly and easily in cultivation.

Epiphytic in rain forest and cloud forest, 600–1500 m (2000–5000 ft.)

Colombia, Ecuador

Kegeliella Mansfeld

TRIBE: Maxillarieae

SUBTRIBE: Stanhopeinae

ETYMOLOGY: Diminutive of *Kegelia*, the name (no longer in use) of a genus established by H. G. Reichenbach in honor of Hermann Aribert Heinrich Kegel (1819–1856), a gardener at Halle University, Germany

DISTRIBUTION: 3 or perhaps 4 species in the West Indies, Central and northern South America

Sympodial epiphytes related to *Gongora* with ovoid, angular, somewhat compressed pseudobulbs, 1- to 3-leaved at apex. Leaves petiolate, elliptic, plicate. Inflorescences basal, pendent, unbranched, few- to many-flowered. Flowers small to medium-sized; sepals free, spreading, the outside covered with glandular hairs; petals smaller than sepals; lip fleshy or membranous, trilobed, with an erect, fleshy callus; side lobes large, erect or spreading, midlobe small. Column long, arched, broadly winged towards the apex; pollinia 2.

CULTIVATION: Because of the pendent inflorescences, plants should be grown on a raft or in a basket in a sphagnum moss and bark mixture. They require intermediate to warm conditions, light shade, and high humidity. They should be watered throughout the year, but less often in winter.

Kegeliella kupperi Mansfeld

Pseudobulbs 2–3 cm long, 2-leaved at apex. Leaves elliptic, to 8 × 6 cm, dark green above, purplish underneath. Inflorescence pendent, to 30 cm long, covered with blackish hairs, 4- to 8-flowered. Flowers ca. 2.5 cm in diameter; sepals and petals greenish, white or pale pink, heavily barred and blotched with maroon; lip clawed, greenish. Column green.

Epiphytic on mossy tree trunks in wet forest, 100–800 m (330–2640 ft.)

Costa Rica, Colombia, Panama

SIMILAR SPECIES: *Kegeliella atropilosa* L. O. Williams & A. H. Heller from Mexico and Central America has a subsessile lip ± parallel to the column.

Koellensteinia Reichenbach f.

TRIBE: Maxillarieae

SUBTRIBE: Zygopetalinae

ETYMOLOGY: Named for the Austrian Captain Kellner von Koellenstein

DISTRIBUTION: 17 species in Central and South America

Terrestrial or epiphytic plants related to *Zygopetalum*. Stems short, leafy, usually forming a pseudobulb, 1- to 3-leaved. Leaves petiolate, linear to oblong. Inflorescences lateral, branched or unbranched, few- to many-flowered. Flowers small to medium-sized; sepals and petals subsimilar, free, spreading; lip trilobed, articulated to the column-foot. Column short, sometimes winged; pollinia 2 or 4.

CULTIVATION: Plants require intermediate conditions, moderate shade, and high humidity. They are usually grown potted in a free-draining bark mixture and should not be allowed to dry out completely for any length of time.

Kefersteinia lactea

Kefersteinia mystacina

Kefersteinia ocellata

Kegeliella kupperi

Koellensteinia graminea (Lindley) Reichenbach f.

SYN. *Aganisia graminea* (Lindley) N. E. Brown

Stems short, not pseudobulbous. Leaves 1–3, to 26 × 1 cm, grasslike. Inflorescence to 25 cm tall, 1- to several-flowered, usually unbranched. Flowers 1–2 cm in diameter, creamy yellow to yellowish pink with maroon bars. Lip side lobes erect, midlobe fan-shaped with a fleshy, bilobed callus.

Epiphytic in shade in wet forest, 50–1000 m (165–3300 ft.)

West Indies, South America

Lacaena Lindley

TRIBE: Maxillarieae

SUBTRIBE: Stanhopeinae

ETYMOLOGY: From Greek, an alternative name for Helen of Troy

DISTRIBUTION: 2 species from Mexico to Colombia

Epiphytes, sometimes lithophytes, with ridged, clustered pseudobulbs, 2- to 4-leaved at the apex. Leaves large, petiolate, plicate. Inflorescences basal, unbranched. Flowers fleshy, showy; sepals spreading, lateral sepals joined at the base to the column-foot to form a short mentum; petals smaller than sepals; lip hinged to column-foot, trilobed. Column ± club-shaped, pollinia 2.

CULTIVATION: Grow plants in baskets in a coarse bark compost, like *Stanhopea* and *Acineta*. They require intermediate conditions and moderate shade, and should be watered and fertilized freely while in growth. While plants are resting, move them to a brighter position and spray only enough to stop the pseudobulbs shriveling.

Lacaena bicolor Lindley

Pseudobulbs to 11 × 6 cm, 3- or 4-leaved. Leaves to 45 × 11 cm, petiole ca. 6 cm long. Inflorescence to 50 cm long, many-flowered. Peduncle, ovary, and outside of flowers with brown scurfy hairs. Flowers to 5 cm across, widely bell-shaped, whitish or yellow-green with purple marks and spots, with a rather unpleasant scent; lip side lobes erect, midlobe deflexed, not clawed, callus deep purple.

Epiphytic in wet forest, ca. 900 m (3000 ft.)

Mexico, Central America, Colombia

Lacaena spectabilis (Klotzsch) Reichenbach f.

Pseudobulbs ovoid, ca. 6 × 3 cm, 2- or 3-leaved. Leaves to 30 × 5 cm. Inflorescence 25–30 cm long, 15- to 20-flowered. Flowers ca. 4 cm across, creamy white spotted with red; lip midlobe clawed, without a purple blotch.

Epiphytic in rain forest, 1000–1700 m (3300–5600 ft.)

Mexico, Central America

Laelia Lindley

SYN. *Schomburgkia* Lindley

TRIBE: Epidendreae

SUBTRIBE: Laeliinae

ETYMOLOGY: Named for Laelia, one of the Vestal Virgins of ancient Rome

DISTRIBUTION: More than 20 species from Mexico to Central America

Epiphytes or lithophytes; pseudobulbs sometimes stalked, globose to club-shaped, laterally compressed, smooth or grooved, covered with papery sheaths, 1- to 3-leaved at apex. Leaves leathery or fleshy, sometimes purple-tinged. Inflorescences terminal, the flowers often clustered near the apex. Flowers resupinate or non-resupinate, showy, sometimes scented; sepals and petals spreading, free, subsimilar or the sepals narrower, the margins sometimes undulate; lip trilobed, side lobes upcurved, often forming a tube round the column, midlobe flat or recurved, the margins often crisped or undulate. Pollinia 8.

There have been many changes recently in the nomenclature of this group of orchids. Following DNA analysis, Brazilian species formerly in *Laelia*, which have for long been recognized as not very closely related to the Mexican and Central American species, have been placed in *Sophronitis*. Most species of *Schomburgkia*, several of which were originally described in *Laelia*, have been moved to that genus (others have been placed in *Myrmecophila*). It remains to be seen if these changes will be generally accepted.

Species of *Laelia* (both those currently accepted and others now in different genera), have been widely involved in intergeneric hybridization with related genera such as *Cattleya* and *Brassia*.

CULTIVATION: Most species can be grown at intermediate temperatures in a standard bark-based compost. They need light shade and should be allowed to dry out between waterings, which helps to promote flowering. After flowering, they should be kept drier although not so dry that the pseudobulbs start to shrivel. When repotting is necessary, it should be done when new roots are just starting to grow.

Laelia anceps Lindley

Pseudobulbs 5–7 cm tall, ovoid, laterally compressed, 1- or 2-leaved. Leaves strap-shaped, ca. 15 cm long. Inflorescence 30–70 cm tall, 2- to 5-flowered. Flowers 8–10 cm across, usually pale to mid violet-pink, the lip white in the throat with yellow lines, midlobe deep purple, but many color forms exist. Petals twice as wide as sepals. Flowering in winter.

Epiphytic in woodland and forest and on scattered trees, often in strong light, 500–1500 m (1650–5000 ft.)

Mexico, Guatemala

Laelia autumnalis (Lexarza) Lindley

Pseudobulbs to 15 cm long, club-shaped, grooved, 2- or 3-leaved. Leaves fleshy, 10–15 cm long. Inflorescence to 60 cm tall, 3- to 6-flowered. Flowers scented, 8–10 cm across, pink-purple, the lip pinkish

Koellensteinia graminea

Laelia anceps

Lacaena bicolor. R. Parsons

Laelia albida

Laelia furfuracea

Laelia gouldiana

white with a purple tip, yellow in the center. Flowering in autumn.

Epiphytic in submontane and montane woodland in fairly good light and lithophytic on mossy rocks, 1500–2600 m (5000–8600 ft.)

Mexico

SIMILAR SPECIES: *Laelia albida* Bateman ex Lindley has smaller, paler flowers than *L. autumnalis* and flowers in winter. *Laelia furfuracea* Lindley has light purple flowers with a deep purple lip and the ovary has scurfy hairs; it grows at altitudes of 2500–3000 m (8250–9900 ft.). *Laelia gouldiana* Reichenbach f. has flowers to 8 cm across, with wider petals than *L. autumnalis* and flowers later. All these come from Mexico.

Laelia rosea (Linden ex Lindley) C. Schweinfurth

SYN. *Schomburgkia rosea* Linden ex Lindley

Pseudobulbs to 15 cm long, 2-leaved. Leaves to 25 × 6 cm. Inflorescence to 55 cm long, densely few- to several-flowered; floral bracts pale pink, ca. 4 cm long. Flowers ca. 4 cm across; sepals and petals deep red-purple, narrow, the margins undulate, lip pink, with yellow keels.

Epiphytic or lithophytic

Colombia, Guyana, Venezuela

SIMILAR SPECIES: *Laelia splendida* (Schlechter) L. O. Williams (syn. *Schomburgkia splendida* Schlechter), from Colombia and Ecuador, has flowers 10 cm across and deep pink floral bracts ca. 9 cm long.

Laelia rubescens Lindley

Pseudobulbs ca. 7 × 4 cm, ovoid or oblong, compressed, 1-leafed, rarely 2-leaved. Leaves ca. 15 × 4 cm. Inflorescence to 75 cm tall, few- to several-flowered near the top. Flowers to 7 cm across, scented, pale mauve to pinkish purple, lip with a central purple blotch, trilobed at about the middle, disc with 2 or 3 ridges, midlobe with undulate margins, the apex truncate or acute.

Epiphytic or lithophytic in dry and wet woodland, in full sun, 0–1650 m (5410 ft.)

Mexico, Central America

Laelia speciosa (Kunth) Schlechter

Pseudobulbs to 6 cm long, 1-leafed. Leaves oblong, to 15 cm long. Inflorescence 12–15 cm long, 1- to 4-flowered. Flowers 12–18 cm across, pink-violet, lip white, streaked with deep violet, violet at tip. The humidity should not be too high and a dry rest is essential. Flowering spring–summer.

Epiphytic in open oak woodland in rather dry areas, 1400–2400 m (4600–7900 ft.)

Mexico

Laelia superbiens Lindley

SYN. *Schomburgkia superbiens* (Lindley) Rolfe

Pseudobulbs to 30 cm long, 1- or 2-leaved. Inflorescence to 80 cm long or more, many-flowered. Flowers 12–13 cm across, violet-purple, sepals and petals narrow, the margins undulate, lip with 5 yellow keels.

Epiphytic in open forest or terrestrial in ravines, to 2000 m (6600 ft.)

Mexico, Guatemala, Honduras

Laelia undulata (Lindley) L. O. Williams

SYN. *Schomburgkia undulata* Lindley

Pseudobulbs to 25 × 5 cm, club-shaped, grooved, 2-leaved. Leaves to 30 × 5 cm. Inflorescence to 1.5 m long, many-flowered. Flowers to 5 cm across, deep maroon-purple, sepals and petals narrow, undulate, twisted, lip rose-purple with 3–5 white keels.

Epiphytic or lithophytic in semi-deciduous forest, 200–300 m (660–1000 ft.)

Colombia, Trinidad, Venezuela

Lankesterella Ames

TRIBE: Cranichideae

SUBTRIBE: Spiranthinae

ETYMOLOGY: Named for Charles H. Lankester (1879–1969), an English

Laelia rosea

Laelia splendida

Laelia superbiens

Laelia rubescens

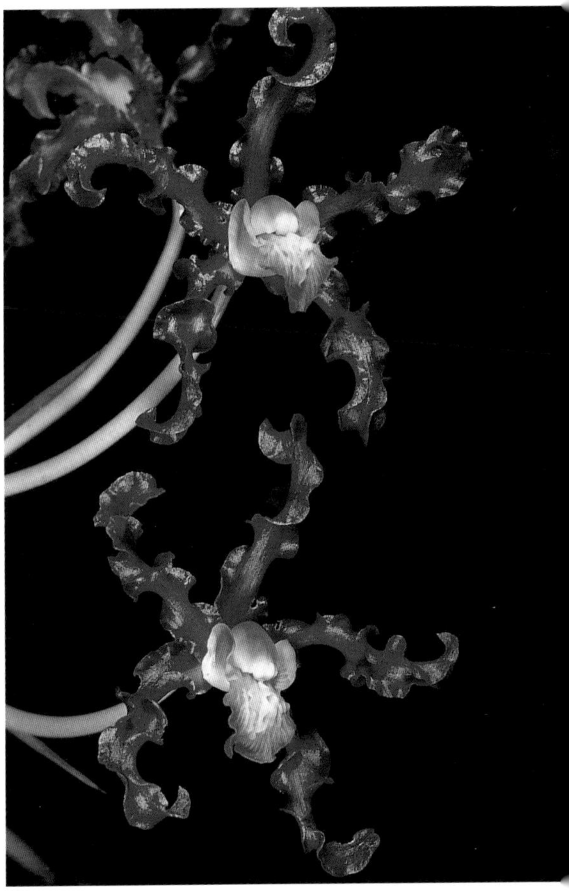

Laelia undulata

orchid grower who lived in Costa Rica

DISTRIBUTION: 12 species in Central and South America

Small epiphytes with fleshy, pubescent roots. Leaves evergreen, petiolate, in a basal rosette. Inflorescences densely hairy, usually arching or pendent, 1-sided, 1- to few-flowered. Flowers green or green and white; lateral sepals joined at base forming a spur with the base of the lip and the column-foot; petals joined in the lower half to the dorsal sepal; lip concave at the base, recurved at about the middle. Pollinia 4.

CULTIVATION: Because of the pendulous inflorescences, plants are usually mounted on bark with a pad of moss at the roots. They require intermediate conditions with good air movement and high humidity all year round.

Lankesterella orthantha (Kraenzlin) Garay

Leaves to 2.5 × 1 cm. Inflorescence 2.5–10 cm long, loosely 1- to 10-flowered. Flowers drooping, not opening widely, about 1 cm long; sepals green, hairy on the outside, petals and lip white.

Epiphytic in moss and lichen on trees in rain forest, 1500–1800 m (5000–6000 ft.)

Costa Rica, Colombia, Ecuador, Peru, Venezuela

Leochilus Knowles & Westcott

TRIBE: Maxillarieae

SUBTRIBE: Oncidiinae

ETYMOLOGY: From Greek *leios*, smooth, and *cheilos*, lip

DISTRIBUTION: 11 species in Mexico, the West Indies, Central and South America

Small epiphytes, often twig epiphytes, with clustered, ovoid, laterally compressed pseudobulbs covered with leafy sheaths, 1- or 2-leaved at apex. Inflorescences basal, branched or unbranched, loosely few- to many-flowered. Flowers small; sepals and petals subsimilar, spreading, free or partly joined; lip entire or trilobed, longer than other parts, with a fleshy callus. Pollinia 2.

CULTIVATION: Most species grow in wet forest at altitudes from 100 to 700 m (330–2300 ft.). They can be grown in intermediate conditions, in pots or preferably mounted, and should be watered throughout the year.

Leochilus carinatus (Lindley) Knowles & Westcott

SYN. *Oncidium carinatum* Lindley

Pseudobulbs ovoid, to 2.5 cm long, usually 2-leaved. Leaves to 12 × 1.5 cm. Inflorescence erect or pendent, to 15 cm long, several- to many-flowered. Flowers scented, to 2 cm long; sepals greenish yellow; petals creamy yellow striped with brown; lip pale yellow with brown spots.

Epiphytic on twigs and small branches in tropical deciduous forest

Mexico

Leochilus labiatus (Swartz) Kuntze

SYN. *Oncidium labiatum* (Swartz) Reichenbach f.

Pseudobulbs ovoid, to 2 cm long, 1-leafed. Leaves to 7 × 2 cm. Inflorescence unbranched, 6–9 cm long, few-flowered. Flowers ca. 12 mm long, translucent yellow or greenish flushed with reddish brown; lip yellow.

Twig epiphyte in tropical rain forest and plantations, 200–1300 m (660–4300 ft.)

Mexico, Central and South America, West Indies

Leochilus oncidioides Knowles & Westcott

SYN. *Rodriguezia maculata* Lindley

Pseudobulbs to 5 cm long, 1- or 2-leaved. Leaves to 17 × 3 cm. Inflorescence to 16 cm long, arching or pendent, few- to many-flowered. Flowers scented, ca. 10 mm long, pale green tinged with red.

Epiphytic on twigs and small branches in riverine forest and deciduous forest, 500–1500 m (1650–5000 ft.)

Mexico, Central America

Lepanthes Swartz

TRIBE: Epidendreae

SUBTRIBE: Pleurothallidinae

ETYMOLOGY: From Greek *lepis*, scale, and *anthos*, flower, thought to refer to the small, scalelike flowers

DISTRIBUTION: More than 800 species from Mexico, the West Indies, Central and South America

Dwarf epiphytes or lithophytes with a short, creeping rhizome and slender, tufted stems (ramicauls), clad in ribbed, thickened sheaths with ciliate margins, usually 1-leafed at the apex. Leaves varying in shape and texture, sometimes attractively patterned and velvety textured. Inflorescences unbranched, 1- to many-flowered, often lying flat on the leaf surface. Flowers small, in a wide range of colors; sepals subequal, the laterals often joined to form a synsepal; petals lobed, smaller than sepals; lip entire, bilobed or trilobed.

CULTIVATION: Species are not easy to cultivate. They can be grown mounted on bark or in small pots in a fine bark or a sphagnum-perlite compost, but require cool, shady, humid, airy conditions and must never be allowed to dry out. Because of this, they are grown most successfully in enclosed cases.

Lepanthes calodictyon Hooker

Stems 2.5–5 cm long. Leaves to 4 × 2.5 cm, elliptic to almost round with undulate or scalloped margins, bright green with a satiny appearance, with a dense network of purplish veins. Inflorescence 1- to several-flowered, the flowers open in succession. Flowers very small, red and yellow.

Epiphytic in wet forest and plantations, 750–1400 m (2460–4600 ft.)

Colombia, Ecuador

Lankesterella orthantha

Leochilus carinatus

Leochilus oncidioides

Lepanthes sp. in wild

Lepanthes calodictyon

Lepanthes escobariana Garay
Inflorescence shorter than leaf, few-flowered, the flowers open in succession. Flowers to 15 mm long, sepals yellow-orange, without tails, the lateral sepals with a broad red-purple streak.
Epiphytic in cloud forest
Colombia

Lepanthes exaltata Luer & R. Escobar
Inflorescence longer than leaf; flowers relatively large, flat, yellowish green flushed with purple-red; petals and lip red.
Epiphytic in cloud forest
Colombia

Lepanthes felis Luer & R. Escobar
Stems 1.5–4.5 cm long. Leaves to 2 × 1.4 cm, purplish beneath. Inflorescence ca. 2 cm long, on top of a leaf, with several flowers set close together and opening in succession. Flowers relatively large, to 2 cm long; sepals yellow, flushed and veined with red-purple, joined at the base forming a deep cup; petals bright green. The 2 green petals look like a cat's eyes, giving rise to the species name.
Epiphytic in cloud forest, 1900–2500 m (6300–8250 ft.)
Colombia

Lepanthes gargantua Reichenbach f.
The largest species in the genus with stems to 30 cm tall. Inflorescence to 6 cm tall, densely many-flowered, the flowers open in succession. Flowers to 3 cm across; sepals broad, yellow, without tails; lip peach to pink.
Epiphytic in forest, 900–3400 m (3000–11,200 ft.)
Colombia, Ecuador, Peru

Lepanthes ligiae Luer & R. Escobar
Flowers ca. 18 mm long, open in succession, yellow-green with a red lip.
Epiphytic in cloud forest, 1500–2000 m (5000–6600 ft.)
Colombia

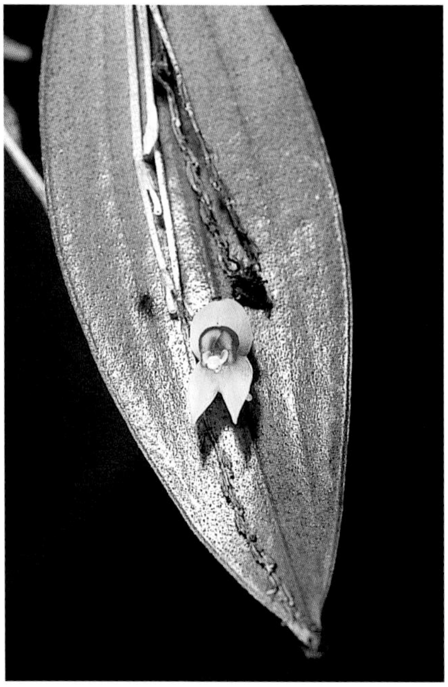
Lepanthes exaltata

Lepanthes lindleyana Oersted & Reichenbach f.
SYN. *Lepanthes micrantha* Ames
Stems 1–6 cm long. Leaves to 4 × 1 cm. Inflorescence dense, the flowers open in succession. Flowers small, distichous; sepals and petals yellowish; petals and lip orange or purple.
Epiphytic in cloud forest and oak forest, 1350–3000 m (4500–9900 ft.)
Costa Rica, Nicaragua, Panama, Colombia, Venezuela

Lepanthes telipogoniflora Schuiteman & A. de Wilde
Flowers large, flat, almost round, 15 × 15 mm, orange with a red lip.
Epiphytic in forest, ca. 500 m (1650 ft.)
Colombia

Lepanthopsis (Cogniaux) Ames

TRIBE: Epidendreae
SUBTRIBE: Pleurothallidinae
ETYMOLOGY: From *Lepanthes* and Greek *opsis*, like, meaning resembling *Lepanthes*
DISTRIBUTION: About 50 species in Florida, the West Indies, Central and South America

Dwarf epiphytes, usually tufted, sometimes scandent. Stems slender, clad in ribbed, tubular sheaths enlarged at the opening, 1-leafed. Leaves elliptical, sometimes flushed with purple. Inflorescences unbranched, 1- to many-flowered. Flowers distichous or secund, flat or cup-shaped; sepals and petals thin-textured; dorsal sepal free or joined at the base to laterals, lateral sepals partly joined; petals unlobed, lip entire or more rarely trilobed, fleshy.
CULTIVATION: Many species are twig epiphytes growing in wet forest or cloud forest and require cool or intermediate, shady conditions with high humidity all year round. They are usually grown mounted.

Lepanthopsis astrophora (Reichenbach f. ex Kraenzlin) Garay
Plants medium or large for genus. Stems 2–7 cm long. Leaves to 2.5 × 1.5 cm. Inflorescence to 17 cm long, loosely several-flowered with up to 6 flowers open at a time. Flowers resupinate, small, pale or bright violet, opening wide.
Epiphytic in forest, 730–1650 m (2400–5410 ft.)
Venezuela

Lepanthopsis floripecten (Reichenbach f.) Ames
Plants medium to large. Stems 2–10 cm long, enclosed in 4–8 dark sheaths. Leaves to 4.5 × 1.7 cm, with a short petiole. Inflorescence ca. 8 cm long, densely many-flowered, the flowers in 2 rows, open together. Flowers yellow-green or yellow-orange flushed with purple or brown.
Epiphytic in forest, 950–2000 m (3100–6600 ft.)
Mexico, Central and South America

Lepanthopsis vinacea C. Schweinfurth
Small to medium plants. Stems 1.5–9.5 cm long. Leaves to 2.5 × 1 cm. Inflorescence to 8 cm long, densely many-flowered, the flowers in 2 rows, open together. Flowers small, bright purple.

Lepanthes escobariana

Lepanthes felis

Lepanthes gargantua

Lepanthes ligiae

Lepanthes telipogoniflora

Lepanthopsis astrophora

Lepanthopsis floripecten

Lepanthopsis vinacea

Epiphytic in forest, 865–2000 m (2850–6600 ft.)
Ecuador, Venezuela

Leptotes Lindley

TRIBE: Epidendreae
SUBTRIBE: Laeliinae
ETYMOLOGY: From Greek *leptotes*, delicacy or gracefulness
DISTRIBUTION: 7 species in South America

Small epiphytes with short, cylindrical pseudobulbs, 1-leafed at apex. Leaves fleshy, terete, usually grooved on upper surface. Inflorescences terminal, unbranched, few-flowered. Flowers large for the size of plant; sepals and petals free, subsimilar; lip joined to the base of the column, trilobed, side lobes spreading, midlobe sometimes fleshy. Pollinia 6, of which 2 are large and 4 small.

CULTIVATION: The flowers are better displayed when plants are mounted, but plants can be grown in pots in a free-draining compost in shady, intermediate or cool conditions. The compost should be allowed to dry out between waterings as the new growth is prone to rot. After flowering, plants should be kept drier.

Leptotes bicolor Lindley

Plants pendulous; pseudobulbs to 3 cm long. Leaves to 10 × 1 cm, grooved above, dark green, suberect or recurved. Inflorescence shorter than leaves, 1- to 4-flowered. Flowers scented, to 5 cm across; sepals and petals white; lip deep pink or purple, midlobe heart-shaped.

Epiphytic low down on tree trunks in rain forest, 700–1100 m (2300–3600 ft.)
Brazil, Paraguay

Leptotes unicolor Barbosa Rodrigues

Pseudobulbs to 1.5 cm long. Leaves to 5.5 × 0.8 cm, deeply grooved above. Inflorescence pendent, 1- or 2-flowered. Flowers scented, nodding, not opening wide, pale pink or white flushed with pink; sepals and petals 25 mm long.

Leptotes tenuis

Epiphytic on tree trunks
Argentina, Brazil, Paraguay

SIMILAR SPECIES: *Leptotes tenuis* Reichenbach f. from Brazil has yellow sepals and petals, the lip white with a purplish blotch.

Liparis L. C. Richard

TRIBE: Malaxideae
ETYMOLOGY: From Greek *liparos*, shiny or greasy, referring to the glossy leaves of the type species, *Liparis loeselii* (Linnaeus) Richard
DISTRIBUTION: About 320 species, occurring worldwide in tropical and temperate areas

Sympodial terrestrial, lithophytic, or epiphytic plants with small to large pseudobulbs. Leaves 1 to several, thin-textured and plicate, or smooth and stiff, or leathery. Inflorescences terminal, erect, unbranched. Flowers yellow, green, orange, red-brown, or purple, usually small; dorsal sepal usually erect, lateral sepals sometimes partly joined; petals free, often linear and reflexed; lip entire or bilobed, often deflexed, not spurred. Column arched, winged at apex; pollinia 4, in 2 pairs.

CULTIVATION: Most species are easily grown in intermediate conditions. Epiphytic species can be potted in a bark mix, terrestrials in a free-draining mixture based on fine bark or composted bark. Most species require a shady, humid position; deciduous species should be kept more or less dry until new growth starts.

Liparis bowkeri Harvey

SYN. *Liparis neglecta* Schlechter

Pseudobulbs conical, to 7 cm tall, 2- to 5-leaved. Leaves to 12 × 6 cm, ovate, plicate, light green. Inflorescence to 20 cm long, loosely several-flowered. Flowers 10–15 mm across, yellow or yellow-green turning orange with age.

Terrestrial in woodland and evergreen forest, occasionally a low-level epiphyte, 1200–2700 m (4000–8900 ft.)
Tropical Africa, South Africa

Liparis condylobulbon Reichenbach f.

Pseudobulbs to 14 × 2 cm, 2-leaved, well-spaced on rhizome. Leaves ca. 15 × 2.5 cm. Inflorescence erect, to 20 cm long, densely many-flowered. Flowers small, green.

Lithophytic and epiphytic, to 1500 m (5000 ft.)
Taiwan, Indo-China to southwestern Pacific and Australia

Liparis crenulata (Blume) Lindley

Pseudobulbs 4–9 cm long, ovoid, set well apart on rhizome, 2- or 3-leaved. Leaves to 33 × 5 cm. Inflorescence longer than leaves, loosely many-flowered. Sepals and petals brownish, reflexed; lip brick red, recurved in the middle.

Epiphytic in submontane and montane forest, 700–2200 m (2300–7260 ft.)
Java, Sumatra

Liparis liliifolia (Linnaeus) Richard ex Lindley

Pseudobulbs ovoid, 2 × 1 cm, 2-leaved. Leaves to 18 × 6 cm, glossy green, midrib prominent below. Inflorescence to 25 cm tall, several- to many-flowered. Flowers ca. 1 cm across, sepals pale green, petals purple, lip pale purple with darker veins. This species is hardy and can be grown outside.

Leptotes bicolor

Leptotes unicolor

Liparis liliifolia

Liparis condylobulbon

Terrestrial on stream banks in an open woodland

Canada, United States

Liparis nervosa (Thunberg) Lindley

SYN. *Liparis elata* Lindley, *L. guineensis* Lindley

Pseudobulbs conical, to 4 cm tall., 2- or 3-leaved. Leaves to 35 × 9 cm, ovate, plicate. Inflorescence to 60 cm tall, densely many-flowered. Flowers small, greenish, the lip greenish purple or maroon-purple.

Terrestrial in woodland or in grassland, in shade or full sun, 500–1800 m (1650–6000 ft.)

Tropical Africa, America, Asia, probably one of the world's most widespread orchids

Liparis nigra Seidenfaden

SYN. *Liparis macrantha* Rolfe ex Hemsley

Pseudobulbs narrowly cylindrical, to 20 cm tall, with several leaves. Leaves to 15 × 6 cm, ovate, pleated. Inflorescence 25–35 cm tall, occasionally more, red-purple, densely many-flowered. Flowers ca. 2 cm across, deep purple-red; lip more or less square, ca. 15 mm long and wide.

Terrestrial in humid shade among rocks, 500–1600 m (1650–5300 ft.)

China, Indochina, Taiwan

Liparis nutans (Ames) Ames

Pseudobulbs to 3 cm long, pear-shaped, 1-leafed. Leaves to 30 × 3 cm. Inflorescence erect, shorter than leaves; peduncle winged, rachis ca. 5 cm long, nodding, densely many-flowered. Flowers ca. 1 cm across, brick red; lip fan-shaped.

Epiphytic or terrestrial in shade of forest

Philippines

Liparis viridiflora (Blume) Lindley

Pseudobulbs cylindrical or ovoid, to 18 × 2 cm, set close together, 2-leaved. Leaves to 25 × 3 cm. Inflorescence to 50 cm tall, densely many-flowered. Flowers small, greenish white or greenish yellow.

Epiphytic or lithophytic in forest or shaded valleys, 200–2300 m (660–7600 ft.)

Widespread in tropical and subtropical Asia

Listrostachys Reichenbach f.

TRIBE: Vandeae

SUBTRIBE: Angraecinae

ETYMOLOGY: From Greek *listron*, spade, and *stachys*, spike or ear of corn

DISTRIBUTION: 1 species in Africa, and perhaps another in Réunion

Robust plants; stem to ca. 15 cm long, covered with old woody leaf bases. Leaves numerous, distichous, linear or strap-shaped. Inflorescence axillary, spreading, densely many-flowered, the flowers set in 2 rows. Flowers small.

In the past, many African epiphytes were classified in *Listrostachys*, but almost all have been moved to other genera.

CULTIVATION: Plants can be potted in an open bark-based compost or mounted. They need intermediate to warm conditions, high humidity, and moderate to heavy shade. Flowers of *Listrostachys pertusa* can often be pollinated by running one's finger along a row of flowers; the pollinia stick to fingertips and some get transferred to the stigmas of other flowers.

Listrostachys pertusa (Lindley) Reichenbach f.

Leaves to 35 × 2 cm, linear, folded, stiff in texture, dark green. Inflorescences 2–4, arising from lower leaf axils, to 30 cm long, densely many-flowered, most open together. Flowers small, white with a green blotch at the mouth of the spur, sometimes dotted with red; sepals and petals subsimilar, spreading, lip 7–8 mm long with a basal claw separating the mouth of the spur from the column, the blade ± rectangular; spur green or reddish, 4–5 mm long, the tip inflated. Flowering in late summer.

Epiphytic in evergreen forest, 500–600 m (1650–2000 ft.)

West and Central Africa

Lockhartia Hooker

TRIBE: Maxillarieae

SUBTRIBE: Oncidiinae

ETYMOLOGY: Named for David Lockhart (1818–1846), first superintendent of Trinidad Botanic Gardens

DISTRIBUTION: 26 species in Mexico, Central and South America

Small to medium-sized sympodial epiphytes, lacking pseudobulbs. Stems leafy, erect or pendent. Leaves distichous, laterally flattened, the bases overlapping. Inflorescences axillary, sometimes branched, few- to many-flowered. Flowers smallish, usually white or yellow; sepals and petals free, subsimilar, spreading or reflexed; lip longer than sepals, entire or lobed.

CULTIVATION: Plants should be mounted or grown in a fine bark mixture in small pots, which need to be suspended for species with pendent stems. They require intermediate temperatures, light shade, and high humidity. Plants should not be allowed to dry out completely but need less water while not in active growth.

Lockhartia amoena Endres & Reichenbach f.

Stems erect or pendent, 10–40 cm long. Leaves triangular, to 3.5 × 1 cm. Inflorescence 3–5 cm long, branched, few-flowered. Flowers 2 cm across, yellow, lip marked with reddish brown, trilobed, the midlobe ± square, with 4 lobules.

Epiphytic in rain forest and cloud forest, 300–1700 m (1000–5600 ft.)

Costa Rica, Guatemala, Ecuador, Peru

Liparis nervosa. E. la Croix

Liparis nigra

Liparis nutans

Lockhartia amoena

Listrostachys pertusa

Lockhartia imbricata

Lockhartia imbricata (Lamarck) Hoehne
SYN. *Lockhartia biserra* (Richard) Christenson & Garay, *L. elegans* Hooker
Stems 8–30 cm long, erect or pendent. Flowers 12–15 mm across, yellow with purple or maroon spots and marks, lip trilobed.

Epiphytic in humid forest, 50–500 m (165–1650 ft.)

Trinidad, South America

Lockhartia oerstedii Reichenbach f.
Stems 10–30 cm long, usually erect. Leaves triangular, to 4 cm long. Inflorescence short, pendent, branched, 1- to several-flowered. Flowers ca. 2 cm across, yellow, lip with red-brown markings, 5-lobed, midlobe emarginate.

Epiphytic in rain forest, 1000–2100 m (3300–6900 ft.)

Mexico, Costa Rica, Guyana, Colombia

SIMILAR SPECIES: *Lockhartia serra* Reichenbach f. from Ecuador has a trilobed lip with incurved side lobes and a broad midlobe.

Lockhartia parthenocomos (Reichenbach f.) Reichenbach f.
SYN. *Lockhartia longifolia* Schlechter
Stems pendent, to 35 cm long. Leaves triangular, to 4 cm long. Inflorescence short, 1- to few-flowered. Flowers 1 cm across, yellow, the lip dotted with purple.

Epiphytic in montane forest and cloud forest, 350–2600 m (1150–8600 ft.)

South America

Lockhartia pittieri Schlechter
Stems spreading to pendent, to 25 cm long. Leaves narrowly triangular, to 3 × 0.7 cm. Inflorescence 1–1.5 cm long, branched, several-flowered. Flowers small, yellow, lip oblong, deeply emarginate, with a brown callus.

Epiphytic in wet forest, 0–800 m (2640 ft.)

Belize, Costa Rica, Guyana, Panama, Ecuador

Ludisia A. Richard

SYN. *Haemaria* Lindley
TRIBE: Cranichideae
SUBTRIBE: Goodyerinae
ETYMOLOGY: Derivation obscure, but possibly after Ludis, the subject of a Greek elegy written by her widower (because of the dark-colored leaves)
DISTRIBUTION: 1 species in China, Southeast Asia, and Indonesia

Terrestrial or lithophyte with a creeping, fleshy rhizome, rooting at the nodes. Stems erect or prostrate, several-leaved. Leaves in a loose rosette or scattered on stem, ovate with a short petiole and a sheathing base. Inflorescence terminal, pubescent, unbranched, several- to many-flowered. Flowers twisted asymmetrically; dorsal sepal and petals forming hood, lateral sepals reflexed; lip with a saccate base, the apex bilobed.

CULTIVATION: Although its flowers are attractive, *Ludisia discolor* is cultivated for its beautifully marked leaves and is the most easily grown of the jewel orchids. It does well in intermediate conditions, in shade, potted in a humus-rich compost, and kept moist throughout the year. It is often grown as a house plant. Shoots that have flowered die back when the flowers are over and plants can then be repotted and divided. Some forms have erect stems, while others are more straggly.

Ludisia discolor (Ker Gawler) A. Richard
SYN. *Haemaria discolor* (Ker Gawler) Lindley
Leaves 5–9 cm long, ovate, with a velvety texture, the upper surface bronze to olive-black, usually with 5 red longitudinal veins and faint cross-veining, but the coloring, particularly the degree of veining, is variable. There is a form with white veins. Inflorescence 15–20 cm long. Flowers white, 1.5–2 cm across, the anther yellow.

Terrestrial or lithophytic in damp places in shade of forest, 500–1000 m (1650–3300 ft.)

China, Southeast Asia, Indonesia

Lueddemannia Linden & Reichenbach f.

TRIBE: Maxillarieae
SUBTRIBE: Stanhopeinae
ETYMOLOGY: Named for Mr. Lueddeman, an orchid-growing friend of Reichenbach and Linden
DISTRIBUTION: 1 species in South America

Robust epiphytes with clustered, ovoid pseudobulbs with 1 node, 2- to 4-leaved at apex. Leaves large, pleated. Inflorescence arising from base of pseudobulb, pendent, many-flowered, unbranched. Flowers fleshy; sepals free, spreading, petals slightly smaller; lip clawed, trilobed at apex, the claw with a toothlike callus. Pollinia 2.

CULTIVATION: Grow in baskets at intermediate temperatures, with moderate shade and plenty of water while in growth. Decrease the amount of water while plants are resting.

Lockhartia oerstedii

Lockhartia serra

Ludisia discolor

Lueddemannia pescatorei (Lindley) Linden & Reichenbach f.

SYN: *Cycnoches pescatorei* Lindley, *L. lehmannii* Reichenbach f.

Pseudobulbs to 13 × 7 cm, ovoid, slightly compressed. Leaves to 40 × 9 cm, lanceolate, acute. Inflorescence pendent, 50–100 cm long, densely many-flowered. Flowers scented, about 5 cm across; sepals reddish brown; petals and lip golden yellow, marked with red, the claw of the lip with a maroon, hairy tooth.

Epiphytic in submontane rain forest, 1300–1600 m (4300–5300 ft.)

Colombia, Ecuador, Peru, Venezuela

Lueddemannia pescatorei. R. Parsons

Luisia Gaudichaud

TRIBE: Vandeae

SUBTRIBE: Aeridinae

ETYMOLOGY: Named for Don Luis de Torres, a 19th-century Portuguese botanist

DISTRIBUTION: About 40 species in tropical and subtropical Asia as far as the West Pacific

Monopodial epiphytes with slender stems, often branched at the base, rooting only at the base. Leaves alternate, terete, fleshy, dark green. Inflorescences arising along stem, short, unbranched, few- to several-flowered. Flowers fleshy; sepals and petals subsimilar, spreading or pointing forwards; lip deflexed, usually larger and darker in color than sepals and petals, entire or trilobed. Pollinia 2.

CULTIVATION: Plants can be grown either mounted or in pots in a standard, free-draining epiphyte compost. They require intermediate to warm conditions, good light, and water throughout the year, although they should dry out between waterings.

Luisia brachystachys (Lindley) Blume

Stem erect, 20–30 cm tall, sometimes branched, covered by leaf sheaths. Leaves to 12 cm long, 12 mm across. Inflorescence arising opposite leaves, short, 4- to 5-flowered. Flowers small, yellow or yellow-green tinged with purplish.

Epiphytic in forest, usually on tree trunks, 500–1900 m (1650–6300 ft.)

Himalayas to China and Indochina

SIMILAR SPECIES: *Luisia megasepala* Hayata from Taiwan has larger, ill-smelling flowers with green sepals and petals and a black lip.

Luisia tristis (G. Forster) Hooker f.

SYN. *Luisia teretifolia* Gaudichaud, *L. zeylanica* Lindley

Plants 20–30 cm tall. Leaves to 15 × 0.5 cm. Inflorescence 2- to 4-flowered. Flowers small, pendent, green mottled with purple, lip deep purple, triangular to heart-shaped, obscurely trilobed at the tip.

Epiphytic in tropical and subtropical forest, 400–3050 m (1320–10,050 ft.)

Tropical Asia to West Pacific

Lycaste Lindley

TRIBE: Maxillarieae

SUBTRIBE: Maxillariinae

ETYMOLOGY: Named for a beautiful woman from Crete, wife of Butes, in the era of classical Greece

DISTRIBUTION: About 36 species and some natural hybrids in Mexico, Central and South America

Medium to large epiphytes, lithophytes, or terrestrials, with fairly large, usually ovate pseudobulbs, with apical spines in those that are deciduous before commencing the new growth. Leaves large, plicate. Inflorescences arising from the base of a pseudobulb, erect or spreading, 1-flowered, occasionally 2-flowered. Flowers showy, some scented, appearing from the base of the most recently matured pseudobulb with the start of the new growth; sepals spreading, subsimilar; petals usually smaller, usually projecting forwards, the upper margins overlapping; lip trilobed, side lobes erect, midlobe large, decurved, the edges entire. Pollinia 4, in unequal pairs on a long, straight stipe.

Many intrageneric hybrids exist. Species have also been hybridized with *Anguloa* and *Ida* to give the hybrid genera ×*Angulocaste* and ×*Lycida*.

CULTIVATION: Plants should be grown in pots in a free-draining compost; a mixture of equal parts of perlite or bark and chopped sphagnum is suitable. Most require intermediate temperatures (*Lycaste skinneri* must be grown cool), high humidity, good air movement, light shade, and plenty of water while growing. They should be kept drier after the leaves fall, with only enough water given to prevent the pseudobulbs shriveling. Careful watering is necessary when the new growths appear as the young leaves are easily damaged by water.

Lycaste aromatica (Graham) Lindley

Pseudobulbs to 11 × 6 cm with 2–4 short spines. Leaves to 60 × 15 cm, deciduous. Inflorescence to 10 cm long. Flowers to 6 cm across, scented, yellow, the lip spotted with orange; callus widely expanded and concave at the apex.

Lycaste brevispatha

Lycaste bradeorum

Luisia brachystachys

Lycaste aromatica

Epiphytic in damp forest, occasionally lithophytic on limestone, to 1850 m (6100 ft.)

Mexico, Nicaragua, possibly Honduras and El Salvador

SIMILAR SPECIES: *Lycaste cochleata* Lindley, from Mexico, Guatemala, Belize, El Salvador, and Nicaragua, has smaller flowers with greenish yellow sepals, orange petals, and the lip saccate at base with a fleshy, concave callus. *Lycaste consobrina* Reichenbach f. from Mexico, Nicaragua, and Guatemala has larger flowers and a broader lip with a huge truncate, protruding, concave fleshy callus. *Lycaste crinita* Lindley from Mexico has smaller flowers, not fragrant, with a very hairy lip.

Lycaste bradeorum Schlechter

Pseudobulbs to 11 × 6 cm, with conspicuous apical spines. Leaves 2–3, deciduous, to 60 × 18 cm. Inflorescence to 11 cm. Flowers up to 7 cm across, scented; sepals greenish yellow, petals and lip orange-yellow with a tapering tongue-shaped callus

Epiphytic in very wet forest, 800–1200 m (2640–4000 ft.)

Costa Rica, Guyana, Honduras, Nicaragua, El Salvador

Lycaste brevispatha Klotzsch

Pseudobulbs 9.5 × 4 cm, with apical spines. Leaves deciduous, 35 × 8.5 cm. Inflorescence 7–10 cm long. Flowers to 6.5 cm across, not scented; sepals pale green with pink central suffusion, petals white tinged with pink, lip white with pink spots, obscurely trilobed with a small, flat callus.

Epiphytic in rain forest, 700–1800 m (2300–6000 ft.)

Costa Rica, Panama

SIMILAR SPECIES: *Lycaste candida* Lindley from Costa Rica, Nicaragua, and Panama has identical coloring but the lip is distinctly trilobed, with a narrow, linear, grooved callus.

Lycaste campbellii C. Schweinfurth

Pseudobulbs with long spines. Leaves deciduous. Flowers small, smelling of old-fashioned soap, 2–4 cm across; sepals yellow-green; petals and lip yellow with narrow, concave callus.

Epiphytic in shade near sea level

Panama, Colombia

Lycaste cruenta (Lindley) Lindley

Pseudobulbs spiny, to 16 cm long. Leaves deciduous, to 65 × 20 cm. Inflorescence 7–17 cm long. Flowers to 10 cm across with a spicy scent, sepals yellow-green, petals bright yellow; lip yellow, base saccate with a dark red blotch; callus short, vestigial. It is a parent of several natural hybrids.

Epiphytic on large branches, or lithophytic, 1800–2200 m (6000–7260 ft.)

Mexico, Guatemala, El Salvador, Guyana

Lycaste deppei (Loddiges) Lindley

Pseudobulbs to 9 × 7 cm, with vestigial spines. Leaves not deciduous until after flowering, to 53 × 13 cm. Inflorescence to 17 cm long. Flowers 9 cm across, peppermint scented; sepals green with red-brown spotting; petals white; lip orange with red spots.

Epiphytic and lithophytic in submontane forest, 1100–1700 m (3630–5500 ft.)

Mexico, Guatemala, Nicaragua, El Salvador, Honduras

Lycaste lasioglossa Reichenbach f.

Pseudobulbs to 10 × 6 cm, lacking spines. Leaves not deciduous until after flowering, to 90 × 11 cm. Inflorescence to 25 cm long. Flowers not scented, ca. 14 cm across; sepals brown, petals yellow, lip densely hairy, yellow with red markings.

Terrestrial at ca. 1800 m (6000 ft.)

Mexico (probably extinct), Honduras, Guatemala, El Salvador Described as *Lycaste macropogon* Reichenbach f. in Costa Rica in 1888, where it is now not known.

Lycaste leucantha Klotzsch

Pseudobulbs to 8.5 cm long, with vestigial or no spines. Leaves not deciduous until after flowering, to 45 × 8 cm. Inflorescence to 15 cm long. Flowers to 8 cm across; sepals pale green; petals and lip white, occasionally scented.

Epiphytic in rain forest and cloud forest, 850–1700 m (2800–5600 ft.)

Costa Rica, Panama, possibly Nicaragua

Lycaste macrophylla (Poeppig & Endlicher) Lindley

Pseudobulbs to 12 cm long, without spines. Leaves not deciduous until after flowering, to 80 × 15 cm.

Lycaste cruenta

Inflorescence 14–30 cm long. Flowers nodding, scented, 9–11 cm across, very variable in color, but sepals most often reddish brown, petals and lip cream or yellow, often marked with pink or red. The callus is tonguelike. Several subspecies and varieties are recognized.

Terrestrial in forest, 500–2400 m (1650–7900 ft.)

Costa Rica, Nicaragua, Panama, Colombia, Ecuador, Venezuela, Peru, Bolivia

SIMILAR SPECIES: *Lycaste dowiana* Endres & Reichenbach f., from Costa Rica, Nicaragua, and Panama, is a small-growing plant with small flowers, brown sepals, cream petals and lip, a much shorter peduncle, and a narrow, raised callus. It flowers sequentially all summer.

Lycaste skinneri (Bateman) Lindley

A beautiful but very variable species. Pseudobulbs without spines. Leaves to 75 × 15 cm, not deciduous until after flowering. Inflorescence to 30 cm long. Flowers very showy, to 17 cm across, not fragrant; sepals and petals white or pink, lip usually deeper pink marked dark pink, rarely white. In cultivation this species requires cool, humid conditions.

Epiphytic or lithophytic in cloud forest, 1300–2100 m (4300–6900 ft.)

Mexico, Honduras, El Salvador, Guatemala (national flower)

Lycaste tricolor (Klotzsch) Reichenbach f.

Pseudobulbs to 8 × 4 cm, without spines, 3-leaved at apex and with 2 or 3 sheaths. Leaves deciduous, to 60 × 14 cm. Inflorescence 6–7 cm tall. Flowers to 6 cm across, not scented; sepals pale beige; petals and lip pale pink.

Epiphytic in rain forest and cloud forest, 600–1150 m (2000–3800 ft.)

Costa Rica, Belize, and previously in Panama (not now)

Lycaste deppei

Lycaste lasioglossa

Lycaste macrophylla

Lycaste skinneri

Lycaste tricolor

Lycomormium Reichenbach f.

TRIBE: Maxillarieae
SUBTRIBE: Coelopsidinae
ETYMOLOGY: From Greek *lykos*, wolf, and *mormo*, hobgoblin, referring to the bizarre look of the flowers
DISTRIBUTION: 5 species in Colombia, Ecuador, and Peru

Large epiphytes or terrestrials with clustered, ovoid, ribbed pseudobulbs, 2- or 3-leafed at apex, enclosed by leafy sheaths when young. Leaves large, plicate, thin-textured, petiolate. Inflorescences basal, pendent. Flowers fleshy, dorsal sepal and petals free, forming a hood over the column, lateral sepals joined at the base to the column-foot; lip divided into a lobed hypochile and a stiff epichile. Column stout, without winged; pollinia 4.

CULTIVATION: Because of the pendent inflorescences, plants must be grown in baskets like *Stanhopea*. They require intermediate temperatures and moderate shade, with plenty of water while growing. After growth is complete, they should be kept drier.

Lycomormium fiskei H. R. Sweet

Inflorescence ca. 15 cm long, several-flowered. Flowers 2.5 cm across, very fleshy; sepals and petals pink or cream with darker spots, lip whitish with reddish spots.

Terrestrial in submontane and montane forest, 1300–1700 m (4300–5600 ft.)

Ecuador, Peru

Lyperanthus R. Brown

TRIBE: Diurideae
SUBTRIBE: Megastylidinae
ETYMOLOGY: From Greek *lypros*, poor, and *anthos*, flower, referring to the dull colors of the flowers
DISTRIBUTION: 2 species in Australia

Terrestrials with ovoid tubers forming new tubers at the ends of long stolons. Leaf single, basal, linear-lanceolate, stiff, leathery, erect. Inflorescences unbranched, 1- to few-flowered; floral bracts leafy, sheathing. Flowers resupinate, dull in color; sepals and petals free, leathery in texture, dorsal sepal forming a hood over the column, lateral sepals narrower than dorsal sepal, petals similar to lateral sepals; lip trilobed, without a spur, with crowded calli. Flowers appear in spring after the leaf has fully grown.

CULTIVATION: Plants are relatively easily cultivated. They should be grown in a free-draining terrestrial compost based on loam, grit or sharp sand, leaf mold, or fine bark. Pots should be kept in a cool, open situation. Plants are kept dry while dormant. When new shoots appear in autumn, they should be watered with care. Tubers need to be quite large before they flower.

Lycomormium fiskei

Lyperanthus suaveolens. J. Stewart

Lyperanthus serratus Lindley
Leaf to 3.5 × 1.5 cm. Inflorescence to 35 cm tall, 3- to 7-flowered. Flowers to 4.5 cm across, pale green to reddish brown, the surface of the midlobe covered with white calli.

Forms loose colonies in open woodland, dense shrub, and coastal vegetation

Southwestern Australia

Lyperanthus suaveolens R. Brown
Leaf to 20 × 1.2 cm. Inflorescence to 45 cm tall, 2- to 8-flowered. Flowers scented, long-lasting, to 3 cm across, yellow-brown to dark reddish brown, lip midlobe yellow.

Forms colonies in woodland and heathland, on well-drained soil, 0–1000 m (3300 ft.)

Eastern Australia, Tasmania

Macodes (Blume) Lindley

TRIBE: Cranichideae
SUBTRIBE: Goodyerinae
ETYMOLOGY: From Greek *makros*, long, and *-odes*, resembling, referring to the long midlobe of the lip
DISTRIBUTION: About 10 species occurring from Malaysia to the Pacific Islands

Evergreen terrestrial plants with short, erect, fleshy stems arising from a short, fleshy, creeping rhizome. Leaves several, usually in loose rosettes. Inflorescences erect. Flowers small, nonresupinate, rather dull-colored; lateral sepals free, dorsal sepal joined to petals; lip trilobed, saccate at base. Pollinia 2.

This is one of several genera known collectively as "jewel orchids," which are grown for the beauty of their leaves rather than their flowers.

CULTIVATION: Grow in a shallow pan in a free-draining terrestrial compost in intermediate to warm, humid, shady conditions. It is better to water from below to avoid getting water on the leaves.

Macodes petola. E. la Croix

Macodes petola (Blume) Lindley
Leaves several in a loose rosette, to 9 × 7 cm, broadly ovate, dark green with 5 longitudinal pale silvery-green veins and numerous cross veins. Raceme to 25 cm tall, many-flowered. Flowers small, brownish with a white lip. The most widely grown species.

In shade in damp forests at low to mid altitudes

Sumatra to the Philippines

Macodes sanderiana Rolfe
Leaves to 7 × 5 cm, broadly ovate to almost round, bright green or bronze-green with a network of golden veins, the underside purple-tinged. Inflorescence 18–20 cm tall. Flowers brownish with a white lip.

In shade on forest floor and in humus on rocks, 350–800 m (1150–2640 ft.)

Papua New Guinea

Macradenia R. Brown

TRIBE: Maxillarieae
SUBTRIBE: Oncidiinae
ETYMOLOGY: From Greek *makros*, long, and *aden*, gland, referring to the long stipe
DISTRIBUTION: 11 species in Florida, Central and South America, and the West Indies

Small to medium-sized epiphytes; pseudobulbs cylindrical or narrowly ovoid, enclosed in several grayish, papery sheaths, 1-leafed at apex. Inflorescences basal, unbranched, erect or pendent, loosely or densely few- to many-flowered. Sepals and petals subsimilar, spreading, sometimes reflexed at the tips, lip trilobed, side lobes clasping column, midlobe spreading. Pollinia 2.

CULTIVATION: Plants can be mounted or grown in pots or baskets in a free-draining compost. They require intermediate temperatures, shade, and high humidity and should be watered throughout the year.

Macradenia brassavolae Reichenbach f.
SYN. *Macradenia modesta* (Rolfe) Rolfe
Pseudobulbs to 4.5 × 1 cm. Leaves to 20 × 3 cm. Inflorescence pendent, to 25 cm long, 10–30-flowered. Flowers 2–3 cm across, maroon or brown with a yellow margin, lip white with maroon-red stripes.

Epiphytic in wet lowland forest, 0–200 m (660 ft.)

Mexico, Central and South America

Macradenia lutescens R. Brown
Pseudobulbs to 6 × 1 cm. Leaves to 15 × 3 cm. Inflorescence pendent, to 18 cm long, laxly few- to many-flowered. Flowers ca. 2.5 cm across, yellowish or greenish marked with purple-brown, lip white with purple markings.

Epiphytic in wet lowland forest, 50–600 m (165–2000 ft.)

Florida, Central and South America, West Indies

Macroclinium Barbosa Rodrigues ex Pfitzer

TRIBE: Maxillarieae
SUBTRIBE: Oncidiinae
ETYMOLOGY: From Greek *macro*, long or large, and *klinion*, little bed, referring to the prominent clinandrium
DISTRIBUTION: 40 species from Mexico to Brazil

Dwarf epiphytes related to *Notylia* with small pseudobulbs covered with sheaths, some leaf-bearing, 1-leafed at apex. Leaves thick-textured, laterally compressed, often covered with red or brown warts. Inflorescences basal or axillary, usually longer than leaves, erect or pendent, usually with the flowers crowded at the end. Flowers large for the size of plant, pinkish to purple; sepals and petals subsimilar; lip clawed at the base, sometimes lobed. Column long, with a small, narrow stigma; pollinia 2.

CULTIVATION: Most species are twig epiphytes and may be short-lived. They like good light and high humidity and should not be allowed to dry out for long.

Macroclinium aurorae Dodson
Leaves dark green covered with reddish warts. Inflorescence 3–4 cm long, rather densely 9- to 15-flowered. Sepals and petals linear, drooping, pale pink tinged with purple at the tips; lip blade elliptic.

Twig epiphyte, ca. 700 m (2300 ft)

Peru

Malaxis Solander ex Swartz

TRIBE: Malaxideae
ETYMOLOGY: From Greek *malaxo*, to soften, referring to the usually soft-textured leaves
DISTRIBUTION: About 300 species in tropical, subtropical, and occasionally temperate regions of Europe, Asia, North and South America

Terrestrial, rarely epiphytic, usually small plants with fleshy stems, often creeping and pseudobulbous. Leaves thin-textured or fleshy, usually plicate, the edge often undulate, sometimes attractively colored. Inflorescences erect, unbranched. Flowers small, often nonresupinate, green, yellowish, brown, pinkish, or purple; dorsal sepal free, lateral sepals free or joined; petals free, often narrower than sepals; lip entire or lobed, lacking a spur and callus, larger than the sepals and petals, the margins often finely toothed. Column short and stout, pollinia 4.

Malaxis differs from *Liparis* in having a short and stout rather than elongate and arched column and in the lip being flat or concave rather than bent down in the middle.

CULTIVATION: Few species of *Malaxis* are in cultivation. Temperate species such as *M. monophyllos* can be grown in a cool greenhouse or alpine house. Tropical species require intermediate to warm conditions with high humidity and heavy shade. They need a free-draining compost with a high organic content. Deciduous

Macradenia brassavolae

Macroclinium aurorae

species should be kept drier while resting.

Malaxis calophylla (Reichenbach f.) Kuntze

SYN. *Malaxis scottii* (Hooker f.) Kuntze

Stem short, erect, 2- or 3-leaved. Leaves to 12 × 4.5 cm, yellow-green with a bronze central patch. Inflorescence 20–25 cm tall, many-flowered. Flowers small, pale pink or creamy yellow.

Terrestrial in hill forest, ca. 1100 m (3600 ft.)

Sikkim to Borneo

SIMILAR SPECIES: *Malaxis discolor* (Lindley) Kuntze from Sri Lanka, *M. lowii* (E. Morren) Ames from Borneo, and *M. metallica* (Reichenbach f.) Kuntze from Borneo also have leaves flushed with bronze or purple.

Malaxis monophyllos (Linnaeus) Swartz

Pseudobulbs small, covered with sheaths, stem 10–30 cm tall; leaf 1 (rarely 2), to 10 × 5 cm. Inflorescence to 15 cm tall, densely many-flowered; flowers small, yellow-green, nonresupinate.

Var. *brachypoda* (A. Gray) P. Morris & Eames (syn. *Malaxis brachypoda* (A. Gray) Fernald) has resupinate flowers and comes from Canada and the United States.

Damp places in semi-shade on base-rich soil, to 1600 m (5300 ft.)

Temperate Europe to Philippines

Malaxis lowii

Masdevallia Ruíz & Pavón

TRIBE: Epidendreae
SUBTRIBE: Pleurothallidinae
ETYMOLOGY: Named for José Masdevall (d. 1801), a Spanish physician and botanist
DISTRIBUTION: More than 500 species in Mexico, Central and South America, with most in the Andes

Epiphytic, lithophytic, or terrestrial plants, usually small, with a short creeping rhizome and no pseudobulbs. Stems usually erect, enclosed by overlapping sheaths at the base, 1-leafed at the apex. Leaves leathery, elliptic to obovate, with a short petiole. Inflorescences arising at the junctions of leaf and stem (where there is a thickened ring of tissue, the annulus), 1- to several-flowered. Peduncle round or triangular in cross-section. Sepals showy, usually joined for part of their length, often with apical tails; petals much smaller than sepals; lip small, hinged to column-foot. Pollinia 2.

Masdevallia has been the subject of 5 monographs by Carlyle Luer. In the index to Part 5 (Luer 2003), Luer divided *Masdevallia* into 12 subgenera, 29 sections, and 21 subsections, but in a more recent volume (Luer 2006) he split *Masdevallia* into 18 genera. I have not followed that treatment here.

Most species are rather similar vegetatively, differing mainly in size. More than 500 hybrids of *Masdevallia* have been registered and hybrids also exist with species of *Dracula*, giving the hybrid genus ×*Dracuvallia*.

CULTIVATION: Most species grow at high altitudes in cloud forest in the Andes where they are covered in mist for part of almost every day and there is frequent rain. So in cultivation, they require cool conditions, high humidity, moderate to heavy shade, and good air movement. Species from lower altitudes will grow at intermediate temperatures, but shade, high humidity, and good air movement are always necessary. Plants are usually grown in small pots, in a free-draining compost based on fine bark or in a chopped sphagnum-perlite mixture. They should not be allowed to remain dry for any length of time, but if kept too wet, the roots rot and the leaves are shed.

Masdevallia agaster Luer

Small, tufted plants. Inflorescence 1.5–2.5 cm long, 1-flowered. Sepals joined for most of their length forming a tubular flower, yellow-orange outside, the free parts white and papillose inside, with orange tails 24–26 mm long.

Epiphytic in cloud forest, 1500–2000 m (5000–6600 ft.)

Ecuador

Masdevallia amabilis Reichenbach f. & Warszewicz

Medium to large plant. Leaves to 17 cm long. Inflorescence 15–40 cm long, erect or horizontal, 1-flowered. Flowers variable in size and color, yellow, orange, white, or purple; sepals joined in the basal half to form a narrow tube; tails 5–15 mm long.

Terrestrial or lithophytic in scrub, in semi-arid areas, 2600–3800 m (8600–12,550 ft.)

Peru

Masdevallia angulata Reichenbach f.

Robust plants. Stems to 6.5 cm long. Leaves 8–18 cm long. Inflorescence to 6 cm long, erect, horizontal or pendent, 1-flowered. Flowers large, fleshy, with an unpleasant smell, sepals forming a deep cup, yellow marked and flushed with purple-red; tails 15–37 mm long.

Epiphytic or lithophytic in cloud forest or terrestrial on roadside banks, 1500–2060 m (5000–6800 ft.)

Colombia, Ecuador

Masdevallia ayabacana Luer

Medium to large plant. Leaves 10–23 cm long. Inflorescence 20–35 cm long, erect, horizontal or pendent, with few flowers open in succession. Sepals deep purple-red with orange to green tails to 6 cm long; petals and lip yellow, dotted with purple.

Epiphytic, ca. 1200 m (4000 ft.)

Peru

Masdevallia barlaeana Reichenbach f.

Medium-sized plant. Inflorescence 15–20 cm long, 1-flowered. Flowers bright orange-red or purple-red, ca. 35 mm long, sepals joined for about two-thirds of their length into a narrow tube, then forming a broad blade; tail of dorsal sepal 3 cm long, lateral sepals with tails about half as long.

Terrestrial in exposed, rocky areas, 2200–3600 m (7260–12,000 ft.)

Peru

Masdevallia bicolor Reichenbach f.

Plants medium-sized, variable. Inflorescence to 13 cm long, 2- or 3-flowered. Sepals joined for part of their length; dorsal sepal green, yellow, or orange, lateral sepals deep purple; tails yellow-green, 7–27 mm long.

Epiphytic or terrestrial in forest, 1100–2500 m (3600–8250 ft.)

Bolivia, Colombia, Ecuador, Peru, Venezuela

Masdevallia caesia Roezl

Large, pendent plants. Leaves to 45 cm long, blue-green. Inflorescence 2–5 cm long, 1-flowered. Flowers 12 cm across, yellow, mottled with red-brown; sepals joined at the base to form a cup, with slender, orange tails to 9 cm long; lip warty, deep purple. Luer refers to *M. caesia*, the only pendent species known to date, as "perhaps the most distinct species of the genus."

Epiphytic in humid forest, 1600–2000 m (5300–6600 ft.)

Colombia

Masdevallia caloptera Reichenbach f.

SYN. *Masdevallia biflora* Regel

Medium-sized plants. Leaves to 11 cm long. Inflorescence 3–18 cm tall, loose-

Masdevallia amabilis

Masdevallia angulata

Masdevallia ayabacana

Masdevallia agaster

Masdevallia bicolor

ly several-flowered, the flowers open together. Flowers small; sepals white, each with 2 purple veins, 7–10 mm long with yellow tails 6–9 mm long.

Epiphytic in wooded gullies, 2750–3200 m (9075–10,500 ft.)

Peru

SIMILAR SPECIES: *Masdevallia polysticta* Reichenbach f. from Ecuador and Peru has slightly larger flowers with longer tails, with purple spots rather than purple veins.

Masdevallia caudata Lindley

Medium-sized. Inflorescence to 9 cm long, 1-flowered. Flowers large, to 15 cm across, cup-shaped, sepals white to yellow, flushed or dotted with purple or brown; tails 4–7 cm long.

Epiphytic in forest, 1700–2800 m (5600–9240 ft.)

Colombia, Venezuela

Masdevallia chaparensis T. Hashimoto

Medium to large; leaves to 13 cm long. Inflorescence to 12 cm long, 1-flowered. Flowers large, white to pink, heavily spotted with purple with slender, greenish tails 3–4 cm long.

Epiphytic in forest, 2300–2800 m (7600–9250 ft.)

Bolivia

Masdevallia coccinea Linden ex Lindley

SYN. *Masdevallia harryana* Reichenbach f., *M. militaris* Reichenbach f.

Large plants. Leaves 10–30 cm long. Inflorescence 25–60 cm tall, 1-flowered. Flowers large, showy, variable in color, red, purple, orange, or white; sepals joined for ca. 20 cm at base to form a tube, dorsal sepal to 40 mm long with a reflexed tail 3–5 cm long, lateral sepals to 60 mm long, the apices acute.

Terrestrial in forest on mountain slopes, 2000–3600 m (6600–12,000 ft.)

Colombia

Masdevallia colossus Luer

Large plants. Leaves 10–18 cm long. Inflorescence to 12 cm long, 1-flowered. Flowers large with an unpleasant smell, fleshy, yellow-green dotted with brown with slender, brown tails 6–7 cm long.

Epiphytic in cloud forest, 1700–2200 m (5600–7260 ft.)

Ecuador, Peru

Masdevallia constricta Poeppig & Endlicher

SYN. *Masdevallia urosalpinx* Luer

Medium-sized plants. Leaves to 11 cm long. Inflorescence to 6 cm long, 1-flowered. Sepals white, veined and flushed with orange, joined for most of their length into an arched tube, constricted towards the mouth; tails yellow, 4–4.5 cm long, that of the dorsal sepal erect, those of the laterals deflexed.

Epiphytic in cloud forest, 1500–1700 m (5000–5600 ft.)

Ecuador, Peru

Masdevallia coriacea Lindley

Medium to large plants. Leaves to 20 × 2.5 cm. Inflorescence 10–24 cm long, 1-flowered, the peduncle marked with purple. Flowers large, fleshy, greenish white or cream, dotted with purple along the veins; sepals joined for 15 mm at base; sepals 35–40 mm long, tails greenish, 10–15 mm long.

Terrestrial in grassland, 2200–3550 m (7260–11,700 ft.)

Colombia, Ecuador, Peru

Masdevallia datura Luer & R. Vasquez

Medium-sized plants. Leaves to 16 × 4 cm. Inflorescence shorter than leaves, 1-flowered. Flowers large, funnel-shaped, white with some yellow veining; tails slender, yellow, to 6.5 cm long.

Masdevallia caloptera

Masdevallia polysticta

Masdevallia caudata

Masdevallia chaparensis

Masdevallia colossus

Masdevallia coccinea

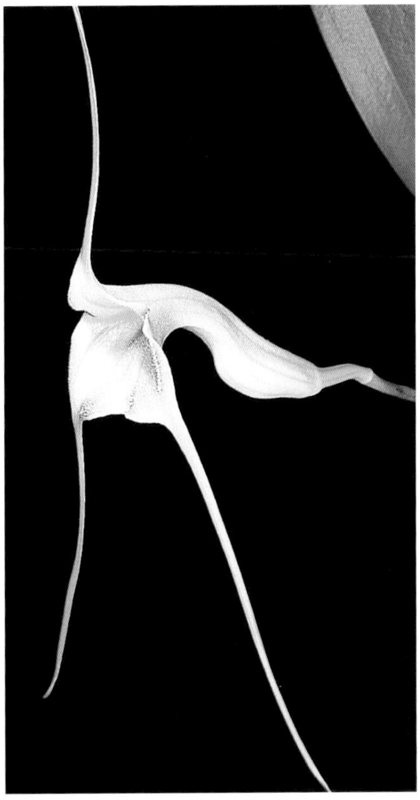
Masdevallia constricta

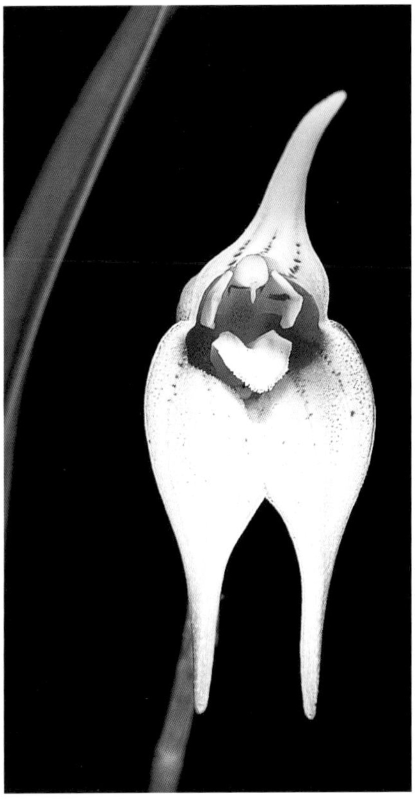
Masdevallia coriacea

Epiphytic in cloud forest, 1800–2500 m (6000–8250 ft.)
Bolivia

Masdevallia davisii Reichenbach f.
Medium-sized plants. Leaves to 18 × 2 cm. Inflorescence to 25 cm long, 1-flowered. Flowers large, ca. 45 mm long, showy, bright yellow or orange-yellow with a brown spot at the base. Sepaline tube cylindrical, curved, ca. 15 mm long; dorsal sepal with greenish tail 20 mm long, tails of lateral sepals 4 mm long.
Terrestrial or lithophytic on exposed, rocky slopes, 3000–3600 m (9,900–12,000)
Peru

Masdevallia decumana Königer
Small plants. Leaves to 5 × 2 cm. Inflorescence 3–5 cm long, 1-flowered. Flowers large; dorsal sepal yellow, dotted with purple-brown and flushed with purple at the base, joined for 4 mm to form an open cup; lateral sepals much larger than the dorsal sepal, greenish white dotted with purple, all sepals with white tails 2.5–5 cm long.
Epiphytic in cloud forest, 1450–2100 m (4800–6900 ft.)
Ecuador, Peru

Masdevallia elephanticeps Reichenbach f. & Warszewicz
Large plants. Leaves 10–30 cm long. Inflorescence to 6 cm long, 1-flowered. Flower very large and fleshy with an unpleasant smell, yellow to yellow-green, sometimes flushed with purple, to 5 cm long plus yellow tails to 6.5 cm long.
Epiphytic in cloud forest, 1970–3030 m (6500–10,000 ft.)
Colombia
SIMILAR SPECIES: *Masdevallia macrura* Reichenbach f., also from Colombia, is as large vegetatively but has even bigger purple, reddish brown, or yellow-brown flowers with tails to 15 cm long. The flowers are the largest in the genus.

Masdevallia floribunda Lindley
Small to medium plants. Leaves to 13 × 2 cm. Inflorescence to 12 cm long, 1-flowered. Flowers ca. 4 cm diameter, white, pale yellow, or pink, spotted and flushed with purple; sepals joined for ca. 5 mm at base, tail of dorsal sepal to 15 mm long, of lateral sepals to 10 mm long. This species has the most northerly distribution in the genus.
Epiphytic in forest, 130–1500 m (430–5000 ft.)
Mexico, Guatemala, Belize, Honduras, Costa Rica, Colombia

Masdevallia gilbertoi Luer & R. Escobar
Medium-sized plants. Leaves to 13 × 3 cm. Inflorescence to 10 cm long, 1-flowered. Flowers showy, white, flushed with orange at the base and marked with purple; tails to 5.5 cm long, slender, that of the dorsal sepal pointing forwards, those of the lateral sepals reflexed.
Epiphytic in forest, 2000–2300 m (6600–7600 ft.)
Colombia

Masdevallia glandulosa Königer
Medium-sized plants. Leaves to 12 cm long. Inflorescence 4–5 cm long, 1-flowered. Sepals bright pink, yellow at the base, glandular-hairy inside, joined to form a conical tube; tails slender, 3.5 cm long.

Masdevallia davisii

Masdevallia decumana

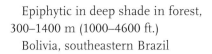

Epiphytic on mossy trunks in cloud forest, 1200–1800 m (4000–6000 ft.)
Ecuador, Peru

Masdevallia ignea Reichenbach f.
Relatively large plants. Leaves to 20 cm long. Inflorescence 18–32 cm long, 1-flowered. Flowers showy, 5 cm long, variable in color, yellow, orange, or red; sepals joined for half their length to form a narrow tube.

Terrestrial in humus on forest floor, 3000–3100 m (9,900–10,200 ft.)
Colombia

Masdevallia infracta Lindley
Medium-sized plants. Inflorescence to 25 cm long, 1- to 5-flowered, the flowers open in succession. Flowers white to yellow flushed with purple, sometimes all purple; tube bell-shaped, ca. 13 mm long, tails 3–4 cm long.

Epiphytic in deep shade in forest, 300–1400 m (1000–4600 ft.)
Bolivia, southeastern Brazil

Masdevallia limax Luer
Small to medium plants. Leaves to 8 × 2 cm. Inflorescence to 5 cm long, 1-flowered. Flowers bright orange, tubular, arched, swollen on the underside, ca. 20 mm long with slender tails 7–13 mm long.

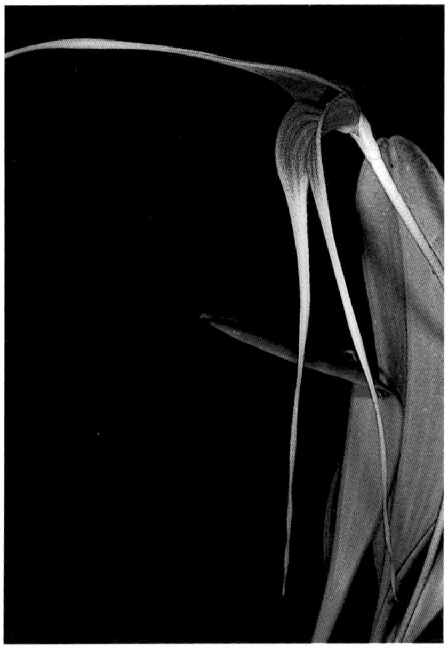

Masdevallia macrura

Masdevallia gilbertoi

Masdevallia ignea

Masdevallia glandulosa

Masdevallia infracta

Masdevallia limax

Masdevallia hirtzii

Masdevallia ophioglossa

Epiphytic in wet forest, 1450–2200 m (4800–7260 ft.)

Ecuador

SIMILAR SPECIES: *Masdevallia hirtzii* Luer & Andreetta, also from Ecuador, has an arched sepaline tube not swollen below, with a wide mouth.

Masdevallia livingstoneana Reichenbach f. & Roezl

Medium-sized plants. Inflorescence ca. 6 cm long, 1-flowered, sometimes 2-flowered, the flowers open in succession. Flowers fleshy, yellow-white or greenish white, flushed with purple; sepaline tube short, free parts of sepals ± triangular, acute, the margins recurved. This predominantly low-altitude species requires temperatures in cultivation on the warm side of intermediate.

Epiphytic in forest, 0–800 m (2800 ft.)

Panama, Costa Rica, Colombia

Masdevallia minuta Lindley

Small plants. Leaves to 6 cm long. Inflorescence to 6 cm long, 1-flowered. Flowers white, sepals 10–20 mm long, including yellow tails 4–7 mm long.

Epiphytic on tree trunks, 100–1000 m (330–3300 ft.)

Central and South America

Masdevallia nidifica Reichenbach f.

Small plants. Leaves to 6 cm long. Inflorescence 3–6 cm long, 1-flowered, peduncle very slender. Flowers translucent white to pink, flushed with reddish purple, sepals partly joined to form a tube, tails ca. 2.5 cm long.

Epiphytic in cloud forest, 900–2000 m (3000–6600 ft.)

Costa Rica, Nicaragua, Panama, Colombia, Ecuador

Masdevallia ophioglossa Reichenbach f.

Small plants. Leaves to 7 cm long. Inflorescence 1-flowered. Flowers small, white; sepals partly joined to form a tube, tails short, thick, and yellowish.

Epiphytic in cloud forest, 1800–2150 m (6000–7100 ft.)

Ecuador

Masdevallia ova-avis Luer

Robust plants. Leaves to 21 × 4.5 cm. Inflorescence horizontal, ca. 25 cm long, densely 6- to 9-flowered, the flowers open together. Sepals gray-purple, mottled with purple and purple-brown, dorsal sepal orbicular, very concave; tails orange, to 16 mm long. The flowers are said to resemble birds' eggs.

Epiphytic in forest and terrestrial by roadside, 2000–2600 m (6600–8600 ft.)

Ecuador

Masdevallia pachyura Reichenbach f.

Medium-sized plants. Leaves to 13 × 2.5 cm. Inflorescence 8–20 cm long, laxly 3- to 8-flowered, the flowers open together. Flowers widely cup-shaped, fleshy, white to yellowish dotted with purple; sepals 10–15 mm long, tails 5–7 mm long.

Epiphytic in cloud forest, 1600–2600 m (5300–8600 ft.)

Ecuador

Masdevallia picturata Reichenbach f.

A small to medium, variable species. Leaves to 7.5 cm long. Inflorescence to 10 cm long, 1–flowered. Sepals 8–15 mm long, white, sometimes

Masdevallia minuta

Masdevallia nidifica

Masdevallia ova-avis

Masdevallia pachyura

Masdevallia picturata

Masdevallia prodigiosa

Masdevallia rosea

with green or yellow tinge, spotted with purple, with very slender white, green, or purple tails 2–7 cm long; dorsal sepal free, lateral sepals joined for 1–3 mm at base.

Epiphytic in cloud forest or terrestrial by roadside, 1500–3000 m (5000–9900 ft.)

Central and South America

Masdevallia prodigiosa Königer
Small to medium plants. Leaves to 7 × 2 cm. Inflorescence ± horizontal, 3–6 cm long, 1-flowered. Flowers large; sepals deep yellow to bright orange forming a shallow cup, dorsal sepal concave, tails slender, to 6 cm long, those on lateral sepals reflexed.

Epiphytic in forest, 2000–2100 m (6600–6900 ft.)

Peru

Masdevallia reichenbachiana Endres ex Reichenbach f.
Medium-sized plants. Leaves to 12 × 2.5 cm. Inflorescence ca. 15 cm long, 1- to 3-flowered, the flower open in succession. Flowers whitish tinged with purple; sepaline tube conical, arched; tail of dorsal sepal 3–4 cm long, reflexed, tails of lateral sepals 2–3 cm long, decurved.

Epiphytic in rain forest and cloud forest, 1500–2000 m (5000–6600 ft.)

Costa Rica

Masdevallia rosea Lindley
Medium-sized plants. Leaves to 18 × 4 cm. Inflorescence 10–15 cm tall, 1-flowered. Flowers showy, sepals bright pink, orange at base, partly joined into an arched tube; lateral sepals ca. 6 cm long with tails 15 mm long.

Epiphytic in cloud forest, 2500–3200 m (8250–10,500 ft.)

Colombia, Ecuador

Masdevallia saltatrix Reichenbach f.
Small plants. Leaves to 11 × 4 cm. Inflorescence 2–6 cm tall, 1-flowered. Flowers erect, ± tubular, S-shaped, red-purple outside, yellow dotted with red inside; tails recurved, to 25 mm long.

Epiphytic in forest, 1800–2000 m (6000–6600 ft.)

Colombia

Masdevallia schlimii Linden ex Lindley
SYN. *Masdevallia polyantha* Lindley
Large plants. Stems to 6 cm long. Leaves 10–21 cm long. Inflorescence 30–40 cm long, loosely 4- to 6-flowered, the flowers open together. Sepals joined at the base forming a cylindrical tube, dorsal sepal yellow, tail 4–5 cm long; lateral sepals purple brown, joined for most of their length, tails 3–4 cm long.

Epiphytic in forest, 1800–3200 m (6000–10,500 ft.)

Colombia, Venezuela

Masdevallia schroederiana Sander ex Veitch
Medium to large plants. Leaves 7–12 cm long. Inflorescence to 12 cm long, few-flowered, the flowers open in succession. Sepals white or greenish white flushed with purple, dorsal sepal flushed with orange inside, partly joined to form a cup-shaped tube; tails white, 5–8 cm long; petals pink.

Epiphytic in cloud forest, 1850–1900 m (6100–6300 ft.)

Costa Rica

Masdevallia strobelii Sweet & Garay
Small plants. Leaves to 6 × 1.7 cm. Inflorescence to 4.5 cm long, 1-flowered. Sepals joined for most of their length into a cylindrical tube, bright orange at base, white towards tip, covered with dense glandular hairs

Masdevallia saltatrix

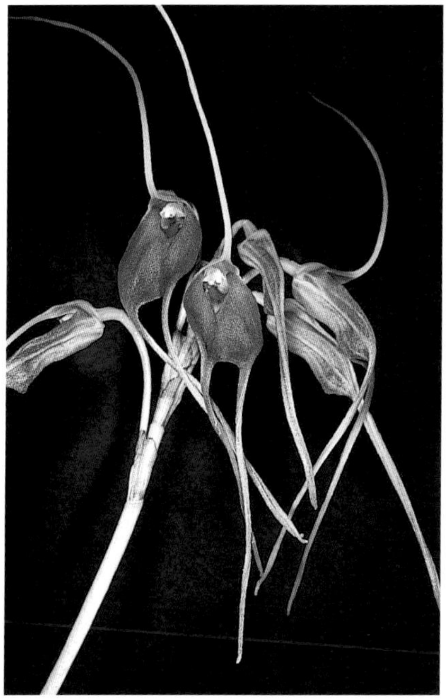

Masdevallia schlimii

Masdevallia schroederiana

Masdevallia strobelii

inside; tails orange-yellow, 3–4 cm long.

Epiphytic in forest and on fence posts, sometimes in open sun, 1400–1500 m (4600–5000 ft.)

Ecuador

Masdevallia tovarensis Reichenbach f.

Medium-sized plants. Leaves to 14 × 3 cm. Inflorescence to 18 cm long, ca. 8-flowered with several open together. Flowers to 3.5 cm across, glistening white; sepaline tube short, dorsal sepal tail slender, erect, ca. 3 cm long; lateral sepal tails ca. 1 cm long. The peduncle should not be cut off after flowering as it may flower again the following year.

Epiphytic in forest, 1600–2000 m (5300–6600 ft.)

Venezuela

Masdevallia triangularis Lindley

Medium-sized plants. Leaves to 12 × 3 cm. Inflorescence 6–12 cm tall, 1-flowered. Flowers wide open, more or less flat, ca. 12 cm across, yellow dotted with red; tails purplish, to 4.5 cm long.

Epiphytic in cloud forest, 500–2600 m (1650–8600 ft.)

Colombia, Ecuador, Venezuela

Masdevallia tovarensis

Masdevallia uniflora Ruíz & Pavón

Medium to large plants. Leaves to 22 × 4 cm. Inflorescence 15–30 cm long, 1-flowered. Sepals white, flushed with bright pink, joined for 10–12 mm to form an open cup; tails 8–17 cm long, green or maroon. This was the first species known to Europeans and is the type species of the genus.

Epiphytic, lithophytic, or terrestrial in cloud forest, 2900–3000 m (9600–9900 ft.)

Peru

Masdevallia veitchiana Reichenbach f.

Medium to large plants. Leaves to 18 × 2 cm. Inflorescence 30–60 cm long, 1-flowered. Flowers showy, to 8 cm across, sepals bright red or orange with purple hairs inside, 50–55 mm long, joined at base for ca. 22 mm into a cylindrical tube; tails to 3 cm long.

Terrestrial or lithophytic in full sun, 2300–3900 m (7600–12,870 ft.)

Peru

Masdevallia xanthina Reichenbach f.

Small to medium-sized plants. Leaves to 8 × 3 cm. Inflorescence 4–6 cm long, 1-flowered. Flowers wide open, cream to yellow with a purple spot at base of lateral sepals; tails to 4.5 cm long.

Epiphytic in forest, 1500–2800 m (5000–9250 ft.)

Colombia, Ecuador

Masdevallia yungasensis T. Hashimoto

Small to medium-sized plants. Leaves to 12 cm long. Inflorescence to 7 cm long, 1-flowered. Flowers showy, white or pink with purple veins or yellow with brown veins; sepals partly joined to form a wide open tube; tails yellow or green, 3.5–4 cm long.

Epiphytic in forest, 1800–3250 m (6000–10,725 ft.)

Bolivia

Maxillaria Ruíz & Pavón

TRIBE: Maxillarieae

SUBTRIBE: Maxillariinae

ETYMOLOGY: From Latin *maxilla*, jaw, referring to a supposed resemblance of column and lip to the jaws of an insect

DISTRIBUTION: More than 550 species in tropical America and the West Indies, with 1 species in Florida

Sympodial epiphytic, lithophytic, occasionally terrestrial herbs. Rhizome long or short; pseudobulbs large, small or almost absent, clustered or set well apart, sometimes enclosed in sheaths some of which may be leaf-bearing, 1- or 2-leaved at the apex. Inflorescences 1-flowered, clustered or solitary. Flowers large or small, sometimes showy, red, brownish, yellow, white, or blotched; sepals free, subsimilar, usually spreading, lateral sepals joined at the base to the column-foot and forming a mentum with it; petals free, similar to dorsal sepal but usually smaller; lip attached to column-foot, entire or trilobed. Column stout, erect, with a distinct foot; pollinia 4, waxy, attached to a curved viscidium.

CULTIVATION: With such a large genus, cultivation requirements vary but most prefer cool to intermediate conditions, light shade, and high humidity with plenty of water while in growth and only a short winter rest. Most do well in pots with a fine to medium bark mix, but the more straggling species are better in baskets. The higher the altitude at which the species grows, the cooler the conditions required in cultivation, but many species apparently have a considerable altitudinal range, which suggests that they are not too fussy about temperature.

Masdevallia triangularis

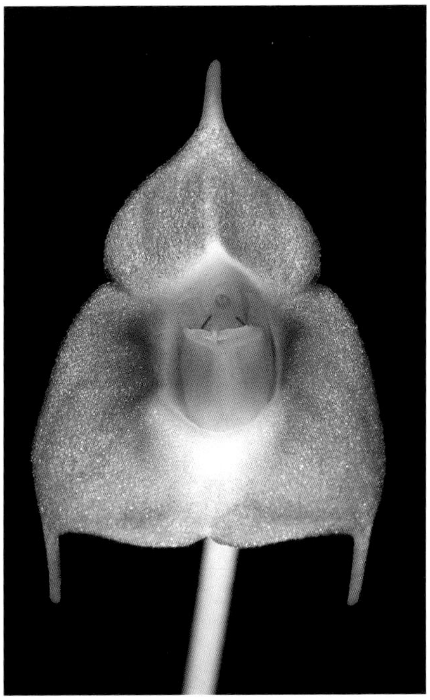

Masdevallia uniflora

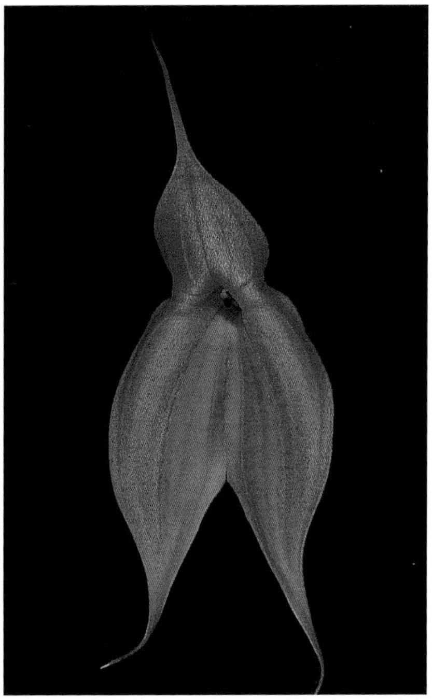

Masdevallia veitchiana

Masdevallia xanthina

Masdevallia yungasensis

Maxillaria acuminata Lindley
Pseudobulbs ovate, flattened, to 3 cm long, well-spaced on creeping rhizome, 2-leaved. Leaves to 10 × 1 cm, oblong. Flowers ca. 3 cm across, yellow, the sepals spreading, acuminate.

Epiphytic in wet submontane and montane forest, 450–2700 m (1500–8900 ft.)

Western South America

Maxillaria arachnites Reichenbach f.
Pseudobulbs small, flattened, 1- to 3-leaved. Leaves lanceolate, to 25 × 3 cm. Inflorescence to 15 cm long. Flowers 10–11 cm across; sepals yellow-green, lanceolate, acuminate; petals white, similar but smaller; lip golden yellow, 17 × 10 mm, trilobed near apex, the margins finely toothed.

Epiphytic or lithophytic, 1000–3000 m (3300–9900 ft.)

Venezuela, Colombia, Ecuador

Maxillaria arbuscula (Lindley) Reichenbach f.
Rhizome branched, slender, with or without pseudobulbs. Leaves distichous, ca. 2 cm long, narrowly strap-shaped. Flowers almost round, ca. 1 cm across; sepals and petals white, dotted with red; lip mostly deep red, the tip fleshy.

Terrestrial, 2500–3100 m (8250–10,200 ft.)

Ecuador, Peru

Maxillaria coccinea (Jacquin) L. O. Williams
Robust plants, the rhizome covered with papery sheaths. Pseudobulbs to 4 cm long, ovoid, flattened, 1-leafed. Leaves to 35 × 2.5 cm, linear. Inflorescences clustered, to 6 cm long. Flowers bright red or pink; sepals to 12 mm long.

Epiphytic on trunks and branches in dense forest, 140–1200 m (460–4000 ft.)

West Indies, Colombia, Venezuela

Maxillaria cogniauxiana Hoehne
Small plants forming drooping tufts. Pseudobulbs clustered, cylindrical, to 2 cm tall. Leaves 2, ca. 3 × 1.5 cm, linear-lanceolate, keeled. Flowers ca. 2 cm across, orange, heavily blotched with maroon.

Mid to high-level epiphyte in forest, to 1400 m (4600 ft.)

Southern and southeastern Brazil

SIMILAR SPECIES: *Maxillaria plebeja* Reichenbach f. is like a smaller version of *M. cogniauxiana* with brownish-green flowers. *Maxillaria acicularis* Herbert has longer, needle-shaped leaves and yellow flowers. Both of these also come from southeastern Brazil.

Maxillaria cucullata Lindley
Pseudobulbs 4–5 cm long, elliptic, 1-leafed. Leaves to 20 cm long, strap-shaped. Inflorescence to 13 cm long. Flowers dark brown; sepals and petals 25–28 mm long; lip trilobed.

Epiphytic, lithophytic, or terrestrial in rain forest and cloud forest, 700–3300 m (2300–10,900 ft.)

Mexico, Central America

Maxillaria discolor (Loddiges ex Lindley) Reichenbach f.
Pseudobulbs clustered. Leaves 10–35 cm long, the underside often purplish. Inflorescence 4–5 cm long. Flowers waxy, apricot, sometimes spotted with maroon, lip orange with maroon spots; sepals spreading, ca. 22 mm long; lip obscurely trilobed, fleshy, with a longitudinal hairy callus.

Epiphytic in shade of lowland to submontane forest, 100–1600 m (330–5300 ft.)

Central and South America

Maxillaria arachnites

Maxillaria cogniauxiana

Maxillaria discolor

Maxillaria acuminata

Maxillaria arbuscula

Maxillaria coccinea

Maxillaria cucullata

Maxillaria elegantula Rolfe

SYN. *Maxillaria dichroma* Rolfe

Rhizome creeping; pseudobulbs ovoid, compressed, to 6 cm long, 1-leafed at apex but with some large basal sheaths, the topmost often leafy. Leaf to 30 × 5.5 cm; petiole to 20 cm long. Inflorescence to 25 cm long. Flowers large, showy, 5–8 cm across, white tinged with purple-brown. Sepals and petals spreading, lip 17 mm long, ovate, obscurely trilobed.

Epiphytic in open woodland, 400–2550 m (1320–8400 ft.)

Ecuador, Peru

Maxillaria grandiflora (Kunth) Lindley

Pseudobulbs to 6 cm long, ovoid, compressed, 1-leafed at apex but with several leaf-bearing sheaths when young. Leaves petiolate, to 30 × 5 cm, elliptic to strap-shaped. Inflorescence 12–25 cm tall. Flowers to 10 cm across, showy, milky white, fleshy, slightly nodding.

Epiphytic or lithophytic in forest, often on steep slopes, 800–3000 m (2640–9900 ft.)

Bolivia, Colombia, Ecuador, Peru, Venezuela

Maxillaria grandiflora

Maxillaria kautskyi Pabst

Slender plants; pseudobulbs ± globose, ca. 15 × 15 mm, wrinkled, 2-leaved, set close together. Leaves to 25 × 5 mm, narrowly linear. Inflorescence short; flowers to 3 cm diameter, yellow, the lip spotted purple near tip.

Epiphytic in submontane forest

Brazil

Maxillaria kautskyi

Maxillaria lepidota Lindley

SYN. *Maxillaria pertusa* Lindley, *M. saxicola* Schlechter

Pseudobulbs to 5 cm long, ovoid, clustered, covered with sheaths, 1-leafed at apex. Leaves linear, to 35 × 2 cm. Inflorescence to 12 cm long. Flowers showy, spidery, scented; sepals and petals yellow with red marks at base, lip creamy yellow, marked with maroon; sepals 6–7 cm long, lanceolate, acuminate; lip 20 × 12 mm, fleshy, the midlobe farinose. Requires cool or intermediate conditions.

Epiphytic in cloud forest, ca. 1400 m (4600 ft.)

Colombia, Ecuador, Peru, Venezuela

Maxillaria luteoalba Lindley
Pseudobulbs clustered, ovoid, compressed, brown, covered with scarious sheaths, 1-leafed at apex. Leaves to 50 × 5 cm, narrowly strap-shaped. Inflorescence to 12 cm long. Flowers large, showy, ca. 10 cm across, white and yellow, the lip side lobes with purple-brown veins. Needs intermediate conditions and fairly good light.

Epiphytic in rain forest, 100–800 m (330–2640 ft.)

Costa Rica, Colombia, Ecuador

SIMILAR SPECIES: *Maxillaria setigera* Lindley (syn. *M. callichroma* Reichenbach f.), from western South America to Guyana, is a sun-loving species with similar white and yellow flowers, 10–15 cm across.

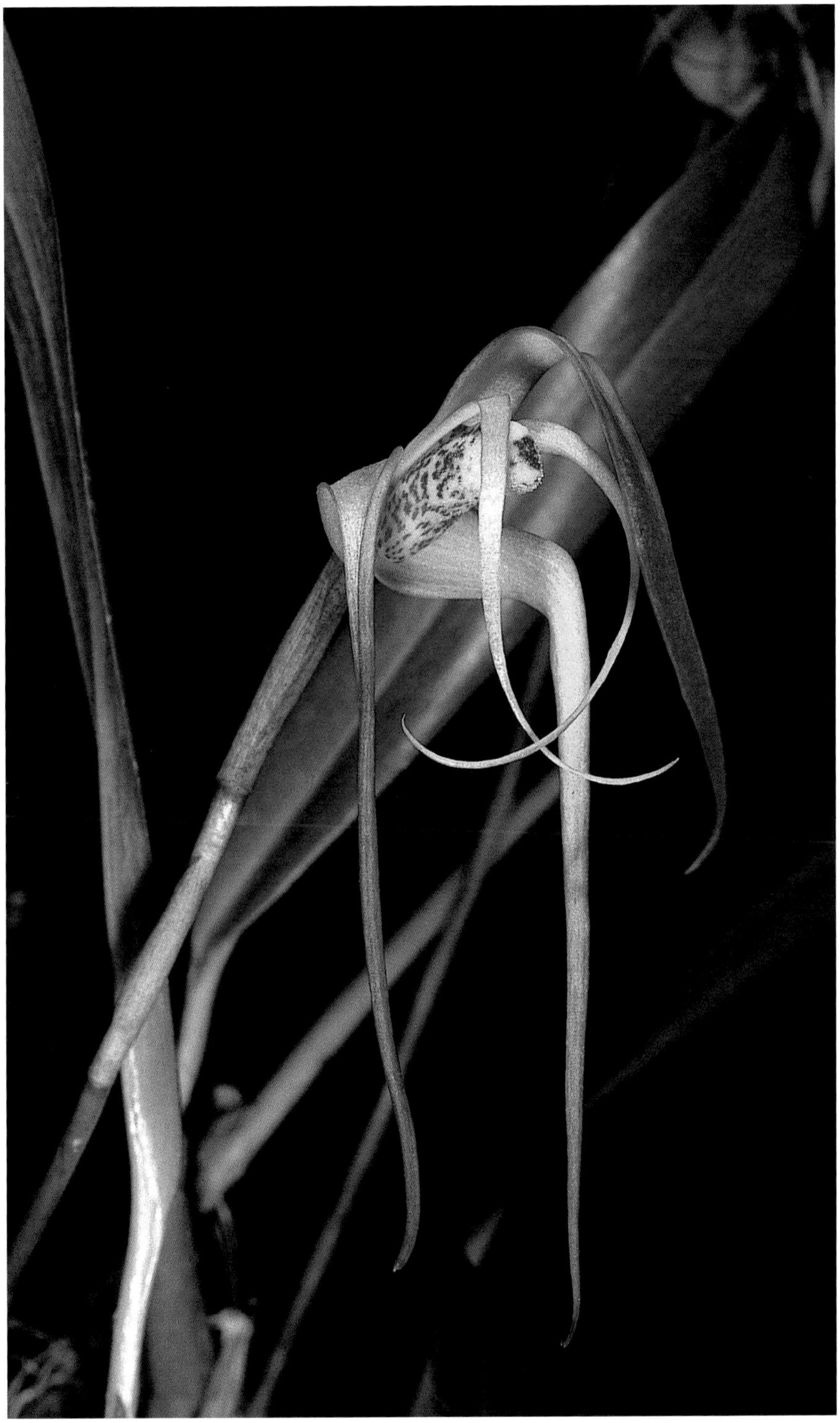

Maxillaria lepidota

Maxillaria lutescens Scheidweiler
SYN. *Maxillaria camaridii* Reichenbach f.
Rhizome elongated, erect or pendent, branched, covered in gray sheaths. Pseudobulbs to 8 cm long, ovoid, compressed, 1- or 2-leaved at apex. Inflorescence short. Flowers scented, ca. 6 cm across, white, the lip midlobe yellow.

Epiphytic in humid forest, 40–1200 m (130–4000 ft.)

Widespread in tropical America

Maxillaria meleagris Lindley
SYN. *Maxillaria lindeniana* A. Richard, *M. punctostriata* Reichenbach f.
Pseudobulbs clustered, to 5.5 × 2 cm, ellipsoid to ovoid, compressed, 1-leafed

Maxillaria meleagris

at apex. Leaves to 40 cm long, less than 2 cm wide, linear. Inflorescence to 8 cm long. Flowers variable in size and color, to 5 cm across, usually yellowish mottled with dark red.

Epiphytic in rain forest and cloud forest, 1500–2450 m (5000–8100 ft.)

Mexico to Venezuela

Maxillaria nasuta Reichenbach f.

SYN. *Maxillaria brevipedunculata* Ames & C. Schweinfurth

Medium to large plants; pseudobulbs to 9 cm long, bilaterally flattened, clustered, 1-leafed at apex. Leaves linear, to 60 cm long. Inflorescence to 8 cm long. Flowers ca. 8 cm across, yellow-green flushed with maroon, the lip mostly maroon, yellow at the tip.

Epiphytic, lithophytic, or terrestrial in rain forest and cloud forest, often in open places, 200–1800 m (660–6000 ft.)

Mexico to South America

Maxillaria nigrescens Lindley

Pseudobulbs elongated, the base covered with gray sheaths, 1-leafed at the apex. Leaves linear, stiff, to 35 cm long. Inflorescence to 15 cm long. Flowers large, rather spidery, sepals and petals dark red, the base of the sepals yellowish; sepals to 60 mm long; lip to 17 mm long, dark maroon. Prefers cool conditions and bright light.

Epiphytic in rain forest, 1500–2700 m (5000–8900 ft.)

Colombia, Peru, Venezuela

Maxillaria ochroleuca Loddiges ex Lindley

Pseudobulbs clustered, to 8 cm long, 1-leafed at apex and with 1 or 2 leaf-bearing sheaths at the base. Leaves linear, to 45 cm long. Inflorescences to 16 cm long, arising in clusters from axils of the basal sheathing leaves. Flowers ca. 5 cm across, strongly scented; sepals and petals white, turning yellow towards apex; lip white, the midlobe orange, fleshy, rough-textured.

Maxillaria splendens

Epiphytic, lithophytic or terrestrial in lowland to submontane forest, 400–1800 m (1320–6000 ft.)

Ecuador, Peru, Brazil

SIMILAR SPECIES: *Maxillaria splendens* Poeppig & Endlicher from Peru has white flowers with a yellow lip midlobe.

Maxillaria parkeri Hooker

Medium to large plants; pseudobulbs clustered, subglobose, ca. 3 cm high and wide, with large, spotted sheaths at the base. Leaves to 50 cm long, narrowly strap-shaped. Inflorescence ca. 7 cm tall. Flowers ca. 6 cm across; sepals yellow, petals white with maroon veining, lip orange-yellow with a white margin, trilobed at about halfway.

Epiphytic in rain forest, 50–900 m (165–3000 ft.)

Central America to Brazil

SIMILAR SPECIES: *Maxillaria loretoensis* C. Schweinfurth from Brazil, Peru, and Venezuela has narrower leaves and sepals.

Maxillaria picta Hooker

SYN. *Maxillaria consanguinea* Klotzsch

Pseudobulbs to 6 cm long, ovoid, compressed, ribbed, set close together, 1- or 2-leaved at apex. Leaves to 30 cm long, strap-shaped. Inflorescence 12–20 cm tall. Flowers ca. 5 cm across; sepals and petals pale yellow outside, golden yellow inside, spotted and banded with purple-brown; lip creamy-white spotted with purple-red.

Epiphytic (rarely lithophytic) in forest, 1100–1400 m (3600–4600 ft.)

Brazil, Argentina

SIMILAR SPECIES: *Maxillaria punctulata* Klotzsch (syn. *M. marginata* Fenzl, *M. crassipes* Kraenzlin, *M. tricolor* Lindley), from Nicaragua to Brazil, Peru, and Venezuela, differs mainly in having smaller flowers, more distinctly marked on the edges of the floral parts. *Maxillaria ubatubana* Hoehne from Brazil, is a larger plant with flowers ca. 7 cm across.

Maxillaria parahybunensis Cogniaux

A small, tufted species; pseudobulbs less than 1 cm long. Leaves 2–3 cm long, elliptic. Flowers borne at base of plants, 1 cm across, brownish. Prefers cool, shaded conditions in cultivation.

Epiphytic in shade in montane forest

Brazil

Maxillaria porphyrostele Reichenbach f.

Pseudobulbs clustered, 4–5 cm long, ellipsoid, 2-leaved at apex. Leaves to 20 cm long, narrowly strap-shaped. Inflorescences clustered, to 8 cm long; flowers 4 cm across, yellow, the lip with purple veining on the side lobes.

Epiphytic in montane forest

Brazil

Maxillaria nasuta

Maxillaria ochroleuca

Maxillaria picta

Maxillaria porphyrostele

Maxillaria porrecta Lindley
SYN. *Maxillaria brunnea* Linden & Reichenbach f.

A variable species, forming clumps. Pseudobulbs to 6 cm long, ovoid, 1-leafed at apex. Leaves 25–45 cm long, linear to elliptic. Inflorescence 8–17 cm long. Flowers ca. 3 cm across, yellowish, tinged with purplish at apex of sepals and petals; lip creamy yellow.

Epiphytic, lithophytic, or rarely terrestrial in wet submontane to cloud forest, often in open places, 500–1800 m (1650–6000 ft.)

Widespread in tropical America from Nicaragua to Ecuador and Peru

Maxillaria reichenheimiana Endres & Reichenbach f.

Small, tufted plants. Pseudobulbs clustered, subglobose, ca. 1.5 cm long, 1-leafed at apex. Leaves to 4 cm long, elliptic, blue-green dotted with gray or white. Inflorescence 5 cm long. Flowers large for size of plant; sepals to 35 mm long, orange flushed with maroon; petals yellowish; lip midlobe yellow, side lobes maroon.

Epiphytic in submontane forest, 600–1400 m (2000–4600 ft.)

Trinidad, Central and South America

Maxillaria rufescens Lindley

A variable small to medium-sized species. Pseudobulbs clustered, 1.5–6 cm long, subglobose to ovoid, 1-leafed at apex. Leaves 4–30 × 3–6 cm, elliptic to strap-shaped. Inflorescence to 5 cm long. Flowers 3–4 cm across, greenish brown, dull yellow, or maroon with a strong vanilla scent.

Epiphytic, rarely lithophytic, in submontane forest, 50–2000 m (165–6600 ft.)

Widespread in Central and South America

Maxillaria sanderiana Reichenbach f. ex Sander

Medium-sized to large plants. Pseudobulbs clustered, to 5 cm long, subglobose or ovoid, 1-leafed at apex. Leaves to 40 cm long, narrowly oblong, with a petiole to 20 cm long. Peduncles to 25 cm long, sometimes in clusters, covered with sheaths. Flowers large, fleshy, scented, showy, to 15 cm across, white, the sepals red at the base, petals flecked with red. Requires cool to intermediate conditions.

Epiphytic in wet forest or lithophytic on stony slopes, 1200–2500 m (4000–8250 ft.)

Ecuador, Peru

Maxillaria sophronitis (Reichenbach f.) Garay

Rhizome long, creeping, covered with brown sheaths. Pseudobulbs to 1.5 cm long, subglobose, 1-leafed at apex. Leaves to 2 cm long, elliptic. Inflorescence ca. 4 cm long. Flowers bright red or orange-red, somewhat cup-shaped; sepals to 13 mm long. With its creeping habit, this species is better mounted, in intermediate conditions with good light.

Maxillaria reichenheimiana

Maxillaria rufescens

Epiphytic in forest, 750–1700 m (2460–5600 ft.)
Venezuela

Maxillaria striata Rolfe

Pseudobulbs clustered, to 8 cm long, oblong or ovoid, with some leaf-bearing sheaths at the base, 1-leafed at apex. Leaves to 24 cm long, oblong or elliptic, with a petiole to 10 cm long. Inflorescence to 30 cm long. Flowers showy, large, to 13 cm across, greenish yellow with purple stripes, lip white in center.

Epiphytic in wet submontane and montane forest, 1500–2200 m (5000–6600 ft.)

Ecuador, Peru

Maxillaria tenuifolia Lindley

Pseudobulbs 2–3 cm long, set up to 5 cm apart on an ascending rhizome. leaves to 35 × 1 cm, linear, dark green. Inflorescence to 5 cm long; flowers to 5 cm across, with a coconut scent, deep red, mottled with yellow in the center; lip yellow marked with red. Requires intermediate to warm conditions.

Epiphytic in rain forest and semi-deciduous forest, 50–600 m (165–2000 ft.)

Mexico, Central America

SIMILAR SPECIES: *Maxillaria sanguinea* Rolfe, from Costa Rica and Panama, has flowers with a fruity scent, a broader lip, usually white at the tip, and leaves less than 3 mm wide.

Maxillaria triloris E. Morren

Medium to large plants. Pseudobulbs clustered, to 6 cm tall, ovoid, with papery sheaths at the base, 1-leafed at apex. Leaves to 40 × 6 cm, narrowly strap-shaped. Inflorescence to 12 cm tall. Flowers large, 11–12 cm across, scented; sepals and petals yellow, white at the base; lip side lobes with maroon veins, midlobe yellow, the margin white, undulate.

Epiphytic at altitudes of 800–1800 m (2600–6000 ft.)

Ecuador, Venezuela

Maxillaria sanderiana

Maxillaria sanguinea

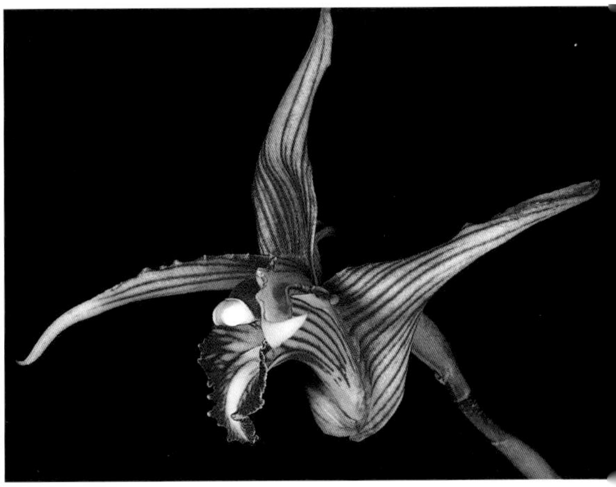

Maxillaria striata

Maxillaria sophronitis

Maxillaria tenuifolia

Maxillaria triloris

Maxillaria uncata Lindley
Rhizome long, pendent, covered with red-brown sheaths. Pseudobulbs minute, 1-leafed at apex. Leaves to 8 cm long, linear, stiff, fleshy. Flowers arising from rhizome sheaths, greenish white, sometimes flushed with maroon; sepals and petals projecting forwards, sepals to 14 mm long, lip obscurely trilobed.

Epiphytic, rarely lithophytic, in wet rain forest, 0–1300 m (4300 ft.)

South America

Maxillaria variabilis Bateman ex Lindley
SYN. *Maxillaria curtipes* Hooker
Rhizome elongated. Pseudobulbs to 4 × 2 cm, set 3–6 cm apart, 1-leafed. Leaves narrow, 15–25 cm long. Inflorescences in small groups, 2–3 cm long. Flowers buff-yellow to dark red; sepals and petals to 16 mm long; lip obscurely trilobed with a shiny purple-brown callus in the center.

Epiphytic, lithophytic, or often terrestrial in rain forest, 500–2500 m (1650–8250 ft.)

Mexico to Ecuador

Mediocalcar J. J. Smith

TRIBE: Podochileae
SUBTRIBE: Eriinae
ETYMOLOGY: From Latin *medius*, middle, and *calcar*, spur, referring to the saccate middle part of the lip
DISTRIBUTION: 17 species in the Pacific Islands, with most in New Guinea

Dwarf epiphytes with a creeping rhizome. Pseudobulbs ± cylindrical, 1- to 5-leaved at apex. Leaves fleshy, linear to lanceolate. Inflorescences terminal, 1-flowered. Flowers small, urn-shaped or bell-shaped; sepals joined for most of their length; petals small, hidden inside sepals; lip entire or obscurely trilobed, saccate. Column short; pollinia 8.

CULTIVATION: With their creeping rhizomes, plants should be mounted. They need intermediate conditions, moderate to heavy shade, and high

Maxillaria uncata

Maxillaria variabilis

Mediocalcar decoratum

humidity and should be watered throughout the year.

Mediocalcar decoratum Schuiteman

Dwarf plants forming mats. Pseudobulbs to 2 × 0.6 cm. Leaves fleshy, linear, to 2.5 cm long. Inflorescence very short. Flowers 8–10 mm long, bell-shaped, orange-red; sepals and petals with yellow tips.

Epiphytic in shade in submontane and montane forest, 900–2000 m (3000–6600 ft.)

New Guinea

Meiracyllium Reichenbach f.

TRIBE: Epidendreae

SUBTRIBE: Laeliinae

ETYMOLOGY: From Greek *meirakyllion*, little fellow, presumably referring to the dwarf, creeping habit

DISTRIBUTION: 2 species in Mexico and Guatemala

Small epiphytes or lithophytes with creeping rhizomes covered by scarious sheaths. Secondary stems short, erect, 1-leafed. Leaf sessile, short, and broad. Inflorescences terminal, several-flowered. Flowers small, purple; sepals spreading, petals narrower than sepals; lip entire, attached to base of column, saccate. Column short; pollinia 8, waxy, in 2 groups.

CULTIVATION: Both species do well in an intermediate greenhouse. With the creeping rhizome, they are better mounted than in pots, although small baskets are suitable. They need only light shade and plenty of moisture and high humidity during the growth and flowering period, but should be kept cooler and drier while at rest. Good ventilation all year round is important.

Meiracyllium trinasutum Reichenbach f.

SYN. *Meiracyllium wendlandii* Reichenbach f.

Leaf to 5 × 3.5 cm, orbicular to elliptic. Inflorescence short, erect, 1- to

4-flowered. Flowers purple, ca. 25 mm across; sepals and petals oblong to elliptic, to 10 mm long; lip saccate at base.

Epiphytic in seasonally dry forest and woodland, occasionally in lower montane rain forest, 450–1500 m (1500–5000 ft.)

Mexico to El Salvador

SIMILAR SPECIES: *Meiracyllium gemma* Reichenbach f., endemic to Mexico, where it grows in pine forest at 400–1000 m (1320–3300 ft.), has larger flowers with sepals and petals 15–17 mm long.

Mexicoa Garay

TRIBE: Maxillarieae
SUBTRIBE: Oncidiinae
ETYMOLOGY: Named for the country of origin
DISTRIBUTION: 1 species in Mexico

Small epiphytes, forming clumps; pseudobulbs ovoid or conical, 1- or 2-leaved at apex, with 1 basal, leafy sheath. Inflorescence basal, appearing with new growth, laxly few-flowered. Flowers showy; sepals and petals subsimilar; lip hinged to column-foot, trilobed, not spurred. Column without wings; pollinia 2.

CULTIVATION: Plants can be potted in a standard epiphyte mix or mounted. They require cool to intermediate temperatures, shade, and high humidity.

Mexicoa ghiesbreghtiana (A. Richard & Galeotti) Garay

SYN. *Oncidium ghiesbreghtiana* A. Richard & Galeotti

Pseudobulbs ca. 4 × 2 cm. Leaves to 15 × 1.5 cm, linear. Inflorescence 14–20 cm long, 3- to 6-flowered. Flowers 3–4 cm long; sepals and petals yellow, heavily veined with red-brown, sepals spreading, petals projecting forward; lip yellow, midlobe emarginate, callus linear, bifid, orange-yellow.

Epiphytic in humid forest, 1400–2300 m (4600–7600 ft.)

Mexico

Mexipedium V. A. Albert & M. W. Chase

SUBFAMILY: Cypripedioideae
ETYMOLOGY: From Mexico and Greek *pedilon*, a shoe or slipper
DISTRIBUTION: 1 species in Mexico

Small lithophyte forming colonies. Rhizome long, covered with sheaths, the growths usually ca. 20 cm apart. Leaves 5 to 8, leathery, folded at base. Inflorescence terminal, with 1 branch, 3- or 7-flowered, the flowers open in succession. Flowers relatively small, thin-textured; sepals pubescent outside, dorsal forming a hood over lip, lateral sepals joined forming a synsepal; petals incurved, lip forming a subglobose pouch.

CULTIVATION: Plants can be grown in intermediate conditions in a mixture that is free-draining but does not dry out too quickly. This usually consists of a mixture of bark or coconut husk with an inert material such as perlite or pumice. Plants need good air movement and moderate shade.

Meiracyllium trinasutum

Because the shoots are well-spaced out, cultivation has proved to be most successful when each shoot is potted up separately, leading to a network of pots joined by runners. If desired, plants can be propagated by cutting a runner once the new growth has become established, but multigrowth plants are more vigorous.

Mexipedium xerophyticum

(Soto Arenas, Salazar & Hágsater) V. A. Albert & M. W. Chase

SYN. *Phragmipedium xerophyticum* Soto Arenas, Salazar & Hágsater

Leaves ca. 6 × 1 cm, strap-shaped, clear green above, pale below. Inflorescence 5–14 cm tall. Flowers 2–2.5 cm across, white, with fine brownish hairs on the outside of the sepals.

Lithophytic on limestone rocks surrounded by stunted trees, ca. 300 m (1000 ft.)

Southern Mexico (Oaxaca)

Microcoelia Lindley

TRIBE: Vandeae

SUBTRIBE: Aerangidinae

ETYMOLOGY: From Greek *mikros*, small, and *koilia*, abdomen, referring to the globose spur of the type species, *Microcoelia exilis*

DISTRIBUTION: About 30 species in Africa and Madagascar

Leafless epiphytes, rarely lithophytes. Stems usually short, rarely long, roots elongate, silvery when dry, greenish when wet, slender or fairly stout, sometimes dorsiventrally flattened, in some species clinging to the bark of the host tree, in others mainly aerial. Inflorescences unbranched. Flowers small; sepals and petals subsimilar, usually spreading; lip entire or obscurely trilobed, spurred at the base.

CULTIVATION: As all photosynthesis is carried out by the roots, potting is not an option. Plants should be mounted on fairly smooth bark and hung up in intermediate conditions with moderate shade and high humidity. It is possible that these species are rather intolerant of fungicide. Although the flowers are small, they are attractive little plants.

Microcoelia aphylla (Thouars) Summerhayes

SYN. *Solenangis aphylla* (Thouars) Summerhayes

Stems to 40 cm long, scandent, climbing on twigs and branches.

Mexicoa ghiesbreghtiana

Mexipedium xerophyticum. J. Hermans

Roots numerous, along stem. Inflorescences numerous on stem, 1–3 cm long, 8- to 16-flowered. Flowers small, white, the parts tipped with reddish brown; spur curved, swollen at apex, 4–5 mm long.

Epiphytic in thicket, 0–300 m (1000 ft.)

East Africa, Madagascar, Mauritius, Réunion

Microcoelia bulbocalcarata L. Jonsson

Roots few, to 50 cm long, 2 mm diameter. Inflorescences several, to 2 cm long, several-flowered. Flowers white, the lip with a green patch; spur to 11 mm long, swollen at the base and apex, constricted in the middle.

Epiphytic in understory of dense forest, in heavy shade, 1680–1950 m (5550–6430 ft.)

Rwanda, Uganda, São Tomé

Microcoelia corallina Summerhayes

Roots fairly short, forming a mound. Inflorescence 2–3 cm long, densely to about 15-flowered, the flowers held at about the same level. Ovary and pedicel salmon-pink, sepals and petals white with a salmon-pink mid line, column and spur salmon-red; spur ca 6 mm long, swollen in apical half. Flowers autumn. This species needs good light.

Epiphytic in hot, dry open woodland, often near a river, 200–670 m (660–2200 ft.)

Kenya, Tanzania, Malawi, Mozambique

Microcoelia exilis Lindley

Roots numerous, branched, silvery-gray, forming a tangled mass. Inflorescence to 25 cm long, densely many-flowered. Flowers tiny, white, with a greenish, globose spur.

Epiphytic usually in thicket and dryish woodland, 0–1800 m (6000 ft.)

Widespread in East and Central Africa, Madagascar

Microcoelia gilpinae (Reichenbach f. & S. Moore) Summerhayes

Roots long, slender. Inflorescence 1.5–3.5 cm long, densely 8- to 12-flowered. Flowers bright orange; sepals ca. 5 mm long; spur 7 mm long.

Epiphytic in understory in forest, 100–1800 m (330–6000 ft.)

Madagascar

Microcoelia stolzii (Schlechter) Summerhayes

Roots silvery green, to 30 cm long, 2–3 mm thick. Inflorescence to 12 cm long, densely many-flowered. Flowers glistening white, tip of spur and anther-cap yellow. Sepals, petals, and lip to 4 mm long, spur conical, to 3 mm long.

Epiphytic in forest and high-rainfall woodland, 800–2450 m (2640–8100 ft.)

East Africa

SIMILAR SPECIES: *Microcoelia globulosa* (Hochstetter) L. Jonsson (syn. *M. guyoniana* (Reichenbach f.) Summerhayes) is widespread in Africa and has a looser, fewer-flowered inflorescence.

Micropera Lindley

SYN. *Camarotis* Lindley

TRIBE: Vandeae

SUBTRIBE: Aeridinae

ETYMOLOGY: From Greek *mikros*, small, and *pera*, sac, referring to the saccate lip

DISTRIBUTION: About 20 species in Asia and Australia

Monopodial, sometimes scandent, epiphytes. Roots numerous, along stem. Leaves linear. Inflorescences arising on stems opposite leaves; flowers

Microcoelia bulbocalcarata. E. la Croix

Microcoelia corallina. E. la Croix

small, fleshy, nonresupinate. Lateral sepals shortly joined at base; lip saccate with a callus on the back wall of the spur and often a bilobed callus on the front wall. Column long and twisted; pollinia 4, in 2 unequal pairs.
CULTIVATION: Most species are easily grown in pots or baskets in a standard, medium, epiphyte compost. They require intermediate to warm conditions with only light shade and should be watered throughout the year.

Micropera obtusa (Lindley) Tang & Wang

Stem erect, branched, 15–20 cm tall. Leaves to 12 × 1 cm. Inflorescence spreading, loosely 10–15-flowered, with only a few open together. Pedicel and ovary with scurfy hairs. Flowers 12–18 mm across; sepals and petals pink; lip yellow or white with yellow markings.

Epiphytic in tropical and subtropical forest, ca. 410 m (1350 ft.)

Northeastern India, Myanmar, Thailand

SIMILAR SPECIES: *Micropera rostrata* (Roxburgh) N. P. Balakrishnan (syn. *Camarotis rostrata* (Roxburgh) Reichenbach f., *Camarotis purpurea* Lindley, *Micropera purpurea* (Lindley)

Microcoelia stolzii. E. la Croix

Microcoelia exilis. E. la Croix

Microcoelia gilpinae. J. Hermans

Micropera rostrata

Pradhan) from India and Bangladesh has a purple lip and a glabrous pedicel and ovary.

Micropera philippinensis (Lindley) Garay

Stems erect, to 40 cm tall. Leaves to 15 × 1.5 cm. Inflorescence erect, to 20-flowered. Flowers white or cream, ca. 10 mm long.

Epiphytic in forest to 850 m (2800 ft.) Philippines

Microterangis Senghas

TRIBE: Vandeae

SUBTRIBE: Aerangidinae

ETYMOLOGY: From Greek *microteros*, smaller, and *angos*, vessel, referring to the spur

DISTRIBUTION: 7 species in Madagascar and Comoro Islands

Stems short, leafy. Inflorescences simple, densely many-flowered. Flowers very small; straw yellow, orange, or reddish brown; sepals and petals similar, spreading; lip entire, sometimes dentate at tip, spurred. Column very short; pollinia 2, stipes and viscidium 1.

Species in this genus were formerly classified as *Chamaeangis*.

CULTIVATION: *Microterangis* species grow better mounted on a bark slab than in a pot. They require shady, humid conditions with good air movement, at intermediate to warm temperatures.

Microterangis hariotiana (Kraenzlin) Senghas

SYN. *Chamaeangis hariotiana* (Kraenzlin) Schlechter

Leaves several, 5–15 × 1.5–4 cm, bright green, elliptic. Racemes several, pendent, 10–20 cm long, densely many-flowered. Flowers tiny, orange or reddish brown, but because of their numbers, showy in spite of their small size. Flowering summer.

Epiphytic in humid forest, 0–500 m (1650 ft.)

Comoro Islands

SIMILAR SPECIES: *Microterangis boutonii* (Reichenbach f.) Senghas, also from the Comoro Islands, has the lip 3-toothed at the apex.

Microtis R. Brown

ONION ORCHIDS

TRIBE: Diurideae

SUBTRIBE: Prasophyllinae

ETYMOLOGY: From Greek *micros*, small and *ous*, ear, thought to refer to the column wings

DISTRIBUTION: 18 species from East Asia, Australia, and New Zealand

Slender terrestrials with globose tubers and a single long, narrow leaf. Inflorescences erect, unbranched, densely few- to many-flowered. Flowers small, usually green, yellow-green or greenish white; sepals and petals free, the dorsal sepal forming a hood with the petals, lateral sepals spreading; lip entire, differing in size, shape and color from sepals and petals.

The common name is given because the leaves look like onion seedlings.

CULTIVATION: Grow in a standard terrestrial mixture in cool conditions in semi-shade and water freely while in growth, with weak doses of fertilizer. When the plants become dormant after flowering, they should be kept dry; this is the time to repot them if necessary. Species that form colonies are easily grown.

Microtis parviflora R. Brown

SLENDER ONION ORCHID

Leaf to 40 cm long, linear, hollow. Inflorescence to 50 cm tall, densely several- to many-flowered. Flowers green or yellow-green, ca. 3 mm across; lip heart-shaped, the margin entire.

Forms colonies in damp areas in grassland and open patches in forest

Australia, New Zealand, New Caledonia

SIMILAR SPECIES: *Microtis unifolia* (G. Forster) Reichenbach f., COMMON ONION ORCHID, from Australia, New Zealand, New Caledonia, Indonesia, the Philippines, China, and Japan has an oblong lip with a callus near the notched apex. *Microtis arenaria* Lindley from Victoria and Tasmania is about 50 cm tall and grows in coastal heath, woodland, and wet grassland.

Miltonia Lindley

SYN. *Anneliesia* Brieger & Lückel

TRIBE: Maxillarieae

SUBTRIBE: Oncidiinae

ETYMOLOGY: Named for Viscount Milton (1786–1857), a keen orchid grower

DISTRIBUTION: 11 species and about 4 natural hybrids in South America, mainly Brazil

Pseudobulbs usually ovoid to oblong, somewhat compressed, subtended by distichous, sometimes leafy sheaths, 2-leaved at apex, set on a creeping rhizome. Leaves linear or strap-shaped. Inflorescences axillary, usually unbranched, erect or arching, 1- to many-flowered. Flowers showy; sepals and petals spreading, subsimilar or petals wider; lip unlobed, often fan-shaped or fiddle-shaped. Pollinia 2.

CULTIVATION: Grow potted in an open mixture, in intermediate conditions and light to moderate shade, with plenty of water while they are in active growth, less while resting.

Miltonia clowesii Lindley

Pseudobulbs to 10 cm long. Leaves to 45 × 2.5 cm, pale green. Inflorescence unbranched, to 4 cm tall, several-flowered, the flowers open in succession 2 or 3 at a time. Flowers 5–8 cm across, yellowish, barred and blotched with red-brown; lip white with a large purple blotch towards the base. Flowers autumn.

Epiphytic in coastal forest, 0–900 m (3000 ft.)

Eastern Brazil

SIMILAR SPECIES: *Miltonia candida* Lindley has brownish sepals and petals spotted and tipped with yellow

Microterangis hariotiana. J. Hermans

Microtis arenaria. R. Parsons

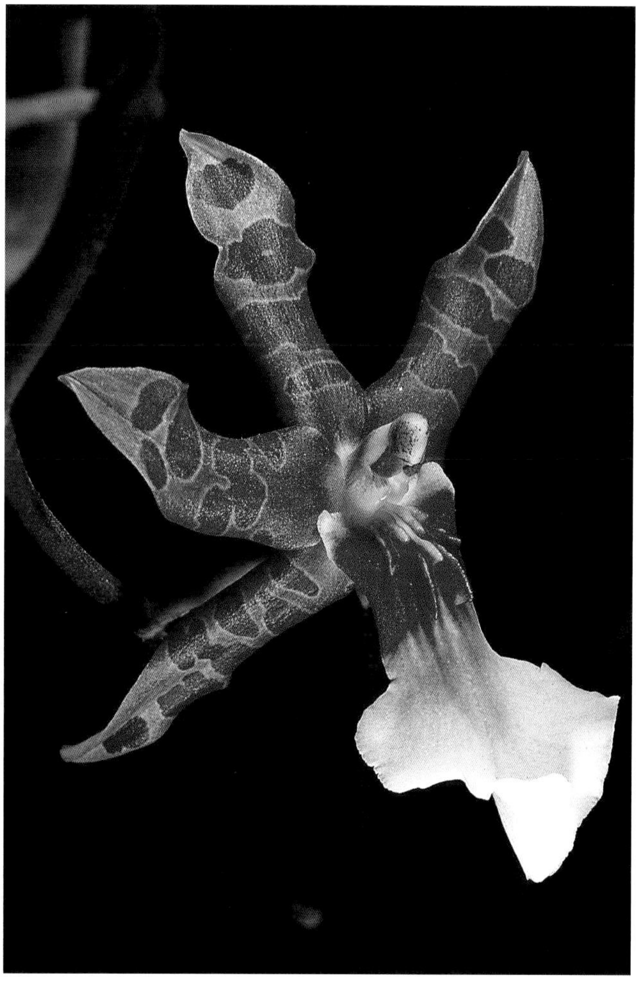
Miltonia clowesii

and a white lip with 2 red marks in the throat, enfolding the column at the base.

Miltonia cuneata Lindley
Pseudobulbs compressed, to 10 cm long. Leaves to 45 × 2.5 cm, dark green. Raceme to 45 cm tall, 7- to 10-flowered. Flowers 5–8 cm across; sepals and petals creamy yellow, heavily barred with chocolate brown; lip white, fan-shaped, with a basal callus of 2 ridges. Flowering winter–spring.

Epiphytic in submontane forest, 800–1000 m (2640–3300 ft.)

Brazil

Miltonia flavescens Lindley
Pseudobulbs to 12 cm long. Leaves to 35 × 1.5 cm. Inflorescence unbranched, 7- to 10-flowered, the flowers open together. Peduncle flattened. Flowers scented, to 7.5 cm across, straw yellow, lip with red spots; sepals and petals narrow, to 50 × 5 mm; lip ovate to oblong, the edges undulate. Flowering summer–autumn.

Epiphytic in submontane forest, ca. 800 m (2640 ft.)

Argentina, Brazil, Paraguay, Peru

Miltonia moreliana A. Richard
SYN. *Miltonia spectabilis* Lindley var. *moreliana* (A. Richard) Henfrey
Pseudobulbs yellowish, laterally compressed, to 10 cm long. Leaves 10–15 cm long, narrowly strap-shaped, yellow-green. Inflorescence to 25 cm long, 1-flowered. Flowers flat, to 10 cm across; sepals and petals plum-purple; lip pink, heavily veined with purple.

Epiphytic in forest

Brazil

Miltonia regnellii Reichenbach f.
Pseudobulbs to 9 cm long. Leaves to 30 × 1.5 cm. Inflorescence to 40 cm long, unbranched, 3- to 5-flowered. Flowers to 7.5 cm across, white flushed with pink or lilac, lip lilac-pink, the margins white. Flowering in autumn.

Epiphytic in submontane rain forest, 300–800 m (1000–2640 ft.)

Eastern Brazil

Miltonia spectabilis Lindley
Pseudobulbs to 7 cm long, leaves to 13 × 2 cm, yellow-green. Inflorescence to 25 cm tall, the peduncle flattened, 1-flowered. Flowers to 10 cm across, sepals and petals white tinged with pink at the base, lip violet-pink with darker veins, callus yellow, with 3 ridges. Flowering in autumn.

Epiphytic in forest, ca. 800 m (2640 ft.)

Brazil

Miltonioides Brieger & Lückel

TRIBE: Maxillarieae
SUBTRIBE: Oncidiinae
ETYMOLOGY: Named for the resemblance to *Miltonia*
DISTRIBUTION: 7 species from Mexico to South America

Large epiphytes, occasionally lithophytes; pseudobulbs laterally compressed, subtended by leafy sheaths, 1- to 2-leaved at apex. Inflorescences axillary from basal sheaths, unbranched, loosely few-flowered. Flowers showy; sepals and petals free, subsimilar, spreading, lip oblong or fiddle-shaped, deflexed at right angles to column, usually with recurved margins, usually 2-colored. Column erect, sometimes winged; pollinia 2.

CULTIVATION: Plants should be potted in an fairly coarse, free-draining mixture, in intermediate conditions and light to moderate shade. They need plenty of water while in active growth, less while resting.

Miltonioides reichenheimii (Linden & Reichenbach f.) Brieger & Lückel
SYN. *Odontoglossum reichenheimii* Linden & Reichenbach f., *Oncidium reichenheimii* (Linden & Reichenbach f.) Garay & Stacy
Pseudobulbs to 12 × 6 cm. Leaves to 45 × 5.5 cm. Inflorescence ca. 1 m long, many-flowered. Flowers fleshy, ca. 7.5 cm across; sepals and petals yellow, heavily blotched with reddish brown; lip white towards the apex, the basal half pink with a 3-ridged callus. Column not winged.

Epiphytic in forest, 1200–2300 m (4000–7600 ft.)

Mexico

SIMILAR SPECIES: *Miltonioides laevis* (Lindley) Brieger & Lückel from Mexico and Guatemala has a 2-ridged basal callus and a winged column.

Miltoniopsis Godefroy-Lebeuf

PANSY ORCHID
TRIBE: Maxillarieae
SUBTRIBE: Oncidiinae
ETYMOLOGY: From *Miltonia*, and Greek *-opsis*, resembling
DISTRIBUTION: 5 species from Central and western South America

Epiphytes or lithophytes with clustered, laterally flattened pseudobulbs, 1-leafed at apex and subtended by several leaf-bearing sheaths. Leaves linear to strap-shaped, usually pale green or gray-green. Inflorescences axillary, unbranched, erect or arching, 1- to few-flowered. Flowers large, showy, flat; sepals and petals subsimilar, spreading, the petals somewhat reflexed at the middle; lip large, flat, auriculate at base, joined to the column by a central keel. Column short; pollinia 2.

Species of *Miltoniopsis* used to be classed as *Miltonia* (to which they are not very closely related) and are still known as *Miltonia* for hybrid registration. There are many *Miltoniopsis* hybrids and the genus has been extensively used in intergeneric hybridization with *Oncidium* and its relatives.

CULTIVATION: Most species grow in rain forest and cloud forest at fairly high altitudes and need cool to inter-

Miltonia flavescens

Miltonia spectabilis

Miltonioides reichenheimii

mediate, humid, shady conditions. They are grown in pots in a medium compost and should be given plenty of water while growing. They need less while resting but should not dry out completely; in dry conditions, the leaves develop transverse concertina-like folds.

Miltoniopsis phalaenopsis (Lindley & Reichenbach f.) Garay & Dunsterville

Leaves to 22 × 0.5 cm, pale green. Inflorescence shorter than leaves, 3- to 5-flowered. Flowers 5–6.5 cm across; sepals and petals pure white, lip white with purple or red blotches and streaks, trilobed, the midlobe fan-shaped, emarginate, with a 3-toothed callus with a yellow spot on each side.

Epiphytic in rain forest and cloud forest, 1200–1500 m (4000–5000 ft.)

Colombia

Miltoniopsis roezlii (Reichenbach f.) Godefroy-Lebeuf

SYN. *Miltoniopsis santanae* Garay & Dunsterville

Leaves to 30 × 1.5 cm, pale green. Inflorescence to 30 cm long, 2- to 5-flowered. Flowers 8–10 cm across, white sometimes with a purple blotch at the base of each petal; lip orange-yellow at the base, slightly broader than long, with 2 hornlike auricles at the base.

Epiphytic in submontane forest, 600–1200 m (2000–4000 ft.)

Colombia, Ecuador, Panama, Venezuela

Miltoniopsis vexillaria (Reichenbach f.) Godefroy-Lebeuf

Leaves to 25 × 2.5 cm, gray-green. Inflorescence to 30 cm long, loosely 4- to 6-flowered. Flowers to 10 cm across; sepals and petals pink, or white flushed with pink; lip broadly fan-shaped, emarginate, white or pale pink, maroon at base with maroon striping and a yellow callus.

Epiphytic in wet submontane and montane forest, 1100–2200 m (3600–7260 ft.)

Colombia, Ecuador, Peru

Miltoniopsis warszewiczii (Reichenbach f.) Garay & Dunsterville

Leaves pale green, to 30 cm long. Inflorescence to 30 × 2.5 cm, loosely 3- to 6-flowered. Flowers 6–7 cm across, white, with a light pinkish-purple blotch at the base of each segment and a yellow callus; lip 3.5 cm long and broad, ± fiddle-shaped.

Epiphytic in rain forest and cloud forest, 1300–1800 m (4300–6000 ft.)

Costa Rica, Guyana, Nicaragua, Panama

Mormodes Lindley

TRIBE: Cymbidieae

SUBTRIBE: Catasetinae

ETYMOLOGY: From Greek *mormo*, phantom or hideous monster, and *oides*, like, referring to the strange flowers

DISTRIBUTION: 70–80 species in Mexico, Central and South America

Pseudobulbs fleshy, oblong to cylindrical, several-leaved. Leaves distichous, long, plicate. Inflorescences lateral from the nodes of the pseudobulbs, unbranched, erect, arching or pendulous, few- to many-flowered. Flowers may be male, female, or bisexual; fleshy, often variable in color; sepals and petals free, similar, spreading or reflexed; lip joined to base of column, entire or trilobed, sometimes pubescent, often reflexed. Column erect, twisted, without wings or a foot; pollinia 2 or 4.

CULTIVATION: *Mormodes* plants are usually grown in pots or baskets, in a free-draining epiphyte compost, although they can be mounted, at intermediate temperatures. They need plenty of water and fertilizer while in active growth as well as good light and ventilation. When they become dormant, they should be kept dry, and in a cooler and darker place.

Mormodes buccinator Lindley

Pseudobulbs clustered, to 20 × 4 cm. Leaves to 40 × 6 cm. Inflorescence to 50 cm tall, erect or arching, few- to several-flowered. Flowers to 6.5 cm across, scented, variable in color from pinkish green with a cream lip to yellow; lip curved over column, the margins recurved.

Epiphytic in forest, 450–1500 m (1500–5000 ft.)

Mexico, Central and South America

Mormodes colossus Reichenbach f.

Pseudobulbs cylindrical, to 30 × 4.5 cm. Leaves to 30 cm long. Inflorescence to 60 cm, arching, densely many-flowered. Flowers scented, long-lasting, to 12 cm across. Sepals and petals green, yellowish or cream, sometimes tinged with pink at the base, lip brown or yellow, with a few red dots near base; lip with a short claw, side margins recurved.

Epiphytic in rain forest, 400–1600 m (1320–5300 ft.)

Costa Rica, Panama

Mormodes hookeri Lemaire

Pseudobulbs cylindrical, to 10 cm long. Inflorescence short, erect, few-flowered. Flowers scented, to 4 cm across, purple-red to dark red-brown; sepals and petals reflexed, lip pubescent, rarely glabrous in male flowers.

Epiphytic in rain forest, ca. 1000 m (3300 ft.)

Costa Rica, Panama

Mormodes ignea Lindley & Paxton

Pseudobulbs cylindrical. Inflorescence erect to arching, to 60 cm long, few- to several-flowered, produced after leaves have fallen. Flowers 5–6 cm across, scented, bright orange dotted with red.

Epiphytic in forest, 250–1200 m

Costa Rica, Colombia, Panama

Mormodes warszewiczii
Klotzsch

SYN. *Mormodes revoluta* Rolfe, *M. wolteriana* Kraenzlin, *M. hirsutissima* F. E. L. Miranda

A variable species. Pseudobulbs to 16 × 5 cm. Inflorescence to 50 cm long, several-flowered. Flowers variable in size and color, usually green, yellowish, or maroon, spotted and striped with purple-brown; sepals 2–13 cm long; lip to 3 cm long, pubescent.

Epiphytic in wet forest, 400–1200 m (1320–4000 ft.)

Bolivia, Brazil, Peru

Miltoniopsis phalaenopsis

Miltoniopsis roezlii

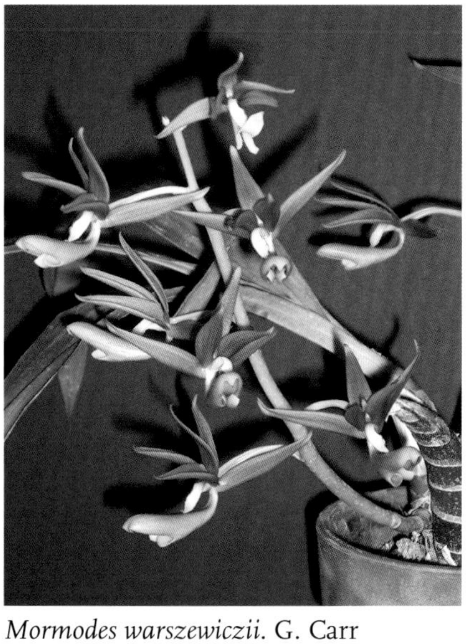

Mormodes warszewiczii. G. Carr

Mormodes ignea. G. Carr

Mormolyca Fenzl

TRIBE: Maxillarieae
SUBTRIBE: Maxillariinae
ETYMOLOGY: From Greek *mormolyca*, hobgobin, referring to the strange look of the flowers
DISTRIBUTION: 8 species in Mexico, Central and South America

Pseudobulbs fleshy, 1-leafed at apex, set on a short rhizome. Leaves leathery, erect. Inflorescence basal, 1-flowered; sepals and petals free, spreading, similar, but the petals slightly smaller; lip suberect, trilobed, side lobes erect, small, midlobe large, decurved. Column without foot; pollinia 4.

CULTIVATION: Plants can be grown in pots or baskets in a standard, free-draining epiphyte compost or mounted on slabs. Most require intermediate temperatures, light to moderate shade, and high humidity. They need less water while resting but should not be allowed to dry out completely.

Mormolyca gracilipes (Schlechter) Garay & Wirth

Pseudobulbs to 3 × 1 cm, compressed. Leaves to 8 × 2 cm, strap-shaped. Inflorescence to 23 cm long. Sepals and petals yellow-brown to salmon-pink, sepals ca. 34 mm long, lanceolate, acuminate; lip 11 × 8 mm, green to yellow-brown spotted with maroon or purple. This Andean species likes fairly cool conditions.

Epiphytic in wet forest, 1000–2700 m (3300–8900 ft.)

Colombia, Ecuador, Peru

Mormolyca peruviana C. Schweinfurth

Pseudobulbs clustered, to 2 cm long. Leaves to 14 × 1 cm. Inflorescence 8–12 cm long. Flowers to 3 cm across, yellow, the lip often with purple markings.

Epiphytic in wet forest, 650–1800 m (2150–6000 ft.)

Peru

Mormolyca ringens (Lindley) Schlechter

SYN. *Mormolyca lineolata* Fenzl

Pseudobulbs to 4 × 3 cm. Leaves to 25 × 3.5 cm. Inflorescence to 35 cm long. Flowers 3–4 cm long, yellow, striped with maroon-purple, lip midlobe reddish brown, sometimes edged with yellow. This species requires temperatures on the warm side of intermediate.

Epiphytic in wet forest, 0–950 m (3100 ft.)

Mexico, Central America

Myoxanthus Poeppig & Endlicher

TRIBE: Epidendreae
SUBTRIBE: Pleurothallidinae
ETYMOLOGY: From Greek *myoxus*, dormouse and *anthos*, flower; the reference is obscure
DISTRIBUTION: Almost 50 species in Mexico, Central and South America

Creeping or tufted epiphytic, lithophytic or terrestrial plants with the rhizome usually covered in scurfy sheaths. Stems erect, enclosed in several tubular sheaths, 1-leafed. Inflorescences in clusters, 1-flowered, the flowers open together or in succession. Flowers small, resupinate; sepals fleshy, often hairy; dorsal sepal free or joined to lateral sepals; lateral sepals free or joined to form a synsepal; petals fleshy, often thickened at apex; lip fleshy, hinged to column-foot, entire or trilobed. Column winged or toothed; pollinia 2 or 4.

CULTIVATION: *Myoxanthus* species can be found at altitudes from near sea level to over 3000 m (9840 ft.), in habitats from lowland scrub to cloud forest, so it is important to know the origin of a plant. However, most species do well in a cool greenhouse. Like most pleurothallids, these species require shade and high humidity all year round.

Myoxanthus fimbriatus Luer & Hirtz

Rhizome scandent, rooting at the nodes. Stems to 22 cm long. Leaves to 13 cm × 7 mm. Flowers ca. 7 mm long, purple-brown sometimes with a green margin; sepals long and narrow, petals fringed, ovate at base, then long and narrow; lip dark purple, 2 mm long.

Epiphytic in forest, 1100–1500 m (3630–5000 ft.)

Ecuador, Peru

Myoxanthus mejiae (Garay & Dunsterville) Luer

Plants tufted, with stout stems to 45 cm long. Leaves to 16 × 4.5 cm. Flowers 7–8 mm long, pale brown tinged with red; petals constricted in the middle, the apex thickened like a club; lip dark purple, decurved, thickened at the apex.

Epiphytic in cloud forest, ca. 2000 m (6600 ft.)

Venezuela

Myoxanthus uxorius (Luer) Luer

Large plants, tufted or creeping. Stems purplish, 20–35 cm long. Leaves stiff, dark green flushed with purple, to 23 × 1 cm. Flowers to 8 mm long, yellow, the lip flushed with brown.

Epiphytic in cloud forest, 1800–2700 m (6000–8900 ft.)

Colombia, Ecuador

Myrmecophila Rolfe

TRIBE: Epidendreae
SUBTRIBE: Laeliinae
ETYMOLOGY: From Greek *myrmex*, ant, and *phila*, loving, referring to the association of these plants with ants
DISTRIBUTION: 10 species from Mexico to Venezuela and in the Caribbean

Large epiphytic or terrestrial plants. Pseudobulbs conical to cylindrical, 1- to 5-leaved at apex, hollow, usually inhabited by ants, which come and go through holes near

Mormolyca gracilipes

Mormolyca peruviana

Myoxanthus fimbriatus

Myoxanthus mejiae

Myoxanthus uxorius

the base of the pseudobulb. Leaves fleshy or leathery, usually elliptical. Inflorescences terminal with a long peduncle, branched or unbranched, erect, arching or spreading, many-flowered, the flowers open in succession a few at a time. Flowers showy; sepals and petals usually undulate, the petals usually narrower, lip entire or trilobed, the midlobe smaller than the side lobes and sometimes deeply emarginate or bilobed. Pollinia 8, in 2 groups of 4.

CULTIVATION: These are large plants which take up a lot of space in a greenhouse but do well outdoors in tropical and subtropical gardens. They can be grown in pots or baskets in a coarse, free-draining bark-based compost in warm conditions and require good light and plenty of water while growing. They should be kept almost dry while resting. They will grow without an ant colony.

Myrmecophila tibicinis

(Bateman ex Lindley) Rolfe

SYN. *Laelia tibicinis* (Bateman ex Lindley) L. O. Williams, *Schomburgkia tibicinis* (Bateman ex Lindley) Bateman

Myrmecophila tibicinis

Pseudobulbs to 55 × 4 cm, cylindrical, ribbed, 3- or 4-leaved. Leaves ca. 25 × 6 cm, oblong. Inflorescence to 2.5 m tall or more, usually branched, the flowers near the apex. Flowers to 8 cm across, maroon or purple; lip side lobes curved up round column, midlobe not clawed, fan-shaped, emarginate.

Epiphytic or terrestrial on trees and shrubs in dry and wet woodland, 0–600 m (2000 ft.)

Mexico, Central America

SIMILAR SPECIES: *Myrmecophila brysiana* (Lemaire) G. C. Kennedy (syn. *Schomburgkia brysiana* Lemaire) from Central America and the West Indies has a shorter inflorescence with yellow flowers flushed with orange-brown; the lip midlobe is clawed and marked with purple.

Mystacidium Lindley

TRIBE: Vandeae

SUBTRIBE: Aerangidinae

ETYMOLOGY: From Greek *mystax*, moustache, probably referring to the papillose rostellum

DISTRIBUTION: 10 species in east tropical Africa and South Africa

Small, short-stemmed monopodial epiphytes with many relatively stout

Mystacidium braybonae

roots, often gray-green with white streaks. Leaves distichous, usually strap-shaped, sometimes deciduous. Inflorescences axillary, several- to many-flowered. Flowers white or translucent yellow-green or whitish green; sepals and petals subsimilar, lanceolate, acute, usually spreading; lip entire or trilobed near the base, spurred, the spur tapering from a wider mouth.

CULTIVATION: Species of *Mystacidium* grow best when mounted on bark or a small branch, as the roots tend to rot in pots. The small species with greenish flowers, such as *M. tanganyikense*, need heavy shade and high humidity throughout the year, while the larger white-flowered species require more light and should be kept drier after flowering, particularly if the leaves are lost. All will grow at intermediate temperatures.

Mystacidium braybonae Summerhayes

Leaves to 6 × 1 cm, dark green. Inflorescences several, pendent, to 5 cm long, 5- to 10-flowered. Flowers white, to 2 cm across, rather bell-shaped; lip trilobed, midlobe triangular, spur to 25 mm long.

Epiphytic in forest

South Africa (Zoutspansberg Mountains)

Mystacidium capense (Linnaeus f.) Schlechter

Leaves 4–10, strap-shaped, to 12 × 2 cm, dark green. Inflorescences several, arching or pendent, to 15-flowered, the flowers in 2 rows. Flowers white, starry, 2–3 cm across; lip trilobed, spur 4–6 cm long. Flowering spring–summer.

Epiphytic in lowland and montane forest and also in thorn scrub, often in hot, dry areas

South Africa, Swaziland

SIMILAR SPECIES: *Mystacidium venosum* Harvey ex Rolfe is usually slightly smaller and flowers in winter in the wild and sometimes when leafless.

Neobathiea Schlechter

TRIBE: Vandeae

SUBTRIBE: Angraecinae

ETYMOLOGY: Named for Henri Perrier de la Bâthie (1873–1958), a French botanist who wrote the account of Orchidaceae in *Flore de Madagascar*

DISTRIBUTION: 5 species in Madagascar, with 1 also in the Comoro Islands

Mystacidium capense

Mystacidium venosum

Small or medium-sized, usually short-stemmed epiphytes. Leaves strap-shaped to elliptic. Inflorescences unbranched, 1- to several-flowered. Flowers white, green, or rarely yellow; sepals and petals free, spreading, subsimilar; lip larger than other parts, entire or trilobed; spur long and slender with a wide mouth.
CULTIVATION: Plants need intermediate temperatures, moderate shade, high humidity, and good ventilation, but should be kept drier in winter. They do well mounted but can also be grown in a small pot with a free-draining compost.

Neobathiea grandidierana (Reichenbach f.) Garay

SYN. *Neobathiea filicornu* Schlechter
Stem short. Leaves to 5 × 1 cm, linear or elliptic, the apex unequally bilobed. Inflorescence slightly shorter than the leaves, 1-flowered. Flowers 2–2.5 cm across, white or greenish white, turning yellow with age; lip entire, ovate, 2 × 1 cm; spur very slender from a wide mouth, 12–15 cm long. Flowering summer.

Humid evergreen forest, 1400–1500 m (4600–5000 ft.)

Madagascar, Comoro Islands

Neobathiea perrieri (Schlechter) Schlechter

Stem short. Leaves to 7 × 2 cm, oblong, the margins undulate, the apex unequally bilobed. Inflorescence 5–10 cm long, 1- or 2-flowered. Sepals and petals greenish, reflexed, lanceolate to spathulate, ca. 22 × 3 mm. Lip white, trilobed, 20 mm long and wide, the midlobe largest; spur 10–12 cm long, very slender from a wide mouth.

Evergreen and semi-deciduous forest, in dryish areas

Madagascar

Neobenthamia Rolfe

TRIBE: Vandeae
SUBTRIBE: Polystachyinae
ETYMOLOGY: Named for British botanist George Bentham (1800–1884)
DISTRIBUTION: 1 species in Tanzania
Stems canelike. straggling, branched, leafy. Inflorescence terminal, usually branched, densely many-flowered. Sepals and petals ± spreading, subequal. Lip fleshy, entire. Pollinia 4, in 2 pairs.

This monospecific genus is related to *Polystachya* but has resupinate flowers and a completely different growth habit.
CULTIVATION: Plants grow easily at intermediate temperatures, potted in a coarse, free-draining bark mixture but need strong light if they are to flower. With their tall, straggling growth, they should be staked.

Neobenthamia gracilis Rolfe

Stems 90–200 cm tall, often with roots at the nodes. Leaves to 28 × 2 cm, grasslike. Inflorescence to 6 cm long and wide. Flowers to 2 cm across, scented, white, the lip with a yellow area in the center edged with pink dots.

Lithophytic or terrestrial on exposed rock faces or on mossy ledges, 450–1800 m (1500–6000 ft.)

Tanzania (Nguru and Uluguru Mountains)

Neocogniauxia Schlechter

TRIBE: Epidendreae
SUBTRIBE: Pleurothallidinae
ETYMOLOGY: From Greek *neos*, new, and for the Belgian botanist Célestin Alfred Cogniaux (1841–1916)
DISTRIBUTION: 2 species in Hispaniola and Jamaica
Dwarf epiphytes forming tufts. Pseudobulbs stemlike, slender, cylindrical, erect, covered by 1–3 tubular, speckled sheaths, 1- to 2-leaved at apex. Leaves leathery, linear-lanceolate to linear-oblong. Inflorescences erect or arching, 1-flowered, rarely 2-flowered. Flowers resupinate, showy; sepals and petals spreading, lip smaller, entire or obscurely trilobed, clasping the column. Pollinia 8.
CULTIVATION: Species of *Neocogniauxia* can be tricky in cultivation. Plants are usually grown potted in a free-draining compost. They require cool conditions, light shade, high humidity, and plenty of air movement. They must not dry out completely.

Neocogniauxia monophylla (Grisebach) Schlechter

Pseudobulbs to 9 cm tall, 1-leafed at apex. Leaves to 10 × 1 cm, linear-oblong. Inflorescence to 30 cm tall, arching, with several sheathing, purple-spotted bracts. Flowers to 5 cm across, bright orange-red; lip shallowly trilobed, the disc papillose; anther-cap purple. Flowers autumn–winter.

Epiphytic in forest, 1200–1300 m (4000–4300 ft.)

Jamaica

SIMILAR SPECIES: *Neocogniauxia hexaptera* (Cogniaux) Schlechter from Hispaniola has 2-leaved pseudobulbs, slightly smaller orange-red flowers, the ovary with 6 wings.

Neofinetia Hu

TRIBE: Vandeae
SUBTRIBE: Aeridinae
ETYMOLOGY: Named for Achille Finet (1862–1913), a French botanist who worked on Chinese and Japanese orchids
DISTRIBUTION: 3 species in China, Korea, Japan, Ryukyu Islands
Monopodial epiphytes or lithophytes with short stems, often branching at base. Leaves distichous, overlapping at the base, stiff, narrowly strap-shaped. Inflorescences axillary, erect, unbranched, few- to several-flowered. Flowers white or pinkish; sepals and petals free, similar; lip trilobed, spurred at the base.
CULTIVATION: Plants are grown in small pots in a rather fine bark mix or in sphagnum in cool to intermediate conditions, with moderate shade and high humidity. They should be

Neobathiea grandidierana

Neobenthamia gracilis

watered throughout the year but kept drier in winter.

Neofinetia falcata (Thunberg) Hu
Stem short, branching and rooting at base. Leaves to 12 × 1 cm, dark green, slightly recurved. Inflorescence to 10-flowered. Sepals, petals, and lip ca. 1 cm long; lip side lobes erect, midlobe strap-shaped; spur very slender, curved, to 5 cm long.

This species is widely grown in Japan, where many cultivars, some with variegated leaves, have been developed.

Epiphytic or lithophytic in forest, 900–1300 m (3000–4300 ft.)

China, Korea, Japan, Ryukyu Islands
SIMILAR SPECIES: *Neofinetia richardsiana* Christenson from China (Sichuan)

Neofinetia falcata

Neocogniauxia monophylla. R. Parsons

has dense, few-flowered inflorescences with smaller flowers and a spur 1 cm long. A third species, *N. xichangensis* Z. J. Liu & S. C. Chen, was also described from Sichuan in 2004.

Neogardneria Schlechter ex Garay

TRIBE: Maxillarieae

SUBTRIBE: Zygopetalinae

ETYMOLOGY: Named for Scottish plant collector George Gardner (1812–1849)

DISTRIBUTION: 1 species in southeastern Brazil

Sympodial epiphytes; pseudobulbs ovoid, 2-leaved at apex. Leaves plicate. Inflorescence arising with new growth, erect or arching, loosely few-flowered. Flowers scented; sepals and petals free, subsimilar, spreading; lip trilobed, with a short basal claw. Pollinia 4, in unequal pairs.

CULTIVATION: Plants are grown potted in a free-draining, bark-based mixture at intermediate temperatures, in moderate to heavy shade. They should be watered freely while in growth but kept almost dry when resting. They dislike high humidity.

Neogardneria murrayana (Gardner ex Hooker) Schlechter ex Garay

SYN. *Neogardneria binotii* (De Wildeman) Hoehne, *Zygopetalum murrayanum* Gardner ex Hooker

Pseudobulbs ovoid, clustered, to 4 cm long. Leaves to 20 × 3 cm, elliptical. Inflorescence 9–25 cm long, 2- to 5-flowered. Flowers ca. 5 cm across; sepals and petals green, lip white with purple marks on the side lobes and a fan-shaped callus between the lobes.

Low-level epiphyte in dense forest and on mountain ridges, 1200–1600 m (4000–5300 ft.)

Southeastern Brazil

Neogyna Reichenbach f.

TRIBE: Arethuseae

SUBTRIBE: Coelogyninae

ETYMOLOGY: From Greek *neo*, new and *gyne*, woman

DISTRIBUTION: 1 species in Nepal, Bhutan, India, China, Myanmar, Thailand, and Laos

Epiphytes or lithophytes closely related to *Coelogyne*, with narrowly ovoid to conical pseudobulbs covered in sheaths, 2-leaved at apex. Leaves petiolate. Inflorescence terminal on a young pseudobulb, pendent, unbranched. Flowers large, bell-shaped; sepals and petals similar, joined and saccate at the base; lip trilobed, funnel-shaped, lacking a spur. Column long, curved; pollinia 4.

CULTIVATION: As for *Coelogyne*. Grow in pots or baskets in a coarse bark-based compost, in good light with plenty of water while growing, although the compost should be allowed to dry out between waterings. Plants should be kept dry while resting, although they should be sprayed occasionally to prevent the pseudobulbs from shriveling. A dry rest seems to be necessary to promote flowering. This species has an exceptionally wide altitudinal range and so should not be too fussy about temperature in cultivation.

Neogyna gardneriana (Lindley) Reichenbach f.

Pseudobulbs to 15 × 2 cm. Leaves 15–40 × 7–9 cm. Inflorescence 6- to 12-flowered, peduncle with several sheaths. Flowers 4–4.5 cm long, white with 2 or 3 yellow keels on the lip.

Epiphytic in forest and lithophytic on shady rocks, 600–3550 m (2000–11,700 ft.)

Nepal, Bhutan, India, China, Myanmar, Thailand, Laos

Neomoorea Rolfe

TRIBE: Maxillarieae

SUBTRIBE: Zygopetalinae

ETYMOLOGY: Named for Frederick W. Moore (1857–1950), curator of the Glasnevin Botanic Garden in Dublin

DISTRIBUTION: 1 species in Colombia, Ecuador, and Panama

Large, sympodial epiphyte with ovoid pseudobulbs, 2-leaved at apex. Inflorescence basal, unbranched, erect or arching. Flowers large, showy, waxy, scented; sepals and petals subsimilar, spreading; lip hinged to the column-foot, trilobed, Pollinia 4, in unequal pairs.

CULTIVATION: Plants should be potted in a coarse, free-draining compost. They require intermediate conditions, moderate shade and humidity, and plenty of water and fertilizer while in growth, although care should be taken not to let water lie on the young leaves. When the pseudobulbs are mature, plants should be kept almost dry until growth starts again.

Neogyna gardneriana

Neogardneria murrayana

Neomoorea wallisii (Reichenbach f.) Schlechter

SYN. *Neomoorea irrorata* (Rolfe) Rolfe

Pseudobulbs to 11 × 6 cm, compressed. Roots of 2 types, long and creeping and short and erect, forming a mat at the base of the plant. Leaves to 75 × 13 cm, plicate, elliptic. Inflorescence 15–45 cm long, few- to 12-flowered. Flowers 6–7 cm across, sepals and petals reddish brown, white at the base; lip pale yellow with purple-brown markings, midlobe yellow, spotted red.

Epiphytic in forest at fairly low altitudes

Colombia, Ecuador, Panama

Nephelaphyllum Blume

TRIBE: Collabieae

ETYMOLOGY: From Greek *nephele*, cloud, and *phyllon*, leaf, referring to the hazy look of the leaves

DISTRIBUTION: About 11 species from the Himalayas through Southeast Asia to the Philippines

Terrestrial plants with creeping, fleshy rhizomes and slender, 1-leafed pseudobulbs. Leaves petiolate, the blade ovate or heart-shaped, often mottled. Inflorescences erect, unbranched, few- to several-flowered; flowers nonresupinate; sepals and petals subsimilar, spreading or reflexed; lip entire or trilobed with a short spur.

CULTIVATION: Grow in shallow pans in a free-draining compost based on fine bark, perlite or pumice, and sphagnum in warm to intermediate, shady conditions. Plants should be kept moist throughout the year but not too wet, or the fleshy rhizomes will rot.

Nephelaphyllum pulchrum Blume

Pseudobulbs ± cylindrical, 2.5 cm long, set 2.5 cm apart. Leaves heart-shaped, to 10 × 6 cm, yellow-green with dark green veins and mottling, purple underneath. Inflorescence to ca. 17 cm long, densely up to 15-flowered. Flowers scented, 25 mm across; sepals and petals deflexed, pale green, purple-veined on the outside; lip white, tinged with green and yellow towards the base; spur 3 mm long.

Nephelaphyllum pulchrum. J. Hermans

Neomoorea wallisi

Terrestrial in moist forest, 300–1500 m (1000–5000 ft.)

Malaysia to Indonesia

Nidema Britton & Millspaugh

TRIBE: Epidendreae

SUBTRIBE: Laeliinae

ETYMOLOGY: An anagram of *Dinema*, a related genus

DISTRIBUTION: 2 species in tropical South and Central America and the West Indies

Sympodial epiphytes with pseudobulbs set on long, creeping rhizomes. Leaves linear, 1 or 2 per pseudobulb. Inflorescences terminal on the pseudobulb, appearing with the new growth, erect, few-flowered. Flowers small with conspicuous bracts; sepals and petals free, spreading, the petals slightly smaller; lip entire, lacking a spur, hinged to the column-foot. Pollinia 4, of 2 different sizes.

CULTIVATION: Grow mounted or in a shallow pan in a bark mixture. Plants need intermediate temperatures and plenty of moisture while growing but should be kept drier, although not completely dry, when resting.

Nidema boothii (Lindley) Schlechter

SYN. *Epidendrum boothii* (Lindley) L. O. Williams

Pseudobulbs to 6 cm long, 1- or 2-leaved. Leaves linear, to 25 cm long, dark, glossy green. Inflorescence to 15 cm long, few-flowered. Flowers creamy white or greenish white, ca. 4 cm across.

Rain forest, 0–1500 m (5000 ft.)

West Indies, Central America and South America

SIMILAR SPECIES: *Nidema ottonis* (Reichenbach f.) Britton & Millspaugh (syn. *Epidendrum ottonis* Reichenbach f.), from Central America and the West Indies, has shorter leaves and flowers of about half the size.

Nidema boothii

Notylia Lindley

TRIBE: Maxillarieae

SUBTRIBE: Oncidiinae

ETYMOLOGY: From Greek *notos*, back, and *tylos*, hump, referring to the shape of the column apex

DISTRIBUTION: 56 species in Mexico, Central and South America, and Trinidad

Small epiphytes, usually with pseudobulbs, 1-leafed at apex, and with sheathing leaves at the base. Inflorescences basal or axillary, arching or pendent, sometimes branched, few- to many-flowered. Flowers small; sepals and petals subsimilar, erect or spreading, the lateral sepals sometimes joined; lip clawed, entire or lobed. Pollinia 2.

CULTIVATION: Plants should be grown in baskets or on rafts, in intermediate conditions, in moderate shade, with high humidity throughout the year.

Notylia barkeri Lindley

Pseudobulbs clustered, ovoid, flattened, to 3 × 1 cm. Leaves elliptic, pale green, to 20 × 5 cm. Inflorescence arching to pendent, to 30 cm long, densely many-flowered. Flowers small, white to greenish, the petals sometimes dotted with yellow, slightly scented.

Epiphytic in forest, scrub, and plantations, to 1600 m (5300 ft.)

Mexico, Central America

Notylia pentachne Reichenbach f.
Pseudobulbs to 3 × 1 cm. Leaves to 20 × 5 cm. Inflorescence pendent, to 35 cm long, many-flowered. Flowers ca. 15 mm across, sepals joined to form a synsepal, greenish or yellow-green, petals white or pale green with 2 or 3 orange spots, lip white, with a long claw.

Epiphytic, usually on twigs, in rain forest, 700–800 m (2300–2640 ft.)

Colombia, Panama, Venezuela

Notylia venezuelana Schlechter
Pseudobulbs conical, ca. 2 cm long. Leaves to 12 × 4 cm. Inflorescence much longer than leaves, densely many-flowered. Flowers ca. 1 cm across; lateral sepals joined for about two-thirds of their length; lip 5–6 mm long, arrow-shaped.

Venezuela

Oberonia Lindley

TRIBE: Malaxideae

ETYMOLOGY: Named after Oberon, the fairy king

DISTRIBUTION: 150–200 species in Southeast Asia, Malaysia, and the Philippines, with 1 species in Africa, Madagascar, and the Mascarene Islands

Sympodial, short-stemmed epiphytes lacking pseudobulbs, usually forming clumps, often pendent. Leaves laterally flattened and irislike, fleshy, often overlapping at the base. Inflorescences terminal, unbranched, densely many-flowered. Flowers very small, nonresupinate; sepals and petals free, spreading; lip entire or trilobed. Pollinia 4.

Many species are similar in appearance.

CULTIVATION: Plants should be mounted, preferably with a moisture-retaining material like sphagnum tied over the fine roots. They need intermediate temperatures, light to moderate shade, high humidity, and good ventilation.

Oberonia disticha (Lamarck) Schlechter
Plants pendent. Leaves 7–8, to 15 × 1 cm, pale green, fleshy, decreasing in size towards top of stem. Inflorescence 3–10 cm long, densely many-flowered. Flowers yellow-ochre to orange.

Epiphytic in evergreen forest and wet woodland, 470–1250 m (1540–4100 ft.)

Throughout tropical Africa, South Africa, Madagascar, Comoro Islands, Mascarene Islands

Oberonia iridifolia (Roxburgh) Lindley
Plants pendent. Leaves 3–7, to 25 × 2.5 cm, fleshy, light green, forming a fan. Inflorescence longer than leaves, very densely many-flowered. Flowers pale green or greenish yellow, all open together.

Epiphytic in dryish forest, 0–500 m (1650 ft.)

Widespread from Himalayas to the Pacific Islands

Octomeria R. Brown

TRIBE: Epidendreae

SUBTRIBE: Pleurothallidinae

ETYMOLOGY: From Greek *okto*, eight, and *meros*, part, referring to the 8 pollinia

DISTRIBUTION: About 150 species in Central and South America and the West Indies

Epiphytes or lithophytes with a creeping or ascending rhizome. Stems enclosed by overlapping, tubular sheaths, 1-leafed at the apex. Leaves fleshy or leathery, flat or terete. Inflorescences axillary, arising in clusters, 1- to many-flowered. Flowers usually small; sepals and petals subsimilar, petals usually slightly smaller; lip shorter than sepals and petals, entire or trilobed, hinged to the column-foot, the disc usually with 2 longitudinal ridges. Pollinia 8, in 2 pairs.

CULTIVATION: Most species succeed in intermediate conditions with high humidity and light shade. They can be grown in pots or baskets in a fine bark mixture or mounted on a slab.

Octomeria graminifolia (Linnaeus) R. Brown
Rhizome creeping. Stems to 7 cm long. Leaves linear, fleshy, to 10 × 1 cm. Inflorescence 1- or 2-flowered. Flowers pale yellow to greenish, lip lamellae purple; sepals ca. 8 mm long.

Epiphytic in wet forest, 50–100 m (165–330 ft.)

Central America, West Indies

Octomeria grandiflora Lindley
Stems to 20 cm long. Leaves leathery, linear, to 20 × 1.5 cm. Inflorescence 1- or 2-flowered. Flowers to 2 cm across, translucent white to pale yellow, lip marked with purple.

Epiphytic in wet forest, 500–2500 m (1650–8250 ft.)

West Indies, South America

Odontoglossum Kunth

TRIBE: Maxillarieae

SUBTRIBE: Oncidiinae

ETYMOLOGY: From Greek *odontos*, tooth, and *glossa*, tongue, referring to processes on the lip

DISTRIBUTION: Almost 70 species in western South America

Medium to large epiphytes or lithophytes. Pseudobulbs clustered, compressed, covered by distichous, sometimes leaf-bearing sheaths, 1- to 3-leaved at apex. Leaves leathery or fleshy. Inflorescences basal, erect or arching, branched or unbranched, few- to many-flowered. Flowers often large and showy, not spurred; sepals and petals spreading, subsimilar but with the petals often shorter, lateral sepals sometimes joined at the base; lip entire or trilobed, the base parallel to the column, side lobes spreading or erect, midlobe deflexed, callus usually of toothed, fleshy lamellae.

Odontoglossum is very closely related to *Oncidium* and several species have gone back and forth between the genera. Other species originally described in *Odontoglossum* have been transferred to other genera, such as *Cyrtochilum, Rhynchostele,* and *Rossioglossum.*

Species of *Odontoglossum* have been much hybridized, both within the genus and with other related genera. With *Cochlioda* and *Miltonia,* it has given rise to the hybrid genus ×*Vuylstekeara,* one of the most widely grown of all orchid hybrid genera.

CULTIVATION: Most species grow at high altitudes and require cool conditions in cultivation with moderate shade and high humidity all year round. They need plenty of water while actively growing, less while resting but should not be allowed to dry out for long. They are grown potted in a fine to medium epiphyte compost.

Oberonia disticha. E. la Croix

Notylia venezuelana

Octomeria grandiflora

Odontoglossum blandum

Reichenbach f.

Pseudobulbs ca. 3 × 2 cm, 2-leaved. Leaves to 25 × 2.5 cm. Inflorescence arching, ca. 25 cm long, densely several-flowered. Flowers scented, to 4.5 cm across, white spotted with purple or red-purple; sepals and petals narrow, long acuminate; lip ovate, emarginate, the margins undulate; callus yellow. Flowering spring and summer.

Epiphytic in forest in the Andes, 1700–2700 m (5600–8900 ft.)

Ecuador, Peru

Odontoglossum cirrhosum

Lindley

Pseudobulbs to 8 cm long, 1-leafed. Leaves to 30 × 3 cm. Inflorescence to 60 cm long, sometimes branched, loosely many-flowered. Flowers to 10 cm across, white with reddish spots, the lip yellow at the base; sepals narrow, long acuminate, petals slightly shorter and broader; lip trilobed near the base, midlobe decurved, narrow, long acuminate; disc with 2 S-shaped horns. Flowering spring.

Epiphytic in forest in the Andes, 1700–2600 m (5600–8600 ft.)

Colombia, Ecuador

Odontoglossum crinitum

Reichenbach f.

Pseudobulbs ovate with sharp margins, 1-leafed at the apex. Inflorescence to 20 cm long, few- to several-flowered. Flowers 5 cm across; sepals and petals yellow with red-brown blotches, narrow, acute; lip white with maroon markings, midlobe covered with long white hairs; callus maroon.

Epiphytic in cloud forest, 1800–3100 m (6000–10,200 ft.)

Colombia, Ecuador

Odontoglossum crispum

Lindley

Pseudobulbs 7–8 cm long, 2-leaved. Leaves to 40 × 3 cm. Inflorescence to 50 cm long, densely several-flowered.

Odontoglossum blandum

Odontoglossum cirrhosum

Odontoglossum cruentum

Flowers to 8.5 cm across, variable in color, usually white or pale pink blotched with red or purple, disc yellow; sepal and petals rounded, margins of all parts crisped and undulate. Flowers mainly in winter.

Epiphytic, 2200–3000 m (7260–9900 ft.)

Colombia

SIMILAR SPECIES: *Odontoglossum nobile* Reichenbach f. (syn. *O. pescatorei* Linden ex Lindley), also from Colombia, has flowers 6 cm across, sepals and petals usually white to pale pink without spots.

Odontoglossum crocidipterum Reichenbach f.

Pseudobulbs to 6 × 3 cm, sometimes purple-spotted, 2-leaved at apex. Inflorescence sometimes branched, ca. 20 cm long. Flowers scented, 5–6 cm across, white or yellow spotted with red-brown or dark brown; sepals, petals, and lip narrow, acuminate. Flowering in winter.

Two subspecies are recognized. Subsp. *crocidipterum* has white or yellow flowers spotted with red-brown or dark brown. Subsp. *dormanianum* (Reichenbach f.) Bockemühl (syn. *Odontoglossum dormanianum* Reichenbach f.) from northwestern Venezuela has white flowers.

Epiphytic in montane forest

Colombia, Venezuela

Odontoglossum cruentum Reichenbach f.

Pseudobulbs to 7 × 3.5 cm, 2-leaved at apex. Leaves to 22 × 2 cm. Inflorescence to 45 cm long, usually unbranched, loosely many-flowered. Flowers 5 cm across, sepals and

Odontoglossum crinitum

petals yellow-green with some large maroon or brown blotches, lip yellow with a maroon or brown blotch in the middle, callus white; sepals and petals narrow, acute; lip deflexed, oblong to elliptic. Flowering spring.

Epiphytic in cloud forest, 2000–2500 m (6600–8250 ft.)

Ecuador, Peru

Odontoglossum gloriosum Linden & Reichenbach f.

Inflorescence to 50 cm long, many-flowered. Flowers scented, to 7 cm across, pale yellow with purple-brown spots; sepals and petals narrow, acuminate; lip ovate, the apex acuminate; callus white. Flowering spring–summer.

Epiphytic in cloud forest, 2000–3000 m (6600–9900 ft.)

Colombia

SIMILAR SPECIES: *Odontoglossum odoratum* Lindley from Colombia and Venezuela has slightly smaller flowers in spring.

Odontoglossum harryanum Reichenbach f.

Pseudobulbs to 8 cm long, 2-leaved at apex. Leaves to 44 × 4 cm. Inflorescence unbranched, to 1 m long, several-flowered. Flowers 9–12.5 cm across, sepals and petals yellow marked with brown, lip white with purple lines at the base and a yellow, fringed callus. Flowering summer–autumn.

Epiphytic on margins of montane forest, 1800–2300 m (6000–7600 ft.)

Ecuador, Peru

Odontoglossum lindleyanum Reichenbach & Warszewicz

Pseudobulbs to 7.5 × 3 cm, 2-leaved. Leaves to 30 × 2 cm. Inflorescence arching, sometimes branched, to 35 cm long, several-flowered. Flowers scented, 5–7 cm across, starry, sepals and petals yellow with large red-brown blotches, lip red-brown, yellow at the tip, white at the base.

Epiphytic at margins and in clearings in montane forest, 1800–2400 m (6000–7900 ft.)

Colombia, Ecuador, Venezuela

Odontoglossum naevium Lindley

Pseudobulbs 4–8 cm long, 2-leaved. Leaves 15–40 cm long. Inflorescence ca. 25 cm long, to 12-flowered. Flowers 8 cm across, starry, white with purple spots; sepals and petals narrow, long acuminate, lip with a yellow callus. Column white, wings fringed. Flowering spring–summer.

Epiphytic in cloud forest, 1200–1400 m (4000–4600 ft.)

Colombia, Guyana, Venezuela

Odontoglossum sanguineum (Reichenbach f.) Dalström

SYN. *Cochlioda sanguinea* (Reichenbach f.) Bentham, *Symphyglossum sanguineum* (Reichenbach f.) Schlechter, *Mesospinidium sanguineum* Reichenbach f.

Pseudobulbs clustered, 2-leaved. Leaves linear, to 22 cm long. Inflorescence to 50 cm long, arching or pendent, loosely many-flowered. Flowers ca. 3 cm across, rose-red, the lip white at the base.

Epiphytic in wet forest, 1000–2500 m (3300–8250 ft.)

Ecuador, Peru

Odontoglossum schillerianum Reichenbach f.

Pseudobulbs to 7 cm long, 1- or 2-leaved at apex. Leaves to 30 × 3 cm. Inflorescence branched, to 35 cm long, several- to many-flowered. Flowers scented, to 5 cm across; sepals and petals yellow spotted with red-brown or maroon, lip purple-brown, white at the base, the tip yellow, midlobe pubescent. Flowering winter–spring.

Epiphytic in forest, 2000–2700 m (6600–8900 ft.)

Venezuela

Odontoglossum spectatissimum Lindley

SYN. *Odontoglossum triumphans* Reichenbach f.

Pseudobulbs to 10 × 4 cm, 2-leaved at apex. Leaves to 40 × 4 cm. Inflorescence sometimes branched, arching, to 90 cm long, several-flowered. Flowers 7.5–10 cm across; sepals and petals golden-yellow marked with cinnamon brown, lip white or pale yellow with a large red-brown central blotch; callus with 2 teeth. Flowering spring.

Epiphytic in montane forest, 1500–3200 ft (5,000–10,500 ft.)

Colombia, Ecuador, Venezuela

Odontoglossum odoratum

Odontoglossum harryanum

Odontoglossum sanguineum

Odontoglossum schillerianum

Odontoglossum spectatissimum

Oeceoclades Lindley

SYN. *Eulophidium* Pfitzer
TRIBE: Cymbidieae
SUBTRIBE: Cyrtopodiinae
ETYMOLOGY: From Greek *oikeios*, private, and *klados*, branch; the reference is obscure
DISTRIBUTION: Almost 40 species in Africa, Madagascar, and the Comoro Islands with 1 species also in tropical and subtropical America and the West Indies

Terrestrial orchids with prominent pseudobulbs, 1- to 3-leaved at apex. Leaves thick and leathery or fleshy, usually petiolate, often attractively colored and mottled. Inflorescences basal, branched or unbranched. Flowers resupinate, thin-textured; sepals usually longer than petals, free, usually spreading, lip 3- to 4-lobed, usually spurred, often with a basal callus. Pollinia 2.

Oeceoclades is closely related to *Eulophia* and some botanists consider them synonymous.

CULTIVATION: Species of *Oeceoclades* have rather few, fleshy roots which rot easily, so it is important to water carefully. Many grow in dry habitats in the wild, but often near a river or the coast, so that humidity may be high. They require intermediate to warm conditions and should be potted in a free-draining mixture based on bark, leaf mold, and grit or sharp sand. Good ventilation is important and water on the leaves should be avoided. In most species the leaves last for at least 2 seasons. While plants are resting, give only enough water to prevent shriveling. Plants with pink or purple leaves need full sunlight, others require light to moderate shade.

Oeceoclades decaryana (H. Perrier) Garay & P. Taylor

Pseudobulbs 2–4 cm long, 2-leaved. Leaves to 25 × 2 cm, linear, gray-green with blue-gray and pale gray blotches. Inflorescence 20–40 cm tall, unbranched, 10- to 20-flowered. Flowers 3.5–4 cm long; sepals and petals dark olive green with purple or red veins, lip 4-lobed, yellow or cream with purple or red veins.

Among rocks in shade of riverine forest or thicket, to 900 m (3000 ft.)

East and South Africa, Madagascar

Oeceoclades gracillima (Schlechter) Garay & P. Taylor

SYN. *Oeceoclades roseovariegata* (Senghas) Garay & P. Taylor

Pseudobulbs ovoid, 2–3 cm long, 2-leaved. Leaves to 4 × 3.5 cm, ovate, prostrate, the edges undulate, deep purple mottled with pink. Inflorescence sometimes with a few branches, to 55 cm tall, loosely many-flowered. Flowers smallish, sepals and petals green, flushed with purple outside, lip white with red spots, trilobed, midlobe emarginate.

Among rocks in semi-deciduous forest

Madagascar

Oeceoclades decaryana. J. Hermans

Oeceoclades lonchophylla

(Reichenbach f.) Garay & P. Taylor
Pseudobulbs 4–5 cm long, conical, 1-leafed. Leaves green with undulate margins; leaf blade 12 × 3.5 cm; petiole as long as or longer than leaf blade. Inflorescence 30–45 cm tall, sometimes with a few short branches, many-flowered. Flowers smallish, green or creamy yellow, with green spots, tinged with purple; lip trilobed, midlobe deeply emarginate.

Coastal forest, 0–200 m (660 ft.)

East and South Africa, Comoro Islands

Oeceoclades maculata (Lindley) Lindley

Pseudobulbs 2–4 cm long, 1-leafed. Leaves 10–30 × 3–5 cm, stiff-textured, glossy gray-green mottled with dark green. Inflorescence 20–30 cm tall, usually unbranched. Flowers ca. 2 cm long; sepals and petals pinkish or straw-colored; lip greenish white with 2 red blotches in the center, trilobed, midlobe emarginate.

In leaf litter in thickets or in rocky scrub, usually in hot, rather dry areas to 1200 m (4000 ft.)

Tropical Africa, United States (Florida), Central and South America, West Indies

Oeceoclades maculata

Oeceoclades saundersiana

(Reichenbach f.) Garay & P. Taylor
Pseudobulbs 8–15 cm long, narrowly conical, 2-leaved. Leaves elliptic, dark glossy green; leaf blade 12–20 cm long; petioles almost as long as leaf blades. Inflorescence to 30 cm long, sometimes with a few short branches, several- to many-flowered. Flowers 3–4 cm long, greenish yellow flushed with purple and with purple veins, lip usually paler, less heavily veined, 4-lobed. This species needs more shade and watering than most.

In shade of damp forest and thicket, to 1200 m (4000 ft.)

Tropical Africa

Oeonia Lindley

TRIBE: Vandeae
SUBTRIBE: Angraecinae
ETYMOLOGY: From Greek *oionos*, a bird of prey, referring to appearance of flowers
DISTRIBUTION: 5 species in Madagascar and the Mascarene Islands

Stems long, slender, branched, leafy with numerous roots. Leaves distichous, ovate to oblong. Inflorescences longer than leaves, few- to several-flowered. Flowers white, green, or yellow-green, the lip often marked with red; sepals and petals subsimilar, ± spreading; lip 3- to 6-lobed, the basal lobes clasping the column; spur short, cylindrical or slightly swollen.

CULTIVATION: Plants grow well mounted on a slab of cork where the aerial roots can spread freely. They can also be potted in a coarse, free-draining compost with a moss pole to climb. They require intermediate temperatures, moderate shade, and high humidity.

Oeonia rosea Ridley
SYN. *Oeonia oncidiiflora* Kraenzlin
Stems to 80 cm long, usually branched. Leaves to 5 × 2.5 cm, ovate. Inflorescence to 15 cm long, unbranched, loosely 2- to 7-flowered. Flowers 2.5 cm across; sepals and petals green, oblong; lip white, red in the throat, 20–25 mm long and wide, 4-lobed, the apical lobes broad and rounded; spur 5–20 mm long.

Epiphytic in mossy, humid evergreen forest, 500–2000 m (1650–6600 ft.)

Madagascar

Oeonia volucris (Thouars) Durand & Schinz
Stems long, thin, branched, erect or pendent. Leaves to 25 × 8 mm, ovate or elliptic. Inflorescence simple, 30–40 cm long, loosely few-flowered. Flowers white, greenish in throat, ca. 3 cm across; sepals and petals spreading, obovate; lip 25–30 mm long, trilobed, the midlobe deeply emarginate.

Epiphytic in coastal forest; humid evergreen forest, 0–1500 m (5000 ft.)

Madagascar, Mauritius, Réunion

Oeoniella Schlechter

TRIBE: Vandeae
SUBTRIBE: Aerangidinae
ETYMOLOGY: Diminutive of *Oeonia*
DISTRIBUTION: 2 species in Madagascar, Comoro Islands, Mascarene Islands, and Seychelles

Monopodial epiphytes with long, often branched, leafy stems and numerous roots. Inflorescences unbranched, long or short, few- to several-flowered. Flowers white or white and green; sepals and petals free; lip funnel-shaped, trilobed near the apex, with a short, conical spur. Pollinia and stipites 2, viscidium 1.

CULTIVATION: Because of their elongated stems, plants should be potted in a coarse bark mix with a moss pole to climb, or mounted on a bark slab. They need intermediate to warm temperatures, high humidity, good ventilation, and moderate shade.

Oeoniella polystachys (Thouars) Schlechter
Stem branched, usually about 15 cm long but up sometimes up to 60 cm. Leaves narrowly oblong, 3–10 cm long. Inflorescence arising on stem opposite leaves, erect or arching, 15–25 cm long, several- to many-flowered. Flowers scented, white, 2–4 cm in diameter; lip trilobed near the apex, the midlobe narrow, acuminate, the side lobes broad, wavy-edged; spur 4 mm long.

Coastal forest

Madagascar, Comoro Islands, Mascarene Islands, Seychelles

SIMILAR SPECIES: *Oeoniella aphrodite* (Balfour f. & S. Moore) Schlechter has slightly smaller flowers and is known only from the Seychelles and the island of Rodrigues.

Oncidium Swartz

TRIBE: Maxillarieae
SUBTRIBE: Oncidiinae
ETYMOLOGY: From Greek *onkos*, mass, referring to the fleshy calli on the lip of many species
DISTRIBUTION: About 270 species in tropical and subtropical America

Epiphytic, lithophytic, or terrestrial plants with a short or long rhizome;

Oeonia rosea

Oeoniella polystachys

pseudobulbs of various sizes and shapes, subtended by distichous sheaths, 1- to 4-leaved. Inflorescences basal, often branched and very long, erect, arching or pendent, few- to many-flowered. Flowers often showy, frequently yellow and brown; sepals subsimilar; petals often larger; lip at right angles to column, entire or trilobed with a basal, fleshy, papillose or pubescent callus; side lobes small to large, spreading or reflexed, midlobe spreading, emarginate. Column short and stout with wings or auricles on either side, pollinia 2.

Numerous species of *Oncidium* have recently been transferred to other genera, some widely accepted and others less so.

Species of *Oncidium* have been widely hybridized, both within the genus and with other related genera. CULTIVATION: Most species grow well in intermediate conditions in pots of well-drained, standard epiphyte compost with plenty of water while in growth and a drier period in winter. Species from higher altitudes require cool conditions; this is mentioned in the text. Many species have very long inflorescences; these can be tied to a trellis or a long stick.

Oncidium altissimum (Jacquin) Swartz

Pseudobulbs clustered, to 10 cm long, compressed, 1- or 2-leaved at apex. Leaves to 80 × 8 cm. Inflorescence to 3 m long, branched towards the apex, many-flowered. Flowers 2.5–3.5 cm across; sepals and petals yellow to yellow-green, blotched and barred with maroon; lip yellow with a maroon-brown blotch at the base, midlobe kidney-shaped.

High-level epiphyte in forest, 30–850 m (100–2800 ft.)

Lesser Antilles

Oncidium barbatum Lindley

A dwarf species with pseudobulbs to 6.5 cm long, 1-leafed. Leaves to 10 × 2.5 cm. Inflorescence branched, to 50 cm long, laxly few-flowered. Flowers to 2.5 cm across; sepals and petals yellow barred and blotched with brown; lip bright yellow with red spots on the callus, deeply trilobed, side lobes as large as midlobe; callus round, fringed, with 5 teeth.

Epiphytic at medium altitudes

Bolivia, Brazil

SIMILAR SPECIES: *Oncidium fimbriatum* Lindley, from Argentina, Brazil, and Paraguay, has longer inflorescences and slightly smaller flowers with the sepals joined at the base.

Oncidium barbatum

Oncidium fimbriatum

Oncidium baueri Lindley

Pseudobulbs to 15 × 4 cm, compressed, 2-leaved, set on a long creeping rhizome. Leaves 20–50 cm long. Inflorescence much branched, to 3 m long, many-flowered. Flowers 3 cm across, waxy, long-lasting, pale to bright yellow with brown bars on the sepals and petals, lip with a red-brown central blotch.

Epiphytic, lithophytic, or terrestrial in evergreen or deciduous forest, 0–1200 m (4000 ft.)

Central and South America

Oncidium bifolium Sims

Small plants with pseudobulbs to 4 × 2 cm, 2-leaved, rarely 1-leafed. Leaves to 12 × 1.5 cm. Inflorescence arching, usually unbranched, to 35 cm long, loosely to 20-flowered. Flowers 2–3 cm across; sepals and petals yellow with red-brown markings, lip golden-yellow with red-brown marks on the callus, midlobe large, clawed then kidney-shaped, deeply emarginate. Column wings finely toothed.

Epiphytic in forest, 1000–3000 m (3300–9900 ft.)

Argentina, Bolivia, Brazil, Paraguay, Uruguay

SIMILAR SPECIES: *Oncidium flexuosum* Loddiges from Argentina, Brazil, and Paraguay is epiphytic in marshy forest at 500–800 m (1650–2640 ft.). It has slightly smaller flowers and shorter petals more regularly barred with red-brown.

Oncidium blanchetii Reichenbach f.

Pseudobulbs clustered, to 8 cm long, 2-leaved. Leaves erect, rigid, to 50 × 3 cm. Inflorescence 30–200 cm tall, branched, many-flowered. Flowers 2.5 cm across; sepals and petals small, yellow barred with red-brown; lip yellow, trilobed, with a warty callus; midlobe much larger than side lobes, kidney-shaped, emarginate.

Oncidium bifolium

Oncidium cheirophorum

Oncidium flexuosum

Terrestrial in montane grassland, scrub, and regenerating forest, 1200–2000 m (4000–6600 ft.)

Brazil

Oncidium cheirophorum

Reichenbach f.

Pseudobulbs to 3 cm long, conical to almost round, 1- or 2-leaved. Leaves to 20 × 1.5 cm. Inflorescence 10–25 cm long, branched, densely many-flowered in the upper part. Flowers scented, to 1.5 cm across, bright yellow; callus white with 3–5 fleshy teeth.

Epiphytic in rain forest and cloud forest, 600–2000 m (2000–6600 ft.)

Central and South America

Oncidium cornigerum Lindley

Pseudobulbs to 15 × 3 cm. Leaves rather lax, to 23 × 4 cm. Inflorescence to 75 cm long, many-flowered, the flowers borne towards the top. Flowers 2 cm across, slightly cup-shaped; sepals and petals bright yellow with red-brown spots and bars, lip bright yellow, fiddle-shaped, midlobe almost round, the margins crisped.

Low-level epiphyte in primary forest, usually near a river, 1000–1200 m (3300–4000 ft.)

Brazil, Paraguay

Oncidium crispum Loddiges ex Lindley

Pseudobulbs dark brown, ribbed, compressed, to 8 × 5 cm, 2-leaved. Leaves to 30 × 5 cm. Inflorescence to 1 m tall, much-branched, many-flowered. Flowers 8–10 cm across, red-brown, sometimes spotted with yellow, lip yellow at the base and with a yellow callus; all parts with crisped and undulate margins. This species prefers cool conditions in cultivation.

Epiphytic at mid and high levels in forest, in fairly good light, to 1400 m (4600 ft.)

Brazil

Oncidium divaricatum Lindley

SYN. *Oncidium pulvinatum* Lindley

Pseudobulbs to 5 cm long, strongly compressed, 1-leafed. Leaves to 30 × 8 cm. Inflorescence much branched, to 2 m long, many-flowered, peduncle purple. Flowers to 2.5 cm across, yellow blotched with brown; petals larger than sepals; lip trilobed, side lobes large, spreading, the margins finely toothed, midlobe smaller, transversely oblong; callus cushionlike, 4-lobed. Column wings rounded.

Epiphytic in moist forest, ca. 1500 m (5000 ft.)

Argentina, Brazil, Paraguay

Oncidium ensatum Lindley

SYN. *Oncidium floridanum* Ames

Pseudobulbs to 10 × 5 cm, 2-leaved. Leaves to 100 × 3 cm, yellowish green. Inflorescence to 2 m tall, many-flowered. Flowers to 3 cm across, sepals and petals yellow, sometimes marked with greenish brown; lip side lobes small, midlobe clawed, then kidney-shaped, emarginate, callus white.

Terrestrial in wet woodland, thicket, and open grassland, 550–600 m (1800–2000 ft.)

United States (Florida), Mexico, Cuba, Central and South America

Oncidium excavatum Lindley

Large plants with clustered pseudobulbs to 18 cm long, 1- or 2-leaved. Leaves to 50 × 4 cm. Inflorescence to 1.5 m tall, branched, erect or arching, loosely many-flowered. Flowers to 3.5 cm across; sepals and petals bright yellow, blotched and barred with red-brown towards the base, the petals larger than the sepals; lip side lobes small, yellow barred with brown, midlobe large, yellow, red at the base, deeply emarginate, with a callus of 4 warty lines.

Terrestrial on steep slopes in wet forest, 2400–2700 m (7900–8900 ft.)

Bolivia, Colombia, Ecuador, Peru

Oncidium forbesii Hooker

Pseudobulbs oblong, to 8 × 4 cm, 1- or 2-leaved. Leaves to 25 × 4 cm. Inflorescence 15–70 cm long, usually unbranched, many-flowered. Flowers 5–6 cm across, red-brown, irregularly bordered with yellow; petals larger and broader than sepals; lip side lobes small, midlobe clawed, fan-shaped, bilobed; callus warty, 5-lobed.

Epiphytic and terrestrial in forest and woodland, 800–1600 m (2640–5300 ft.)

Brazil

SIMILAR SPECIES: *Oncidium gardneri* Lindley from Brazil has yellower flowers and tends to grow at higher altitudes. In cultivation it requires more shade, lower humidity, and cooler temperatures than *O. forbesii.*

Oncidium fuscatum Reichenbach f.

SYN. *Miltonia warszewiczii* Reichenbach f.

Pseudobulbs to 12 cm long, clustered, compressed, 1-leafed at apex. Leaves to 33 × 3.5 cm. Inflorescence to 50 cm long, usually branched, many-flowered. Flowers 5 cm across, all parts with undulate margins; sepals and petals red-brown, tipped with white or yellow; lip pinkish purple with white margins, midlobe almost round, deeply emarginate. Column wings round, purple.

Epiphytic at fairly low altitudes

Brazil, Colombia, Ecuador, Peru

Oncidium hastatum (Bateman) Lindley

Pseudobulbs to 11 × 6 cm, compressed, 2-leaved. Leaves to 40 × 3 cm. Inflorescence branched, to 1.5 m long, many-flowered. Flowers 4–5 cm across; sepals and petals yellow to yellow-green, thickly blotched and barred with maroon; lip arrow-shaped, side lobes spreading, white, midlobe purple; callus 4-lobed, white with purple lines.

Epiphytic or lithophytic in pine forest, ca. 2000 m (6600 ft.)

Mexico

Oncidium hastilabium (Lindley) Beer

Pseudobulbs to 6 × 4 cm, compressed, 1- or 2-leaved. Leaves to 35 × 4 cm. Inflorescence to 80 cm long, many-flowered. Flowers to 7.5 cm

Oncidium divaricatum

Oncidium crispum

Oncidium forbesii

Oncidium fuscatum

Oncidium hastatum

Oncidium hastilabium

Oncidium leucochilum

across, scented, long-lasting; sepals and petals pale yellow or pale green barred with red-brown; lip white or pale pink, the base purple; side lobes small, curved, acute, midlobe clawed, heart-shaped.

Epiphytic in forest, ca. 1500 m (5000 ft.)

Colombia, Ecuador, Peru, Venezuela

Oncidium klotzschianum Reichenbach f.

SYN. *Oncidium obryzatum* Reichenbach f. & Warszewicz

Pseudobulbs to 6 × 3 cm, grooved and compressed, 1- or 2-leaved at the apex. Leaves to 30 × 3.5 cm. Inflorescence 45–100 cm long, branched, many-flowered. Flowers ca. 4 cm across, yellow, blotched with red-brown at the base of the sepals, petals, and lip; lip side lobes spreading, midlobe kidney-shaped, emarginate; callus with 3 apical lobes.

Epiphytic in rain forest and cloud forest, 700–1600 m (2300–5300 ft.)

Central and South America

Oncidium leucochilum Bateman ex Lindley

Pseudobulbs to 13 × 6 cm, compressed, ribbed, 1- or 2-leaved. Leaves to 60 × 4.5 cm. Inflorescence to 3 m long, branched, many-flowered. Flowers to 3.5 cm across; sepals and

Oncidium longipes

petals yellow to pale green, heavily blotched with purple-brown; lip white, tinged with pink or yellow.

Epiphytic in oak and juniper forest, 1500–2200 m (5000–7260 ft.)

Mexico, Guyana, Honduras

Oncidium longipes Lindley

Pseudobulbs ca. 3 × 1 cm, 1- or 2-leaved, set on a creeping rhizome. Leaves ca. 10 × 2 cm. Inflorescence unbranched, to 15 cm long, 2- to 5-flowered. Flowers 2–3.5 cm across, yellow-brown or light reddish brown barred and tipped with yellow; lip bright yellow with red spots on and around the callus; side lobes spreading, rounded, midlobe clawed then kidney-shaped.

High-level epiphyte in primary forest at low altitudes

Argentina, Brazil, Paraguay, Uruguay

Oncidium maculatum (Lindley) Lindley

Pseudobulbs to 10 × 4 cm, strongly compressed, 2-leaved. Leaves to 25 × 5 cm. Inflorescence usually branched, to 1 m tall, many-flowered. Flowers to 5 cm across; sepals and petals brownish to yellow-green heavily blotched with dark purple-brown; lip side lobes small, midlobe white tipped with yellow, the margins undulate; callus of 4 keels, streaked with purple.

Epiphytic in wet forest, 800–2000 m (2640–6600 ft.)

Mexico, Central America

Oncidium marshallianum Reichenbach f.

Pseudobulbs 15 × 4 cm, slightly compressed, 2-leaved. Leaves to 30 × 4 cm. Inflorescence branched, 75–180 cm tall, many-flowered. Flowers variable in size and color, to 5.5 cm across; sepals light yellow with red-brown bars, petals bright yellow with red-brown spots towards the base, lip bright yellow, deeply emarginate, the claw and callus spotted with orange-red.

Epiphytic in forest, sometimes terrestrial in low scrub, 1000–1500 m (3300–5000 ft.)

Southeastern Brazil

Oncidium ornithorhynchum Kunth

Pseudobulbs to 6 × 3 cm, 2-leaved at apex. Leaves to 25 × 3 cm. Inflorescence arching, to 50 cm long, branched, many-flowered. Flowers to 2.5 cm across, scented; sepals and petals white, pink or lilac-purple, the lip darker; side lobes small, midlobe clawed, ± fan-shaped, emarginate; callus yellow or orange. This pretty species does better in cool conditions.

Oncidium maculatum

Oncidium ornithorhynchum

Epiphytic in cloud forest, 1000–1500 m (3300–5000 ft.), occasionally in low-altitude rain forest

Mexico, Central and South America

Oncidium raniferum Lindley

Pseudobulbs to 6.5 × 2 cm, 2-leaved at apex. Leaves to 17 × 1.5 cm. Inflorescence erect, to 35 cm tall, with many spreading branches, many-flowered. Flowers to 1.5 cm across; sepals and petals small, yellow spotted with brown; lip yellow spotted and striped with brown, side lobes rounded, toothed, midlobe fan-shaped, deeply emarginate; callus red-brown. Column wings with brown stripes.

Epiphytic

Brazil

Oncidium sarcodes Lindley

Pseudobulbs to 15 × 3 cm, ± spindle-shaped, 2- or 3-leaved at apex. Leaves to 25 × 5 cm. Inflorescence arching, to 1.8 m tall, branched, many-flowered. Flowers to 5 cm across, long-lasting; sepals and petals glossy chestnut-brown with a yellow margin, lip bright yellow with red-brown spots at the base, side lobes small, midlobe transversely oblong, emarginate; callus white or yellow with red-brown spots. This species requires cool temperatures and seems to do better mounted.

Epiphytic

Brazil

Oncidium sphacelatum Lindley

Pseudobulbs to 15 × 5 cm, ovoid, compressed with sharp edges, 2- or 3-leaved. Leaves 25–100 cm long. Inflorescence branched, to 1.5 m tall, many-flowered. Flowers 3 cm across, bright yellow, sepals and petals with brown or maroon spots on the lower half, lip with a red-brown blotch in front of the callus, midlobe transversely oblong, emarginate, the edges undulate.

Epiphytic in lowland rain forest, rarely terrestrial in humus, 50–200 m (165–660 ft.)

Mexico, Central America, Venezuela

Oncidium tigratum Reichenbach f. & Warszewicz

Pseudobulbs to 10 × 4 cm, compressed, 2-leaved at apex. Leaves to 20 × 3.5 cm. Inflorescence to 40 cm long with short branches, many-flowered. Flowers ca. 2.5 cm across; sepals and petals bright yellow marked with brown or red, lip bright yellow with brown bands at the base; side lobes earlike, midlobe kidney-shaped; callus white, warty. Column yellow tinged with purple, wings yellow with red-brown markings.

Colombia, Ecuador, Peru

Oncidium tigrinum Lexarza

Pseudobulbs to 10 × 6 cm, compressed, 2- or 3-leaved at apex. Leaves to 45 × 2.5 cm. Inflorescence branched, erect, 60–90 cm long, many-flowered. Flowers ca. 7.5 cm across, scented; sepals and petals bright yellow, heavily blotched and barred with dark brown, lip yellow, side lobes earlike, midlobe with a narrow claw then broadly oblong, emarginate; callus with 3 keels ending in blunt teeth. This species does better in cool conditions.

Oncidium sarcodes

Oncidium tigratum

Oncidium unguiculatum

Epiphytic in oak forest, 2000–2500 m (6600–8250 ft.)

Mexico

SIMILAR SPECIES: *Oncidium unguiculatum* Lindley from Mexico has a lip with a much longer claw to the midlobe and darker marks on sepals and petals.

Oncidium warszewiczii Reichenbach f.

Pseudobulbs to 9 × 5 cm, ovoid, compressed, 2-leaved. Leaves to 30 × 3 cm. Inflorescence 25–50 cm long, unbranched, arching, 6- to 12-flowered. Flowers to 3 cm across, golden yellow with a few red-brown spots around the callus and at the base of the petals; lip side lobes small, midlobe kidney-shaped to almost round; callus with 5 small teeth.

Epiphytic in rain forest and oak forest, 1200–2900 m (4000–9500 ft.)

Costa Rica, Panama, Colombia

Ophrys Linnaeus

TRIBE: Orchideae

SUBTRIBE: Orchidinae

ETYMOLOGY: From Greek *ophrys*, eyebrow, probably referring to the hairy lip

DISTRIBUTION: Probably about 20–30 species in Europe, North Africa, and the Middle East

Terrestrial herbs with 2, rarely 3, globose or ellipsoid tubers. Leaves basal and along stem. Inflorescences erect, unbranched, few- to several-flowered. Sepals spreading, glabrous, green, yellow-green, or pink; petals usually smaller than sepals; lip rather obscurely trilobed, lacking a spur, often hairy but with a central, blue or gray shiny area (speculum).

Estimates of the number of species in this genus vary from 16 to 251. Some authors take a broad concept while others recognize almost every variant at specific level.

CULTIVATION: Most species are native to the Mediterranean region and are usually cultivated in pots in an alpine house. They need a free-draining, calcareous soil and should be kept dry after flowering, when the leaves have withered.

Ophrys apifera Hudson

BEE ORCHID

Stem 15–50 cm tall; basal leaves lanceolate, acute. Inflorescence laxly 2- to 10-flowered. Flowers 2–3 cm across; sepals pale to deep pink; petals small, greenish; lip 12–15 mm long, convex, the pointed tip reflexed, with small, hairy side lobes; midlobe velvety red-brown with U-shaped yellow markings. Several forms and varieties have been described. Flowering midspring–midsummer.

Grassland and scrub, usually on calcareous soil; a colonizer of open habitats such as old quarries and road verges

Europe, North Africa, Near East

SIMILAR SPECIES: *Ophrys fuciflora* (Crantz) Moench has triangular pink petals and a squarer lip.

Ophrys insectifera Linnaeus

FLY ORCHID

Slender plant to 50 cm tall. Leaves 7–10, linear-lanceolate, basal and along the stem. Inflorescence loosely 2- to 14-flowered. Flowers small, sepals yellow-green, petals purple-brown, antennae-like; lip velvety red-brown with an iridescent blue band across the middle. Flowering late spring–summer.

Open woodland on calcareous soil

Europe, as far north as Scandinavia

Ophrys lutea Cavanilles

YELLOW BEE ORCHID

Leaves 3–6 in a basal rosette, to 9 × 2.5 cm, with 1 or 2 stem leaves above. Raceme 10–30 cm tall, loosely 1- to 7-flowered; bracts longer than ovary. Flowers ca. 2 cm across; sepals and petals yellow-green, petals much shorter than sepals; lip distinctly trilobed, ca. 2 cm long, oblong, deep brown to purple-black with a yellow margin; speculum iridescent bluish gray. Flowering late winter–late spring.

Open woodland, poor grassland, on base-rich, usually calcareous soils

Mediterranean region

Ophrys tenthredinifera Willdenow

SAWFLY ORCHID

Leaves 3–5 in a basal rosette, to 12 × 3.5 cm, with 1–4 sheathing leaves on stem. Inflorescence 10–45 cm tall, loosely 3- to 8-flowered. Flowers 2.5 cm across; sepals and petals lilac or pink; sepals broadly ovate, petals triangular, much smaller. Lip velvety brownish purple with a yellow to light brown, hairy margin; speculum small, blue-gray edged with yellow. Flowering late spring–early summer.

Open pine woods, poor grassland, scrub, on basic or slightly acid soils

Mediterranean region

Orchis Linnaeus

TRIBE: Orchideae

SUBTRIBE: Orchidinae

ETYMOLOGY: From Greek *orchis*, testicle, referring to the shape of the tubers

DISTRIBUTION: More than 20 species from Europe, particularly from around the Mediterranean, North Africa, and temperate Asia.

Ophrys fuciflora

Ophrys apifera

Ophrys insectifera

Ophrys lutea

Small to medium-sized terrestrial plants with 2, occasionally 3, globose to ellipsoid tubers. Leaves basal, rosulate, spotted or unspotted. Inflorescences unbranched, terminal, cylindrical, usually densely several- to many-flowered. Flowers purple, red, pink, yellow, or white, sometimes scented; floral bracts membranous, never leafy; sepals and petals free, subsimilar, lateral sepals spreading or forming a hood with the dorsal sepal and petals; lip usually trilobed with the midlobe often itself divided; usually spurred, the spur slender or saccate.

Species of *Orchis* interbreed readily, as many natural hybrids have been recorded. Recent DNA work has led to several species previously included here being moved to other genera such as *Anacamptis* and *Neotinea*.

CULTIVATION: Some species, for example, *Orchis mascula*, will become naturalized if planted in temperate gardens, but others are better in an alpine house. They are usually grown in pans, in a free-draining terrestrial compost with added lime if the species grows naturally in calcareous soils. After the leaves die back, plants should be kept dry until signs of new growth appear.

Orchis mascula Linnaeus

EARLY PURPLE ORCHID

Stem erect, 20–60 cm tall. Leaves 3–5 towards base, glossy dark green, usually spotted with purple. Inflorescence densely up to about 20-flowered. Flowers purple or pinkish purple; dorsal sepal forming hood with petals, lateral sepals spreading or reflexed; lip 8–15 mm long, white in center with purple spots; midlobe notched, longer than side lobes; spur 10–15 mm long, cylindrical, slightly upcurved. Flowering spring–summer.

Most often in broad-leaved woodland, but also in open grassland, on calcareous, neutral or even slightly acid soils

Europe, North Africa, Middle East

Orchis militaris Linnaeus

MILITARY ORCHID

Stem 20–65 cm tall. Basal leaves 3–5, elliptic, to 18 × 5 cm. Inflorescence fairly densely many-flowered. Sepals and petals forming a hood, pale pink outside, purple veined inside; lip to 15 mm long, the midlobe divided again, pink or purplish, paler in center with tufts of reddish hairs forming spots; spur cylindrical, decurved.

Open woodland, grassland, and scrub, on calcareous soil

Europe; rare in England

Orchis purpurea Hudson

LADY ORCHID

Stem 30–90 cm tall. Basal leaves 3–6, to 20 × 7 cm, glossy green, semi-erect. Inflorescence densely many-flowered. Sepals and petals brownish red, forming a hood; lip white or pale pink with tufts of hair forming purple spots, trilobed, side lobes narrow, midlobe broadly triangular, notched, to 2 cm long and broad; spur short, curved. Flowering late spring–early summer.

Woodland, on well-drained, chalky soil

Europe, North Africa

Ornithocephalus Hooker

TRIBE: Maxillarieae

SUBTRIBE: Oncidiinae

ETYMOLOGY: From Greek *ornis*, bird, and *kephale*, head, referring to the column apex, thought to resemble a bird's head

DISTRIBUTION: About 47 species in Mexico, Central and South America, and the West Indies

Small, sympodial epiphytes without pseudobulbs. Stems short, covered by overlapping leaf sheaths. Leaves fleshy, laterally flattened, arranged in a fan, articulated to the sheaths. Inflorescences axillary, unbranched, few- to many-flowered. Flowers small, white, greenish white or greenish yellow; sepals and petals free, subsimilar, spreading or reflexed; lip entire or

Orchis militaris

Orchis purpurea

Orchis mascula

trilobed, with a fleshy callus near the base. Pollinia 4.

CULTIVATION: Plants can be grown either mounted or in a small pot in a fine epiphyte compost. They require intermediate, shady conditions, good ventilation, and high humidity. The roots should be allowed to dry between waterings but should not remain dry for any length of time.

Ornithocephalus bicornis

Lindley

Leaves to 7 × 1.2 cm, lanceolate. Inflorescence about same length as leaves, few- to many-flowered, rachis densely hairy. Flowers ca. 5 mm across, greenish white or greenish yellow.

Epiphytic in tropical rain forest, to 1000 m (3300 ft.)

Mexico, Central and South America, West Indies

Ornithocephalus ciliatus

Lindley

Leaves ca. 4 × 1 cm. Inflorescence usually shorter than leaves, few-flowered. Flowers ca. 7 mm across, whitish, the lip cream with 5 green veins. See photo on page 15.

Epiphytic in forest

Trinidad, South America

Ornithocephalus gladiatus

Hooker

SYN. *Ornithocephalus falcatus* Focke, *O. bonplandii* Reichenbach f.

Plants usually pendent. Leaves numerous, linear, to 10 × 0.6 cm. Inflorescence to 11 cm long, many-flowered. Flowers 5 mm across, white with a greenish lip.

Epiphytic in plantations and forest, 0–1800 m (6000 ft.)

Central and South America, West Indies

SIMILAR SPECIES: *Ornithocephalus inflexus* Lindley (syn. *O. tonduzii* Schlechter) from Mexico and Central America is not usually pendent and has a concave lip.

Ornithocephalus bicornis

Ornithocephalus ciliatus

Ornithocephalus gladiatus

Ornithochilus (Lindley) Wallich ex Bentham

TRIBE: Vandeae

SUBTRIBE: Aeridinae

ETYMOLOGY: From Greek *ornis*, bird, and *cheilos*, lip, referring to the birdlike lip

DISTRIBUTION: 3 species in tropical and subtropical Asia

Small monopodial epiphytes related to *Aerides*. Stem short. Leaves fleshy. Inflorescences axillary, usually branched, many-flowered. Flowers small to medium-sized; sepals and petals free, sepals larger and broader than petals. Lip hypochile spurred at the end near the epichile; epichile trilobed, the margins fringed or finely toothed. Column small, without a foot; pollinia 4, in 2 pairs.

CULTIVATION: With their long, pendent inflorescences, plants should be mounted or grown in a suspended pot. They require intermediate temperatures, moderate shade, and high humidity throughout the year.

Ornithochilus difformis (Lindley) Wallich ex Bentham

SYN. *Ornithochilus fuscus* Wallich ex Lindley

Stem 1–8 cm long. Leaves several, to 18 × 5 cm, fleshy, elliptic, unequally and acutely bilobed at the apex. Inflorescence to 45 cm long, usually with spreading branches, many-flowered. Flowers ca. 1 cm across; sepals and petals yellow or green with red-brown streaks; lip maroon with yellow markings or greenish white with purple streaks, the margins deeply fringed, with a central ridge; spur maroon and green, 3–5 cm long, curved down at right angles.

Var. *difformis* occurs from the Himalayas to western Malesia. Var. *kinabaluensis* J. J. Wood, A. L. Lamb & Shim has green and white flowers and is endemic to Mt. Kinabalu in Borneo where it grows in forest at 1400–1500 m (4600–5000 ft.)

Epiphytic on tree trunks in woodland, 600–2000 m (2000–6600 ft.)

Ornithochilus difformis

Himalayas to western Malesia, Borneo

Ornithophora Barbosa Rodrigues

TRIBE: Maxillarieae
SUBTRIBE: Oncidiinae
ETYMOLOGY: From Greek *ornis*, bird, and *phoros*, bearing, referring to the appearance of the column
DISTRIBUTION: 1 species in Brazil

Small epiphyte with narrowly ovoid pseudobulbs, 2-leaved at apex, with distichous basal leafy sheaths, set along a thin, creeping rhizome. Inflorescence arising from axils of sheaths, unbranched, several-flowered. Flowers small, sepals and petals free, subsimilar; lip clawed, lacking a spur, blade transversely semi-circular with 4 ridges at the base and a trilobed callus on the claw. Column slender, without wings; pollinia 2.

CULTIVATION: With their creeping habit, plants do well in a small basket in a fine bark-based compost, in intermediate, shady conditions. They need to be watered or sprayed throughout the year.

Ornithophora radicans

Ornithophora radicans (Linden & Reichenbach f.) Garay & Pabst

SYN. *Sigmatostalix radicans* Linden & Reichenbach f., *Ornithophora quadricolor* Barbosa Rodrigues

Leaves linear, grasslike, to ca. 10 cm long. Inflorescence to 10 cm long, 8- to 11-flowered. Flowers 8–10 mm across, greenish white, lip white with a yellow callus; column purple.

Epiphytic in wet forest
Brazil

Osmoglossum Schlechter

TRIBE: Maxillarieae
SUBTRIBE: Oncidiinae
ETYMOLOGY: From Greek *osme*, odor, and *glossa*, tongue, referring to the scent of the type species
DISTRIBUTION: 5 species in Mexico, El Salvador, Guyana, Panama, Colombia, and Ecuador

Pseudobulbs ovoid, clustered, enclosed in distichous leafy sheaths, 1- to 2-leaved at the apex. Leaves narrow. Inflorescence arising from sheath axils, unbranched. Flowers showy, mainly white; sepals and petals spreading, subsimilar; lip deflexed, joined to column at base, with a callus of 3 fleshy ridges. Column lacking a foot; pollinia 2.

CULTIVATION: Plants are grown in pots in a free-draining fine to medium epiphyte mixture, in intermediate conditions with moderate shade. They should be kept drier and cooler when resting.

Osmoglossum pulchellum (Bateman ex Lindley) Schlechter

SYN. *Odontoglossum pulchellum* Bateman ex Lindley, *Cuitlauzina pulchella* (Bateman ex Lindley) Dressler & N. H. Williams

Pseudobulbs ovoid, ridged, to 10 × 3.5 cm. Leaves to 50 × 1.5 cm,

Osmoglossum pulchellum

narrowly strap-shaped. Inflorescence to 50 cm long, erect or somewhat pendent, loosely few- to several-flowered. Flowers 3–3.5 cm across, scented, white tinged with pink below, lip fiddle-shaped, white, deflexed after the callus; callus of 3 ridges, yellow spotted with red.

Epiphytic in oak forest and cloud forest, 1500–2200 m (5000–7260 ft)

Mexico, El Salvador, Guyana

Otochilus Lindley

TRIBE: Arethuseae
SUBTRIBE: Coelogyninae
ETYMOLOGY: From Greek *otos*, ear, and *cheilos*, lip, referring to the earlike side lobes of the lip
DISTRIBUTION: 5 species from Nepal to China and Southeast Asia

Creeping epiphytes with cylindrical pseudobulbs, superposed (that is, arising from below the apex of the previous one and so forming chains), 2-leaved at apex. Leaves linear to elliptic, pleated, thin-textured. Inflorescences terminal on pseudobulb, unbranched, laxly few- to many-flowered. Flowers medium-sized; sepals and petals subsimilar, narrow, free, spreading; lip saccate at base, trilobed; side lobes earlike, midlobe oblong.

CULTIVATION: Because of their trailing habit, plants should be grown mounted or in hanging baskets. They require intermediate conditions, moderate shade, and plenty of water while in growth.

Otochilus fuscus Lindley

Pseudobulbs cylindrical, to 8 × 1.5 cm, forming a pendent chain. Leaves linear, 10–20 cm long. Inflorescence 12–17 cm long, arching or pendent, laxly many-flowered, the peduncle covered with overlapping sheaths. Flowers scented, 14–16 mm across, white, the base of the lip pink, column orange-brown; sepals and petals linear; lip 4–6 mm long, midlobe oblong, acute, deflexed.

Subtropical hillside forest, 780–2500 m (2600–8250 ft.)

Bhutan, India, Nepal, Cambodia, Myanmar, Thailand, Vietnam

Otoglossum (Schlechter) Garay & Dunsterville

TRIBE: Maxillarieae
SUBTRIBE: Oncidiinae
ETYMOLOGY: From Greek *otos*, ear and *glossa*, tongue, referring to the earlike lip side lobes
DISTRIBUTION: 13 species in Central and South America

Medium to large epiphytic, lithophytic, or terrestrial plants with a thin creeping or ascending rhizome. Pseudobulbs well-spaced out on rhizome, 1- to 3-leaved at apex, with 2 pairs of leaf-bearing sheaths at the base. Leaves fleshy. Inflorescences unbranched with a long peduncle; flowers showy, usually clustered. Sepals and petals spreading, subsimilar, usually with the margins undulate; lip joined to the column-foot, trilobed, deflexed. Pollinia 2.

CULTIVATION: The scandent habit makes these plants awkward to cultivate, but they can be grown in pots in a free-draining epiphyte compost with a moss pole to climb. They require cool conditions with high humidity, light shade, and good ventilation. They should be given plenty of water while growing but kept much drier when not in active growth.

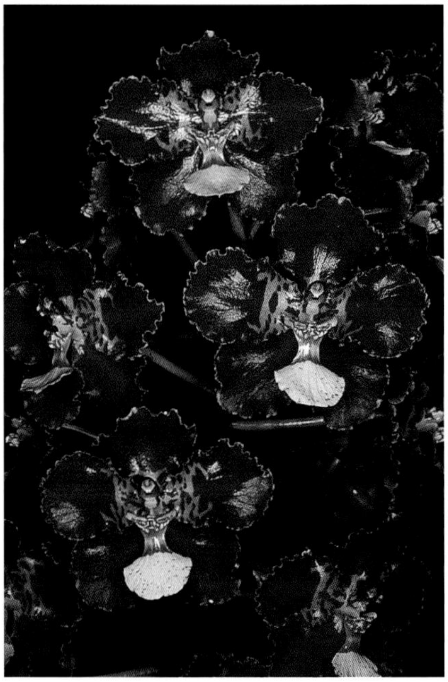

Otoglossum brevifolium. R. Parsons

Otoglossum brevifolium (Lindley) Garay & Dunsterville

SYN. *Otoglossum chiriquense* (Reichenbach f.) Garay & Dunsterville, *Odontoglossum chiriquense* Reichenbach f.

Pseudobulbs almost round, compressed, 1-leafed at apex. Leaves to 30 × 9 cm, thick-textured. Inflorescence to 60 cm long, usually erect, several-flowered. Flowers 4–5 cm across, chestnut brown, yellow at the base and on the margins; lip golden yellow, the midlobe notched or bilobed at the apex.

Epiphytic in rain forest and cloud forest or terrestrial on steep banks, 800–2800 m (2640–9250 ft.)

Central and South America

Otoglossum coronarium (Lindley) Garay & Dunsterville

SYN. *Odontoglossum coronarium* Lindley

Pseudobulbs 2- or 3-leaved at apex. Inflorescence to 1 m tall, 7- to 11-flowered. Flowers to 6 cm across, yellow blotched with red-brown; lip yellow.

Epiphytic in wet forest or terrestrial on steep banks, 800–3000 m (2640–9900 ft.)

Ecuador

Otochilus fuscus. F. Bronsema

Otoglossum coronarium. R. Parsons

Otostylis Schlechter

TRIBE: Maxillarieae
SUBTRIBE: Zygopetalinae
ETYMOLOGY: From the Greek *otos*, ear, and *stylis*, column, referring to the conspicuous wings on the column
DISTRIBUTION: 4 species in South America and Trinidad

Terrestrials with small, ovoid pseudobulbs, usually hidden by leaf bases and sheaths. Leaves several, petiolate, lanceolate, pleated. Inflorescences axillary, unbranched, erect with a long peduncle, several- to many-flowered. Flowers showy, mostly white, long-lasting; sepals and petals free, subsimilar, spreading; lip entire or obscurely trilobed with a transverse callus at the base. Column winged, with a short foot; pollinia 4, viscidium 1.

CULTIVATION: Species of *Otostylis* are uncommon in cultivation, the most widely grown being *O. brachystalix*. They require a free-draining terrestrial compost, good light and air movement in intermediate conditions and should be kept almost dry while dormant.

Otostylis brachystalix (Reichenbach f.) Schlechter

SYN. *Aganisia brachystalix* (Reichenbach f.) Rolfe, *Zygopetalum brachystalix* Reichenbach f.

Pseudobulbs ovoid, to 2 cm long. Leaves to 70 × 5 cm, narrowly lanceolate. Inflorescence erect, 70–90 cm long, many-flowered. Flowers 2.5–3 cm across, white, the lip yellow in the center.

This attractive species is difficult to cultivate. In Trinidad, where it has a very limited distribution and is protected, it grows in tropical savanna, which is alternately very wet and very dry, and is situated over a hard pan that prevents drainage during the wet season and access to subsoil water in the dry season.

Seasonally wet savannah, 800–1700 m (2640–5600 ft.)

Brazil, Colombia, Guyana, Peru, Trinidad, Venezuela

SIMILAR SPECIES: *Otostylis lepida* (Linden & Reichenbach f.) Schlechter, from Brazil, Guiana, and Venezuela, has the tips of the sepals and petals often tinged with pink and has a W-shaped callus.

Otostylis brachystalix. S. Laurent

Pabstia Garay

SYN. *Colax* Lindley
TRIBE: Maxillarieae
SUBTRIBE: Zygopetalinae
ETYMOLOGY: Named for Guido Pabst, an authority on Brazilian orchids
DISTRIBUTION: 5 species in southeastern Brazil

Pseudobulbs ovoid, 2-leaved at apex and with leafy sheathing bracts at the base. Leaves lanceolate, plicate. Inflorescences basal, few-flowered. Flowers large, showy; sepals and petals free, subsimilar; lip shorter than other parts, entire or trilobed, clawed, with a fleshy basal callus. Pollinia 4.

CULTIVATION: Grow in pots in a medium epiphyte mix in intermediate, shaded conditions with high humidity and plenty of water while growing. Give less water while plants are resting but do not allow them to dry out completely.

Pabstia jugosa (Lindley) Garay

Pseudobulbs to 7 × 3 cm. Leaves to 45 × 7 cm, dark green, thin-textured. Inflorescence erect, 20–25 cm tall, 1- to 6-flowered. Flowers 5–7.5 cm across, scented, fleshy, long-lasting; sepals and petals spreading, white or greenish white, the petals blotched or barred with purple or maroon; lip trilobed, white or greenish white heavily marked with purple or maroon.

Epiphytic at low levels on trunks and low branches in wet forest or lithophytic in wet gullies, always in heavy shade, ca. 700 m (2300 ft.)

Southeastern Brazil

Pabstia jugosa

Panisea (Lindley) Lindley

TRIBE: Arethuseae
SUBTRIBE: Coelogyninae
ETYMOLOGY: From Greek *pan*, all, and *isos*, equal, referring to the similarity of flower segments
DISTRIBUTION: 8 species in northeastern India and Southeast Asia

Small epiphytic or lithophytic plants with short, branched rhizomes. Pseudobulbs ovoid, 1- or 2-leaved at apex. Leaves narrowly elliptic to linear. Inflorescences lateral, unbranched, 1- to several-flowered. Flowers small to medium-sized; sepals and petals free, subsimilar; lip entire or trilobed, with or without a callus, clawed at the base, the claw with a sigmoid curve.

CULTIVATION: Grow in intermediate conditions with moderate shade, in pots in a medium bark mix or mounted on a bark slab. Plants should be watered freely while in growth but kept drier in winter while resting.

Panisea demissa (D. Don) Pfitzer

Pseudobulbs clustered, ovoid, to 4 cm long, 1- or 2-leaved at apex. Leaves lanceolate, to 4 × 1.5 cm. Inflorescence curving down, laxly 5- to 8-flowered. Flowers 10–12 mm across, white; lip entire, with a sigmoid bend at the base, lacking a callus. This high-altitude species requires cool conditions.

Epiphytic in forest, 1900–3300 m (6300–10,900 ft.)

Bhutan, China, India, Myanmar, Nepal, Laos, Thailand, Vietnam

Panisea uniflora Lindley

Plants 10–20 cm tall, the rhizome covered with overlapping scales. Pseudobulbs 1.5–3.5 cm long, 2-leaved. Leaves linear, 5–15 cm long. Inflorescence erect, 1-flowered, ca. 2 cm long. Flowers 20–25 mm across, apricot or yellowish, the lip obscurely trilobed, slightly darker with 3–7 orange or brown blotches.

Epiphytic or lithophytic in humid forest, 250–1500 m (825–5000 ft.)

Bhutan, Nepal, India, Myanmar, Laos, Thailand, Vietnam

SIMILAR SPECIES: *Panisea albiflora* (Ridley) Seidenfaden has few-flowered inflorescences with drooping, white flowers. It comes from Vietnam where it grows in montane forest at 1300–2900 m (4300–9500 ft.).

Paphinia Lindley

TRIBE: Maxillarieae
SUBTRIBE: Stanhopeinae
ETYMOLOGY: Named for Paphia, the Aphrodite in Cyprus
DISTRIBUTION: 16 species in Central and South America and Trinidad

Epiphytic, rarely terrestrial, plants with small pseudobulbs covered with distichous papery sheaths when young. Leaves large, pleated, thin-textured. Inflorescences basal, usually pendent, unbranched, few-flowered. Flowers large, showy, short-lived; sepals and petals ± spreading, subsimilar but the petals smaller, lateral sepals joined to column-foot; lip joined to apex of column-foot, clawed, trilobed; side lobes erect, midlobe triangular to arrow-shaped; disc with a fleshy callus and sometimes glandular hairs. Pollinia 2.

CULTIVATION: Plants can be grown mounted or in baskets in an open, bark-based compost in intermediate conditions with moderate shade. Unlike *Stanhopea* species, they need to be watered throughout the year.

Paphinia cristata (Lindley) Lindley

Leaves to 25 × 4.5 cm, Inflorescence to 15 cm long, pendent, 1- to 3-flowered. Flowers to 10 cm across, reddish brown with white or yellowish striping; lip purple-brown, the claw white.

Epiphytic in wet forest, 50–1000 m (165–3300 ft.)

Trinidad, South America

Paphinia lindeniana Reichenbach f.

Leaves to 27 × 7 cm. Inflorescence to 10 cm long, pendent, to 8-flowered. Flowers ca. 10 cm across, purple-brown with white markings.

Epiphytic in wet forest, 50–600 m (165–2000 ft.)

Brazil, Colombia, Peru, Venezuela

Paphiopedilum Pfitzer

SUBFAMILY: Cypripedioideae
ETYMOLOGY: From Paphos, the birthplace of Aphrodite, and Greek *pedilon*, slipper
DISTRIBUTION: More than 70 species in tropical Asia

Sympodial plants without pseudobulbs, usually terrestrial but sometimes epiphytic or lithophytic. Stems short, roots thick. Leaves several, usually forming a fan, strap-shaped, oblong or elliptic, folded at base, plain green or mottled dark and light green, sometimes flushed with purple underneath. Inflorescences terminal, 1- to several-flowered. Flowers large, usually showy; dorsal sepal erect or forming a hood over lip, usually ovate; lateral sepals joined to form a concave synsepal; petals free, spreading or pendent, often hairy; lip forming a deep slipper-shaped or urn-shaped pouch, hairy inside, sometimes hairy outside. Column short, stalked, with a fleshy staminode (derived from a sterile stamen) behind which are 2 fertile anthers and a stalked stigma. The shape of the staminode is a useful taxonomic feature. The ovary has 1 loculus, a distinguishing feature from *Phragmipedium*, where the ovary is trilocular.

At present, 3 subgenera are recognized: *Parvisepalum* with 5 species, *Brachypetalum* with about 4 species, and subgenus *Paphiopedilum*, which is divided into 5 sections, with the remainder.

Many species have been used in hybridization. The first artificial *Paphiopedilum* hybrid, *Paph.* Harrisianum (*Paph. villosum* × *Paph. barbatum*) was made by John Dominy and first flowered in 1869. Now, more than 10,000 hybrids have been registered.

CULTIVATION: Paphiopedilums are the most widely cultivated of the slipper orchids and most are relatively easily grown. Although, as in any large genus, species have varying preferences, almost all species will do well in an intermediate greenhouse. As a general rule, species with mottled leaves require warmer conditions than those with plain green leaves and single flowers, while plain-leaved species with multiple flowers also need fairly warm, bright conditions. All need high humidity and moderate shade—as with other orchids, too much shade results in dark green, luxuriant-looking leaves but poor flowering, while too much light leads to yellowish leaves. Plants need water throughout the year, but as the roots quickly rot if the compost remains too wet, they need a free-draining mixture, usually based on medium bark, perlite, and charcoal. Chopped coconut husk also seems to be suitable and some people are very successful with inorganic materials such as rockwool. Most species grow in limestone areas and for these, a small amount of dolomite added to the compost is helpful. While in growth, plants benefit from regular applications of dilute fertilizer but this is not necessary in winter. Plants should not be divided unless absolutely necessary as many do not flower well until there are a number of growths.

Paphinia cristata

Panisea uniflora. J. Hermans

Panisea albiflora. H. Oakeley

Paphiopedilum acmodontum

Schoser ex M. W. Wood

Leaves mottled, to 18 × 4 cm. Inflorescence to 25 cm tall, 1-flowered. Flowers ca. 7 cm across; dorsal sepal white with vertical purple stripes, synsepal white with green and purple stripes; petals spreading, green and white, pink towards the apex, with purple veins and spots in the basal half; pouch bronze or olive green.

Terrestrial, to 1000 m (3300 ft.)

Philippines

SIMILAR SPECIES: *Paphiopedilum argus* (Reichenbach f.) Stein, also from the Philippines, has larger flowers with more heavily-spotted petals.

Paphiopedilum appletonianum (Gower) Rolfe

Leaves to 25 × 4 cm, obscurely mottled above, tinged with purple at base below. Inflorescence to 48 cm tall, 1-flowered, rarely 2-flowered. Flowers 6–10 cm across; sepals greenish white or light green with darker green veining; petals spathulate, twisted in apical half, green and purple with maroon-black spots on basal half; lip yellow-ochre to light purple with darker veins.

Terrestrial on forest floor, 450–1500 m (1500–5000 ft.)

China, Cambodia, Laos, Thailand, Vietnam

Paphiopedilum armeniacum

S. C. Chen & F. Y. Liu

Rhizome long with growths about 5 cm apart. Leaves to 15 × 2.5 cm, strongly mottled with light and dark bluish green above, heavily spotted with purple below. Inflorescence to 60 cm tall, 1-flowered. Flowers 6–11 cm across, bright golden yellow, the staminode with red veins; lip almost globose. Flowers autumn or early spring.

Terrestrial and lithophytic in open woodland on limestone soil, 1200–2050 m (4000–6700 ft.)

China (western Yunnan)

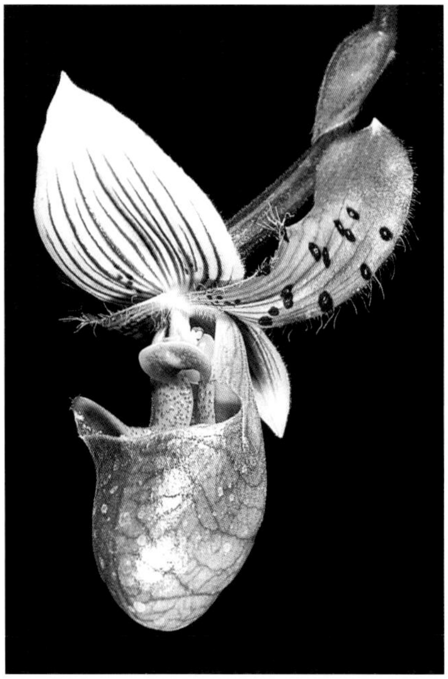

Paphiopedilum argus

Paphiopedilum bellatulum

(Reichenbach f.) Stein

Leaves to 14 × 5 cm, dark green with pale mottling above, purple-spotted below. Inflorescence to 5 cm long, 1-flowered, occasionally 2-flowered. Flowers 5.5–8 cm across, slightly bell-shaped, white or creamy yellow with many large, maroon-purple spots; lip relatively small, ellipsoid.

Terrestrial or lithophytic in shade on steep limestone slopes, 900–1500 m (3000–5000 ft.)

China, Myanmar, Thailand

Paphiopedilum callosum

(Reichenbach f.) Stein

Leaves to 20 × 5 cm, mottled pale and dark green. Inflorescence to 40 cm tall, purple with purple hairs, 1-flowered, occasionally 2-flowered. Flowers 8–11 cm across; sepals white veined with purple and green, petals deflexed, white to yellow-green, pink towards the apex, with purple and green veins and with maroon warts mainly on the upper margin; pouch green flushed maroon; staminode green, flushed with purple.

Var. *sublaeve* (Reichenbach f.) P. J. Cribb has smaller flowers with relatively broader petals. Var. *potentianum* (O. Gruss & J. Röth) P. J. Cribb has a narrower dorsal sepal and petals without warts on the upper margins.

Terrestrial in leaf litter in forest, 300–1300 m (1000–4300 ft.)

Cambodia, Laos, Malaya, Thailand

SIMILAR SPECIES: *Paphiopedilum barbatum* (Lindley) Pfitzer from Malaysia, Penang Island, and Sumatra has more richly colored flowers. *Paphiopedilum lawrenceanum* (Reichenbach f.) Pfitzer from Borneo has more strongly tessellated leaves and larger, more richly colored flowers.

Paphiopedilum charlesworthii

(Rolfe) Pfitzer

Leaves to 15 × 3 cm, plain green above, purple-spotted near the base below. Inflorescence 8–15 cm long, 1-flowered. Flowers to 8 cm across; dorsal sepal pink with darker veins, rarely white; petals yellow-green with red-brown reticulate veining; pouch pinkish brown with darker veins; staminode white. The pink dorsal sepal is very distinctive. One collector comments that the temperature in the area in Myanmar where this species grows falls to below freezing in winter.

Lithophytic and terrestrial on limestone hills, 1200–1600 m (4000–5300 ft.)

China, Myanmar, Thailand

Paphiopedilum concolor

(Bateman) Pfitzer

Leaves to 14 × 4 cm, mottled dark and light green above, purple-spotted below. Inflorescence to 8 cm long, 1- or 2-flowered. Flowers 5.5–7 cm across, yellow or cream covered with fine purple dots; lip ellipsoid.

Terrestrial in sandy places and on limestone hills, 90–1000 m (300–3300 ft.)

Southwestern China, Cambodia, Laos, Myanmar, Thailand, Vietnam

SIMILAR SPECIES: *Paphiopedilum niveum* (Reichenbach f.) Stein, from northern Malaysia and southern Thailand,

Paphiopedilum appletonianum

Paphiopedilum armeniacum

Paphiopedilum barbatum

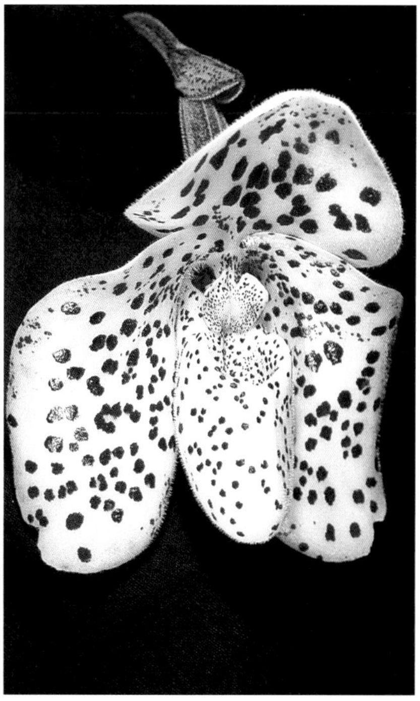

Paphiopedilum bellatulum

where it grows on limestone from sea level to 200 m (660 ft.), has a taller inflorescence (15–20 cm), smaller, white flowers only lightly spotted with purple, and a smaller lip.

Paphiopedilum dayanum

(Lindley) Stein

Leaves to 21 × 5 cm, strongly tessellated with dark green, the base blue-green or yellow-green. Inflorescence to 5 cm long, purple with purple hairs, 1-flowered. Flowers to 15.5 cm across; sepals white with green veins, the dorsal sepal relatively long and narrow; petals purplish, lip deep maroon-purple; staminode green with darker veins.

Terrestrial in leaf litter, 300–1450 m (1000–4800 ft.)

Borneo (Sabah)

SIMILAR SPECIES: *Paphiopedilum javanicum* (Reinwardt ex Lindley) Pfitzer from Borneo (Sabah, Sarawak), Java, Bali, Flores, and Sumatra, where it grows terrestrially in deep shade of forest at 950–2000 m (3100–6600 ft.), has smaller flowers differing in color and shape of sepals, petals, and staminode.

Paphiopedilum delenatii

Guillaumin

Leaves to 11 × 4 cm, mottled dark and pale green above, purple-spotted below. Inflorescence to 22 cm tall, 1- or 2-flowered. Flowers 7–8 cm across, pale to deep pink, the pouch usually darker, with red and yellow markings on the staminode. This species grows in the wild on acid soil and so should not have dolomite added to the compost. Flowering in early spring.

Terrestrial in crevices on steep, granite slopes under open woodland, 800–1500 m (2640–5000 ft.)

Vietnam

Paphiopedilum druryi

(Beddome) Stein

Plants with creeping rhizomes, forming large clumps. Leaves to 30 × 4 cm, light green with darker veins. Inflorescence to 25 cm long, peduncle purple, 1-flowered. Flowers 6–6.5 cm across, yellow or greenish yellow, the dorsal sepal and petals with a central maroon line; pouch yellow.

Terrestrial or lithophytic in full sun or light shade on rocky slopes, 1400–1600 m (4600–5300 ft.)

Southern India

Paphiopedilum fairrieanum

(Lindley) Stein

Leaves to 28 × 3 cm, green, faintly mottled with darker green. Inflorescence with purplish hairs, to 45 cm long, 1-flowered, occasionally 2-flowered. Flowers variable in size, usually 9–10 cm across; sepals and petals white, veined with green and purple, the petals deflexed, curving up again at the tips; lip yellowish veined and flushed with purple, staminode yellow with green and purple veins.

Terrestrial and lithophytic on limestone outcrops on grassy slopes, 1400–2200 m (4600–7260 ft.)

Bhutan, Sikkim, northeastern India

Paphiopedilum godefroyae

(Godefroy-Lebeuf) Stein

Leaves to 14 × 3 cm, mottled dark and light green above, usually purple-spotted below. Inflorescence to 8 cm tall, purple, pubescent, 1- or 2-flowered. Flowers 4.5–9 cm across, white or cream, usually purple-spotted, lip often with fewer spots than the sepals and petals.

Terrestrial and lithophytic on limestone, 0–100 m (330 ft.)

Thailand

Paphiopedilum henryanum

Braem

SYN. *Paphiopedilum dollii* Lückel

Leaves to 17 × 2.5 cm, plain green. Inflorescence to 15 cm long, 1-flowered. Flowers 5 cm across; sepals yellow with dark maroon spots, with purple hairs on the outside; petals yellow and purple with maroon spots mainly in the basal half; pouch purple-pink with a yellow margin; staminode yellow with a purple spot in the middle. Flowers autumn.

Terrestrial on slopes and cliffs, 1000–1200 m (3300–4000 ft.)

China, Vietnam

Paphiopedilum hirsutissimum

(Lindley ex Hooker) Stein

Leaves narrowly strap-shaped, to 45 × 2 cm, green, with some purple spotting underneath. Inflorescence to 25 cm long, densely covered with long hairs, 1-flowered. Flowers 11–14 cm across; sepals pale yellow or greenish, heavily flushed with brown; petals pubescent, yellow with purple-brown spots in the basal half, purple-pink in the apical half, partly twisted in the middle,

Paphiopedilum concolor

Paphiopedilum niveum

Paphiopedilum javanicum

Paphiopedilum fairrieanum

Paphiopedilum delenatii

Paphiopedilum godefroyae

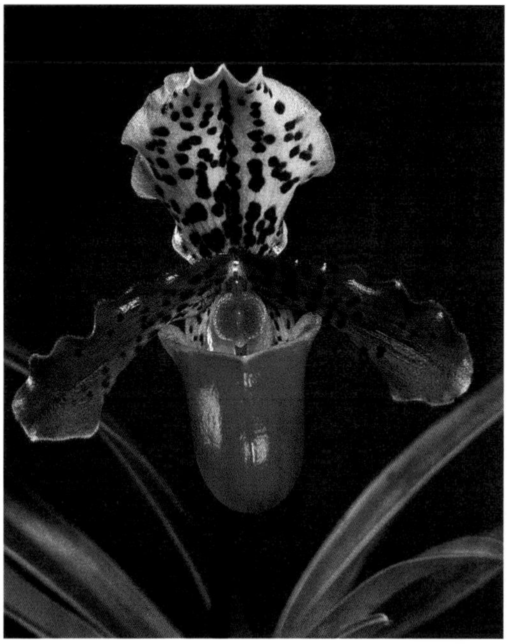

Paphiopedilum henryanum. E. la Croix

Paphiopedilum hirsutissimum

the lower margins strongly undulate; pouch pale yellow or pale green with some purple dots; staminode pale yellow, glossy brown in the center, with purple spots towards the base.

Var. *esquirolei* (Schlechter) Karasawa & K. Saito (syn. *Paphiopedilum esquirolei* Schlechter) has large flowers, 13–16 cm across. It comes from China, Thailand, Laos, and Vietnam, where it grows on limestone cliffs at 450–1800 m (1500–6000 ft.).

Epiphytic or lithophytic, 200–1800 m (660–6000 ft.)

Northeastern India, Myanmar

Paphiopedilum insigne (Wallich ex Lindley) Pfitzer

Leaves to 32 × 3 cm, green above, purple spotted near base below. Inflorescence to 25 cm tall, 1-flowered. Flowers 7–12 cm across; dorsal sepal pale green with raised maroon spots inside and a white margin, synsepal green with brown spots; petals yellow-brown with red-brown veining; pouch yellow flushed and veined with purple-brown; staminode yellow.

This is a variable species and several color forms have been described, including var. *sanderianum* Rolfe with bright yellow and white flowers and var. *sanderae* Reichenbach f. with green-veined yellow flowers.

Terrestrial and lithophytic on limestone outcrops near rivers, 1000–1500 m (3300–5000 ft.)

Northeastern India

SIMILAR SPECIES: *Paphiopedilum exul* (Ridley) Rolfe from Thailand, where it grows as a lithophyte or terrestrial near the sea at altitudes of 0–50 m (165 ft.), has a shorter inflorescence and a smaller flower with the synsepal almost as large as the dorsal sepal. *Paphiopedilum gratrixianum* (Masters) Rolfe from Laos and Vietnam also tends to have smaller flowers than *P. insigne* with fewer and larger spots on the dorsal sepal.

Paphiopedilum lowii (Lindley) Stein

Leaves to 40 × 6 cm, linear to strap-shaped, plain green. Flowers 9–16.5 cm across; sepals pale green, the dorsal with purple markings on the basal half; petals spathulate, twisted in the middle, yellow with maroon spots, the apical third pinkish purple; pouch yellow-brown with maroon veins.

Epiphytic, rarely lithophytic, in riverine forest and rain forest, 250–1600 m (825–5300 ft.)

Borneo, Java, peninsular Malaysia, Sulawesi, Sumatra

Paphiopedilum malipoense S. C. Chen & Z. H. Tsi

Rhizome long and creeping, leaves to 20 × 4 cm, dark green with paler mottling above, marked with purple below. Inflorescence to 30 cm long, 1-flowered. Flowers 8–12 cm across, apple-scented. Sepals and petals apple-green, striped and spotted with

Paphiopedilum insigne

Paphiopedilum gratrixianum

Paphiopedilum lowii

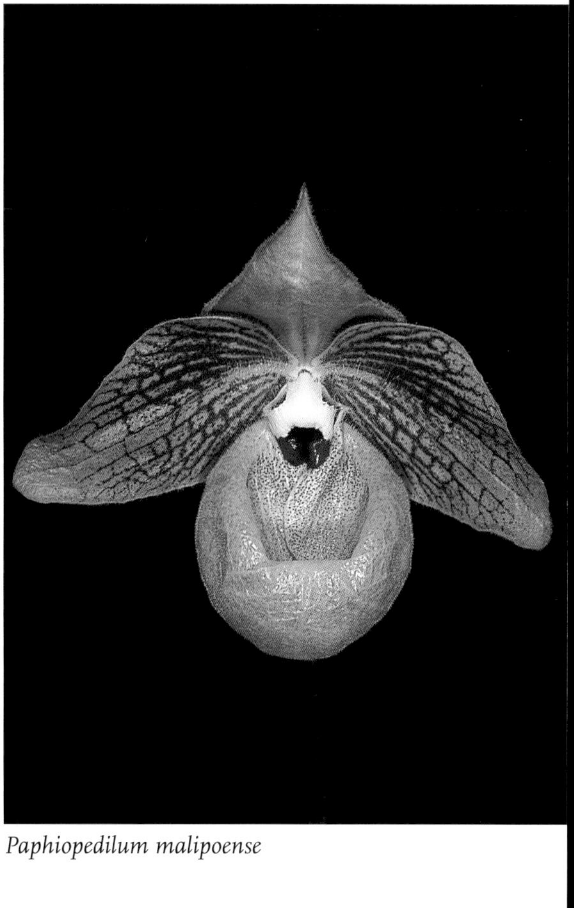

Paphiopedilum malipoense

purple; pouch gray-green with purple spots inside. Staminode white and maroon.

Var. *jackii* (H. S. Hui) Averyanov (syn. *Paphiopedilum jackii* H. S. Hua) from China differs in having narrower petals, a green lip, and a white staminode with a green central mark. Var. *hiepii* (Averyanov) P. J. Cribb (syn. *P. hiepii* Averyanov) from Vietnam has longer and narrower sepals and petals, a smaller lip, and a white staminode with a purple center.

Terrestrial in mixed forest on limestone, 500–1300 m (1650–4300 ft.)

China, Vietnam

Paphiopedilum micranthum T. Tang & F. T. Wang

Leaves to 15 × 5 cm, mottled dark and light green above, purple-spotted below. Inflorescence to 20 cm tall, 1-flowered. Flowers 6–9 cm across, thin-textured; sepals and petals yellow-pink veined with red-purple; lip large, very inflated, pink, paler at the base, with purple spots inside; staminode vertically folded, white and yellow, spotted red.

Terrestrial in deep shade in thin soil on limestone hills, 450–1550 m (1500–5100 ft.)

Southwestern China

Paphiopedilum parishii (Reichenbach f.) Stein

Leaves strap-shaped, to 45 × 7.5 cm, green. Inflorescence arching, 30–50 cm long, 2- to 9-flowered. Flowers 9–10.5 cm across; sepals cream to yellow-green with darker veins; petals ± pendent, linear, the basal part green with dark maroon spots on the lower margin, the apical half maroon-black, spirally twisted.

Epiphytic or sometimes lithophytic on mossy branches and boulders, 1200–2200 m (4000–7260 ft.)

Southwestern China, Myanmar, Thailand

Paphiopedilum philippinense (Reichenbach f.) Stein

Leaves strap-shaped, V-shaped in cross-section, plain green, to 50 × 5.5 cm. Inflorescence to 50 cm long, 2- to 5-flowered. Flowers to 8.5 cm across; sepals white with maroon stripes; petals long and tapering, 6–17 cm long, 5–7 mm wide, twisted, white or yellow at the base, then maroon with dark marginal warts; pouch and staminode yellow.

Terrestrial or lithophytic on limestone, often in an open situation, 0–500 m (1650 ft.)

Borneo, Philippines

Paphiopedilum primulinum M. W. Wood & P. Taylor

Leaves oblong, to 17 × 4 cm, green. Inflorescence to ca. 40 cm long, with many flowers open in succession. Flowers 6.5–8 cm across, pale to bright yellow with green sepals; petals ciliate on margins; staminode green.

Var. *purpurascens* (M. W. Wood) P. J. Cribb has purple-spotted petals and a purple-flushed lip.

Lithophytic in scrub on limestone, 0–500 m (1650 ft.)

Northern Sumatra

Paphiopedilum rothschildianum (Reichenbach f.) Stein

Leaves linear, to 60 × 5 cm, plain green. Inflorescence to ca. 50 cm long, 2- to 6-flowered. Flowers 14–30 cm across; sepals cream or yellow with maroon veins; petals cream or yellow, marked and striped with maroon-brown, held horizontally, 8–14 cm long, the margins hairy; pouch yellow, flushed with purple. This spectacular species is known from only three sites and is extinct from one of them, thanks to overcollection and habitat destruction. It is a parent of many fine hybrids.

Terrestrial or lithophytic on ledges of limestone cliffs, in shaded and open situations, 600–1200 m (2000–4000 ft.)

Borneo (Sabah, Mt. Kinabalu)

SIMILAR SPECIES: *Paphiopedilum adductum* Asher from the Philippines has decurved rather than spreading petals and a small staminode that does not completely cover the stigma.

Paphiopedilum sanderianum (Reichenbach f.) Stein

Leaves linear, to 45 × 5 cm, glossy green. Inflorescence ± horizontal, 2- to 5-flowered. Flowers ca. 7 cm across and 95 cm long; sepals yellow with maroon stripes; petals cream or yellow, covered with maroon warts and hairs, ribbonlike, pendent, spiraling, to 90 cm long; lip yellow, veined and flushed with brown. This extraordinary species has been overcollected and is now rare in the wild.

Lithophytic on vertical limestone cliffs, 50–900 m (165–3000 ft.)

Borneo (Sarawak)

Paphiopedilum spicerianum (Reichenbach f.) Pfitzer

Leaves to 30 × 6 cm, dark green, purple-spotted at the base on the underside. Inflorescence to 35 cm tall, 1- or 2-flowered. Flowers 5–7 cm across; dorsal sepal white, midvein maroon, curving forwards, the margins recurved so that it lies ± horizontally over the flower; synsepal greenish white; petals yellow-green, midvein purplish, the upper edge very undulate; pouch green flushed with brown; staminode white flushed with purple, yellow in center.

Lithophytic or terrestrial on limestone outcrops and cliffs, 300–1300 m (1000–4300 ft.)

Northeastern India, northwestern Myanmar

Paphiopedilum sukhakulii Schoser & Senghas

Leaves to 13 × 4.5 cm, mottled dark green and yellow-green. Inflorescence

Paphiopedilum micranthum

Paphiopedilum philippinense

Paphiopedilum primulinum

Paphiopedilum rothschildianum

1-flowered, purple covered with fine white hairs. Flower 11–14 cm across; sepals white with green veins, purple-spotted at base; petals green, densely spotted with maroon, the edges ciliate, held ± horizontally; pouch green, veined and flushed with maroon-purple.

Terrestrial in humus-rich soil in shade of forest, often by streams, on mountain slopes to 1000 m (3300 ft.)

Northeastern Thailand

SIMILAR SPECIES: *Paphiopedilum wardii* Summerhayes from northern Myanmar and possibly China has leaves mottled with purple on the underside and smaller flowers with deflexed, purplish petals and a differently shaped staminode.

Paphiopedilum venustum

(Wallich ex Sims) Pfitzer

Leaves to 25 × 5.5 cm, mottled dark and gray-green, purple-spotted below. Inflorescence to 24 cm long, 1-flowered, occasionally 2-flowered. Flowers 8–9 cm across; sepals white with green veins; petals white, veined green, flushed with purple towards the tips, with a few large, dark maroon warts; pouch yellow with green veins, flushed with purple. This was the first species of *Paphiopedilum* to be introduced to cultivation; it was described and illustrated in *Curtis's Botanical Magazine* as *Cypripedium venustum* in 1820.

Terrestrial on cliff ledges and in leaf litter under trees in very wet areas, 60–1350 m (200–4500 ft.)

Northeastern India, Bhutan, Sikkim, Bangladesh

Paphiopedilum victoria-regina

(Sander) M. W. Wood

SYN. *Paphiopedilum chamberlainianum* (Sander) Stein, *P. kalinae* Braem

Leaves oblong, to 30 × 10 cm, green. Inflorescence arching, to 60 cm long, with many flowers open in succession. Flowers 8–10 cm across; sepals greenish with purple veins, the dorsal flushed with purple at the base; petals yellow blotched with dark maroon, horizontal, twisted, the margins ciliate; pouch pink with purple spots, the margin white.

Lithophytic on cliffs, 800–1600 m (2640–5280 ft.)

Sumatra

SIMILAR SPECIES: *Paphiopedilum victoria-mariae* (Sander ex Masters) Rolfe also from Sumatra, where it grows at 1500–2000 m (5000–6600 ft.), has leaves mottled with darker green, flushed with purple below, flowers in which the dorsal sepal lacks deep maroon stripes, petals without purple blotches, and a lip lacking spots.

Paphiopedilum vietnamense

Gruss & Perner

Leaves to 20 × 7 cm, glossy, mottled dark green and gray-green above, flushed with purple below. Inflorescence to 25 cm long, 1- or 2-flowered. Flowers 10–12 cm across; sepals white or pink flushed with purple-pink towards the apex; petals white, pink or purple, flushed with purple in the apical two-thirds; pouch white, pink or purple with a purple blotch on the front, spotted with purple inside; staminode yellow with a white margin and green center. This beautiful species was described in 1999.

Lithophytic or terrestrial in wet evergreen forest on limestone, 350–550 m (1150–1800 ft.)

Vietnam

Paphiopedilum villosum

(Lindley) Stein

Leaves to 42 × 4 cm, green above, the underside purple-spotted at the base. Inflorescence to 24 cm long, 1-flowered, the peduncle with long purple hairs. Flowers 7.5–13.5 cm across. Dorsal sepal green, maroon in the center, the margin white; synsepal pale green; petals red-brown with a central purplish stripe; pouch yellow-ochre, flushed with reddish pink; staminode yellow with a green or yellow central knob.

Var. *boxallii* (Reichenbach f.) Pfitzer from Myanmar has large purple spots on the dorsal sepal and petals marked with purple. Var. *annamense* Rolfe has smaller flowers and narrower leaves.

Epiphytic, rarely lithophytic, in mixed forest, 1100–2000 m (3600–6600 ft.)

Northeastern India, Myanmar, Thailand

Papilionanthe Schlechter

TRIBE: Vandeae

SUBTRIBE: Aeridinae

ETYMOLOGY: From Greek *papilio*, butterfly, and *anthe*, flower

DISTRIBUTION: 11 species from India to China and Indonesia

Monopodial epiphytes or terrestrials related to *Vanda* with erect or scrambling stems, sometimes branched at the base. Leaves distichous, terete, the upper surface slightly grooved. Inflorescences axillary, 1- to several-flowered. Flowers large, showy; sepals and petals free, spreading, subsimilar; lip trilobed with a conical spur.

Species of *Papilionanthe* have been widely used in hybridization but are still known as *Vanda* for registration purposes. *Papilionanthe hookeriana* and *P. teres* are the parents of *Vanda* Miss Joaquim, the national flower of Singapore.

CULTIVATION: Plants can be grown in baskets or in beds with poles to climb up, in a coarse epiphyte mix. They require full sunlight and, for most species, warm conditions with plenty of water and fertilizer. They tend to flower off and on throughout the year.

Papilionanthe hookeriana

(Reichenbach f.) Schlechter

SYN. *Vanda hookeriana* Reichenbach f.

Stems erect or scrambling, to ca. 2 m long. Leaves to 10 cm long. Inflorescence to 30 cm long, 2- to 12-flowered. Flowers 4–6 cm across, sepals and petals white to pale

Paphiopedilum sukhakulii

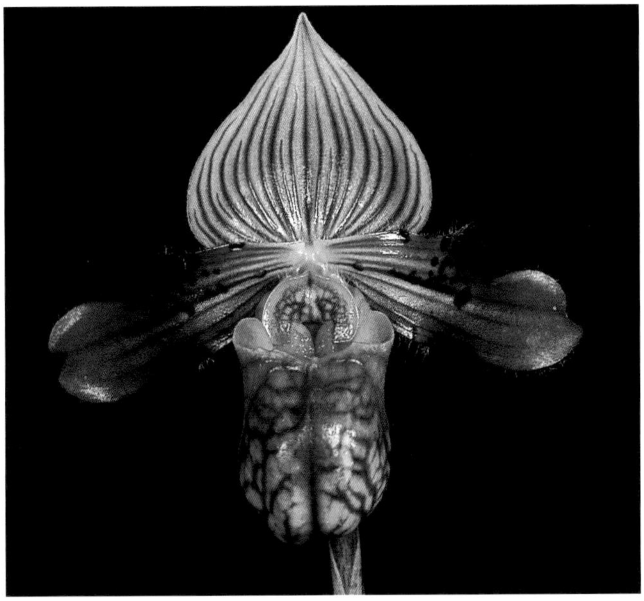

Paphiopedilum venustum

Paphiopedilum villosum

Paphiopedilum victoria-regina

Paphiopedilum wardii

mauve, lip pink, heavily blotched with red-purple.

Epiphytic, often on *Pandanus*, or lithophytic in low-lying, swampy areas

Indochina to Sumatra and Borneo

Papilionanthe teres (Roxburgh) Schlechter

SYN. *Vanda teres* (Roxburgh) Lindley

Stems scrambling, branched, more than 1 m long. Leaves fleshy, to 18 × 0.8 cm. Inflorescence 15–30 cm long, 2- to 6-flowered. Flowers 5 cm across, sepals and petals white tinged with pink or magenta, lip purple-red, yellow-brown at the base, lip midlobe fan-shaped.

Epiphytic on tree trunks in forest and at forest edge, ca. 600 m (2000 ft.)

China, India, Laos, Myanmar, Thailand, Vietnam

Papilionanthe vandarum (Reichenbach f.) Garay

Stems to 2 m long, slender, forming tangled clumps. Leaves to 12 cm long with a sharp point. Inflorescence to 8 cm long, 1- to 5-flowered. Flowers night-scented, to 5 cm across, white, flushed with light purple at the base, sepals and petals and lip with undulate margins; spur slender, to 2 cm long. This species needs cool conditions in cultivation.

Epiphytic in woodland, 1600–1750 m (5300–5800 ft.)

India to southern China

Papperitzia Reichenbach f.

TRIBE: Maxillarieae

SUBTRIBE: Oncidiinae

ETYMOLOGY: Named for William Papperitz, a friend of H. G. Reichenbach

DISTRIBUTION: 1 species in Mexico

Dwarf plants with small pseudobulbs covered in sheaths, 1-leafed at apex. Inflorescence basal, erect or arching, several-flowered. Dorsal sepal free, forming a hood, lateral sepals joined; petals free, pointing forwards.

CULTIVATION: Requires intermediate conditions, light shade, good air movement, and high humidity throughout the year. Plants are usually mounted and should not be allowed to dry out. Like many twig epiphytes, they tend to be short-lived in cultivation, as is probably the case in the wild.

Papperitzia leiboldii (Reichenbach f.) Reichenbach f.

Pseudobulbs clustered, laterally flattened, to 1 cm tall. Leaves to 7 cm tall, linear, stiff-textured. Flowers ca. 15 mm across, pale green, the lip whitish; lip hairy inside, saccate at base, with a trilobed callus.

Twig epiphyte in mountain rain forest, 600–900 m (2000–3000 ft.)

Mexico

Paraphalaenopsis A. D. Hawkes

TRIBE: Vandeae

SUBTRIBE: Aeridinae

ETYMOLOGY: From Greek *para*, beside, and *Phalaenopsis*

DISTRIBUTION: 4 species and 1 natural hybrid in Borneo

Large, short-stemmed monopodial plants, usually pendent. Leaves cylindrical, grooved on the upper surface. Inflorescences axillary, few- to several-flowered. Flowers showy; sepals and petals spreading; lip trilobed, side lobes erect, midlobe narrow with a broader, bilobed or forked apex. Pollinia 2.

Species of *Paraphalaenopsis* have been used in hybridization. Until recently, they were registered as *Phalaenopsis*.

CULTIVATION: Plants require similar warm, humid conditions to *Phalaenopsis*, but with rather more light, although they should not be exposed to direct sunlight. Because of the long, pendent leaves, they are better grown mounted or in baskets rather than in pots.

Paraphalaenopsis denevei (J. J. Smith) A. D. Hawkes

SYN. *Phalaenopsis denevei* J. J. Smith

Leaves 3–6, to 70 × 1 cm. Inflorescence 3- to 15-flowered. Flowers ca. 5 cm across, yellow-green or yellow-brown; lip white with red dots.

Epiphytic in low-altitude riverine forest

Borneo (Kalimantan)

Paraphalaenopsis labukensis Shim, A. L. Lamb & C. L. Chan

Leaves to 2 m long. Inflorescence to 15-flowered. Flowers scented, reddish brown margined with yellow.

Epiphytic in hill forest, 500–1000 m (1650–3300 ft.)

Borneo (Sabah)

Paraphalaenopsis laycockii (M. R. Henderson) A. D. Hawkes

SYN. *Phalaenopsis laycockii* M. R. Henderson

Leaves to 1 m long. Inflorescence densely to 15-flowered. Flowers 7–8 cm across, pale lilac; lip marked with yellow.

Epiphytic in lowland and hill forest

Borneo (Kalimantan)

Paraphalaenopsis serpentilingua (J. J. Smith) A. D. Hawkes

SYN. *Phalaenopsis serpentilingua* J. J. Smith

Leaves to 30 cm long. Inflorescence erect, to 7-flowered. Flowers 2–3 cm across, white tinged with lilac-pink; lip yellow with purple bands.

Lithophytic on mossy rocks at low altitudes

Borneo (Kalimantan)

Pecteilis Rafinesque

TRIBE: Orchideae

SUBTRIBE: Orchidinae

ETYMOLOGY: From Greek *pectein*, a comb, referring to the deeply cut side lobes of the lip in some species

DISTRIBUTION: 5 species in tropical Asia

Terrestrials with large tubers. Leaves on stem, sometimes also in a basal rosette. Flowers showy, mostly white; sepals entire, forming a hood over

Papilionanthe teres

Papilionanthe vandarum

Papperitzia leiboldii

Paraphalaenopsis labukensis. H. Oakeley

the column; petals smaller, entire; lip decurved, trilobed, side lobes usually deeply fringed, midlobe entire; spur pendent, long. Anthers widely spaced, stigmas sessile.

Pecteilis is very close to *Habenaria* (and several species shuttle back and forth between the 2 genera), but it differs in details of the column.

CULTIVATION: Species of *Pecteilis* can be grown in a free-draining terrestrial compost in cool to intermediate conditions. They die back after flowering and should be kept almost, but not completely dry. If dry for too long, the tubers shrivel.

Pecteilis hawkesiana (King & Pantling) C. S. Kumar

SYN. *Pecteilis sagarikii* Seidenfaden

DUCK ORCHID

Leaves in basal rosette, ovate, to 12 × 9 cm. Inflorescence to 25 cm tall, few-flowered. Flowers white or cream, scented; sepals and petals suberect; lip obscurely trilobed at base, the lobes not fringed, midlobe 2–5 cm long, usually bright yellow, sometimes cream; spur 3–5 cm long, slender, pendent. Flowering in autumn.

Terrestrial

Myanmar, Thailand

Pecteilis susannae (Linnaeus) Rafinesque

SYN. *Habenaria susannae* (Linnaeus) R. Brown

Leaves on stem, to 12 × 5 cm. Inflorescence to 75 cm tall, few-flowered. Flowers white, night-scented, 6–7 cm long; sepals and petals suberect; lip trilobed at base, side lobes triangular, fringed; spur 9–14 cm long. Flowering summer.

Terrestrial in grassland, 1000–2000 m (3300–6600 ft.)

China, Malesia

Pelatantheria Ridley

TRIBE: Vandeae

SUBTRIBE: Aeridinae

ETYMOLOGY: From Greek *pelates*, approaching, and *anthera*, anther; the reference is obscure

DISTRIBUTION: 7 species in Asia from India to Malesia

Monopodial epiphytes or lithophytes with long, slender, branched, leafy stems. Leaves oblong. Inflorescences lateral, short, unbranched. Flowers small to medium; sepals and petals subsimilar; lip spurred with a callus in the mouth of the spur, trilobed; side lobes joined to column, midlobe flat, with a toothed callus. Column short, pollinia 2.

CULTIVATION: Grow in pots in a medium bark-based compost, with a moss pole to support the stem and for the roots to cling to. Plants require intermediate conditions, moderate shade, and high humidity.

Pelatantheria rivesii (Guillaumin) Tang & F. T. Wang

Stem ca. 1 m long, leafy, with many roots. Leaves to 4 × 1.5 cm. Inflorescence 2- to 7-flowered. Flowers small, less than 1 cm across; sepals and petals yellow-green with 2 or 3 maroon stripes, lip white, the midlobe pink.

Epiphytic or lithophytic in evergreen forest, 700–1100 m (2300–3600 ft.)

China, Laos, Vietnam

Peristeria Hooker

TRIBE: Maxillarieae

SUBTRIBE: Coeliopsidinae

ETYMOLOGY: From Greek *peristeria*, a dove, referring to the appearance of the column

DISTRIBUTION: 11 species in Central and South America and Trinidad

Large epiphytes or terrestrials related to *Acineta*; pseudobulbs fleshy, 1- to several-leaved. Leaves large, petiolate, plicate. Inflorescences basal, erect or pendent, unbranched, many-flowered, the flowers open in succession. Flowers showy, fleshy, almost globose, scented; sepals and petals ± orbicular, the petals smaller, lateral sepals joined at the base; lip trilobed, continuous with the column, side lobes erect, midlobe hinged at base. Column short, stout, lacking a foot; pollinia 2.

CULTIVATION: Grow in intermediate to warm conditions, in shade, with water throughout the year. Species with pendent inflorescences should be grown in baskets, in a standard epiphyte mixture. *Peristeria elata*, the only species with an erect inflorescence, can be grown in a large pot, in a well-drained terrestrial compost.

Peristeria elata Hooker

DOVE ORCHID; HOLY GHOST ORCHID

Pseudobulbs to 12 × 8 cm, 3- to 5-leaved at apex. Leaves 30–100 × 6–12 cm. Inflorescence 70–130 cm long, erect, many-flowered, with 2–4 flowers open together. Flowers 5 cm across, cup-shaped, strongly scented, waxy, white; lip side lobes spotted with red.

Terrestrial in rain forest, often among rocks, 0–1300 m (4300 ft.)

Costa Rica, Panama (national flower), Colombia, Ecuador, Venezuela

Peristeria elata

Pecteilis hawkesiana, showing yellow midlobe. R. Parsons

Pecteilis hawkesiana, showing white midlobe. P. O'Byrne

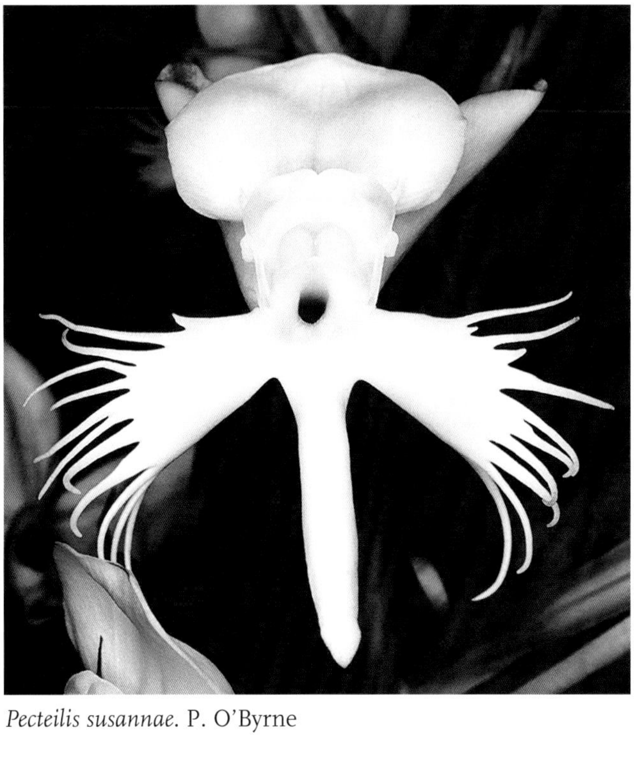

Pecteilis susannae. P. O'Byrne

Pelatantheria rivesii

Pescatoria Reichenbach f.

SYN. *Bollea* Reichenbach f.
TRIBE: Maxillarieae
SUBTRIBE: Zygopetalinae
ETYMOLOGY: Named for V. Pescatore, a French orchid grower
DISTRIBUTION: 25 species in Central and South America

Epiphytes related to *Zygopetalum*, lacking pseudobulbs. Leaves plicate, thin-textured, distichous, forming a fan. Inflorescences arising from axils of basal sheaths, 1-flowered, short, erect or arching. Flowers showy, often scented; sepals fleshy, dorsal sepal free, laterals joined at the base; petals similar to sepals but narrower; lip fleshy, trilobed, narrowing to a basal claw continuous with the column-foot; side lobes small, midlobe convex, disc with a prominent callus of several keels. Pollinia 4.

The name is sometimes spelled *Pescatorea*, but Reichenbach used *Pescatoria* in his original description.

CULTIVATION: Plants are usually grown in pots in a medium, free-draining compost. They require intermediate conditions, moderate to heavy shade, good ventilation, and high humidity all year round. They should not be allowed to dry out completely.

Pescatoria cerina (Lindley & Paxton) Reichenbach f.

Large plants. Leaves to 60 × 5 cm. Inflorescence to 10 cm tall. Flowers to 7 cm across, scented, sepals and petals white or pale yellow, lip yellow, the callus marked with red-brown; anther-cap violet.

Epiphytic in rain forest, 700–1600 m (2300–5300 ft.)

Costa Rica, Panama

SIMILAR SPECIES: *Pescatoria bella* Reichenbach f. from Colombia has white and violet flowers to 9 cm across.

Pescatoria coelestis (Reichenbach f.) Dressler

SYN. *Bollea coelestis* (Reichenbach f.) Reichenbach f.

Pescatoria violacea

Leaves 6–10, forming a fan, to 30 × 5 cm, pale green, thin-textured. Inflorescence to 16 cm long. Flowers 8–10 cm across, waxy, long-lasting, scented, violet, cream at the tips and at the base; sepals and petals obovate, lip recurved with a yellow callus. Column deep violet.

Epiphytic in cloud forest, 900–1900 m (3000–6300 ft.)

Colombia

SIMILAR SPECIES: *Pescatoria violacea* (Lindley) Dressler (syn. *Bollea violacea* (Lindley) Reichenbach f.) from northern South America to Brazil has violet flowers with a purple callus and narrower sepals and petals. *Pescatoria lawrenceana* (Reichenbach f.) Dressler (syn. *Bollea lawrenceana* Reichenbach f.) from Colombia and Ecuador has inflorescences to 12 cm long, cream flowers to 8 cm across blotched with violet towards the tips, and a white column with a violet anther.

Pescatoria hemixantha (Reichenbach f.) Dressler

SYN. *Bollea hemixantha* Reichenbach f.

Leaves to 30 × 4 cm, forming a fan. Flowers 7–8 cm across; sepals and petals yellowish white; lip pale yellow with a bright yellow callus. Column broad, hoodlike, white with purple marks.

Epiphytic in wet forest, 100–1300 m (330–4300 ft.)

Brazil, Colombia, Guyana, Venezuela

Pescatoria lehmannii Reichenbach f.

Leaves to 45 × 5 cm. Inflorescence to 15 cm long, often growing horizontally. Flowers 8–9 cm across, scented; sepals and petals white marked with purple or maroon; lip dark purple, the apical part with long, purple or white hairs.

Epiphytic on mossy branches in wet forest and cloud forest, 500–1350 m (1650–4500 ft.)

Ecuador

Phaius Loureiro

TRIBE: Collabieae
ETYMOLOGY: From Greek *phios*, gray, probably referring to how the flowers darken when damaged
DISTRIBUTION: About 40 species in Africa, Madagascar, Asia, Australia, and the Pacific Islands

Terrestrial plants with pseudobulbous or canelike leafy stems. Leaves large, plicate. Inflorescences basal or axillary, unbranched. Flowers often showy; sepals and petals free, similar, usually spreading; lip free or joined to column at base, simple or trilobed, with a basal spur and a keeled callus. Pollinia 8, in 2 groups of 4.

Flowers turn blue-black when damaged or as they fade, Indigo dyes have been extracted from various parts of some species.

CULTIVATION: Plants are usually easily grown in a well-drained but humus-rich compost in shaded, humid, intermediate to warm conditions. They need plenty of water and fertilizer in spring and summer while in active growth but should be kept drier in autumn and winter. Many species, particularly *Phaius tankervilleae*, do well in tropical and subtropical gardens.

Phaius flavus (Blume) Lindley

SYN. *Phaius maculatus* Lindley

Plants 40–100 cm tall. Pseudobulbs to 15 × 6 cm. Leaves 30–60 × 5–20 cm, green with yellow or white spots. Inflorescence densely many-flowered.

Pescatoria cerina

Phaius flavus

Pescatoria coelestis

Pescatoria lehmannii

Phaius tankervilleae

Flowers 6–8 cm across, yellow, occasionally white; lip trilobed with orange or brown markings; spur conical to 8 mm long.

Terrestrial or on mossy logs in scrub, 660–3350 m (2170–11,050 ft.)

India, Malaysia, Pacific Islands

Phaius tankervilleae (Banks ex l'Héritier) Blume

Large plants to 2 m tall. Pseudobulbs to 6 cm long. Leaves petiolate, 30–100 × 3–8 cm, thin-textured. Inflorescence 10- to 20-flowered. Flowers showy, 10–12.5 cm across, variable in color; sepals and petals white, yellowish, green, pink, or red, edged with yellow; lip trilobed, tubular, pink to maroon inside, yellow at base, outside white; midlobe red, orange, or pink and white; spur slender, to 15 mm long.

Terrestrial in grassland and open forest, 350–1600 m (1150–5300 ft.)

Subtropical and tropical Asia to the Pacific Islands

Phalaenopsis Blume

SYN. *Doritis* Lindley, *Kingidium* P. F. Hunt

TRIBE: Vandeae

SUBTRIBE: Aeridinae

ETYMOLOGY: From Greek *phalaina*, moth, and *opsis*, like, meaning resembling a moth

DISTRIBUTION: More than 60 species and several natural hybrids in tropical Asia to the Pacific Islands and Australia

Short-stemmed, monopodial plants, usually epiphytic but occasionally lithophytic or terrestrial. Leaves distichous, sometimes deciduous, few to several, usually broadly obovate, oval or oblong, fleshy, sometimes flushed with purple or mottled with gray or silver. Inflorescences axillary, branched or unbranched, erect, arching, or pendent, few- to many-flowered. Flowers long-lasting, usually showy, sometimes scented; sepals and petals free, spreading, subsimilar but the petals usually larger; lip trilobed, side lobes usually erect, midlobe sometimes with 2 hornlike or threadlike projections at the apex. Column stout, pollinia 2 or 4.

Species with 4 pollinia were previously included in the genera *Doritis* and *Kingidium*.

Species of *Phalaenopsis* have been widely used in hybridization and these hybrids are now probably the most widely grown orchids in the world, being increasingly sold as house plants. The earliest hybrids were derived from *Phal. amabilis* and *Phal. aphrodite* but now many other species are involved. More hybrids of *Phalaenopsis* are currently being registered than of any other orchid.

CULTIVATION: Most *Phalaenopsis* species and hybrids require intermediate to warm temperatures, moderate to heavy shade, and high humidity. They are usually grown potted in an open, bark-based compost; clear plastic pots are often used as the roots are photosynthetic. Watering should be done with care; if water lodges in the crown of the plant, it will quickly rot, particularly if temperatures are lower than ideal. Plants are free-flowering, which is part of their attraction, but do, however, need a drop in temperature of 5–8°C (10–15°F) at night to initiate flowering. Inflorescences should not be cut off when flowering is over (as long as they remain green) as they often produce a branch from a node and flower again. These orchids do very well as house plants provided they are not exposed to direct sunlight for any length of time.

Phalaenopsis amabilis (Linnaeus) Blume

SYN. *Phalaenopsis grandiflora* Lindley

Leaves glossy green, to 50 × 10 cm. Inflorescence arching, to ca. 1 m long, with or without a few branches. Flowers to 10 cm across, scented, white, sometimes flushed with pink, the lip and callus marked with red and yellow; lip clawed, midlobe cross-shaped, with 2 tendrils at the apex.

Epiphytic in forest, 0–1500 m (5000 ft.)

Malesia to Australia

SIMILAR SPECIES: *Phalaenopsis aphrodite* Reichenbach f. from Taiwan and the Philippines, has a ± triangular lip midlobe and a different callus.

Phalaenopsis amabilis

Phalaenopsis aphrodite

Phalaenopsis deliciosa

Phalaenopsis equestris

Phalaenopsis cornu-cervi

(Breda) Blume & Reichenbach f.

Stem 5–10 cm long. Leaves glossy bright green, to 22 × 4 cm. Inflorescence to 40 cm long, branched, the rachis flattened with flowers alternating, opening 1 at a time. Flowers ca. 2.5 cm across, yellow, blotched and barred with red-brown; lip midlobe yellow, anchor-shaped, side lobes mostly red-brown.

Epiphytic in lowland and riverine forest, 0–750 m (2460 ft.)

Southeast Asia

Phalaenopsis deliciosa

Reichenbach f.

SYN. *Kingidium deliciosum* (Reichenbach f.) Sweet

Leaves dark green, to 16 × 4 cm, the margins usually undulate. Inflorescence branched, to 20 cm long, many-flowered. Flowers 1.5–2 cm across; sepals and petals white or yellow, sometimes flushed with pink at the base; lip rose-pink with darker veining, saccate at the base; midlobe wedge-shaped, emarginate. Pollinia 4.

Epiphytic in lowland, riverine forest, to 600 m (2000 ft.)

India, Malesia

Phalaenopsis equestris

(Schauer) Reichenbach f.

Leaves ± oblong, to 20 × 6.5 cm, dark green sometimes flushed with purple below. Inflorescence arched, to 30 cm long, sometimes branched, densely many-flowered. Flowers to 4 cm across, variable in both size and color; sepals and petals usually white or pale pink flushed with deeper pink, lip deep pink or purple-red, the callus white or yellow. Among others, a pure white form exists (forma *alba*), also one that is white with a yellow lip (f. *aurea*).

Epiphytic in forest, 0–300 m (1000 ft.)

Taiwan, Philippines

Phalaenopsis cornu-cervi

Phalaenopsis fasciata

Phalaenopsis gigantea

Phalaenopsis fasciata

Reichenbach f.

Leaves bright green, to 20 × 6 cm. Inflorescence erect or arching, longer than the leaves. Flowers to 4 cm across, fleshy, waxy, scented; sepals and petals yellow heavily barred with red-brown; lip white, side lobes orange, apex of midlobe pink to magenta.

Epiphytic in forest, 0–300 m (1000 ft.)

Philippines

Phalaenopsis gigantea J. J. Smith

Leaves 5–6, pendent, to 68 × 25 cm. Inflorescence pendent, sometimes with a few branches, to 40 cm long. Flowers to 5 cm across, scented; sepals and petals cream to pale yellow, heavily barred with maroon-brown; lip white, midlobe with 6 longitudinal purple stripes.

Epiphytic in lowland and hill forest, 0–900 m (3000 ft.)

Borneo

Phalaenopsis lobbii

(Reichenbach f.) H. Sweet

A dwarf species. Leaves to 13 × 5 cm. Inflorescence erect, to 10 cm long, several-flowered. Flowers 1.5–2 cm across; lip white, midlobe with 2 broad, red-brown vertical stripes. This small species is often mounted.

Epiphytic in lowland, evergreen forest, 350–1200 m (1150–4000 ft.)

India, Myanmar, Vietnam

Phalaenopsis lueddemanniana

Reichenbach f.

Leaves to 30 × 9 cm. Inflorescence erect or arching, often branched, to 30 cm long. Flowers fleshy, scented, long-lasting, 4–6 cm across, variable in color; sepals and petals usually white, barred with magenta or purple-brown; lip carmine red, yellow at the base, with papillae at the junction of the lobes, side lobes erect, midlobe oblong, abruptly constricted near the apex.

Epiphytic in forest, to 500 m (1650 ft.)

Philippines

SIMILAR SPECIES: *Phalaenopsis hieroglyphica* (Reichenbach f.) Sweet (syn. *P. lueddemanniana* var. *hieroglyphica* Reichenbach f.), also from the Philippines, has larger flowers and no constriction near the midlobe apex.

Phalaenopsis mannii

Reichenbach f.

Leaves to 35 × 7 cm, oblong or elliptic. Inflorescence arching or pendent, to 45 cm long, sometimes branched, many-flowered. Flowers waxy, long-lasting, ca. 4 cm across; sepals and petals yellow, blotched and barred with reddish brown; lip midlobe white, anchor-shaped.

Epiphytic in evergreen forest, often near a stream, 500–1500 m (1650–5000 ft.)

India, Nepal, China, Myanmar, Vietnam

Phalaenopsis mariae Burbridge ex R. Warner & H. Williams

Leaves oblong, to 40 × 10 cm. Inflorescence pendent, branched or unbranched, to 60 cm long, several- to many-flowered. Flowers 4–5 cm across; sepals and petals cream, barred and blotched with pink, light purple, or red-brown; lip mauve-pink to purple, midlobe hairy towards the apex.

Epiphytic in heavy shade, 100–1000 m (330–3300 ft.)

Borneo, Philippines

Phalaenopsis pulcherrima

(Lindley) J. J. Smith

SYN. *Doritis pulcherrima* Lindley

Terrestrial plants branching at the base to form clumps. Leaves to 15 × 3 cm. Inflorescence erect, unbranched, to 60 cm long, many-flowered.

Phalaenopsis mannii

Phalaenopsis pulcherrima

Phalaenopsis lobbii

Phalaenopsis lueddemanniana

Flowers to 5 cm across, bright magenta; lip midlobe with 3 lobules, the side lobules orange, the disc white. This species requires more light than most other *Phalaenopsis* species; failure to flower is usually due to lack of light.

Terrestrial in sandy soil or lithophytic, 100–1200 m (330–4000 ft.)

India to Malesia

Phalaenopsis schilleriana Reichenbach f.

Leaves elliptic, to 45 × 11 cm, dark green mottled with silver-gray above, purple below. Inflorescence branched, pendent, many-flowered. Flowers faintly scented, white, pink, or mauve, 7–8 cm across; lip midlobe anchor-shaped at the tip.

Epiphytic in forest, 0–800 m (2640 ft.)

Philippines

Phalaenopsis stuartiana Reichenbach f.

Leaves to 35 × 8 cm, dark green mottled with silver-gray above, flushed with purple below. Inflorescence branched, pendent, to 60 cm long, many-flowered. Flowers to 6 cm across, faintly scented, white, the lower halves of the lateral sepals and the lip greenish yellow with brown spots; apex of lip anchor-shaped.

Epiphytic in lowland forest, 0–300 m (1000 ft.)

Philippines

Phalaenopsis violacea H. Witte

Leaves to 25 × 12 cm, pale to mid green. Inflorescence arching, 1- or 2-flowered, the flowers open in succession. Flowers 3.5–5 cm across, scented, deep pink, the tips of the sepals and petals white or pale green, the lower margins of the lateral sepals and the lip midlobe deeper pink, side lobes and callus yellow.

Epiphytic in forest, ca. 150 m (500 ft.)

Malaysia, Sumatra

SIMILAR SPECIES: *Phalaenopsis bellina* (Reichenbach f.) Christenson from Borneo was included in *P. violacea*. It differs in its very strong, lemon fragrance, in having greenish-white flowers with the lateral sepals flushed with purple and a purple lip, and in having sepals and petals of a slightly different shape.

Pholidota Lindley ex Hooker

TRIBE: Arethuseae

SUBTRIBE: Coelogyninae

ETYMOLOGY: From Greek *pholidotus*, covered in scales, referring to the overlapping floral bracts

DISTRIBUTION: About 30 species throughout Asia and into Australia

Epiphytic, lithophytic, or terrestrial plants with a creeping or pendent rhizome; pseudobulbs clustered, spaced apart, or forming chains, cylindrical to conical, with basal sheaths, 1- to 2-leaved at apex. Inflorescences unbranched, many-flowered, appearing before, with or after the new growth, usually pendent, sometimes spiral, with prominent, overlapping bracts. Flowers in 2 rows, small, white to brownish, usually not opening wide; sepals ovate to oblong; petals ovate to linear; lip straight or S-shaped, the base saccate.

CULTIVATION: Plants are most successful potted in a standard bark-based compost, as they flower better when slightly pot-bound. Most require intermediate conditions with light to moderate shade and plenty of water while growing. They should be kept much drier while resting, but the pseudobulbs should not be allowed to shrivel. Pots need to be suspended when the plants are in flower.

Pholidota articulata Lindley

Pseudobulbs cylindrical, 4–12 cm long, one growing from near the top of another, forming a chain, 2-leaved. Leaves to 20 × 5 cm. Inflorescence apical, to 18 cm long, several- to many-flowered, the bracts falling as the flowers open. Flowers scented, greenish white to pink; lip brownish

Phalaenopsis schilleriana

Phalaenopsis bellina

Pholidota articulata

yellow with 5 ridges towards the base.

Epiphytic or lithophytic in forest, 800–2500 m (2640–8250 ft.)

India, China, Southeast Asia to Sulawesi

Pholidota chinensis Lindley

Pseudobulbs ovoid, to 8 cm long, set close together, 2-leaved at apex. Leaves to 22 × 6 cm. Inflorescence to 30 cm long, several- to many-flowered. Flowers ca. 1 cm long, greenish white to buff.

Epiphytic or lithophytic in forest, 100–2500 m (330–8250 ft.)

China, Myanmar, Vietnam

Pholidota imbricata Hooker

Pseudobulbs clustered, cylindrical, to 8 cm long, 1-leafed at apex. Leaves to 50 × 10 cm. Inflorescence pendent, spiraling, to 30 cm long, many-flowered. Flowers white, sometimes pink-tinged, partly concealed by light brown, papery bracts. The most widely grown species.

Epiphytic or lithophytic in forest, 1000–2700 m (3300–8900 ft.)

Widespread in tropical Asia

Phragmipedium Rolfe

SUBFAMILY: Cypripedioideae

ETYMOLOGY: From Greek *phragma*, partition, and *pedilon*, slipper, referring to the tripartite ovary and the slipper-shaped lip

DISTRIBUTION: More than 20 species in Mexico, Central and South America

Terrestrial, lithophytic, or sometimes epiphytic plants with fibrous roots and short, leafy stems. Leaves distichous, arranged in a fan, flat but folded at base, usually strap-shaped, mid to dark green. Inflorescences terminal, sometimes branched, few- to many-flowered, peduncle and rachis hairy. Flowers large, deciduous; dorsal sepal erect or forming a hood, lateral sepals joined to form a synsepal; petals free, broad and spreading or narrow and pendent; lip forming a deep, inflated pouch, the margins inrolled. Column short, stout, fertile stamens 2, staminode varying in shape.

Phragmipedium species and hybrids were less popular in cultivation than their Asian relatives, *Paphiopedilum*, but with the discovery of the bright red *Phrag. besseae* in 1981 and its involvement in the production of some splendid hybrids, this began to change. The popularity of the genus increased further with the discovery in 2001 of the even more spectacular *Phrag. kovachii*.

CULTIVATION: Most species of *Phragmipedium* grow in seepage areas and require more moisture throughout the year than paphiopedilums. They will grow in intermediate conditions with light to moderate shade in a free-draining compost based on bark, coconut chips, or rockwool. The mixture should not have added dolomite. Many growers are successful when they stand the pots in shallow water.

Phragmipedium besseae Dodson & J. Kuhn

Inflorescence to 60 cm long, sometimes branched. Flowers 4–7 cm across, bright scarlet, the lip tinged with yellow; petals elliptical, spreading. A yellow form ('Flavum') exists.

Var. *dalessandroi* (Dodson & O. Gruss) A. Moon & P. J. Cribb (syn. *Phragmipedium dalessandroi* Dodson & O. Gruss) from northern Ecuador is a more compact plant. It has apricot-red flowers with narrower, drooping petals.

Terrestrial in wet forest or lithophytic on cliff faces, 1000–1500 m (3300–5000 ft.)

Ecuador, northern Peru

Pholidota imbricata

Phragmipedium caudatum (Lindley) Rolfe

Leaves to 60 × 6 cm. Inflorescence 40–80 cm tall, with 2–6 flowers open together. Flowers yellow-green to yellow-brown marked and veined with reddish brown; petals pendent, twisted, to 50 cm long.

Terrestrial on grassy slopes or lithophytic on cliffs, 800–2500 m (2640–8250 ft.)

Bolivia, Peru

Pholidota chinensis

Phragmipedium besseae

Phragmipedium caudatum

Phragmipedium lindenii

SIMILAR SPECIES: *Phragmipedium lindenii* (Lindley) Dressler & N. Williams from Colombia, Ecuador, and Peru has a petalloid lip.

Phragmipedium kovachii J. T. Atwood, Dalström & R. Fernández

SYN. *Phragmipedium peruvianum* Christenson

Leaves several, distichous, narrowly strap-shaped, usually ca. 30 × 4–5 cm. Inflorescence ca. 30 cm tall, the stem purplish and pubescent, usually with 1 flower open at a time, rarely with 2 or 3. Flowers large, 15–20 cm across; sepals greenish, streaked with purple, petals almost round, raspberry to purple; lip rich purple.

Usually in 15–20 cm of soil overlying rock, in areas of high humidity, 1800–2200 m (6000–7260 ft.)

Northeastern Peru

Phragmipedium longifolium (Warszewicz & Reichenbach f.) Rolfe

Leaves to 75 × 4 cm. Inflorescence 35–75 cm tall, with several flowers open in succession. Flowers ca. 20 cm across, green marked with red or violet; petals spreading or deflexed, to 12 × 1 cm, slightly twisted; pouch yellow-green flushed with purple.

Terrestrial or lithophytic in wet forest, especially on cliff slopes, 500–1500 m (1650–5000 ft.)

Costa Rica, Colombia, Ecuador

Phragmipedium pearcei (Reichenbach f.) Rauh & Senghas

Leaves linear, to 25 cm long. Inflorescence to 30 cm tall, with several flowers open in succession; sepals and petals green with maroon veins, petals ca. 7 cm long, pendulous, linear, twisted; pouch yellow or yellow-green with purple veins.

Terrestrial or lithophytic, often near a river, 300–1200 m (1000–4000 ft.)

Ecuador, Peru

Phragmipedium schlimii (Linden & Reichenbach f.) Rolfe

Inflorescence sometimes branched, to 50 cm tall, 5- to 10-flowered. Flowers 4–7.5 cm across; sepals and petals white flushed with pink, petals spreading, ovate; lip rose-pink. With *P. longifolium*, this is a parent of the old but still widely grown hybrid *P.* Sedenii.

Terrestrial or lithophytic in wet areas, 1400–1900 m (4600–6300 ft.)

Colombia

Phymatidium Lindley

TRIBE: Maxillarieae

SUBTRIBE: Oncidiinae

ETYMOLOGY: From Greek *phyma*, growth, and the Latin diminutive *-idium*, referring to the small size of the plants

DISTRIBUTION: 10 species in southern and southeastern Brazil

Dwarf epiphytes with short, leafy stems. Leaves linear, slender, spirally arranged or in a fan. Inflorescences usually longer than leaves, many-flowered. Flowers small, white, distichous; sepals and petals free, spreading, subsimilar but the petals narrower; lip clawed, entire, without a spur, with a fleshy callus. Column long, slender; pollinia 4.

CULTIVATION: Plants can be grown potted in a fine compost or mounted. They require intermediate, shady conditions with high humidity throughout the year.

Phymatidium falcifolium Lindley

SYN. *Phymatidium tillandsioides* Barbosa Rodrigues

Leaves numerous, spirally arranged, 3–6 cm long, up to 1 mm wide. Inflorescences erect, loosely 3- to 10-flowered. Flowers less than 1 cm across, white with a green mark on the lip; lip ovate, truncate, the edges finely toothed. Plants have an interesting appearance, resembling the bromeliad *Tillandsia usneoides* (Spanish moss).

Low-level epiphyte in humid forest, usually near water, 1000–1300 m (3300–4300 ft.)

Southern and southeastern Brazil

Platanthera Richard

TRIBE: Orchideae

SUBTRIBE: Orchidinae

ETYMOLOGY: From Greek *platys*, wide, and *anthera*, anther

DISTRIBUTION: About 130 species in Europe, North Africa, Asia, and North and Central America

Terrestrial herbs with tubers or fleshy roots. Stem erect. Leaves unspotted, often 2 or 3 at base of plant with sheaths along stem. Inflorescences cylindrical, usually few- to several-flowered. Flowers small or medium-sized, often scented, white, greenish, yellow, orange, or pink; dorsal sepal usually forming a hood with petals, lateral sepals spreading or recurved; lip entire or trilobed, the margins sometimes deeply fringed, spurred at the base.

CULTIVATION: Some species of *Platanthera* will grow in temperate gardens, in woodland or in grass, depending on the natural habitat. Others can be grown in a cool greenhouse or alpine house in a standard terrestrial compost, keeping the

Phragmipedium kovachii

Phragmipedium longifolium

Phragmipedium pearcei

Phragmipedium schlimii

Phymatidium falcifolium

plants dry after the leaves die back until new growth appears in spring.

Platanthera bifolia (Linnaeus) Richard

LESSER BUTTERFLY ORCHID

Slender plants to ca. 50 cm high with 2 ovoid tubers. Leaves 2, ± basal, ovate, glossy green. Inflorescence fairly densely few- to many-flowered. Flowers scented, white, tinged with green; lateral sepals spreading; lip strap-shaped, to 12 mm long; spur slender, ca. 25 mm long. Pollinia set close together and parallel to each other, covering the mouth of the spur. Flowering late spring–summer.

Acid moorland, woodland

Europe, North Africa, Asia

SIMILAR SPECIES: *Platanthera chlorantha* (Custer) Reichenbach f., GREATER BUTTERFLY ORCHID, has a similar distribution (although not extending as far east in Asia) but usually grows on basic soil. The spike tends to be looser and wider. The main distinguishing character is the position of the pollinia, which are close together at the top but diverge rather than lying parallel, showing the mouth of the spur. Flowering summer.

Platanthera ciliaris (Linnaeus) Lindley

Stem erect, leafy, 70–100 cm tall. Leaves 5–30 × 1–5 cm, glossy green. Inflorescence densely or loosely many-flowered. Flowers yellow or bright orange; dorsal sepal forming a hood with the petals, lateral sepals reflexed; lip to 25 mm long, entire, deeply fringed, spur slender, 2.5–3.5 cm long. Flowering summer–autumn.

Fields, woodland and bogs, in full sun or partial shade

Eastern and southeastern United States

SIMILAR SPECIES: *Platanthera blephariglottis* (Willdenow) Lindley, also from the eastern United States, is a shorter plant with white flowers. It usually grows in wet areas.

Platanthera grandiflora (Bigelow) Lindley

LARGE PURPLE FRINGED ORCHID

Robust plants to 120 cm tall. Leaves several, along stem. Inflorescence 30- to 60-flowered. Flowers showy, 20–25 mm across, pale to deep purple; lip 18 × 25 mm, flat, trilobed, the side lobes spreading, all lobes deeply fringed; spur slender, to 25 mm long. Flowering summer.

Bogs, damp open woodland, to 1800 m (6000 ft.)

Eastern United States and Canada north to Newfoundland

SIMILAR SPECIES: *Platanthera psychodes* (Linnaeus) Lindley, LESSER PURPLE FRINGED ORCHID, with a similar distribution, has smaller flowers, with the lip less deeply cut. It usually flowers about 2 weeks earlier than *P. grandiflora.*

Platanthera integra (Nuttall) A. Gray ex L. C. Beck

Stem to 60 cm tall with 1 or 2 leaves 5–20 cm long near the base, grading

Platanthera grandiflora. R. Parsons

Platystele compacta

into bracts up the stem. Inflorescence densely many-flowered. Flowers small, yellow; lip entire, strap-shaped, the edge finely toothed but not fringed; spur short and slender. Flowering summer–autumn.

Wet meadows, pinewoods

Eastern and southeastern United States

Platanthera japonica (Thunberg) Lindley

Plants to 60 cm tall with fleshy roots. Leaves lanceolate, to 16 cm long, borne along stem. Inflorescence loosely 10- to 20-flowered. Flowers white, turning yellowish with age; lip fleshy, narrowly strap-shaped, entire, to 20 mm long, 2 mm wide; spur slender, pointing down, to 6 cm long. Flowering summer.

In forests or on grassy slopes, 800–2500 m (2640–8250 ft.)

China, Japan, Korea

Platystele Schlechter

TRIBE: Epidendreae

SUBTRIBE: Pleurothallidinae

ETYMOLOGY: From Greek *platys*, broad, and *stele*, column

DISTRIBUTION: More than 90 species in Mexico, Central and South America

Small epiphytic, lithophytic, or terrestrial plants, tufted or creeping. Stems erect, enclosed in overlapping sheaths, 1-leafed at apex. Leaves petiolate. Inflorescences unbranched, sometimes zigzag, with tubular floral bracts. Flowers small; sepals and petals usually spreading, subsimilar, thin-textured, the sepals sometimes tailed, the lateral sepals sometimes joined at the base; lip very small, fleshy, entire, the base joined to the column-foot. Pollinia 2.

CULTIVATION: These little plants need high humidity all year round. They can be grown mounted or potted in a fine bark mix in cool or intermediate conditions.

Platystele compacta (Ames) Ames

Stems very short, covered in white sheaths. Leaves to 5 × 0.5 cm. Inflorescence to 10 cm long, densely many-flowered, the flowers open together and in succession; peduncle threadlike. Flowers minute, translucent pale green or yellow; lip orange.

Epiphytic in wet forest, 350–2500 m (1150–8250 ft.)

Mexico, Central America

Platystele jungermannioides (Schlechter) Garay

Tiny creeping plant with 1 root at each node, eventually forming a mosslike mat. Stems 0.3 mm long.

Platanthera bifolia. E. la Croix

Platanthera chlorantha. E. la Croix

Platanthera ciliaris. R. Parsons

Leaves to 2.5 mm long. Inflorescence to 5 mm long, 2- or 3-flowered. Flowers minute, translucent yellow-green; lip light brown. This species is a candidate for the role of the world's smallest orchid.

Epiphytic in cloud forest, 200–1000 m (660–3300 ft.)

Mexico, Costa Rica, Guatemala, Panama

Platystele oxyglossa (Schlechter) Garay

Small tufted plants with stems 3–5 mm long, enclosed in a sheath. Leaves to 3.5 cm long. Inflorescence to 4 cm long, with several flowers open in succession. Flowers variable in size; sepals 1–5 mm long, pale yellow-green, sometimes flushed with purple; lip purple-red, brown, or green. This is the most widespread species in the genus.

Epiphytic in rain forest and cloud forest, 200–2000 m (660–6600 ft.)

Mexico, Central and South America

Platystele oxyglossa

Platystele stellaris Luer

Small, tufted plants. Leaves 2–3 cm long. Inflorescence to 15 cm long, with few flowers open in succession. Flowers starry, ca. 3 cm across; sepals and petals translucent light tan with red-brown midvein, long acuminate; lip red-brown.

Epiphytic in cloud forest, 2100–2400 m (6900–7900 ft.)

Ecuador

Plectorrhiza Dockrill

TRIBE: Vandeae

SUBTRIBE: Aeridinae

ETYMOLOGY: From Greek *plektos*, twisted, and *rhiza*, root

DISTRIBUTION: 3 species, 2 in eastern Australia and 1 on Lord Howe Island

Monopodial epiphytes with long, usually branched, leafy stems and many tangled, wiry roots. Inflorescences arising on stem, unbranched, few- to several-flowered. Flowers small, scented; sepals and petals free, spreading, subsimilar; lip joined to column base, trilobed, spurred with a hairy callus near the spur opening.

CULTIVATION: With their straggling habit, plants are better mounted. They require intermediate conditions in light shade with plenty of air movement and humidity. In subtropical climates, they do well attached to garden trees.

Plectorrhiza tridentata (Lindley) Dockrill

TANGLE ORCHID

Stems flattened, to 30 cm long. Leaves to 10 × 1.5 cm, ± sickle-shaped, acute. Inflorescence to 12 cm long, loosely 3- to 15-flowered. Flowers ca. 8 mm across, strongly scented, green or brownish with a white lip; spur ca. 3 cm long. Flowering summer.

Epiphytic on outer branches of trees in rain forest and in gullies, 50–900 m (165–3000 ft.)

Australia (New South Wales, Queensland, Victoria)

Plectrelminthus Rafinesque

TRIBE: Vandeae

SUBTRIBE: Aerangidinae

ETYMOLOGY: From Greek *plektron*, spur, and *helmins*, worm

DISTRIBUTION: 1 species in West Africa

Large epiphyte with short stem and stout roots. Leaves numerous. Inflorescences arising from lower leaf axis, several-flowered, pendent. Flowers with lips pointing upwards; sepals and petals spreading, subsimilar; spur long. Column long, the anther-cap beaked.

CULTIVATION: Because of the long roots, plants do best in a basket in a coarse, free-draining bark-based mixture. They require warm temperatures, good light, and high humidity.

Plectrelminthus caudatus (Lindley) Summerhayes

Leaves to 35 × 3 cm, narrowly strap-shaped, yellowish green. Inflorescence to 80 cm long, 4- to 12-flowered, the rachis zigzag. Flowers

Plectrelminthus caudatus

Plectorrhiza tridentata. R. Parsons

fleshy, scented; sepals and petals yellow-green, sometimes tinged with bronze; lip white; sepals 35–50 mm long, lanceolate, acute, the laterals joined at the base behind the spur; petals slightly shorter; lip to 60 mm long, including a basal claw to 15 mm long and an apical acumen 15 mm long, the blade ovate, the claw with 2 projections about halfway along that meet to form a V.

High-level epiphyte in low-altitude forest

West and Central Africa

Plectrophora H. Focke

TRIBE: Maxillarieae
SUBTRIBE: Oncidiinae
ETYMOLOGY: From Greek *plektron*, spur, and *phoros*, bearing
DISTRIBUTION: 10 species in Central and South America

Twig epiphytes forming tufts; pseudobulbs small, laterally flattened, 1-leafed at the apex, with 2–4 leafy sheaths at the base. Inflorescences arising from axils of sheaths, shorter than leaves, 1- to 3-flowered. Flowers fleshy, large for size of plants, green, yellowish, or white; sepals subequal, lateral sepals basally forming a long, narrow spur; petals broader than sepals; lip entire or with shallow lobes, funnel-shaped at the base with 2 spurs running into the sepal spur. Pollinia 2.

CULTIVATION: Grow plants mounted or in small pots in a fine epiphyte compost, in intermediate to warm conditions with good light and high humidity. They need plenty of water while in active growth, less while resting.

Plectrophora alata (Rolfe) Garay

SYN. *Trichocentrum alatum* Rolfe

Pseudobulbs to 1.5 cm long, Leaves strap-shaped, to 12 × 1 cm. Flowers 3.5 cm across, creamy white, yellow, or orange in the throat; lip ± square, emarginate, edges undulate; spur 4–5 cm long.

Epiphytic in rain forest, 600–800 m (2000–2640 ft.)

Costa Rica, Guyana, Panama, Colombia

Plectrophora iridifolia H. Focke

Leaves laterally flattened, 4–7 cm long. Flowers white or greenish white, not opening wide; sepals to 13 mm long; lip 14–18 mm long, funnel-shaped with yellow or orange stripes or dots; spur 20–25 mm long.

Twig epiphyte in rain forest or scrub, 50–500 m (165–1650 ft.)

Bolivia, Brazil, Colombia, Ecuador, Peru, Venezuela

Pleione D. Don

TRIBE: Arethuseae
SUBTRIBE: Coelogyninae
ETYMOLOGY: From Greek Pleione, mother of Pleiades
DISTRIBUTION: More than 20 species and several natural hybrids from northern India, China, Myanmar, Thailand, Laos, and Vietnam

Dwarf, deciduous epiphytes, lithophytes, or terrestrials; pseudobulbs annual, usually clustered, ovoid, conical, or pear-shaped, 1- to 2-leaved at apex. Leaves thin-textured, pleated, petiolate. Inflorescences arising from base of pseudobulb, erect, 1- to 2-flowered. Flowers showy, white, pink, mauve, or magenta, occasionally yellow, the lip marked with red, brown, or yellow; sepals and petals subsimilar, free, spreading, lip ± tubular, entire or obscurely trilobed, the apical margin often fringed or toothed, with a callus of lines of lamellae or hairs inside.

Many beautiful intrageneric hybrids and cultivars are now available.

CULTIVATION: Pleiones are cultivated both by orchid growers and alpine enthusiasts. They are almost hardy but dislike winter wet and so are usually grown in a cool glasshouse, alpine house, or cold frame. They do well on windowsills indoors. They should be kept dry and cool (just frost-free) in winter and are usually repotted towards the end of this resting period. Plants are grown in pans or shallow pots in a mixture of fine orchid bark, perlite, and sphagnum moss. When the young growths appear in early spring, they should be brought into a warmer but shady place and careful watering should be started. Plants should be watered and fertilized until the leaves have died back, some months after flowering has finished.

Pleione bulbocodioides (Franchet) Rolfe

SYN. *Pleione pogonioides* Rolfe

A variable species. Pseudobulbs conical, ca. 2.5 cm long, 1-leafed. Leaf ca. 15 × 2.5 cm, developing after flowering. Inflorescence to 20 cm long, 1- or rarely 2-flowered. Flowers 7–9 cm across, pink to deep red-purple; lip to 45 mm long, with darker marks, the margins fringed; callus of 4 or 5 lamellae. Flowering spring.

Terrestrial, or lithophytic on and among mossy rocks, 900–3600 m (3000–12,000 ft.)

Widespread in China

Pleione ×*confusa* P. Cribb & C. Z. Tang

This natural hybrid between *P. forrestii* Schlechter and *P. albiflora* P. Cribb & C. Z. Tang has been widely misidentified as *P. forrestii*. Pseudobulbs conical, 20–25 mm long and wide, 1-leafed at apex. Leaf 10–15 × 3–4 cm. Inflorescence 2–5 cm tall, 1-flowered. Flowers scented, primrose-yellow with red spots on the lip; sepals and petals to 42 mm long; lip to 32 mm long, the base saccate, the apical margins fringed; callus of 4–6 undulate, dissected lamellae. Flowering spring.

Terrestrial or lithophytic on mossy rocks, 2200–3200 m (7260–10,500 ft.)

China (Yunnan)

SIMILAR SPECIES: *Pleione forrestii* Schlechter, from Yunnan and northern Myanmar, has slightly smaller flowers and entire lip lamellae.

Plectrophora alata

Pleione formosana

Pleione formosana Hayata
Pseudobulbs ovoid, to 30 mm long, green or purple, 1-leafed at apex. Leaf to 25 cm long. Inflorescence 7–12 cm tall, 1-flowered, sometimes 2-flowered. Flowers white to pink, the lip with yellow, reddish, or brown marks; sepals and petals to 60 mm long; lip to 55 mm long, emarginate, the apical margins fringed; callus of 2–5 interrupted lamellae. Flowering spring. This is the commonest species in cultivation and among the hardiest and most easily grown.

Terrestrial, lithophytic, or epiphytic, but usually on rocks in submontane and montane forest, 500–2500 m (1650–8250 ft.)

China, Taiwan

SIMILAR SPECIES: *Pleione pleionoides* (Schlechter) Braem & Mohr (syn. *P. speciosa* Ames & Schlechter) has more richly colored, usually larger, flowers, with a callus of 2–4 yellow, toothed ridges. This attractive species is better known by its synonym, *P. speciosa*.

Pleione praecox (J. E. Smith) D. Don
Pseudobulbs top-shaped, 15–30 mm long, 10–15 mm wide, green mottled with red-brown or purple, 2-leaved at apex, rarely 1-leafed. Leaves to 16 × 7 cm, elliptic, acuminate. Inflorescence 8–13 cm tall, 1- or 2-flowered, usually appearing after leaves have fallen; sepals and petals to 70 cm long; lip to 50 mm long, emarginate, the margins toothed or cut; callus of 3–5 lines of papillae. Flowering in autumn.

Terrestrial or lithophytic among or on mossy rocks on rocky slopes, occasionally epiphytic, 1200–3400 m (4000–11,200 ft.)

Bhutan, China, India, Myanmar, Thailand, Vietnam

SIMILAR SPECIES: *Pleione maculata* (Lindley) Lindley, with a similar distribution, is another autumn-flowering species with smaller, white flowers, the lip with purple blotches, and plain green pseudobulbs. *Pleione ×lagenaria* Lindley is believed to be a natural hybrid between these 2 species and is intermediate in character.

Pleione praecox

Pleurothallis R. Brown

TRIBE: Epidendreae
SUBTRIBE: Pleurothallidinae
ETYMOLOGY: From Greek *pleuron*, rib, and *thallos*, shoot, referring to the thin stems
DISTRIBUTION: About 1000 species in Mexico, Central and South America, and the West Indies

Epiphytic, lithophytic, or terrestrial plants, tufted or creeping. Stems usually erect, enclosed in tubular sheaths, 1-leafed at apex. Leaves with or without a petiole, of various shapes. Inflorescences usually terminal, unbranched, arising from a spathe, 1- to many-flowered. Flowers small; sepals subequal, lateral sepals joined for part or all of their length to form a synsepal; petals smaller than sepals; lip entire or trilobed, sometimes clawed. Column sometimes winged; pollinia 2.

Pleione maculata

In the past few years, as a result of DNA analysis, many species of *Pleurothallis* have been moved to other genera such as *Stelis* and *Specklinia*, and there may well be more readjustments of genera to come.

CULTIVATION: Most species of *Pleurothallis* require high humidity, moderate shade, and good ventilation all year round. They can be mounted or grown in pots in a fine bark-based compost in cool to intermediate conditions, depending on their origin. Many species flower off and on throughout the year.

Pleurothallis allenii (Linnaeus) O. Williams

Small plant. Leaves elliptical. Inflorescence 1-flowered. Flowers ca. 1 cm long, purple, edged in yellow; lateral sepals joined to the tips.

Epiphytic in forest, 550–1000 m (1800–3300 ft.)

Panama

Pleurothallis cordata (Ruíz & Pavón) Lindley

Leaves heart-shaped. Inflorescence 1-flowered, although several usually arise together, the flowers lying on top of the leaf. Flowers small, variable in color, deep purple to orange with a purple lip.

Epiphytic or lithophytic in forest, 500–3100 m (1650–10,200 ft.)

Bolivia, Colombia, Ecuador, Peru, Venezuela

Pleurothallis crocodiliceps Reichenbach f.

Stems flattened towards apex. Leaves to 12 × 5 cm, ovate. Inflorescence to 6 cm long, arising in a cluster, each 1-flowered. Flowers ca. 1 cm long,

Pleurothallis allenii

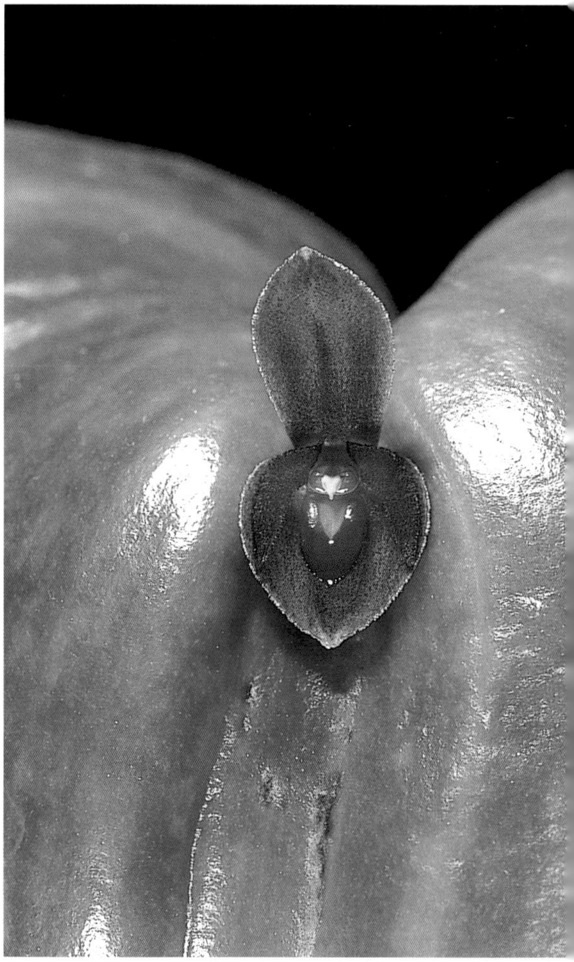

Pleurothallis cordata

Pleurothallis crocodiliceps

white or yellow, sometimes with purple marks; lip deep purple.

Epiphytic in rain forest and cloud forest, 900–1900 m (3000–6300 ft.)

Mexico, Central and South America

Pleurothallis gargantua Luer

One of the largest species, 25–55 cm tall, with heart-shaped leaves to 30 × 15 cm. Inflorescence 1-flowered, the flower lying on top of the leaf. Flowers ca. 7.5 cm long (probably the largest in the genus), deep purple, the dorsal sepal sometimes pink with darker stripes.

Terrestrial in steep forest, ca. 1500–2500 m (5000—8250 ft.)

Ecuador

Pleurothallis imperialis Luer

A robust species, 25–45 cm tall. Leaves large, heart-shaped. Flowers lying on top of leaf, 4–6 cm long; dorsal sepal yellow flushed with purple-pink at the base, lying over flower, synsepal purple.

Epiphytic in forest or terrestrial on roadsides, 300–2200 m (1000–7260 ft.)

Ecuador

Pleurothallis loranthophylla Reichenbach f.

Leaves petiolate, to 10 × 3.5 cm. Inflorescence 10–15 cm long, arching, loosely many-flowered, the flowers open together. Flowers ca. 2 cm long, translucent yellow heavily marked with purple.

Epiphytic in rain forest and cloud forest, 600–2050 m (2000–6700 ft.)

Central and South America

Pleurothallis marthae Luer & R. Escobar

Plants 12–18 cm tall, with heart-shaped leaves held horizontally. Inflorescence 1-flowered but several arise together so that a group of flowers lie on each leaf. Flowers ca. 5 cm long, not opening wide, variable in color but usually pale to deep pink.

Epiphytic in forest

Colombia

Pleurothallis palliolata Ames

Plants 8–17 cm tall. Leaves horizontal, ovate, to 10 × 4 cm. Inflorescence 1-flowered. Flowers ca. 15 mm long; sepals yellow, lined with red-brown, the dorsal sepal very concave; petals and lip red.

Epiphytic in rain forest and cloud forest, 1000–2100 m (3300–6900 ft.)

Costa Rica, Panama

Pleurothallis platystachys Regel

Inflorescence to 25 cm long, many-flowered. Flowers distichous, all open together, partly concealed by bracts; sepals yellow; petals and lip purple.

Epiphytic in rain forest, 80–1650 m (260–5410 ft.)

Brazil

Pleurothallis pruinosa Lindley

Stems to 8 cm long. Leaves to 5 × 1 cm. Inflorescence 2–4 cm long, loosely few-flowered, the flowers open together. Flowers ca. 6 mm across, pale yellow to greenish.

Epiphytic in plantations and rain forest, 150–2700 m (500–8900 ft.)

Central and South America, West Indies

Pleurothallis gargantua

Pleurothallis imperialis

Pleurothallis loranthophylla

Pleurothallis palliolata

Pleurothallis ruscifolia

Pleurothallis ruscifolia (Jacquin) R. Brown
Stems to 40 cm tall. Leaves erect, to 30 × 6 cm. Inflorescence to 20 cm long, pendent, few-flowered, several arising together. Flowers to 2 cm long, pale green to pale yellow. This is the type species of the genus.
Epiphytic in rain forest and cloud forest, 0–2000 m (6600 ft.)
Central and South America, West Indies

Pleurothallis secunda Poeppig & Endlicher
Inflorescence to 20 cm long, several-flowered. Flowers ca. 15 mm long, pale pink with darker lines.
Epiphytic in forest, 600–3200 m (2,000–10,500 ft.)
South America

Pleurothallopsis Porto & Brade

SYN. *Restrepiopsis* Luer
TRIBE: Epidendreae
SUBTRIBE: Pleurothallidinae
ETYMOLOGY: From *Pleurothallis* and Greek *opsis*, like, meaning resembling *Pleurothallis*
DISTRIBUTION: 16 species in Central and South America
Epiphytic, lithophytic, or terrestrial plants, tufted or creeping, the stems enclosed in tubular, funnel-shaped sheaths, 1-leafed. Inflorescences 1-flowered or in clusters, the flowers open in succession. Flowers resupinate, usually thin-textured; dorsal sepal free, laterals joined to form a synsepal; lip trilobed, hinged to the column-foot. Pollinia 4 or 8.
CULTIVATION: As for *Pleurothallis*. Most species require high humidity, moderate shade, and good ventilation all year round. They can be mounted or grown in pots in a fine bark-based compost in cool to intermediate conditions, depending on their origin. Many species flower off and on throughout the year.

Pleurothallis secunda

Pleurothallopsis inaequalis (Luer & R. Escobar) Pridgeon & M. W. Chase

SYN. *Restrepiopsis inaequalis* Luer & R. Escobar

Stems to 13 cm tall, enclosed in 5–7 brown, ribbed sheaths. Leaves to 4.5 × 2 cm. Inflorescence a cluster of single flowers open in succession. Flowers 10–12 mm long, white to yellow-green with purple-brown veins.

Epiphytic in forest, 1500–2400 m (5000–7900 ft.)

Colombia, Ecuador

Pleurothallopsis norae (Garay & Dunsterville) Pridgeon & M. W. Chase

SYN. *Restrepiopsis norae* Garay & Dunsterville

Stems 1–3.5 cm long. Leaves elliptic, flushed with purple, 1–2.5 mm long. Inflorescence ca. 1 cm long, a cluster of single flowers open in succession. Flowers very small, greenish white flushed with pink on the mid veins.

Epiphytic in forest, 1400–2600 m (4600–8600 ft.)

Colombia, Ecuador, Venezuela

Pleurothallopsis tubulosa (Lindley) Pridgeon & M. W. Chase

SYN. *Pleurothallis tubulosa* Lindley, *Restrepiopsis tubulosa* (Lindley) Luer

Stems 2–12 cm long, enclosed in brown, ribbed sheaths. Leaves to 6 × 3 cm. Inflorescence a cluster of single flowers open in succession. Flowers ca. 8 mm long, white to green, sometimes flushed or veined in brown or purple.

Epiphytic or terrestrial in cloud forest, 1500–3600 m (5000–12,000 ft.)

Costa Rica, Panama, Colombia, Ecuador, Venezuela

Pleurothallopsis inaequalis

Pleurothallopsis norae

Podangis Schlechter

TRIBE: Vandeae

SUBTRIBE: Aerangidinae

ETYMOLOGY: From Greek *podos*, foot, and *angos*, vessel, referring to the lobed tip of the spur

DISTRIBUTION: 1 species in West and Central Africa

Stem short, sometimes branching at the base. Leaves fleshy, bilaterally flattened, forming a fan. Inflorescence unbranched, shorter than leaves, arising below leaves and from lower leaf axils. Sepals and petals subsimilar; lip entire, ovate, concave, spurred. Column short and stout; pollinia and stipites 2.

CULTIVATION: Careful watering is needed whether plants are grown in pots or mounted, as the flowers turn brown if they get wet. In pots there is also a tendency to rot unless the compost dries out between waterings. This species requires intermediate to warm temperatures, shade, and high humidity.

Podangis dactyloceras Schlechter

Leaves several, 10–15 cm long, 5–10 mm wide, sword-shaped, dark green, glossy. Racemes to 5 cm long, 2- to 20-flowered, the flowers set close together. Pedicel and ovary 20–25 mm long. Flowers small, bell-shaped, translucent white with a dark green anther-cap; spur 9–11 mm long, tapering from a wide mouth then enlarged and usually lobed at the apex. Flowering summer.

Epiphytic in evergreen forest, 750–1600 m (2460–5300 ft.)

West and Central Africa

Pleurothallopsis tubulosa

Podangis dactyloceras. E. la Croix

Polycycnis Reichenbach f.

TRIBE: Maxillarieae
SUBTRIBE: Stanhopeinae
ETYMOLOGY: From Greek *polys*, many, and *kyknos*, swan, referring to the appearance of the flowers
DISTRIBUTION: 17 species in Central and South America

Epiphytes, sometimes terrestrial on embankments, related to *Stanhopea*; pseudobulbs short, ovoid to cylindrical, with basal sheaths, 1- to 3-leaved at apex. Leaves large, plicate, petiolate. Inflorescences basal, usually pendent but sometimes erect, few- to many-flowered. Flowers showy; sepals and petals free, spreading or reflexed, subsimilar but the petals smaller; lip joined to base of column, spreading, trilobed, side lobes narrow, midlobe entire or obscurely trilobed. Column long, slender, arching; pollinia 2.

CULTIVATION: As most species have pendent inflorescences, they are usually grown mounted or in baskets, in a coarse, free-draining bark-based compost. They require intermediate temperatures, moderate shade, high humidity, and plenty of water while in active growth. They should be kept much drier when resting.

Polycycnis barbata (Lindley) Reichenbach f.

Pseudobulbs to 6 × 3 cm, ovoid, ridged, 1-leafed. Leaves ca. 30 × 15 cm with a petiole 8 cm long. Inflorescence 30–50 cm long, pendent, many-flowered. Flowers ca. 5 cm across, thin-textured, creamy yellow barred and spotted with purple-red; lip white spotted with red or purple.

Epiphytic in rain forest, 800–1200 m (2640–4000 ft.)

Costa Rica, Panama, Colombia, Venezuela

Polycycnis barbata

Polycycnis muscifera (Lindley & Paxton) Reichenbach f.

Pseudobulbs to 6 cm long, 1-leafed. Leaves to 27 × 10 cm, with a petiole ca. 10 cm long. Inflorescence 20–30 cm long, erect or arching, many-flowered. Flowers 3–4 cm across, clear yellow marked with red-brown.

Epiphytic in rain forest, 900–1200 m (3000–4000 ft.)

Central and South America

Polystachya Hooker

TRIBE: Vandeae
SUBTRIBE: Polystachyinae
ETYMOLOGY: From Greek *polys*, many, and *stachys*, spike or ear of grain
DISTRIBUTION: More than 150 species, mostly in Africa but also in America, the West Indies, and Asia

Small to medium-sized plants, most epiphytic, sometimes lithophytic, rarely terrestrial, usually with well-defined pseudobulbs but sometimes with reedlike stems. Leaves 1 to several, in some species deciduous. Inflorescences terminal on pseudobulb or stem, simple or branched, 1- to many-flowered. Flowers small to medium-sized, usually scented, sometimes pubescent, nonresupinate, often bell-shaped; lateral sepals oblique, joined to the column-foot to form a chinlike mentum; dorsal sepal

Polycycnis muscifera

Polystachya bella

smaller; petals small; lip usually trilobed, rarely entire, often fleshy and recurved. Column short and stout, pollinia 2.

CULTIVATION: Most species are easily grown and, as they are compact and free-flowering, deserve to be more widely cultivated. They can be mounted but most have fine roots that dry out quickly and are usually more successful in pots in a medium bark mixture. Deciduous species should be kept more or less dry until new growth appears, others should be watered all year round, although less freely in winter. Most species will grow in intermediate conditions, with light shade. Many species flower off and on throughout the year.

Polystachya affinis Lindley
Pseudobulbs coinlike, to 5 cm diameter, lying flat on the substrate, 2- or 3-leaved. Leaves to 11 × 2 cm, deciduous. Inflorescence arching or pendent, often branched, to ca. 40 cm long, many-flowered. Flowers scented, red-brown edged with yellow.

Epiphytic in evergreen forest, 600–1350 m (2000–4500 ft.)

West and Central Africa

Polystachya bella Summerhayes
Pseudobulbs to 4 × 2.5 cm, ellipsoid, somewhat flattened, set close on an ascending rhizome. Leaves to 16 × 3 cm, glossy dark green. Inflorescence erect, to 25 cm long, sometimes with a few branches, densely many-flowered. Flowers golden-yellow to orange, lateral sepals to 17 mm long. This species does well if given a moss pole to climb on.

Epiphytic in forest, 1800–1950 m (6000–6430 ft.)

Kenya

SIMILAR SPECIES: *Polystachya laurentii* De Wildeman from DR Congo, Rwanda, and Uganda has white flowers with a yellow mark on the lip. The 2 species may well be synonymous, in which case *P. laurentii* would be the valid name.

Polystachya campyloglossa Rolfe

Pseudobulbs small, ± globose, 2- or 3-leaved. Leaves to 10 × 2 cm. Inflorescence erect, longer than leaves, 2- to 6-flowered. Flowers strongly scented; sepals green to yellow; lip white with purple veins on the side lobes.

Epiphytic in forest and wet woodland, 1100–2700 m (3600–8900 ft.)

East Africa

Polystachya concreta (Jacquin) Garay & Sweet

SYN. *Polystachya flavescens* (Lindley) J. J. Smith, *P. luteola* (Swartz) Hooker

Pseudobulbs to 5 × 1 cm, conical, 3- to 5-leaved. Leaves to 30 × 5 cm. Inflorescence branched, 30–50 cm tall, many-flowered. Flowers small, fleshy, yellow or greenish yellow.

Epiphytic, sometimes lithophytic, in woodland, 200–1000 m (660–3300 ft.)

United States (Florida), Central and South America, Asia

SIMILAR SPECIES: *Polystachya foliosa* (Hooker f.) Reichenbach f. from tropical America has a shorter column-foot and differently shaped lip side lobes; the flowers sometimes self-pollinate without opening. *Polystachya tessellata* Lindley and *P. modesta* Reichenbach f. from tropical Africa are sometimes considered synonymous with *P. concreta* but differ in the details of their lips; also *P. tessellata* has slightly larger flowers in a range of colors from white, yellow, and green to pink.

Polystachya tessellata. E. la Croix

Polystachya campyloglossa. E. la Croix

Polystachya lawrenceana. E. la Croix

Polystachya cultriformis
(Thouars) Sprengel

SYN. *Polystachya gerrardii* Harvey

Pseudobulbs conical, to 10 × 1 cm, 1-leafed at apex. Leaves to 35 × 5 cm. Inflorescence longer than leaves, branched, many-flowered. Flowers ca. 8 mm long, usually white but sometimes yellow, green, pink, or purple.

Epiphytic in forest, 500–2900 m (1650–9500 ft.)

Tropical Africa, Madagascar, Mascarene Islands, Seychelles

Polystachya galeata (Swartz) Reichenbach f.

SYN. *Polystachya grandiflora* Lindley ex Hooker

Pseudobulbs to 14 cm long, cylindrical, 1-leafed at apex. Leaves to 25 × 3 cm, leathery. Inflorescence usually shorter than leaves, unbranched, several-flowered. Flowers to 22 mm long, the largest in the genus, green or yellow-green, usually flushed with purple.

Epiphytic in evergreen forest, 400–1000 m (1320–3300 ft.)

West Africa

Polystachya lawrenceana
Kraenzlin

Pseudobulbs conical, to 5 cm long. Leaves to 15 × 2 cm, lax. Inflorescence arching, to 16 cm long, loosely to ca. 10-flowered. Flowers fleshy, 10–12 mm long; sepals bronze-green flushed with maroon; lip fleshy, pale to bright pink. This rare species does well in cultivation.

Lithophytic on exposed rock faces, 1350–1600 m (4500–5300 ft.)

Malawi

Polystachya cultriformis

Polystachya galeata

Polystachya longiscapa Summerhayes

Pseudobulbs to 10 × 3 cm, conical, forming a chain. Leaves several, 20–36 × 1.5–2.5 cm, grasslike, arching. Inflorescence to 90 cm tall, with a few branches, several-flowered. Flowers wide open, 4–5 cm across, pale pink to lilac. In cultivation, this species needs good light.

Lithophytic on rock faces

Tanzania

SIMILAR SPECIES: *Polystachya dendrobiiflora* Reichenbach f. (syn. *P. tayloriana* Rendle) is a more widespread species that is smaller in all parts and grows terrestrially or epiphytically.

Polystachya odorata Lindley

Pseudobulbs to 4 cm long, conical. Leaves to 25 × 4 cm. Inflorescence longer than leaves, branched, many-flowered. Flowers small, scented, white or yellow.

Epiphytic in evergreen forest, 900–1350 m (3000–4500 ft.)

West and Central Africa

Polystachya dendrobiiflora. E. la Croix

Polystachya ottoniana Reichenbach f.

Pseudobulbs to 2.5 cm long, ovoid, asymmetric, forming chains, 2- or 3-leaved. Leaves to 13 × 1 cm. Inflorescence shorter than leaves, 1- to 2-flowered. Flowers bell-shaped, 10–12 mm long, usually white but sometimes pink, green, or yellow, lip white with a yellow central line.

Epiphytic or lithophytic in forest and woodland, 0–1800 m (6000 ft.)

Mozambique, South Africa, Swaziland

Polystachya paniculata (Swartz) Rolfe

Pseudobulbs cylindrical, stout, to 18 × 2 cm, Leaves several, to 30 × 3.5 cm, strap-shaped, sometimes with purple marks. Inflorescence to 20 cm long, much branched, many-flowered. Flowers small, vermilion red or orange with red marks. This striking species likes warmer conditions than most.

Epiphytic in rain forest, 900–1150 m (3000–3800 ft.)

West and Central Africa

Polystachya pubescens (Lindley) Reichenbach f.

Pseudobulbs 2–3 cm long, conical, forming clumps. Leaves several, 5–10 cm long, dark green, elliptic. Inflorescence pubescent, to 12 cm tall, 7- to 12-flowered. Flowers opening wide, to 2 cm across, bright golden yellow, the lateral sepals with red-brown longitudinal lines on upper half. Flowering autumn–early winter.

Epiphytic or lithophytic in woodland

South Africa, Swaziland

Polystachya zambesiaca Rolfe

Pseudobulbs to 2 × 1 cm, oblong, 2- or 3-leaved. Leaves to 8 × 1.5 cm, often purple-edged. Inflorescence 5–8 cm long, 3- to 20-flowered. Flowers ca. 12 mm long, yellow or yellow-green, lip white or yellow, side lobes purple-veined.

Epiphytic or lithophytic in woodland and on rocky hills, 900–2000 m (3000–6600 ft.)

East Africa

Pomatocalpa Breda

TRIBE: Vandeae

SUBTRIBE: Aeridinae

ETYMOLOGY: From Greek *pomatos*, flask, and *kalpe*, pitcher, referring to the shape of the lip

DISTRIBUTION: About 30 species in tropical and subtropical Asia to the Pacific Islands and Australia

Monopodial epiphytes with long or short stems. Leaves oblong or strap-shaped. Inflorescences axillary, often branched, erect or pendent, many-flowered. Flowers small; sepals and petals free, spreading, subequal; lip trilobed, the base of the side lobes joined to column-foot; spur saccate with a tonguelike projection on the back wall. Pollinia 4, in 2 pairs.

CULTIVATION: Most species are grown in pots or baskets in a free-draining, bark-based compost, in warm temperatures with bright light and plenty of water throughout the year. Small species can be mounted.

Pomatocalpa bicolor (Lindley) J. J. Smith

Stem erect, to 30 cm tall. Leaves strap-shaped, to 13 × 3 cm. Inflorescence erect, sometimes branched, to 30 cm long, ca. 20-flowered. Flowers 1.5 cm across, cream to yellowish with purple markings.

Epiphytic in forest or lithophytic, to 500 m (1650 ft.)

Philippines

Pomatocalpa spicatum Breda, Kuhl & Hasselt

Stem 2–3 cm long. Leaves to 20 × 5 cm. Inflorescence to 15 cm long, arching or pendent, occasionally branched, densely many-flowered. Flowers ca. 1 cm across, sepals and petals yellow with maroon markings, lip white or pale yellow.

Polystachya pubescens. E. la Croix

Polystachya odorata. E. la Croix

Polystachya zambesiaca. E. la Croix

Pomatocalpa spicatum

Epiphytic on tree trunks, or lithophytic, in submontane forest, to 1000 m (3300 ft.)

Himalayas to Malesia

Ponerorchis Reichenbach f.

TRIBE: Orchideae

SUBTRIBE: Orchidinae

ETYMOLOGY: From Greek *poneros*, worthless, and *orchis*, orchid—an inappropriate name!

DISTRIBUTION: About 20 species in Asia, most in Himalayas, China, and Japan

Small terrestrials with globose or oblong tubers. Leaves 1 or 2, usually at or near base of stem. Inflorescences several-flowered. Flowers pale to deep pink, purple, or rarely yellow; dorsal sepal often forming a hood with petals, lateral sepals spreading; lip trilobed, without a callus, spurred.

Some hybridization has been done with other species in the genus, but it is cultivars of *Ponerorchis graminifolia* that are most widely grown.

CULTIVATION: *Ponerorchis graminifolia* is widely grown in Japan and many cultivars have been developed, showing great variation in flower color and shape. Plants can be grown in an alpine house or cool greenhouse, where they are protected from frost. They require deep pots as the roots grow vertically and a light, free-draining compost and should be repotted annually. Plants are dormant in winter and should be kept dry although the air should be humid otherwise the tubers shrivel. Watering and fertilizing start when the new growth appears in spring and should continue until the leaves die back in autumn or early winter.

Ponerorchis graminifolia Reichenbach f.

Stems slender, 8–15 cm tall. Leaves grasslike, to 12 × 0.8 cm. Inflorescence unbranched, secund, few- to several-flowered. Flowers ca. 13 mm long, 6 mm across (often much larger in cultivated forms), white or pink spotted with deep pink or magenta; dorsal sepals and petals forming a hood; lip trilobed, lobes all spreading.

In cracks and among moss on rocks and cliffs, up to 100 m (330 ft.)

Japan

Ponthieva R. Brown

TRIBE: Cranichideae

SUBTRIBE: Cranichidinae

ETYMOLOGY: Named for Henri de Ponthieu, a French merchant who sent plants from the West Indies to Joseph Banks in 1778

DISTRIBUTION: About 30 species in tropical and subtropical America

Terrestrials or epiphytes with fleshy roots, lacking pseudobulbs. Leaves several, often in a rosette. Inflorescences terminal, unbranched; bracts leafy, shorter than flowers. Flowers nonresupinate; sepals pubescent, free or rarely with lateral sepals joined, the dorsal smaller than the laterals; petals small, asymmetrical, joined at the base to the sides of the column; lip fleshy, small, entire or trilobed, joined to the column at the base. Column short and stout; pollinia 4.

CULTIVATION: Species of *Ponthieva* can be grown in pans in an acid, free-draining terrestrial compost. They require intermediate to warm conditions, fairly heavy shade, and high humidity. Less water should be given after flowering has finished, but plants should not dry out completely.

Ponthieva maculata Lindley

Leaves basal, to 28 × 5 cm. Inflorescence to 30 cm tall, loosely several-flowered. Flowers relatively showy, dorsal sepal and petals bronze or yellow, barred with brown or maroon, lateral sepals white spotted with green or maroon; lip red or greenish red, with white markings.

Epiphytic, occasionally terrestrial, in forest, to 2500 m (8250 ft.)

Colombia, Ecuador, Venezuela

Ponthieva racemosa (Walter) C. Mohr

Leaves in a rosette, to 16 × 5 cm with a petiole 2–4 cm long. Inflorescence 20–50 cm tall, several- to many-flowered. Flowers 8–12 mm across, pale green, the lip white, green in the center.

Terrestrial in grassy areas in wet woodland, 600–2000 m (2000–6600 ft.)

Southern United States to South America

Porpax Lindley

TRIBE: Podochileae

SUBTRIBE: Eriinae

ETYMOLOGY: From Greek *porpax*, a shield handle, referring to shape of either leaves or pseudobulbs

DISTRIBUTION: 13 species in tropical Asia

Dwarf epiphytes or lithophytes with a creeping rhizome. Pseudobulbs ovoid to spherical, dorsiventrally flattened, covered with sheaths that disintegrate to form a network, 2-leaved, the leaves appearing with or after flowers. Inflorescences terminal, usually 1-flowered. Flowers small, bell-shaped; sepals joined to form a tube, petals free; lip entire or obscurely trilobed, V-shaped in cross-section.

CULTIVATION: Plants are more successful when mounted. They require intermediate conditions, moderate shade, high humidity, and plenty of water while actively growing.

Porpax meirax (C. S. P. Parish & Reichenbach f.) King & Pantling

SYN. *Eria meirax* (C. S. P. Parish & Reichenbach f.) N. E. Brown

Pseudobulbs clustered, round, flattened, to 10 mm across. Leaves to 2.5 cm long, elliptic to oblong, appearing after the flowers. Flowers ca. 10 mm long, dull brown, the sepals joined

Ponerorchis graminifolia. E. la Croix

Porpax meirax. R. Parsons

Ponthieva maculata

almost to the tips; lip obscurely trilobed, midlobe oblong.

Epiphytic on mossy branches in evergreen forest, sometimes lithophytic on mossy rocks

Myanmar

Porroglossum Schlechter

TRIBE: Epidendreae

SUBTRIBE: Pleurothallidinae

ETYMOLOGY: From Greek *porro*, forward, and *glossa*, referring to the position of the lip

DISTRIBUTION: More than 30 species in the Andes in Bolivia, Colombia, Ecuador, Peru, and Venezuela

Small epiphytic or terrestrial plants, tufted or creeping; pseudobulbs absent, stems erect, the base enclosed in tubular sheaths, 1-leafed at apex. Leaves petiolate. Inflorescences unbranched, few- to several-flowered, the flowers open in succession. Flowers resupinate or nonresupinate; sepals joined to about halfway to form a cup, the apices usually prolonged into tails; petals small; lip spoon-shaped, with a claw arched round the top of the column-foot and joined to it. Column winged, with a prominent foot; pollinia 2.

Many species were originally described in *Masdevallia*. *Porroglossum* has a specialized pollination mechanism. The lip is touch-sensitive and when an insect lands on it, it snaps upwards so that the insect comes in contact with the pollinia. The lip gradually returns to the open position. For a full description of this, see Luer (1987) in the "monographs" section of the bibliography.

CULTIVATION: Species of *Porroglossum* require cool to intermediate conditions, moderate shade, good ventilation, and high humidity all year round. They grow better in clay pots, which keep the roots cooler in hot weather, in a compost of 2 parts fine or medium bark, 1 part sphagnum, and 1 part charcoal. They can also be grown mounted if the humidity can be kept high enough. Plants should not be allowed to get too wet but must not dry out completely.

Porroglossum amethystinum (Reichenbach f.) Garay

Leaves to 10 cm long. Inflorescences 15–25 cm long, few-flowered. Flowers bright pink, dorsal sepal with a short tail, lateral sepals with long, slender, orange tails; lip white dotted with purple, purple-black near the tip.

Epiphytic in forest and terrestrial on roadside banks, ca. 2000 m (6600 ft.)

Ecuador

Porroglossum muscosum (Reichenbach f.) Schlechter

Variable, medium-sized plants. Stems 1–4 cm long. Leaves warty, to 15 cm long, green tinged with purple. Inflorescence 15–25 cm long, densely few-flowered, peduncle densely hairy. Flowers usually pale yellow-green with brown veins but sometimes pink or orange with darker veins; tails slender, 10–30 mm long; lip with a maroon blotch near tip. This is the most widespread species.

Epiphytic in cloud forest or terrestrial on roadside banks, 1000–2700 m (3300–8900 ft.)

Colombia, Ecuador, Venezuela

SIMILAR SPECIES: *Porroglossum echidnum* (Reichenbach f.) Garay from Colombia is a larger plant with the sepal tails thickened at the tips.

Porroglossum olivaceum Sweet

Stems to 1.5 cm long. Leaves 5–10 cm long, slightly warty. Inflorescence 10–25 cm tall, densely several-flowered. Flowers yellowish brown with darker veins; dorsal sepal with a short, reflexed tail, lateral sepals with long, slender, horizontal tails; lip yellow or white, spotted with purple.

Epiphytic in cloud forest, occasionally terrestrial on roadside banks, 1500–2000 m (5000–6600 ft.)

Colombia, Ecuador

Prasophyllum R. Brown

LEEK ORCHIDS

TRIBE: Diurideae

SUBTRIBE: Prasophyllinae

ETYMOLOGY: From Greek *prason*, leek, and *phyllon*, leaf

DISTRIBUTION: More than 100 species in southern and eastern Australia and New Zealand

Often robust terrestrials with subterranean tubers and 1 erect, cylindrical leaf. Inflorescences unbranched, few- to many-flowered. Flowers nonresupinate, often dull-colored, scented; dorsal sepal free, broader than the laterals; lateral sepals free or partly joined; petals free, usually unlike sepals; lip unlobed, often with undulate margins, thin-textured with a large, fleshy callus. Pollinia 4.

CULTIVATION: Plants are dormant in summer. Most species are stimulated into flowering by fire, and some will only flower after burning. Many species are difficult to grow, particularly to bring into flower, but colony-forming species such as *Prasophyllum australe* are easier. They require cool greenhouse or alpine house conditions with moderate shade where they can be grown in pans in a free-draining terrestrial compost with plenty of water while growing but kept dry while dormant.

Prasophyllum australe R. Brown

Leaf to 35 cm long. Inflorescence to 60 cm tall, densely many-flowered. Flowers ca. 15 mm across, strongly scented, white or yellowish suffused and striped with red-brown and green; lip white, strongly recurved.

Forms colonies in wet, grassy places in open forest at mid altitudes

Southeastern Australia, Tasmania

Prasophyllum elatum R. Brown

Leaf to 1.2 m long. Inflorescence to 1.5 m tall, densely many-flowered. Flowers scented, ca. 1.6 cm across,

Porroglossum amethystinum

Porroglossum olivaceum

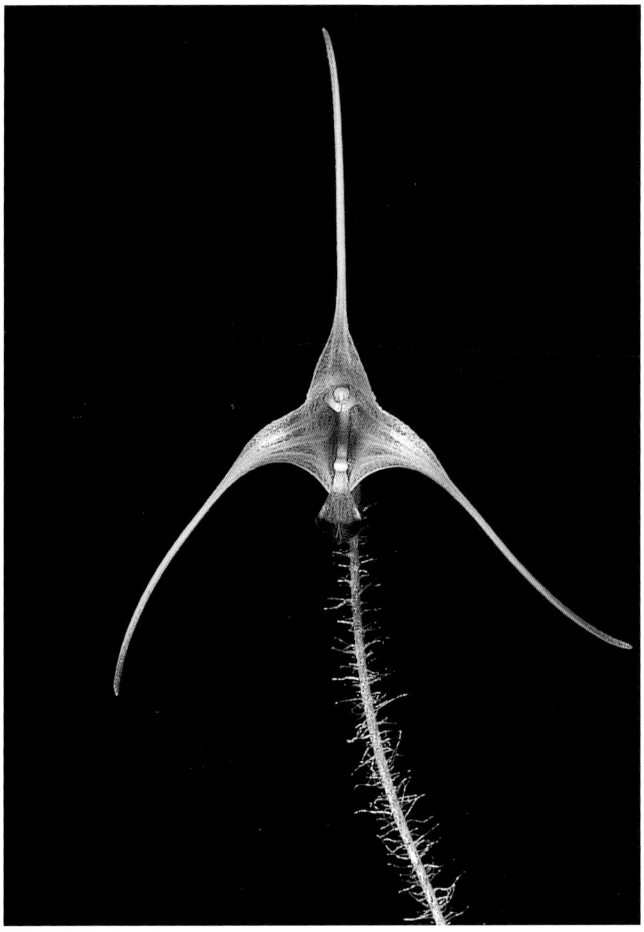
Porroglossum muscosum

Porroglossum echidnum

Prasophyllum elatum. J. Stewart

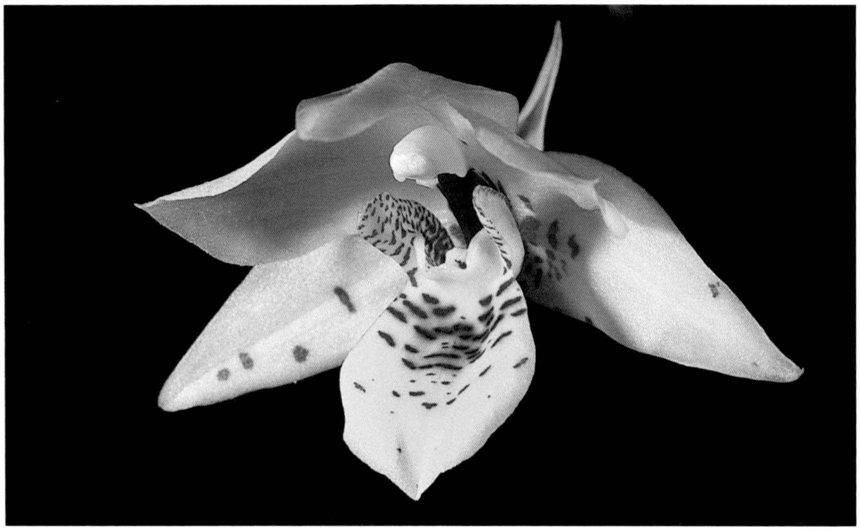

Promenaea guttata

pale yellow-green, brownish, or purple-black, the lip white, recurved, the margins crisped.

Most often in low scrub and heaths near coast

Widespread in Australia

Promenaea Lindley

TRIBE: Maxillarieae

SUBTRIBE: Zygopetalinae

ETYMOLOGY: Named for Promeneia, a priestess or prophetess of Dodona mentioned by Herodotus

DISTRIBUTION: 18 species in Brazil

Small sympodial epiphytes; pseudobulbs clustered, ovoid, compressed, 1- to 3-leaved at apex. Leaves to ca. 10 cm long, light green, often thin-textured, slightly plicate. Inflorescences arising from base of pseudobulb, horizontal or pendent, usually shorter than leaves, 1- to 2-flowered. Flowers medium-sized, fleshy, showy; sepals and petals subsimilar, free, spreading; lateral sepals joined to column-foot forming a short mentum; lip trilobed with a lobed or warty callus on disc; side lobes narrow, clasping the column, midlobe spreading. Column fleshy with a short foot, pollinia 4.

CULTIVATION: Promenaeas do best grown in pots or baskets in a free-draining fine bark mix in cool to intermediate temperatures, light shade, and moderately high humidity. They should be allowed to dry out between waterings but not for long, and care should be taken that water does not lie in the new growths.

Promenaea guttata

(Reichenbach f.) Reichenbach f. Leaves 7–8 cm long. Inflorescence ca. 7 cm long, horizontal or pendent, 1-flowered. Flowers ca. 4 cm across; sepals and petals cream to light green, barred with maroon; lip bright yellow with red-brown lines at the base. Flowering summer.

Epiphytic in cloud forest

Brazil

Promenaea stapelioides (Lindley) Lindley

Leaves to 10 cm long, ovate-lanceolate to oblong. Inflorescence ca. 5 cm long. Flowers scented, to 5 cm diameter; sepals and petals cream to buff with broken lines of maroon-brown (like flowers of the African succulent *Stapelia*); lip deep purple, the midlobe ovate to almost round. Column pale yellow. Flowering summer.

Epiphytic or lithophytic on mossy rocks in cool montane forest

Brazil

Promenaea xanthina (Lindley) Lindley

SYN. *Maxillaria xanthina* Lindley, *Promenaea citrina* D. Don

Leaves to 7 cm long, gray-green, rather fleshy. Inflorescence 5–10 cm long, 1- or 2-flowered. Flowers to 5 cm across, scented, long-lasting; sepals and petals primrose yellow; lip deeper yellow, midlobe oblong, side lobes with a few reddish spots; callus fleshy, trilobed. Column dotted with red.

Epiphytic on tree trunks in submontane forest, 1200–1500 m (4000–5000 ft.)

Brazil

Prosthechea Knowles & Westcott

SYN. *Anacheilium* Hoffmannsegg, *Euchile* (Dressler & G. E. Pollard) Withner

TRIBE: Epidendreae

SUBTRIBE: Laeliinae

ETYMOLOGY: From Greek *prostheke*, appendage, referring to the tissue on the back of the column of the type species, *P. glauca* Knowles & Westcott

DISTRIBUTION: More than 100 species from Florida south to Central and South America and the West Indies

Epiphytes or lithophytes with spindle-shaped, often flattened, pseudobulbs. Leaves 1–5, often glaucous. Inflorescences unbranched, usually with a basal sheath. Flowers usually nonresupinate; lip joined to lower half of column; callus usually a thick pad. Column without wings or a foot, the apex with 3 teeth; pollinia 4. Capsule with 3 wings or 3 sharp angles. (*Encyclia* capsules do not have wings or angles.)

Although the name *Prosthechea* was proposed in 1838, until recently the species have been classified in *Encyclia* and are still better known by

Promenaea stapelioides

Promenaea xanthina

that name. DNA analysis indicates that they should be treated as a separate genus.

CULTIVATION: Most species are easily grown and do well in intermediate temperatures with good light. They are usually grown potted in a standard epiphyte compost and need plenty of water while growing but should dry out between waterings.

Prosthechea boothiana (Lindley) W. E. Higgins

SYN. *Encyclia boothiana* (Lindley) Dressler

Pseudobulbs to 3 × 3 cm, circular, flattened, 2- or 3-leaved. Leaves to 1 cm long. Inflorescence to 25 cm long, few-flowered, basal sheath to 6 cm long. Flowers ca. 2 cm across, greenish yellow with red-brown blotches; lip with a white callus.

Epiphytic in rather dry forest, 0–100 m (330 ft.)

United States (Florida), Mexico, Central America, West Indies

Prosthechea brassavolae (Reichenbach f.) W. E. Higgins

SYN. *Encyclia brassavolae* (Reichenbach f.) Dressler, *Panarica brassavolae* (Reichenbach f.) Withner & P. A. Harding

Pseudobulbs to 20 × 5 cm, 2- or 3-leaved, set well apart on rhizome. Leaves to 28 × 5 cm. Inflorescence to 50 cm long, to ca. 15-flowered. Flowers showy, to 10 cm across; sepals and petals long and narrow, yellow-green to greenish tan; lip clawed, unlobed, pinkish purple, white at the base. This attractive, high-altitude species does better in cool conditions.

Epiphytic in rain forest and cloud forest, 900–2600 m (3000–8600 ft.)

Mexico to Panama

Prosthechea chacaoensis (Reichenbach f.) W. E. Higgins

SYN. *Anacheilium chacaoense* (Reichenbach f.) Withner & P. A. Harding, *Encyclia chacaoensis* (Reichenbach f.) Dressler & Pollard

Pseudobulbs to 10 × 5 cm, slightly flattened, gray-green, 2- or 3-leaved. Leaves to 30 × 5 cm, pale green. Inflorescence to 10 cm long, 2- to several-flowered. Flowers 4 cm across, scented, nonresupinate; sepals and petals pale green, lip shell-shaped, white with purple veins.

Epiphytic in moist forest, 0–900 m (3000 ft.)

Central and South America

Prosthechea citrina (Lexarza) W. E. Higgins

SYN. *Encyclia citrina* (Lexarza) Dressler, *Euchile citrina* (Lexarza) Withner

Plants pendent with pseudobulbs to 6 × 3 cm, 2- to 4-leaved. Leaves to 16 × 4 cm, gray-green. Inflorescence to 10 cm long, 1- or 2-flowered. Flowers 7–9 cm across, waxy, long-lasting, strongly scented, not opening widely, lemon yellow, the lip deeper yellow with a paler margin. With their pendent habit, plants should be mounted; they need cool to intermediate temperatures and a dry rest in winter.

Epiphytic in oak and pine forest, 1300–2600 m (4300–8600 ft.)

Mexico

Prosthechea cochleata (Linnaeus) W. E. Higgins

SYN. *Anacheilium cochleatum* (Linnaeus) Hoffmannsegg, *Encyclia cochleata* (Linnaeus) Lemée

COCKLESHELL ORCHID, CLAMSHELL ORCHID

Pseudobulbs to 20 × 5 cm, ovoid to ellipsoid, 1- to 3-leaved. Leaves to 40 × 5 cm. Inflorescence to 50 cm tall, few- to many-flowered. Flowers nonresupinate; sepals and petals pale green to yellow-green, to 7 cm long, less than 1 cm wide, deflexed, twisted; lip to 2.5 cm long, 3 cm wide, shell-shaped, deep purple-black with yellowish veins, white with purple veins at the base. This is the national flower of Belize.

Epiphytic in wet, broad-leaved forest, 450–1000 m (1500–3300 ft.)

United States (Florida), Mexico, Central and South America, West Indies

Prosthechea fragrans (Swartz) W. E. Higgins

SYN. *Anacheilium fragrans* (Swartz) Acuña, *Encyclia fragrans* (Swartz) Lemée

Pseudobulbs to 13 cm long, shortly stalked, well-spaced on rhizome, 1- or 2-leaved. Leaves to 30 × 5 cm, pale green. Inflorescence few-flowered. Flowers 2–4 cm across, scented, white, creamy or greenish; lip purple-veined, broadly ovate, apiculate, concave, to 20 × 12 mm.

Epiphytic in rain forest, 0–1000 m (3300 ft.)

Central and South America, West Indies

Prosthechea mariae (Ames) W. E. Higgins

SYN. *Encyclia mariae* (Ames) Hoehne, *Euchile mariae* (Ames) Withner

Pendulous plants with pseudobulbs to 4 × 3 cm, 2- or 3-leaved. Leaves to 18 × 3 cm, gray-green or olive green. Inflorescence to 20 cm long, few-flowered. Flowers 5–8 cm across, lime green, the lip white, marked with green in the center. In cultivation, this species requires conditions similar to *E. citrina*.

Epiphytic in dryish forest, 1000–1200 m (3000–4000 ft.)

Mexico

Prosthechea ochracea (Lindley) W. E. Higgins

SYN. *Encyclia ochracea* (Lindley) Dressler

Pseudobulbs to 10 × 1 cm, 2- or 3-leaved. Leaves to 25 × 1.5 cm. Inflorescence to 12 cm tall, densely several- to many-flowered. Flowers ca. 2 cm across, slightly cup-shaped, yellow-brown; lip white or yellow with red spots, the side lobes bigger than the midlobe.

Prosthechea brassavolae

Prosthechea citrina

Prosthechea cochleata

Prosthechea mariae

Prosthechea ochracea

Epiphytic in rain forest, 1600–1900 m (5300–6300 ft.)

Mexico, Central America

Prosthechea prismatocarpa (Reichenbach f.) W. E. Higgins

SYN. *Encyclia prismatocarpa* (Reichenbach f.) Dressler, *Panarica prismatocarpa* (Reichenbach f.) Withner & P. A. Harding

Pseudobulbs to 20 cm long, pear-shaped, 2- or 3-leaved. Leaves to 30 × 5 cm. Inflorescence 15–45 cm tall, many-flowered. Flowers to 5 cm across, scented; sepals and petals greenish cream to greenish yellow blotched with deep purple; lip mid-lobe lilac-purple; margins white.

Epiphytic in rain forest and cloud forest, 100–2450 m (330–8100 ft.)

Central and South America

Prosthechea pygmaea (Hooker) W. E. Higgins

SYN. *Encyclia pygmaea* (Hooker) Dressler

Pseudobulbs to 50 × 8 mm, 2-leaved, set 3–5 cm apart on creeping rhizome. Leaves to 10 × 2 cm. Inflorescence 1-flowered. Flowers to 12 mm across, scented, cream to pale green tinged with lilac or yellow-brown, lip white with 1–3 purple streaks. One of the smallest species.

Moist forest and cloud forest, 50–1800 m (165–6000 ft.)

United States (Florida), Mexico, West Indies, Central and South America

Prosthechea radiata (Lindley) W. E. Higgins

SYN. *Anacheilium radiatum* (Lindley) Pabst, Moutinho & A. V. Pinto, *Encyclia radiata* (Lindley) Dressler

Pseudobulbs to 16 × 4 cm, 2- or 3-leaved, set 2–3 cm apart on a creeping rhizome. Leaves to 30 × 3 cm. Inflorescence to 20 cm long with few to several flowers in a cluster. Flowers strongly scented, nonresupinate, cream or pale green; lip concave, veined with purple.

Epiphytic in forest, 150–2000 m (500–6600 ft.)

Mexico, Central America

Prosthechea vitellina (Lindley) W. E. Higgins

SYN. *Encyclia vitellina* (Lindley) Dressler

Pseudobulbs to 6 cm tall, 1- to 3-leaved. Leaves to 24 × 5 cm, gray-green. Inflorescence to 40 cm tall. Flowers showy, ca. 4 cm across, orange-red to scarlet; lip orange or yellow. This popular species does best in cool conditions.

Epiphytic in scrub woodland and cloud forest, 1400–2600 m (4600–8600 ft.)

Mexico, El Salvador, Guatemala

Pseudolaelia Porto & Brade

TRIBE: Epidendreae

SUBTRIBE: Laeliinae

ETYMOLOGY: From Greek *pseudo*, false, and *Laelia*, as the genus resembles *Laelia* in having 8 pollinia

DISTRIBUTION: 10 species in Brazil

Epiphytes or lithophytes with spindle-shaped pseudobulbs, 2- to 7-leaved at apex, set apart on a creeping rhizome. Leaves sometimes purplish. Inflorescences terminal, long, unbranched, several-flowered. Flowers 2–5 cm across, pink or yellowish; sepals and petals free, subsimilar; lip joined to base of column, trilobed, midlobe with or without a ridged callus. Column stout; pollinia 8.

CULTIVATION: I can find no information on cultivation of these species. I would expect them to grow potted in a free-draining, bark-based compost in good light, with plenty of water while growing but with a dry resting period.

Pseudolaelia vellozicola (Hoehne) Porto & Brade

SYN. *Schomburgkia vellozicola* Hoehne

Leaves several. Inflorescence to 150 cm tall, to 15-flowered, the flowers near the apex of the stem. Flowers ca. 4 cm across, pink; lip with a yellow-and-white ridged callus.

Lithophytic and epiphytic on *Vellozia* species, 1000–1400 m (3300–4600 ft.)

Eastern Brazil

Psychilis Rafinesque

TRIBE: Epidendreae

SUBTRIBE: Laeliinae

ETYMOLOGY: From Greek *psyche*, butterfly, and *cheilos*, lip

DISTRIBUTION: 15 species in the Caribbean islands

Epiphytes or lithophytes with a short rhizome covered in papery sheaths; pseudobulbs of various shapes, 1- to 3-leaved at apex. Leaves leathery, the margins sometimes finely toothed. Inflorescences erect, sometimes

Prosthechea prismatocarpa

Pseudolaelia vellozicola. C. van den Berg

Prosthechea radiata

Prosthechea vitellina

Psychilis olivacea

branched, covered in overlapping papery sheaths. Flowers clustered, several open at a time in succession over a long period, usually pink or purple; sepals and petals free, spreading or reflexed; lip trilobed, clawed, with a callus at the base and a grooved callus on the midlobe. Pollinia 4.

CULTIVATION: Plants require intermediate to warm conditions with bright light and high humidity. They do not need frequent watering and should be kept almost dry while resting. They seem to be most successfully grown in baskets in a coarse, free-draining compost or mounted on a slab. In the wild most species grow at fairly low altitudes, 0–1000 m (3300 ft.), in habitats from dry, thorny scrub to pine woodland.

Psychilis bifida (Aublet) Sauleda
SYN. *Epidendrum bifidum* Aublet, *Encyclia bifida* (Aublet) Britton & Wilson
Pseudobulbs slender, pear-shaped or cylindrical, to 10 cm long, Leaves 15–25 × 1–2 cm. Inflorescence to 1.5 m tall, to 25-flowered. Flowers showy, ca. 3 cm across, pale rose-red; sepals and petals oblanceolate; lip ca. 24 mm long and wide, midlobe deeply emarginate.
Hispaniola

Psychilis olivacea (Cogniaux) Sauleda
SYN. *Epidendrum olivaceum* Cogniaux, *Encyclia olivacea* (Cogniaux) Beckner
Leaves narrow, to 21 × 1.5 cm, the margins finely toothed. Inflorescence to 65 cm long with a few branches. Flowers showy, 5 cm across; sepals and petals ovate, yellowish green; lip deep purple-red.
Hispaniola

Psychopsiella Lückel & Braem

TRIBE: Maxillarieae
SUBTRIBE: Oncidiinae
ETYMOLOGY: Diminutive of *Psychopsis*
DISTRIBUTION: 1 species in Brazil and Venezuela

Dwarf plants with an ascending rhizome and small, heart-shaped, bilaterally flattened pseudobulbs, 1-leafed at the apex, both pseudobulbs and leaves lying flat on the substrate. Inflorescences basal, much longer than the leaf, few-flowered. Flowers relatively large, showy; sepals and petals free, spreading, petals larger than sepals; lip trilobed, saccate at the base, midlobe much larger than side lobes.

CULTIVATION: Because of their distinctive growth habit, plants must be mounted. They require intermediate conditions, moderate shade, and high humidity. They should be given less water when not in active growth.

Psychopsiella limminghei (E. Morren ex Lindley) Lückel & Braem
SYN. *Oncidium limminghei* E. Morren ex Lindley
Pseudobulbs 1–2 × 1–1.5 cm. Leaves elliptic, to 3.5 × 3 cm, mottled with darker green and red. Inflorescence wiry, ca. 15 cm long, 1- to 3-flowered. Flowers 3–4 cm across; sepals and petals dark red-brown with some yellow-green banding, particularly on the petals; lip to 20 mm long and wide, yellow mottled with red-brown, side lobes spreading, midlobe ± kidney-shaped.
Brazil, Venezuela

Psychopsis Rafinesque

BUTTERFLY ORCHIDS
TRIBE: Maxillarieae
SUBTRIBE: Oncidiinae
ETYMOLOGY: From Greek *psyche*, butterfly, and *opsis*, like, meaning resembling a butterfly
DISTRIBUTION: 4 species in Central and South America

Pseudobulbs clustered, laterally compressed, enclosed in thin sheaths at the base, 1-leafed at apex. Leaves stiff, erect, often mottled with red. Inflorescences basal, erect, unbranched, the flowers produced singly in succession over a long period. Flowers showy; dorsal sepal

Psychopsiella limminghei

and petals erect, narrow at the base and broader at the tips; lateral sepals broader, spreading, often with undulate margins; lip large, trilobed, with basal calli. Pollinia 2.

CULTIVATION: Plants can be grown either potted in a coarse epiphyte mix or mounted on a bark slab. They need a bright, airy situation in intermediate to warm conditions and should be watered freely while in growth but kept cooler while resting, when they only need to be misted every few days. Old flower spikes should not be cut off as they sometimes flower again.

Psychopsis krameriana (Reichenbach f.) H. G. Jones
SYN. *Oncidium kramerianum* Reichenbach f., *O. nodosum* E. Morren
Pseudobulbs to 4 × 4 cm. Leaves to 15 × 6.5 cm, mottled with maroon.

Inflorescence 30–90 cm tall. Flowers to 12 cm long; sepals and petals red-brown edged and banded with yellow; lip deep red-brown with a prominent purple-brown callus.

Epiphytic in wet woodland, 50–800 m (165–2640 ft.)

Costa Rica to Ecuador

Psychopsis papilio (Lindley) H. G. Jones

SYN. *Oncidium papilio* Lindley, *Psychopsis picta* Rafinesque

Pseudobulbs to 5 cm long. Leaves to 25 × 7 cm, mottled with red-brown. Inflorescence erect, to 1 m tall. Flowers to 15 cm long; sepals and petals purple mottled with yellow; lip yellow, the side lobes spotted and edged with orange-brown.

Epiphytic in rain forest, 800–1000 m (2640–3300 ft.)

Central and South America, Trinidad

Pteroceras Hasskarl

TRIBE: Vandeae

SUBTRIBE: Aeridinae

ETYMOLOGY: From Greek *ptero*, wing, and *ceras*, horn, referring to appendages at the base of the lip

DISTRIBUTION: About 25 species from India to southern China and Malesia

Small, monopodial epiphytes, usually with short stems. Inflorescences few- to many-flowered. Flowers smallish, short-lived; sepals and petals free, spreading, the lateral sepals often broader than the petals; lip fleshy, mobile, spurred, trilobed, side lobes larger than midlobe. Column short and stout with a long foot; pollinia 2.

CULTIVATION: Plants are usually mounted but can be potted in a standard bark mix. They require intermediate conditions and high humidity and should not be allowed to dry out completely.

Pteroceras leopardinum (Parish & Reichenbach f.) Seidenfaden & Smitinand

SYN. *Thrixspermum leopardinum* Parish & Reichenbach f.

Stems erect, to 10 cm long. Leaves several, distichous, to 14 × 2 cm. Inflorescence ca. 6 cm long, to 10-flowered. Flowers small, fleshy; sepals and petals yellow with brown-

Psychopsis krameriana

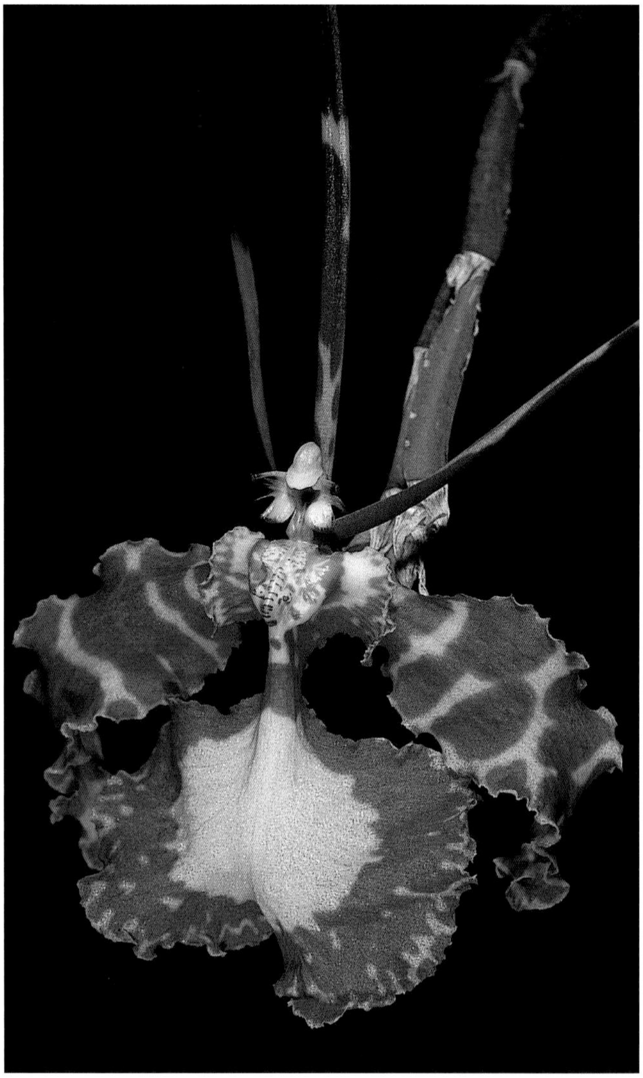

Psychopsis papilio

ish or purple spots; lip white with purple-brown spots on side lobes; spur saccate, hairy inside.

Epiphytic in woodland, 450–1700 m (1500–5600 ft.)

Widespread from India to Southeast Asia

Pteroceras semiteretifolium H. A. Pederson

Miniature plant, Leaves short, fleshy, slightly curved, borne in a fan. Inflorescence 1-flowered. Flowers opening wide, ca. 2 cm across, white, sometimes flushed with pink; lip side lobes marked with purple.

Twig epiphyte in lowland evergreen forest

Vietnam

Pteroceras teres (Blume) Holttum

Pendent plants with stems to 25 cm long. Leaves several, to 19 × 3 cm. Inflorescence few- to many-flowered. Flowers resupinate, scented, ca. 8 mm long; sepals and petals yellow, spotted and barred with red-brown; lip yellow, side lobes erect, linear, midlobe with 2 small calli; spur cylindrical, swollen at apex.

Epiphytic in evergreen forest

Widespread from India to Southeast Asia

Pterostylis R. Brown

GREENHOODS

TRIBE: Cranichideae

SUBTRIBE: Pterostylidinae

ETYMOLOGY: From Greek *pteron*, wing, and *stylos*, pillar, referring to the prominent wings on the column

DISTRIBUTION: About 200 species, mostly in Australia, with some in New Zealand and the West Pacific

Small, deciduous terrestrials with globose tubers, sometimes stoloniferous. Leaves either in a basal rosette or bractlike on stem. Inflorescences 1- to many-flowered. Flowers resupinate, green, sometimes tinged or striped with purple or red-brown; dorsal sepal arched, forming a galea (hood) with the petals, enclosing the column; lateral sepals fused at the base, the tips free, usually erect and overtopping the galea but deflexed in some species; lip motile, clawed, sometimes with a slender basal appendage.

CULTIVATION: Species of *Pterostylis* are the most widely cultivated of Australian terrestrial orchids; those that form colonies are easily grown. They require cool conditions such as an alpine house and do well in a standard, free-draining terrestrial mix, with several tubers planted in 1 pot. Of the colony-forming species, those with leaves in a rosette flower in winter and spring, while those with leaves along the stem flower in autumn. All should be kept dry while dormant; careful watering should start when the leaves appear. Plants quickly increase vegetatively and should be

Pteroceras semiteretifolium

Pterostylis curta. E. la Croix

repotted at least every 2 years, otherwise they become overcrowded.

Pterostylis baptistii Fitzgerald
Leaves ovate, to 8 × 2.5 cm, in a rosette. Inflorescence to 40 cm tall, 1-flowered. Flowers to 6 cm long, the largest in the genus, translucent white, flushed and marked with green and brown; lateral sepals free for ca. 35 mm at the tip, the free parts filiform, protruding behind the galea.

Forms colonies in high-rainfall forest and thicket

Eastern Australia

Pterostylis curta R. Brown
Leaves ovate, to 10 × 3 cm, in a rosette. Inflorescence 10–30 cm tall, 1-flowered. Flowers ca. 35 mm long, whitish striped with green and flushed with green and brown; free parts of lateral sepals ca. 12 mm long, lying beside the hood but not overtopping it; lip to 20 mm long, brown, twisted at the apex.

Forms dense colonies usually in open forest, often near a stream

Eastern and southeastern Australia, New Caledonia

Pterostylis nutans R. Brown
PARROT'S BEAK ORCHID
Leaves ovate, to 9 × 3 cm, forming a rosette. Inflorescence to 30 cm tall, 1- or 2-flowered. Flowers nodding, to 25 mm long, translucent with green stripes, sometimes reddish towards the tips; free parts of lateral sepals protruding beyond galea; lip recurved, to 15 mm long, green with a red-brown median ridge.

Forms colonies in grassland and in coastal scrub

Eastern and southeastern Australia, New Zealand (North Island)

Pterostylis ophioglossa R. Brown
SNAKE-TONGUE GREENHOOD
Leaves in rosette, to 4 × 1.5 cm. Inflorescence to 25 cm long, 1-flow-

Pterostylis ophioglossa

Pterostylis recurva. H. Oakeley

ered. Flowers erect or nodding, ca. 30 mm long, white, flushed with green, brown, or reddish; lip prominent, deeply notched.

Common in coastal scrub, open forest, and forest edge

Australia (Queensland, New South Wales), New Caledonia

Pterostylis pedunculata R. Brown

MAROONHOOD

Leaves ovate, petiolate, to 4 × 2 cm, forming a rosette. Inflorescence to 25 cm tall, 1- or 2-flowered. Flowers to 20 mm long, green and white at the base, then suffused with deep reddish brown; free points of lateral sepals 30 mm long, protruding well above the hood.

Forms colonies at a range of altitudes, often in gullies among ferns, sometimes on mossy logs

Southeastern Australia

Pterostylis recurva Bentham

JUG ORCHID

Inflorescence to 60 cm tall, wiry, with several stem leaves to 5 cm long, 1- to 3-flowered. Flowers to 35 mm long, translucent white striped and flushed with green and brown, funnel-shaped; petals spreading, lateral sepals free in the apical half, the free parts becoming filiform, decurved; lip ca. 15 mm long, reddish. Although this species does not form colonies, it is not difficult to cultivate.

Widespread in woodland and dense scrub

Southwestern Western Australia

Quekettia Lindley

TRIBE: Maxillarieae
SUBTRIBE: Oncidiinae
ETYMOLOGY: Named for Edwin J. Quekett (1808–1847), lecturer in botany at London Hospital
DISTRIBUTION: 4 species in South America

Twig epiphytes with long, wiry roots; pseudobulbs very small, laterally compressed, enclosed in overlapping sheaths, sometimes leafy, 1-leafed at apex. Leaves ± terete. Inflorescences axillary, branched or unbranched. Flowers minute; dorsal sepal free; lateral sepals joined at the base; petals like dorsal sepal or broader; lip entire, joined to column base. Column lacking a foot, winged at the apex; pollinia 2.

CULTIVATION: These little species should be most successful mounted, in warm to intermediate temperatures, with bright light, good air movement, and high humidity all year round.

Quekettia microscopica Lindley

SYN. *Quekettia chrysantha* Barbosa Rodrigues

Inflorescence shorter than leaves, few- to several-flowered. Flowers minute; sepals and petals bright yellow-green; lip golden yellow with 2 maroon spots near apex.

Twig epiphyte in rain forest, often in full sun, 50–500 m (165–1650 ft.)

Brazil, French Guiana, Guyana, Surinam, Venezuela

Quekettia microscopica. M. Campacci

Rangaeris Summerhayes

TRIBE: Vandeae
SUBTRIBE: Aerangidinae
ETYMOLOGY: A near anagram of *Aerangis*, a related genus
DISTRIBUTION: 6 species in Africa

Monopodial epiphytes, occasionally lithophytes, with long or short stems. Leaves linear, strap-shaped, oblong or bilaterally flattened. Inflorescences axillary, unbranched, few to many-flowered. Flowers usually white, scented, turning apricot with age; lip entire or trilobed, spurred at the base; spur usually long and slender.

Rangaeris is a disparate genus and it will be surprising if future DNA work does not lead to some of the species being moved to other genera.

CULTIVATION: All species require intermediate to warm conditions, high

Rangaeris amaniensis

humidity, and moderate shade. Less water should be given while plants are resting. The smaller species do well mounted; others can be grown in pots or baskets in a coarse, free-draining mixture.

Rangaeris amaniensis

(Kraenzlin) Summerhayes
Stems woody, to 45 cm long; roots stout. Leaves to 12 × 1.5 cm, strap-shaped, folded at base. Inflorescence to 20 cm long, 5- to 13-flowered. Flowers white; sepals 10–25 mm long, spreading or recurved, petals slightly smaller; lip obscurely trilobed; spur to 16 cm long, slender, pendent. This species does best in a basket.

Montane forest or open woodland, 1050–2600 m (3500–8600 ft.)

East Africa

Rangaeris muscicola

Rangaeris muscicola

(Reichenbach f.) Summerhayes
Stem short. Leaves several, in a fan, to 18 × 2 cm, strap-shaped, folded, slightly recurved. Inflorescences usually 2 per plant, to 30 cm long, several- to many-flowered. Flowers white, ca. 15 mm across; sepals and petals spreading, lanceolate to elliptic; lip entire, ovate; spur to 9 cm long, very slender. Does best mounted.

Evergreen forest or woodland, sometimes lithophytic, 600–2200 m (2000–7260 ft.)

Widespread in Africa

Rangaeris rhipsalisocia

(Reichenbach f.) Summerhayes
Stems short. Leaves several, in a fan, to 12 × 1 cm, bilaterally flattened. Inflorescence to 10 cm long, 9- or 10-flowered. Flowers white, bell-shaped; sepals to 11 mm long; lip entire, to 10 mm long, spur to 15 mm long, the apex hooked forwards. Does best mounted as it rots easily.

Evergreen forest, 100–200 m (330–660 ft.)

West and Central Africa

Renanthera Loureiro

TRIBE: Vandeae
SUBTRIBE: Aeridinae
ETYMOLOGY: From Greek *renes*, kidneys, and *anthera*, anther, referring to the kidney-shaped pollinia
DISTRIBUTION: 20 species in Asia from India to the Pacific Islands

Large or medium-sized, monopodial epiphytic, occasionally terrestrial plants. Stems stout, sometimes scandent, leaves distichous, oblong or strap-shaped. Inflorescences branched or unbranched, many-flowered. Flowers showy, red, orange, or yellow, often spotted; dorsal sepal and petals subsimilar, oblanceolate; lateral sepals larger, usually spathulate; lip much smaller, trilobed, the base saccate; side lobes erect, midlobe often reflexed. Pollinia 4, kidney-shaped.

Renanthera citrina

CULTIVATION: Plants require conditions similar to *Vanda*—bright light, warm or intermediate to warm temperatures, and plenty of water. The smaller species can be grown in pots, but larger ones do better in baskets, with supporting wire if necessary.

Renanthera bella J. J. Wood

One of the smaller species; leaves leathery, semi-terete, 10–12 cm long, 1 cm wide. Inflorescence unbranched, pendent, 10–15-flowered. Flowers 5–6 cm across, red or deep pink with darker spots. This species is often confused with *R. monachica*.

Epiphytic in hill forest, 800–1100 m (2640–3600 ft.)

Borneo

Renanthera citrina Averyanov

Plants 20–45 cm tall; leaves leathery, light green, 7–10 cm long. Inflorescence erect, branched up to 50 flowered. Flowers 6–7 cm across, lemon yellow with scattered raspberry pink spots on the sepals and petals. Lip geniculate with a bright yellow spot in center. Flowering spring.

Epiphytic in forest, 600–1000 m (2000–3300 ft.)

Vietnam

Renanthera coccinea Loureiro

The type species of the genus and the commonest in cultivation. Large plants to 2 m tall with a scrambling stem. Leaves oblong, 7–9 cm long. Inflorescence erect, branched, many-flowered. Flowers 5–7 cm across, bright red. Dorsal sepal and petals dotted with lighter red, lateral sepals unspotted; lip dark red with a big white blotch in the center.

Epiphytic or terrestrial at edge of forest or in open woodland, ca. 1400 m (4600 ft.)

China, Vietnam, Laos, Thailand, Myanmar

Renanthera imschootiana Rolfe

Plants to about 1.7 m tall; leaves to 12 × 2 cm. Inflorescence branched, arching with the weight of the many flowers. Flowers 7–8 cm across, the largest in the genus, flame red, the lip darker red with a bright yellow blotch in the center.

Epiphytic in forest up to 500 m (1650 ft.)

Myanmar, China, India

Renanthera matutina Blume

SYN. *Renanthera angustifolia* Hooker

Plants about 1 m tall. Leaves narrow, 10–20 cm long. Inflorescence branched, pendent, many-flowered. Flowers 4–5 cm across, long-lasting, light red with darker spots, lip yellow-orange and white.

Epiphytic in lowland forest, 100–600 m (330–2000 ft.)

Borneo, Java, peninsular Malaysia, Philippines, Sumatra

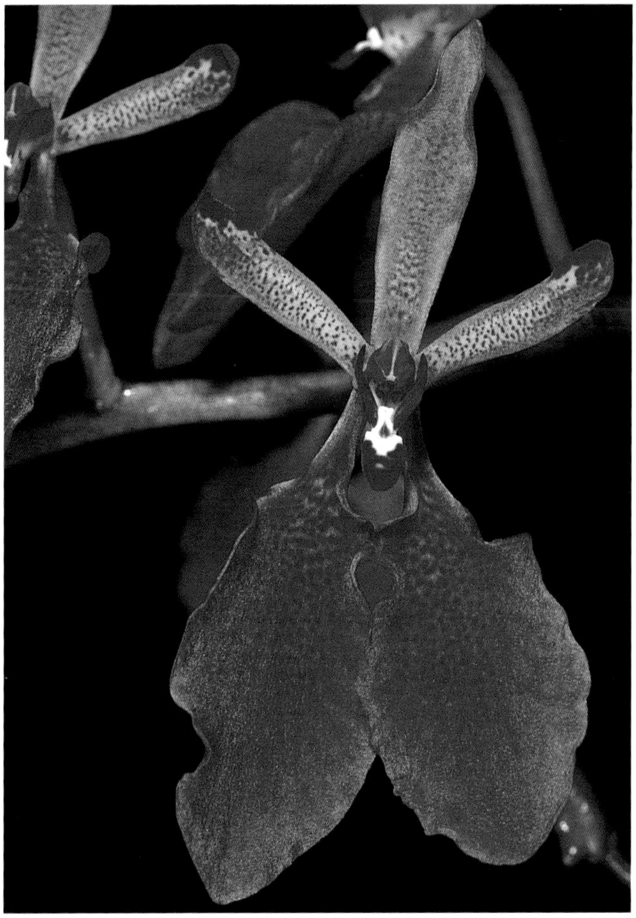

Renanthera imschootiana

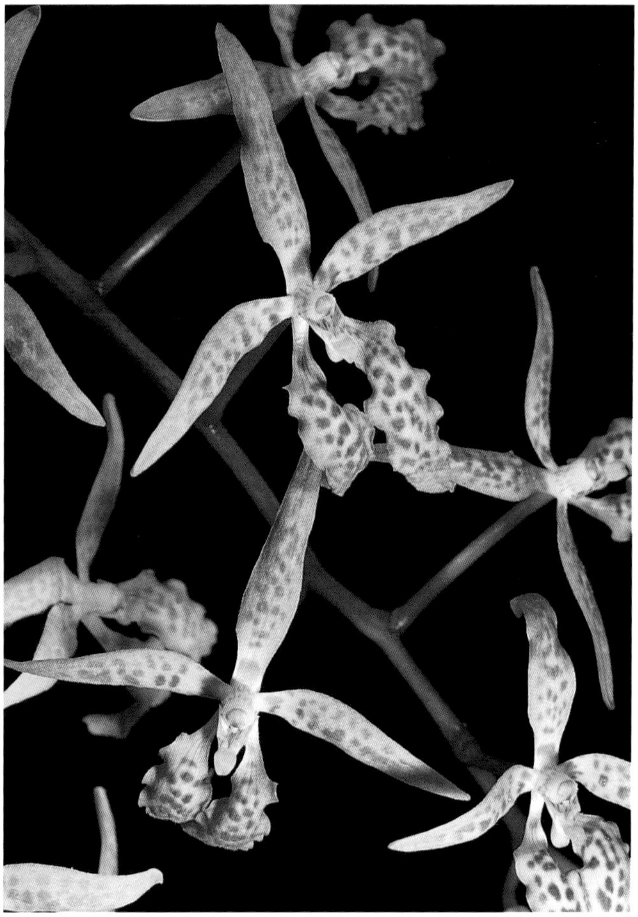

Renanthera matutina

Renanthera monachica

Renanthera storei

Renanthera monachica Ames
Erect plants to 50 cm tall. Leaves semi-terete, 8–12 cm long, often dark green on upper surface and violet-purple below. Inflorescence unbranched, pendulous, to about 50-flowered. Flowers ca. 4 cm across, yellow to light orange with red spots, long-lasting, open in autumn. *R. monachica* cannot withstand temperatures below 15°C.

Epiphytic in forest up to 500 m (1650 ft.)

Endemic to the Philippines

Renanthera storei Reichenbach f.
One of the largest in the genus, to 4 m high. Leaves leathery, 10–12 × 3 cm. Inflorescence branched, pendulous, with over 100 bright red, unspotted flowers about 6 cm across. The spathulate lateral sepals are very wide at the tips; the dark red lip has a white central blotch.

Epiphytic in bright light up to 1000 m (3300 ft.)

Endemic to the Philippines

Restrepia Kunth

TRIBE: Epidendreae
SUBTRIBE: Pleurothallidinae
ETYMOLOGY: Named for José Manuel Restrepo (b. 1782), a Colombian botanist
DISTRIBUTION: About 50 species in Mexico, Central and South America

Small, tufted epiphytes with erect stems enclosed in overlapping, papery, often spotted, sheaths, 1-leafed at apex. Leaves fleshy or leathery, often flushed with purple on the underside. Inflorescences usually arising in clusters at the junction of stem and leaf, 1-flowered. Flowers small to large, often lying on the leaves; dorsal sepal free, erect, narrow, the apex enlarged; lateral sepals joined for most of their length to form a boat-shaped synsepal; petals like dorsal sepal but smaller; lip hinged to base of column, entire or trilobed, the apex bilobed. Pollinia 4.

CULTIVATION: Species of *Restrepia* are epiphytic in rain forest and cloud forest at altitudes from 350 to 3500 m (1150–11,550 ft.). They require cool to intermediate conditions, good ventilation and high humidity all year round. They can be grown potted in a fine epiphyte compost or mounted, if the humidity is sufficiently high.

Restrepia antennifera Kunth
Stems to 23 cm long. Leaves to 10 × 5 cm. Flowers lying on back of leaf, peduncle 4–9 cm long; sepals to 5 cm long, yellow, veined and dotted with purple; petals translucent white, narrowly linear, to 3 cm long.

Epiphytic in forest, 1500–3500 m (5000–11,500 ft.)

Colombia, Venezuela

SIMILAR SPECIES: *Restrepia guttulata* Lindley from Colombia, Ecuador, and Venezuela has the synsepal spotted with purple.

Restrepia aristulifera Garay & Dunsterville
Stems stout, 6–25 cm tall. Leaves to 9 × 4 cm. Peduncle 3–5 cm long, Sepals ca. 25 mm long, dorsal sepal translu-

Restrepia antennifera

Restrepia aristulifera

Restrepia guttulata

cent white with a red midvein, lateral sepals pale yellow with red-purple spots on the apical half and red-purple veins on the basal half.

Epiphytic in cloud forest, 2200–2800 m (7260–9250 ft.)

Colombia, Venezuela

Restrepia dodsonii Luer
Small plants; stems to 5 cm long, leaves 2–4 × 1–2.5 cm. Peduncle 2–4 cm long, sepals pinkish white, the laterals with rows of purple dots, to 24 mm long; petals translucent white; lip margins toothed.

Epiphytic in plantations and forest, 1400–1700 m (4600–5600 ft.)

Ecuador

Restrepia elegans Karsten
Stems 2–8 cm long; leaves to 6 × 3 cm. Peduncle 3–5 cm long; sepals

Restrepia dodsonii

18–24 cm long, dorsal sepal translucent white with a purple midvein; lateral sepals yellowish, spotted with brown or purple.

Epiphytic in forest, 1400–2750 m (4600–9075 ft.)

Venezuela

Restrepia muscifera (Lindley) Reichenbach f.

A variable species; stems 2.5–17 cm long, the lower sheaths black-spotted. Leaves to 8 × 3.5 cm. Peduncle 7–20 mm long; sepals 8–15 mm long, white, yellow or pink, spotted with purple, the lateral sepals bifid with rounded lobes.

Epiphytic in rain forest and cloud forest, 600–2700 m (2000–8900 ft.)

Mexico, Central America, Colombia, Ecuador

Restrepia pelyx Luer & R. Escobar

Stems 4–13 cm long, the lower sheaths spotted with brownish purple. Leaves to 8 × 4 cm. Peduncle erect, 4–5 cm long. Sepals thin-textured, dorsal sepal translucent white with a red-purple midvein, lateral sepals forming a concave synsepal 21–26 mm long, yellow or tan with red or brown spots; lip spotted with purple or yellow.

Epiphytic in forest, 2000–2700 m (6600–8900 ft.)

Colombia, Venezuela

Restrepiella Garay & Dunsterville

TRIBE: Epidendreae

SUBTRIBE: Pleurothallidinae

ETYMOLOGY: Diminutive of *Restrepia*

DISTRIBUTION: 1 species in Mexico to Costa Rica

Small, tufted epiphyte. Stems stout, with a tubular sheath near the middle and 2 or 3 overlapping sheaths at the base, 1-leafed at apex.

Restrepia elegans

Restrepia muscifera

Leaves thick and leathery, petiolate. Inflorescences 1-flowered but several arising in a cluster from a spathe at the junction of leaf and stem; sepals fleshy, pubescent on outside, dorsal sepal free, lateral sepals joined into a synsepal, notched at apex; petals small, covered with papillae; lip with 2 lobules at base, hinged to column-foot, with a longitudinal keel. Pollinia 4.

CULTIVATION: As for *Restrepia*, but at intermediate rather than cool temperatures. Grow either potted in a fine epiphyte compost or, if the humidity is sufficiently high, mounted. Plants require intermediate conditions, good ventilation, and high humidity all year round.

Restrepiella ophiocephala

(Lindley) Garay & Dunsterville

Stems to 20 cm long; leaves 10–20 × 3–4 cm. Inflorescence short. Flowers opening wide, 3–4 cm long; sepals fleshy, greenish or yellowish spotted and flushed with purple-red.

Epiphytic in humid lowland forest and in plantations, 450–1200 m (1500–4000 ft.)

Mexico, Belize, Guatemala, El Salvador, Nicaragua, Costa Rica

Rhipidoglossum

Schlechter

TRIBE: Vandeae

SUBTRIBE: Aerangidinae

ETYMOLOGY: From Greek *rhipis*, fan, and *glossum*, tongue, referring to the lip shape in most species

DISTRIBUTION: About 35 species on mainland Africa and islands off the west coast

Long or short-stemmed plants with numerous roots, often with white streaks more noticeable when wet. Inflorescences unbranched. Flowers usually small, translucent; sepals

Restrepia pelyx

Restrepiella ophiocephala

and petals spreading, petals usually shorter and broader than sepals; lip spurred, often broader than long. Column short; pollinia 2, each with its own stipes and viscidium.

The genus *Rhipidoglossum* was established in 1918 by German botanist Rudolf Schlechter but until recently, most botanists placed it in synonymy with *Diaphananthe*, which Schlechter had described 4 years earlier. However, recent DNA work indicates that the genera should be kept separate in spite of their similar appearance. The most important difference is that in *Diaphananthe* each pollinium has its own stipes but they share a common viscidium while in *Rhipidoglossum* there are 2 viscidia. *Rhipidoglossum* species tend to have smaller flowers (except *R. kamerunense*), and most species of *Diaphananthe* have a peg-like callus on the lip in the mouth of the spur, which is lacking in *Rhipidoglossum*.

CULTIVATION: Short-stemmed species grow well in pots in a medium bark-based compost, but those with long stems do better mounted on bark. Most require intermediate conditions with fairly heavy shade and high humidity. While not in growth, they should be kept drier but not allowed to dry out completely.

Rhipidoglossum kamerunense (Schlechter) Garay

SYN. *Diaphananthe kamerunensis* (Schlechter) Schlechter

Robust, short-stemmed plants with stout roots. Leaves several, to 36 × 5.5 cm, oblanceolate, unequally and obtusely bilobed at apex. Inflorescence pendent, 10–12 cm long, 5–10-flowered, the peduncle covered with loose, papery bracts 10–15 mm long. Flowers 3–4 cm across (the largest in the genus), pale green or pale yellow. Petals suborbicular, the margins fringed. Lip to 20 × 24 mm, fan-shaped, trilobed near the apex, the midlobe toothlike, the apical margin fringed; spur 12–14 mm long.

Epiphytic in forest and woodland, 1000–1800 m (3300–6000 ft.)

West and Central Africa

Rhipidoglossum rutilum (Reichenbach f.) Schlechter

SYN. *Diaphananthe rutila* (Reichenbach f.) Summerhayes

Stem to 40 cm long, usually pendent. Roots numerous, the growing tips often purple. Leaves to 12 × 2 cm, linear or strap-shaped, dark olive-green, often purple-tinged. Inflorescences arising along stem, 5–20 cm long, densely many-flowered. Flowers ca. 6 mm across, purplish brown, occasionally cream. Lip to 4 × 5 mm, fan-shaped; spur slender, 4–8 mm long, incurved.

Epiphytic, often at low levels, in evergreen and riverine forest, 550–2200 m (1800–7260 ft.)

Widespread in tropical Africa

Rhipidoglossum xanthopollinium (Reichenbach f.) Schlechter

SYN. *Diaphananthe xanthopollinia* (Reichenbach f.) Summerhayes

Rather variable. Stem usually long, to 30 cm, but sometimes remaining short. Roots numerous, 4–5 mm diameter. Leaves several to many, to 15 × 2.5 cm, strap-shaped, sometimes fleshy and V-shaped in cross-section. Racemes arising along stem, to 9 cm long, densely many-flowered. Flowers small, creamy yellow or straw orange, lilac-scented. Flowering spring–summer.

Epiphytic in submontane and riverine forest and woodland, 600–1800 m (2000–6000 ft.)

East and Central Africa, South Africa

SIMILAR SPECIES: *Rhipidoglossum pulchellum* (Summerhayes) Garay, from West, Central, and East Africa, has pale yellow flowers twice as large as those of *R. xanthopollinium*.

Rhyncholaelia Schlechter

TRIBE: Epidendreae

SUBTRIBE: Laeliinae

ETYMOLOGY: From Greek *rhynchos*, beak, and *Laelia*, referring to the beak separating the ovary from the rest of the flower

DISTRIBUTION: 2 species in Mexico and Central America

Pseudobulbs long, club-shaped, 1-leafed at apex. Leaves thick, fleshy, gray-green. Inflorescence 1-flowered. Flowers large, showy, scented, long-lasting; sepals spreading, free, similar, petals broader; lip funnel-shaped, enclosing column at base, margins entire or fringed. Column club-shaped; pollinia 8.

Both species of *Rhyncholaelia* have been much used in hybridization with related genera.

CULTIVATION: Both species are easily grown in similar conditions to *Cattleya*, in pots or baskets in a coarse, free-draining compost, in bright light with good air movement. They should be kept much drier in the resting season.

Rhyncholaelia digbyana (Lindley) Schlechter

SYN. *Brassavola digbyana* Lindley

Pseudobulbs to 21 cm long, 2 cm wide, with papery whitish sheaths. Leaves to 20 × 5 cm, sometimes tinged with purple. Inflorescence to 14 cm long. Flowers to 18 cm across, strongly scented; sepals and petals pale green; lip white, the margins deeply fringed.

Epiphytic in rather dry forest and thicket at low altitudes

Mexico, Central America

Rhyncholaelia glauca (Lindley) Schlechter

SYN. *Brassavola glauca* Lindley

Pseudobulbs to 8 cm long. Leaves to 13 × 3.5 cm. Inflorescence to 10 cm long. Flowers to 12.5 cm across; sepals and petals white or pale green, flushed with mauve on the outside;

pidoglossum rutilum

pidoglossum pulchellum. E. la Croix

Rhyncholaelia glauca

lip pale green or white, rounded, the margins undulate, with a pink or purple mark at the base.

Epiphytic or occasionally terrestrial in humid forest, 600–1600 m (2000–5300 ft.)

Mexico to Colombia

Rhynchostele Reichenbach f.

SYN. *Lemboglossum* Halbinger
TRIBE: Maxillarieae
SUBTRIBE: Oncidiinae
ETYMOLOGY: From Greek *rhynchos*, beak, and *stele*, column
DISTRIBUTION: 15 species in Mexico, Central America, and Venezuela

Epiphytic, lithophytic, or rarely terrestrial plants with clustered, ovoid, laterally compressed pseudobulbs, 1- to 3-leaved at apex and with basal sheaths. Inflorescences basal, sometimes with a few branches, few- to many-flowered. Flowers large, showy; sepals and petals free, spreading, subsimilar; lip with a short claw joined to the column at the base, with a fleshy callus on the claw; blade spreading. Column long and slender.

CULTIVATION: Plants are usually grown in pots in a standard epiphyte compost. Most grow in humid, high-altitude forest and so require cool to intermediate temperatures, light to moderate shade, and plenty of water while in growth. While resting they should be kept cooler and drier.

Rhynchostele bictoniensis

(Bateman) Soto Arenas & Salazar
SYN. *Odontoglossum bictoniense* (Bateman) Lindley, *Lemboglossum bictoniense* Bateman

Pseudobulbs ca. 6 × 3 cm, 2- or 3-leaved, with 3–4 basal sheaths. Leaves to 45 × 5.5 cm, strap-shaped. Inflorescence to 80 cm tall, many-flowered. Flowers to 5 cm across, sometimes scented; sepals and petals pale green or yellow-green with red-brown markings; lip ± heart-shaped, white or pink, the edges undulate.

Epiphytic in cloud forest, 2000–2500 m (6600–8250 ft.)

Mexico, Central America

Rhynchostele bictoniensis

Rhynchostele cervantesii

Rhynchostele cervantesii

(Lexarza) Soto Arenas & Salazar
SYN. *Odontoglossum cervantesii* Lexarza, *Lemboglossum cervantesii* (Lexarza) Halbinger

Pseudobulbs to 6 × 3 cm, angled. Leaves to 15 × 3 cm. Inflorescence to 30 cm tall, covered with brownish sheaths, several-flowered. Flowers 3.5–7 cm across, scented; sepals and petals white or pink with irregular red-brown bands in basal half; lip white or pink with purple stripes at the base.

Epiphytic in evergreen cloud forest and lithophytic on cliffs, 1400–3200 m (4,600–10,500 ft.)

Mexico

Rhynchostele cordata (Lindley)

Soto Arenas & Salazar
SYN. *Odontoglossum cordatum* Lindley, *Lemboglossum cordatum* (Lindley) Halbinger

Pseudobulbs to 8 × 3.5 cm, 1-leafed at the apex and with 2 basal sheaths. Leaves to 23 × 5 cm. Inflorescence 25–60 cm tall, many-flowered. Flowers 4–8 cm across; sepals and petals long acuminate, yellow blotched and barred with red-brown; lip heart-shaped, acuminate, white blotched with red-brown.

Epiphytic in cloud forest, 1000–3100 m (3300–10,200 ft.)

Mexico, Central America

SIMILAR SPECIES: *Rhynchostele maculata* (Lexarza) Soto Arenas & Salazar (syn. *Odontoglossum maculatum* Lexarza, *Lemboglossum maculatum* (Lexarza) Halbinger), also from Mexico and Central America, has acute or shortly acuminate petals.

Rhynchostele rossii (Lindley)

Soto Arenas & Salazar
SYN. *Odontoglossum rossii* Lindley, *Lemboglossum rossii* (Lindley) Halbinger

Pseudobulbs to 6 × 3.5 cm. Leaves to 14 × 3 cm. Inflorescence to 20 cm long, erect or arching, 1- to 4-flowered. Flowers 5–8 cm across; sepals and petals white, pale pink, or pale

Rhynchostele cordata

Rhynchostele maculata

Rhynchostele rossii

Rhynchostylis gigantea

yellow, sepals and base of petals mottled with red-brown; lip white, heart-shaped, the edges crisped. Column pinkish mauve.

Epiphytic in cloud forest, 2000–3000 m (6600–9900 ft.)

Mexico, Central America

Rhynchostylis Blume

FOXTAIL ORCHIDS

TRIBE: Vandeae

SUBTRIBE: Aeridinae

ETYMOLOGY: From Greek *rhynchos*, beak, and *stylos*, column

DISTRIBUTION: 4 species in tropical Asia

Robust epiphytes or lithophytes with short, stout stems and thick roots. Leaves distichous, fleshy, narrowly strap-shaped. Inflorescences erect, arching or pendent, cylindrical, many-flowered. Flowers showy; sepals and petals spreading, the petals broader; lip joined to base of column-foot, entire or obscurely trilobed, saccate or with a laterally flattened spur. Column short and stout, pollinia 2.

CULTIVATION: Plants are usually grown in hanging baskets so that the roots are not confined. They require intermediate to warm conditions, high humidity, and moderate shade. They need plenty of water while in active growth, but when there are no green growing tips on the roots, they should be given much less water.

Rhynchostylis coelestis

(Reichenbach f.) Reichenbach f. ex H. J. Veitch

Stem to 20 cm long. Leaves to 20 cm long. Inflorescence erect. Flowers to 2 cm across, waxy, white; tips of the sepals, petals, and lip violet-blue.

This species and *Rhynchostylis gigantea* have been hybridized with *Vanda* to give the hybrid genus ×*Rhynchovanda*.

Epiphytic in rather dry forest and open woodland, 0–700 m (2300 ft.)

Cambodia, Thailand, Vietnam

Rhynchostylis gigantea

(Lindley) Ridley

Stem stout, to 15 cm long, roots to 18 mm in diameter. Leaves to 40 × 4.5 cm. Inflorescence arching or pendent, 15–30 cm long, densely many-flowered. Flowers 3 cm across; sepals and petals white with reddish-purple marks; lip red-purple with darker veins; spur 5 mm long with white hairs inside.

Epiphytic on tree trunks in open woodland and lowland forest, to 1000 m (3300 ft.)

China to Malesia

Rhynchostylis retusa (Linnaeus) Blume

Stem 3–10 cm long, covered in old leaf bases. Leaves 20–40 × 2–4 cm. Inflorescence 25–45 cm long, pendent, densely many-flowered. Flowers 1.5–2 cm across; sepals and petals white, spotted with pink; lip white at the base, pink in the apical half; spur 6–8 mm long.

Rhynchostylis retusa

Robiquetia succisa

Epiphytic on tree trunks in open woodland or at forest edge, 300–1400 m (1000–4600 ft.)

Tropical Asia

Robiquetia Gaudichaud

TRIBE: Vandeae

SUBTRIBE: Aeridinae

ETYMOLOGY: Named for Pierre Robiquet, a French chemist

DISTRIBUTION: About 40 species in tropical and subtropical Asia

Epiphytes with long or short stems. Leaves distichous. Inflorescences axillary, sometimes branched, usually pendent, many-flowered. Flowers small, in a range of colors from white to yellow and red; sepals and petals free, dorsal sepal usually forming a hood over the column; lip trilobed, rather fleshy, spurred. Column short and stout; pollinia 2.

CULTIVATION: Plants can be grown in pots or baskets or mounted. They require intermediate to warm temperatures, light to moderate shade, and plenty of water while in active growth. They need less water while resting but should not dry out completely for long.

Robiquetia spathulata (Blume) J. J. Smith

Stems pendent, 50–100 cm long. Leaves oblong, to 20 × 4 cm. Inflorescence 8–18 cm long, densely many-flowered. Flowers 5–13 mm across, yellow with red-brown or purplish blotches on the sepals and petals, lip with smaller spots; spur club-shaped, ca. 5 mm long.

Epiphytic in forest and riverine forest, 0–1400 m (4600 ft.)

Eastern Himalayas to Malesia

Robiquetia succisa (Lindley) Seidenfaden & Garay

SYN. *Robiquetia paniculata* (Lindley) J. J. Smith

Stem to 1 m long, pendent. Leaves oblong, to 12 × 2.5 cm. Inflorescence branched, to 23 cm long, fairly densely many-flowered. Flowers 7–9 mm across, yellow or greenish yellow, sometimes with red-brown dots; spur club-shaped, 3–4 mm long.

Epiphytic in open woodland or lithophytic on cliffs, 500–1800 m (1650–6000 ft.)

Himalayas to China and Indochina

Rodriguezia Ruíz & Pavón

TRIBE: Maxillarieae
SUBTRIBE: Oncidiinae
ETYMOLOGY: Name for Spanish botanist, Don Manuelo Rodriguez
DISTRIBUTION: About 40 species in Central and South America

Small, sympodial epiphytes with small pseudobulbs hidden in leafy sheaths, 1- to 2-leaved at apex, set close together or well-spaced on a scandent rhizome. Roots long and fine. Inflorescences lateral, unbranched, often pendent. Flowers relatively large, with the dorsal sepal and petals forming a hood; lateral sepals usually spreading; lip clawed with a short spur and an obovate blade with crests on the disc.

CULTIVATION: Most species of *Rodriguezia* are twig epiphytes and grow well mounted on slabs of bark or coconut. They need good light and regular water throughout the year, but should dry out between waterings. Mist freely while in growth, but new growths are prone to fungal attack so good air movement is important. In winter, the minimum temperature should not be less than 12–15°C (54–59°F).

Rodriguezia batemanii Poeppig & Endlicher

The largest species in the genus, 20–25 cm tall, with pseudobulbs set close together on a climbing rhizome. Inflorescence arching or pendent, 3- to 10-flowered. Flowers to 7 cm across, white, usually tinged with pink or purple; sepals and petals spreading; lip broad with an undulate margin and a yellow callus; spur incurved. Flowering in spring; last for about a month.

Epiphytic in rain forest, 50–200 m (165–660 ft.)

Brazil, Ecuador, Peru, Venezuela

Rodriguezia batemanii

Rodriguezia candida Bateman ex Lindley

Plants creeping or scandent. Pseudobulbs compressed, to 5 cm tall, 1-leafed. Leaves to 15 cm long, oblong or lanceolate. Raceme arching or pendent, few-flowered. Flowers large, scented, white with a yellow mark on the lip; dorsal sepal 30 mm long, lateral sepals joined; lip fan-shaped, to 54 mm long.

Epiphytic in rain forest, 200–500 m (660–1650 ft.)

Brazil, Guyana, Venezuela

Rodriguezia decora (Lemaire) Reichenbach f.

A small, scandent species with compressed pseudobulbs set 3–5 cm apart. Leaves leathery. Inflorescence pendent. Flowers ca. 3.5 cm across, white, dotted with pink, more or less tubular with the bilobed lip protruding. Flowering summer–autumn; last for 2 to 3 weeks.

Epiphytic in rain forest

Southeastern Brazil

SIMILAR SPECIES: *Rodriguezia satipoana* Dodson & D. E. Bennett from Peru.

Rodriguezia granadensis (Lindley) Reichenbach f.

A small species ca. 10 cm tall. Pseudobulbs 1-leafed. Inflorescence spreading, 3- to 7-flowered. Flowers to 3 cm across, crystalline white with yellow marks on the lip; spur to 2 cm long. Flowering spring–summer; may last for over a month.

Epiphytic in rain forest

Columbia, Ecuador

Rodriguezia lanceolata Ruíz & Pavón

SYN. *Rodriguezia secunda* Kunth

This species is the commonest in cultivation. Leaves narrow. Inflorescence spreading or pendent, to 20-flowered. Flowers showy, ca. 2.5 cm across, pink to deep red. Flowering in summer; last for 3 to 4 weeks.

Epiphytic in rain forest and riparian forest, 50–900 m (165–3000 ft.)

Widespread in Central and South America

Rodriguezia decora

Rodriguezia lanceolata

Rodriguezia granadensis

Rodriguezia leeana Reichenbach f.

Leaves leathery, V-shaped in section. Inflorescence arching or pendent. Flowers to 4 cm across, white flushed with pink towards the base; lip marked with yellow.

Epiphytic in rain forest, 50–200 m (165–660 ft.)

Brazil, Ecuador, Peru, Surinam, Venezuela

Rodriguezia venusta (Linden ex Lemaire) Reichenbach f.

Plants 12–18 cm tall. Pseudobulbs 1-leafed. Inflorescence pendent, 5- to 8-flowered. Flowers to 3.5 cm across, fragrant, white; lip emarginate, with a bright yellow callus; spur recurved. Flowering in spring; last for a month.

Epiphytic in rain forest

Brazil, Peru

Rossioglossum (Schlechter) Garay & G. C. Kennedy

TRIBE: Maxillarieae

SUBTRIBE: Oncidiinae

ETYMOLOGY: Named for J. Ross, who collected orchids in Mexico in the 1830s

DISTRIBUTION: 6 species in Mexico and Central America

Medium-sized to large epiphytes with clustered, ovoid pseudobulbs, 2-leaved at apex. Leaves large, petiolate. Inflorescences lateral, unbranched, laxly few- to several-flowered. Flowers large, showy; sepals and petals spreading, subsimilar or the petals broader; lip rather obscurely trilobed with a prominent callus; side lobes small, earlike, midlobe large.

CULTIVATION: Plants are most successful potted in a medium grade epiphyte compost at cool to intermediate temperatures. They need bright light and plenty of water while in growth. Once the pseudobulbs are mature, they should be kept cooler and drier, with only enough water given to prevent the pseudobulbs shriveling. Most flower in autumn and winter.

Rossioglossum grande (Lindley) Garay & G. C. Kennedy

SYN. *Odontoglossum grande* Lindley

CLOWN ORCHID

Pseudobulbs to 10 × 6 cm, with sharp angles. Leaves to 40 × 6.5 cm. Inflorescence to 30 cm tall, 2- to 8-flowered. Flowers ca. 15 cm across; sepals yellow with red-brown bars and blotches, petals red-brown in basal half, yellow in apical half; lip creamy white or pale yellow, midlobe ± orbicular, the margins crisped. A yellow form is known as f. *aureum*.

Epiphytic in wet, deciduous forest, 1400–2700 m (4600–8900 ft.)

Mexico, Central America

SIMILAR SPECIES: *Rossioglossum insleayi* (Baker ex Lindley) Garay & G. C. Kennedy (syn *Oncidium insleayi* Baker ex Lindley, *Odontoglossum insleayi* (Baker ex Lindley) Lindley) from Mexico has smaller flowers with the edges of the sepals and petals rolled back and the base of the petals barred instead of solid brown. *Rossioglossum williamsianum* (Reichenbach f.) Garay & G. C. Kennedy (syn. *Odontoglossum williamsianum* Reichenbach f.) from Mexico and Guatemala has slightly smaller flowers and shorter, broader, paddle-shaped petals.

Rossioglossum hagsaterianum Soto Arenas

Flowers 9–16 cm across; sepals and petals glossy chocolate brown, sometimes with yellow margins and tips; lip flaring abruptly from a narrow base, yellow, with red-brown blotches around the margin and bars at the base. A form with pure yellow flowers is known as f. *aureum*.

Epiphytic, 1300–2000 m (4300–6600 ft.)

Mexico

SIMILAR SPECIES: *Rossioglossum splendens* (Reichenbach f.) Garay & G. C. Kennedy (syn. *Odontoglossum splendens* (Reichenbach f.) G. C. Kennedy & Garay), also from Mexico, has slightly smaller flowers and a lip with a gradually tapering base.

Rossioglossum schlieperianum (Reichenbach f.) Garay & G. C. Kennedy

SYN. *Odontoglossum schlieperianum* Reichenbach f.

Pseudobulbs to 6 × 3 cm, 2-leaved at apex. Leaves to 30 × 7 cm. Inflorescence arching, 20–40 cm long, several-flowered. Flowers 7–10 cm across, yellow or greenish yellow barred with reddish brown in the basal halves of the parts; callus bright yellow with red marks. A yellow form of this species is known as f. *flavidum*.

Epiphytic in rain forest and cloud forest, 1400–2000 m (4600–6600 ft.)

Costa Rica, Panama

Rudolfiella Hoehne

TRIBE: Maxillarieae

SUBTRIBE: Zygopetalinae

ETYMOLOGY: Named for German taxonomist Rudolf Schlechter (1872–1925)

DISTRIBUTION: 6 species in Central and South America and Trinidad

Medium-sized sympodial epiphytes. Pseudobulbs round to ovoid, flattened, 1-leafed at apex. Leaves petiolate, plicate. Inflorescences lateral, unbranched, loosely few- to several-flowered. Flowers showy; sepals and petals free, spreading or cup-shaped; lateral sepals joined to column-foot to form a mentum; lip clawed, trilobed, with a fleshy callus in the center. Pollinia 4.

CULTIVATION: Grow plants potted in a free-draining, medium bark-based mixture. They require intermediate temperatures, moderate shade, and plenty of water while in growth. When resting, they should be kept cooler and much drier.

Rodriguezia venusta

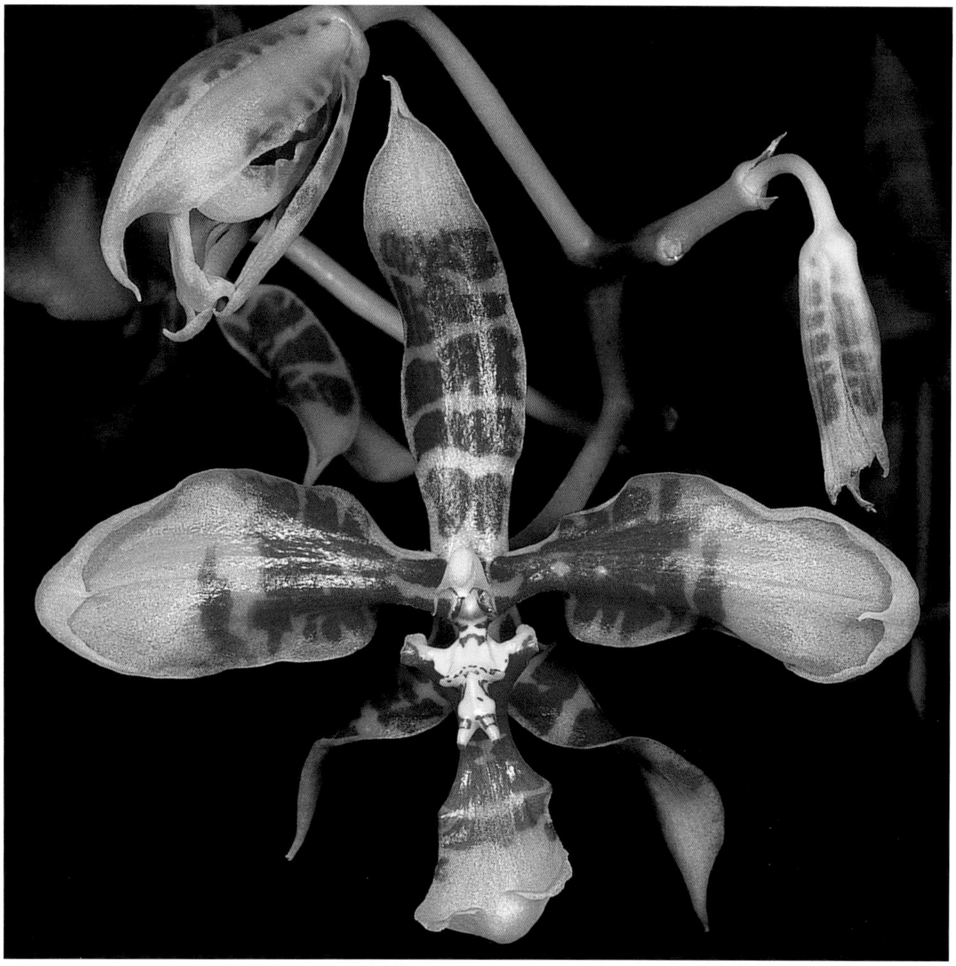

Rossioglossum schlieperianum

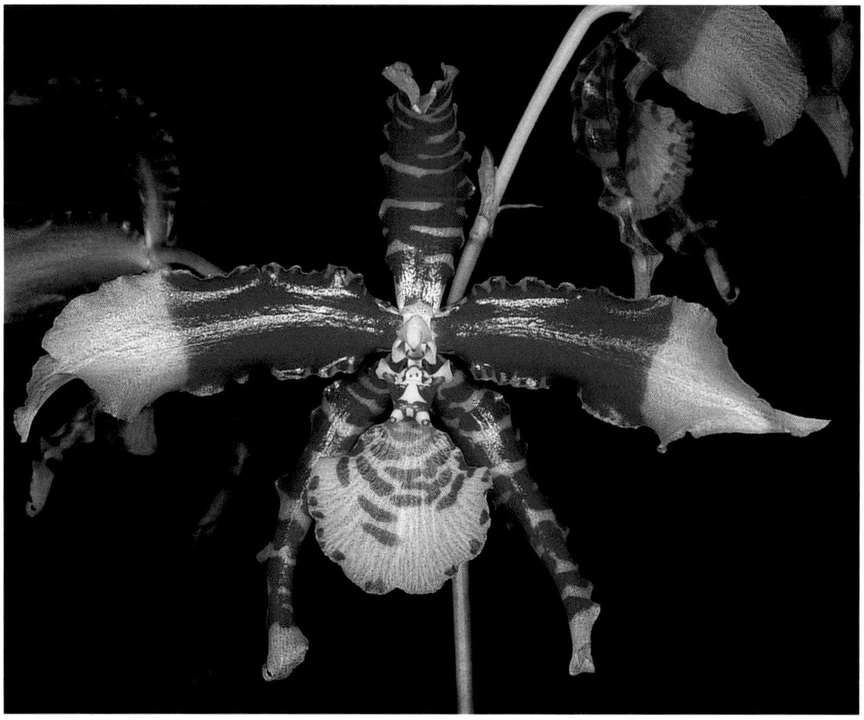

Rossioglossum grande

Rossioglossum insleayi

Rudolfiella aurantiaca

Sarcochilus ceciliae

Sarcochilus falcatus

Rudolfiella aurantiaca (Lindley) Hoehne

SYN. *Bifrenaria aurantiaca* Lindley

Pseudobulbs clustered, ovoid, flattened, ca. 5 × 4 cm. Leaves 10–37 cm × 3–5 cm. Inflorescence to 30 cm long, laxly about 15-flowered. Flowers ca. 4 cm across, long-lasting, orange or yellowish orange, blotched with brown; lip claw as long as the blade, trilobed in the middle with a trilobed, pubescent callus.

Epiphytic in rain forest, 50–1100 m (165–3600 ft.)

Brazil, Ecuador, Guyana, Peru, Trinidad, Venezuela

Sarcochilus R. Brown

TRIBE: Vandeae

SUBTRIBE: Aeridinae

ETYMOLOGY: From Greek *sarcos*, fleshy, and *cheilos*, lip

DISTRIBUTION: 25 species in Australasia and the Pacific Islands

Monopodial epiphytes and lithophytes. Stem short, often branched at the base. Leaves usually distichous, fleshy. Inflorescences axillary, unbranched, few- to many-flowered. Flowers fleshy, sepals and petals subsimilar; lip trilobed, mobile, with a small, sometimes saccate, spur at the base; disc with a grooved callus.

About 100 hybrids involving *Sarcochilus* exist, most intrageneric.

CULTIVATION: The epiphytic species usually do better mounted on bark, while the lithophytes, which are more robust, do well in pots and baskets in a coarse, free-draining compost. All like high humidity and cool or intermediate conditions, while good air movement is essential.

Sarcochilus ceciliae F. Mueller

Stems to 10 cm long, erect, branched at base. Leaves several, to 8 × 1 cm, linear, channeled, often with darker spots. Inflorescence erect, to 20 cm long, 6- to 15-flowered. Flowers 6–10 mm across, pink, rarely white, the lip with a yellow callus, midlobe densely hairy. In cultivation, this species requires good light and intermediate temperatures.

Lithophytic, usually in hollows or crevices where litter is present, in both exposed and shaded situations, usually above 500 m (1650 ft.)

Australia (Queensland to northern New South Wales)

Sarcochilus falcatus R. Brown

ORANGE-BLOSSOM ORCHID

Stems short, sparsely branched at base. Leaves several, to 16 × 2 cm, strap-shaped, curved, often yellowish green. Racemes arching to pendent, to 18 cm long, 3- to 12-flowered. Flowers ca. 30 mm across, strongly scented, white or cream, the sepals sometimes striped with purple on the outside, waxy-textured; sepals and petals spreading; lip small, marked with yellow or orange; spur thin, pointing forwards.

Epiphytic in humid areas where air movement is good

Australia (Queensland to Victoria)

Sarcochilus fitzgeraldii F. Mueller

Robust lithophyte with stems to 60 cm long, much branched, often pendent. Leaves several, to 20 × 1.5 cm, linear, fleshy. Racemes to 20 cm long, arching or pendent, 4- to 15-flowered. Flowers ca. 30 mm across, white or pink with red spots in the center; sepals and petals spreading; lip short, yellow; spur blunt, pointing forwards.

Lithophytic in moist, shaded places such as ravines and gorges

Australia (southeastern Queensland to northeastern New South Wales)

SIMILAR SPECIES: *Sarcochilus hartmannii* F. Mueller has a similar distribution. It is a more erect plant, the lip side lobes are broader, and it tends to grow in more exposed situations, thus requiring more light in cultivation. *Sarcochilus* Fitzhart is an artificial hybrid of the last 2 species.

Sarcoglottis Presl

TRIBE: Cranichideae

SUBTRIBE: Spiranthinae

ETYMOLOGY: From Greek *sarcos*, flesh, and *glottis*, tongue, referring to the texture of the lip

DISTRIBUTION: About 45 species in Mexico, Central and South America, and the West Indies

Terrestrial plants with many fleshy, cylindrical roots in a dense cluster, sometimes with several clusters set along a creeping rhizome. Leaves several, in a basal rosette, usually petiolate, green, often marked with white stripes and dots, occasionally reddish brown with green dots. Inflorescences pubescent,

Sarcochilus hartmannii

Sarcoglottis sp. in Ecuador. R. Parsons

unbranched, few- to many-flowered, sometimes appearing before leaves. Flowers fleshy, small to medium-sized, sometimes scented; sepals pubescent on the outside, dorsal sepal and petals forming a hood over the column; lateral sepals partly joined, forming an internal nectary; lip enclosing the column at the base, blade usually recurved. Column-foot much longer than the column.

CULTIVATION: Species of *Sarcoglottis* are cultivated for their attractive leaves. They should be grown in shallow pans in a humus-rich terrestrial compost. They need intermediate to warm conditions and plenty of water while growing. When plants are dormant, they should be kept much drier but not allowed to dry out completely or the roots will shrivel.

Sarcoglottis sceptrodes

(Reichenbach f.) Schlechter

SYN. *Sarcoglottis hunteriana* Schlechter

Leaves numerous, elliptic, petiolate, to 25 × 7 cm, green with silvery white stripes and spots. Inflorescence to 70 cm long, several-flowered. Flowers ca. 4 cm long, lemon-scented, not opening wide, yellow-green with dark green veins; lateral sepals horizontal or upcurved, undulate, obtuse.

Terrestrial in wet woodland, 0–800 m (2640 ft.)

Mexico, Central America

SIMILAR SPECIES: *Sarcoglottis acaulis* (J. E. Smith) Schlechter from Central and South America has down-curved, acute lateral sepals.

Satyrium Swartz

TRIBE: Diseae

SUBTRIBE: Satyriinae

ETYMOLOGY: From Greek *satyrion*, the two-horned satyr, referring to the twin spurs

DISTRIBUTION: More than 80 species, most in Africa but with some in Madagascar and Asia

Slender or robust terrestrial herbs with globose, ovoid, or ellipsoid tubers. Leaves either on flowering stem or on a separate sterile shoot with only sheathing leaves on flowering stem. Inflorescences unbranched, densely or loosely few- to many-flowered; floral bracts often large, sometimes colored. Flowers nonresupinate (lip at the top), relatively small, in a wide range of colors, often showy; sepals and petals subsimilar, joined at the base to each other and the lip; lip forming a hood with a wide or narrow mouth, bearing 2 spurs, long and slender or short and saccate. Column erect, inside lip; pollinia 2.

CULTIVATION: Species of *Satyrium* are not widely grown, partly because they are difficult to obtain. All have a definite dormant period, whether they are summer- or winter-growing. While dormant, they should be kept dry and watering should not start until the new growth is visible above the soil; watering should be stopped when the leaves start to turn yellow and die back. Plants require an open, free-draining compost usually containing river sand. Most like good light and cool conditions. For further information on growing African species, see Wodrich (1997) in the "cultural" section of the bibliography.

Satyrium carneum (Aiton) R. Brown

Robust plants 30–80 cm tall. Basal leaves 2, ovate, to 23 cm long, tightly pressed to the ground. Flowering stem with several sheathing leaves; spike densely many-flowered. Flowers pink, relatively large, the sepals to 18 mm long; spurs 1.5–2 cm long, parallel to the ovary. Flowering in spring; summer dormant.

Winter rainfall area, in fynbos on coastal hills, 15–300 m (50–1000 ft.)

South Africa (southwestern Cape)

Satyrium coriifolium Swartz

Robust plants 20–75 cm tall. Leaves borne on stem, towards the base, to 15 cm long, erect or spreading,

Satyrium carneum. J. Stewart

Satyrium coriifolium. E. la Croix

elliptic. Inflorescence densely many-flowered. Flowers bright orange or bright yellow; sepals to 13 mm long; lip bent forwards with a 2-mm-long flap over the mouth, spurs 9–12 mm long, lying along ovary. Flowering early spring; summer dormant.

Winter rainfall area, on sandy soil and clay, 0–750 m (2460 ft.)

South Africa (from southwestern to eastern Cape)

Satyrium erectum Lindley

Robust plants 10–50 cm tall. Basal leaves 2, almost round, 4–16 cm long, pressed to the ground. Flowering stem with several sheathing leaves; spike densely several- to many-flowered. Flowers strongly and sweetly scented, pale to deep pink with darker marks on the petals and lip; sepals to 12 mm long; spurs 7–9 mm long. Flowering usually in spring; summer dormant.

Winter rainfall area on dry sandy or clay soil, 150–1500 m (500–5000 ft.)

South Africa (Namaqualand to western Cape)

Satyrium nepalense D. Don

Erect terrestrial plants 15–70 cm tall. Leaves semi-erect or spreading, 10–25 × 5–10 cm, oblong, rather fleshy. Flowering stem stout, with some sheathing leaves; spike densely many-flowered, the bracts longer than the flowers. Flowers scented, bright pink, rarely white, to 16 mm across; spurs 10–16 mm long, longer than ovary. Flowering summer; winter dormant. This attractive species is hardy in some temperate gardens but is usually grown in an alpine house.

Var. *ciliatum* (Lindley) Hooker f. (syn. *Satyrium ciliatum* Lindley) from Bhutan, China, Nepal, and Tibet, has ciliate sepals and petals and a spur less than 1 cm long.

Open montane grassland and in forest clearings, 1500–4100 m (5000–13,500 ft.)

Bhutan, India, Myanmar, Sri Lanka

Scaphosepalum Pfitzer

TRIBE: Epidendreae

SUBTRIBE: Pleurothallidinae

ETYMOLOGY: From Greek *skaphos*, something hollowed out, and *sepalum*, sepal, referring to the concave sepals

DISTRIBUTION: About 45 species in Mexico, Central and South America, with most in the Colombian and Ecuadorean Andes

Small tufted or creeping epiphytic, lithophytic, or terrestrial plants. Stem erect, enclosed by papery sheaths, 1-leafed at apex. Leaves petiolate, leathery, elliptical to obovate. Inflorescences unbranched, erect or pendent, few to many-flowered, the flowers open in succession. Flowers small, nonresupinate, often cup-shaped, sepals fleshy, sometimes hairy, usually with tails; dorsal sepal free, lateral sepals joined into a synsepal with 2 fleshy calli near the apices; petals and lip small; lip entire or obscurely trilobed, hinged to the column-foot. Column with 2 dentate wings at apex. Pollinia 2.

CULTIVATION: Plants require cool to intermediate conditions, heavy shade, high humidity throughout the year, and good air movement. They can be mounted on a slab or grown in a pot, in a sphagnum-perlite or fine bark mixture. It is important that the temperature does not rise above 25°C (77°F).

Scaphosepalum antenniferum Rolfe

One of the larger species with stems 2–5 cm long and leaves to 27 × 6.5 cm. Inflorescence to 30 cm tall, many-flowered, with 2 or 3 flowers open at a time; peduncle stout and warty. Flowers green or yellow-green, tinged with purple; lateral sepals with an ovate blade 15 × 9–10 mm and slender, down-curved tails 10–12 mm long.

Epiphytic or terrestrial in montane forest, 1500–2550 m (5000–8400 ft.)

Colombia, Ecuador, Peru

Scaphosepalum breve Reichenbach f.

Stems 1–3 cm long, forming tufts. Leaves to 15 × 2 cm, narrowly elliptic. Racemes 5–25 cm long, loosely several- to many-flowered; peduncle ± horizontal, slender and warty. Flowers yellow-green marked with purple; sepals 25 mm long including down-curved tails about as long as the blades.

Epiphytic in montane forest, 1000–2200 m (3300–7260 ft.)

Bolivia, Colombia, Ecuador, Guyana, Venezuela

SIMILAR SPECIES: *Scaphosepalum rapax* Luer from Ecuador, where it is epiphytic in wet forest at 450–600 m (1500–2000 ft.), is much smaller and has purple, prickly flowers.

Scaphosepalum grande Kraenzlin

SYN. *Scaphosepalum escobarianum* Garay

Stems slender, to 5 cm long. Leaves to 20 × 5.5 cm, including a petiole to 7 cm long. Inflorescence ca. 30

Satyrium erectum. J. Stewart

Scaphosepalum antenniferum

Scaphosepalum rapax

Scaphosepalum breve

Scaphosepalum grande

cm long, several- to many-flowered. Flowers greenish white flushed with purple; lateral sepals with an ovoid blade 11 mm long, tails deflexed, 11–15 mm long.

Epiphytic in forest, 1200–1500 m (4000–5000 ft.)

Colombia

Scaphosepalum microdactylum Rolfe

Stems 1–2 cm long. Leaves 4–18 cm long including a petiole 1–7 cm long. Inflorescence ± horizontal, successively many-flowered, to 15 cm long. Flowers pale yellow or yellow-green, flushed or spotted with reddish brown; lateral sepals 5–8 mm long, including an apiculus 1 mm long.

Epiphytic or terrestrial in forest, 0–2300 m (7600 ft.)

Mexico, Costa Rica, Guatemala, Honduras, Nicaragua, Panama, Colombia

Scaphosepalum ovulare Luer

Stems slender, 4–6 mm long, forming tufts. Leaves 1.5–4 cm long, including a petiole 3–15 mm long. Inflorescence ± pendulous, 2–4 cm long, few-flowered. Flowers yellow, sometimes flushed and spotted with purple or all purple; lateral sepals 4–5 mm long, lacking tails.

Epiphytic in wet forest, 600–1200 m (2000–4000 ft.)

Ecuador

Scaphosepalum swertiifolium (Reichenbach f.) Rolfe

Tufted epiphyte with stems 2–3 cm long. Leaves ca. 20 × 4 cm, including a petiole to 10 cm long. Inflorescence to 15 cm long, several- to many-flowered. Flowers white or pale yellow with red or brown marks; lateral sepals to 5 cm long, including spreading tails ca. 4 cm long.

Epiphytic in forest, 750–2300 m (2460–7600 ft.)

Colombia, Ecuador

Scaphosepalum microdactylum

Scaphosepalum ovulare

Scaphosepalum swertiifolium

Scaphosepalum verrucosum

Scaphosepalum verrucosum (Reichenbach f.) Pfitzer

SYN. *Scaphosepalum ochthodes* (Reichenbach f.) Pfitzer

Stems to 3 cm long, forming tufts or creeping. Leaves to 13 × 3 cm, including a petiole 1–4 cm long. Inflorescence erect, 20–50 cm long, many-flowered, the peduncle finely warty. Flowers small, fleshy, yellow or yellow-green marked with reddish brown or purple; lateral sepals 7.5–8.5 mm long, including tails 1.5 mm long.

Epiphytic, lithophytic, or terrestrial in forest, woodland, and by roadside, 1800–2850 m (6000–9400 ft.)

Colombia

Scaphyglottis Poeppig & Endlicher

TRIBE: Epidendreae

SUBTRIBE: Laeliinae

ETYMOLOGY: From Greek *scaphe*, bowl, and *glottis*, tongue, referring to the concave lip

DISTRIBUTION: About 60 species in Mexico, Central and South America, and the West Indies

Epiphytes or lithophytes; stems usually forming pseudobulbs, either arising direct from the rhizome or from the apex of an older pseudobulb, forming a branched chain. Leaves apical, 1–3. Inflorescences unbranched, sometimes in clusters (fascicles). Flowers small, sepals and petals free, subsimilar, but the petals usually wider; lip hinged to column-foot, entire or trilobed, sometimes with calli. Pollinia 4 or 6.

CULTIVATION: Plants can be grown potted in a standard bark-based epiphyte compost or mounted, at intermediate temperatures with good air movement. They should be watered throughout the year, although with less given when the plants are not in active growth.

Scaphyglottis pulchella

(Schlechter) L. O. Williams

Pseudobulbs slender, sometimes superposed, enlarged towards the top, 2-leaved at the apex. Leaves to 22 × 1.5 cm. Inflorescence 1- or 2-flowered. Flowers ca. 2.5 cm across, greenish white or pale green, lip ± rectangular, white with violet streaks.

Epiphytic in rain forest and cloud forest, 700–1500 m (2300–5000 ft.)

Costa Rica, Panama

Scaphyglottis stellata Loddiges ex Lindley

SYN. *Scaphyglottis amethystina* (Reichenbach f.) Schlechter

Pseudobulbs with a short stem, sometimes superposed, to 12 × 1 cm, 2-leaved at apex. Leaves to 12 × 1 cm. Inflorescence short, 2- or 3-flowered, in terminal clusters. Flowers 10–15 mm across, white to violet-pink; lip trilobed, fan-shaped.

Epiphytic in wet woodland, 0–1500 m (5000 ft.)

Central and South America

Schlimmia Planchet & Linden

TRIBE: Maxillarieae

SUBTRIBE: Stanhopeinae

ETYMOLOGY: Named for Louis Schlim, who collected orchids in South America for his cousin Jean Linden

DISTRIBUTION: 8 species in the northern Andes of South America

Epiphytes or terrestrials with clustered, ovoid pseudobulbs, 1-leafed at the apex, with overlapping distichous sheaths at the base. Leaves petiolate, pleated. Inflorescences basal, pendent, few-flowered. Flowers bell-shaped; dorsal sepal free, forming a hood over the column with the petals; lateral sepals joined forming a saccate, helmet-shaped mentum; lip small, in 2 parts, the hypochile broad,

Scaphyglottis pulchella

the epichile small, heart-shaped. Column winged, pollinia 2.

CULTIVATION: Because of the pendent inflorescences, plants should be grown in baskets in an open but moisture-retentive compost. They require cool to intermediate temperatures, shade, and high humidity. They should be watered throughout the year, with less given in winter, but should not dry out completely.

Schlimmia alpina Reichenbach f. & Warszewicz

Pseudobulbs to 5 × 1.5 cm. Leaves to 30 × 10 cm. Inflorescence to 15 cm long, 3- to 5-flowered, peduncle purple. Flowers ca. 5 cm long, waxy, scented, white to greenish white with pink spots at the base; lip with a yellow swelling at the base.

Terrestrial on rocky mountain slopes in wet forest, 1000–1500 m (3300–5000 ft.)

Colombia, Ecuador

SIMILAR SPECIES: *Schlimmia trifida* Reichenbach f. from Colombia, Ecuador, and Venezuela differs in details of the column.

Schlimmia alpina

Schoenorchis Blume

TRIBE: Vandeae

SUBTRIBE: Aeridinae

ETYMOLOGY: From Greek *schoinos*, reed, and *orchis*, orchid, referring to the rushlike leaves

DISTRIBUTION: 26 species in tropical and subtropical Asia

Monopodial epiphytes with short or long stems, rooting at the base. Leaves narrow, flat or cylindrical. Inflorescences simple or branched, many-flowered. Flowers small, white to purple; sepals and petals free, subsimilar, not spreading; lip trilobed, spurred with a callus at the mouth of the spur, midlobe fleshy, side lobes erect.

CULTIVATION: Plants should be mounted so that those with long stems can climb or hang down. They need intermediate to warm temperatures, high humidity, and moderate shade, with plenty of water while plants are in active growth.

Schoenorchis gemmata (Lindley) J. J. Smith

Stem pendent, leafy, 5–20 cm long. Leaves linear, somewhat curved, to 13 cm long. Inflorescence arching or pendulous, longer than leaves, branched, many-flowered. Flowers 3–4 mm across, purple, the tips of the sepals and midlobe of lip white.

Epiphytic on tree trunks in forest, 200–2000 m (660–6600 ft.)

Assam to China and Indochina

Schoenorchis juncifolia
Reinwardt ex Blume

Stems branched, pendent, to 1 m long. Leaves terete, 8–16 cm long. Inflorescence 6–7 cm long, many-flowered. Flowers ca. 6 mm long, white flushed with purple.

Epiphytic in submontane forest, ca. 1500 m (5000 ft.)

Borneo, Java, Sumatra

Schoenorchis micrantha
Reinwardt ex Blume

SYN. *Schoenorchis densiflora* Schlechter

Stem branched, 5–15 cm long. Leaves distichous, terete, curved, ca. 2 cm long, 2 mm wide. Inflorescence ca. 2 cm long, many-flowered. Flowers very small, white, turning yellowish as they age.

Epiphytic in submontane and riverine forest, 0–1500 m (5000 ft.)

Indochina to the southwest Pacific and Australia

Scuticaria Lindley

TRIBE: Maxillarieae

SUBTRIBE: Zygopetalinae

Scuticaria steelei. R. Parsons

ETYMOLOGY: From Latin *scutica*, a lash, referring to the whiplike leaves

DISTRIBUTION: 9 species from Central and South America

Sympodial epiphytes with a short or creeping rhizome; pseudobulbs small, 1-leafed at the apex. Leaves long, pendent, fleshy, more or less cylindrical but grooved on the upper surface. Inflorescences lateral, 1- to few-flowered. Flowers showy; sepals and petals subsimilar, free, spreading; lip trilobed; side lobes erect, midlobe rounded or emarginate.

CULTIVATION: Because of their long, pendent leaves, *Scuticaria* species are usually grown mounted on a vertical bark slab but can be grown in a suspended pot in a standard bark-based compost. They should be given intermediate temperatures, moderate shade, and high humidity. They need plenty of water while growing, but should be kept drier after flowering.

Scuticaria hadwenii (Lindley) Hooker

Leaves to 45 × 1 cm. Inflorescence arching or pendent, to 5 cm long, 1- or 2-flowered. Flowers 6–8 cm across, scented, long-lasting; sepals and petals green, greenish yellow, or yellow with purple-brown bars and blotches; lip 3.5 × 3 cm, white or pale yellow with purplish spots, suborbicular or ovate, concave, hairy inside. Flowering spring–autumn.

Epiphytic in primary scrub forest, over 1500 m (5000 ft.)

Brazil, Guyana

Scuticaria steelei (Hooker) Lindley

Pseudobulbs to 3 cm long. Leaves to 160 × 1 cm, occasionally even longer. Raceme short, 1- to 3-flowered. Flowers 7–8 cm across, scented, waxy, long-lasting, yellow or greenish yellow with reddish or maroon-brown irregular marks; lip whitish or cream with reddish streaks, emarginate; callus bright yellow or orange.

Epiphytic in rain forest and scrub, often near a river, 100–1200 m (330–4000 ft.)

Central and South America

Sedirea Garay & H. Sweet

TRIBE: Vandeae

SUBTRIBE: Aeridinae

ETYMOLOGY: The name of the related genus *Aerides* spelled backwards

DISTRIBUTION: 2 species in China, Korea, and Japan

Short-stemmed, monopodial epiphytes, branching at the base when older, with stout, fleshy roots. Leaves several. Inflorescences axillary, unbranched, several-flowered. Flowers fleshy, scented; sepals and petals subsimilar, spreading or slightly cupped; lip trilobed with a basal spur.

CULTIVATION: Grow mounted or in pots in a medium epiphyte compost in a cool or intermediate greenhouse, in a humid, partially shaded situation. Keep drier in winter, but do not let plants dry out completely.

Sedirea japonica (Linden & Reichenbach f.) Garay & H. Sweet

Leaves 5–8, strap-shaped, 5–15 cm long, keeled. Raceme to 15 cm long, 2–12-flowered. Flowers scented, somewhat cupped, 2.5–3 cm across, greenish white, the lateral sepals with purplish bars on the basal half; lip with pink-purple spots and bars; midlobe obovate to spathulate; spur conical, tapering.

Epiphytic in pine forest

Japan, Korea, Ryukyu Islands

Sedirea subparishii (Z. H. Tsi) Christenson

Leaves to 19 × 3.5 cm. Inflorescence to 10 cm long, several-flowered. Flowers pale yellow-green spotted with maroon; sepals to 2 cm long; lip white to yellow-green, the lip midlobe narrowly oblong, sometimes red-purple; spur 1 cm long.

Epiphytic on tree trunks on wooded hillsides, 700–1400 m (2300–4600 ft.)

Southern China

Scuticaria hadwenii. R. Parsons

Schoenorchis juncifolia

Sedirea japonica

Seidenfadenia Garay

TRIBE: Vandeae
SUBTRIBE: Aeridinae
ETYMOLOGY: Named for the Danish diplomat and taxonomist Gunnar Seidenfaden (1908–2001)
DISTRIBUTION: 1 species in Myanmar

Stems short, leafy; roots numerous, fleshy. Leaves long, semi-cylindrical. Inflorescence axillary, unbranched. Sepals and petals free, spreading, subsimilar; lip trilobed, lacking a callus, spurred at the base, the side lobes very small, midlobe flat. Column short and fleshy, pollinia 2.

Seidenfadenia differs from *Aerides* and *Rhynchostylis* mainly in the details of the rostellum, which projects above the column.

CULTIVATION: Plants of *Seidenfadenia* do better when mounted. They require intermediate temperatures, bright light, and plenty of water during the growing period. While resting, they should be kept cooler and drier.

Seidenfadenia mitrata (Reichenbach f.) Garay

SYN. *Aerides mitrata* Reichenbach f.

Leaves to 60 × 0.5 cm, pendent, grooved on the upper side. Inflorescence to 25 cm long, densely several- to many-flowered, ± erect. Flowers showy, 12–20 mm across, scented; sepals and petals white, sometimes tinged with purple, lip magenta-purple; spur 4–5 mm long, bilaterally flattened, parallel to midlobe.

Epiphytic in monsoon forest, 100–800 m (330–2640 ft.)

Myanmar

Serapias Linnaeus

TONGUE ORCHIDS
TRIBE: Orchideae
SUBTRIBE: Orchidinae
ETYMOLOGY: From Serapis, an Egyptian god
DISTRIBUTION: About 15 species and many natural hybrids in Europe, mainly around the Mediterranean, North Africa, and the Middle East

Terrestrial plants with 2 to 5 globose, unlobed tubers. Leaves borne along stem, linear to lanceolate, erect or semi-erect. Inflorescences several-flowered, with prominent bracts as long as or longer than the flowers. Flowers usually dull red or purplish, heavily veined; sepals and petals forming a hood; lip large, trilobed, the midlobe tonguelike, lacking a spur.

CULTIVATION: In northern Europe, species of *Serapias* are usually grown in pots with a standard, free-draining terrestrial compost in an alpine house or cold frame. In southern Europe and other temperate areas they can be naturalized in a garden.

Serapias cordigera Linnaeus

Stems 15–50 cm tall. Leaves several to 15 cm long. Inflorescence densely 5- to 15-flowered, bracts tinged with purple. Sepals to 2.5 cm long, grayish purple. Lip to 7 cm long, purple or maroon, side lobes concealed in the hood, midlobe prominent, heart-shaped. Flowering spring–summer.

Grassland and light woodland, often on base-rich soil, to 1000 m (3300 ft.)

Mediterranean area, North Africa

Serapias neglecta De Notaris

Stem 10–30 cm long. Leaves 4–10, semi-erect, 5–11 cm long, sometimes folded. Inflorescence rather densely few- to several-flowered; sepals and petals yellow-green to lilac; lip to 5 cm long, midlobe red-brown to yellow, heart-shaped. Flowering late spring–early summer.

Open woodland, damp meadows, often on acid soil, to 600 m (2000 ft.)

Southern Europe

Serapias vomeracea (Burman f.) Briquet

Stem 20–60 cm tall. Leaves several, 6–20 cm long, semi-erect. Raceme loosely 3- to 10-flowered, the bracts much longer than the flowers. Sepals and petals grayish lilac with darker veins. Lip 2–4 cm long, densely hairy, rust-red to violet-brown. Flowering spring–summer.

Open woodland, damp grassland, usually on basic soil, to 1000 m (3300 ft.)

Southern Europe

Sievekingia Reichenbach f.

TRIBE: Maxillarieae
SUBTRIBE: Stanhopeinae
ETYMOLOGY: Named for Dr. Sieveking, mayor of Hamburg, where Reichenbach was living at the time
DISTRIBUTION: 16 species in Central and South America

Smallish epiphytes or lithophytes with clustered, ovoid pseudobulbs surrounded by overlapping basal sheaths, 1- or 2-leaved at apex. Leaves petiolate, pleated. Inflorescences basal, pendent, long or short, few- to many-flowered towards the apex. Sepals and petals free, spreading, subsimilar; lip entire or trilobed, margins sometimes fringed, with a basal callus. Column sometimes winged, pollinia 2.

CULTIVATION: Because of the pendent inflorescences, plants should be grown mounted or in baskets. They require intermediate temperatures with moderate shade and should be watered throughout the year.

Sievekingia fimbriata Reichenbach f.

Pseudobulbs ca. 3.5 × 2 cm. Leaves 10–20 × 3.5–6.5 cm, plus a petiole 4–6 cm long. Inflorescences usually several per plant, 6–8 cm long, 8- to 10-flowered. Flowers scented, 2–3 cm across, orange-yellow with red marks; petals irregularly fringed or toothed, lip trilobed, with a basal, hairy callus, midlobe fringed.

Epiphytic in rain forest and cloud forest, 800–1200 m (2640–4000 ft.)

Costa Rica, Panama

Sievekingia reichenbachiana Rolfe

Pseudobulb to 3.5 cm long. Leaves to 30 × 3.5 cm. Inflorescence 5–10

Serapias vomeracea

Seidenfadenia mitrata

Sievekingia fimbriata

cm long, densely 3- to 9-flowered. Flowers nonresupinate, 5 cm across; sepals pale yellow, petals yellow with purple spots at the base, deeply fringed; lip trilobed, the margins deeply fringed.

Epiphytic in wet forest or lithophytic on embankments, 300–1400 m (1000–4600 ft.)

Ecuador

Sievekingia suavis Reichenbach f.

Pseudobulbs to 4 × 2 cm. Leaves to 20 × 4 cm. Inflorescence 4–6 cm long, 6- to 12-flowered. Flowers 2–2.5 cm across; sepals yellow, petals and lip orange; lip marked with red inside, callus 3-ridged; all margins entire.

Epiphytic in rain forest and cloud forest, 200–900 m (660–3000 ft.)

Costa Rica, Nicaragua, Panama

Sigmatostalix Reichenbach f.

TRIBE: Maxillarieae
SUBTRIBE: Oncidiinae
ETYMOLOGY: From Greek *sigma*, the letter *S*, and *stalix*, stake, referring to the S-shaped column
DISTRIBUTION: About 50 species in Mexico, Central and South America

Small epiphytes with a short, creeping rhizome. Pseudobulbs usually clustered, small, angled, 1- or 2-leaved at apex, usually with some basal sheathing leaves. Inflorescences arising from base of pseudobulbs, usually longer than leaves, unbranched, few to many-flowered. Flowers small, thin-textured; sepals and petals subsimilar, spreading or reflexed; lip sometimes clawed, entire or lobed. Column slender, pollinia 2.

CULTIVATION: Most species grow easily in small pots in a fine to medium epiphyte compost or mounted on slabs or rafts. They require intermediate conditions, moderate shade, and high humidity throughout the year.

Sigmatostalix graminea (Poeppig & Endlicher) Reichenbach f.

SYN. *Sigmatostalix pusilla* Schlechter

Pseudobulbs small and slender, 7–12 mm long, 1-leafed at the apex and with several basal, leafy sheaths. Leaves 3–5 cm long, 2 mm wide. Inflorescence 3–6 cm long, laxly few-flowered. Flowers ca. 5 mm across, pale yellow spotted or striped with purple.

Epiphytic in wet forest, 600–1600 m (2000–5300 ft.)

Ecuador, Peru

Sigmatostalix picta Reichenbach f.

Pseudobulbs to 3 × 1.5 cm. Leaves to 12 cm long, 12 mm wide, often dark green or reddish brown. Inflorescence 7–30 cm long. Flowers to 15 mm long, yellow or yellow-green with red or red-brown marks, or red-brown with yellow spots; sepals and petals reflexed, lip clawed, blade oblong to kidney-shaped.

Epiphytic in rain forest and cloud forest, 700–1750 m (2300–5800 ft.)

Mexico, Central and South America

Smitinandia Holttum

TRIBE: Vandeae
SUBTRIBE: Aeridinae
ETYMOLOGY: Named for Tem Smitinand, coauthor of *Orchids of Thailand* (1959–1963)
DISTRIBUTION: 3 species in tropical Asia

Small monopodial epiphytes. Leaves distichous, articulated to persistent sheaths, unequally bilobed at the tips. Inflorescences lateral, unbranched, densely many-flowered. Flowers small; sepals and petals free, subsimilar; lip trilobed, with the mouth of the spur almost closed by a fleshy wall-like callus at the base of the lip. Pollinia 4, in 2 pairs.

CULTIVATION: Plants can be grown in small pots or baskets, in a standard bark-based epiphyte compost. They require intermediate to warm conditions with only light shade and moisture throughout the year.

Smitinandia micrantha (Lindley) Holttum

SYN. *Saccolabium micranthum* Lindley, *Cleisostoma micrantha* (Lindley) King & Pantling

Stem 4–6 cm long, several-leaved. Leaves oblong, to 11 × 2 cm. Inflorescence arching or pendent, densely many-flowered. Flowers 3–4 mm across, long-lasting; sepals and petals white, usually tinged with pink; lip marked with deeper violet-pink.

Epiphytic in forest, 270–1000 m (870–3300 ft.)

Himalayas to Malaysia

Sobennikoffia Schlechter

TRIBE: Vandeae
SUBTRIBE: Angraecinae
ETYMOLOGY: Named by Rudolf Schlechter in honor of his wife, whose maiden name was Sobennikoff
DISTRIBUTION: 4 species from Madagascar

Robust terrestrial, lithophytic or epiphytic plants. Stem short or long. Leaves distichous, leathery or fleshy. Inflorescences axillary, suberect or spreading, few- to several-flowered. Flowers white or white and green, turning yellow or apricot as they age; sepals and petals free, spreading, the tips sometimes recurved, subsimilar; lip trilobed near the apex, with a funnel-shaped base tapering into a spur. Pollinia 2.

CULTIVATION: These plants are not easy to cultivate, both leaves and roots having a tendency to rot. In spite of sometimes being terrestrial or lithophytic, they are likely to do better in a free-draining, epiphyte compost and should dry out between waterings and be kept drier in the resting season. Intermediate temperatures are suitable.

Sobennikoffia humbertiana H. Perrier

Stem 10–50 cm long with up to 15 leaves towards apex. Leaves strap-shaped, to 25 × 2.5 cm. Inflorescence

Sievekingia reichenbachiana

Sigmatostalix graminea

Sigmatostalix picta

Smitinandia micrantha

Sobennikoffia humbertiana. J. Hermans

Sobennikoffia robusta. J. Hermans

longer than leaves, 5- to 9-flowered. Flowers ca. 4 cm across; lip trilobed near apex, side lobes small, midlobe 10–12 mm long; spur 2–2.5 cm long.

Epiphytic in humid evergreen forest, lithophytic in dry forest, 400–1200 m (1320–4000 ft.)

Madagascar

Sobennikoffia robusta (Schlechter) Schlechter

Stem 25–40 cm long. Leaves numerous, strap-shaped, to 35 × 3.5 cm. Inflorescence erect, to 50 cm long, to 15-flowered. Flowers ca. 4 cm across; lip trilobed at apex, midlobe slightly longer than side lobes; spur 4.5–5 cm long, ± erect.

Epiphytic or lithophytic in seasonally dry woodland and scrub, 1500–2000 m (5000–6600 ft.)

Madagascar

Sobralia Ruíz & Pavón

TRIBE: Sobralieae

ETYMOLOGY: Named for Francisco Sobral, a Spanish botanist and physician

DISTRIBUTION: About 100 species in Mexico, Central and South America

Terrestrial, rarely epiphytic, plants with fleshy roots and leafy, reedlike stems forming clumps. Leaves alternate, ribbed. Inflorescences terminal or lateral, unbranched, the flowers open in succession and often lasting for only 1 day. Flowers large, showy, sometimes scented; sepals and petals spreading, subsimilar; lip entire or trilobed, joined to the column at the base, ± funnel-shaped, spreading and crisped near the apex. Column long, the apex trilobed; pollinia 8.

CULTIVATION: Plants should be potted in a free-draining mixture of coarse bark and leaf mold, in intermediate to warm conditions. They require only light shade and plenty of water and fertilizer while in active growth. When resting, they should be kept just moist. They are good landscape plants for tropical and subtropical gardens.

Sobralia candida (Poeppig & Endlicher) Reichenbach f.

Stems to 90 cm long. Leaves to 22 × 3 cm, linear. Inflorescence 1-flowered. Flowers to 3 cm across, white or cream, the lip white or pale salmon, sometimes with reddish spots near the apex.

Epiphytic or terrestrial in forest, 700–1700 m (2300–5600 ft.)

Colombia, Ecuador, Peru, Venezuela

Sobralia decora Bateman

Plants to 1.3 m tall. Leaves to 24 × 10 cm, the sheaths with black hairs. Inflorescence short, few-flowered. Flowers scented, to 10 cm across; sepals and petals white or pale mauve, lip pale to deep rose-purple; disc yellow and red.

Epiphytic on trees and logs in moist forest, sometimes terrestrial, 0–600 m (2000 ft.)

Mexico, Central and South America

Sobralia dichotoma Ruíz & Pavón

Stems to 3 m tall, occasionally branched. Leaves to 35 × 9 cm. Inflorescence loosely few- to many-flowered. Flowers to 10 cm across, fleshy, scented, white outside, red to violet inside; lip with several yellow keels.

Terrestrial in open woodland, 750–2800 m (2460–9250 ft.)

Bolivia, Colombia, Ecuador, Peru, Venezuela

Sobralia dichotoma

Sobralia fragrans Lindley
Plants to 45 cm tall. Stem rather flattened. Leaves to 25 × 5 cm. Inflorescence 1- to 3-flowered. Flowers to 7.5 cm across, scented; sepals and petals cream or greenish white, the sepals sometimes pink-tinged; lip yellow or white with yellow-orange veins, apex deeply fringed; disc orange-yellow with toothed keels.

Epiphytic in wet forest, 0–1050 m (3500 ft.)

Mexico, Central and South America

Sobralia macrantha Lindley
Plants to 2 m tall, leaves to 35 × 10 cm. Inflorescence several-flowered. Flowers to 25 cm across, scented, variable in color, sepals and petals usually pink-mauve to rose purple, lip rose-purple, white at the base, yellow in the center, the margin crisped and undulate. This is the most widely cultivated species in the genus.

Terrestrial on slopes and rock outcrops in open pine woodland, 50–1000 m (165–3300 ft.)

Mexico, Central America

SIMILAR SPECIES: *Sobralia leucoxantha* Reichenbach f. from Central America has smaller flowers, white with a yellow throat.

Sobralia rosea Poeppig & Endlicher
Stems to 2 m tall. Inflorescence long, zigzag, several-flowered, the flowers open in succession. Flowers ca. 9 cm across; sepals and petals pale pink, lip deeper pink with magenta veins, yellow in the throat, very frilly-edged.

Terrestrial on grassy slopes in wet forest, 200–3300 m (660–10,900 ft.)

Colombia, Ecuador, Peru, Venezuela

Sobralia violacea Linden ex Lindley
Stems 45–200 cm tall. Leaves to 27 × 7 cm. Inflorescence conelike, several-flowered. Flowers to 13 cm across, fleshy, scented, sepals usually deep purple-pink, the petals slightly paler, lip orange-yellow towards the base, the margins purple, crisped.

Terrestrial in rain forest, 500–1700 m (1650–5600 ft.)

Central and South America

Sophronitis Lindley

SYN. *Hoffmannseggella* H. G. Jones, *Hadrolaelia* Chiron & V. P. Castro, *Dungsia* Chiron & V. P. Castro, *Microlaelia* Chiron & V. P. Castro

TRIBE: Epidendreae

SUBTRIBE: Laeliinae

ETYMOLOGY: From Greek *sophron*, modest, referring to the small flowers of the type species

DISTRIBUTION: About 60 species in South America from Brazil to northern Argentina

Epiphytic, lithophytic, or terrestrial plants. Pseudobulbs usually club-shaped to cylindrical, 1-leafed, occasionally 2-leaved, at apex. Leaves

Sobralia fragrans

leathery or fleshy. Inflorescence unbranched, few to several-flowered, sometimes subtended by a spathe. Flowers resupinate, usually scented, showy, white, pink, red, orange, yellow, brownish, or green. Sepals free, petals sometimes subsimilar, sometimes broader with undulate edges. Lip trilobed, side lobes usually enclosing column. Pollinia 8.

Most of these species were originally described under *Laelia*. However, it has long been recognized that the Brazilian laelias were not very closely related to the Mexican laelias. As the type species of the genus (*Laelia anceps*) comes from Mexico, new names had to be found for the Brazilian species. There has been considerable disagreement as to how these should be treated, with some botanists splitting what were previously the Brazilian laelias into several smaller genera. Here, I have followed the treatment in *Genera Orchidacearum*, volume 4, which treats them as a fairly broadly defined *Sophronitis*. A full explanation of this is given in the book (Pridgeon et al. 2005, p. 315).

Sobralia rosea

Sobralia macrantha

Many species have different color forms which have often been given varietal or cultivar names. They have been widely used in hybridization with species of *Cattleya* and within the genus *Sophronitis*, particularly *Soph. cernua* and *Soph. coccinea*, which transmit their bright red color and compact growth habit to their hybrids.

CULTIVATION: Most species require intermediate temperatures, moderate humidity, and good light. The smaller species can be mounted; otherwise they should be potted in a free-draining epiphyte mixture. They should have plenty of water and fertilizer while growing, but need a dry resting period, with only occasional misting to prevent the pseudobulbs from shriveling.

Sophronitis bradei (Pabst) van den Berg & M. W. Chase

SYN. *Laelia bradei* Pabst, *Hoffmannseggella bradei* (Pabst) Chiron & V. P. Castro

Pseudobulbs cylindrical, to 4 × 1 cm, 2-leaved. Leaves fleshy, ca. 3 × 1.5 cm, with incurved margins. Inflorescence 5–6 cm long, few-flowered. Flowers pale yellow, ca. 2 cm across.

Lithophytic in cracks of rocks, 1200–1300 m (4000–4300 ft.)

Brazil

Sophronitis briegeri Blumenschein

Inflorescence to 25 cm long, 1- to 5-flowered. Flowers 4–5 cm across, pale to deep yellow. Flowering late spring–early summer.

Lithophytic, 1300–1400 m (4300–4600 ft.)

Brazil

Sophronitis cinnabarina (Bateman ex Lindley) van den Berg & M. W. Chase

SYN. *Laelia cinnabarina* Lindley, *Hoffmannseggella cinnabarina* (Lindley) H. G. Jones

Pseudobulbs cylindrical, 10–20 cm tall. Inflorescence 25–50 cm tall, 5- to 15-flowered. Flowers 5–6 cm across, orange-red; sepals and petals linear, curved, lip recurved, the margin undulate. Flowering spring–early summer.

Usually terrestrial in open situations, over 800–1500 m (2640–5000 ft.)

Brazil

Sophronitis coccinea (Lindley) Reichenbach f.

SYN. *Hadrolaelia coccinea* (Lindley) Chiron & V. P. Castro

Pseudobulbs to 4 × 0.6 cm. Leaves to 6 × 2.5 cm, elliptic, dark green often flushed with purple. Inflorescence to 6 cm long, usually 1-flowered. Flowers fleshy, to 7.5 cm across, usually bright scarlet, lip yellow at the base, but occasionally white or magenta. Flowering autumn–winter.

Epiphytic high in forest trees and in cloud forest, 800–1300 m (2640–4300 ft.)

Argentina, Brazil

SIMILAR SPECIES: *Sophronitis cernua* Lindley from Argentina, Brazil, and Paraguay has smaller flowers (ca. 3 cm across) and is epiphytic at lower levels and in drier areas. *Sophronitis mantiqueirae* (Fowlie) Fowlie from Brazil grows in drier forest over 1800 m (6000 ft.)

Sophronitis crispa (Lindley) van den Berg & M. W. Chase

SYN. *Laelia crispa* (Lindley) Reichenbach f., *Hadrolaelia crispa* (Lindley) Chiron & V. P. Castro

Pseudobulbs to 25 cm long, laterally compressed, 1- or 2-leaved. Leaves 15–30 × 5 cm. Inflorescence to 30 cm long, 4- to 7-flowered, subtended by a flattened sheath. Flowers showy, 12 cm across, white, the lip mainly purple, yellow at the base, the margins crisped. Flowering in autumn.

Epiphytic in the upper forks of tall trees in forest remnants, in good light, sometimes lithophytic, 800–1500 m (2640–5000 ft.)

Southeastern Brazil

Sophronitis crispata (Thunberg) van den Berg & M. W. Chase

SYN. *Laelia rupestris* Lindley, *Hoffmannseggella crispata* (Thunberg) H. G. Jones

Pseudobulbs 4–10 cm long, 1-leafed. Leaves to 16 × 3 cm. Flowers 4–5 cm across; sepals and petals rose-pink, lip white in the throat, the midlobe purple.

In humus in fissures of rocks, in good light, 400–800 m (1320–2640 ft.)

Brazil

SIMILAR SPECIES: *Sophronitis ghillanyi* (Pabst) van den Berg & M. W. Chase, also from Brazil, has paler flowers, the lip with a pink margin and a yellow throat with a purple spot at the apex. *Sophronitis longipes* (Reichenbach f.) van den Berg & M. W. Chase (syn. *Laelia longipes* Reichenbach f.) has paler pink flowers and a yellow throat.

Sophronitis fidelensis (Pabst) van den Berg & M. W. Chase

SYN. *Laelia fidelensis* Pabst, *Hadrolaelia fidelensis* (Pabst) Chiron & V. P. Castro

Pseudobulbs ca. 4 × 3 cm, 1-leafed. Leaves to 12 × 4 cm. Inflorescence to 30 cm long, 2- or 3-flowered. Flowers to 12 cm across, lavender-pink, the lip white or yellow in the throat.

Lithophytic

Brazil

Sophronitis harpophylla (Reichenbach f.) van den Berg & M. W. Chase

SYN. *Laelia harpophylla* Reichenbach f., *Dungsia harpophylla* (Reichenbach f.) Chiron & V. P. Castro

Pseudobulbs slender, to 30 cm long, 1- or 2-leaved. Leaves to 20 × 3 cm. Inflorescence shorter than leaves, 3- to 7-flowered. Flowers 5–8 cm across, vermilion red, lip yellow in the center and with a pale margin. Flowering winter–spring. Requires a shorter, less dry rest than most other species.

Epiphytic in shade in humid areas, 500–900 m (1650–3000 ft.)

Brazil

Sophronitis mantiqueirae

Sophronitis cinnabarina

Sophronitis coccinea

Sophronitis cernua

Sophronitis harpophylla

Sophronitis jongheana

Sophronitis jongheana (Reichenbach f.) van den Berg & M. W. Chase

SYN. *Laelia jongheana* Reichenbach f., *Hadrolaelia jongheana* (Reichenbach f.) Chiron & V. P. Castro

Pseudobulb 5 cm long, 1-leafed. Leaves 10–15 cm long. Inflorescence ca. 10 cm long, 1- or 2-flowered. Flowers 12–13 cm across, lilac (rarely white), lip white with a rich yellow throat and a pink margin and side lobes. Flowering in early spring.

Epiphytic in forest remnants, 1300–1600 m (4300–5300 ft.)

Brazil

Sophronitis lobata (Lindley) van den Berg & M. W. Chase

SYN. *Laelia lobata* (Lindley) Veitch, *Hadrolaelia lobata* (Lindley) Chiron & V. P. Castro

Pseudobulbs to 20 cm long, 1-leafed. Leaves to 20 cm long. Inflorescence to 40 cm long, 4- to 7-flowered. Flowers lilac-purple; lip with darker veins, the margin undulate, apex emarginate. Flowering spring.

Lithophytic in coastal areas

Southeastern Brazil

Sophronitis milleri (Blumenschein ex Pabst) van den Berg & M. W. Chase

SYN. *Laelia milleri* Blumenschein ex Pabst, *Hoffmannseggella milleri* (Blumenschein ex Pabst) Chiron & V. P. Castro

Pseudobulbs to 4 cm long. Leaves to 6 × 3 cm. Inflorescence 2- to 6-flowered. Flowers 6 cm across, red or orange-red, lip yellow in the throat, the margin undulate. Flowering summer.

Lithophytic or epiphytic on *Vellozia* species, 800–1300 m (2640–4300 ft.)

Brazil

Sophronitis perrinii (Lindley) van den Berg & M. W. Chase

SYN. *Laelia perrinii* Lindley, *Hadrolaelia perrinii* (Lindley) Chiron & V. P. Castro

Pseudobulbs 15–25 cm long, laterally flattened. Leaves 15–25 cm long. Inflorescence to 25 cm long, 2- to 6-flowered. Flowers 11–14 cm across, pale to deep rose purple, occasionally white, lip magenta, yellow in the throat. Flowering in winter.

Epiphytic, 700–900 m (2300–3000 ft.)

Southeastern Brazil

Sophronitis pumila (Hooker) van den Berg & M. W. Chase

SYN. *Laelia pumila* (Hooker) Reichenbach f., *Hadrolaelia pumila* (Hooker) Chiron & V. P. Castro

Pseudobulbs to 10 cm long, 1-leafed. Leaves to 10 cm long. Inflorescence 7–8 cm long, 1-flowered. Flowers 8–11 cm across, rose-purple; lip deep purple, yellow in the throat. Flowering spring or autumn.

Epiphytic on tall trees in forest, 600–900 m (2000–3000 ft.)

Southern and southeastern Brazil

Sophronitis purpurata (Lindley & Paxton) van den Berg & M. W. Chase

SYN. *Laelia purpurata* Lindley, *Hadrolaelia purpurata* (Lindley & Paxton) Chiron & V. P. Castro

Pseudobulbs spindle-shaped, to 50 cm long, 1-leafed. Leaves to 40 × 5 cm. Inflorescence to 30 cm tall, 2- to 5-flowered. Flowers 15–20 cm across, fleshy, very showy; sepals and petals white or pale pink, lip pink outside and at the apex, throat yellow with purple veins, side lobes and center of midlobe rich purple. Many color forms exist. Flowering spring–summer.

High-level epiphyte in forest, 0–400 m (1320 ft.)

Southern and southeastern Brazil

Sophronitis sincorana (Schlechter) van den Berg & M. W. Chase

SYN. *Laelia sincorana* Schlechter, *Hadrolaelia sincorana* (Schlechter) Chiron & V. P. Castro

Pseudobulbs ca. 2 cm long, almost round, 1-leafed. Inflorescence ca. 6 cm long, 1- or 2-flowered. Flowers to 10 cm across, purple, lip a darker purple with a white patch in the throat, midlobe deeply emarginate. In cultivation, a dry rest is essential.

Lithophytic or epiphytic on *Vellozia* species, in dry areas, 1100–1300 m (3600–4300 ft.)

Brazil

Sophronitis milleri

Sophronitis pumila

Sophronitis purpurata

Sophronitis sincorana

Sophronitis tenebrosa

Sophronitis tenebrosa (Rolfe) van den Berg & M. W. Chase

SYN. *Laelia tenebrosa* Rolfe, *Hadrolaelia tenebrosa* (Rolfe) Chiron & V. P. Castro

Pseudobulbs to 30 cm long, 1-leafed. Leaves to 30 × 6 cm. Inflorescence to 30 cm long, 2- to 4-flowered. Flowers ca. 16 cm across. Sepals and petals bronze, lip rose-purple, darker in the throat, the margins white. Flowering summer.

Epiphytic in shade in rain forest

Brazil

SIMILAR SPECIES: *Sophronitis grandis* (Lindley) van den Berg & M. W. Chase (syn. *Laelia grandis* Lindley) has yellow-brown sepals and petals and a whitish lip veined with purple.

Sophronitis xanthina (Lindley) van den Berg & M. W. Chase

SYN. *Laelia xanthina* Lindley, *Hadrolaelia xanthina* (Lindley) Chiron & V. P. Castro

Pseudobulbs to 25 × 3 cm, 1-leafed. Leaves to 30 × 6 cm, blue-green. Inflorescence ca. 25 cm tall, few-flowered. Flowers to 8 cm across, deep yellow, lip white with a yellow throat and some purple streaks. Flowering spring–summer.

Epiphytic

Brazil

Spathoglottis Blume

TRIBE: Collabieae

ETYMOLOGY: From Greek *spathe*, spathe or broad blade, and *glottis*, tongue, referring to the shape of the lip

DISTRIBUTION: About 40 species from southern India through Asia to Australia

Terrestrial plants related to *Calanthe* and *Phaius* with conical to ovoid pseudobulbs arising from a creeping rhizome. Leaves up to 4, plicate, sheathing at base, lanceolate, mostly evergreen but deciduous in some species. Inflorescences erect, usually tall, unbranched, arising from basal leaf axils, with a long peduncle, few- to many-flowered. Flowers showy; sepals and petals free, spreading, the petals larger than the sepals; lip trilobed, not spurred, the midlobe clawed with 2 small calli at the base of the claw, side lobes narrow, erect. Pollinia 8.

CULTIVATION: Grow in pots in a mixture of 4 parts of leaf mold, 1 part of coarse perlite, and 1 part of coarse river sand or a similar free-draining terrestrial compost. Plants do better with frequent applications of fertilizer during the growing season and plenty of water while in growth. In tropical and subtropical areas, *Spathoglottis* species and hybrids are sometimes grown as garden plants. Possibly because of their size, they are not widely grown in cool-temperate areas where they need an intermediate to warm glasshouse.

Spathoglottis aurea Lindley
Pseudobulbs small, ca. 2.5 cm high. Leaves to 70 × 5 cm, narrowly lanceolate, with petioles ca. 20 cm long. Inflorescence 60 cm tall, 4- to 10-flowered. Flowers to 7 cm across, golden yellow, the lip and calli dotted with crimson. Warm-growing.

Crevices between rocks, 750–1500 m (2460–5000 ft.)

Borneo, Java, Malaysia, Sumatra

Spathoglottis ixioides (D. Don) Lindley
Pseudobulbs small, globose to ovoid, ca. 1.5 cm tall. Leaves 2–3, grasslike, to 20 cm long. Inflorescence shorter than leaves, 1- to 3-flowered. Flowers 2–3 cm across, bright yellow with purple dots at the base of the lip; midlobe obcordate. This is a cool-growing species that can be treated like *Pleione* species in cultivation.

On mossy rocks; roadside banks; 1950–3650 m (6430–12,100 ft.)

Bhutan, Sikkim

Spathoglottis petri Reichenbach f.
Pseudobulbs ovoid. Leaves several, 30–70 × 2.5–8 cm. Inflorescence to 70 cm tall, densely up to 20-flowered near apex. Flowers to 4 cm diameter, lilac-pink to magenta; disc white.

Open, grassy slopes, ca. 700 m (2300 ft.)

Vanuatu, New Caledonia

Spathoglottis plicata Blume
SYN. *Spathoglottis lilacina* Griffith
Pseudobulbs to 7 cm long, 5 cm across. Leaves numerous, 30–120 × 2–7 cm, narrowly lanceolate, with a petiole to 15 cm long. Inflorescence hairy, to 1 m tall, few- to many-flowered. Flowers ca. 2.5 cm across, white, lilac, pink, or purple with a

Sophronitis xanthina

Spathoglottis aurea

yellow callus; lip T-shaped when flat. This is the most widespread and most widely cultivated species, naturalized in some areas.

Damp places, 0–500 m (1650 ft.)

India, Southeast Asia to Philippines

Specklinia Lindley

TRIBE: Epidendreae

SUBTRIBE: Pleurothallidinae

ETYMOLOGY: Named for Veit Rudolf Speckle (d. 1550)

DISTRIBUTION: About 200 species in the West Indies, Central and South America

Small epiphytic, lithophytic, or terrestrial plants, tufted or creeping. Stems erect, enclosed in tubular sheaths, 1-leafed at apex. Leaves usually petiolate, almost round to ovate. Inflorescences unbranched, floral bracts tubular. Dorsal sepal free or joined to lateral sepals to form a cup; lateral sepals sometimes joined to form a synsepal. Petals sometimes with fringed or toothed margins. Column usually winged, with a foot; pollinia 2.

In *Icones Pleurothallidinarum*, volume 28, Luer (2005) established 10 new genera for species in the expanded genus *Specklinia*, but for consistency, I am following the treatment in *Genera Orchidacearum*, volume 4 (Pridgeon et al. 2005), and Kew's *World Checklist of Monocotyledons* (Govaerts 2007).

CULTIVATION: Like *Pleurothallis*, most species of *Specklinia* require high humidity, moderate shade, and good ventilation all year round. They can be mounted or grown in pots in a fine bark-based compost in cool to intermediate conditions, depending on their origin. Many species flower off and on throughout the year.

Specklinia brighamii (S. Watson) Pridgeon & M. W. Chase

SYN. *Pleurothallis brighamii* S. Watson

Leaves to 9 × 1 cm. Inflorescence to 10 cm long, few-flowered, the flowers open in succession. Flowers small, yellow, striped with red-brown or green.

Epiphytic in wet forest, 0–950 m (3100 ft.)

Mexico, Central and South America

Specklinia endotrachys (Reichenbach f.) Pridgeon & M. W. Chase

SYN. *Pleurothallis endotrachys* Reichenbach f., *P. pfavii* Reichenbach f.

Leaves to 17 × 3 cm. Inflorescence ca. 40 cm long, many flowered, the flowers open in succession. Flowers fleshy, ca. 3 cm long; sepals yellow, orange, or red, petals red-brown.

Epiphytic in rain forest and cloud forest, 700–2300 m (2300–7600 ft.)

Mexico, Central and South America

Specklinia grobyi (Bateman ex Lindley) F. Barros

SYN. *Pleurothallis grobyi* Bateman ex Lindley

Dwarf plants. Leaves to 5 × 1 cm, purplish on underside. Inflorescence to 14 cm long, several-flowered, the flowers open together. Flowers small, green, white, or orange, marked with red-purple.

Epiphytic in wet forest, 0–1000 m (3300 ft.)

Mexico, Central and South America

Sphyrarhynchus Mansfeld

TRIBE: Vandeae

SUBTRIBE: Aerangidinae

ETYMOLOGY: From Greek *sphyra*, hammer, and *rhynchos*, beak, referring to the shape of the rostellum

DISTRIBUTION: 1 species in Tanzania

Dwarf monopodial plant. Leaves several. Inflorescence short. Flowers white and green; sepals and petals similar; lip entire, spurred. Column short; pollinia and stipites 2, viscidium 1; rostellum hammer-shaped, bilobed.

CULTIVATION: Plants should be mounted, in intermediate temperatures and given moderate shade and high humidity. They should not be allowed to dry out for long.

Sphyrarhynchus schliebenii Mansfeld

Roots somewhat flattened. Leaves 2–3.5 × 0.5 cm, narrowly elliptic, rather fleshy. Inflorescence 3–4 cm long, densely 6- to 10-flowered. Flowers large for the size of plant, glistening white with a green blotch on the lip; sepals and petals to 14 × 4 mm, lanceolate, acute; lip to 6 × 4 mm, oblong, spur to 8 mm long, swollen at the apex.

Epiphytic in evergreen forest, 900–1600 m (3000–5300 ft.)

Tanzania

Spiranthes Richard

TRIBE: Cranichideae

SUBTRIBE: Spiranthinae

ETYMOLOGY: From Greek *speira*, spiral, and *anthos*, flower, referring to the spiral inflorescences

DISTRIBUTION: A cosmopolitan genus of about 30 species

Terrestrial plants with fleshy roots. Leaves several in a basal rosette, sometimes with a few on flowering stem, sometimes withered by flowering time. Inflorescences erect, unbranched, pubescent, few- to many-flowered, the flowers arranged in a spiral. Flowers ± tubular, the parts usually recurved near the apex, white, green, or pale yellow, rarely pink; sepals and petals narrow, petals sometimes adnate to dorsal sepal, lateral sepals free; lip entire, clawed at the base. Pollinia 2.

CULTIVATION: Several species are hardy in temperate gardens and can be naturalized in grass. Others can be grown in pots in a free-draining terrestrial compost with plenty of organic matter, in cool or intermediate conditions depending on place of origin. Plants should be kept almost dry while resting, when usually no leaves are present, but should not be allowed to dry out completely.

Spathoglottis plicata

Specklinia endotrachys

Specklinia grobyi

Sphyrarhynchus schliebenii. B. Campbell

Spiranthes odorata (Nuttall) Lindley

SYN. *Spiranthes cernua* (Linnaeus) Richard var. *odorata* (Nuttall) Correll

Leaves 3–5, to 50 × 4 cm. Inflorescence to 1 m tall, densely several- to many-flowered. Flowers scented, 10–18 mm long, white or cream, the lip pale yellow or green in the center. The cultivar 'Chadd's Ford' is widely cultivated, usually as *S. cernua* var. *odorata*. It can be grown outside or in an alpine house in cool-temperate regions. Flowering autumn–early winter.

Wet grassland, cypress swamps

Southeastern United States

SIMILAR SPECIES: *Spiranthes cernua* (Linnaeus) Richard from eastern Canada and eastern and central United States is usually a smaller plant with smaller flowers.

Spiranthes sinensis (Persoon) Ames

Leaves to 20 × 1 cm. Inflorescence 15–50 cm tall, densely many-flowered. Flowers ca. 5 mm long, usually magenta pink with a white lip, occasionally pale pink or white. Flowering spring–summer.

Wet rocky areas on rocky slopes, open woodland, 100–3500 m (330–11,500 ft.)

Eastern Europe to Australia

Spiranthes spiralis (Linnaeus) Chevallier

AUTUMN LADY'S TRESSES

Inflorescence 3–20 cm tall, several-flowered, arising from remains of the previous year's rosette, with the next season's rosette beside it. Flowers 5–7 mm long, white, the lip greenish. Flowering in autumn. This species can be naturalized in temperate gardens.

In short turf on calcareous soil; sand dunes; often near sea.

Europe, North Africa, Asia to western Himalayas

Stanhopea Frost

TRIBE: Maxillarieae

SUBTRIBE: Stanhopeinae

ETYMOLOGY: Named for the Earl of Stanhope, president of the London Medico-Botanical Society from 1829 to 1937

DISTRIBUTION: About 60 species and several natural hybrids in Mexico, Central and South America, and Trinidad

Large epiphytic or lithophytic plants. Pseudobulbs ovoid, 1-leafed at apex. Leaves large, petiolate, plicate, usually elliptic. Inflorescences unbranched, basal, pendent, rather loosely few- to several-flowered. Bracts large, papery. Flowers very large, fleshy, showy, strongly scented (usually, but not always, pleasantly), short-lived, rarely lasting for more than 3 to 4 days. Sepals and petals subsimilar, free, spreading or reflexed. Lip complex, divided into a hypochile, mesochile, and epichile, the mesochile often with 2 horns. Column long, sometimes winged; pollinia 2.

Spiranthes odorata. H. Oakeley

Spiranthes sinensis. H. Oakeley

Vegetatively, all species are similar, with heavily veined leaves 40–70 cm long, 15–20 cm wide, with a grooved petiole. Differences lie in the number of flowers on an inflorescence, the size and color of the flowers, and mainly the shape of the lip.

CULTIVATION: Plants must be grown in baskets, wooden or plastic-covered wire lined with sphagnum, with spaces large enough for the inflorescences to come through the bottom. A coarse bark-based compost or a mixture of 2 parts of living sphagnum to 1 part of perlite can be used. Stanhopeas need intermediate conditions, good light, high humidity, plenty of air movement, and plenty of water and fertilizer while in active growth. When the pseudobulbs are mature, they should be kept drier but not allowed to shrivel. Most species flower in summer and early autumn.

Stanhopea anfracta Rolfe

Inflorescence 7- to 13-flowered. Flowers 5–8 cm across; sepals and petals spreading, pale to deep orange; lip orange with a dark brownish eyespot on either side near the base.

Epiphytic in cloud forest, 1000–2200 m (3300–7260 ft.)

Bolivia, Ecuador, Peru

Stanhopea candida Barbosa Rodrigues

Inflorescence ca. 8 cm long, 2- to 4-flowered. Flowers white or ivory, ca. 7 cm across, the lip spotted and tinged with pink, hypochile with 2 marginal horns, mesochile with none.

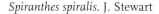

Spiranthes spiralis. J. Stewart

Stanhopea candida

Epiphytic on large branches of trees in wet lowland forest, 150–600 m (500–2000 ft.)

Brazil, Colombia, Peru, Venezuela

Stanhopea cirrhata Lindley
Inflorescence 4–5 cm long, 2-flowered. Flowers to 6 cm across; sepals and petals reflexed, yellow; lip orange, mesochile horns maroon-purple.

Epiphytic in wet forest, 0–700 m (2300 ft.)

Costa Rica, Nicaragua, Panama

Stanhopea costaricensis Reichenbach f.
Inflorescence 12–20 cm long, 5- to 7-flowered. Flowers 9 cm across; sepals and petals spreading or reflexed, cream or pale yellow spotted with red-brown; lip white or cream densely spotted with red-brown, hypochile with 2 dark red-brown eyespots, mesochile horns ca. 25 mm long.

Epiphytic in rain forest and cloud forest, 700–900 m (2300–3000 ft.)

Central America

Stanhopea ecornuta Lemaire
Inflorescence to 20 cm long, 2-flowered. Flowers ca. 6 cm across; sepals and petals white, the base of the petals often purple-spotted, lip golden yellow, spotted and flushed with red on the lower half.

Epiphytic in wet broad-leaved forest, 0–700 m (2300 ft.)

Central America

Stanhopea grandiflora (Loddiges) Lindley
SYN. *Stanhopea eburnea* Lindley
Inflorescence ca. 10 cm long, 2- to 4-flowered. Flowers to 15 cm across, cream dotted with purple-red and with reddish lines on the hypochile; hypochile with a pair of short horns, mesochile with none.

Epiphytic in forest, 100–1000 m (330–3300 ft.)

South America, Trinidad

Stanhopea graveolens Lindley
Inflorescence 3- to 9-flowered. Flowers unpleasantly scented, ca. 8 cm across, cream or greenish white; sepals and petals with purple spots; lip epichile with a large, maroon spot on each side, mesochile with 2 fleshy horns.

Epiphytic in riverine forest, to 2700 m (8900 ft.)

Mexico, Central America

Stanhopea jenischiana Kramer ex Reichenbach f.
Inflorescence to 30 cm long, 4- to 8-flowered. Flowers about 7 cm across, orange-yellow spotted with maroon; sepals and petals reflexed, lip hypochile often with 2 purple-red eyespots. Needs a dry rest to flower well.

Epiphytic in forest, 800–1500 m (2640–5000 ft.)

Colombia, Ecuador, Peru

Stanhopea nigroviolacea (C. Morren) Beer
SYN. *Stanhopea tigrina* Bateman var. *nigroviolacea* C. Morren
Inflorescence ca. 8 cm long, 2- or 3-flowered. Flowers to 18 cm across, vanilla-scented, whitish, greenish yellow or yellow, heavily blotched and spotted with deep purple-red.

Stanhopea ecornuta

Stanhopea grandiflora

Stanhopea jenischiana

Stanhopea nigroviolacea

Epiphytic in forest, 1200–2000 m (4000–6600 ft.)
Mexico

Stanhopea oculata (Loddiges) Lindley
Inflorescence to 50 cm long, 5- to 7-flowered. Flowers vanilla-scented, 10–13 cm across, greenish white or cream, spotted with maroon; lip hypochile yellow with 2 large maroon eye-spots, mesochile with 2 fleshy horns.

Epiphytic on trees or logs in wet broad-leaved forest, or lithophytic, 400–750 m (1320–2460 ft.)
Mexico, Central and South America

Stanhopea pulla Reichenbach f.
Inflorescence 3–4 cm long, 2-flowered. Flowers to 7 cm across (smallest in the genus), creamy yellow; sepals and petals ± reflexed, lip light orange-brown with reddish markings; mesochile lacking horns.

Epiphytic in rain forest, 0–1000 m (3300 ft.)
Costa Rica, Colombia, Panama

Stanhopea tigrina Bateman
Inflorescence to 15 cm long, 2- to 4-flowered. Flowers strongly scented, to 20 cm across, yellow heavily barred and blotched with purple-brown; hypochile golden yellow, dotted with purple-brown; mesochile creamy white, the horns dotted with purple; epichile cream, spotted purple, apex 3-toothed.

Epiphytic in forest, to 1100 m (3600 ft.)
Mexico

Stanhopea wardii Loddiges ex Lindley
Inflorescence to 18 cm long, 3- to 10-flowered. Flowers to 14 cm across, yellow, dotted with purple-red; lip hypochile orange with 2 purple-brown eyespots, mesochile with horns 3–4 cm long.

Epiphytic or lithophytic in rain forest, 400–2700 m (1320–8900 ft.)
Central and South America

Staurochilus Ridley ex Pfitzer

TRIBE: Vandeae
SUBTRIBE: Aeridinae
ETYMOLOGY: From Greek *stauros*, cross, and *chilos*, lip, referring to the cross-shaped lip of the type species, *S. fasciatus*
DISTRIBUTION: About 15 species in Southeast Asia, with most in the Philippines

Robust monopodial epiphytes or lithophytes with long, leafy stems and long, thick roots. Leaves strap-shaped, leathery, in 2 rows. Inflorescences long, erect, usually branched. Flowers showy, long-lasting, scented, usually yellow and brown; sepals and petals spreading; lip fleshy, trilobed, sometimes spurred. Column short and broad; pollinia 4.

Most species have been placed at some time in *Trichoglottis*, but they differ in the long, branched inflorescences and larger flowers.

CULTIVATION: Plants can be grown in pots or baskets in a coarse, free-draining bark-based compost. They like intermediate to warm temperatures, plenty of water while in growth, and good air circulation.

Stanhopea oculata

Staurochilus fasciatus Reichenbach f.
SYN. *Trichoglottis fasciatus* Reichenbach f.
Stems erect, to 75 cm long. Leaves to 15 × 3 cm. Inflorescence 10–17 cm long, 2- to 6-flowered. Flowers ca. 4 cm across; sepals and petals white outside, yellow blotched with red-brown inside; lip not spurred, side lobes erect, midlobe cross-shaped.

Epiphytic in forest and lithophytic on limestone rocks, 400–500 m (1320–1650 ft.)
Widespread in Southeast Asia and the Pacific Islands

Staurochilus ionosmus (Lindley) Schlechter
SYN. *Cleisostoma ionosma* Lindley, *Trichoglottis ionosma* (Lindley) J. J. Smith
Stem erect, to 1 m tall. Leaves arching, to 30 × 2.5 cm. Inflorescence erect, to 25-flowered. Flowers scented, 3 cm across; sepals and petals yellow, blotched with light reddish brown; lip white, spotted with red, the midlobe heart-shaped.

Epiphytic in forest, 300–1300 m (1000–4300 ft.)
Japan, Ryukyu Islands, Taiwan, Philippines

Stelis Swartz

SYN. *Physosiphon* Lindley, *Condylago* Luer
TRIBE: Epidendreae
SUBTRIBE: Pleurothallidinae
ETYMOLOGY: From Greek *stelis*, a name for mistletoe
DISTRIBUTION: More than 700 species in Florida, the West Indies, Mexico, Central and South America

Epiphytic, lithophytic, or terrestrial plants, usually small, tufted or creeping. Stem enclosed in tubular or funnel-shaped sheaths, 1-leafed. Inflorescences unbranched, usually several-flowered, arising from a spathe. Flowers small; sepals ovate or triangular, sometimes hairy, free

Stanhopea tigrina. H. Oakeley

Stanhopea wardii

Staurochilus ionosmus

or partly joined; petals usually half-moon-shaped. Lip fleshy, entire or tri-lobed, hinged to column or column-foot. Pollinia 2.

Many species previously included in *Pleurothallis* were moved to *Stelis* by Pridgeon and Chase in 2001 and many new species are still being described.

CULTIVATION: *Stelis* species occupy a wider range of habitats and altitudes than most of the related pleurothallid genera. However, most species will grow potted in a fine bark-based compost in cool to intermediate conditions in moderate to heavy shade, with good ventilation, and with high humidity throughout the year.

Stelis arcuata (Lindley) Pridgeon & M. W. Chase
SYN. *Pleurothallis arcuata* Lindley, *Specklinia arcuata* (Luer) Luer
Stems to 5 cm long. Leaves to 10 × 2 cm. Inflorescence to 30 cm long, to about 15-flowered. Flowers ca. 10 mm long, dorsal sepal yellow with maroon stripes, lateral sepals joined, deep purple.

Epiphytic in open forest, 1000–1600 m (3300–5300 ft.)

Guyana, Venezuela, Brazil

Stelis argentata Lindley
Stems to 6 cm tall. Leaves to 10 × 2.5 cm. Inflorescence to 20 cm tall, ± secund, many-flowered. Flowers 8 mm across, pale pink to purplish; sepals spreading, orbicular.

Epiphytic in rain forest and cloud forest, 800–1600 m (2640–5300 ft.)

Mexico, Central and South America

Stelis gelida (Lindley) Pridgeon & M. W. Chase
SYN. *Pleurothallis gelida* Lindley, *Specklinia gelida* (Lindley) Luer
Leaves to 25 × 6 cm. Inflorescence erect, to 30 cm long, several-flowered. Flowers small, secund, white, pale yellow or yellow-green.

Epiphytic in rain forest, to 1900 m (6300 ft.)

Stelis argentata

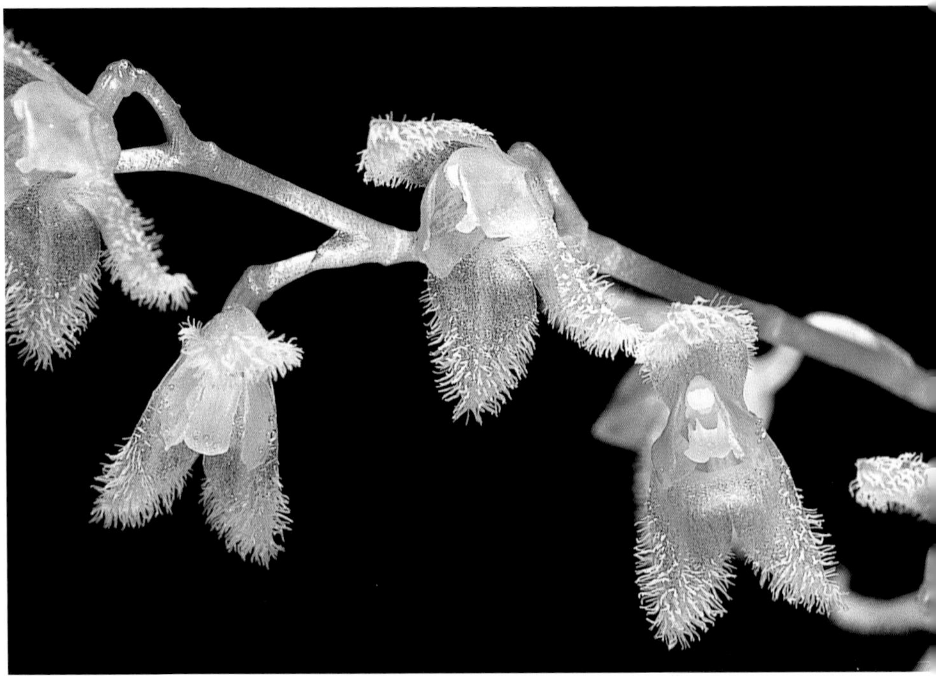

Stelis gelida

United States (Florida), West Indies, Mexico, Central and South America

Stelis megachlamys (Schlechter) Pupulin

SYN. *Pleurothallis tuerckheimii* Schlechter, *P. megachlamys* Schlechter

A large species with stems to 35 cm long. Leaves to 25 × 7 cm. Flowers large, sepals pubescent, ca. 25 long, deep red-brown to purple.

Epiphytic in rain forest and cloud forest, 1000–2050 m (3300–6700 ft.)

Mexico, Central America

Stelis segoviensis (Reichenbach f.) Pridgeon & M. W. Chase

SYN. *Pleurothallis segoviensis* Reichenbach f.

Stems to 6 cm long, forming dense clumps. Leaves to 13 × 1.5 cm. Inflorescence to 20 cm long, secund, few- to several-flowered. Flowers ca. 2 cm long, variable in color, deep purple-red to yellow-green marked with brown.

Epiphytic in rain forest and cloud forest, 600–2000 m (2000–6600 ft.)

Mexico, Central and South America

Stelis villosa (Knowles & Westcott) Pridgeon & M. W. Chase

SYN. *Pleurothallis schiedei* Reichenbach f., *P. hirsuta* Ames

Leaves to 6, ca. 2 cm long. Inflorescence loosely few-flowered, with 1 or 2 flowers open together. Sepals 5–7 mm long, yellow-green mottled with purple, with long, purple hairs inside.

Epiphytic in wet woodland, 1300–1900 m (4300–6300 ft.)

Mexico, Central America

Stenia Lindley

TRIBE: Maxillarieae

SUBTRIBE: Zygopetalinae

ETYMOLOGY: From Greek *stenos*, narrow, referring to the slender pollinia of the genus

DISTRIBUTION: 8 species in Central and South America

Small to medium-sized epiphytes lacking pseudobulbs. Leaves strap-shaped to elliptic, forming a fan, the bases overlapping. Inflorescences basal, 1-flowered. Flowers large and showy but short-lived; sepals and petals spreading, subsimilar, lateral sepals joined to column-foot; lip fleshy, concave or saccate.

Stelis megachlamys

Stelis segoviensis

Stenia calceolaris

CULTIVATION: Plants should be grown in pots in a free-draining epiphyte compost. They require intermediate temperatures and humid, shady conditions. They should be watered throughout the year and not be allowed to dry out.

Stenia calceolaris (Garay) Dodson & Bennett

SYN. *Chaubardiella calceolaris* Garay

Flowers ca. 2.5 cm across, pale green to greenish white dotted with red-brown, the petals more densely spotted than the sepals; lip saccate, whitish with red-brown spots.

Epiphytic in montane forest and cloud forest, 1200–2200 m (4000–7260 ft.)

Ecuador, Peru

Stenia guttata Reichenbach f.

Leaves to 13 × 3.5 cm. Inflorescence ± prostrate, very short. Flowers ca. 5 cm across, yellow-green to straw yellow, spotted with dark purple; lip obscurely trilobed, disc with a transverse callus with 7 teeth.

Epiphytic in wet forest, 800–2100 m (2640–6900 ft.)

Peru

Stenia guttata

Stenia pallida Lindley

Leaves to 15 × 4 cm, stiff, slightly recurved. Inflorescence to 6 cm long, erect or arching. Flowers 4–5 cm across, creamy white to pale greenish yellow; lip obscurely trilobed, deeply saccate at the base, the side lobes dotted with maroon.

Epiphytic in wet forest, 100–500 m (330–1650 ft.)

Trinidad, South America

Stenoglottis Lindley

TRIBE: Orchideae

SUBTRIBE: Orchidinae

ETYMOLOGY: From Greek *stenos*, narrow, and *glottis*, tongue, referring to the narrow lip

DISTRIBUTION: 5 species, possibly more, from South Africa and east tropical Africa

Terrestrial or lithophytic plants, occasionally low-level epiphytes, with swollen, fleshy roots but no tubers. Leaves spotted or unspotted, in basal rosettes. Inflorescences arising from the middle of a rosette, erect, with some scattered sheaths, unbranched, loosely or densely several- to many-flowered. Flowers pink, lilac, or white, often spotted with purple. Sepals shortly joined to column at base, the rest free; petals free, forming a loose hood with the sepals. Lip 3- or 5-lobed, longer than sepals and petals, with or without a spur, the lobes often fringed.

CULTIVATION: Plants should be grown in shallow pans in a free-draining terrestrial mix, in cool to intermediate conditions. When the leaves die back after flowering, the dead remnants should be removed. Keep plants dry until new growth starts to appear, usually after a few weeks, when careful watering can be resumed.

Stenoglottis zambesiaca. E. la Croix

Stenoglottis fimbriata Lindley
Leaves several, to 15 × 1.5 cm, the edges undulate, dark green, spotted with purple-brown (rarely unspotted). Inflorescence 10–40 cm tall, several- to many-flowered. Flowers rose-mauve, spotted with purple; lip 9–15 mm long, lacking a spur, trilobed at about halfway, all lobes usually fringed. Flowering in late summer.

Terrestrial in humus or on fallen logs, or lithophytic on mossy rocks, in shade in forest, to 2200 m (7260 ft.)

South Africa, Swaziland.

SIMILAR SPECIES: *Stenoglottis zambesiaca* Rolfe, from South and East Africa as far north as Malawi and Tanzania, has been confused with *S. fimbriata* in the past but differs in details of the flower. Plants are usually smaller, with paler flowers and less heavily marked leaves.

Stenoglottis longifolia. E. la Croix

Stenoglottis longifolia Hooker f.
Leaves numerous, 9–25 × 1–4 cm, light green, the edges undulate. Inflorescence 30–100 cm tall, densely many-flowered. Flowers pale to deep pink, the lip with some purple spots; sepals to 10 mm long; lip 15–16 mm long, lacking a spur, 5-lobed in the basal third, the lobes usually fringed. The most widely grown species. Flowering in autumn.

Terrestrial in humus or lithophytic on mossy rocks, to 1300 m (4300 ft.)

South Africa

Stenoglottis woodii Schlechter
Leaves numerous, 5–15 × 1–3 cm, bluish green, the edges not undulate. Inflorescence to 40 cm tall, many-flowered. Flowers white or pink, the lip usually with some purple spots; lip 10–14 mm long, trilobed in the apical half, with a slender spur 1.5–3 mm long, straight or slightly curved. Flowering summer.

Terrestrial or lithophytic in rocky areas, to 500 m (1650 ft.)

South Africa, Zimbabwe

SIMILAR SPECIES: *Stenoglottis macloughlinii* (L. Bolus) G. McDonald from South Africa is sometimes considered synonymous with *S. woodii* but has narrower leaves and differs in some details of the flower, including a longer spur.

Stenorrhynchos Richard ex Sprengel

TRIBE: Cranichideae
SUBTRIBE: Spiranthinae
ETYMOLOGY: From Greek *stenos*, narrow, and *rhynchos*, snout, referring to the slender rostellum
DISTRIBUTION: 5 species in Mexico, Central and South America, and the West Indies

Small to large terrestrial, rarely epiphytic, plants with clusters of fleshy roots. Leaves often in a rosette. Inflorescences erect, unbranched, few- to many-flowered with large floral bracts. Flowers small to large, sometimes showy; sepals free, subsimilar, the dorsal forming a hood with the petals, the laterals spreading or erect, saccate at the base; lip entire or trilobed, saccate at the base, then narrowing, the apical part deflexed, the disc often hairy.

CULTIVATION: Plants should be grown in pans in a free-draining, humus-rich terrestrial compost in cool to intermediate, shady conditions. They need to be watered throughout the year, although less frequently in winter.

Stenorrhynchos speciosum (Gmelin) Richard

Leaves in a basal rosette, elliptic to obovate, to 21 × 7 cm, dark green often striped and spotted with silver. Inflorescence to 70 cm tall, densely few- to many-flowered. Bracts to 4 cm long, longer than the flowers, red. Flowers pink to bright red; sepals and petals lanceolate, acuminate; lip obscurely trilobed with 2 fleshy calli at the base.

Epiphytic or terrestrial in rain forest and cloud forest, 1000–2000 m (3300–6600 ft.)

Mexico, Central and South America, Caribbean

Summerhayesia P. J. Cribb

TRIBE: Vandeae

SUBTRIBE: Aerangidinae

ETYMOLOGY: Named for orchid specialist Victor Summerhayes (1892–1974), who worked at the Royal Botanic Gardens, Kew

DISTRIBUTION: 3 species in Africa

Stems short; leaves stiff, linear, folded, forming a fan. Racemes axillary. Flowers nonresupinate (the lip is at the top), fleshy, white to creamy yellow; lateral sepals joined at the base enclosing the spur; lip boat-shaped. Pollinia 2, viscidium 1, slipper-shaped.

CULTIVATION: Plants require intermediate or preferably warm temperatures, light to moderate shade, and plenty of water while in growth, with a drier rest in winter. They can be grown in pots in a coarse bark-based mixture or mounted, which lets the long spurs hang freely.

Stenoglottis woodii

Stenorrhynchos speciosum

Summerhayesia laurentii. E. la Croix

Summerhayesia laurentii (De Wildeman) P. J. Cribb

SYN. *Aerangis laurentii* (De Wildeman) Schlechter

Leaves several, distichous, to 20 × 1 cm. Inflorescence arching or spreading, to 50 cm long, many-flowered. Flowers creamy white with a greenish spur; sepals and petals 8–9 mm long; lip of similar length, boat-shaped; spur 6–8 cm long, pendent, straight, slender.

Epiphytic in rain forest, to 800 m (2640 ft.)

West and Central Africa

Summerhayesia zambesiaca P. J. Cribb

Leaves to 14 × 1.5 cm, recurved, yellow-green. Inflorescence erect or arching, 12–15 cm long, 4- to 5-flowered. Flowers creamy yellow, the outside covered with some short, rusty hairs; sepals and petals 12–14 mm long; lip 12 mm long, boat-shaped; spur 16–20 cm long, pendent, straight, slender.

High-level epiphyte in high-rainfall woodland and in rain forest, occasionally lithophytic, 600–700 m (2000–2300 ft.)

DR Congo, Malawi, Tanzania, Zambia, Zimbabwe

Tainia Blume

SYN. *Ania* Lindley

TRIBE: Collabieae

ETYMOLOGY: From Greek *tainia*, fillet, referring to the long, narrow petals of *T. speciosa*, the type species

DISTRIBUTION: 18 species in tropical Asia

Terrestrial plants, rarely lithophytic or epiphytic. Pseudobulbs cylindrical or ovoid, composed of a single internode, 1-leafed at apex. Leaf petiolate, plicate, elliptic to ovate. Inflorescences usually terminal, sometimes lateral, usually unbranched, the peduncle with tubular sheaths, several- to many-flowered. Sepals and petals subsimilar, spreading; lip entire or trilobed, slightly saccate but not spurred. Pollinia 8 in 4 pairs.

CULTIVATION: Grow plants in clay pots in a well-drained terrestrial compost. They require intermediate to warm conditions and a humid, shaded situation with plenty of water while in growth, less when resting.

Tainia penangiana Hooker f.

SYN. *Tainia hookeriana* King & Pantling, *Ania penangiana* (Hooker f.) Summerhayes

Pseudobulbs conical, to 5 cm tall. Leaf to 50 × 10 cm, elliptic, with a petiole to 35 cm long. Inflorescence to 1 m tall, rather loosely 5- to 25-flowered, the flowers open together. Flowers 2–5 cm across, greenish brown to yellow with reddish stripes, the lip white or cream; sepals and petals spreading; lip trilobed, midlobe suborbicular, apiculate, the margins slightly undulate; spur to 4 mm long.

Terrestrial in tropical evergreen and riverine forest, 500–1000 m (1650–3300 ft.)

Tainia penangiana

Teagueia rex

China, India, Peninsula Malaysia, Thailand, Vietnam

Tainia speciosa Blume

Pseudobulbs to 8 cm long, narrowly rectangular, glossy. Leaf to 20 cm long, ovate-lanceolate, with a petiole to 22 cm long. Inflorescence 35–45 cm long, 3- to 12-flowered, the flowers open together. Flowers to 10 cm across, pale green or yellow-green striped with purple-red, lip creamy yellow, with or without stripes; sepals to 6.5 cm long, petals to 4.5 cm long, all long acuminate; lip entire, to 22 mm long, ovate with a recurved acumen.

Terrestrial in humus in shade of primary forest, 250–1200 m (825–4000 ft.)

Borneo, Java, peninsular Malaysia, Sumatra, Thailand

Teagueia (Luer) Luer

TRIBE: Epidendreae

SUBTRIBE: Pleurothallidinae

ETYMOLOGY: Named for Walter Teague, who found the type species

DISTRIBUTION: 11 species in Colombia and Ecuador

Epiphytic, rarely terrestrial plants, creeping or tufted. Stems erect, 1-leafed at apex. Leaves ovate to elliptical, petiolate. Inflorescences arising laterally from near the stem apex, several-flowered. Flowers relatively large, arranged in 2 rows; floral bracts tubular. Sepals thin-textured, tailed, often pubescent; dorsal sepal free, laterals partly joined. Petals small. Lip heart-shaped, fleshy, concave or channeled, the margins inrolled. Column lacking wings and a foot; pollinia 2.

CULTIVATION: Species of *Teagueia* grow in the Andes of Colombia and Ecuador, in wet forest or cloud forest, at altitudes from 750 to 3000 m (2460–9900 ft.). They require cool, shady conditions with high humidity all year round. They can be mounted on slabs with a pad of moss to retain moisture or potted in a fine epiphyte compost.

Teagueia tentaculata Luer & Hirtz

Leaves to 13 × 3 cm. Inflorescence suberect, to 11 cm long, several-flowered. Flowers light yellow; sepals ca. 33 mm long, ovate at the base, with long, threadlike tails.

Epiphytic in cloud forest, 2400 m (7900 ft.)

Ecuador

SIMILAR SPECIES: *Teagueia rex* (Luer & R. Escobar) Luer (syn. *Platystele rex* Luer & R. Escobar) from Colombia has bright rose-pink flowers with shorter tails (sepals ca. 20 mm long) and a lip with a prominent basal callus.

Telipogon Kunth

TRIBE: Maxillarieae
SUBTRIBE: Oncidiinae
ETYMOLOGY: From Greek *telos*, end, and *pogon*, beard, referring to the hairy column apex
DISTRIBUTION: More than 150 species in Central and South America

Small to medium-sized epiphytes or terrestrials lacking pseudobulbs, often with a creeping rhizome or decumbent stem. Stems short or long, sometimes branching. Leaves few to many, distichous, leathery or fleshy. Inflorescences terminal or lateral, erect, unbranched, 1- to several-flowered. Flowers showy, often large for the size of plant. Sepals free, spreading, subequal; petals much larger than the sepals, spreading, sometimes slightly concave, usually ovate to orbicular, usually with prominent veining; lip similar to petals or broader, with a basal callus. Column short; pollinia 4.

CULTIVATION: These beautiful plants are notoriously difficult to cultivate. Most grow at high altitudes in cloud forest and must have cool conditions with moderate shade, high humidity, and good air movement. They are most likely to succeed if grown in small pots, in a mixture containing sphagnum. They need frequent misting and should not be allowed to dry out.

Telipogon ariasii Dodson & D. E. Bennett

Flowers yellow, veined and barred with red-brown, deep red in center.

Epiphytic in cloud forest, ca. 2800 m (9250 ft.)

Peru

Telipogon costaricensis Schlechter

Stem to 15 cm long. Leaves to 8 cm long. Inflorescence 12–45 cm long, 5- to 11-flowered, the flowers open in succession. Flowers ca. 5 cm across, nonresupinate, yellow, veined with purple-brown, flushed with purple-brown in the center; column and bristles brown.

Epiphytic in very wet forest, 2700–3200 m (8,900–10,500 ft.)

Costa Rica

Telipogon latifolius Kunth

SYN. *Telipogon bruchmuelleri* Reichenbach f.

Stem very short. Leaves to 6 × 1.5 cm. Inflorescence to 8 cm tall, 1- or 2-flowered. Flowers ca. 4 cm across; sepals bright yellow-green, petals and lip paler, the petals flushed with maroon-pink at the base, lip veined with pink; callus maroon; column brown.

Twig epiphyte in cloud forest, 1800–2800 m (6000–9250 ft.)

Colombia, Ecuador, Venezuela

Telipogon nervosus (Linnaeus) Druce

Stem often scrambling, sometimes suberect, 20–40 cm long or more. Leaves ca. 2 × 1 cm. Inflorescence to 30 cm long, 5- to 9-flowered, the flowers open in succession. Flowers ca. 3 cm across; sepals light green, petals and lip greenish yellow, veined with brown or purple, column maroon.

Terrestrial in cloud forest, ca. 2500 m (8250 ft.)

Colombia, Venezuela

SIMILAR SPECIES: *Telipogon pulcher* Reichenbach f. from Colombia and Ecuador has fewer and larger flowers, ca. 5 cm across; the petals and lip are broader and cream with red-brown veins.

Telipogon venustus Schlechter

Inflorescence to 40 cm long. Flowers ca. 1.5 cm across; sepals brownish green, petals and lip yellow-orange with red veins, column red.

Epiphytic in cloud forest, 2000–3300 m (6600—10,900 ft.)

Colombia, Ecuador

Tetramicra Lindley

TRIBE: Epidendreae
SUBTRIBE: Laeliinae
ETYMOLOGY: From Greek *tetra*, 4, and *mikros*, small, possibly referring to the 4 smaller pollinia
DISTRIBUTION: 13 species in the West Indies

Terrestrial, lithophytic, or epiphytic plants with a creeping rhizome. Pseudobulbs small or absent; stems short and stout. Leaves distichous, sometimes semi-terete,. Inflorescences erect, unbranched, the flowers open in succession. Sepals and petals free, spreading; dorsal sepal usually narrower than laterals; lip trilobed, larger than other parts, with prominent, spreading side lobes and a broad midlobe. Pollinia 8 (4 large, 4 small).

CULTIVATION: Because of their scrambling and creeping habit, plants are best mounted. In the wild they usually grow in forest on limestone. They require intermediate to warm conditions, light to moderate shade, and high humidity all year round.

Tetramicra bulbosa Mansfeld

Pseudobulbs ca. 2 cm long, covered in papery sheaths, 2- or 3-leaved. Leaves to 10 × 1 cm, the margins finely toothed. Inflorescence to 35 cm long, few- to several-flowered. Flowers ca. 2 cm across; sepals and petals red-brown, lip bright pink or purple with darker lines on the midlobe.

Lithophytic on limestone, ca. 600 m (2000 ft.)

Hispaniola, Jamaica

Tetramicra canaliculata (Aublet) Urban

Stems ca. 2 cm long, 1- to 4-leaved. Leaves to 18 × 1 cm, linear to almost cylindrical, grooved on the upper side, recurved. Inflorescence erect, to 60 cm tall, few-flowered, the flowers open in succession and long-lasting. Flowers ca. 5 cm across, slightly scented; sepals and petals purplish

Telipogon ariasii

Tetramicra bulbosa

Telipogon latifolius

green, lip bright pink with darker veins and a white disc.

Epiphytic or lithophytic in scrub on rocky hillsides in full exposure.

Bahamas, Hispaniola

SIMILAR SPECIES: *Tetramicra elegans* (Hamilton) Cogniaux (syn. *Cyrtopodium elegans* Hamilton) occurs on several Caribbean islands; it has needlelike leaves and the lip has a yellow disc.

Tetramicra eulophiae Reichenbach f.

Leaves fleshy, cylindrical, to 35 cm long, 3 mm wide. Inflorescence 40–60 cm long, 10- to 15-flowered. Flowers ca. 1.5 cm across; sepals and petals reddish brown; lip ovate, pink with darker veining.

Terrestrial in open areas in pinewoods, 200–700 m (660—2300 ft.)

Cuba

Teuscheria Garay

TRIBE: Maxillarieae

SUBTRIBE: Maxillariinae

ETYMOLOGY: Named for German botanist Heinrich Teuscher (1891–1984)

DISTRIBUTION: 7 species in Mexico, Central and South America

Rhizome short or long, covered in overlapping sheaths. Pseudobulbs small, ovoid, covered with leaf sheaths, 1-leafed at the apex. Leaves narrow, pleated, petiolate. Inflorescences basal, erect or pendent, 1-flowered. Flowers large, fleshy, resupinate or nonresupinate; sepals and petals subsimilar, dorsal sepal and petals free, lateral sepals joined to column-foot forming a mentum; lip joined to column-foot, clawed at the base, trilobed. Pollinia 4.

CULTIVATION: Plants require intermediate conditions, with good light and high humidity. If potted, they need an open, free-draining compost; they flower better if pot-bound and should not be repotted frequently. Species with long rhizomes can be mounted. When growth is complete, plants should be kept dry, with occasional misting to prevent the pseudobulbs from wrinkling.

Teuscheria cornucopia Garay

Rhizome elongate. Inflorescence erect, 7–8 cm long. Flowers ca. 1 cm across, nodding, nonresupinate, mauve-pink, the lip with darker stripes; mentum ascending, curved.

Epiphytic in cloud forest, 1000–1500 m (3300–5000 ft.)

Ecuador

Teuscheria pickiana (Schlechter) Garay

SYN. *Bifrenaria pickiana* Schlechter

Pseudobulbs to 3 × 2 cm, spaced out on rhizome. Leaves to 60 × 3 cm. Inflorescence ca. 3 cm long. Flowers resupinate, ca. 2 cm long, pink, the lip yellow inside.

Epiphytic in rain forest, 50–1000 m (165–3300 ft.)

Belize, Costa Rica, Colombia, Ecuador, Guyana, Mexico

Teuscheria wageneri (Reichenbach f.) Garay

SYN. *Bifrenaria wageneri* Reichenbach f., *Stenocoryne wageneri* (Reichenbach f.) Kraenzlin, *Teuscheria venezuelana* Garay

Pseudobulbs clustered, to 2.5 cm long. Leaves to 35 × 2.5 cm. Inflorescence pendent, to 10 cm long. Flowers opening wide, to 5 cm across; sepals and petals bronze tinged with maroon, lip white, flushed with pink at the margins, with a golden-yellow, powdery callus.

Epiphytic in cloud forest, 1200–1400 m (4000–4600 ft.)

Venezuela

Thelymitra Forster & Forster f.

SUN ORCHIDS

TRIBE: Diurideae

SUBTRIBE: Thelymitrinae

ETYMOLOGY: From Greek *thelys*, female, and *mitra*, cap, referring to the hooded column

DISTRIBUTION: Almost 100 species in Australia, New Zealand, Southeast Asia, and the Pacific Islands

Deciduous terrestrials with paired, ovoid tubers. Leaf single, basal, erect, lanceolate to terete, occasionally hairy, often ribbed. Inflorescences erect, 1- to many-flowered. Flowers resupinate, brightly colored, usually opening only in sunshine; lip usually similar to sepals and petals, not spurred, unlobed, lacking a callus. Column with fused wings forming a hood, sometimes lobed, over the anther, with 2 appendages which may be fringed or hairy.

CULTIVATION: Some species are difficult to maintain in cultivation. In general, they require an acid, free-draining terrestrial compost containing wood shavings. They like bright light and need plenty of water from autumn to spring, when they are growing, and should be kept dry when resting. In temperate areas they do best in a cool house or alpine house.

Thelymitra arenaria Lindley

Leaf 20 × 1.8 cm, lanceolate, fleshy, channeled. Inflorescence to 35 cm tall, 3- to 12-flowered. Flowers ca. 25 mm across, pale blue; column yellow. One of the easier species to cultivate.

Open forest

Tasmania

Thelymitra aristata Lindley

SYN. *Thelymitra grandiflora* Fitzgerald

Leaf to 35 × 2 cm, fleshy, ribbed, often with dark blotches. Inflorescence to 80 cm long, 5- to 30-flowered. Flowers ca. 35 mm across, pale to deep blue or lilac; column apex yellow, column arms with tufts of white or yellow hairs.

Open forest and heathland near coast, often on sandy soil

Southeastern Australia, Tasmania

Thelymitra crinita Lindley

Leaf ovate, to 18 × 4.5 cm. Inflorescence to 75 cm tall, to 12-flowered. Flowers bright blue, ca. 40 mm across; upper part of column covered with black and yellow calli.

Open woodland in sandy soil, usually near coast

Southwestern Western Australia

Thelymitra ixioides Swartz

Leaf linear, to 20 × 1 cm, channeled. Inflorescence to 60 cm tall, several-flowered. Flowers 20–40 mm across, usually deep blue but sometimes pale blue, mauve, pink, or white; sepals sometimes spotted with dark blue; back of column covered with rows of club-shaped glands.

Heath or open woodland, from sea level to high altitudes

Southeastern Australia, New Zealand

SIMILAR SPECIES: *Thelymitra juncifolia* Lindley, from southeastern Australia, has a yellow apical band on the column and flowers up to 20 mm across. It grows well in cultivation.

Thelymitra pauciflora R. Brown

Leaf to 20 × 2 cm, linear, fleshy, channeled, ribbed. Inflorescence to 50 cm tall, to 15-flowered. Flowers 10–20 mm across, pale to bright blue, occasionally pink or white; lip smaller than other parts; column white or blue, the hood sometimes yellow or brown.

Habitat varied, from open forest to heathland, from sea level to high altitudes

Southeastern and southwestern Australia, New Zealand

SIMILAR SPECIES: *Thelymitra nuda* R. Brown differs in column details.

Thunia Reichenbach f.

TRIBE: Arethuseae

SUBTRIBE: Coelogyninae

ETYMOLOGY: Named for Graf von Thun of Tetschin (1786–1873)

DISTRIBUTION: 5 species in India, China, and Southeast Asia

Sympodial orchids, usually terrestrial but sometimes lithophytic or epiphytic. Stems erect, clustered,

Teuscheria cornucopia

Thelymitra aristata. J. Stewart

Thelymitra ixioides. J. Stewart

Thunia alba var. *bracteata*

canelike, biennial, the lower parts covered with sheaths, the upper part leafy. Leaves distichous, thin-textured. Inflorescences terminal; bracts prominent; the flowers short-lived but produced in succession. Flowers large, showy and scented; sepals and petals free, subsimilar; lip trumpet-shaped, the apex frilly.

CULTIVATION: Canes should be potted in a terrestrial mix, watered and fertilized freely while in growth, and kept in shade in intermediate conditions. After flowering, plants should be kept dry in a cool, bright place.

Thunia alba

Thunia alba (Lindley) Reichenbach f.

SYN. *Thunia marshalliana* Reichenbach f.

Plants 30–100 cm tall. Leaves 10–20 cm long, lanceolate or elliptic, thin-textured. Inflorescence to 30 cm long, nodding, 2- to 7-flowered. Flowers often not opening wide, sepals and petals white, lip orange or yellow with purple stripes; sepals 4–7 cm long; lip oblong, tubular; spur 1 cm long, cylindrical, horizontal.

Terrestrial, lithophytic, or epiphytic in forks of trees in submontane forest, 1000–2300 m (3300–7600 ft.)

China, India, Myanmar

Ticoglossum Rodriguez ex Halbinger

TRIBE: Maxillarieae

SUBTRIBE: Oncidiinae

ETYMOLOGY: From Tico, a colloquial name for Costa Ricans, and Greek *glossa*, tongue

DISTRIBUTION: 2 species in Costa Rica

Pseudobulbs clustered, round to ovoid, compressed, with sharp angles, with some leafy basal sheaths, 1-leafed at apex. Leaves petiolate, elliptic to lanceolate. Inflorescences arising from basal sheaths, about as long as the leaves, 1- to few-flowered. Flowers large, showy, white or pink. Sepals and petals free, subsimilar but the petals shortly clawed. Lip with a short claw and a fleshy callus.

Ticoglossum krameri. J. Stewart

Column short, with 2 protuberances beside the stigma; pollinia 2.

CULTIVATION: *Ticoglossum krameri* requires intermediate conditions while *T. oerstedii* does better in cool. Both species are grown potted in a fine to medium epiphyte compost, in light shade with high humidity and good air movement. They need plenty of water while in active growth but should be kept drier while resting.

Ticoglossum krameri

(Reichenbach f.) Rodriguez ex Halbinger

SYN. *Odontoglossum krameri* Reichenbach f.

Pseudobulbs ca. 4 × 3 cm. Leaves to 25 × 4 cm. Inflorescence 15–20 cm long, arching to pendent, 2- or 3-flowered. Flowers to 4.5 cm across, long-lasting, white or pink, lip ± wedge-shaped with a yellow callus spotted with red, with a brown or orange band in front of it.

Epiphytic in rain forest, 400–1200 m (1320–4000 ft.)

Costa Rica, Nicaragua, Panama

SIMILAR SPECIES: *Ticoglossum oerstedii* (Reichenbach f.) Rodriguez ex Halbinger (syn. *Odontoglossum oerstedii* Reichenbach f.) from Costa Rica and Panama has pseudobulbs with rounded edges, a 1- or 2-flowered inflorescence, and white flowers with an orange callus. It grows at higher altitudes, 1600–3100 m (5300–10,230 ft.).

Tolumnia Rafinesque

TRIBE: Maxillarieae

SUBTRIBE: Oncidiinae

ETYMOLOGY: Probably named for Tolumnius, mentioned by Virgil

Ticoglossum oerstedii. R. Parsons

DISTRIBUTION: About 30 species in the West Indies

Small epiphytes and lithophytes lacking pseudobulbs, sometimes stoloniferous. Leaves distichous, fleshy, bilaterally flattened, triangular in cross-section or terete, forming a fan. Inflorescences usually much longer than leaves, branched or unbranched. Flowers large, showy; lateral sepals partly joined, lying behind lip; petals free, larger than sepals; lip much larger than other parts, trilobed, the midlobe often bilobed, with a complicated fleshy callus at the base. Column with prominent wings; pollinia 2.

These plants are still sometimes referred to as equitant oncidiums.

CULTIVATION: *Tolumnia* species should be grown mounted or in baskets or small clay pots in a very open bark mixture. They require warm to intermediate conditions, good to dappled light, high humidity, and good air movement. They will rot if water stays in the growths for any length of time. Stoloniferous species are better mounted. Plants should not be divided frequently as they seem to resent disturbance.

Tolumnia calochila (Cogniaux) Braem

Leaves terete, to 10 cm long, 3 mm wide. Inflorescence to 10 cm long, 2- to 6-flowered. Flowers to 2 cm across; sepals yellow-green, petals and lip bright yellow; lip midlobe heart-shaped, deeply fringed.

Epiphytic in lowland forest in rather dry areas, 0–200 m (660 ft.)

Cayman Islands, Cuba, Hispaniola

Tolumnia pulchella (Hooker) Rafinesque

SYN. *Oncidium pulchellum* Hooker

Leaves to 20 × 4 cm, bilaterally flattened or triangular in cross-section. Inflorescence erect, to 50 cm long, sometimes branched, many-flowered. Flowers to 2.5 cm across, white tinged with pink or magenta; lip midlobe deeply bilobed; callus trilobed, white and yellow.

Epiphytic on small trees or lithophytic on limestone, 120–900 m (400–3000 ft.)

Jamaica

Tolumnia triquetra (Swartz) Nir

SYN. *Oncidium triquetrum* (Swartz) R. Brown

Leaves to 20 × 1 cm. Inflorescence ca. 20 cm long. Flowers to 2 cm across, white or pale yellow, mottled and veined with dark red; lip not bilobed.

Epiphytic in trees in exposed situations, 120–380 m (400–1250 ft.)

Jamaica

Tolumnia variegata (Swartz) Braem

SYN. *Oncidium variegatum* (Swartz) Swartz

Stoloniferous plants. Leaves bilaterally flattened, recurved, the margins slightly serrate, to 15 × 1.5 cm. Inflorescence branched or unbranched, to 45 cm long, several-flowered. Flowers 2–2.5 cm across, white or pale pink marked with brown or purple; lip kidney-shaped, emarginate.

Epiphytic in rather dry woodland, 0–2000 m (6600 ft.)

Cuba, Hispaniola, Leeward Islands, Puerto Rica

SIMILAR SPECIES: *Tolumnia velutina* (Lindley & Paxton) Braem from Cuba is a slightly smaller plant; the lip has a velvety texture. *Tolumnia bahamensis* (Nash) Braem from Florida and the Bahamas has semiterete leaves.

Trias Lindley

TRIBE: Epidendreae

SUBTRIBE: Bulbophyllinae

ETYMOLOGY: From Greek *trias*, 3, referring to the triangular flowers

DISTRIBUTION: 12 species in India and Southeast Asia

Small epiphytes closely related to *Bulbophyllum*. Rhizome creeping; pseudobulbs small, ovoid to subglobose, 1-leafed at apex. Inflorescences basal, 1-flowered, with tubular bracts. Flowers almost triangular, usually large for the size of plant; sepals fleshy, similar, spreading, the laterals joined to the column-foot; petals small; lip narrow, fleshy, mobile. Anther-cap elongated, often cleft.

CULTIVATION: Species of *Trias* should be grown like the smaller species of *Bulbophyllum*, either mounted on a slab or grown in a shallow pan. They require intermediate, shaded conditions, high humidity, and plenty of water while in growth but should be kept drier when resting.

Trias oblonga Lindley

Pseudobulbs to 2 cm long, angled, set close together. Leaves to 3 cm long. Inflorescence about 2.5 cm tall. Flowers yellow-green, to 2.5 cm across.

Epiphytic at moderate altitudes

Myanmar, Thailand

Trias picta (C. S. P. Parish & Reichenbach f.) Hemsley

Pseudobulbs 1–1.5 cm across, ovoid, set ca. 1.5 cm apart. Leaves 5–7 cm long, fleshy, elliptic, acute. Inflorescence 2–4 cm long. Flowers ca. 2 cm across, yellowish heavily spotted and marked with red.

Epiphytic at altitudes around 1000 m (3300 ft.)

India, Thailand, Myanmar

Trichocentrum Poeppig & Endlicher

SYN. *Lophiaris* Rafinesque

TRIBE: Maxillarieae

SUBTRIBE: Oncidiinae

ETYMOLOGY: From Greek *tricho*, hair, and *kentron*, spur, referring to the slender spur of most species

DISTRIBUTION: About 70 species in Mexico and tropical America

Pseudobulbs clustered, very small, with distichous sheaths at the base, 1-leafed at the apex. Leaves fleshy or leathery. Inflorescences arising from sheath axils, 1- to many-flowered. Flowers relatively large; sepals and

Tolumnia calochila

Tolumnia pulchella

Tolumnia variegata

Trias picta

petals free, spreading, subsimilar; lip joined to the column at base, entire or trilobed, spurred at the base, with a fleshy, crested callus. Column short and stout, winged; pollinia 2.

CULTIVATION: Plants can be grown potted in a free-draining compost or the smaller species can be mounted on a slab or raft. They require intermediate conditions, light to moderate shade, and high humidity. They should be watered less often when not actively growing but should not remain dry for long periods.

Trichocentrum candidum Lindley

Leaves stiff and fleshy, to 7 × 2 cm. Inflorescence to 2 cm long, 1- to 3-flowered, the flowers open in succession. Flowers ca. 3.5 cm across, white, the lip with reddish markings at the base.

Epiphytic in wet forest, 800–1000 m (2640–3300 ft.)

Mexico, Central America

Trichocentrum capistratum Linden & Reichenbach f.

SYN. *Trichocentrum panamense* Rolfe

Trichocentrum cebolleta

Leaves to 10 × 2.5 cm, fleshy, elliptic, dark green flushed with purple. Inflorescence 2–4 cm long, few-flowered, the flowers open in succession. Flowers ca. 3.5 cm across, sepals and petals pale green or yellow-green; lip ovate, concave, white, blotched with purple-pink towards the base; spur short, bilobed at the apex.

Epiphytic in rain forest, 500–1100 m (1650–3600 ft.)

Costa Rica, Panama, Colombia, Venezuela

Trichocentrum cavendishianum

(Bateman) M. W. Chase & N. H. Williams

SYN. *Oncidium cavendishianum* Bateman, *Lophiaris cavendishiana* (Bateman) Braem

Leaves to 45 × 13 cm, thick and leathery, flushed with red in strong light. Inflorescence branched, 1–2 m tall, many-flowered. Flowers to 4 cm across, scented; sepals and petals yellow blotched with red-brown; lip bright yellow, deeply trilobed.

Epiphytic, up to 2800 m (9250 ft.)

Mexico, Central America

Trichocentrum pfavii

Trichocentrum cebolleta

(Jacquin) M. W. Chase & N. H. Williams

SYN. *Oncidium cebolleta* (Jacquin) Swartz, *O. longifolium* Lindley

Pseudobulbs to 1.5 cm long, covered in white sheaths. Leaves to 40 × 2.5 cm, cylindrical, grooved on the upper surface. Inflorescence sometimes branched, 75–150 cm long, many-flowered. Flowers to 4 cm across; sepals and petals greenish yellow heavily marked with red-brown, lip bright yellow with a few red-brown marks, deeply trilobed, the midlobe fan-shaped, emarginate.

Epiphytic in rather dry areas, 150–1700 m (500–5600 ft.)

Mexico, Central and South America, West Indies

Trichocentrum pfavii

Reichenbach f.

Leaves 12 × 4 cm, elliptic, fleshy. Inflorescence to 5 cm long, usually 2-flowered. Flowers ca. 4 cm across; sepals and petals white with a red-brown blotch; lip wedge-shaped, white with 1 or 2 red-purple blotches; spur conical, ca. 3 mm long; column wings brown.

Epiphytic in rain forest, 650–1250 m (2100–4100 ft.)

Costa Rica, Panama

Trichocentrum tigrinum

Linden & Reichenbach f.

Leaves to 12 × 3 cm, dark green often spotted with red-brown. Inflorescence to 15 cm long, erect to pendent, 1- or 2-flowered. Flowers ca. 6 cm across; sepals and petals yellow-green spotted and barred with maroon-brown, lip ± rectangular, the apex bilobed,

Trichocentrum tigrinum

white with pinkish-red markings towards the base; callus yellow with 5 keels; spur short. In cultivation, needs good light and a dry winter rest.

Epiphytic in seasonally dry forest
Ecuador, Peru

Trichoceros Kunth

TRIBE: Maxillarieae
SUBTRIBE: Oncidiinae
ETYMOLOGY: From Greek *tricho*, hair, and *keras*, horn, referring to hairy projections on the column
DISTRIBUTION: 9 species in Colombia, Ecuador, and Peru

Small to medium sized epiphytic, lithophytic, or terrestrial plants with long creeping or ascending rhizomes. Pseudobulbs small, covered by overlapping leafy sheaths, 1-leafed at apex. Leaves small, fleshy or leathery. Inflorescences basal, unbranched, usually longer than leaves, loosely few- to several-flowered. Flowers rather insectlike, often nonresupinate; sepals and petals free, spreading, subsimilar; lip usually trilobed, side lobes spreading or erect, midlobe large, usually ovate. Column short and stout, lacking wings and a foot, with dark hairs around the anther.

CULTIVATION: With their scrambling habit, plants should be grown on slabs of bark or tree fern with a pad of moss. They need cool to intermediate conditions, shade, and high humidity. They should be watered throughout the year.

Trichoceros antennifer (Humboldt & Bonpland) Kunth

Leaves gray-green. Inflorescence to 25 cm long, several-flowered, the flowers open in succession. Flowers 2–2.5 cm across; sepals and petals ovate, greenish yellow, sometimes marked with red-brown; lip side lobes narrow and spreading, greenish white barred with maroon, midlobe maroon, sometimes greenish towards apex; column covered with red-brown bristles.

Trichoceros antennifer

Terrestrial or lithophytic on steep, mossy slopes in mist forest, 1800–3000 m (6000–9900 ft.)

Colombia, Ecuador, Peru

Trichoceros muralis Lindley

Flowers ca. 2 cm across; sepals and petals ovate, yellow-green with red-brown longitudinal stripes; lip red-brown, side lobes rounded; column covered in red-brown bristles.

Terrestrial on rather dry, rocky slopes, 2200–3200 m (7,260–10,500 ft.)

Ecuador

Trichoglottis Blume

TRIBE: Vandeae

SUBTRIBE: Aeridinae

ETYMOLOGY: From Greek *tricho*, hair, and *glottis*, tongue, referring to the hairy lip or to the hairy projection in the throat

DISTRIBUTION: More than 60 species from eastern Taiwan, tropical Asia, and the northwestern Pacific Islands

Monopodial epiphytes; stems leafy, elongated, often branched, climbing or pendent. Leaves in 2 rows; inflorescences axillary, 1- to many-flowered. Flowers sometimes showy, sepals and petals spreading, the lateral sepals joined to the column-foot; lip fleshy, partly hairy, saccate or spurred at the base, trilobed, side lobes erect, midlobe entire or trilobed, the spur or sac with a hairy projection from the back wall just below the column. Pollinia 4, unequal, in 2 pairs.

CULTIVATION: Grow in a medium bark compost. The climbing species will need a support such as a moss pole, while pendulous species should be grown in a suspended pot or basket. They require intermediate to warm conditions with moderate shade and high humidity throughout the year and plenty of water while in active growth.

Trichoglottis atropurpurea Reichenbach f.

SYN. *Trichoglottis brachiata* Ames

Stems erect, to ca. 60 cm long. Leaves oblong, to 8 × 4 cm. Inflorescence short, 1-flowered. Flowers to 6 cm across, deep purple, almost black, the lip pink with a yellow throat; lip midlobe trilobed, cross-shaped.

Epiphytic in woodland, 0–300 m (1000 ft.)

Philippines

Trichoglottis philippinensis Lindley

Stems erect, branched, to 60 cm tall. Leaves oblong, to 7 × 3.5 cm.

Trichoceros muralis

Trichoglottis atropurpurea

Inflorescence short, 1-flowered. Flowers 3–4 cm across, scented; sepals and petals greenish yellow, lightly to heavily spotted and blotched with brown; lip white, the midlobe trilobed, cross-shaped.

Epiphytic in woodland to 300 m (1000 ft.)

Borneo, Philippines, Sumatra

Trichoglottis pusilla Teijsmann & Binnendijk

Stems to 12.5 cm long. Leaves strap-shaped, to 12 × 1 cm. Inflorescences ca. 4 cm long, usually 3-flowered. Flowers 2–2.5 cm across, fleshy, with a scent that some people find unpleasant, white, the sepals and petals with horizontal purple stripes; lip trilobed, the midlobe ovate, concave.

Epiphytic in forest, 1000–2000 m (3300–6600 ft.)

Java, Sumatra

Trichopilia Lindley

TRIBE: Maxillarieae

SUBTRIBE: Oncidiinae

ETYMOLOGY: From Greek *tricho*, hair, and *pilion*, cap, referring to hairs on the column around the anther

DISTRIBUTION: About 35 species in Mexico, Central and South America, and the West Indies

Epiphytes with small, laterally compressed, clustered pseudobulbs, 1-leafed at apex. Inflorescences basal, arching or pendent, 1- to several-flowered. Flowers large, showy, often fragrant; sepals and petals spreading, subsimilar, narrow, often twisted or undulate; lip obscurely trilobed, joined to base of column, funnel-shaped then spreading, the margins undulate. Pollinia 2.

CULTIVATION: Grow plants in pots or baskets in a medium bark-based epiphyte compost. They require intermediate conditions, light to moderate shade, and high humidity. They need plenty of water while in growth but should be given a cooler, drier rest.

Trichoglottis pusilla

Trichopilia fragrans

Trichopilia laxa

Trichopilia fragrans (Lindley) Reichenbach f.

Pseudobulbs to 13 × 3 cm. Leaves to 30 × 7 cm. Inflorescence pendent, to 30 cm long, 2- to 5-flowered. Flowers to 12 cm across, scented, long-lasting; sepals and petals white or pale green, lip white with an orange blotch in the center, the blade elliptic, emarginate.

Epiphytic or terrestrial in wet forest, 1200–2800 m (4000–9250 ft.)

South America, West Indies

Trichopilia laxa (Lindley) Reichenbach f.

Pseudobulbs narrow, strongly compressed. Leaves to 30 × 5 cm. Inflorescence to 26 cm long, pendent, 4- to 7-flowered. Flowers not open-

Trichopilia marginata

ing wide, ca. 3.6 cm long; sepals and petals pale green to pinkish; lip pale green, the base white.

Epiphytic in rain forest, 1200–1800 m (4000–6000 ft.)

Colombia, Ecuador, Peru, Venezuela

Trichopilia marginata Henfrey

Pseudobulbs to 14 × 2 cm, narrowly oblong. Leaves to 40 × 5 cm. Inflorescence 3–5 cm long, 1- to few-flowered. Flowers scented, to 10 cm across; sepals and petals reddish brown or flesh pink, the margins pale green; lip red, the margin usually white, tubular, the apex deeply emarginate.

Epiphytic in rain forest, 700–950 m (2300–3100 ft.)

Costa Rica, Nicaragua, Panama, Colombia

Trichopilia suavis Lindley & Paxton

Pseudobulbs to 8 × 6 cm, almost round. Leaves 10–40 × 4–8 cm, oblong or elliptic. Inflorescence 4–6 cm long, 1- to several-flowered. Flowers to 10 cm across, strongly scented; sepals and petals white or cream, sometimes spotted and blotched with rose-lilac or red; lip white or cream with red blotches and orange or brown teeth in the throat.

Epiphytic in rain forest and cloud forest, 400–1600 m (1320–5300 ft.)

Costa Rica, Panama, Colombia

Trichopilia tortilis Lindley

Pseudobulbs to 7 × 2 cm. Leaves to 8 × 4 cm. Inflorescence 4–10 cm long, arching or pendent, 1- or 2-flowered. Flowers to 10 cm across, scented; sepals and petals greenish white with a brown central stripe; lip white, yellow in the center, spotted with pink.

Epiphytic in rain forest, 1100–1500 m (3600–5000 ft.)

Mexico, Central America

Trichopilia suavis

Trichopilia tortilis

Trichopilia turialbae

Trichopilia turialbae

Reichenbach f.

Pseudobulbs to 10 × 3.5 cm. Leaves to 25 × 5 cm. Inflorescence 8–11 cm long, 1- to several-flowered. Flowers to 7.5 cm across, white with orange lines in the throat or clear yellow with orange-brown lines in the throat.

Epiphytic in rain forest, 800–1100 m (2640–3600 ft.)

Costa Rica, Nicaragua, Panama

Trichosalpinx Luer

TRIBE: Epidendreae

SUBTRIBE: Pleurothallidinae

ETYMOLOGY: From Greek *trichos*, hair, and *salpinx*, trumpet, referring to the pubescent stem sheaths

DISTRIBUTION: More than 100 species in the West Indies, Mexico, Central and South America

Epiphytic, lithophytic, or terrestrial plants. Stems enclosed in tubular or funnel-shaped sheaths with pubescent ridges and margins, 1-leafed at apex. Inflorescences 1- to several-flowered. Sepals often tailed and pubescent; dorsal sepal free or joined at the base to the lateral sepals; lateral sepals free or joined to form a synsepal. Petals small, rarely tailed. Lip simple or trilobed, the base hinged to the column-foot. Column winged or hooded; pollinia 2.

CULTIVATION: Plants should be grown either mounted with a small pad of moisture-retaining material at the roots or in small pots of fine-grade epiphyte mixture. Provide medium light levels, cool to intermediate temperatures, and regular watering throughout the year.

Trichosalpinx blaisdellii

(S. Watson) Luer

Stems 3–13 cm long. Leaves to 6 × 3 cm, flushed with purple. Inflorescence to 4 cm long, several-flowered, the flowers open together. Flowers fleshy, rose-purple or red-brown, ca. 10 mm long, lateral sepals joined to about halfway; lip orange-brown to purple, ovate.

Epiphytic in rain forest and cloud forest, 40–1800 m (130–6000 ft.)

Mexico, Central America

SIMILAR SPECIES: *Trichosalpinx ciliaris* (Lindley) Luer (syn. *Specklinia ciliaris* Lindley, *Pleurothallis ciliaris* (Lindley) L. O. Williams) from Mexico, Central and South America has narrower stems and leaves and slightly smaller flowers.

Trichosalpinx trachystoma

(Schlechter) Luer

Stems 2–7 cm long. Leaves to 3.5 × 1.8 cm. Inflorescence 10–12 mm long, 2- to 4-flowered, the flowers open together. Flowers very small, ca. 3 mm long, red-purple, white towards the base; lip spathulate.

Epiphytic in forest, 350–950 m (1150–3150 ft.)

Costa Rica, Guatemala

Tridactyle Schlechter

TRIBE: Vandeae

SUBTRIBE: Aerangidinae

ETYMOLOGY: From Greek *tri*, 3, and *daktylos*, finger, referring to the trilobed lip of most species

DISTRIBUTION: More than 40 species in continental Africa, as far south as coastal South Africa

Monopodial plants with short to long woody stems, erect or pendent, sometimes branched, usually epiphytic but sometimes lithophytic. Roots usually thick, sometimes verrucose. Leaves distichous, usually linear, strap-shaped or oblong, leathery or ± succulent. Inflorescences borne along stem, the flowers in 2 rows, all facing the same way. Flowers small to medium, white, greenish, straw yellow or brownish; sepals and petals subsimilar, spreading; lip spurred, usually but not always trilobed. Column short.

CULTIVATION: Most species grow easily and flower regularly. They do well in pots and baskets in a fairly coarse compost but can be mounted, and most are suited by intermediate conditions, with light shade. Most species come from areas with a seasonal rainfall and benefit from a cooler, drier rest in winter.

Tridactyle anthomaniaca

(Reichenbach f.) Summerhayes

Stems long, pendent, leafy. Leaves narrowly oblong, bilobed at apex, rather fleshy, twisted to face the same way. Inflorescence 10–15 mm long, 2- to 4-flowered. Flowers orange-straw, about 10 mm diameter; lip entire, spur 10–15 mm long.

Epiphytic in high-rainfall woodland and edge of forest, 650–1350 m (2150–4500 ft.)

Widespread in tropical Africa

Tridactyle bicaudata (Lindley) Schlechter

Stems leafy, to ca. 80 cm long, erect or pendent. Leaves strap-shaped. Inflorescence to 13 cm long, about

Trichosalpinx blaisdellii

Trichosalpinx trachystoma

Tridactyle anthomaniaca

Tridactyle bicaudata

Tridactyle tricuspis. E. la Croix

Tridactyle gentilii

20-flowered. Flowers yellowish to yellow-green, about 10 mm across; sepals and petals ovate; lip trilobed at about halfway, midlobe short and triangular, side lobes longer, spreading, fringed at the tips; spur up to 2 cm long.

Epiphytic or lithophytic in forest and woodland, sometimes on exposed rocks, 0–2500 m (8250 ft.)

Widespread in tropical and subtropical Africa

SIMILAR SPECIES: *Tridactyle tricuspis* (Bolus) Schlechter, also widespread in Africa, has flowers with lip side lobes shorter than midlobe and not deeply fringed. *Tridactyle tridactylites* (Rolfe) Schlechter, widespread in Africa, is often lithophytic, with leafy stems to 60 cm long and lip side lobes longer than midlobe.

Tridactyle gentilii (De Wildeman) Schlechter

Stems leafy, to 80 cm long, usually becoming pendent. Leaves strap-shaped, up to 20 cm long. Inflorescence to 5 cm long, 7- to 15-flowered. Flowers scented, greenish white to cream, to 18 mm across, the lip about 10 mm long, trilobed in the middle, midlobe triangular, side lobes longer and deeply fringed at the apex; spur 4–8 cm long.

Epiphytic in forest and woodland, in high rainfall areas, to 2200 m (7260 ft.)

West, Central, and South Africa

Tridactyle tridentata (Harvey) Schlechter

SYN. *Tridactyle bolusii* (Rolfe) Schlechter, *T. teretifolia* Schlechter

Stems woody, 10–50 cm long, erect or pendent, usually branched and rooting at base. Leaves towards top of stem, cylindrical, with or without a groove along the top, dull olive green, the sheaths with dark spots. Inflorescence less than 3 cm long, densely up to 8-flowered. Flowers 6 mm across, straw yellow; lip trilobed near apex, midlobe and side lobes of similar length; spur 6–18 mm long. In cultivation, does better mounted.

Epiphytic in woodland, often in fairly dry areas, 900–2250 m (3000–7300 ft.)

Central, East, and South Africa

Tridactyle truncatiloba Summerhayes

This little known species has the largest flowers in the genus. Stems to 100 cm long, erect or straggling;

Tridactyle truncatiloba. E. la Croix

roots long and smooth. Leaves strap-shaped, about 15 cm long. Inflorescence 10–12 cm long, 7- to 10-flowered, the flowers all facing the same way. Flowers scented, white with a green streak on the lip, 5 cm long from apex of dorsal sepal to tip of lip; lip trilobed at about halfway, midlobe 13 mm long, side lobes spreading, 8 mm long, fringed and truncate at the tips. In cultivation, needs good light.

Lithophytic or terrestrial on embankments, 300–400 m (1000–1320 ft.)

Congo, Gabon

Trigonidium Lindley

TRIBE: Maxillarieae
SUBTRIBE: Maxillariinae
ETYMOLOGY: From Greek *trigonon*, triangle, referring to the appearance of the flowers
DISTRIBUTION: 14 species in Mexico, Central and South America

Epiphytes and lithophytes with long or short rhizomes. Pseudobulbs cylindrical or ovoid with overlapping sheaths at the base, 1- or 2-leaved at apex. Inflorescences basal, erect, 1-flowered, usually as long as or longer than the leaves. Flowers large, often tubular at the base, then the sepals (the showiest part of the flower) spreading or reflexed; petals smaller than sepals; lip smaller than petals, trilobed, not spurred; side lobes erect, midlobe fleshy. Column short, without wings; pollinia 4.

CULTIVATION: Grow in pots or baskets in a standard epiphyte mix, in intermediate conditions with light shade and high humidity. Plants should be kept drier while resting but not so dry that the pseudobulbs shrivel.

Trigonidium egertonianum Bateman ex Lindley

SYN. *Trigonidium brachyglossum* (A. Richard & Galeotti) Schlechter

Pseudobulbs densely clustered, to 7 × 3 cm, ovoid, 2-leaved. Inflorescence arising on mature growths, 25–45 cm long. Flowers bell-shaped, 3–4 cm long; sepals and petals yellow-green to pinkish brown, veined and marked with brown; lip yellow-brown to pinkish brown, with brown veins.

Epiphytic on large branches in wet forest, 0–900 m (3000 ft.)

Central and South America

Trisetella Luer

TRIBE: Epidendreae
SUBTRIBE: Pleurothallidinae
ETYMOLOGY: From Greek *tri*, 3, *seta*, bristle, and the diminutive suffix *-ella*, referring to the slender sepal tails
DISTRIBUTION: More than 20 species in Central and South America

Small, tufted, epiphytic or lithophytic plants. Stems with overlapping tubular sheaths, 1-leafed at apex. Inflorescences unbranched. Flowers

Trigonidium egertonianum

resupinate. Sepals with slender or club-shaped tails; dorsal sepal joined to some extent to the lateral sepals; lateral sepals joined to form a synsepal, the tails arising below the apices. Petals minute; lip ± oblong, hinged at the base to the column-foot, with 2 longitudinal calli. Column hooded but lacking wings; pollinia 2.

CULTIVATION: Most species of *Trisetella* do not grow at very high altitudes and so are easier to cultivate than many of the Pleurothallidinae. They can be grown in small pots in a fine bark or sphagnum-based compost or mounted on a slab—they seem to do well on tree fern. They need cool or intermediate temperatures, depending on their altitude of origin, good air movement, shade, and high humidity all year round.

Trisetella hirtzii Luer

Stems 4–5 mm long. Leaves to 17 × 4 mm. Inflorescence ca. 25 mm long, densely several-flowered, the flowers open in succession. Sepals bright pink, partly joined to form an open cup ca. 10 mm long with tails 10–11 mm long; tail of dorsal sepal orange, tails of lateral sepals white. Petals white. Lip brown.

Trisetella hirtzii

Trisetella hoeijeri

Epiphytic in wet forest, 950–1500 m (3150–5000 ft.)
Ecuador

Trisetella hoeijeri Luer & Hirtz
Leaves to 27 × 2.5 mm. Inflorescence 4–6 cm long, several-flowered, the flowers open in succession. Flowers opening wide, crystalline white with 3 red lines on the lateral sepals; dorsal sepal 4 mm long with a tail 20 mm long, lateral sepals 15 mm long with tails 15 mm long.
Epiphytic in cloud forest, ca. 1800 m (6000 ft.)
Ecuador

Trisetella triaristella (Reichenbach f.) Luer
Leaves to 5 cm long, 2.5 mm wide, narrowly linear. Inflorescence 4–8 cm long, warty, 2- to 5-flowered, the flowers open in succession. Dorsal sepal joined for ca. 2 mm to lateral sepals,

Trisetella triaristella

Trisetella triglochin

Trisetella hoeijeri in habitat.

yellow-orange, ca. 4 mm long with a yellow or purple tail ca. 25 mm long; lateral sepals purple, ca. 19 mm long, joined for most of their length, with tails ca. 20 mm long arising below the apex.

Epiphytic in rain forest, 300–2000 m (1000–6600 ft.)

Costa Rica, Panama, Colombia, Ecuador

SIMILAR SPECIES: *Trisetella triglochin* (Reichenbach f.) Luer from Central and South America has a smooth peduncle and yellow or purple flowers with shorter tails, ca. 12 mm long.

Tuberolabium Yamamoto

SYN. *Trachoma* Garay

TRIBE: Vandeae

SUBTRIBE: Aeridinae

ETYMOLOGY: From Latin *tuber*, tuber, and *labium*, lip, referring to the saccate lip

DISTRIBUTION: About 25 species in Taiwan, tropical Asia, the Pacific Islands, and Australia

Small, short-stemmed monopodial epiphytes. Leaves linear to strap-shaped, often thick-textured. Inflorescences axillary, few- to many-flowered, the rachis sometimes thickened. Flowers usually short-lived, white, yellowish, or greenish with purple or red markings; sepals and petals free, spreading, subsimilar; lip joined to the base of the column, trilobed, side lobes toothlike, midlobe fleshy, saccate. Pollinia 2.

CULTIVATION: Most species are easily grown in intermediate to warm temperatures and light to moderate shade. They should be mounted on bark or potted in a moisture-retentive compost and kept moist throughout the year.

Tuberolabium quisumbingii (L. O. Williams) Christenson

SYN. *Saccolabium quisumbingii* L. O. Williams

Leaves to 10 × 2.5 cm. Inflorescences of similar length, to 20-flowered. Flowers ca. 1.5 cm across, scented; sepals and petals greenish white, lip white with red-purple markings.

Epiphytic in forest, to 300 m (1000 ft.)

Philippines

Tuberolabium rhopalorrhachis (Reichenbach f.) J. J. Wood

Leaves to 11 × 2 cm. Inflorescence 2–4 cm long, several-flowered, 2–4 open at a time. Flowers ca. 8 cm across, white or yellowish with red markings, lip yellow and white, spur white and red.

Epiphytic in forest, 0–1800 m (6000 ft.)

Peninsular Malaysia, Thailand, Borneo, Java, Sumatra, Australia

Tuberolabium stellatum (M. A. Clements, J. J. Wood & D. L. Jones) J. J. Wood

SYN. *Trachoma stellata* M. A. Clements, J. J. Wood & D. L. Jones.

Small, often pendulous plants forming clumps. Stems to 8 cm long. Leaves several, to 15 × 3 cm. Inflorescence 3–4 cm long, to 10-flowered. Flowers starry, to 1 cm across; sepals and petals creamy white with purple marks at the base.

Epiphytic in rain forest

Australia (Queensland)

Vanda Jones ex R. Brown

SYN. *Trudelia* Garay

TRIBE: Vandeae

SUBTRIBE: Aeridinae

ETYMOLOGY: From the Sanskrit name for *Vanda tessellata*

DISTRIBUTION: About 50 species in subtropical and tropical Asia to the Pacific Islands and Australia

Medium to large monopodial epiphytes, occasionally lithophytes. Stem short to long. Leaves distichous, strap-shaped, with bilobed tips. Inflorescences axillary, usually unbranched, few- to many-flowered. Flowers often large and showy; sepals and petals free, usually spreading, subsimilar, often clawed; lip joined to the base of the column, trilobed, spurred or saccate. Column short and stout; pollinia 2.

Many species previously included in *Vanda* have been moved to other genera, including *Holcoglossum*, *Euanthe*, and *Papilionanthe*. *Vanda* species have been widely used in hybridization with other related genera such as *Ascocentrum* and *Neofinetia* and these are of great horticultural value.

CULTIVATION: Species of *Vanda* are most often grown in baskets to allow their long roots to hang freely. In the Far East they are often grown without compost, but in greenhouse conditions they are more successful in a coarse, free-draining bark-based compost. Most species come from low altitudes and require warm temperatures, bright light, and ample water and air movement. If temperatures are low, they should be kept drier. If plants become too tall and leggy, the upper part of the stem, provided it has some roots, can be cut off and replanted.

Vanda alpina (Lindley) Lindley

SYN. *Trudelia alpina* (Lindley) Garay

Stem to 18 cm long; roots basal. Leaves to 16 × 1.5 cm. Inflorescence short, 1- to 3-flowered. Flowers pendent, to 2 cm across; sepals and petals green to yellow-green; lip green with violet stripes, saccate and maroon-purple at the base. Flowering spring–summer. Needs cool to intermediate conditions.

Epiphytic in broad-leaved forest, 1000–2000 m (3300–6600 ft.)

China, India

Vanda coerulea Griffiths ex Lindley

Stem to ca. 25 cm long. Leaves numerous, to 18 × 2 cm. Inflorescence suberect, to about 35 cm long, laxly several-flowered. Flowers ca. 10 cm across, pale violet-blue to

Tuberolabium quisumbingii

Vanda coerulea

purple-blue, tessellated with darker purple. Flowers mostly in autumn in cultivation. Requires cool to intermediate temperatures. This species is a parent, with *Euanthe sanderiana*, of the famous hybrid *Vanda* Rothschildiana, registered in 1931.

Epiphytic on tree trunks in open woodland, 1000–1600 m (3300–5300 ft.)

China, India

Vanda coerulescens Griffiths

Stem 2–8 cm long. Leaves to 12 × 1 cm, slightly fleshy. Inflorescence to 36 cm long, loosely many-flowered. Flowers 3 cm across, sepals and petals white to pale violet blue, lip purple-blue, often with white stripes. Flowering spring–early summer. This species does better in intermediate temperatures.

Epiphytic on tree trunks in open woodland, 300–1600 m (1000–5300 ft.)

China, India

Vanda cristata Wallich ex Lindley

SYN. *Trudelia cristata* (Wallich ex Lindley) Senghas

Stem stout, to 15 cm long. Leaves to 13 × 2 cm, recurved. Inflorescence short, 2- to 6-flowered. Flowers to 5 cm across; sepals and petals yellowish to green, lip yellow to white, with violet-purple or red-brown stripes, with a saccate spur. Flowering spring–summer. Does better in intermediate temperatures.

Epiphytic on tree trunks, 700–2100 m (2300–6900 ft.)

China, India

Vanda cristata

Vanda dearei Reichenbach f.
Stems to 1 m long, sometimes more, older plants branching at the base. Leaves to 45 × 4 cm, thick-textured. Inflorescence to 15 cm long, loosely 4- to 6-flowered. Flowers 4–5 cm across, fleshy, very fragrant, lasting for about a week; sepals and petals cream, yellow or pale yellow flushed with salmon-pink or brown; lip white at base, with red lines at the junction of the lobes, midlobe yellow at apex. Flowers mainly in summer and early autumn. Needs warm temperatures throughout the year.

Epiphytic in riverine forest or lithophytic in rocky places, 0–300 m (1000 ft.)

Borneo, Lesser Sunda Islands

Vanda denisoniana Benson & Reichenbach f.
Medium-sized plants. Inflorescence 15–18 cm long, several-flowered. Flowers 5–6 cm long, strongly scented in the evening; sepals and petals creamy yellow to greenish yellow, sometimes flushed with bronze; lip yellow-green. Flowers mainly in spring.

Epiphytic in forest, 600–750 m (2000–2480 ft.)

China, Indochina

Vanda lamellata Lindley
Stems to 40 cm long. Leaves to about 30 × 1 cm. Inflorescence 20–30 cm long, several-flowered. Flowers ca. 4 cm long, faintly scented; sepals and petals recurved, pale yellow to brownish yellow, lip yellow and white, striped and flushed with red-purple. Flowers off and on throughout the year.

Var. *boxallii* Reichenbach f. has white flowers marked with brown in the center and a purple-pink lip.

Epiphytic in full sun, usually near the coast, 0–300 m (1000 ft.)

China, Borneo, Philippines

Vanda tessellata (Roxburgh) Hooker
SYN. *Vanda roxburghii* R. Brown
Plants usually ca. 60 cm tall. Inflorescence to 30 cm long, 5- to 10-flowered. Flowers scented, 5 cm across; color variable, but usually sepals and petals greenish yellow with brown tessellation, lip side lobes

Vanda lamellata

Vanda tessellata

Vanda tricolor

white, spotted purple, midlobe violet. Flowers mainly in summer.

Epiphytic, ca. 1500 m (5000 ft.)

India to Indochina

Vanda tricolor Lindley

SYN. *Vanda suavis* Lindley

Stems to 45 cm long. Leaves numerous, to 45 × 4 cm. Inflorescence to 25 cm long, several-flowered. Flowers scented, 5–7 cm across; sepals and petals white outside, mottled with red-brown or less usually yellow inside; lip usually mauve, sometimes yellow, the apex emarginate. Flowers mainly in autumn and winter.

Epiphytic on branches in open positions, 700–1600 m (2300–5300 ft.)

Laos, Java, Bali

SIMILAR SPECIES: *Vanda luzonica* Loher from the Philippines has unscented white flowers with purple markings and a purple-pink lip.

Vandopsis Pfitzer

TRIBE: Vandeae

SUBTRIBE: Aeridinae

ETYMOLOGY: From *Vanda* and Greek *opsis*, like, meaning resembling *Vanda*

DISTRIBUTION: 4 species in tropical Asia

Robust, erect plants related to *Vanda* with long stems and fleshy, strap-shaped leaves. Inflorescences sometimes branched, densely many-flowered. Flowers large, showy, fleshy. Sepals and petals free, spreading, subsimilar; lip trilobed, the side lobes attached to the base of the column, midlobe long, fleshy, laterally compressed, keeled. Column short with a basal projection in front; pollinia 4.

CULTIVATION: Because of their large size, plants are best grown in beds but they can be grown in baskets or large pots in a coarse, free-draining epiphyte compost. They require intermediate to warm temperatures, good light, and plenty of water throughout the year.

Vandopsis gigantea (Lindley) Pfitzer

Plants forming large clumps. Stem stout, to 30 cm long. Leaves distichous, fleshy, strap-shaped, to 50 × 7 cm. Inflorescence axillary, pendent, to 40 cm long, densely many-flowered. Flowers to 7 cm across, deep yellow with brownish or purplish spots.

Epiphytic in open woodland or at forest edge, 800–1700 m (2640–5600 ft.)

China to peninsular Malaysia

Vandopsis undulata (Lindley) J. J. Smith

Stem arching or pendent, to 1 m long. Leaves oblong, to 12 cm long. Inflorescence branched or unbranched, to 50 cm long, laxly several-flowered. Flowers scented, 7–8 cm across; sepals and petals white, margins undulate, lip midlobe pale brown or red-brown, side lobes with green and brown stripes.

Epiphytic in forest, 1300–2300 m (4300–7600 ft.)

Vandopsis gigantea

Vandopsis undulata

Bhutan, China, India, Nepal, Sikkim

Vanilla Miller

SUBFAMILY: Vanilloideae

TRIBE: Vanilleae

ETYMOLOGY: From Spanish *vainilla*, a little pod

DISTRIBUTION: More than 100 species throughout the tropics and subtropics, except in Australia

Monopodial plants with climbing or scrambling, vinelike, green, succulent, photosynthetic stems, round or ± square in cross-section, sometimes grooved, often reaching considerable length, with a leaf and roots at each node. In some species, the leaves are reduced to scales, so that plants appear leafless. Leaves when present usually fleshy or leathery. Inflorescences usually axillary, sometimes branched, with few to many flowers opening in succession. Flowers large, showy, white, yellow, or greenish, the lip sometimes marked with purple or orange. Sepals and petals free, subsimilar, spreading or recurved; lip joined to column at base, entire or trilobed, funnel-shaped, the apical margin often undulate. Fruit a long, fleshy capsule with relatively large seeds.

CULTIVATION: Almost all species of *Vanilla* have a similar growth habit, initially rooting in the ground, then scrambling up trees, attached by the nodal roots, or over rocks, rooting where the stem touches the ground. In cultivation, plants should be grown in a pot in a standard bark-based epiphyte compost, then allowed to climb a moss pole or artificial branch or trained along poles suspended from a greenhouse roof. They do not flower until the stems reach a considerable length and sometimes not until the stem is trained horizontally. They require intermediate to warm conditions, preferably the latter, high humidity, and moderate shade. Leafless species tend to occur in seasonally dry areas and need less shade. They are interesting plants to grow in a greenhouse and, when they are trained horizontally, take up relatively little space in spite of their length.

Vanilla aphylla Blume

Stems leafless, reddish green, to about 1 cm thick. Inflorescence about 3-flowered. Flowers ca. 4.5 cm across; sepals and petals pale yellowish green, curving back, lip whitish violet with many long, violet hairs inside.

Trailing over stumps and logs in forest, 50–600 m (165–2000 ft.)

India to Java

Vanilla phalaenopsis Reichenbach f. ex Van Houtte

Stems 1–1.5 cm thick, leafless. Inflorescence unbranched, to 35 cm long, many-flowered. Flowers white, to 15 cm across, white, apricot, pink, or salmon in the throat.

Scrambling in coastal bush

Seychelles

SIMILAR SPECIES: *Vanilla roscheri* Reichenbach f. from East Africa and *V. madagascariensis* Rolfe from Madagascar are leafless species that are sometimes considered synonymous with *V. phalaenopsis.*

Vanilla madagascariensis. J. Hermans

Vanilla planifolia G. Jackson

SYN. *Vanilla fragrans* Salisbury

Stems green, to 1 cm thick. Leaves to 20 × 7 cm, oblong, fleshy, bright green. Inflorescence 5–7 cm long, many-flowered, the flowers open in succession. Flowers ca. 6 cm across, pale yellow-green, the lip covered with yellow hairs inside; capsules 15–25 cm long. This species is the most important source of commercial vanilla and is widely cultivated for the purpose, particularly in Mexico and Madagascar.

Wet woodland, 50–100 m (165–330 ft.)

United States (Florida), Central and South America, West Indies

Vanilla polylepis Summerhayes

Stems 1–1.5 cm thick, succulent, bright green. Leaves fleshy, to 20 × 5 cm. Inflorescence to 5 cm long, several-flowered, with 1–3 open at

Vanilla planifolia with capsules. J. Hermans

Vanilla polylepis. E. la Croix

Vanilla pompona. H. Oakeley

a time. Flowers to 10 cm across, white or greenish white, lip yellow in the throat, usually maroon-purple towards the apex.

Scrambling on riverine trees and rocks, 1200–1500 m (4000–5000 ft.)

East and Central Africa

Vanilla pompona Schiede

Stem to 2 cm thick. Leaves to 30 × 14 cm, fleshy. Inflorescence axillary, to 20 cm long, many-flowered. Flowers 13–14 cm across, sepals and petals pale yellow-green, lip golden-orange.

Wet woodland, 0–600 m (2000 ft.)

Mexico, Central America

Warmingia Reichenbach f.

TRIBE: Maxillarieae

SUBTRIBE: Oncidiinae

ETYMOLOGY: Name for Danish botanist Eugenius Warming (1841–1924), who found the type species

DISTRIBUTION: 5 species in Central and South America

Dwarf epiphytes with small 1-leafed pseudobulbs. Leaves leathery, oblong. Inflorescences arising from base of pseudobulb, unbranched, pendent, few- to many-flowered. Flowers white, ± translucent; sepals and petals subsimilar but the margins of the petals finely toothed; lip trilobed, side lobes short and broad, midlobe long and narrow, disc with 2 calli. Pollinia 2.

CULTIVATION: Because of their pendent inflorescences, plants are better grown mounted. They require intermediate conditions, light to moderate shade, and high humidity. They should be kept drier in winter but not allowed to dry out completely.

Warmingia eugenii Reichenbach f.

Pseudobulbs 4 × 0.4 cm, cylindrical or narrowly conical. Leaves to 10 × 2.5 cm. Inflorescence to 12 cm long, many-flowered. Flowers 2.5–3 cm across, glistening white with a yellow

Warmingia eugenii

callus at the base of the lip; lip side lobes finely toothed.

Epiphytic in wet forest, 0–1000 m (3300 ft.)

Argentina, Brazil

Warrea Lindley

TRIBE: Maxillarieae
SUBTRIBE: Zygopetalinae
ETYMOLOGY: Named for Frederick Warre, who collected orchids in Brazil in 1829
DISTRIBUTION: 4 species in Mexico, Central and South America

Medium to large terrestrials with ellipsoid to ovoid pseudobulbs covered in leaf sheaths, several-leaved. Leaves distichous, plicate. Inflorescences erect, basal, few- to several-flowered. Flowers showy; dorsal sepal free, lateral sepals joined to column-foot; petals similar to sepals but slightly smaller; lip joined to column-foot, entire or trilobed, with a basal callus of 3 to 5 ridges. Pollinia 4.

CULTIVATION: Plants should be grown potted in a free-draining terrestrial compost, in intermediate conditions with moderate shade. They need abundant water while in active growth but should be given much less while resting.

Warrea costaricensis Schlechter

Pseudobulbs narrow, 10–15 cm long, 1-leafed. Leaves to 65 × 8 cm. Inflorescence to 80 cm tall, several-flowered. Flowers to 6.5 cm across, nodding, red-bronze, lip yellow, mottled with red.

Terrestrial in wet forest, 50–900 m (165–3000 ft.)

Costa Rica, Guatemala, Panama

Warrea warreana (Loddiges ex Lindley) C. Schweinfurth

Pseudobulbs 4–12 cm long, 3- to 4-leaved. Leaves to 60 × 10 cm. Inflorescence to 1 m tall, 10- to 12-flowered. Flowers ca. 4 cm across, ± globose, nodding, fleshy, white or yellow-white, lip with a large purple blotch.

Terrestrial in grassland, scrub, and forest, 200–1000 m (660–3300 ft.)

Argentina, Brazil, Bolivia, Colombia, Ecuador, Peru, Venezuela

Warrea warreana

Xylobium colleyi

Xylobium Lindley

TRIBE: Maxillarieae
SUBTRIBE: Maxillariinae
ETYMOLOGY: From Greek *xylon*, wood, and *bios*, life, referring to the epiphytic habit
DISTRIBUTION: More than 30 species in Mexico, Central and South America, and the West Indies

Epiphytic, rarely terrestrial, plants. Pseudobulbs globose to cylindrical, 1- to 3-leaved. Leaves large, plicate, petiolate. Inflorescences basal, unbranched, erect or arching, often short, few- to many-flowered. Sepals and petals free, spreading, subsimilar but petals smaller; lip joined at base to column-foot, simple or trilobed, with a fleshy callus. Column with a distinct foot; pollinia 4.

CULTIVATION: Plants should be potted in an open bark-based compost in intermediate conditions with only light shade. They need plenty of water while growing but should be kept drier when resting.

Xylobium colleyi (Bateman ex Lindley) Rolfe

Pseudobulbs almost round, 2–4 cm long. Leaves 20–70 cm long. Inflorescence often pendent, to 3 cm long, densely several-flowered. Flowers 2–2.5 cm long, yellow-brown with purple spots; said to smell unpleasant.

Epiphytic in very humid woodland, 0–700 m (2300 ft.)

Central and South America, Trinidad

Xylobium foveatum (Lindley) G. Nicholson

Pseudobulbs ovoid, to 8 × 4 cm, 2- or 3-leaved. Leaves to 50 × 5 cm. Inflorescence to 30 cm long, suberect or arching, fairly densely many-flowered. Flowers 2–3 cm across, white or yellow, lip striped with red at the base.

Epiphytic in rain forest, 0–1300 m (4300 ft.)

Mexico, Central and South America, West Indies

Xylobium pallidiflorum (Hooker) G. Nicholson

Pseudobulbs to 18 × 1 cm long, narrowly cylindrical, 1-leafed. Leaves to 40 × 8 cm. Flowers 1–1.5 cm long, pale yellow or pale green, the base of lip and apex of column orange.

Epiphytic in montane forest, ca. 1600 m (5300 ft.)

South America, West Indies

Xylobium squalens (Lindley) Lindley

Pseudobulbs to 8 × 3 cm, 2- or 3-leaved. Leaves ca. 50 × 6 cm. Inflorescence ca. 15 cm long, densely

Xylobium pallidiflorum

flowered towards the apex. Flowers 1–2 cm long, white or yellow, reddish in the center.

Epiphytic in rain forest, 500–900 m (1650–3000 ft.)

Costa Rica, Brazil

Ypsilopus Summerhayes

TRIBE: Vandeae

SUBTRIBE: Aerangidinae

ETYMOLOGY: From Greek *upsilon*, the letter *Y*, and *pous*, foot, referring to the Y-shaped stipe that joins the 2 pollinia to the single viscidium

DISTRIBUTION: 5 species in East Africa from Kenya to South Africa

Short-stemmed plants with thick roots, closely related to *Tridactyle*. Leaves linear, ± in a fan. Inflorescences arising from leaf axils, unbranched. Flowers white or green. Sepals and petals usually spreading, subsimilar, often with some sparse hairs on the outside; lip entire or obscurely trilobed, lacking a callus, spurred at the base.

CULTIVATION: Plants can be potted in a rather coarse, free-draining bark-based compost but tend to be more successful when mounted on bark and given high humidity, light shade and good air movement. They require intermediate conditions but should be kept cooler and drier in winter.

Ypsilopus erectus (P. J. Cribb) P. J. Cribb & J. Stewart

Stem to 6 cm long, often less. Leaves several, in a fan, to 15 × 0.6 cm, partly folded, often recurved. Inflorescence arching, to 20 cm long, 4- to 20-flowered. Flowers 10–12 mm across, white, with scurfy hairs on the outside, ovary and pedicel sometimes pink; lip to 7 × 3 mm, spur slender, to 6 cm long, greenish towards the tip.

Epiphytic, rarely lithophytic, in woodland, 0–2100 m (6900 ft.)

East Africa from Tanzania to South Africa

SIMILAR SPECIES: *Ypsilopus longifolius* (Kraenzlin) Summerhayes from Kenya and Tanzania, where it grows in forest at 1450–2400 m (4800–7900 ft.), has similar flowers but plants are pendent, with linear leaves to 25 cm long.

Zelenkoa M. W. Chase & N. H. Williams

TRIBE: Maxillarieae

SUBTRIBE: Oncidiinae

ETYMOLOGY: Named for Harry Zelenko, a well-known *Oncidium* artist

Ypsilopus erectus. E. la Croix

DISTRIBUTION: 1 species in Central and South America

Small, tufted epiphytes or lithophytes. Pseudobulbs clustered, ovoid, sometimes 1- or 2-leafed at the apex and subtended by 2 or 3 sheaths, the upper 1 or 2 leafy. Leaves lanceolate, the margins sometimes finely toothed towards the base. Inflorescences basal, longer than leaves, usually unbranched, sometimes with a few branches. Flowers resupinate. Sepals free, subequal; petals free, much larger than sepals; lip trilobed, the midlobe much larger than the side lobes, with a large basal callus joined to the column. Column winged; pollinia 2.

CULTIVATION: This species is most successful when mounted as good drainage is essential. Plants require intermediate conditions and good light.

Zelenkoa onusta

Zelenkoa onusta (Lindley) M. W. Chase & N. H. Williams

SYN. *Oncidium onustum* Lindley

Pseudobulbs to 4 cm long, compressed, 1- or 2-leaved. Leaves to 12 × 2 cm. Inflorescence to 50 cm long, sometimes branched, often secund. Flowers to 3 cm across, golden yellow; petals round, the edges undulate; lip trilobed, side lobes small and spreading, midlobe round, deeply emarginate; callus trilobed.

Epiphytic in very dry areas, often on cacti, or lithophytic on cliff faces near coast, depending for moisture on night fog

Panama, Colombia, Ecuador, Peru

Zootrophion Luer

TRIBE: Epidendreae

SUBTRIBE: Pleurothallidinae

ETYMOLOGY: From Greek *zootrophion*, a menagerie

DISTRIBUTION: About 16 species in Central and South America and the West Indies

Small, tufted or creeping plants. Stems enclosed in sheaths, 1-leafed at apex. Leaves petiolate. Inflorescences unbranched, 1- to several-flowered. Flowers erect or nodding. Lateral sepals joined together forming a synsepal, which is joined to the dorsal sepal at the tips and base but free in the middle, forming “windows.” Petals and lip small, enclosed in sepals; lip trilobed, hinged to the column-foot. Pollinia 2.

CULTIVATION: Most species are epiphytic in cloud forest, so high humidity throughout the year is important. Plants should have a daily cycle of being soaked in mist and then partially drying out. Most will grow in intermediate conditions, in light shade, in a bark-sphagnum-perlite mixture, either potted or in a small basket.

Zootrophion atropurpureum (Lindley) Luer

SYN. *Cryptophoranthus atropurpureus* (Lindley) Rolfe

Stems 3–5 cm long. Leaves to 9 × 3 cm. Inflorescence 1-flowered, much shorter than the leaves, sometimes several arising together. Flowers ca. 1.5 cm long, deep purple.

Epiphytic in montane forest, sometimes on fallen logs or terrestrial on banks, 600–1300 m (2000–4300 ft.)

Central and South America, West Indies

Zootrophion dayanum (Reichenbach f.) Luer

SYN. *Cryptophoranthus dayanus* (Reichenbach f.) Rolfe

Stems to 11 cm long. Leaves to 10 × 5.5 cm. Flowers pendent, to 4 cm long, yellow marked with red-purple with large "windows."

Epiphytic in montane forest

Bolivia, Colombia, Ecuador, Peru

Zootrophion endresianum (Kraenzlin) Luer

SYN. *Cryptophoranthus endresianus* Kraenzlin

A relatively large species with broadly elliptical leaves to 14 × 7 cm. Inflorescence 3–4 cm long, several-flowered. Flowers 3–4 cm long, bright yellow spotted and streaked with red.

Epiphytic in rain forest, 600–1200 m (2000–4000 ft.)

Costa Rica, Colombia, Ecuador

Zootrophion vulturiceps (Luer) Luer

SYN. *Cryptophoranthus vulturiceps* Luer

Stems to 7 cm long. Leaves to 12 × 3 cm. Inflorescence ca. 2 cm long, several-flowered, the flowers open in succession. Flowers ca. 3 cm long, sepals pure white, petals and lip yellowish.

Epiphytic in rain forest and cloud forest, 1400–1700 m (4600–5600 ft.)

Costa Rica

Zygopetalum Hooker

TRIBE: Maxillarieae

SUBTRIBE: Zygopetalinae

ETYMOLOGY: From Greek *zygon*, yoke, and *petalon*, petal, assumed to refer to the callus at the base of the lip which appears to held the petals together

DISTRIBUTION: 15 species in Argentina, Bolivia, Brazil, Paraguay, and Peru

Epiphytes or terrestrials with short, stout pseudobulbs with basal, sheathing leaves, 2- or more leaved at the apex. Leaves distichous, pleated. Inflorescences basal, unbranched, 1- to several-flowered. Flowers large or small, usually showy, waxy, often scented. Sepals and petals subsimilar, usually greenish heavily marked with maroon or brown; lip always of a different color, whitish or violet-blue, trilobed, side lobes small, midlobe large and spreading with a prominent callus at the base. Pollinia 4.

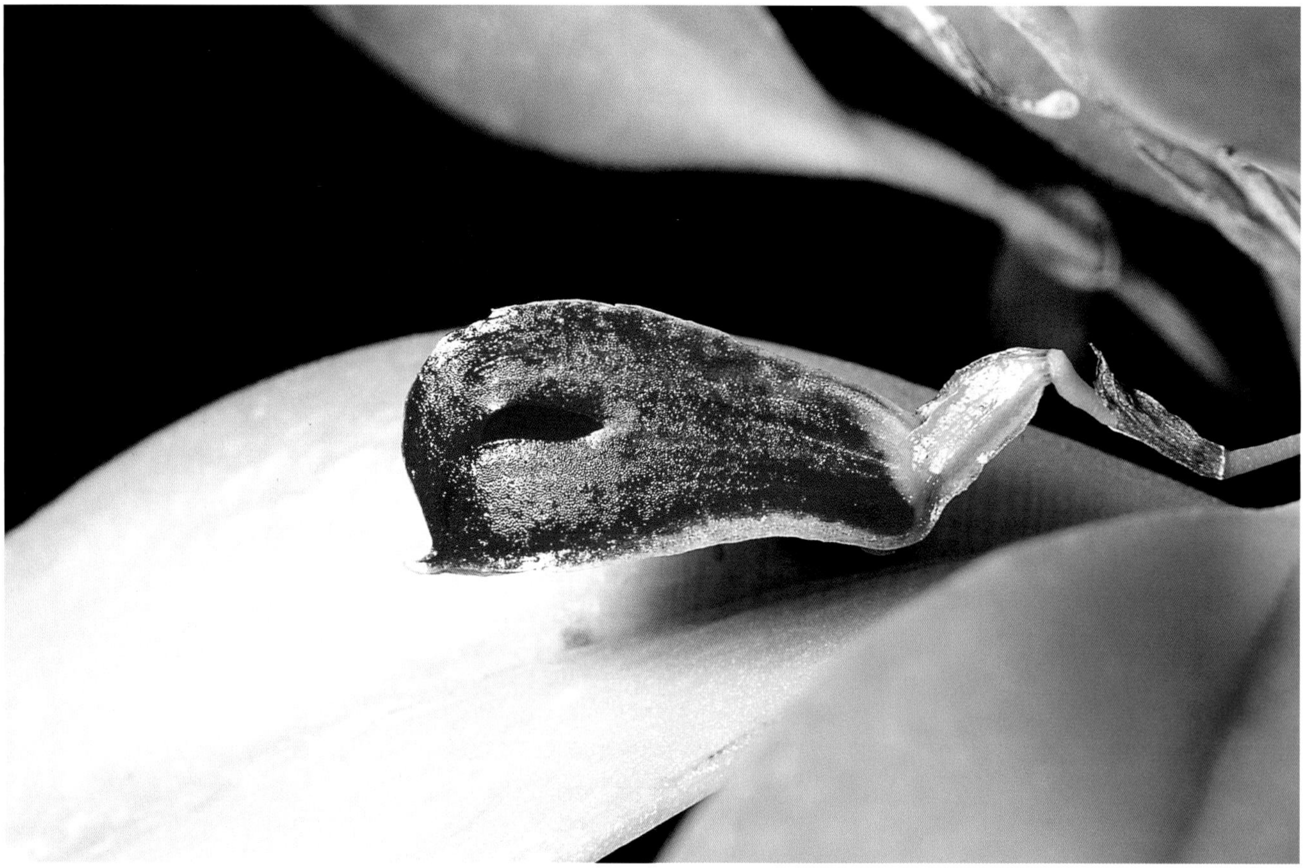

Zootrophion atropurpureum

In recent years, many attractive hybrids have been registered and these plants are becoming very popular in cultivation.

CULTIVATION: Zygopetalums have a large root system and need a fairly large pot. They require intermediate temperatures and an open, free-draining compost, moderate shade, high humidity, and plenty of water and fertilizer while actively growing. They need much less water while resting.

Zygopetalum crinitum Loddiges

Pseudobulbs to 5 cm long with 2–3 basal sheathing leaves, 2-leaved at the apex. Leaves at apex to 35 × 4.5 cm. Inflorescence to 45 cm long, 3- to 7-flowered. Flowers to 9 cm across, scented, long-lasting; sepals and petals yellow-green heavily marked with chestnut-brown; lip broadly wedge-shaped, the margins undulate, white, veined with red or blue-purple.

Usually terrestrial in leaf litter, sometimes epiphytic in forks of trees, 600–1200 m (2000–4000 ft.)

Southern and southeastern Brazil

Zygopetalum maculatum (Kunth) Garay

SYN. *Zygopetalum intermedium* Loddiges ex Lindley, *Z. mackayi* Hooker

Inflorescence to 40 cm long, 8- to 12-flowered. Flowers 4–8 cm across, scented, green or yellow-green blotched with red-brown; lip white with blue-violet lines.

Terrestrial in shade on mountain ridges and roadside banks, 1000–2250 m (3300–7300 ft.)

Bolivia, Brazil, Peru

Zygopetalum maculatum

Zootrophion dayanum

Zygopetalum crinitum

Zygopetalum maxillare Loddiges

Pseudobulbs to 9 × 3 cm, 2- or 3-leaved at apex. Leaves to 45 × 6 cm. Inflorescence to 35 cm long, 5- to 8-flowered. Flowers 6 cm across, scented, long-lasting. Sepals and petals green blotched and barred with brown, lip violet-blue with a purple callus, midlobe almost round, the margins undulate.

Epiphytic on tree ferns in shade of forest, 600–1300 m (2000–4300 ft.)

Argentina, Brazil, Paraguay

Zygopetalum maxillare

Zygosepalum Reichenbach f.

TRIBE: Maxillarieae

SUBTRIBE: Zygopetalinae

ETYMOLOGY: From Greek *zygon*, yoke, and *sepalum*, sepal, referring to the sepals joined at the base

DISTRIBUTION: 8 species in tropical South America

Pseudobulbs often set well apart on a creeping rhizome, 2- or 3-leaved at the apex. Leaves plicate. Inflorescences basal, erect or ± pendent, few-flowered. Flowers large, fleshy, showy. Sepals and petals subsimilar, spreading, the lateral sepals joined at the base. Lip simple or trilobed, with a basal callus. Column winged at the tip, with a short foot; pollinia 4. Anther-cap with a long, beaklike projection, which is among the main distinguishing features from *Zygopetalum*.

CULTIVATION: Because of the creeping rhizome, plants are better mounted on a slab or grown in a basket. Most require intermediate to warm temperatures, moderate shade, and good humidity. They should be kept drier while resting but not allowed to become completely dry.

Zygosepalum labiosum (Richard) C. Schweinfurth

Rhizomes scandent. Leaves to 25 × 5 cm. Inflorescence to 20 cm long, 1- to 3-flowered. Flowers to 10 cm across; sepals and petals greenish flushed with maroon at the base; lip white with a violet callus and violet veining.

Epiphytic in deep shade in forest, ca. 400 m (1320 ft.)

South America

Zygosepalum lindeniae (Rolfe) Garay & Dunsterville

SYN. *Zygopetalum lindeniae* Rolfe

Pseudobulbs ovoid, to 6 cm long, Leaves to 25 × 3 cm. Inflorescence 15–20 cm long. Flowers 8 cm across; sepals and petals greenish with red veins or reddish brown, white at the base; lip white with purple-red veining.

Epiphytic low down on tree trunks in lowland rain forest

South America

Zygosepalum tatei (Ames & C. Schweinfurth) Garay & Dunsterville

SYN. *Zygopetalum tatei* Ames & C. Schweinfurth

Leaves narrow, ca. 15 cm long. Inflorescence 30–50 cm tall, 4- to 6-flowered. Flowers 4–5 cm across; sepals and petals yellowish or green-

Zygosepalum labiosum

ish brown with brown markings; lip white with a purple-pink crest. This species needs cool conditions in cultivation.

Terrestrial (rarely lithophytic or epiphytic) in short, dense vegetation in damp places, 1800–2400 m (6000–7900 ft.)

Brazil, Guyana, Venezuela

Zygostates Lindley

SYN. *Dipteranthus* Barbosa Rodrigues

TRIBE: Oncidiinae

SUBTRIBE: Ornithocephalinae

ETYMOLOGY: From Greek *zygostates*, balance or scales, referring to the staminodes, thought to look like a balance

DISTRIBUTION: 20 species in southern tropical America

Small epiphytes with pseudobulbs lacking or very small and obscure. Leaves fleshy or leathery, forming a fan. Inflorescences lateral, unbranched, few- to many-flowered. Flowers small, translucent, white or greenish yellow. Sepals and petals subsimilar, free, spreading or the sepals reflexed; lip entire, lacking a spur, the margin sometimes toothed, with a fleshy basal callus. Column slender, with 2 club-shaped basal staminodes; pollinia 4.

CULTIVATION: Plants are usually mounted but can be grown in small pots, in intermediate to warm, shaded conditions, with high humidity and good air movement. In the wild, many species are twig epiphytes.

Zygostates apiculata (Lindley) Toscano

SYN. *Dipteranthus planifolius* Reichenbach f., *D. estradae* Dodson, *Ornithocephalus planifolius* Reichenbach f.

Leaves several, to 4 cm long, narrowly lanceolate. Inflorescence pendent, to 9 cm long, ca. 20-flowered. Flowers ca. 7 mm across, yellow or yellow-green.

Epiphytic in low-altitude, seasonally dry forest

Bolivia, Colombia, Ecuador, Peru, Venezuela

Zygostates grandiflora (Lindley) Mansfeld

SYN. *Dipteranthus grandiflorus* (Lindley) Pabst, *Ornithocephalus grandiflorus* Lindley

Inflorescence 12–18 cm long, pendent, densely many-flowered. Flowers relatively large, ca. 2 cm across, white, green towards center.

Epiphytic in forest, to 1000 m (3300 ft.).

Brazil.

Zygostates lunata Lindley

SYN. *Ornithocephalus navicularis* Barbosa Rodrigues

Leaves several, to 7 × 2 cm, oblong-spathulate. Inflorescence arching or pendent, 10–15 cm long, many-flowered. Flowers ca. 8 mm across, sepals and petals yellowish green, the petals with a serrated edge, lip white, the margins fringed, callus yellow.

Epiphytic on mossy trees in mid-altitude forest

Brazil

Zygostates multiflora (Rolfe) Schlechter

Inflorescence pendent, ca. 8 cm long, several-flowered. Flowers small, white, the lip with 2 backward-pointing projections at the base.

Epiphytic on twigs in forest, 1200–1400 m (4000–4600 ft.)

Brazil

Zygostates lunata

Zygostates grandiflora

Zygostates multiflora

GLOSSARY

Acuminate Tapering to a long point
Anther The part of the stamen that bears pollen
Apex The growing point of a stem or root
Apicule A short point at the end of a leaf, bract or perianth segment
Articulated Jointed
Autotrophic Manufacturing its own food
Axil The angle between a leaf and a stem
Axillary inflorescence One arising in the axil of a leaf or leaf base, as opposed to a terminal inflorescence, which comes from the end of a stem
Bract A small leaf at the base of a flower-stalk or an inflorescence
Callus A protuberance or growth, usually on the lip of an orchid
Campanulate Bell-shaped
Capitate Of an inflorescence, forming a dense head
Ciliate With a marginal fringe of fine hairs
Claw The narrow, stalklike base of some sepals, petals, or lips
Cleistogamous A flower that self-pollinates without opening
Clinandrium The part of the column that contains the anther
Clone The asexually produced offspring of a single parent; they will be genetically identical
Column In an orchid, the organ formed by the fusion of stamens, style, and stigma
Cultivar A particular form of a species or hybrid
Disc The central area of the lip, often with calli and crests
Distichous Refers to leaves arranged in two opposite rows
Epichile The terminal part of a lip divided into three parts (for example, in *Stanhopea*)
Epiphyte (adj. **epiphytic**) A plant which grows on another plant, but without obtaining nourishment from it (that is, not a parasite)
Filiform Threadlike
Galea Helmet-shaped hood
Geniculate Bent like a knee
Genus A natural group of closely related species
Glabrous Lacking hairs
Grex A group name for all plants derived from a cross between the same two species or hybrids
Hypochile The basal part of a lip divided into three parts (see *epichile*)
Imbricate Overlapping
Inflorescence Flower and flower-stalk together
Intergeneric Between or among two or more genera
Internode The part of a stem between two nodes
Intrageneric Within one genus
Keiki A small plant arising from the stem, pseudobulb, or inflorescence of a mature plant
Labellum. See *lip*
Lamella A thin plate of tissue
Lamina The blade of a leaf (or a sepal, petal, or lip)
Linear Narrow, with more or less parallel margins
Lip (**labellum**) The unpaired petal of an orchid, usually different from the other two
Lithophyte (adj. **lithophytic**) A plant which grows on rock
Mentum A chinlike projection on a flower, formed by the bases of the lateral sepals and the column-foot
Meristem Undifferentiated tissue, usually from a growing point, which is capable of developing into specialized tissue
Mesochile The middle part of a lip with 3 parts
Monopodial A type of growth which continues indefinitely from a terminal bud
Mycorrhiza Fungi which live in a symbiotic relationship with a plant, usually in the roots
Node The place where a leaf joins a stem
Nonresupinate Refers to a flower that has not twisted, or has twisted through 360 degrees, so that the lip is at the top of the flower
Ovary The part of a flower which contains the ovules and eventually becomes the fruit, containing seed; in orchids, the ovary is inferior, lying below the sepals and petals
Palea Motile projections round the edges of petals in some *Bulbophyllum* species
Panicle A branched inflorescence
Papillose Covered with small, soft protuberances (papillae)
Pedicel The stalk of each individual flower in an inflorescence
Peduncle The stalk of an inflorescence
Perianth The sepals and petals collectively
Petiole A leaf stalk
Photosynthesis The process by which plants manufacture carbohydrates from gases in the presence of sunlight
Plicate Pleated
Pollinarium The male reproductive part of an orchid flower, consisting of the pollinia from an anther with the associated parts, the viscidium (or viscidia) and stipes (or stipites)
Pollinium (plural **pollinia**). Pollen grains cohering into a mass
Protocorm A swollen, tuberlike structure that is the first stage of growth after an orchid seed germinates
Pseudobulb A swollen, bulblike structure at the base of a stem

Pubescent Covered with short, fine hairs
Raceme An unbranched inflorescence of pedicelled flowers
Rachis In orchids, the main axis of an inflorescence above the peduncle, to which the flowers are attached
Resupinate Refers to a flower that has twisted through 180 degrees so that the lip is at the bottom of the flower
Rhizome A stem on or below the ground with roots growing down from it and flowering shoots up
Rugose Rough or wrinkled
Rupicolous Rock-dwelling
Saccate Baglike
Saprophyte (adj. **saprophytic**) A plant, usually without chlorophyll, which obtains its food by the breakdown of dead organic matter in the soil
Scandent Climbing
Scape An erect flower stalk without leaves or bracts
Secund Of flowers arranged on one side of the rachis
Sessile Without a stalk
Sheath The lower part of a leaf clasping a stem
Spathe A conspicuous bract or leaf at the base of an inflorescence
Spathulate (**spatulate**) More or less spoon-shaped
Species A group of similar individuals, the basic unit of classification
Spike An unbranched inflorescence of sessile flowers (in orchids, often used for any unbranched inflorescence)
Spur A slender, usually hollow, extension of part of a flower, usually, but not always, the lip
Stamen The male organ of a flower, which bears the pollen
Staminode An infertile or rudimentary stamen
Stigma The part of the column which receives pollen
Stipe or **stipes** (plural **stipites**) A stalk joining the pollinium to the viscidium
Stolon A running stem which forms roots
Stomata The pores through which a plant's gas exchange takes place
Symbiosis (adj. **symbiotic**). The association of two different organisms which contribute to each other's support
Sympodial A type of growth that is determinate, ending in a potential inflorescence
Synsepal The joined lateral sepals of some orchids
Terete Cylindrical; circular in cross-section
Terrestrial Growing in the ground
Umbel An inflorescence where all the flowers come off at the same point
Unifoliate One-leafed
Velamen An absorbent layer of dead cells covering the roots of many orchids
Verrucose Warty
Viscidium A sticky gland joined to the pollinium or pollinia

BIBLIOGRAPHY

Cultural

Adams, P. B., ed. 1988. *Reproductive Biology of Species Orchids: Principles and Practice.* School of Botany, University of Melbourne; Orchid Species Society of Victoria, Australia.

American Orchid Society. 1995. *Handbook on Orchid Pests and Diseases.* Rev. ed. American Orchid Society, Palm Beach, Florida.

Bechtel, H., P. Cribb, and E. Launert. 1992. *The Manual of Cultivated Orchid Species.* 3d ed. Blandford, London.

Cribb, P. J., and C. Bailes. 1989. *Hardy Orchids.* Helm, London; Timber Press, Portland, Oregon.

Crous, H., and G. Duncan. 2006. *Grow Disas.* SANBI, Kirstenbosch, South Africa.

Fitch, C. M. 1997. *Growing Orchids Under Lights.* American Orchid Society.

Hawkes, A. D. 1965. *Encyclopaedia of Cultivated Orchids.* Faber and Faber, London.

la Croix, I. F. 2000. *Orchid Basics.* Hamlyn, London.

Light, M. 1995. *Growing Orchids in the Caribbean.* Macmillan Education, Oxford.

Nash, N., and I. F. la Croix, eds. 2005. *Flora's Orchids.* Global Book Publishing, New South Wales, Australia; Timber Press, Portland, Oregon.

Northen, R. 1975. *Orchids as House Plants.* Rev. ed. Dover Publications, New York.

Northen, R. 1980. *Miniature Orchids.* Van Nostrand Reinhold, New York.

Northen, R. 1990. *Home Orchid Growing.* 4th ed. Prentice-Hall Press, New York.

Pridgeon, A., ed. 1992. *The Illustrated Encyclopedia of Orchids.* Weldon Publishing, Sydney; Timber Press, Portland, Oregon.

Seaton, P., and M. Ramsay. 2005. *Growing Orchids from Seed.* Royal Botanic Gardens, Kew.

Stewart, J. 2000. *Orchids.* Rev. ed. Timber Press, Portland, Oregon

Stewart, J., and M. Griffiths, eds. 1995. *RHS Manual of Orchids.* Macmillan, London.

Thompson, P. A. 1977. *Orchids from Seed.* London: HMSO.

Tullock, J. 2005. *Growing Hardy Orchids.* Timber Press, Portland, Oregon.

Williams, B., ed. 1980. *Orchids for Everyone.* Salamander Press, London.

Wodrich, K. H. K. 1997. *Growing South African Indigenous Orchids.* A. A. Balkema, Rotterdam.

Geographical

Europe

Allan, B., P. Woods, and S. Clarke. 1993. *Wild Orchids of Scotland.* HMSO, Edinburgh.

Buttler, K. P. 1991. *Field Guide to Orchids of Britain and Europe.* Crowood Press, Swindon.

Davies, P., J. Davies, and A. Huxley. 1983. *Wild Orchids of Britain and Europe.* Chatto and Windus, Hogarth Press, London.

Delforge, P. 2006. *Orchids of Europe, North Africa and the Middle East.* 3d ed. A. and C. Black, London.

Duperrex, P., and D. Tyteca. 1961. *Orchids of Europe.* Blandford Press, London.

Foley, M., and S. Clarke. 2005. *Orchids of the British Isles.* Griffin Press, Cheltenham; Royal Botanic Garden Edinburgh.

Harrap, A., and S. Harrap. 2005. *Orchids of Britain and Ireland.* A. and C. Black, London.

Jacquet, P. 1995. *Une répartition des Orchidées sauvages de France.* 3d ed. Société Française d'Orchidophilie, Paris.

Lang, D. 2004. *Britain's Orchids.* WildGuides, New Basing, Hampshire, England.

Summerhayes, V. S. 1968. *Wild Orchids of Britain.* 2d ed. Collins, London.

Africa

Ball, J. S. 1978. *Southern African Epiphytic Orchids.* Conservation Press, Johannesburg.

Cadet, J. 1989. *Joyaux de nos Forêts: Les Orchidées de la Réunion.* Janine Cadet, Sainte Clotilde, Réunion.

Cribb, P. J. 1984. *Orchidaceae,* part 2. In *Flora of Tropical East Africa,* ed. R. M. Polhill. A. A. Balkema, Rotterdam.

Cribb, P. J. 1989. *Orchidaceae,* part 3. In *Flora of Tropical East Africa,* ed. R. M. Polhill. A. A. Balkema, Rotterdam.

Cribb, P. J., and S. Thomas. 1997. *Orchidaceae.* In *Flora of Ethiopia and Eritrea,* vol. 6, eds. S. Edwards, S. Demissew, and I. Hedberg. National Herbarium, Addis Ababa, Ethiopia; Uppsala University, Sweden.

Demissew, S., P. J. Cribb, and F. Rasmussen. 2004. *Field Guide to Ethiopian Orchids.* Royal Botanic Gardens Kew.

Du Puy, D., P. J. Cribb, J. Bosser, J. Hermans, and C. Hermans. 1999. *The Orchids of Madagascar.* Royal Botanic Gardens Kew.

Geerinck, D. 1984. Orchidaceae, part 1. In *Flore d'Afrique Centrale.* Jardin Botanique National de Belgique, Meise.

Geerinck, D. 1992. Orchidaceae, part 2. In *Flore d'Afrique Centrale.* Jardin Botanique National de Belgique, Meise.

Hermans, J. and C., D. Du Puy, P. J. Cribb, and J. Bosser. 2007. *Orchids of Madagascar*, 2d ed. Royal Botanic Gardens Kew.

la Croix, I. F., and P. J. Cribb. 1995. *Orchidaceae*, part 1. In *Flora Zambesiaca*, vol. 11, part 1, ed. G. V. Pope. Royal Botanic Gardens Kew.

la Croix, I. F., and P. J. Cribb. 1998. *Orchidaceae*, part 2. In *Flora Zambesiaca*, vol. 11, part 2, ed. G. V. Pope. Royal Botanic Gardens Kew.

la Croix, I. F., and E. A. S. la Croix. 1997. *African Orchids in the Wild and in Cultivation*. Timber Press, Portland, Oregon.

la Croix, I. F., E. A. S. la Croix, and T. M. la Croix. 1991. *Orchids of Malawi*. A. A. Balkema, Rotterdam.

Linder, H. P., and H. Kurzweil. 1999. *Orchids of Southern Africa*. A. A. Balkema, Rotterdam.

Moriarty, A. 1975. *Wild Flowers of Malawi*. Purnell, Cape Town, South Africa.

Morris, B. 1970. *The Epiphytic Orchids of Malawi*. The Society of Malawi, Blantyre.

Perez-Vera, F. 2003. *Les Orchidées de Côte d'Ivoire*. Collection Parthénope. Biotope, Mèze, France.

Perrier de la Bâthie, H. 1939. 49e Famille, *Orchidées*, vol. 1. In *Flore de Madagascar*, ed. H. Humbert. Imprimerie Officielle, Tananarive, Madagascar.

Perrier de la Bâthie, H. 1941. 49e Famille, *Orchidées*, vol. 2. In *Flore de Madagascar*, ed. H. Humbert. Imprimerie Officielle, Tananarive, Madagascar.

Piers, F. 1968. *Orchids of East Africa*. J. Cramer, Lehre, Germany.

Pottinger, M. 1983. *African Orchids: A Personal View*. HGH Publications, Wokingham, England.

Segerback, L. B. 1983. *Orchids of Nigeria*. A. A. Balkema, Rotterdam.

Stévart, T., and F. de Oliveira. 2000. *Guide des Orchidées de São Tomé et Principe*. Ecofac, Gabon.

Stewart, J., and B. Campbell. 1970. *Orchids of Tropical Africa*. W. H. Allen, London.

Stewart, J., and B. Campbell. 1996. *Orchids of Kenya*. St. Paul's Bibliographies, Winchester, England.

Stewart, J., and E. F. Hennessy. 1981. *Orchids of Africa*. Macmillan, London.

Stewart, J., J. Hermans, and B. Campbell. 2006. *Angraecoid Orchids*. Timber Press, Portland, Oregon.

Stewart, J., H. P. Linder, E. A. Schelpe, and A. V. Hall. 1982. *Wild Orchids of Southern Africa*. Macmillan South Africa, Johannesburg.

Summerhayes, V. S. 1968a. *Orchidaceae*, part 1. In *Flora of Tropical East Africa*, ed. E. Milne-Redhead and R. M. Polhill. Crown Agents, London.

Summerhayes, V. S. 1968b. *Orchidaceae*. In *Flora of West Tropical Africa*, vol. 3, part 1, ed. F. N. Hepper. Crown Agents, London.

Szlachetko, D. L., and T. S. Olszewski. 1998. *Flore du Cameroun*, 34, *Orchidacées*, vol. 1. MINREST, Yaoundé, Cameroun.

Szlachetko, D. L., and T. S. Olszewski. 2001a. *Flore du Cameroun*, 35, *Orchidacées*, vol. 2. MINREST, Yaoundé, Cameroun.

Szlachetko, D. L., and T. S. Olszewski. 2001b. *Flore du Cameroun*, 36, *Orchidacées*, vol. 3. MINREST, Yaoundé, Cameroun.

Thouars, A.-A. du Petit. 1822. *Orchidées des Iles Australes de l'Afrique*. Paris.

Williamson, G. 1977. *The Orchids of South Central Africa*. J. M. Dent, London.

North America

Brown, P. M. 2002. *Wild Orchids of Florida*. University Press of Florida, Gainesville, Florida.

Brown, P. M. 2004. *Wild Orchids of the Southeastern United States, North of Peninsular Florida*. University Press of Florida, Gainesville, Florida.

Brown, P. M. 2006a. *Wild Orchids of the Pacific Northwest and Canadian Rockies*. University Press of Florida.

Brown, P. M. 2006b. *Wild Orchids of the Prairies and Great Plains Region of North America*. University Press of Florida.

Brown, P. M. 2008. *Wild Orchids of Texas*. University Press of Florida, Gainesville, Florida.

Coleman, R. A. 2002. *The Wild Orchids of Arizona and New Mexico*. Cornell University Press, Ithaca, New York.

Hágsater, E., G. Salazar, R. Jiménez, M. López, and R. Dressler. 2005. *Orchids of Mexico*. Chinoin Productos Farmacéuticos, Mexico City.

Keenan, P. E. 1998. *Wild Orchids Across North America: A Botanical Travelogue*. Timber Press, Portland, Oregon.

Luer, C. A. 1972. *The Native Orchids of Florida*. New York Botanical Garden, New York.

Luer, C. A. 1975. *The Native Orchids of the United States and Canada, Excluding Florida*. New York Botanical Garden, New York.

Central and South America and the Caribbean

Adams, C. D. 1972. *Flowering Plants of Jamaica*. University of the West Indies, Mona, Jamaica.

Carnevali, G., I. M. Ramírez-Morillo, G. A. Romero-González, C. A. Vargas, and E. Foldats. 2003. *Orchidaceae*. In *Flora of the Venezuelan Guayana*, vol. 7, eds. P. E. Berry, K. Yatskievych, and B. K. Holst. Missouri Botanical Garden Press, St. Louis, Missouri.

Chiron, G., and R. Bellone. 2005. *Les orchidées de Guyane français*. Tropicalia, France.

Dodson, C. H., and D. E. Bennett (1989). *Orchids of Peru*. In *Icones Plantarum Tropicarum*, series 2, fasc. 1, 2. Missouri Botanical Garden, St. Louis.

Dodson, C. H., and C. A. Luer. 2005. *Orchidaceae*, part 2, *Aa–Cyrtidiorchis*. In *Flora of Ecuador*, no. 76, eds. G. Harling and L. Andersson. University of Göteborg and Riksmuseum, Stockholm, Sweden.

Dodson, C. H., and P. Marmol de Dodson. 1980–1984. *Orchids of Ecuador*. In *Icones Plantarum Tropicarum* 1–5, 10. Marie Selby Botanic Garden, Florida.

Dodson, C. H., and P. Marmol de Dodson. 1989. *Orchids of Ecuador*. In *Icones Plantarum Tropicarum*, series 2, fasc. 5, 6. Missouri Botanical Garden, St. Louis.

Dodson, C. H., and R. Vásquez. 1989. *Orchids of Bolivia*. In *Icones Plantarum Tropicarum*, series 2, fasc. 3, 4. Missouri Botanical Garden, St. Louis.

Dunsterville, G. C. K., and E. Dunsterville. 1988. *Orchid Hunting in the Lost World (and Elsewhere in Venezuela)*. American Orchid Society, West Palm Beach, Florida.

Dunsterville, G. C. K., and L. A. Garay. 1959–1976. *Venezuelan Orchids Illustrated*, vols. 1–6. André Deutsch, London.

Dunsterville, G. C. K., and L. A. Garay. 1979. *Orchids of Venezuela: An Illustrated Field Guide*. Botanical Museum, Harvard University, Cambridge, Massachusetts.

Escobar, R., ed. 1990. *Native Colombian Orchids*. Vol. 1. Editorial Colina, Medellin.

Feldmann, P., and N. Barré. 2001. *Atlas des Orchidées Sauvage de la Guadeloupe*. CIRAD, Paris

Garay, L. A. 1978. *Orchidaceae*, part 1, *Cypripedioideae, Orchidoideae, Neottioideae*. In *Flora of Ecuador*, no. 9, eds. G. Harling and B. Sparre. University of Göteborg and Riksmuseum, Stockholm, Sweden.

Garay, L. A., and H. R. Sweet. 1974. *Orchidaceae*. In *Flora of the Lesser Antilles*. Arnold Arboretum, Harvard University, Jamaica Plain, Massachusetts.

Hammel, B. E., M. H. Grayum, C. Herrera, and N. Zamorra, eds. 2003. *Manual de Plantas de Costa Rica*. Vol. 3, *Monocotiledoneas (Orchidaceae–Zingiberaceae)*. Missouri Botanical Garden Press, St. Louis, Missouri.

Hoehne, F. C. 1940–1953. *Flora Brasilica—Orchidaceas*. São Paulo, Brazil.

Llamacho, J. O., and J. A. Larramendi. 2005. *The Orchids of Cuba*. Greta Editores, Spain.

McLeish, I., N. R. Pearce, and B. R. Adams. 1995. *Native Orchids of Belize*. A. A. Balkema, Rotterdam.

Miller, D., and R. Warren. 1994. *Orchids of the High Mountain Atlantic Rain Forest of Southeastern Brazil*. Rio Atlantic Forest Project, Salamandra Consultoria Editorial, Rio de Janeiro.

Nir, M. 2000. *Orchidaceae Antillanae*. DAG Media Publishing, New York.

Pabst, G., and F. Dungs. 1975–1977. *Orchidaceae Brasiliensis*. 2 vols. Kurt Schmersow, Hildesheim, Germany.

Schweinfurth, C. 1958–1961. *Orchids of Peru*. Fieldiana 30.

Williams, L., and P. Allen. 1980. *Orchids of Panama*. Missouri Botanical Garden, St. Louis.

Asia

Beaman, T. E., J. J. Wood, R. S. Beaman, and J. H. Beaman. 2001. *Orchids of Sarawak*. Natural History Publications (Borneo) and Royal Botanic Gardens Kew.

Chan, C. L., A. Lamb, P. S. Shim, and J. J. Wood. 1994. *Orchids of Borneo*. Vol. 1, *Introduction and a Selection of Species*. Sabah Society, Kota Kinabalu, Malaysia; Royal Botanic Gardens Kew.

Chen, S., Z. Tsi, and L. Yibo. 1999. *Native Orchids of China in Color*. Science Press, Beijing.

Comber, J. B. 1990. *Orchids of Java*. Royal Botanic Gardens Kew.

Comber, J. B. 2001. *Orchids of Sumatra*. Natural History Publications (Borneo) and Royal Botanic Gardens Kew.

Cootes, J. 2001. *The Orchids of the Philippines*. Timber Press, Portland, Oregon.

Cribb, P. J., and W. A. Whistler. 1996. *Orchids of Samoa*. Royal Botanic Gardens Kew.

Garay, L. A., and H. R. Sweet. 1974. *Orchids of the Southern Ryukyu Islands*. Botanical Museum, Harvard University, Cambridge, Massachusetts.

Holttum, R. E. 1964. *Orchids of Malaya*. 3d ed. Government Printing Office, Singapore.

Lewis, B. A., and P. J. Cribb. 1989. *Orchids of Vanuatu*. Royal Botanic Gardens Kew.

Lewis, B. A., and P. J. Cribb. 1991. *Orchids of the Solomon Islands and Bougainville*. Royal Botanic Gardens Kew.

Lucksom, S. Z. 2007. *The Orchids of Sikkim and North East Himalaya*. Concept, Siliguri, India.

Pearce, N. R., and P. J. Cribb. 2002. *The Orchids of Bhutan*. Royal Botanic Garden Edinburgh; Royal Government of Bhutan

Pradhan, M. 2005. *100 Sikkim Himalayan Orchids*. Spenta Multimedia, Mumbai, India.

Pradhan, U. C., and S. C. Pradhan. 1997. *100 Beautiful Himalayan Orchids and How to Grow Them*. Primulaceae Books, Kalimpong, India.

Pradhan, U. C., and S. C. Pradhan. 2005. *Himalayan Jewel Orchids and How to Grow Them*. Primulaceae Books and Himalayan Orchid Exports.

Schlechter, R. 1982. *The Orchidaceae of German New Guinea*. Australian Orchid Foundation, Melbourne. (Translated from the original German.)

Seidenfaden, G. 1975–1983. *Orchid Genera in Thailand*. Dansk Botanisk Arkiv.

Teoh, E. S. 2005. *Orchids of Asia*. 3d ed. Times Editions-Marshall Cavendish, Singapore.

Valmayor, H. 1984. *Orchidiana Philippiana*. Eugenio Lopez Foundation, Manila, Philippines.

Vermeulen, J. J. 1991. *Orchids of Borneo*. Vol. 2, *Bulbophyllum*. Sabah Society, Kota Kinabalu, Malaysia; Royal Botanic Gardens Kew

Wood, J. J. 1997. *Orchids of Borneo*. Vol. 3, *Dendrobium, Dendrochilum, and Others*. Sabah Society, Kota Kinabalu, Malaysia; Royal Botanic Gardens Kew.

Wood, J. J. 2003. *Orchids of Borneo*. Vol. 4. Sabah Society, Kota Kinabalu, Malaysia; Royal Botanic Gardens Kew.

Wood, J. J., R. S. Beaman, and J. H. Beaman. 1993. *The Plants of Mount Kinabalu: 2: Orchids*. Royal Botanic Gardens Kew.

Wood, J. J., and P. J. Cribb. 1994. *A Checklist of the Orchids of Borneo*. Royal Botanic Gardens Kew.

Australia

Jones, D. L. 1988. *Native Orchids of Australia*. Reed, Australia.

Richards, H., R. Wootton, and R. Datodi. 1988. *Cultivation of Australian Native Orchids*. 2d ed. Australasian Native Orchid Society, Victorian Group, Cheltenham, Victoria.

Riley, J. J., and D. P. Banks. 2002. *Orchids of Australia*. Princeton University Press, Princeton and Oxford

Monographs

Averyanov, L., P. J. Cribb, P. K. Loc, and N. T. Hiep. 2003. *Slipper Orchids of Vietnam*. Royal Botanic Gardens Kew.

Birk, L. A. 2004. *The Paphiopedilum Grower's Manual*. 2d ed. Pisang Press, Santa Barbara, California.

Chadwick, A. A., and A. E. Chadwick. 2006. *The Classic Cattleyas*. Timber Press, Portland, Oregon.

Christenson, E. A. 2001. *Phalaenopsis: A Monograph*. Timber Press, Portland, Oregon.

Clayton, D. 2002. *The Genus Coelogyne. A Synopsis*. Natural History Publications (Borneo) and Royal Botanic Gardens Kew.

Cribb, P. J. 1997a. *The Genus Cypripedium*. Royal Botanic Gardens Kew and Timber Press, Portland, Oregon.

Cribb, P. J. 1997b. *Slipper Orchids of Borneo*. Natural History Publications, Borneo.

Cribb, P. J. 1998. *The Genus Paphiopedilum*. 2d ed. Natural History Publications (Borneo) and Royal Botanic Gardens Kew.

Cribb, P. J., and I. Butterfield. 1999. *The Genus Pleione*. 2d ed. Royal Botanic Gardens Kew.

Du Puy, D., and P. J. Cribb. 2007. *The Genus Cymbidium*. Royal Botanic Gardens Kew.

Garay, L. A., F. Hamer, and E. S. Siegerist. 1994. The genus *Cirrhopetalum* and the genera of the *Bulbophyllum* Alliance. *Nordic Journal of Botany* 14(6): 609–646.

Gerritsen, M. E., and R. Parsons. 2005. *Masdevallias*. Timber Press, Portland, Oregon.

Grove, D. G. 1995. *Vandas and Ascocendas*. Timber Press, Portland, Oregon

Hillerman, F. E., and A. W. Holst. 1986. *An Introduction to the Cultivated Angraecoid Orchids of Madagascar*. Timber Press, Portland, Oregon.

Jonsson, L. 1981. A monograph of the genus *Microcoelia*. *Symbolae Botanique Uppsalienses* 23 (4).

Kelleher, J. 1984. *Intriguing Masdevallias*. HGH Publications, Wokingham, Berkshire.

Lavarack, B, W. Harris, and G. Stocker. 2000. *Dendrobium and Its Relatives*. Timber Press, Portland, Oregon.

Luer, C. A. 1986–2005. *Icones Pleurothallidinarum*. Vols. 1–28. Missouri Botanical Garden, St. Louis, Missouri.

Motes, M. R. 1997. *Vandas: Their Botany, History, and Culture*. Timber Press, Portland, Oregon.

Oakeley, H. 1993. *Lycaste Species: The Essential Guide*. H. F. Oakeley, London.

Schelpe, S., and J. Stewart. (1990). *Dendrobiums: An Introduction to the Species in Cultivation*. Orchid Sundries, Dorset, England.

Siegerist, E. S. 2001. *Bulbophyllums and Their Allies*. Timber Press, Portland, Oregon.

Stewart, J., J. Hermans, and B. Campbell. 2006. *Angraecoid Orchids*. Timber Press, Portland, Oregon

Vermeulen, J. J. 1987. *A Taxonomic Revision of the Continental African Bulbophyllinae*. Orchid Monographs 2. E. J. Brill, Leiden.

Vogelpoel, L. 1985. *Disa uniflora: Its Propagation and Cultivation*. Disa Society of South Africa.

Wood, H. P. 2006. *The Dendrobiums*. Gantner Verlag, Ruggell, Liechtenstein

Wood, J. J. (2001). *Dendrochilum of Borneo*. Natural History Publications (Borneo) and Royal Botanic Gardens Kew.

Zelenko, H., B. D. Zelenko, and J. Warshaw. 1997. *The Pictorial Encyclopedia of Oncidium*. Zai Publications, New York.

Miscellaneous

Brummitt, R. K., and C. E. Powell, eds. 1992. *Authors of Plant Names*. Royal Botanic Gardens Kew.

Darwin, C. 1862. *On the Various Contrivances by which British and Foreign Orchids are Fertilised by Insects*. John Murray, London.

Dressler, R. L. 1981. *The Orchids: Natural History a tion*. Harvard University Press, Cambridge, Massachusetts.

Dressler, R. L. 1993. *Phylogeny and Classification of the Orchid Family*. Dioscorides Press, Portland, Oregon.

Fitch, C. M. 1995. *Orchid Photography*. American Orchid Society, West Palm Beach, Florida.

Govaerts, R. 2007. *World Checklist of Monocotyledons*. The Board of Trustees of the Royal Botanic Gardens, Kew. http://www.kew.org/wcsp/monocots.

Koopowitz, H. 2001. *Orchids and Their Conservation*. Batsford, London.

Mabberley, D. J. 1987. *The Plant Book*. Cambridge University Press.

Pridgeon, A. M. 1996. *Orchids*. Status Survey and Conservation Action Plan. IUCN/SSC Orchid Specialist Group, Gland, Switzerland.

Pridgeon, A. M., P. J. Cribb, M. W. Chase, and F. N. Rasmussen. 1999. *Genera Orchidacearum*. Vol. 1, *General Introduction, Apostasioideae, Cypripedioideae*. Oxford University Press.

Pridgeon, A. M., P. J. Cribb, M. W. Chase, and F. N. Rasmussen. 2001. *Genera Orchidacearum*. Vol. 2, *Orchidoideae* (part 1). Oxford University Press.

Pridgeon, A. M., P. J. Cribb, M. W. Chase, and F. N. Rasmussen. 2003. *Genera Orchidacearum*. Vol. 3, *Orchidoideae* (part 2), *Vanilloideae*. Oxford University Press.

Pridgeon, A. M., P. J. Cribb, M. W. Chase, and F. N. Rasmussen. 2005. *Genera Orchidacearum*. Vol. 4, *Epidendroideae* (part 1). Oxford University Press.

Reinikka, M. A. 1995. *A History of the Orchid*. Rev. ed. Timber Press, Portland, Oregon.

Schlechter, R. 1918. *Attempt at a Natural New Classification of the African Angraecoid Orchids*. Translation by H. J. Katz and J. T. Simmons, 1986. Australian Orchid Foundation, Essendon.

Schultes, R. E., and A. S. Pease. 1963. *Generic Names of Orchids: Their Origin and Meaning*. Academic Press.

INDEX OF COMMON NAMES

INDEX OF SCIENTIFIC NAMES

Accepted names are in *italics*, synonyms in roman. Numbers in **boldface** indicate photo pages.